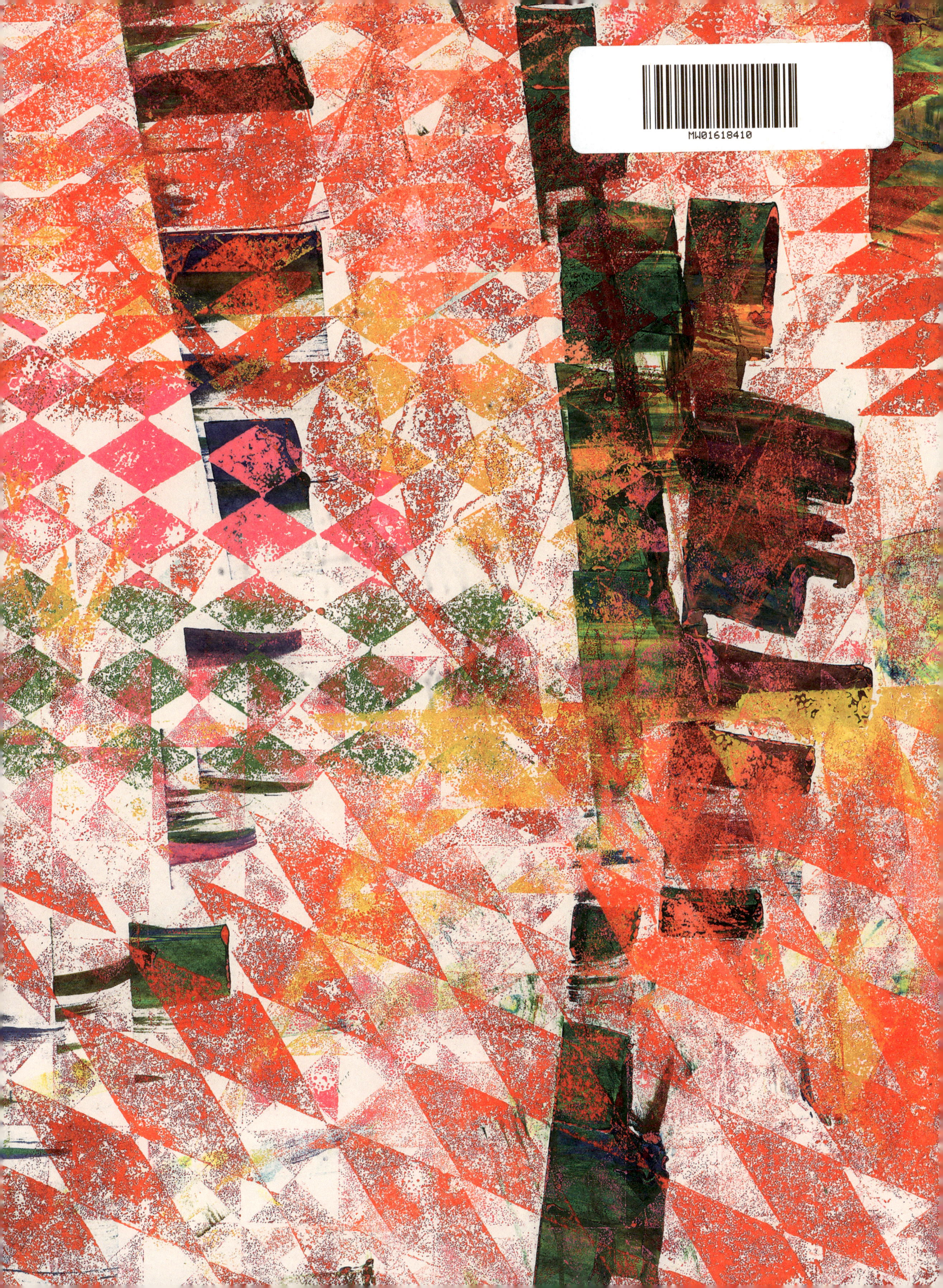
MW01618410

I hope you enjoy
this book

Amos Paul Kennedy Jr

16 November 2024

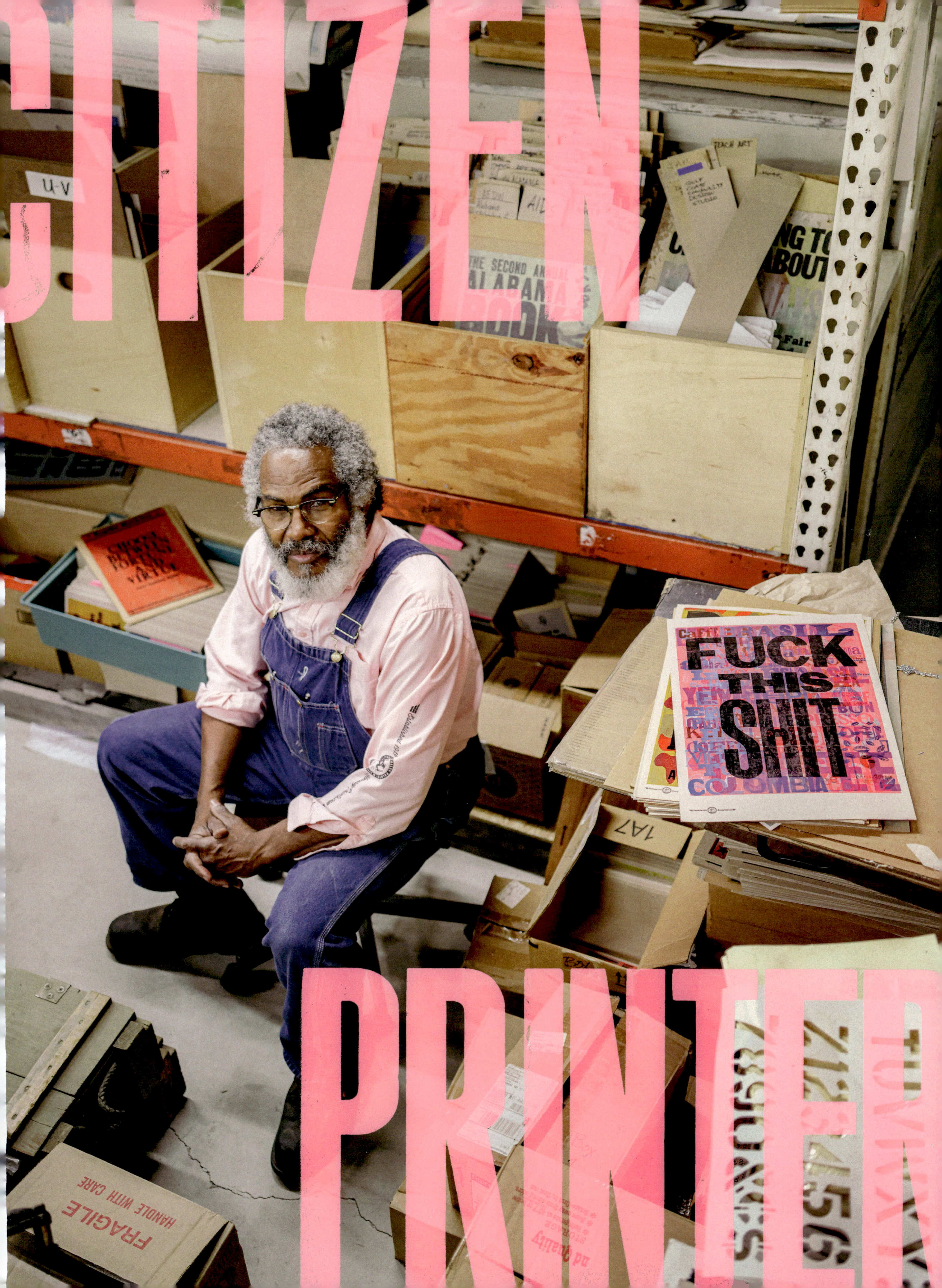
CITIZEN
PRINTER
FUCK THIS SHIT
COLOMBIA
FRAGILE
HANDLE WITH CARE

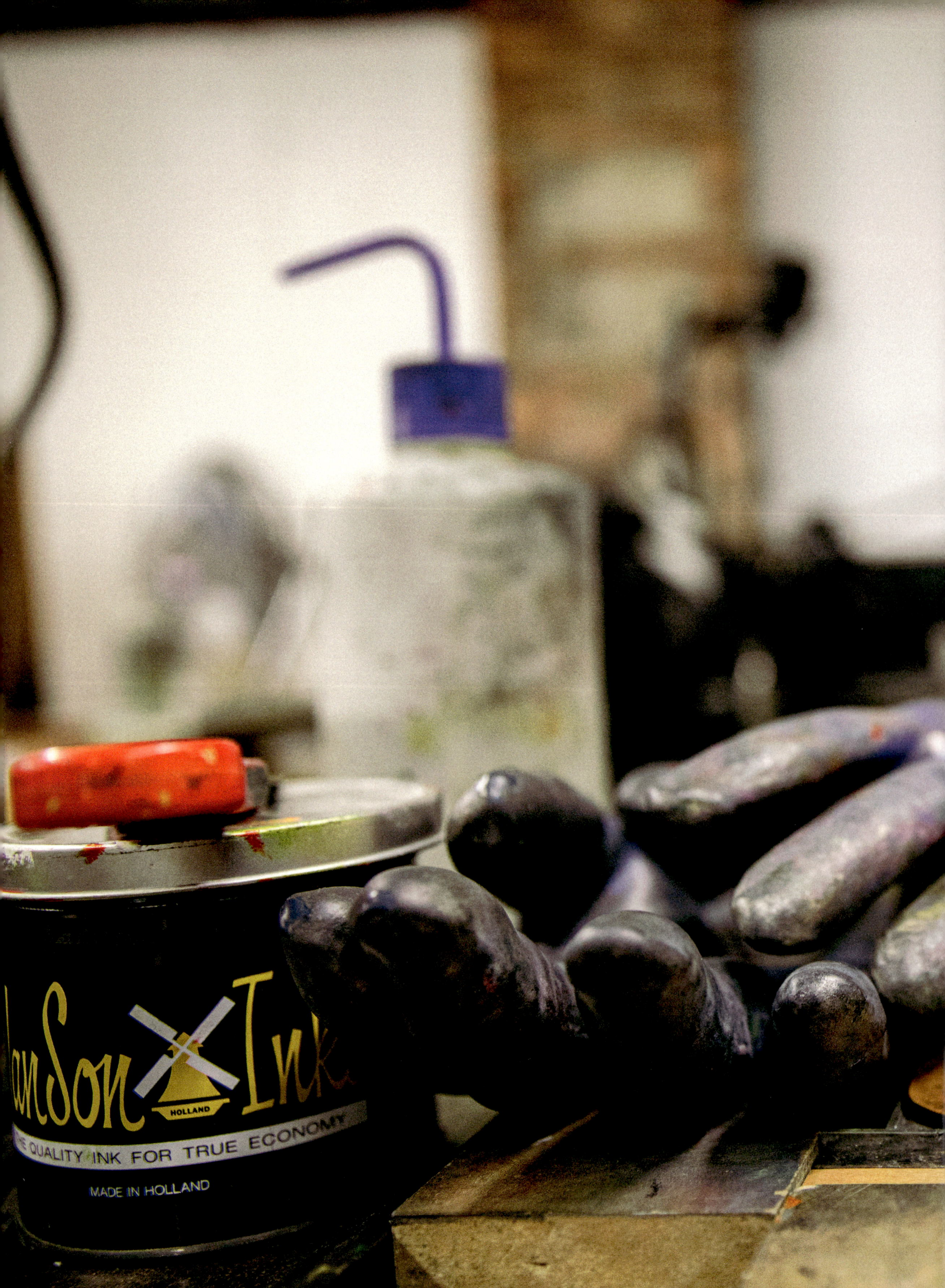
HOLLAND
QUALITY INK FOR TRUE ECONOMY
MADE IN HOLLAND

ALL ARTISTS ARE POLITICAL

Si Kahn

OLD IS AN ATTITUDE.

BE NICE AND LEAVE

Some cause HAPPINESS wherever they go; Others whenever they go.

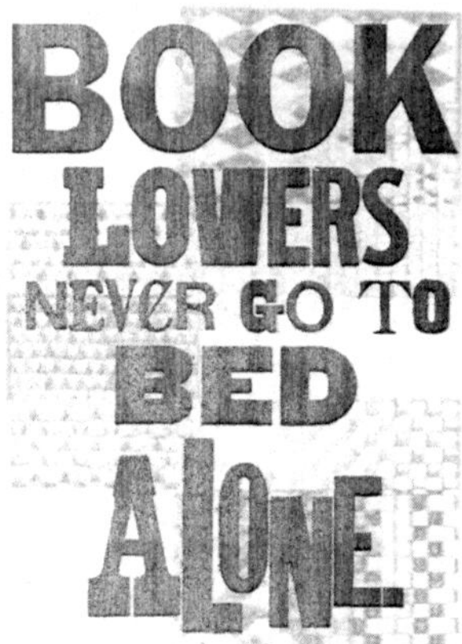

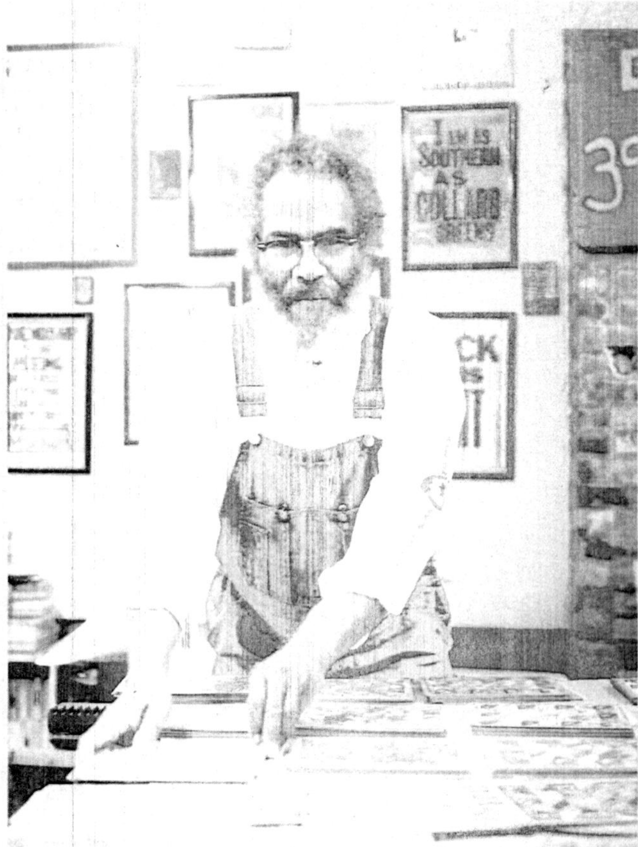

A self-described "humble negro printer," Amos Paul Kennedy, Jr., is internationally recognized for his type-driven messages of social justice and Black power, emblazoned in rhythmically layered and boldly inked prints made for the masses. Borrowing words from civil rights heroes such as Rosa Parks, Fannie Lou Hamer, Frederick Douglass, and Sojourner Truth, Kennedy issues fearless statements on race, capitalism, history, and politics—along with plenty of witty truisms—in his exuberant, colorful, and one-of-a-kind posters and handbills.

A vital monograph on a trailblazing contemporary Black artist, *Citizen Printer* features more than 800 reproductions representing the breadth of Kennedy's letterpress prints (including rarely seen artist's books), plus original portraiture of the maker at work, a powerful manifesto, and a foreword by *New York Times* bestselling author Austin Kleon, all presented in a dynamic and type-forward design from AIGA medalist Gail Anderson and Joe Newton.

With essays by scholars Kelly Walters and Myron M. Beasley, *Citizen Printer* tells Kennedy's inspiring story and contextualizes his work within the entwined legacies of Black printing and Black protest—and offers readers tools for lifting their voices so they too can **agitate, agitate, agitate** for a better TODAY.

AMOS PAUL KENNEDY, JR., was working a corporate job when, at nearly forty, he discovered the art of letterpress printing on a tour of Colonial Williamsburg. Kennedy then devoted himself to the craft, earning an MFA in graphic design at the University of Wisconsin–Madison. He now operates Kennedy Prints!, a letterpress printshop in Detroit. He has been featured in outlets like *Hyperallergic*, the *New York Times*, and the *Economist*, and he has exhibited in dozens of museums and galleries across the United States, including Poster House, the Brooklyn Public Library, the Library of Congress, and the libraries of the Museum of Modern Art and the Metropolitan Museum of Art.

ISBN 978-1-7368633-8-1

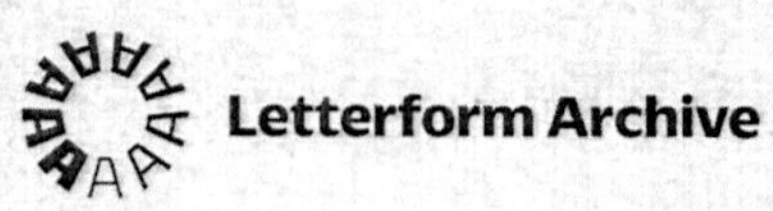

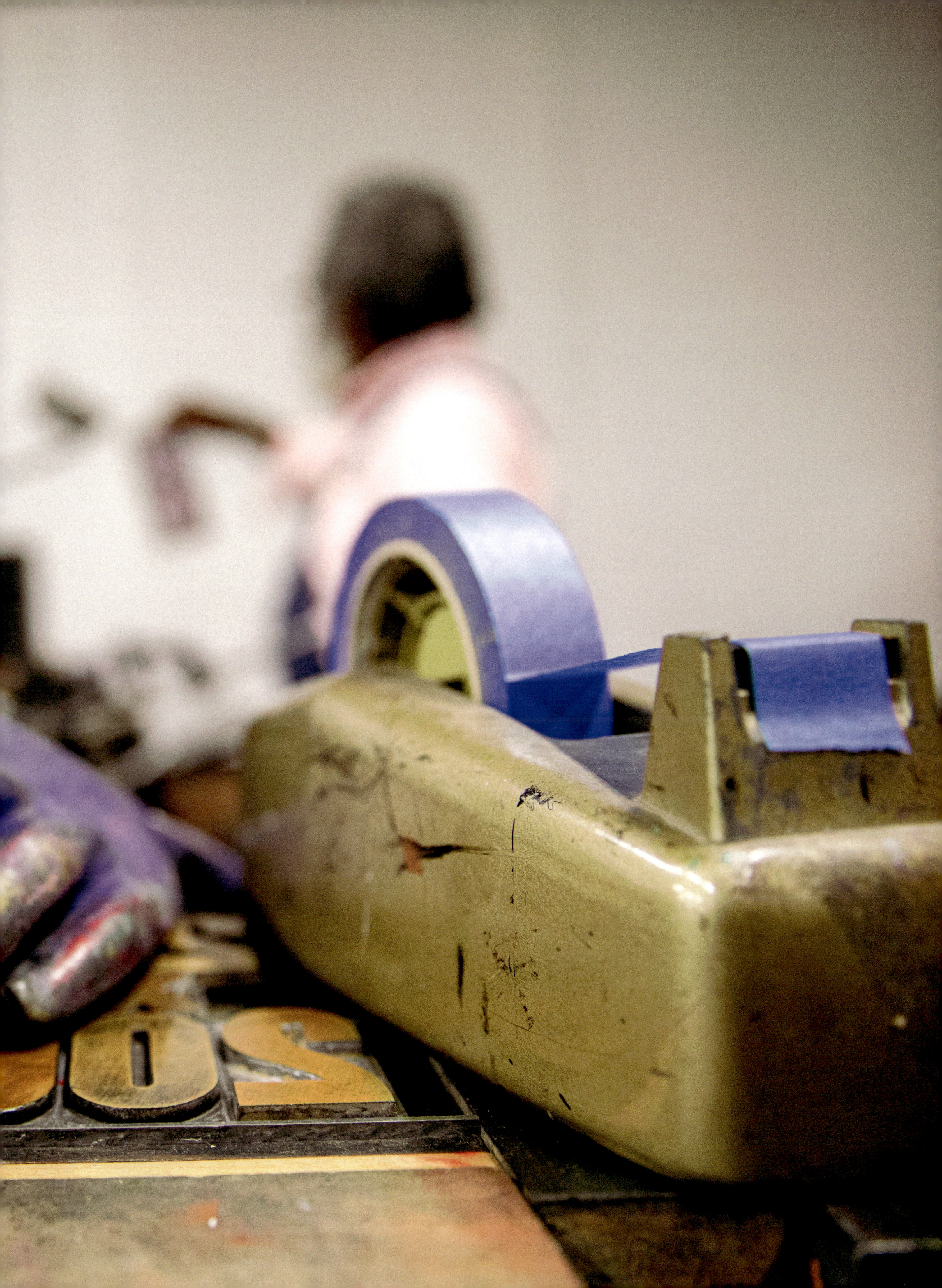

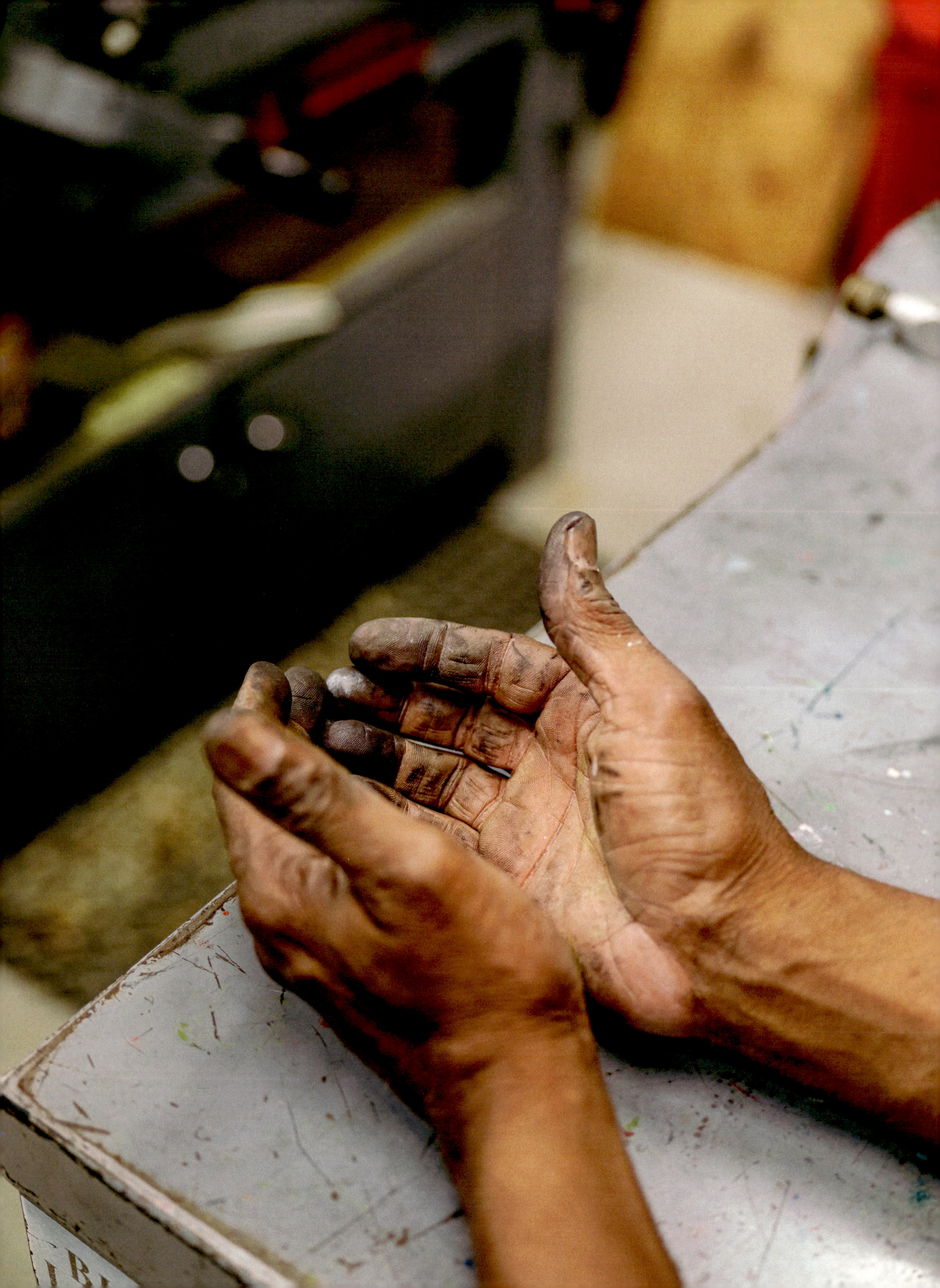

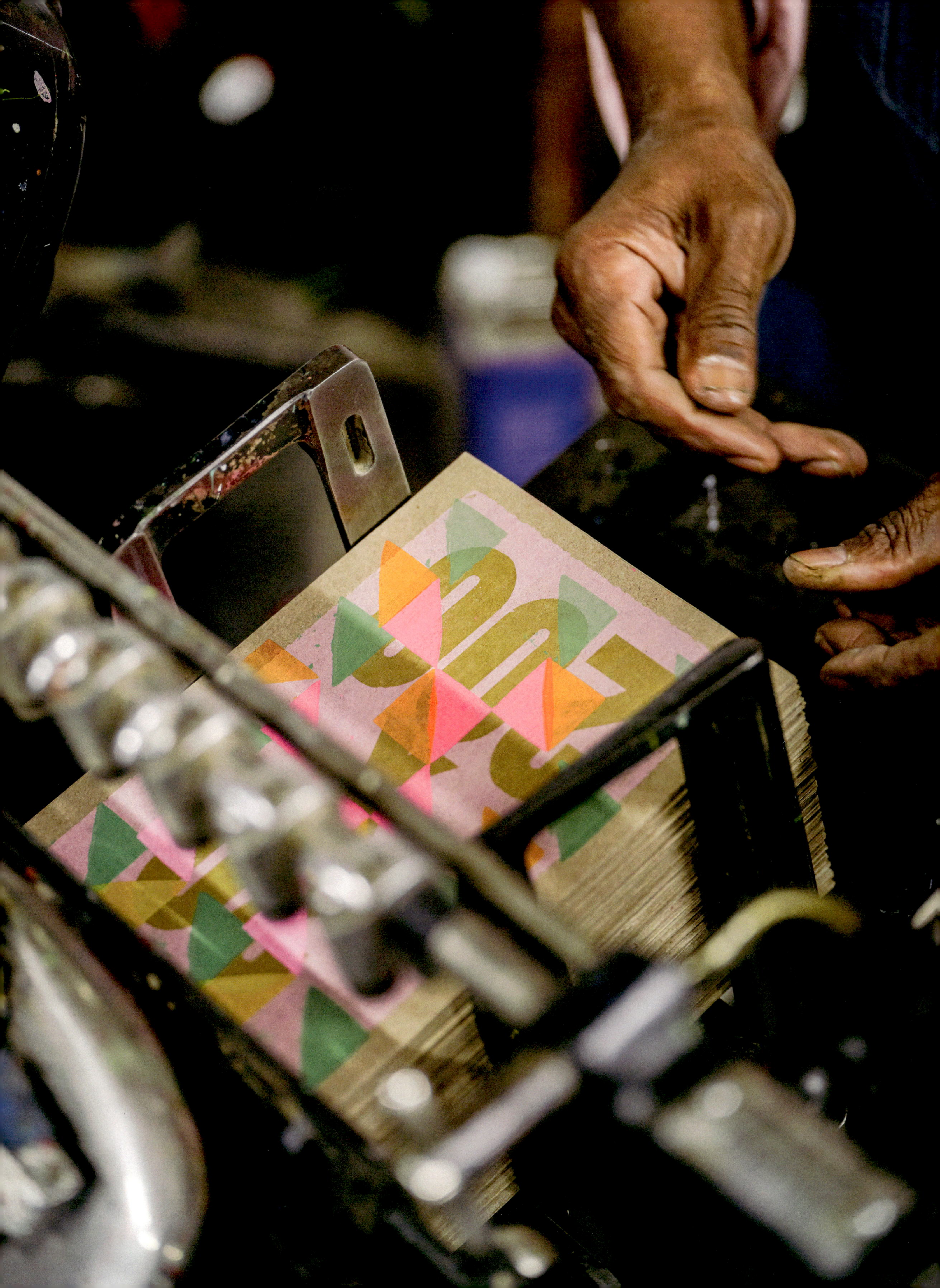

"I do not w
'blackface'
'fine printin
print negro. T
to express n
To do to print
blues and
did to

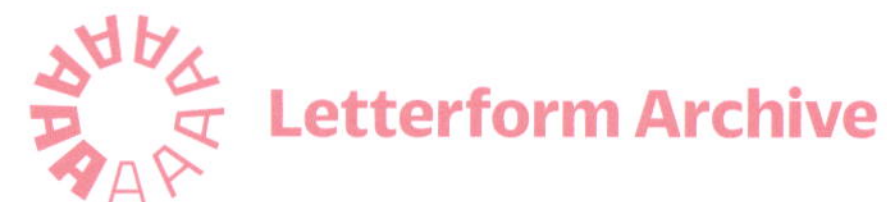

AMOS PAU

ant to put
n so-called
g.' I want to
o use printing
gro culture.
ng what the
spirituals
nusic."

KENNEDY, JR.

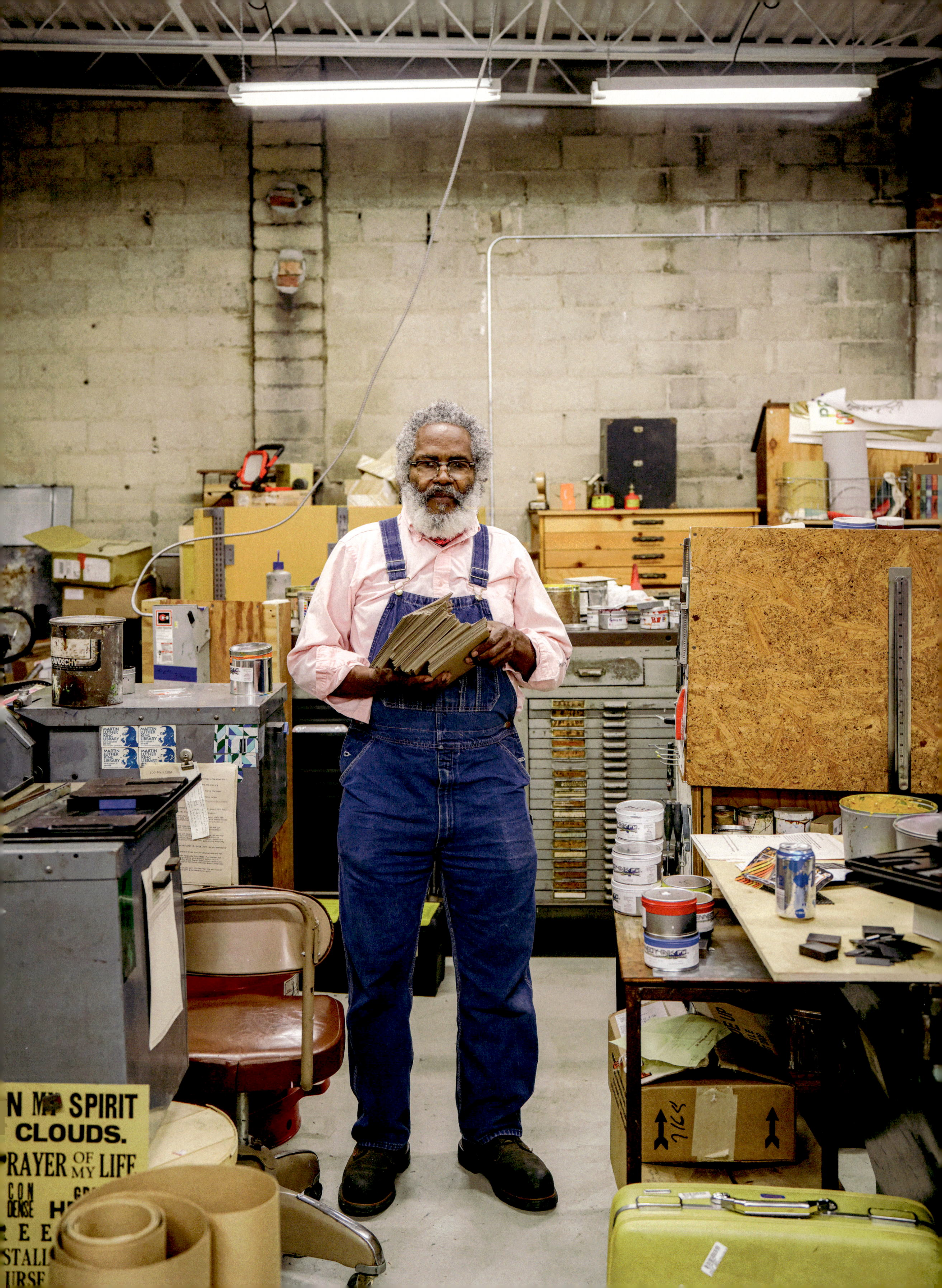
SPIRIT
CLOUDS.
RAYER OF MY LIFE

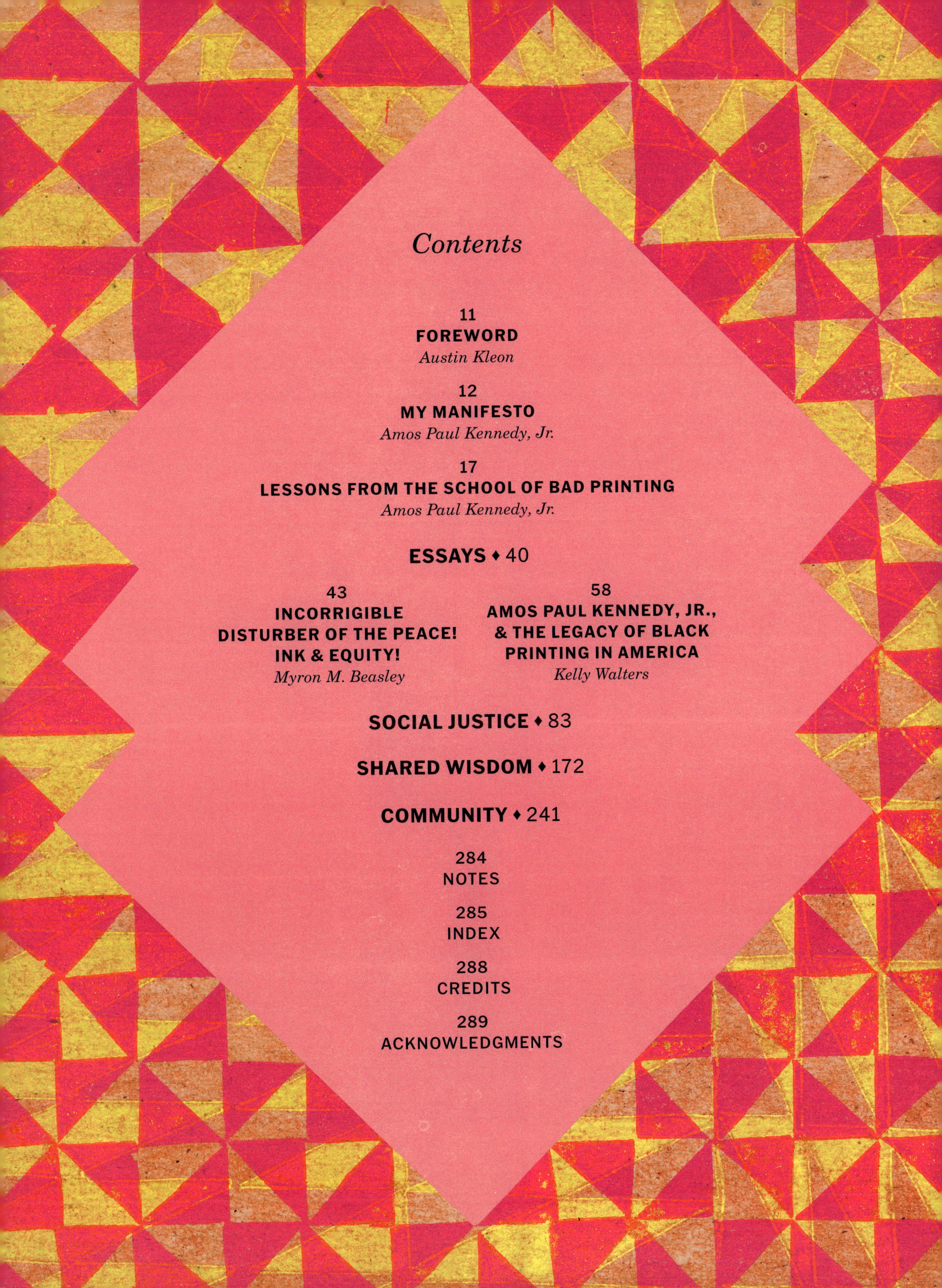

Contents

11
FOREWORD
Austin Kleon

12
MY MANIFESTO
Amos Paul Kennedy, Jr.

17
LESSONS FROM THE SCHOOL OF BAD PRINTING
Amos Paul Kennedy, Jr.

ESSAYS ♦ 40

43
INCORRIGIBLE DISTURBER OF THE PEACE! INK & EQUITY!
Myron M. Beasley

58
AMOS PAUL KENNEDY, JR., & THE LEGACY OF BLACK PRINTING IN AMERICA
Kelly Walters

SOCIAL JUSTICE ♦ 83

SHARED WISDOM ♦ 172

COMMUNITY ♦ 241

284
NOTES

285
INDEX

288
CREDITS

289
ACKNOWLEDGMENTS

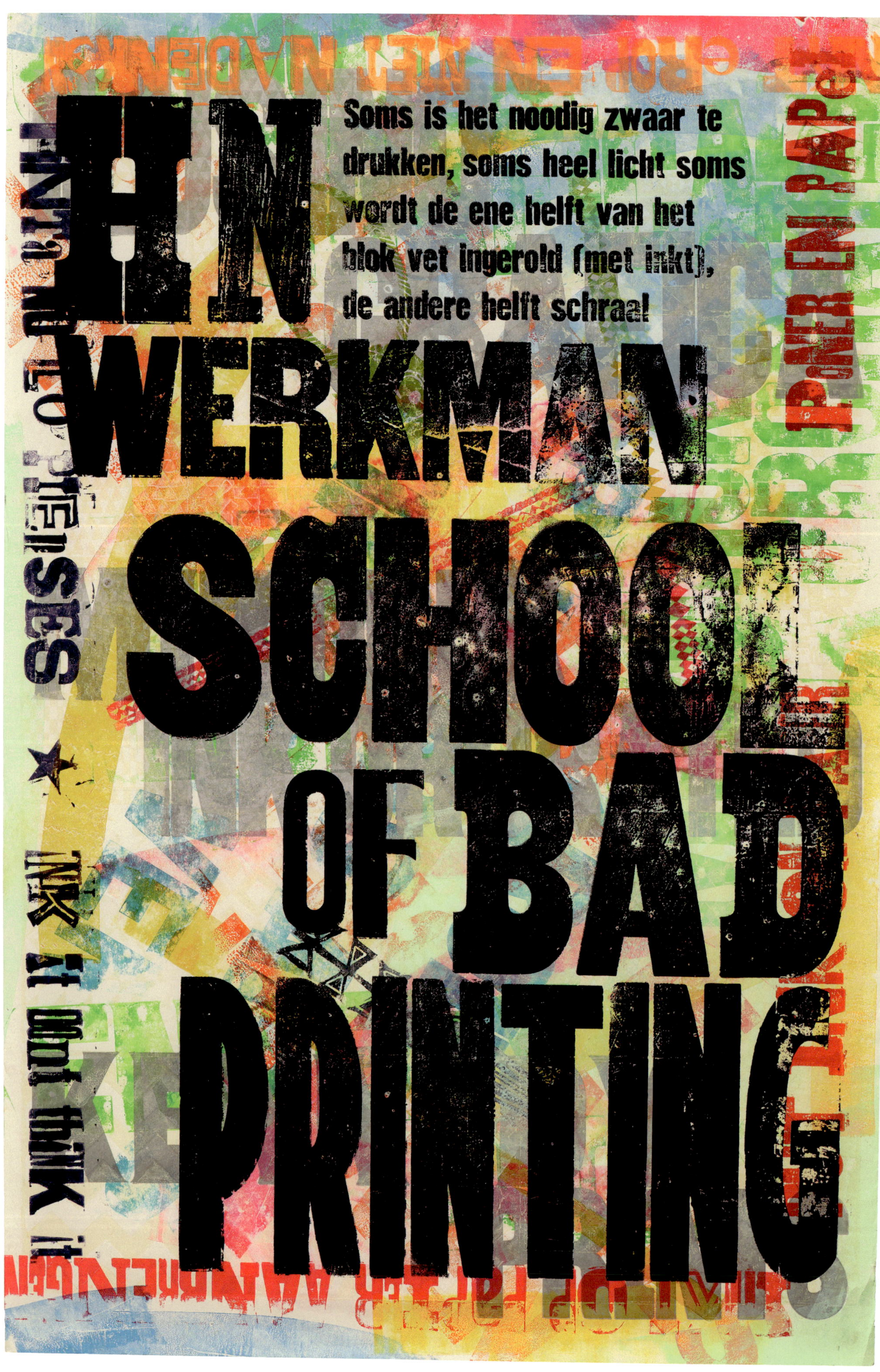
HN
WERKMAN
SCHOOL
OF BAD
PRINTING
Soms is het noodig zwaar te drukken, soms heel licht soms wordt de ene helft van het blok vet ingerold (met inkt), de andere helft schraal
Don't think it ink it

Foreword

Man of Letters

by AUSTIN KLEON

You are holding in your hands a book about Amos Paul Kennedy, Jr., a man who embodies so much of what I love and admire in people who make things.

The first thing that strikes me about Amos is his love of language. He is a man of letters! (I do not consider it an insignificant detail that he was once enrolled in a library science program.) His work is a collection of words. He gathers them from books, aphorisms, proverbs, the mouths of babes, his own mind, and wherever else one receives messages. "I'm just borrowing things," I've heard him say. "I'm putting things together that people left for me."

Kennedy's work is evidence of the head, the heart, and the hands together at play. His is a physical process, done by a human body in time and space with the real materials of ink and chipboard and wood and machinery, pressing them all together into something new. In this digital age, it's inspiring to see someone *using their digits*. Among the many images in this book that bring me joy, my favorite might be the photograph of his ink-stained hands.

He's a great *imperfectionist*, inviting the happy little accidents that make each of his works unique. Every print is "a little off," he says, "because we're all just a little off."

A literature professor will praise a text for having many layers, but in Kennedy's works you can actually see the layers with your eyes.

Kennedy locates himself within a tradition and digs into the past, but there is an irreverence and rowdiness in his work—an infectious, undeniable life force.

"All you have to do is declare yourself crazy," he says. "And do what you want to do."

He is a man who has been willing to walk away from comfort in order to devote himself to his calling. He has said:

> *I don't want more. I want less. I want to have less, so I will have more time to devote to this gift that I have. Because in the final analysis, the only thing that we have that is not renewable is our life. When I am dead, they will still make money. My time, I have decided, is more important. To claim my time to do what I want to do in that time.*[1]

Maybe most important to me is his sense of humor. There's a bad idea in our culture that comedy is not as serious as tragedy, but those in the know will tell you that comedy is humanity's greatest survival mechanism. Laughter is a great means of resistance in the face of struggle, suffering, and death. As bell hooks told us, "We cannot have a meaningful revolution without humor."

Kennedy will not call himself an artist, and I have not used that word so far out of respect for him, but he's as much of an artist as anyone I've ever seen. I suspect he would love the Balinese saying often quoted by another printmaker hero of mine, Corita Kent: "We have no art. We do everything as well as we can." (He might've already printed that one.)

Many times I've known the delight of opening an envelope postmarked Detroit with a Kennedy print inside. To hold a thing in my hands that he's made with his hands makes me want to make things with my hands. I hope you will experience that same joy and inspiration when you turn the pages of this book.

To borrow words from the word borrower who borrowed them: *Proceed and be bold!*

LEFT Amos Paul Kennedy, Jr., *H. N. Werkman School of Bad Printing* (an ode to another great imperfectionist, Dutch expressionist printer Hendrik Nicolaas Werkman), 2018, letterpress on paper, 40½ × 28 inches (102.75 × 71 cm), Detroit.

My Manifesto

I print negro.*

I use printing to express negro culture.

I seek to do to printing what the blues did to music.

I do not put blackface on so-called fine printing or artists' books.

I make books negro. I do not make negro books.

I call for a better world through the power of the poster.

I PRINT FOR THE GLORY OF MY PEOPLES!

To print is to share ideas with people.

Letterpress printing is a technique that for half a millennium has shared ideas. It has democratized knowledge for Western civilization.

Prior to printing, knowledge was passed down orally in stories and song, and written knowledge was in the hands of the authorities—the churches and the kings.

With letterpress printing came the growth of literacy and the expansion of universities in Europe—the industrialization of printing disseminated knowledge to a larger audience than ever before.

It is hard to imagine in today's digital life, but in previous centuries, if you did not have money, you could not reach the masses. The only way to do it without censorship was to own a printing press.

In the 1800s, abolitionists wielded this power to print broadsides and pamphlets that called for an end to enslavement.

Late in the nineteenth century, the Black press used it to expose racist mob violence in the South.

In the twentieth, activists used it to print placards to protest Jim Crow laws.

Black printing helped the civil rights movement to flourish.

I go back to that legacy.

I PRINT FOR THE GLORY OF MY PEOPLES!

But by the time I started printing in 1988, letterpress had been replaced in the pressrooms by offset. It had gone from a commercial craft to an exclusive art.

After 150 years of using movable type to call for equality, negro culture simply moved on from letterpress printing.

This rejection partly explains the absence of negro printed matter preserved in collections today, including posters, fine printing, and artists' books.**

But these disciplines should not be deprived of the brilliance of negro culture.

Nor should negro culture be deprived of the power and legacy of these disciplines.

So I decided to devote my energies to reintroducing letterpress printing into negro culture.

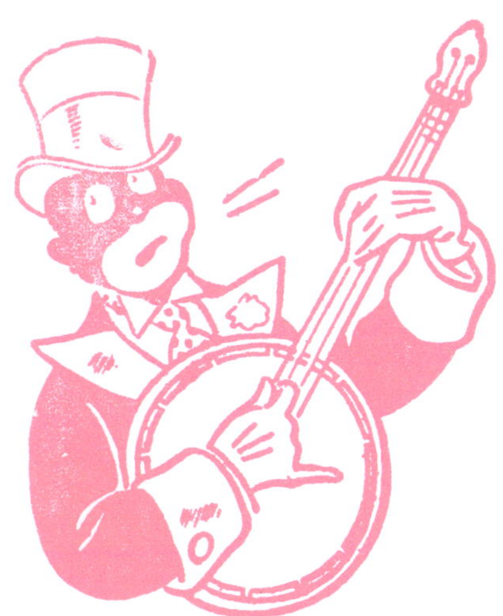

I PRINT FOR THE GLORY OF MY PEOPLES!

Today our culture is attempting to atomize letterpress printing. It is trying to destroy letterpress's populist roots by relegating it to an elitist art form that appears only in fine printing and artists' books.

Letterpress printing is for humanity ☛ The MESSAGE is the medium

Historically, the knowledge shared in letterpress printing has been more important than the physical medium itself.

Fine printing is for the bourgeois ☛ The MEDIUM is the message

This work is produced for a relatively small group of printers and collectors who marvel at the manipulation of the materials. They care more about the medium than the message it carries.***

Artists' books are for the elite ☛ The MEDIUM is the medium

To print for the elite is to place all importance on the object. It is all hand labor and rare materials. The message is exclusion.

I use letterpress printing, but I use it to disrupt the segregated realms of fine printing and artists' books.

My very presence as a negro letterpress printer in these circles exposes the injustices of civilization to those who use fine printing and artists' books to look away from those injustices.

I PRINT FOR THE GLORY OF MY PEOPLES!

Throughout history, the printer has had to choose to either resist or assist in the marginalization of knowledge.****

I MADE THE CHOICE:

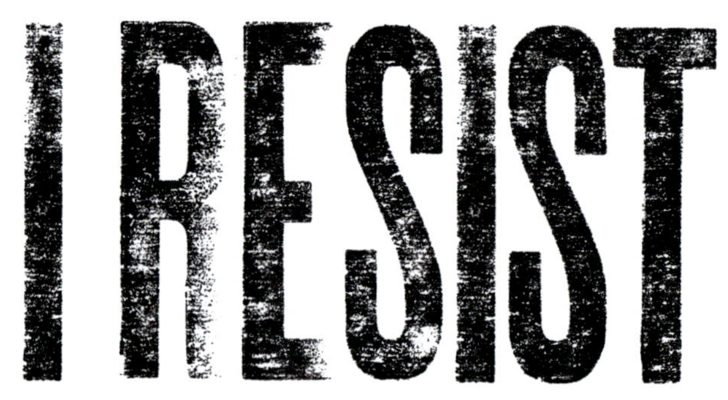

I print POSTERS for the MASSES.

Posters invade your visual space.

They are too loud to ignore.

They are very aggressive.

Posters allow me to put the message in the hands of the people and move on.

I PRINT FOR THE GLORY OF MY PEOPLES!

Understand that, for me, printing is commerce, not capitalism. It is a trade between one who practices a skill and another who values it. This trade directly empowers the skilled worker, not the capitalist who profits off that worker.

Understand that my very existence is protest.

The existence of Black people in America is an act of protest, of survival.

We were supposed to be used up and replaced.

Everything I do is a manifestation of that protest.

Understand that my connection with the universe is most present in the printshop—that my deep love of printing for the masses has led me to a deep connection with ALL.

With time, I have realized that my people are actually ALL peoples.

Some folks have told me that my story has changed their lives—that my decision to leave a life as a business bureaucrat in favor of one as a letterpress printer gave them permission to leave the path they happened to be traveling for the path they truly wanted to travel. "I must go forth," they said.

I feel it is my duty to continue to make these cracks in our inhumane society so that others will have space to live their lives.

And the spaces that they make will expand the cracks for others, just as the space I make expands the cracks made by my ancestors.

One day our growth will rumble down the walls that separate our humanity.

I try to print a world into existence that is as welcoming and nurturing as the universe is to me, and I urge others to

agitate

AGITATE

AGITATE *****

for a world that is welcoming and nurturing to them.

I PRINT FOR THE GLORY OF MY PEOPLES.

—Amos Paul Kennedy, Jr.

*
You may mistake me for African American but I am negro, a descendant of the enslaved peoples of these United States of America. Above my desk, I have this quote from Black Civil War soldier and historian George W. Williams, which appears in volume 1 of his 1883 book, *History of the Negro Race in America from 1619 to 1880: Negroes as Slaves, as Soldiers, and as Citizens*:

> It is not wise, to say the least, for intelligent Negroes in America to seek to drop the word *Negro*. It is a good, strong, and healthy word, and ought to live. It should be covered with glory: let Negroes do it.

**
Another reason is that early ephemera in general was not deemed important enough to keep, but especially early ephemera produced by Black printers.

***
A brilliant satire of fine printing and artists' books appears in Charles Chesnutt's 1904 novella, *Baxter's Procrustes*. In it, an exclusive club of white male collectors fall all over themselves praising a book that—once they actually open it—turns out to be blank.

****
Many printers have run clandestine presses: secret printing operations where they published pamphlets and flyers on behalf of a resistance movement, like the experimental Dutch printer H. N. Werkman during World War II. Werkman not only resisted Nazism—he also broke through a lot of restraints in letterpress printing. There was a rebellion on the social level and a rebellion on the craft level. I think that some of my work is a form of rebellion on the craft level.

*****
Shortly before he died in 1895, the Black statesman and former enslaved person Frederick Douglass was asked what advice he would give to a young person. He said, "Agitate, agitate, agitate!" So I do. AND SO SHOULD YOU.

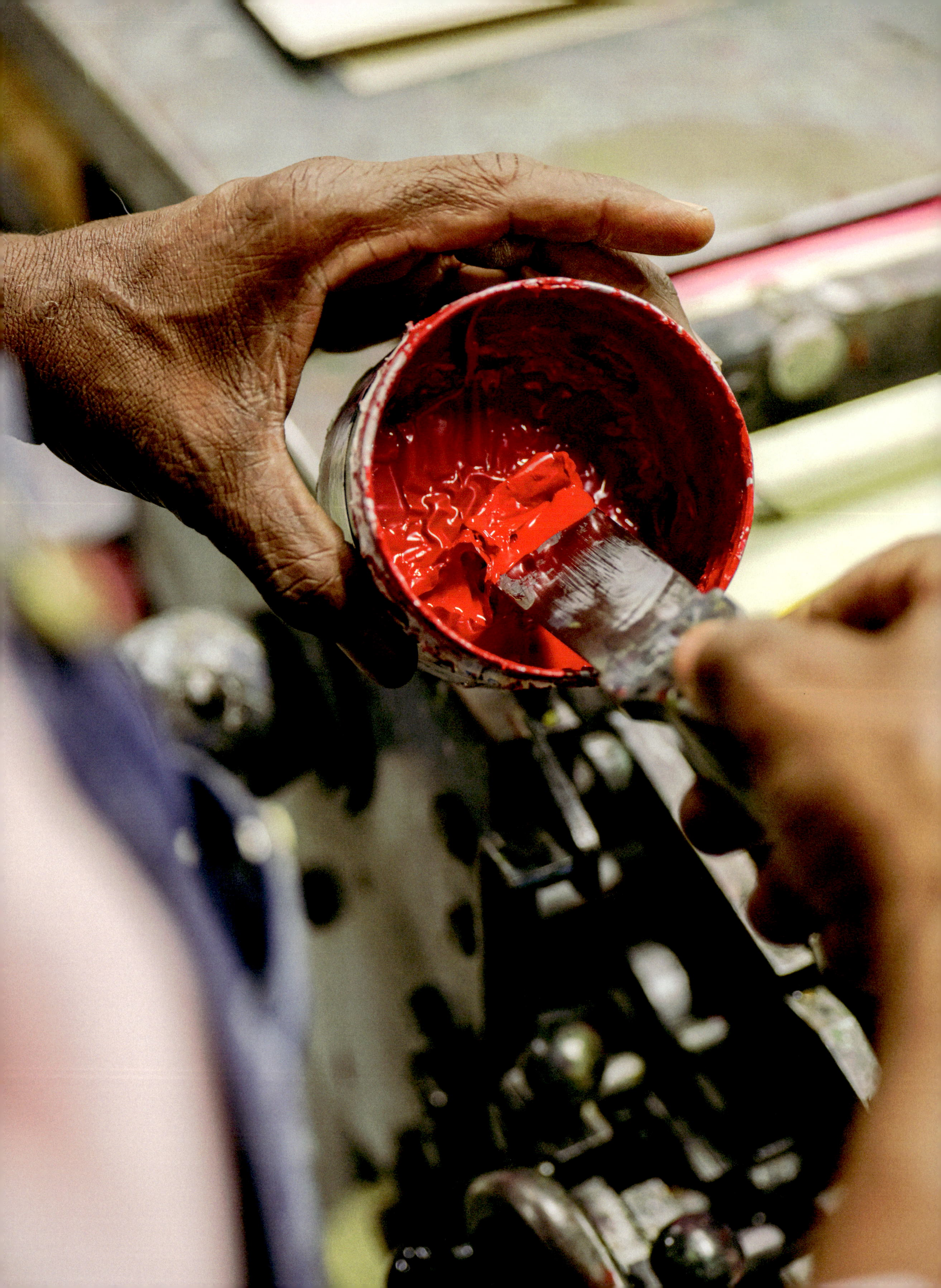

Lessons from the School of Bad Printing

When I discovered letterpress printing, it was like falling off a cliff. But gravity was actually taking care of me that day, because as it turns out, printing is the best thing I can do. Everyone has a calling in life. My calling is to print.

My technique is simple: I put ink on paper. I like to put a lot of ink on paper in a lot of different colors. Most of what I do is in the moment. When I get to the press, the energy that's generated makes things happen. I don't go in with sketches or plans.

Most people don't know what letterpress is anymore, to be candid. Letterpress printing is a form of relief printing in which raised type and illustrations are locked into a configuration on a press bed, inked, and pressed into multiple sheets of paper, transferring the type and imagery onto the sheets to create an edition of prints that look exactly the same. Some experts may nitpick that definition, but that's OK—it gives them something to feel important about.

I like to do letterpress differently, anyway.

You see, as a culture, we have gotten caught up in this idea of perfection, and in this moment of mass manufacturing, perfection means everything is almost all the same. But in the real world, everything is different. And nothing gets more perfect than in the real world. So I believe each print I make should be unique and different. And just a little off because we're all just a little off.

That's why me and my friends Ro Barragán and Jan-Willem van der Looij started up what we call the School of Bad Printing. (I "run" the Detroit branch, while they do their thing in Buenos Aires and the Netherlands, respectively.) Our goal is to make things messy and random. Because that's the way life is. What we consider order is simply randomization that we can understand.

Here is how to get yourself a degree in bad printing:*

- *Work in a rush.*
- *Build up ink in a lot of layers.*
- *Disregard registration and ink density.*
- *Tolerate—no,* celebrate—*the mark of the maker: the patchy type impressions, the ink splashes, your own fingerprints. Put your humanity into it!*
- *INK it, don't THINK it. Just have fun.*

*We don't do degrees, but you can print your own!

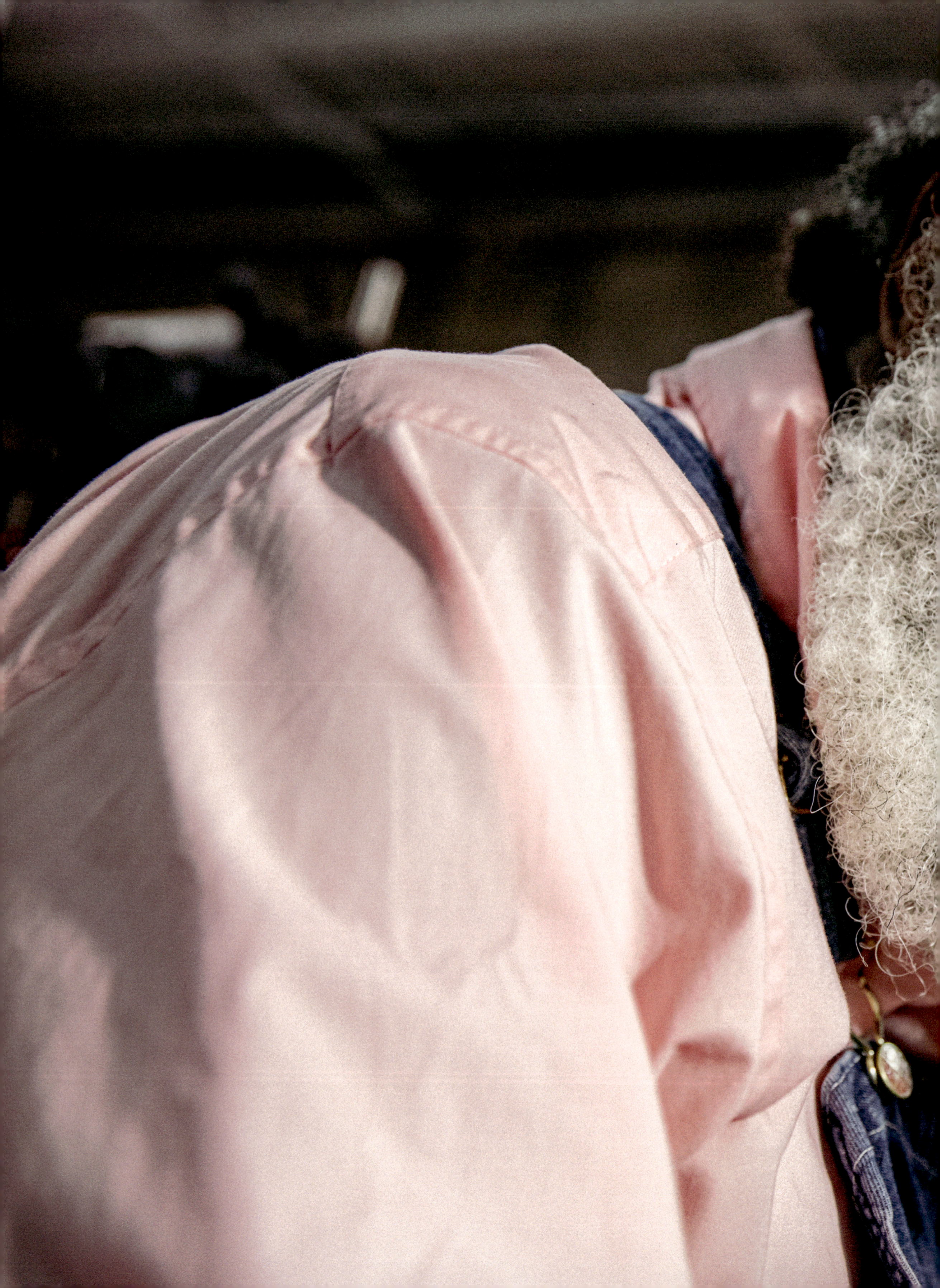

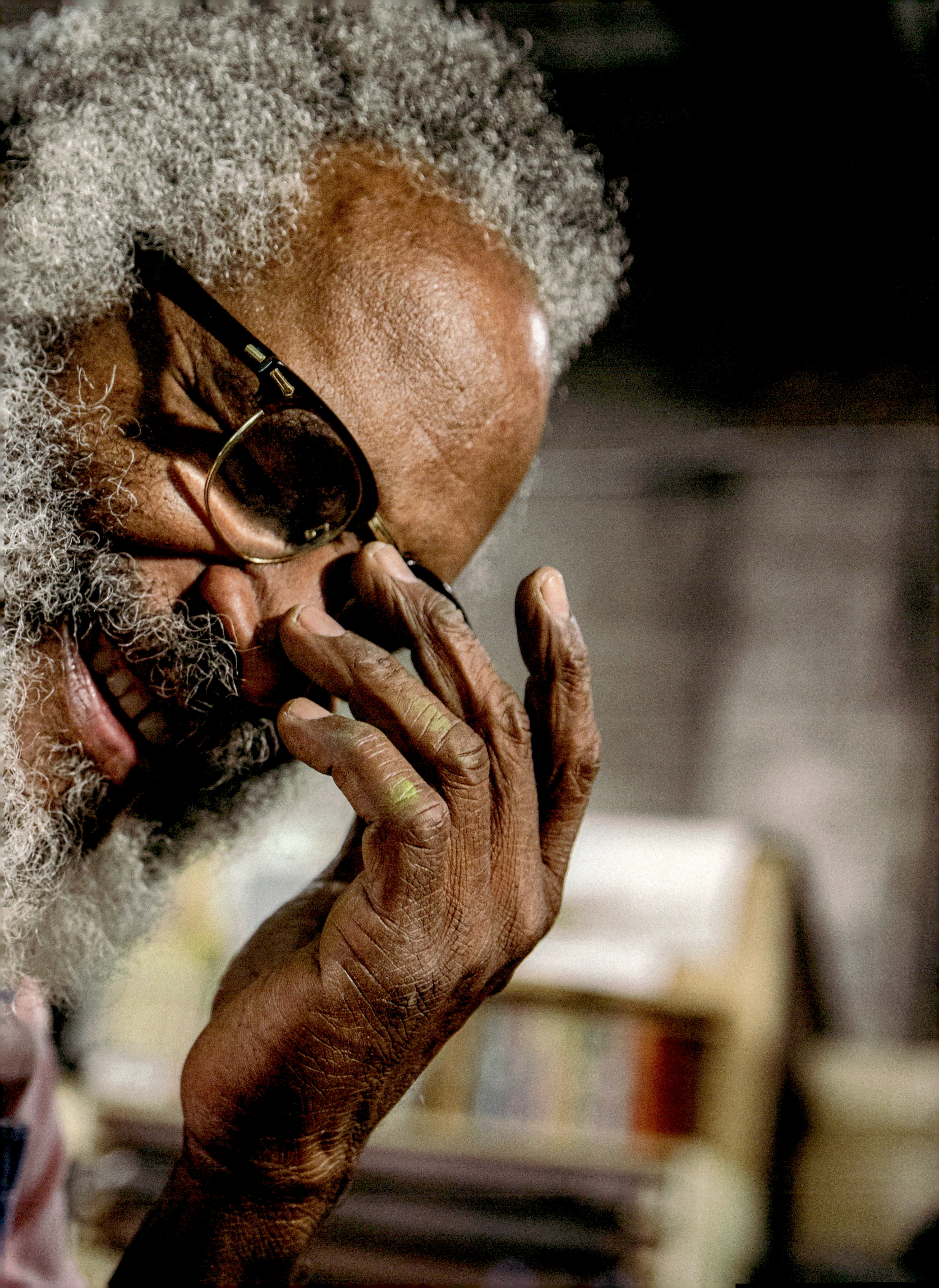

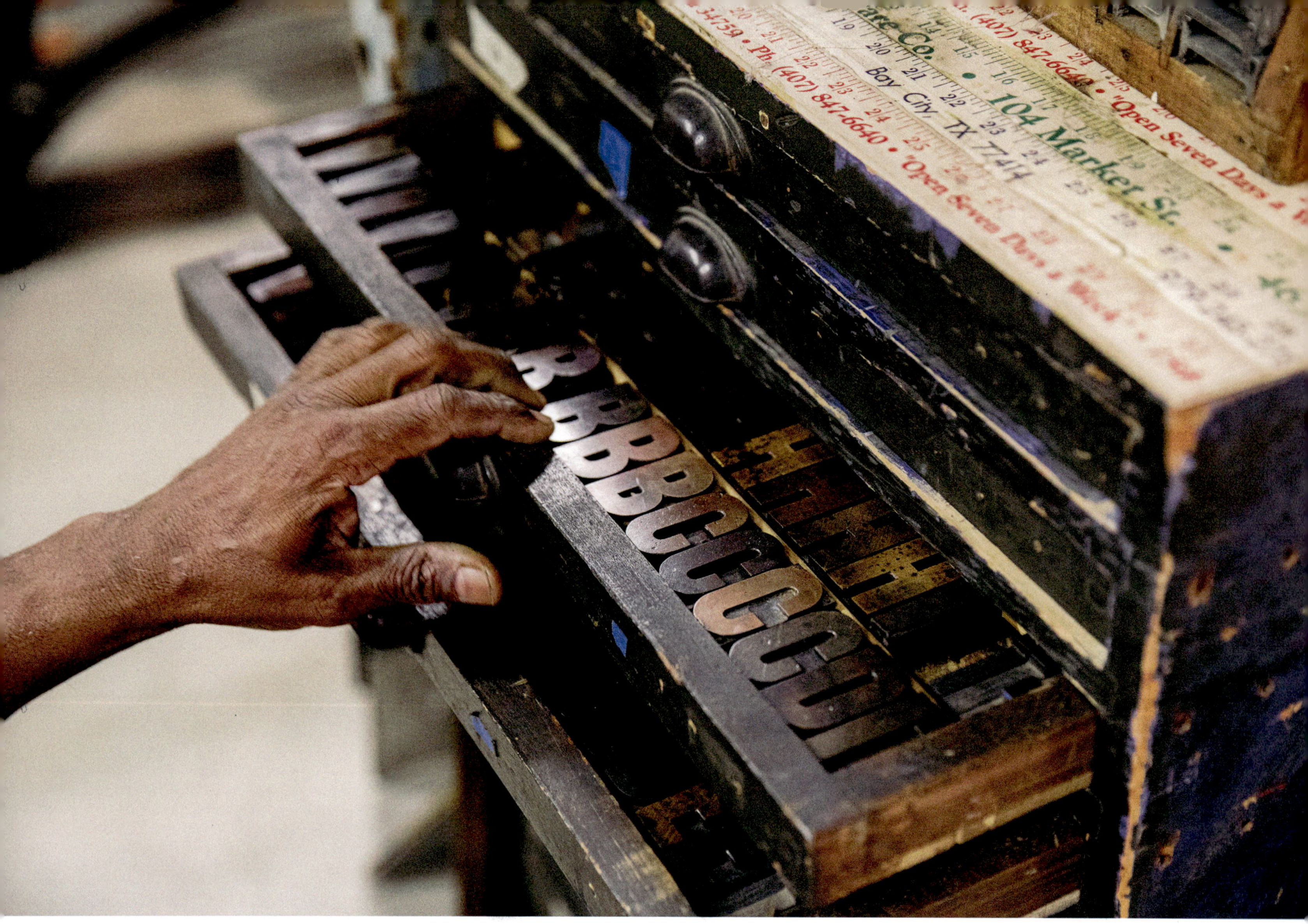

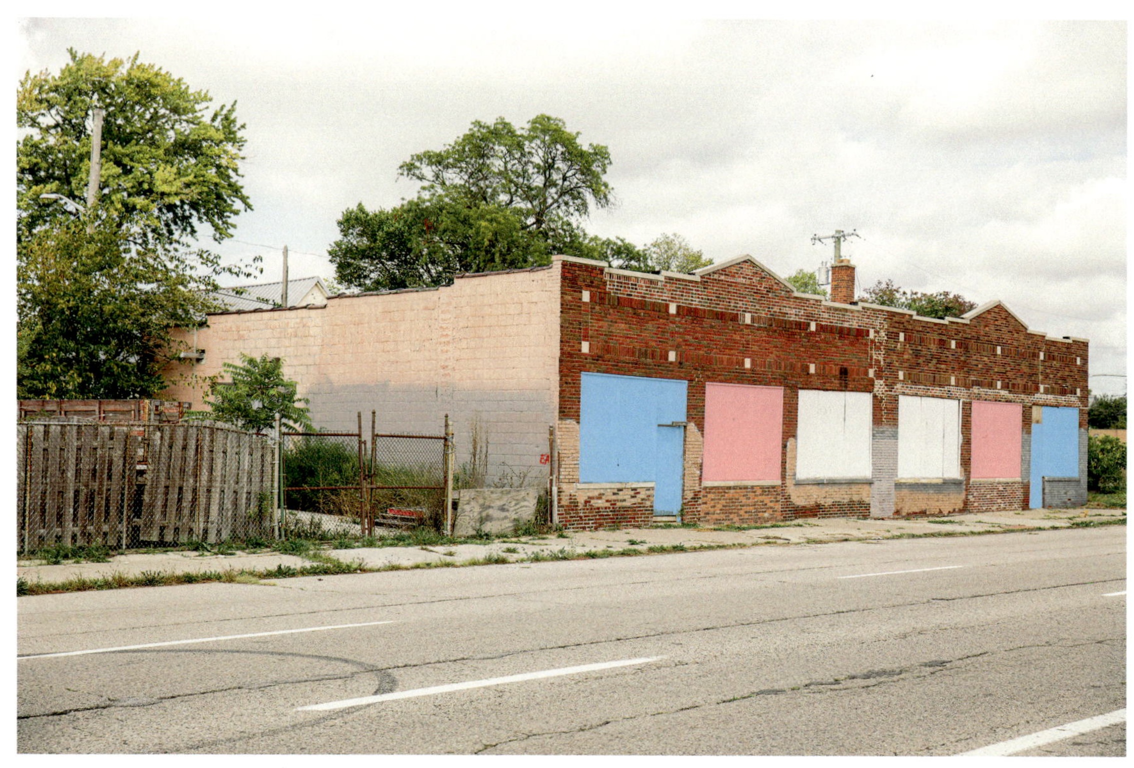

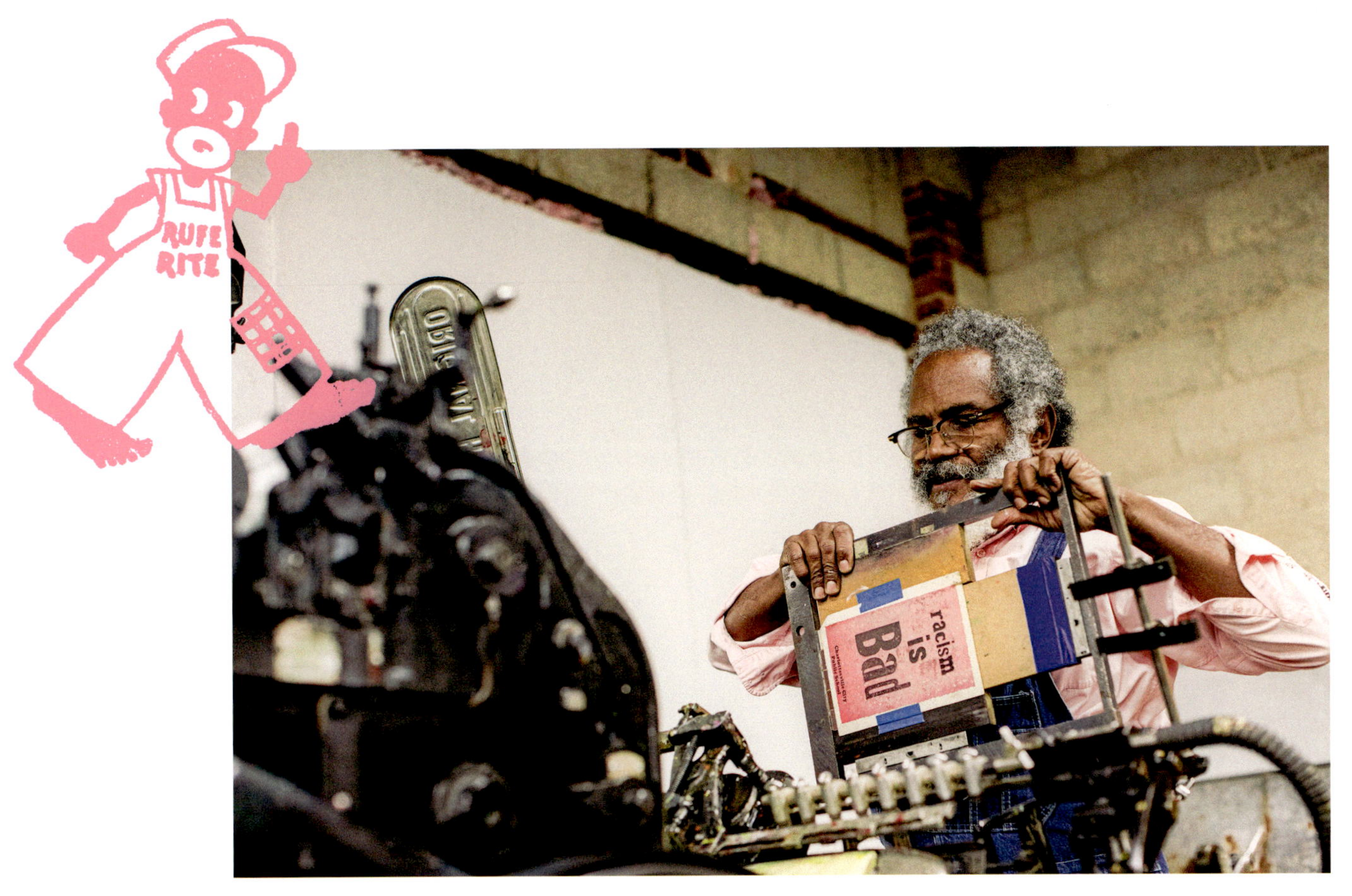
RUFE
RITE
racism
is
Bad

What:
When:
Where:
Who:
IN PERSON!
FESTIVAL
Cake Walk
GROUND
BEEF
4 Family
SALE
CHARITY
BAZAAR
SALE

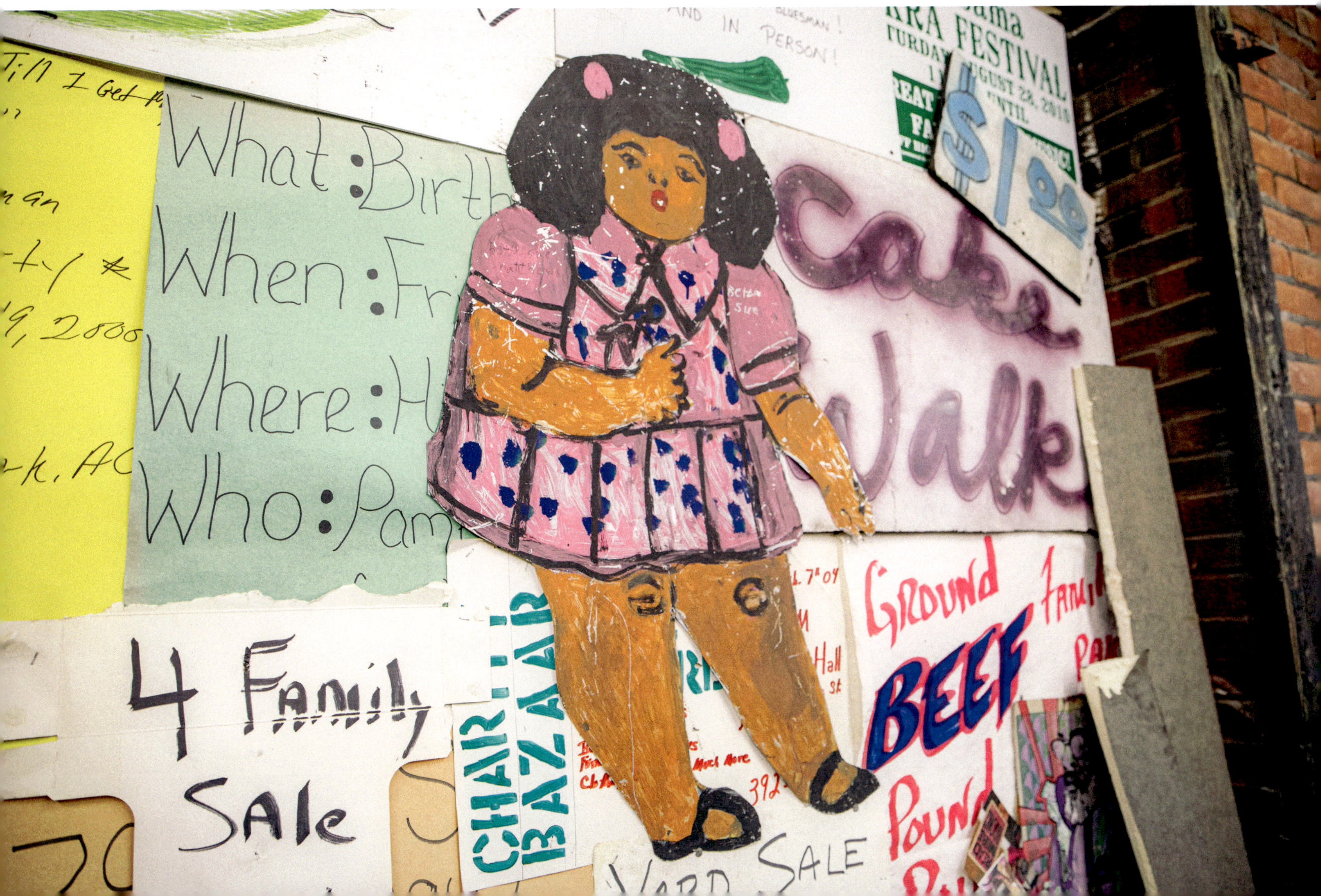

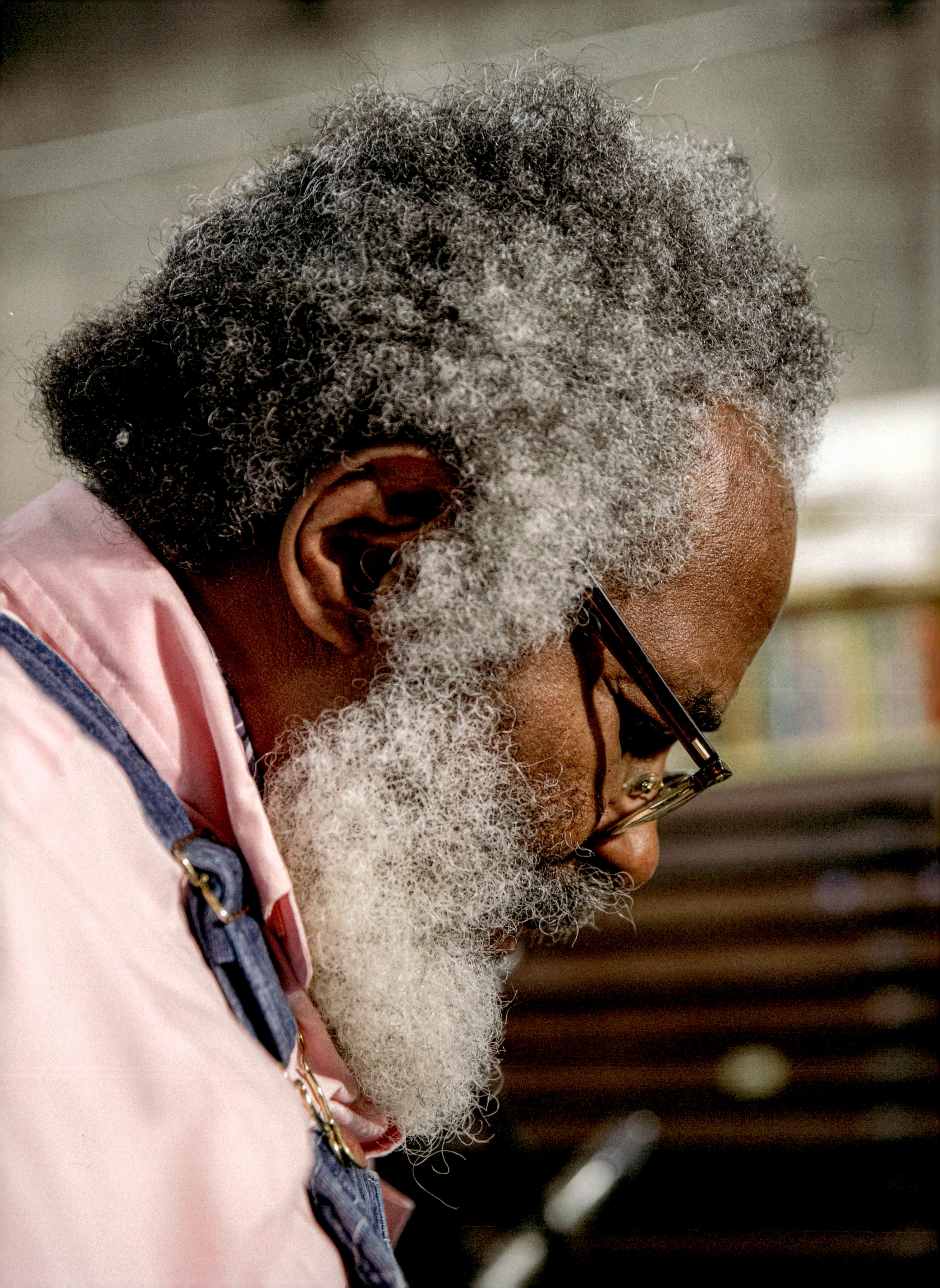

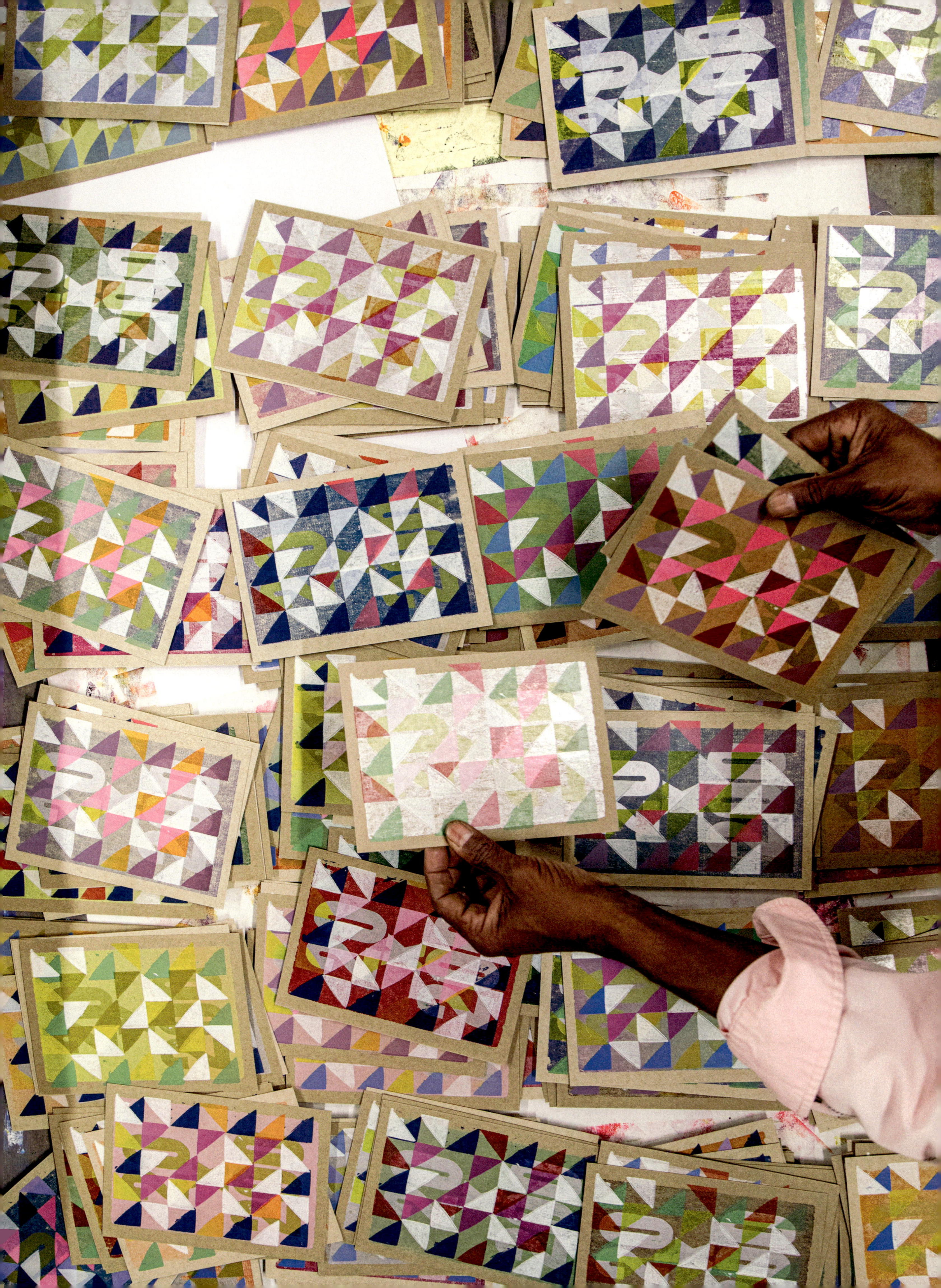

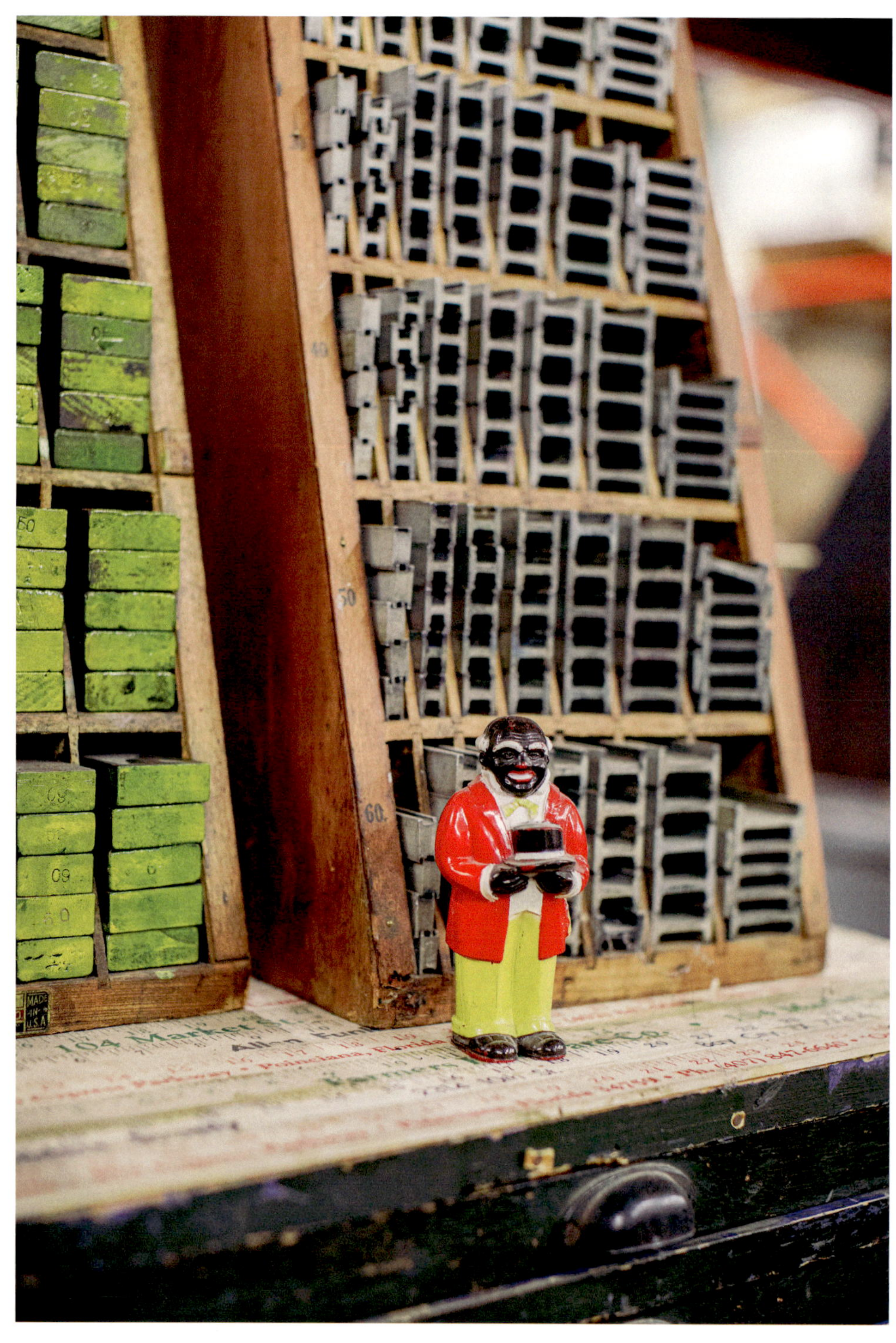

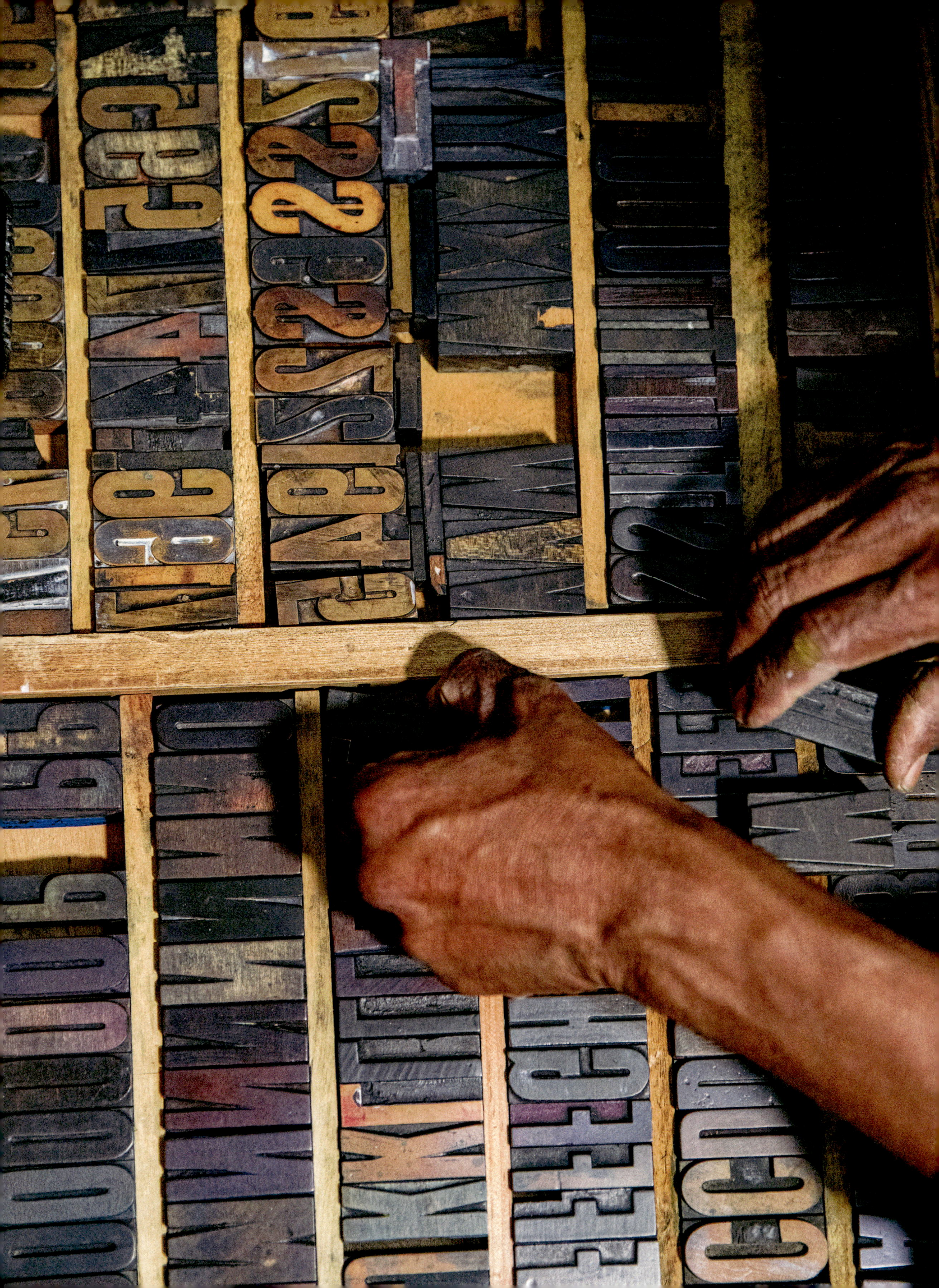

Talking Type

When I started printing, I wanted to put myself in the position of a Black printer in the 1800s, when I would have had to make do with incomplete or battered type, but it still would have gotten the message out.

Type is my main tool, but I wouldn't call myself a typesetter. Type is a thing of beauty in itself, and it should be allowed to do its own thing—to have its own expression.

SELECTING TYPE

I prefer the randomness of orphan type: characters from a bunch of different fonts, some wood, some metal. I tend to work with two kinds: big sans serifs like we see in signs, or calligraphic faces that remind me of the stroke of a broad-edge pen. (I was once a practicing calligrapher, and I am still influenced by the pen.) My wood typefaces are old nameless grotesques—whatever survived from the poster printshops of the nineteenth century. I call them fats and thins. The metal typefaces I rely on the most are Franklin Gothic, Cooper Black, and Lydian.

When I'm picking the type for a print, I think about the message I'm sharing. For the words of humanitarian architect Samuel "Sambo" Mockbee, I used Cooper Black, which I associate with advertising from the 1930s and '40s, when Black culture was defined by the rural South, where Mockbee did his work. It's heavy and quirky, with curved serifs that are very penlike (see pages 208–9). In *Be the Joy That You Seek*, I chose an antique art nouveau typeface from Italy for its sheer ebullience (see page 184).

For the artist's book *Mask*, I digitally printed the text in Rudolf Koch's Neuland, a 1923 typeface often employed to depict Africa as primitive, then hand-carved the words into a Masonite block that I used to print the book itself (see page 87). I was aware of the criticism of Neuland but liked it because it was strong, with plenty of the maker's mark.

For *Strange Fruit*, I chose News Gothic, one of the sans serifs that dominated newspaper headlines in the twentieth century, to rebreak the news of Jim Crow lynchings (see pages 94–97).

MIXING TYPE

I want my type to reflect the diversity of the world. That's why you'll often see black sheep in my prints. Like in *I Am as Southern as Mint Juleps* (see page 226), I use inline wood type for the *L* and *P*. Designed for chromatic printing in the 1800s, these pieces came with a solid mate, and they'd print the inline in one color and the solid in another. I don't have the solids, but I use the inlines for a little funk. I also tried a calligraphic *O* from the typeface Bradley in *I Am as Southern as Collard Greens*, and an upside-down *7* instead of an *L* in *I Am as Southern as Dolly Parton* (see pages 228–29). Why? It's Dolly Parton. Any old *L* won't do.

Even broken or worn-down type gets used in my shop. Damaged type needs to be seen, too.

This is in part because—while I have more than 750 cases of type—I lack a complete set for most of it. But it's also because I print the world I want to live in. And that's a world where there is no segregation, even in the typecase.

SETTING TYPE

Sometimes I use type for **VOICE**. I like my prints to be loud. So I often center my type and set it big to fill the whole sheet to shout whatever it is I'm saying, like in *Ladies, No Fighting in the Bathroom* (see page 260).

One thing I'm known for is my layers: dense typographic backgrounds printed with words that relate to my main message, like in the *Quotations of Rosa Louise Parks* portfolio (see pages 106–11). These are a form of call and response, with the main message on top acting as the call and all the layers underneath as the response. This is to reflect the Black oratory traditions we hear in sermons and civil rights speeches.

Sometimes I use type to show **MOTION**, like the letters joyfully getting down in my dance posters (see pages 204–5), or the up-and-down movement in *If There Is No Struggle, There Is No Progress* (see page 59). Here I am mimicking something I learned in high school chemistry, which is that if the electrons in an atom get bumped out of equilibrium, they agitate to get back to where they belong.

That's what the letters are doing there—agitating, just like we the people need to do to achieve equality.

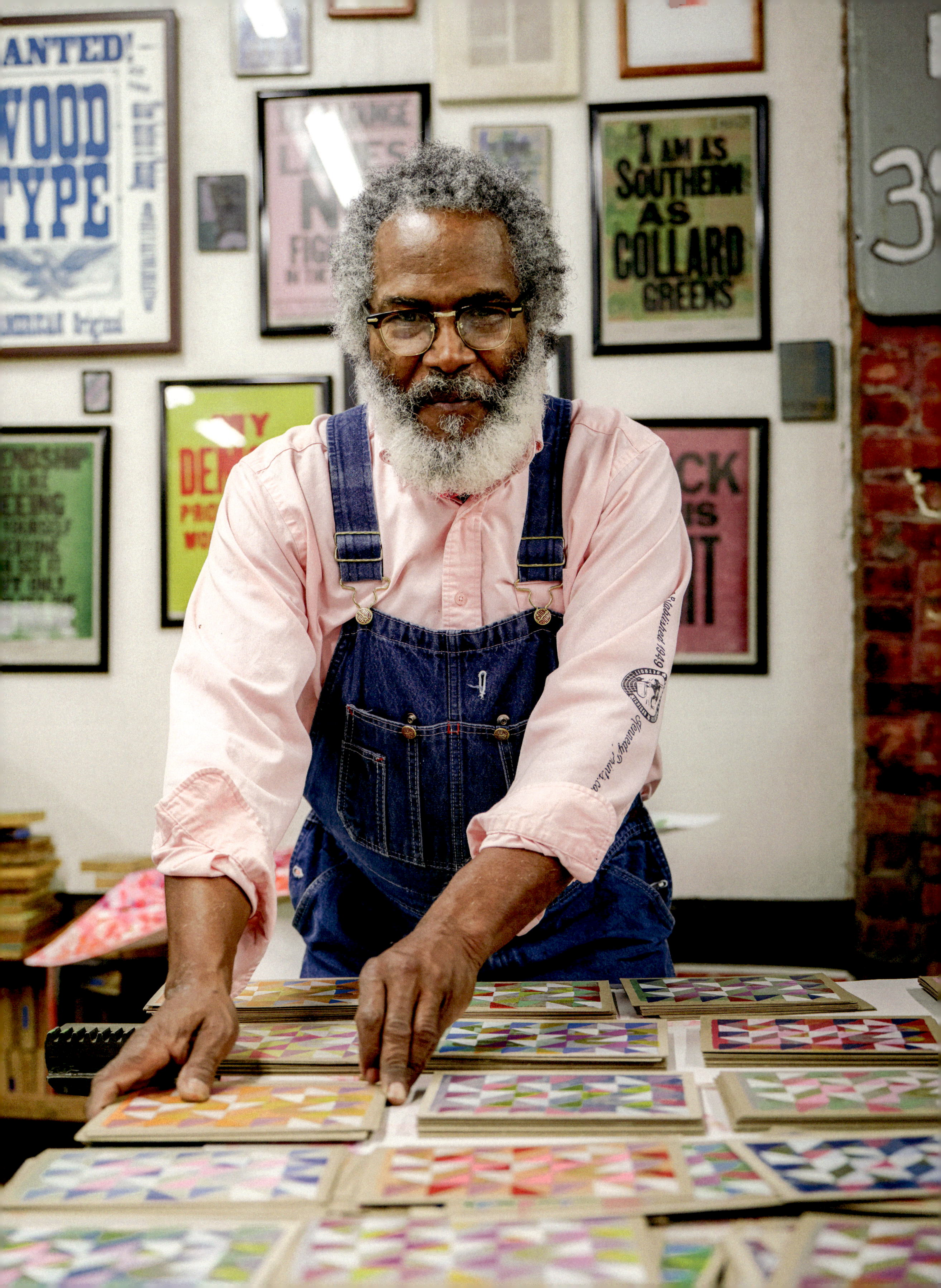
ANTED!
WOOD
TYPE
I AM AS
SOUTHERN
AS
COLLARD
GREENS

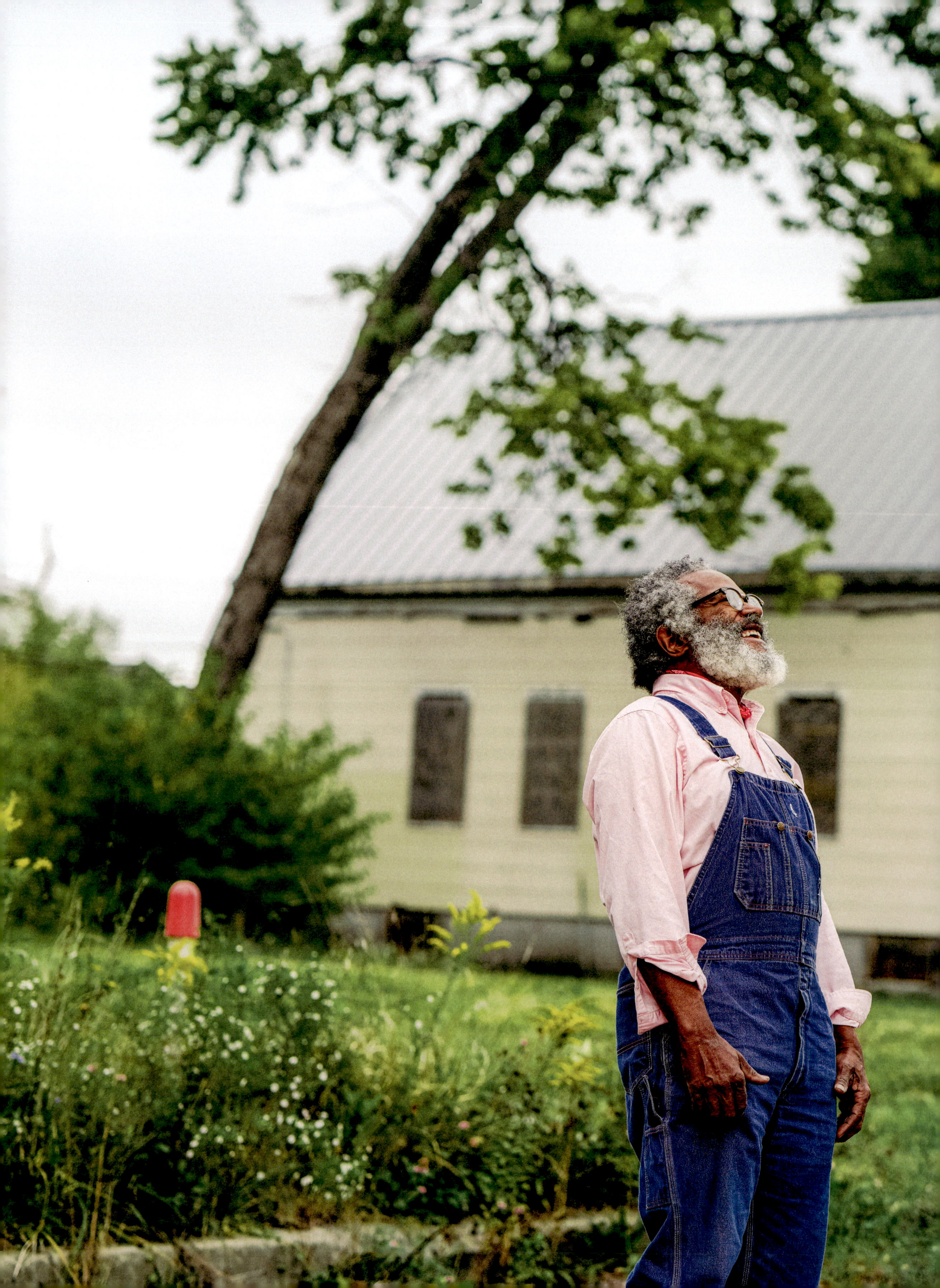

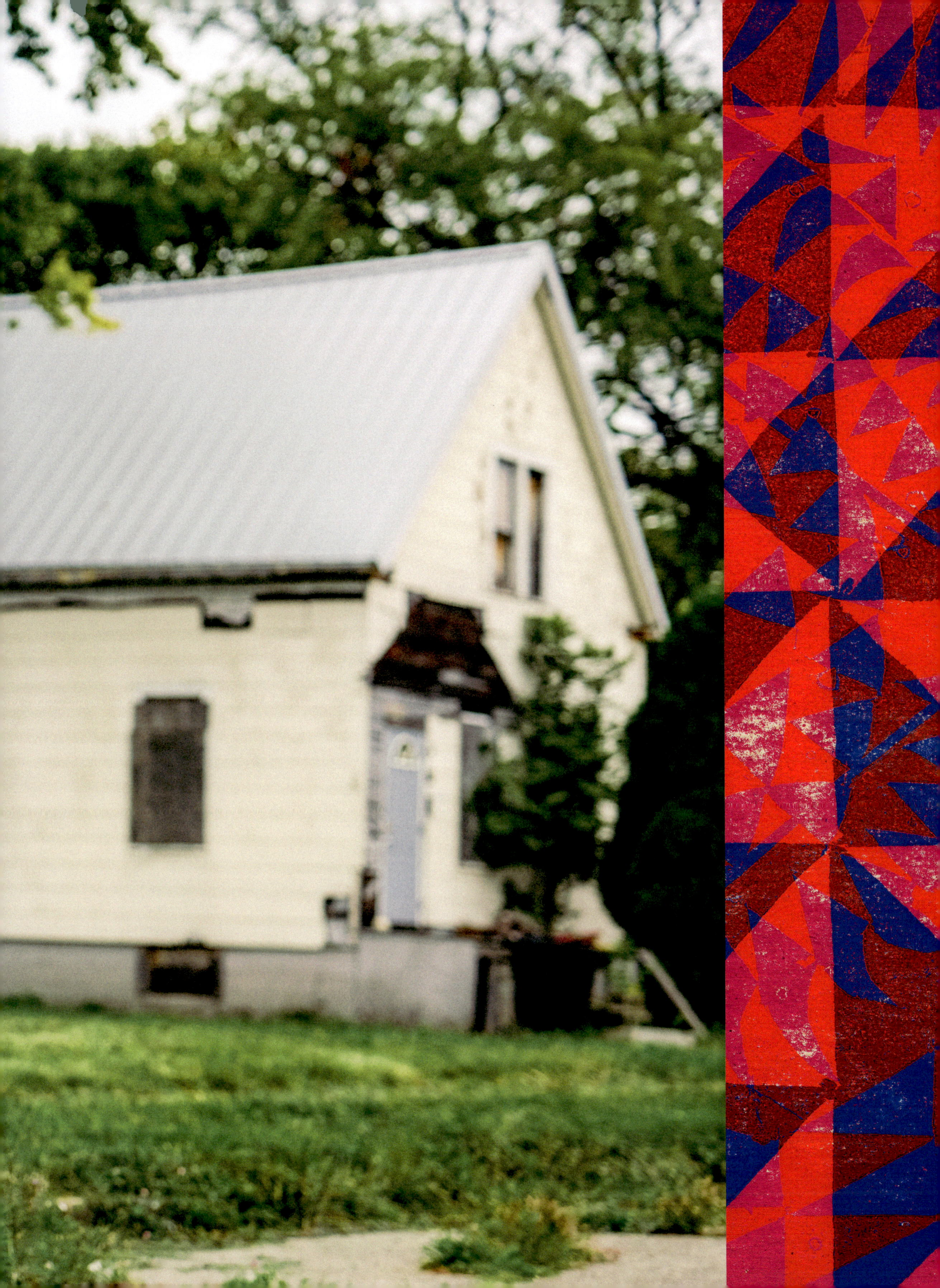

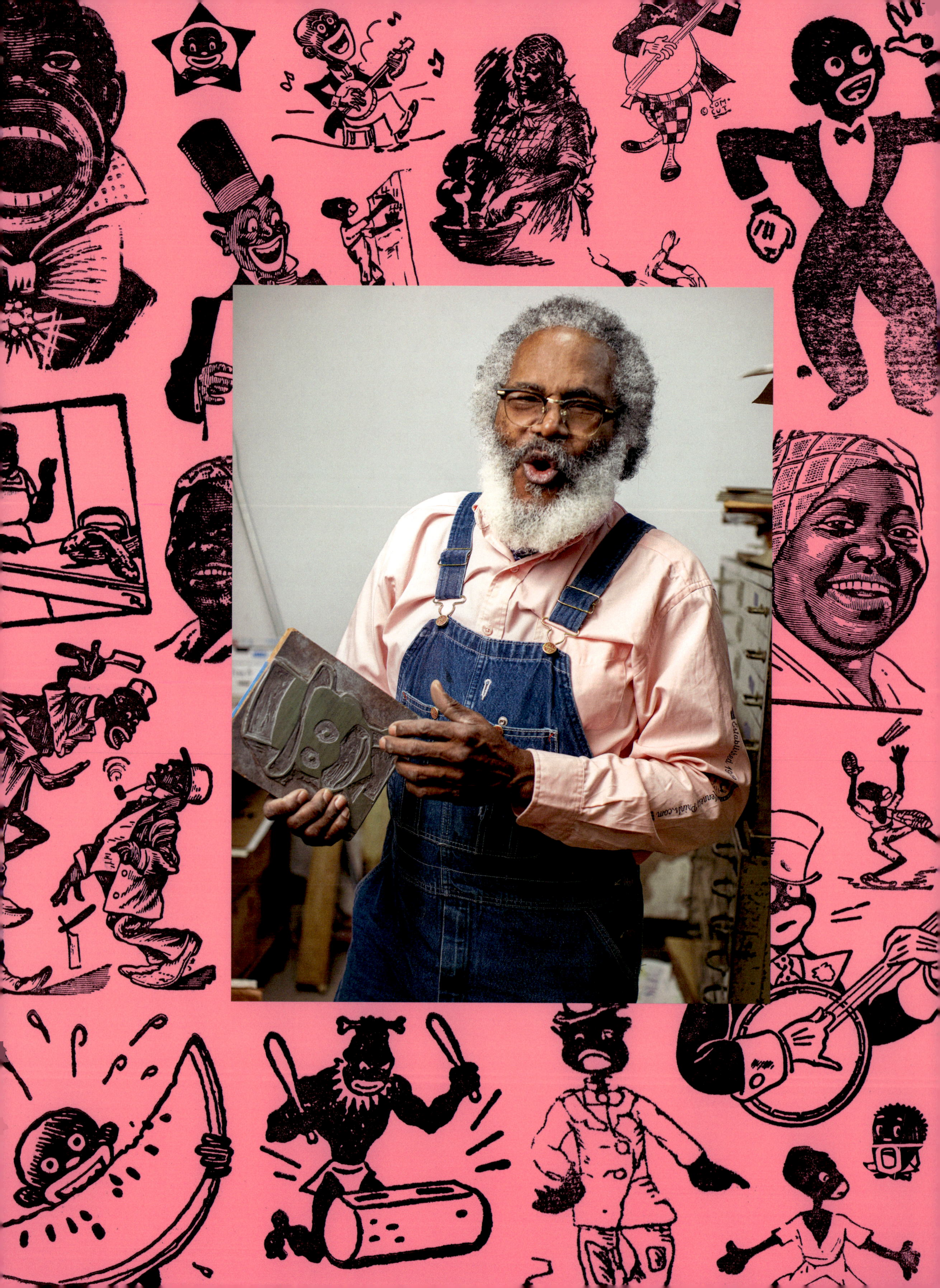

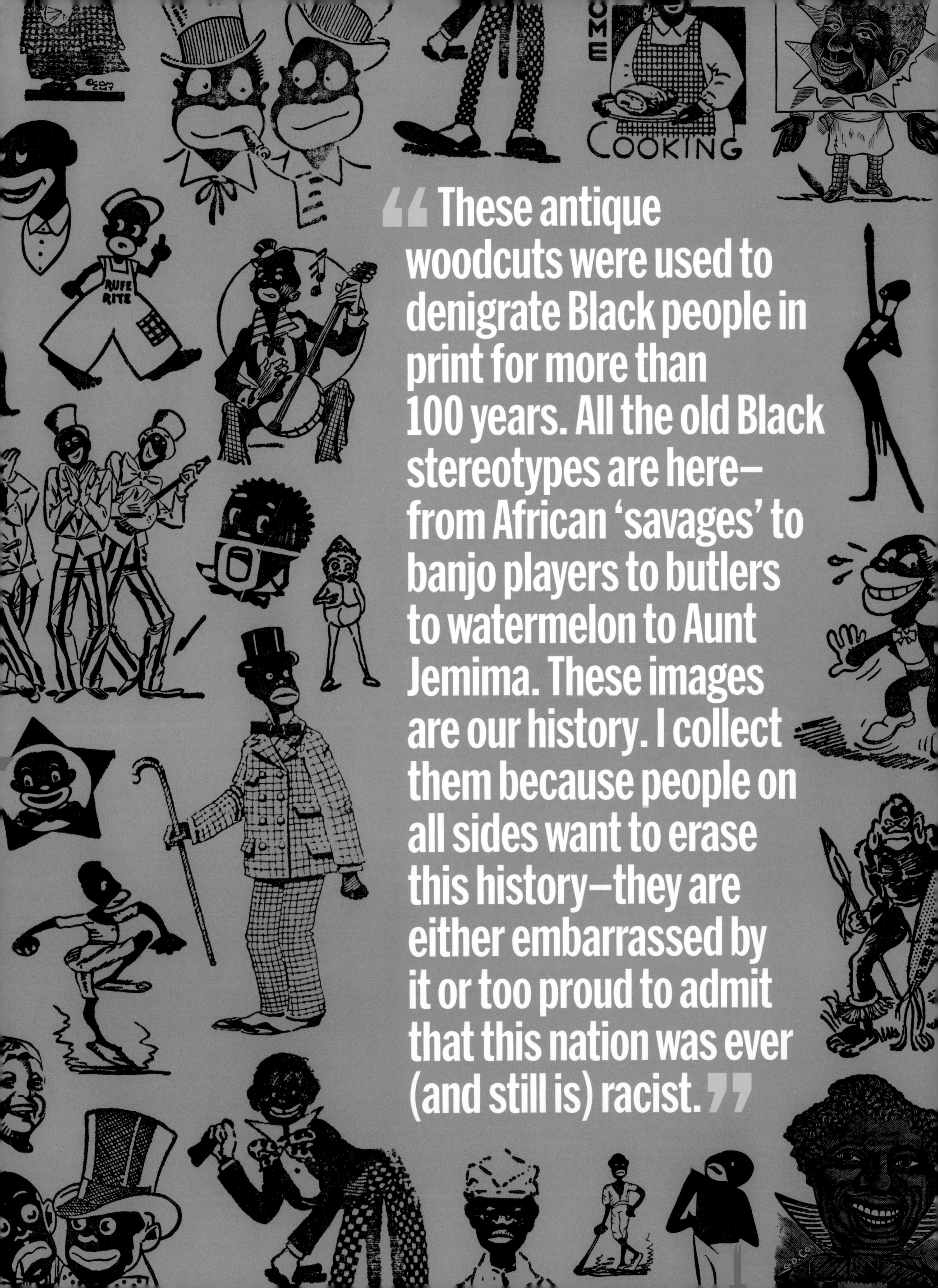

“These antique woodcuts were used to denigrate Black people in print for more than 100 years. All the old Black stereotypes are here—from African ‘savages’ to banjo players to butlers to watermelon to Aunt Jemima. These images are our history. I collect them because people on all sides want to erase this history—they are either embarrassed by it or too proud to admit that this nation was ever (and still is) racist.”

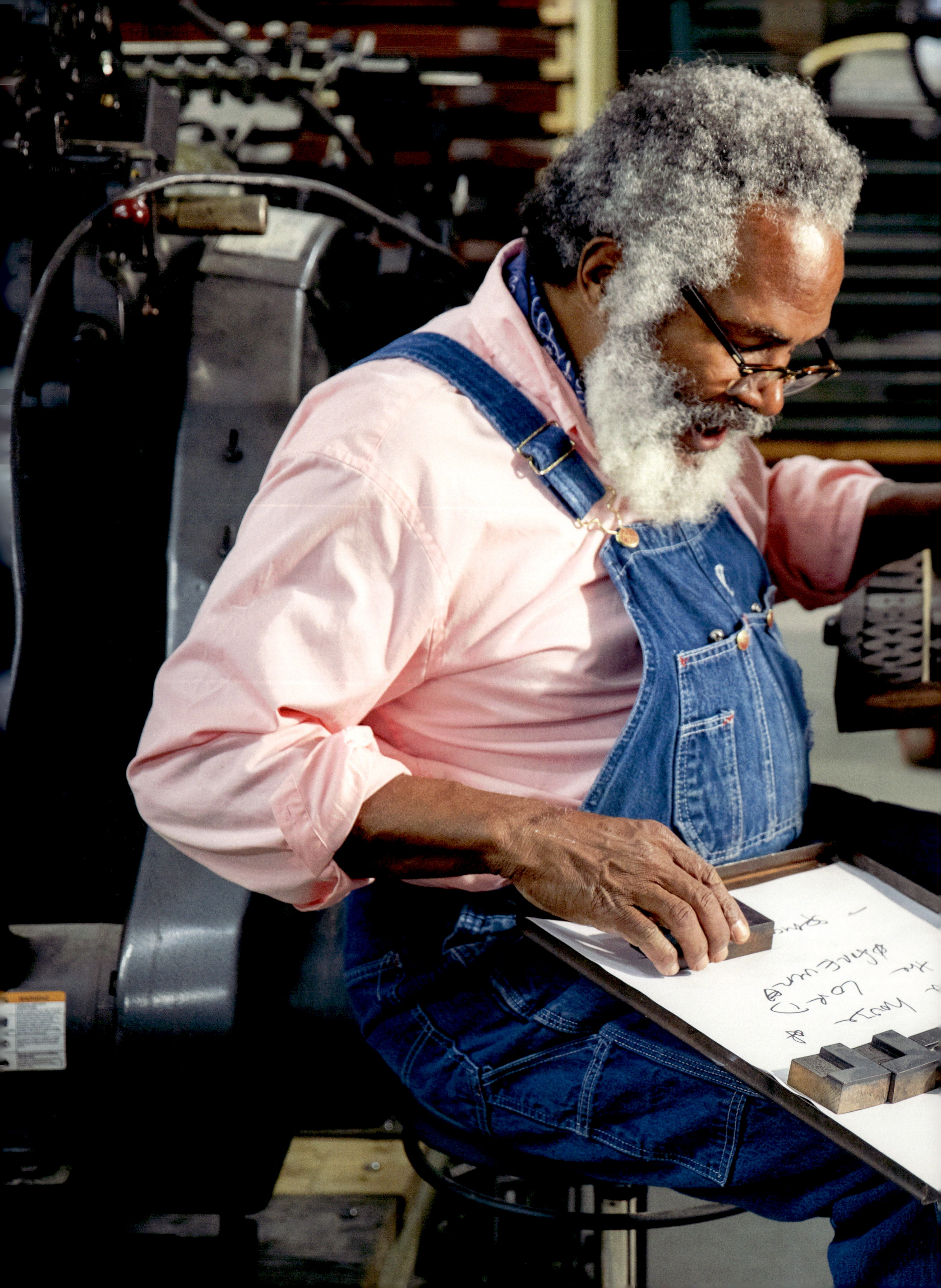

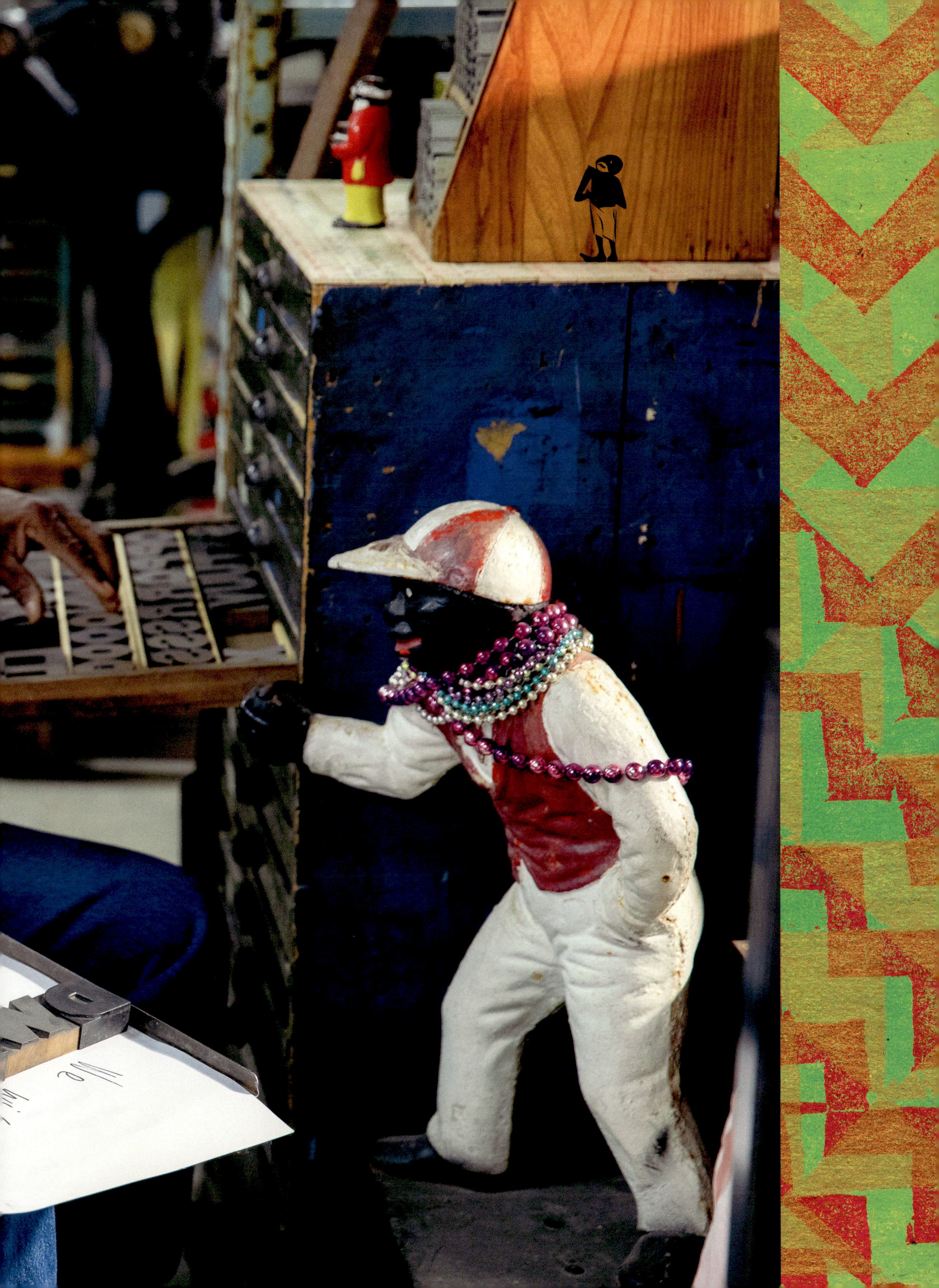

My Secret Sauce (Or My Misunderstanding of What I Do)

0

No two prints should ever be exactly the same! Fight the capitalist scourge of mere duplication. I am not manufacturing. I am PRINTING.

When I do an edition of prints with a multilayered typographic background, I like for each layer to have lots of different type styles and sizes and lots of different colors. So I've come up with this process, which allows for maximum variation—except when I choose to do it in a different way, 'cause this is my printshop, and I do as I please!

STEP 0: HAVE LOTS OF FLAT BACKGROUNDS ON HAND

Before I even start a project, I put together four stacks of paper (1,000 sheets total) with flat backgrounds in four different categories of colors: the three primary colors (red, yellow, and blue) and what I call miscellaneous.

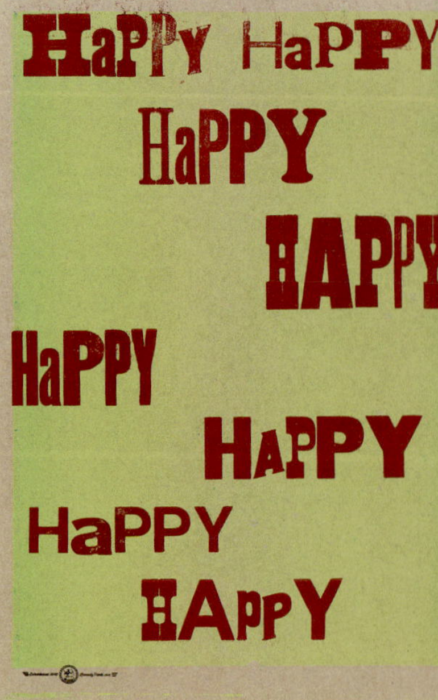

You may be thinking, what about secondary colors, like orange or green? My idea of color is informed by my desire to avoid color theory, so orange backgrounds can go in either the red or yellow stacks, depending on my mood. Green backgrounds can go in either the yellow or blue piles. Are you getting the idea? If not, don't worry. It works for me.

1

Miscellaneous is a grab bag of metallics, or combinations of red, yellow, and blue overprinting each other, or whatever other colors I feel like adding to the pot. Sometimes I throw in patterned backgrounds left over from older jobs, too.

I use a stand-alone rack called a collator to sort the flats so that each color is represented in the four stacks. Now I'm ready to print. Now the magic and/or chaos can begin.

STEP 1: PRINT THE FIRST TYPOGRAPHIC LAYER

Before I print any text for a project, I arrange all the type on separate sheets of plexiglass and stack them so I can see how the individual layers will interact when printed on a single sheet. I do a mix of right- and left-justified text, and I center some, too, so there is ample coverage. I like working a little like a calligrapher, using different-size type to expand or contract a word given what space I have. I also like how using type in various heights and widths makes the letters seem to dance up and down and from side to side. For the first layer of *Always Choose Happy*, I mix serifs with sans serifs, uppercase with lower.

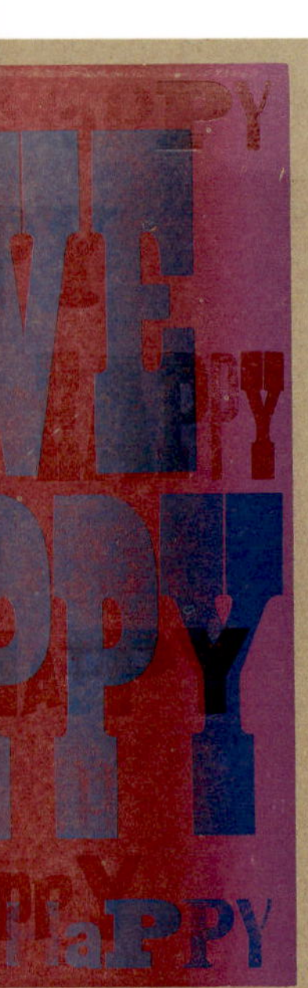

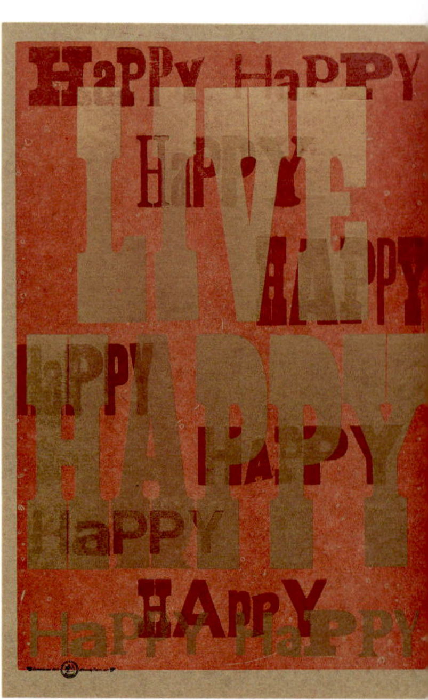

Once I've more or less figured it all out, I transfer the lockup for the first layer to the press and ink the words in the same four categories of colors I used for the flat backgrounds. I don't care if the text stands out, since I'll be adding letters in more colors in the next passes. Again, I sort the prints in the collator, this time so each stack includes all the different background colors and all the different text colors.

2

STEP 2: PRINT THE SECOND TYPOGRAPHIC LAYER

I build up a second layer of words, again using four ink categories. For this step in this particular project, I use a single typeface—a generic Western-style slab serif known as French Clarendon—in one large size, all uppercase letters. I keep sorting the prints the same way to keep a random distribution of color.

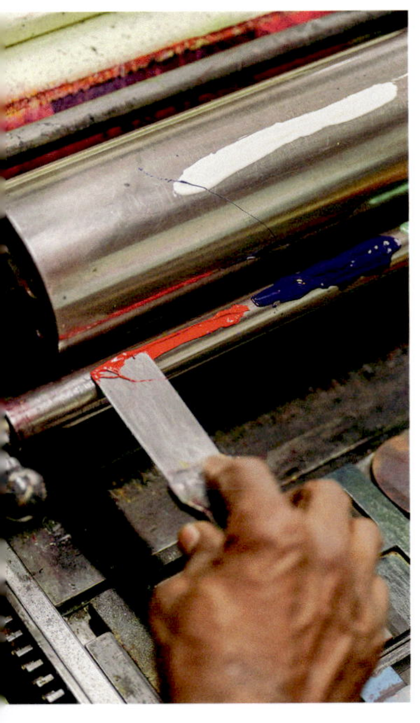

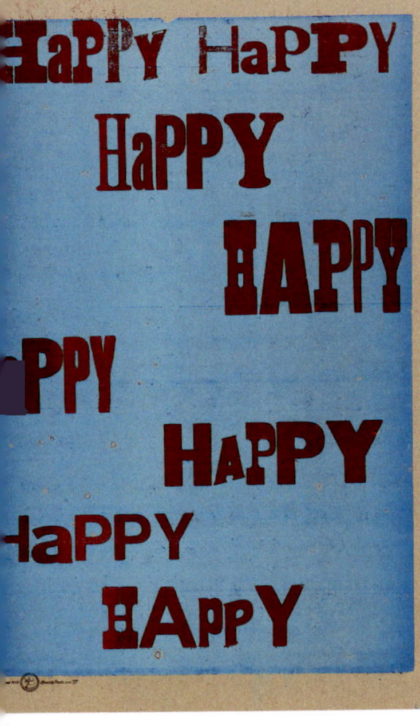
HaPPY HaPPY
HaPPY
HAPPY
HAPPY
HAPPY
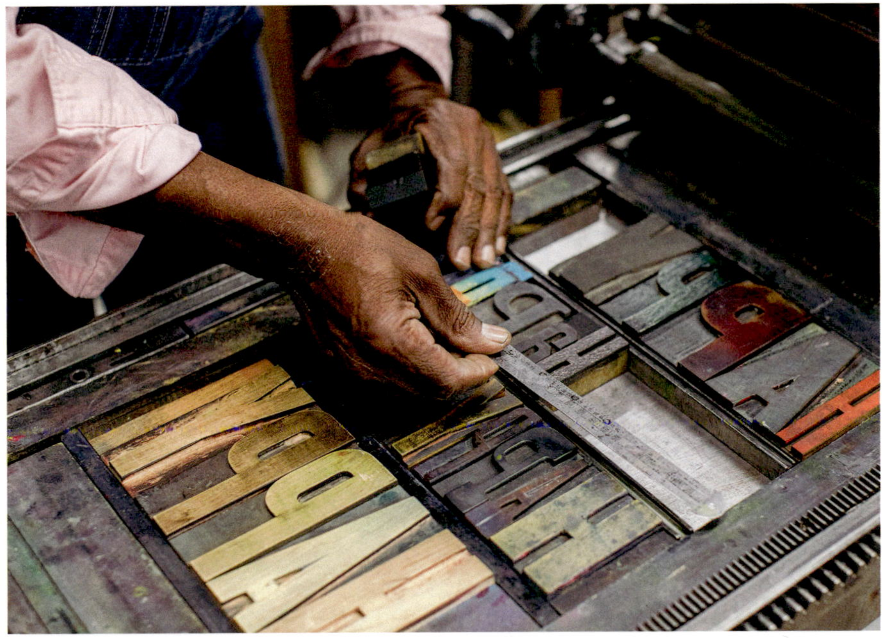
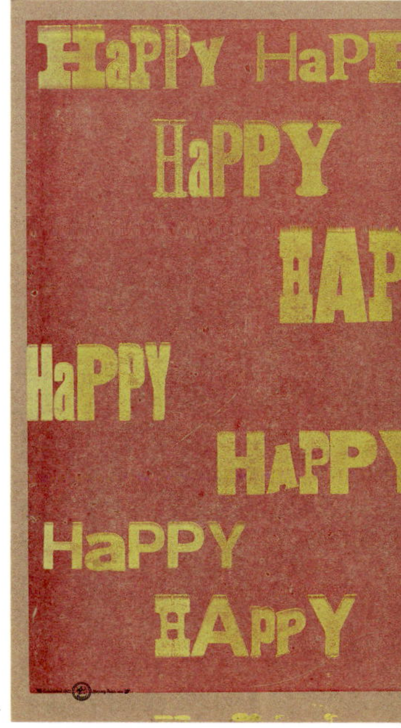
HaPPY
HaPPY
HaPPY
HaPPY
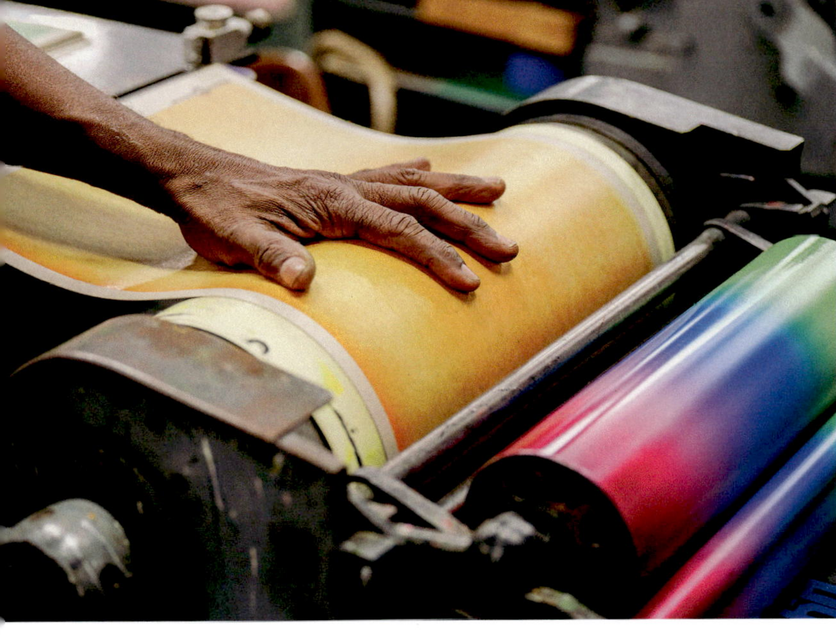
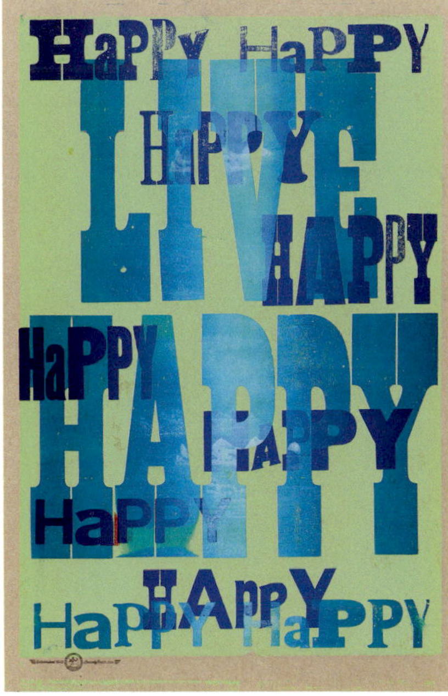
HaPPY HaPPY
LIVE
HAPPY
HaPPY
HAPPY
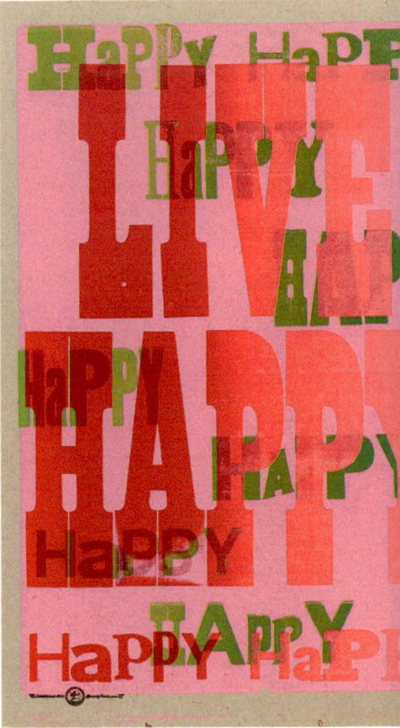
LIVE

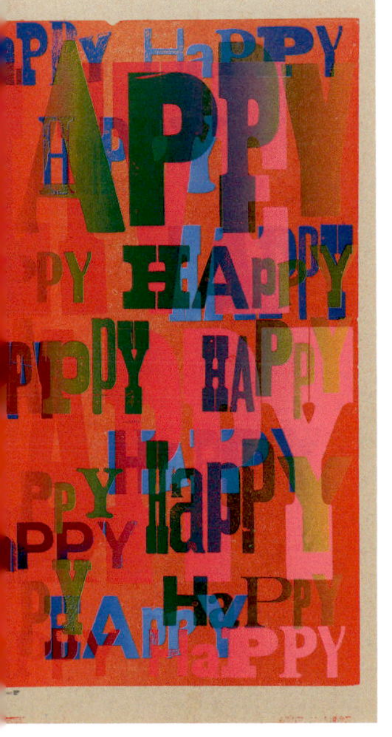

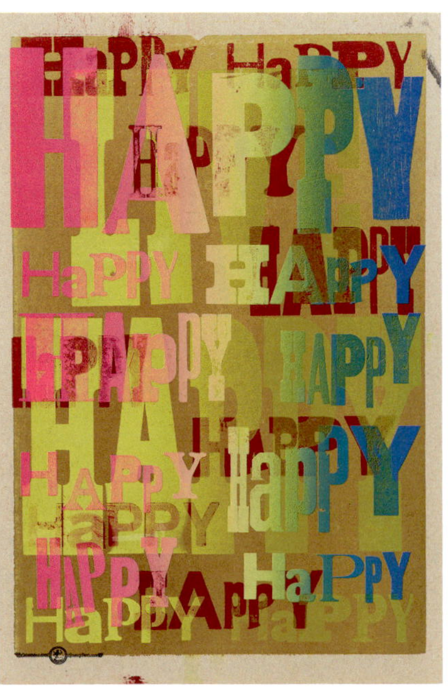
HAPPY

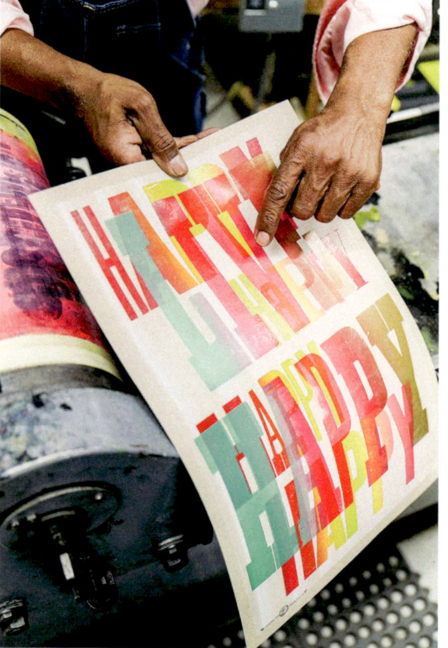

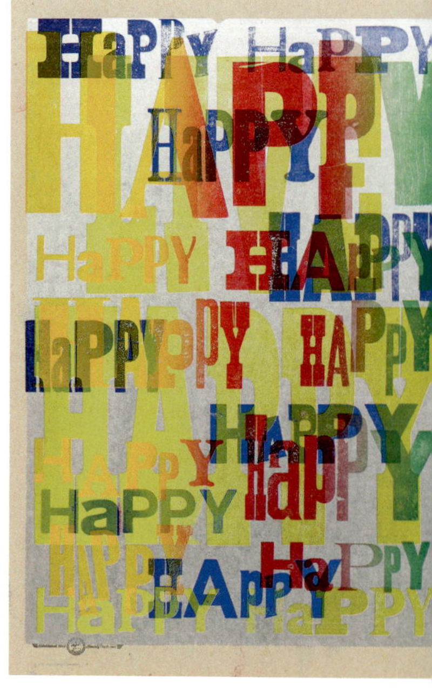
HAPPY

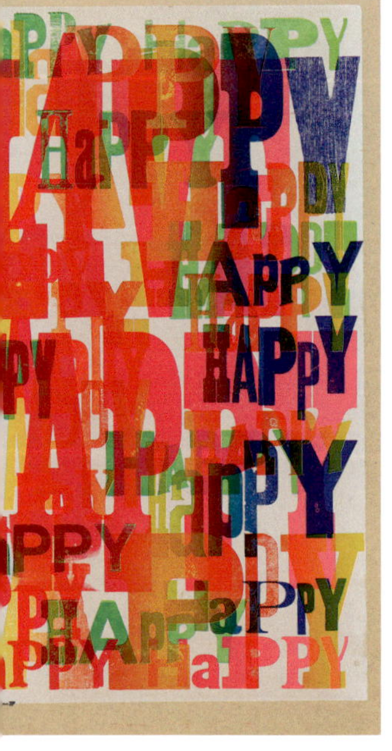

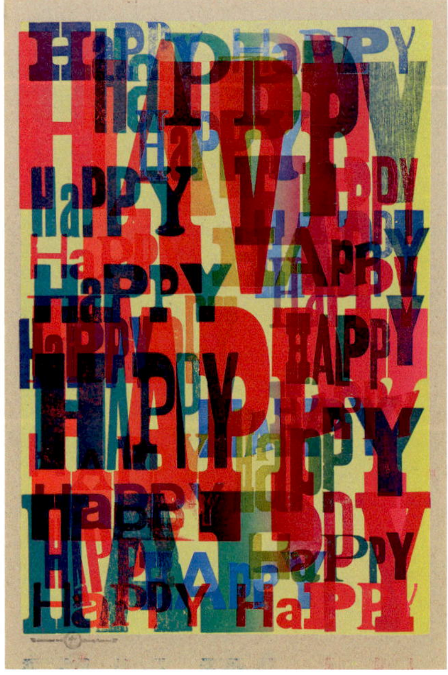

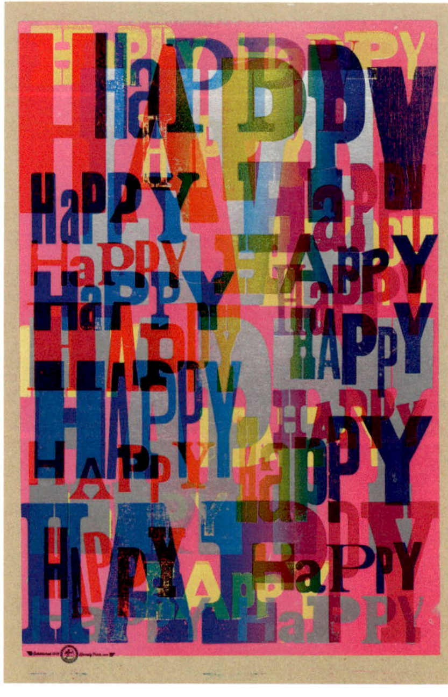

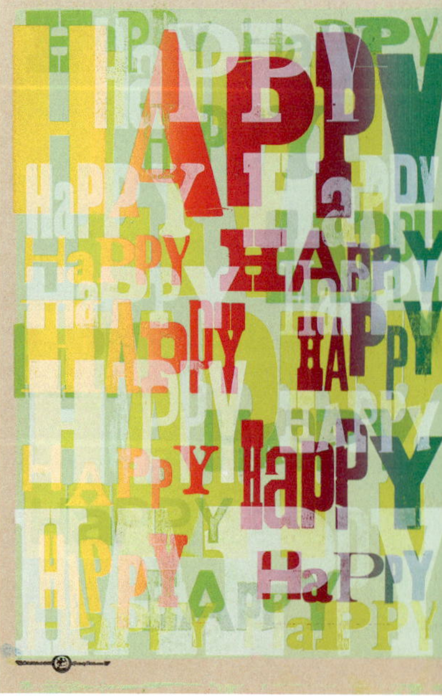

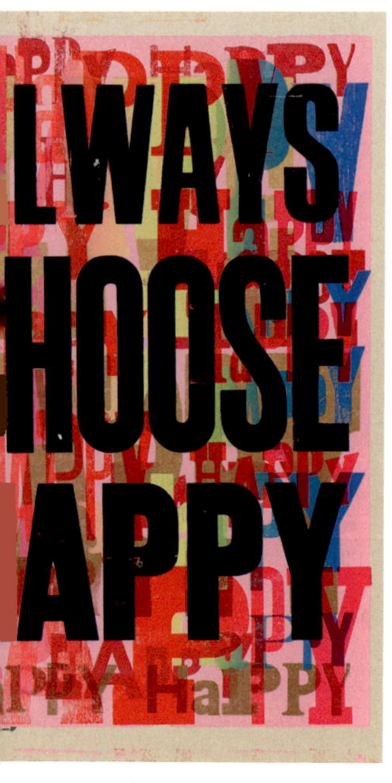
LWAYS
HOOSE
APPY

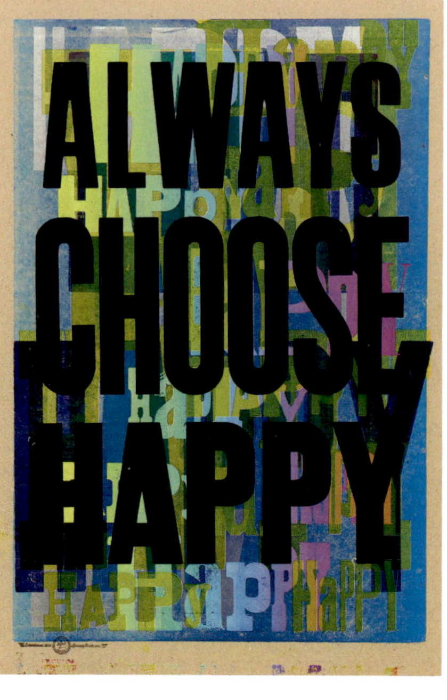
ALWAYS
CHOOSE
HAPPY

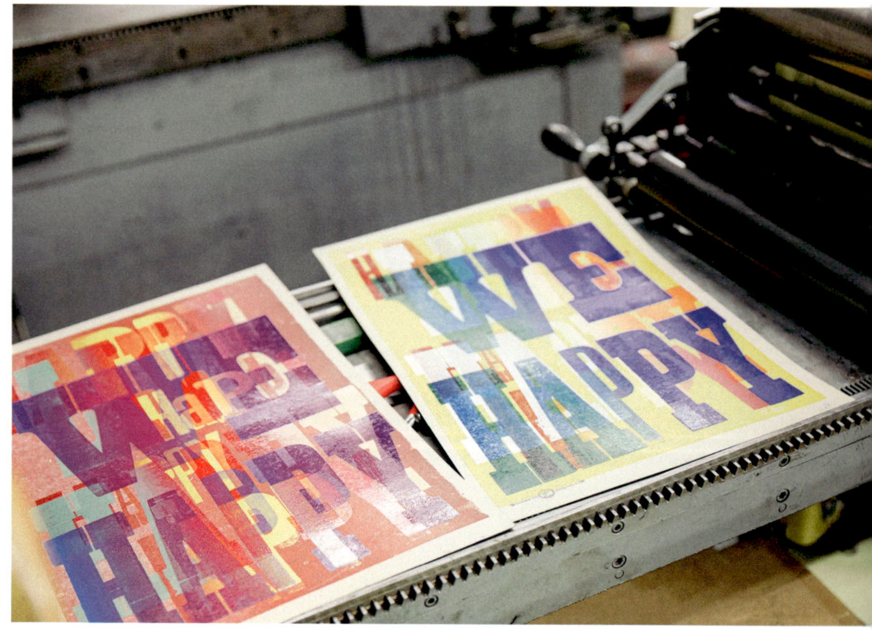

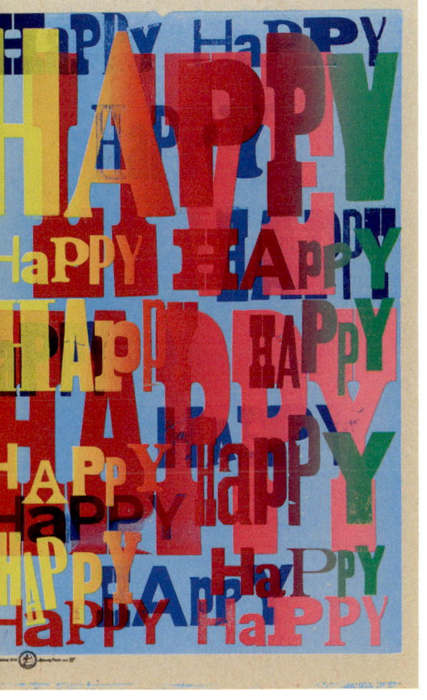

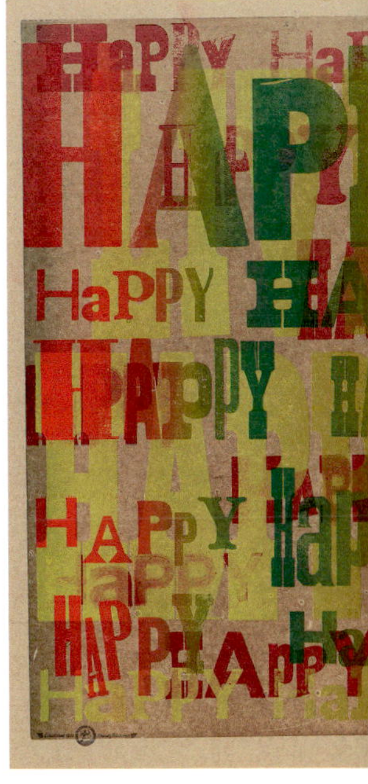

3

STEP 3: PRINT THE THIRD TYPOGRAPHIC LAYER

I do a third layer of "happy," again in many typefaces and sizes so y'all don't get bored with me. I create color gradients using split fountain printing so the type shifts in hue, going from yellow to red to green. I keep mixing the stacks as I go.

STEP 4: PRINT THE FOURTH TYPOGRAPHIC LAYER

I do a fourth layer. I go for maximum coverage of the sheet. It's getting real dense and loud, just the way I like it.

STEP 5: PRINT THE MAIN TEXT

It's time for the main message on top. I do this in black in real big type so folks can make it out. In my work, the image is the positioning of the text on the page. What kind of shape does it make? What is the hierarchy of the words? Usually I center and justify the main message, just like the signs I saw when I was first printing in the South.

Sometimes I work fast and don't wait for a print to dry, so some of the ink gets pulled away. Other times I might let a letter show through and intersect awkwardly with the text on the layer above. But someone is going to love those details.

A designer would fix these faults, and that is why I am not a designer. I disregard a lot of the rules of graphic design. (Let's just say I didn't see much of the Swiss influence down in Alabama.) I prefer the imperfections—the mark of the maker is the most beautiful thing to me. But I am also not an artist. What I do is not an exclusive art. It is PRINTING. But if you give me $20, you can call it what you want!

(You may be wondering, why "Always choose happy"? Happiness is a state of mind that you can make for yourself—that you can will yourself into. Not one that is merely giddy, but one that is reflective and meditative, like that which I experience in the printshop. For when I print, I am truly GALLIVANTING, and I hope that the joy I experience printing gets infused into the printed matter itself, and radiates out wherever that print goes to live.)

4

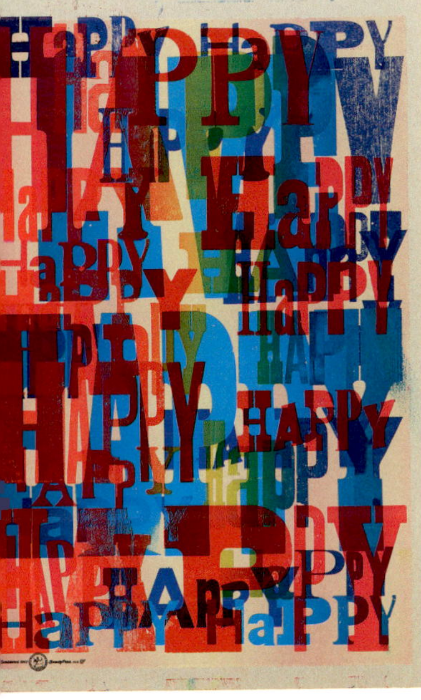

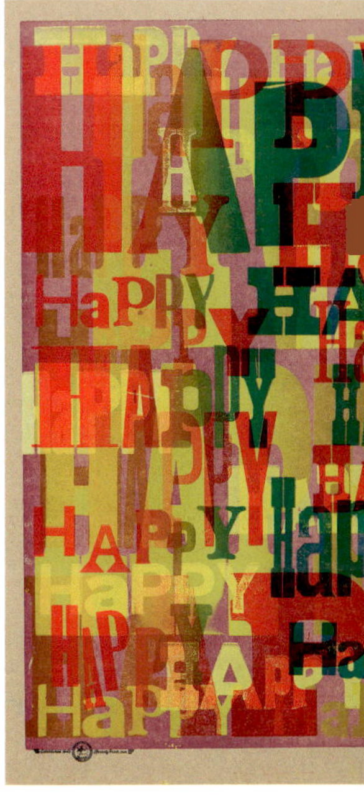

The truth be told, I don't know what I am doing. But I sure enuff enjoy doing it.

5

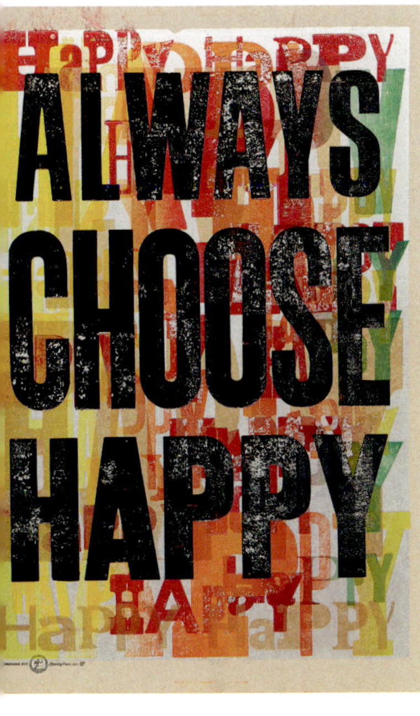

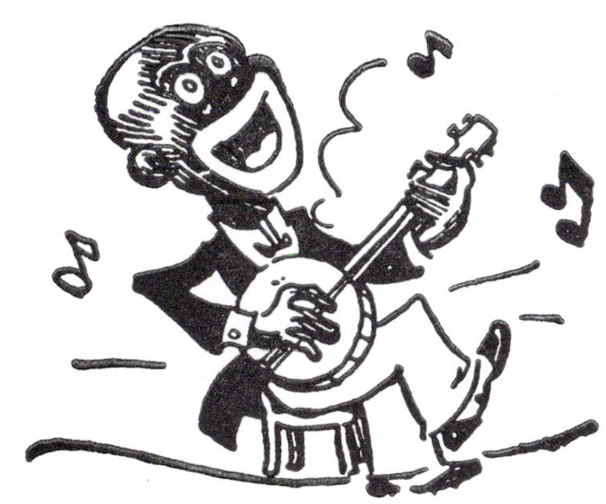

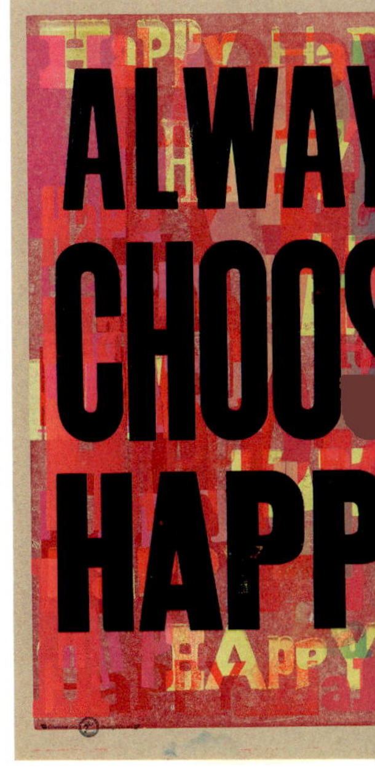

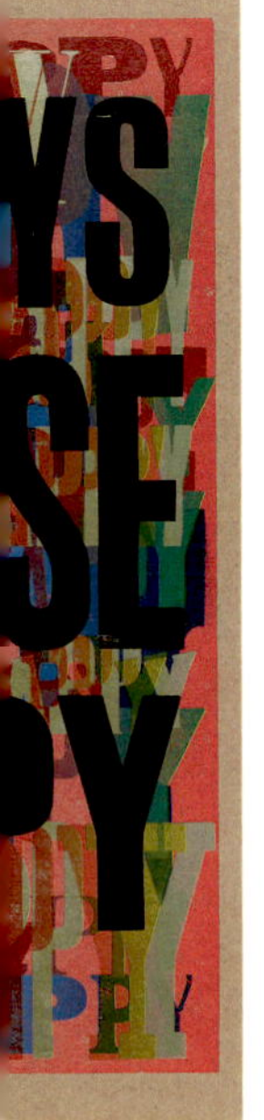
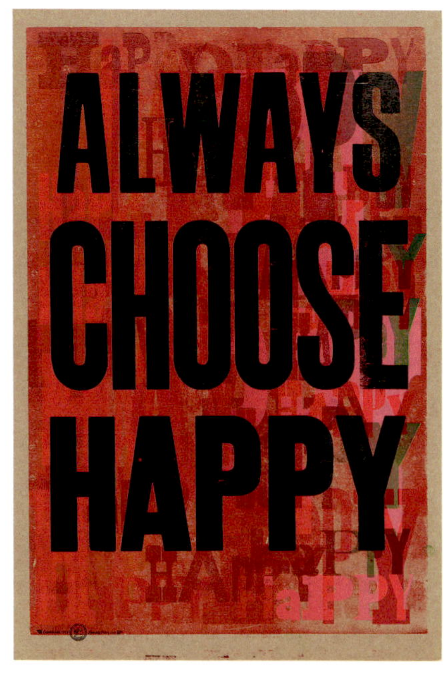
ALWAYS
CHOOSE
HAPPY
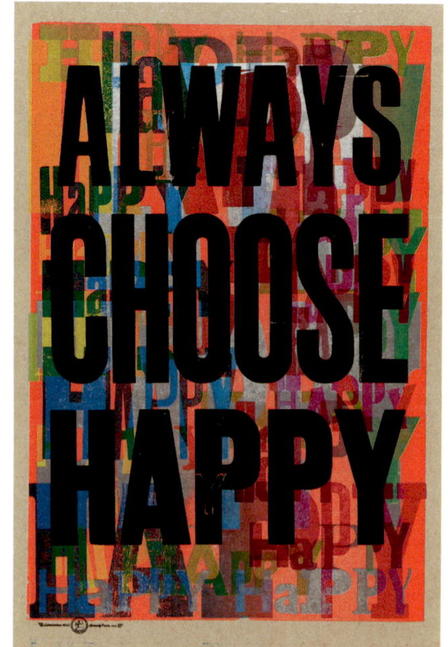
ALWAYS
CHOOSE
HAPPY
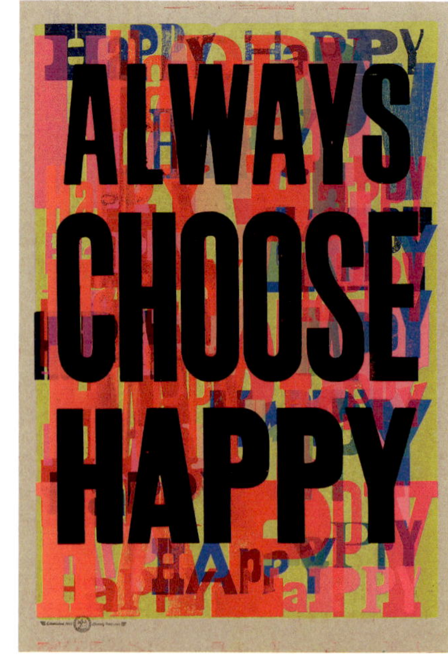
ALWAYS
CHOOSE
HAPPY
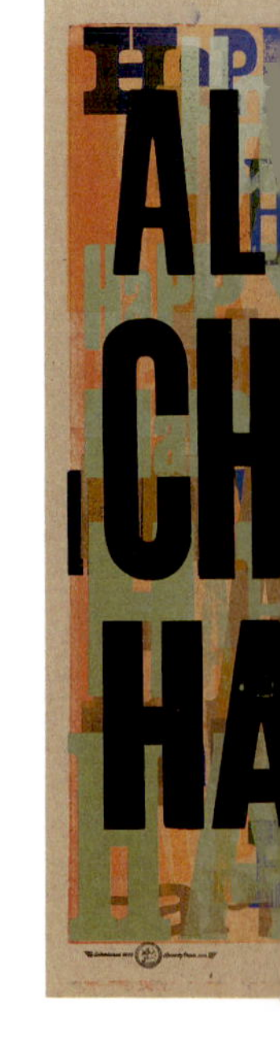
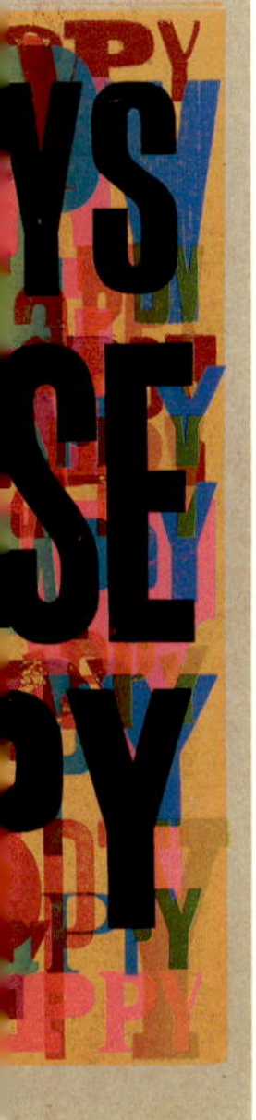
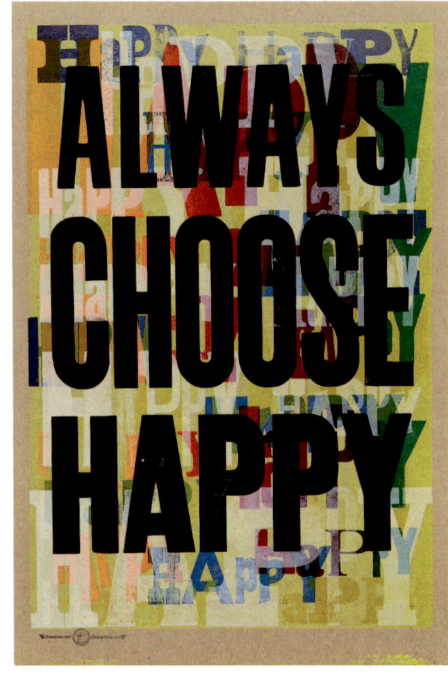
ALWAYS
CHOOSE
HAPPY
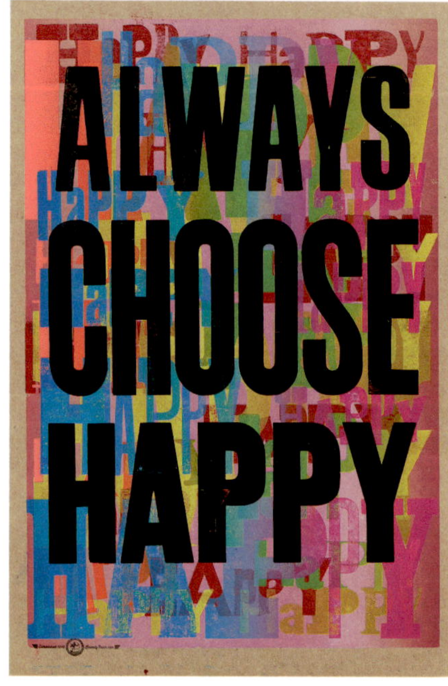
ALWAYS
CHOOSE
HAPPY
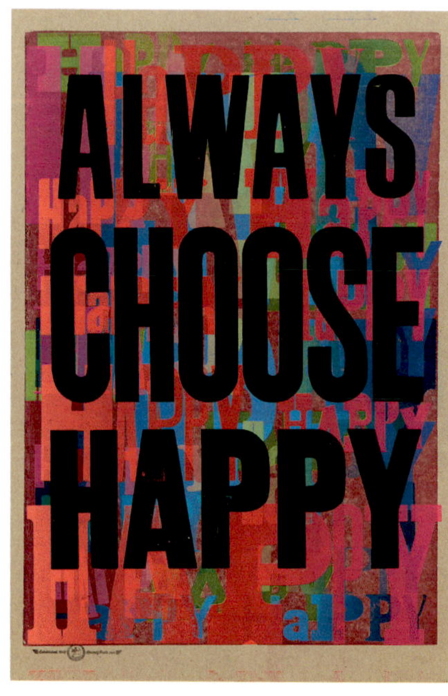
ALWAYS
CHOOSE
HAPPY
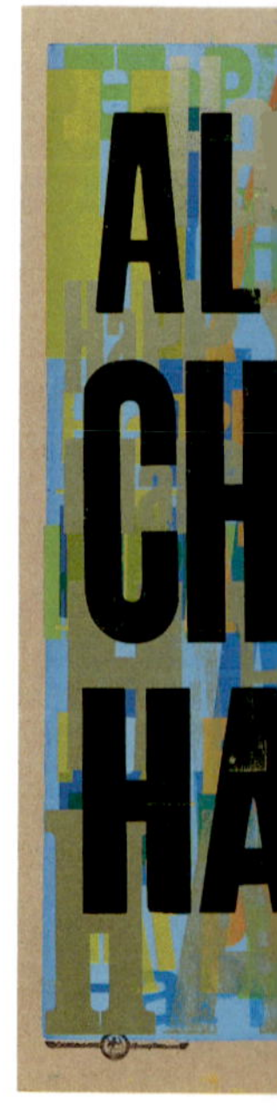
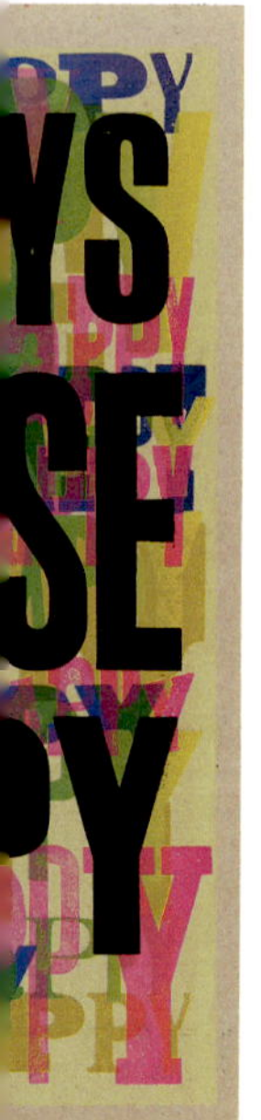
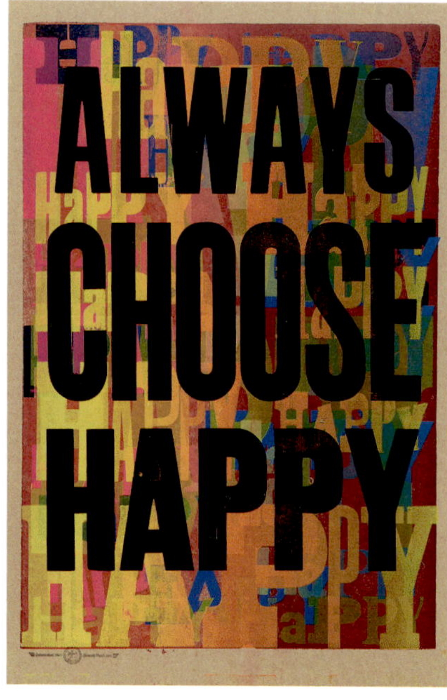
ALWAYS
CHOOSE
HAPPY
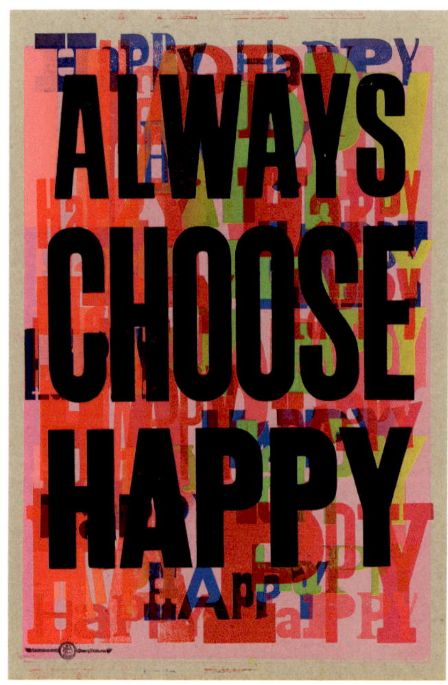
ALWAYS
CHOOSE
HAPPY
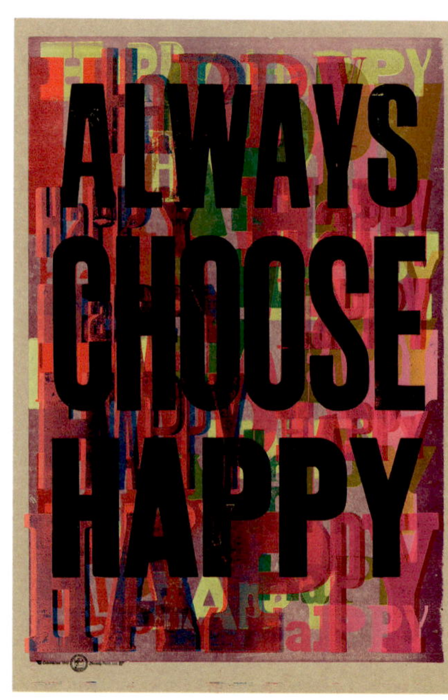
ALWAYS
CHOOSE
HAPPY
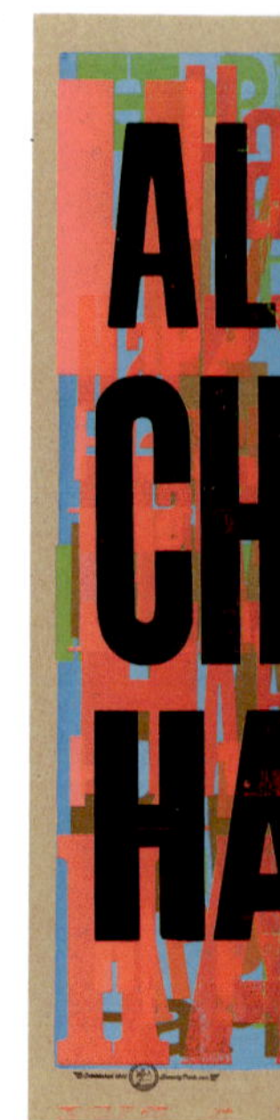

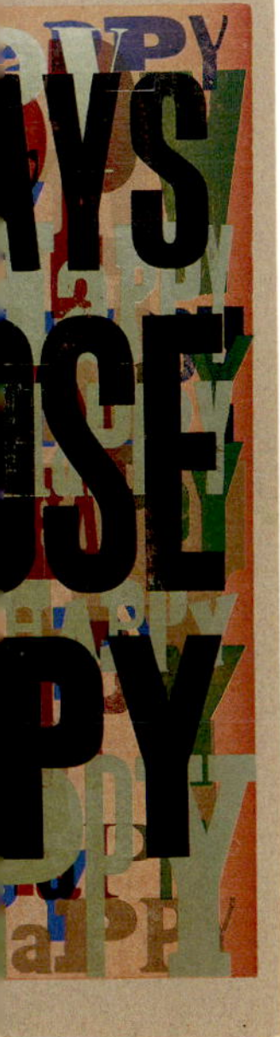

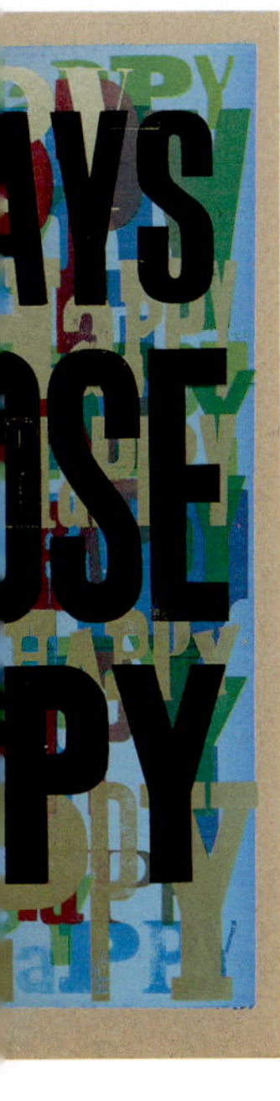

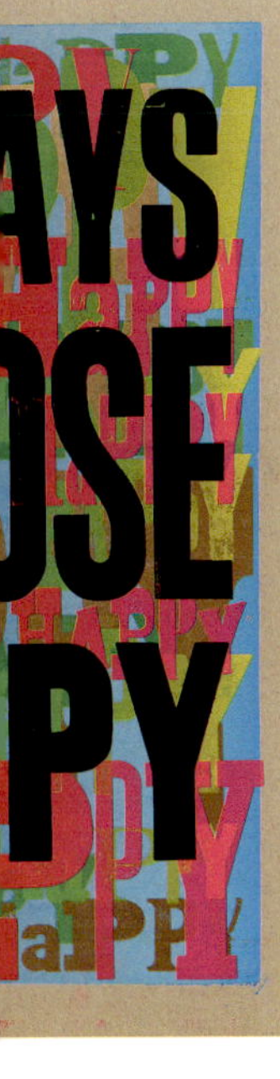

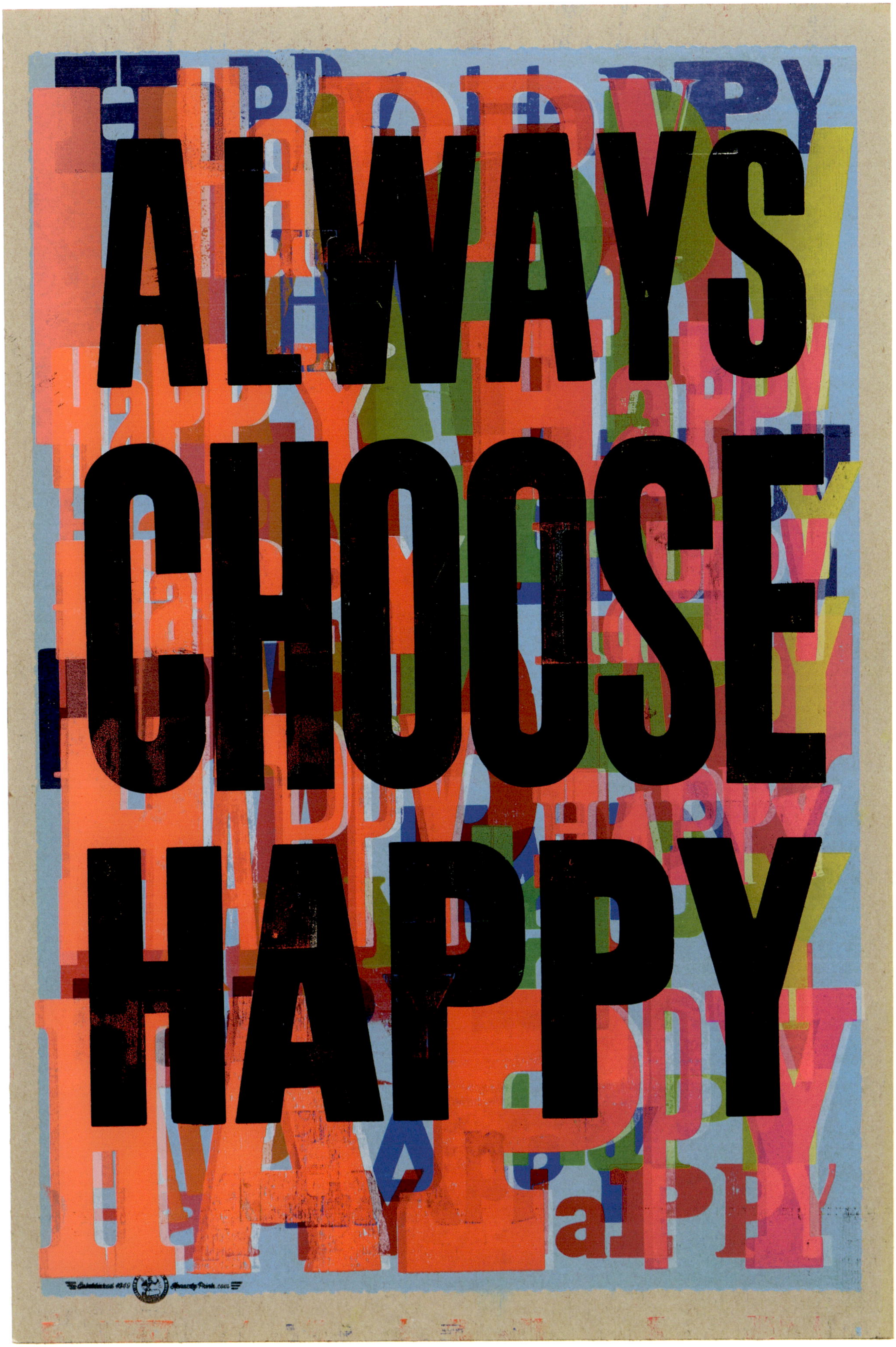

ALWAYS
CHOOSE
HAPPY

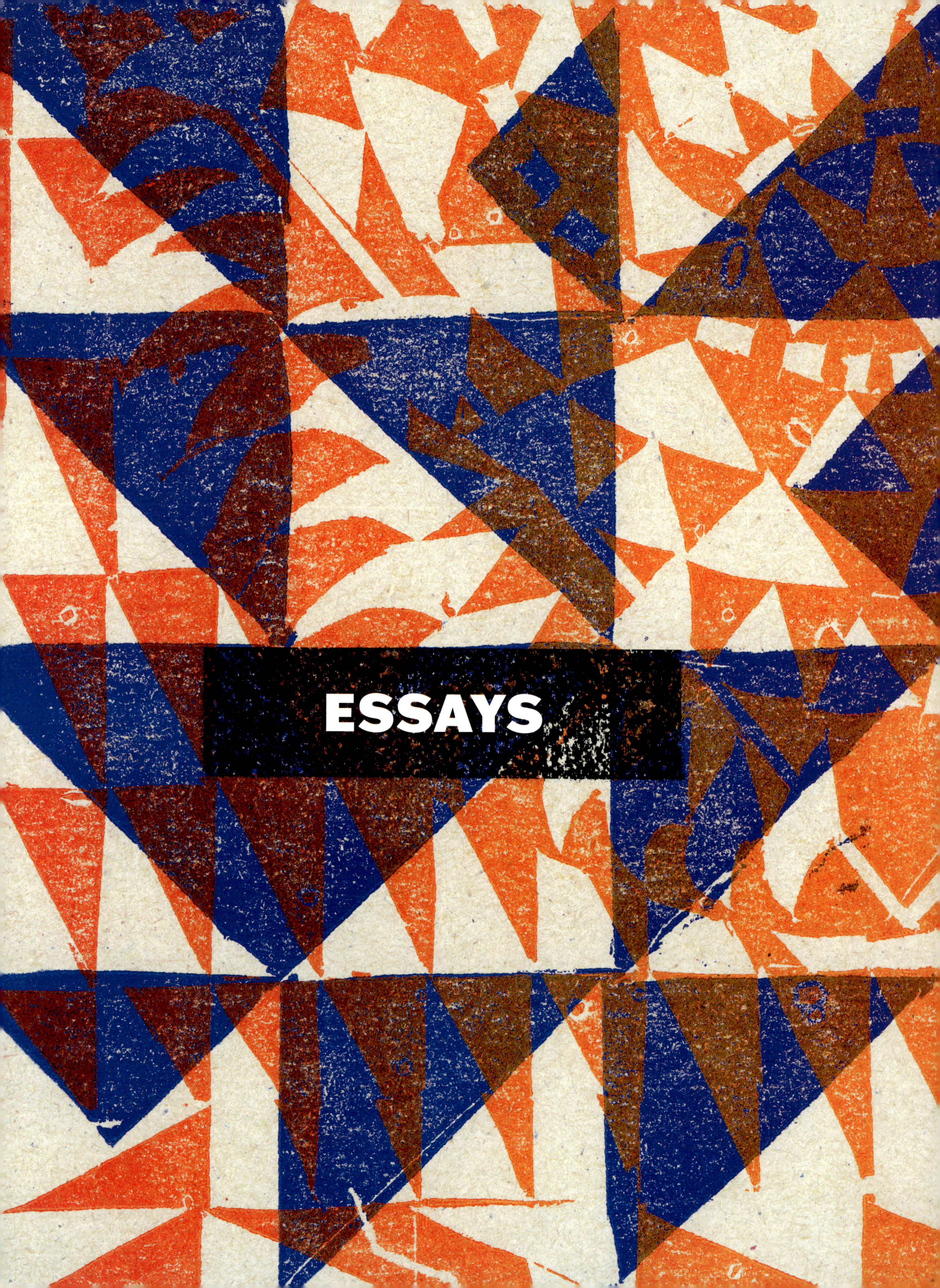
ESSAYS

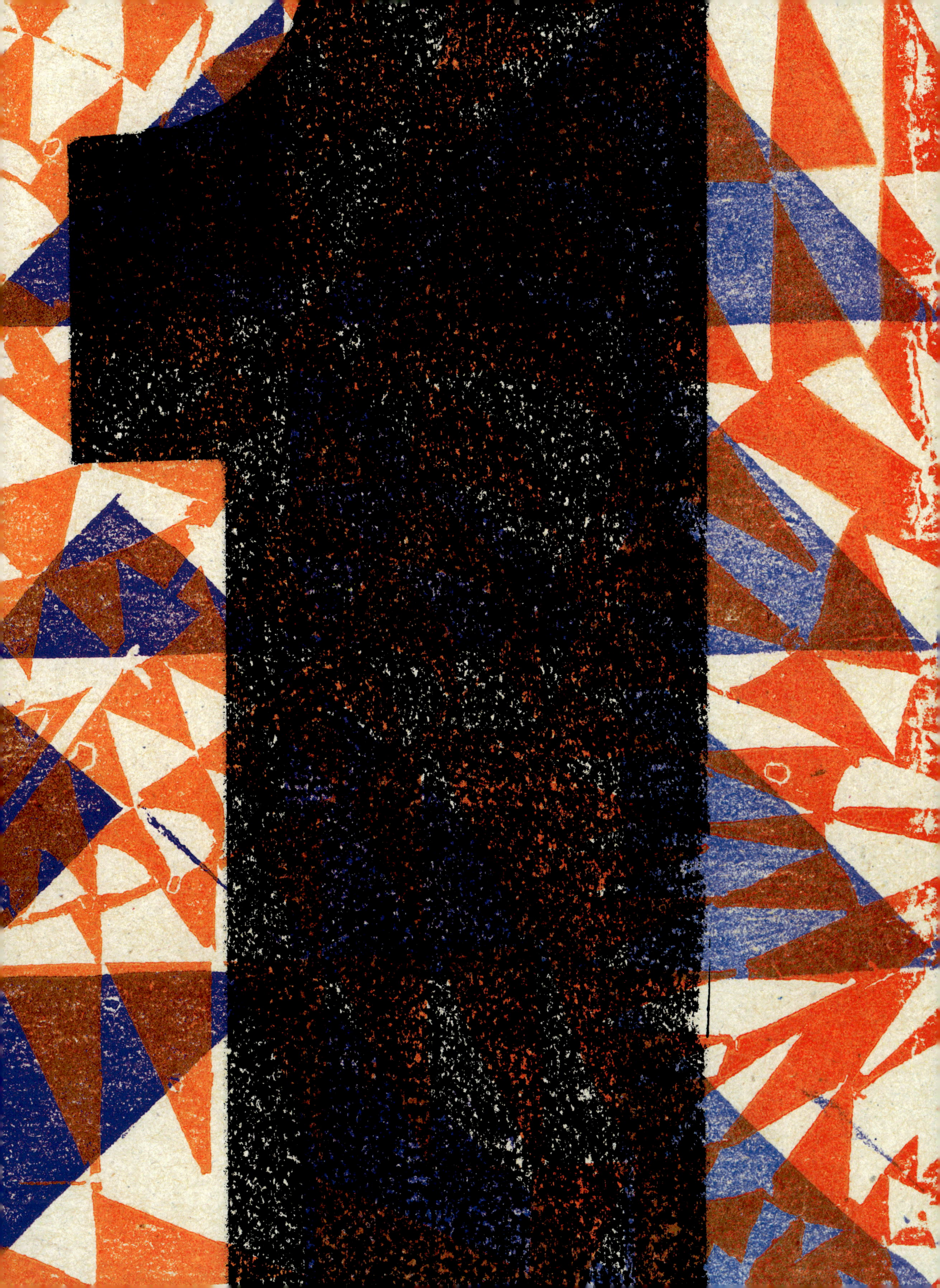

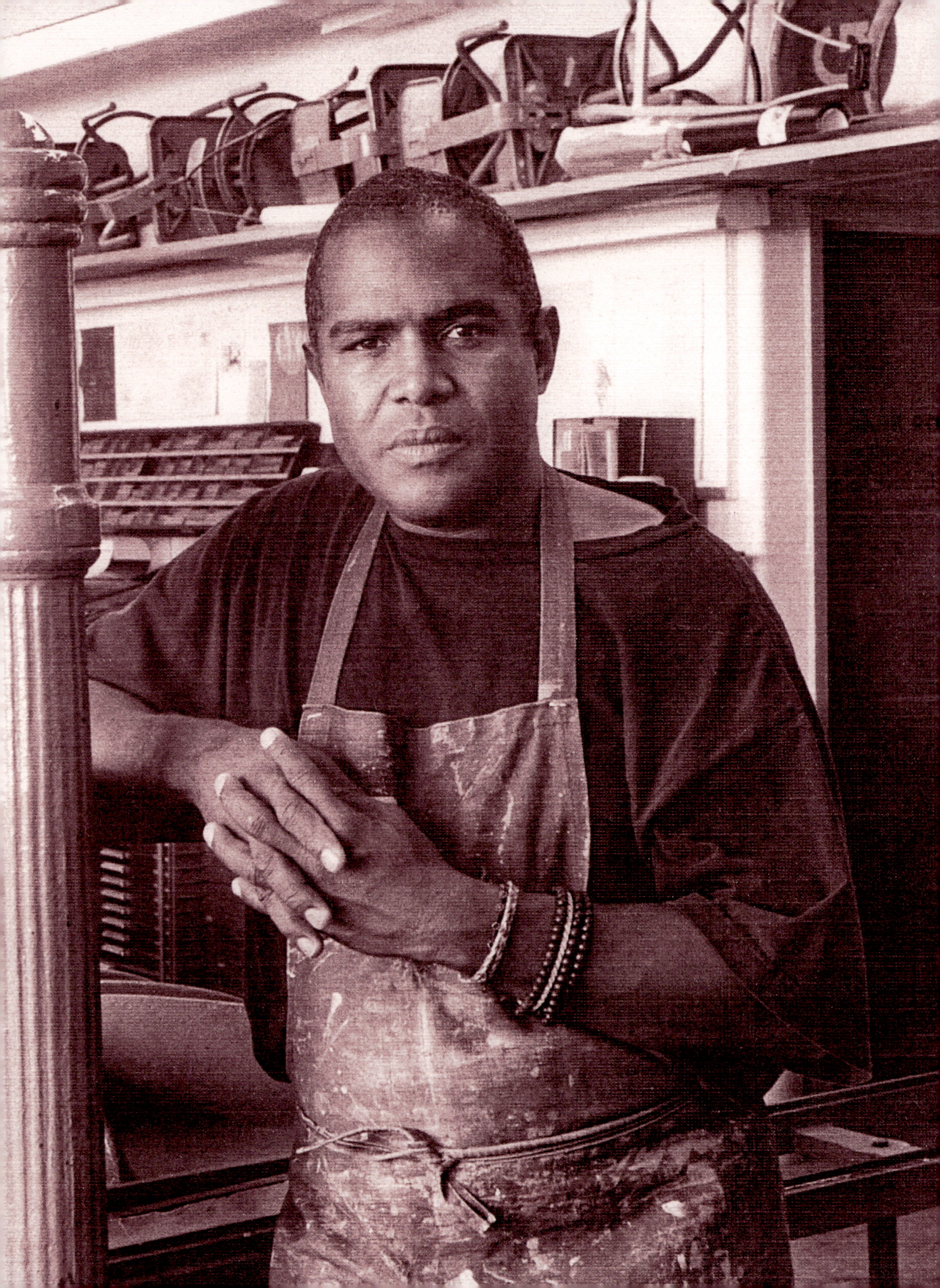

Incorrigible Disturber of the Peace! INK & EQUITY!

by **MYRON M. BEASLEY**

The artist is distinguished from all other responsible actors in society—the politicians, legislators, educators, and scientists—by the fact that he is his own test tube, his own laboratory, working according to very rigorous rules, however unstated these may be, and cannot allow any consideration to supersede his responsibility to reveal all that he can possibly discover concerning the mystery of the human being.

—JAMES BALDWIN, "The Creative Process," 1962

I've always considered myself a social printer, a social activist with a press, whatever you want to call it. I always considered myself as not printing to be pretty. And I like [a saying I overhead one of my students repeat]: "Put the message in the hands of the people and move on." Because the message is more important than putting another brass spacing in the lockup to get just the right look.

—AMOS PAUL KENNEDY, JR., University of Wisconsin–Madison Oral History Program, 2018

LEFT Kennedy in the Indiana University printshop, circa 1998, Bloomington, Indiana.

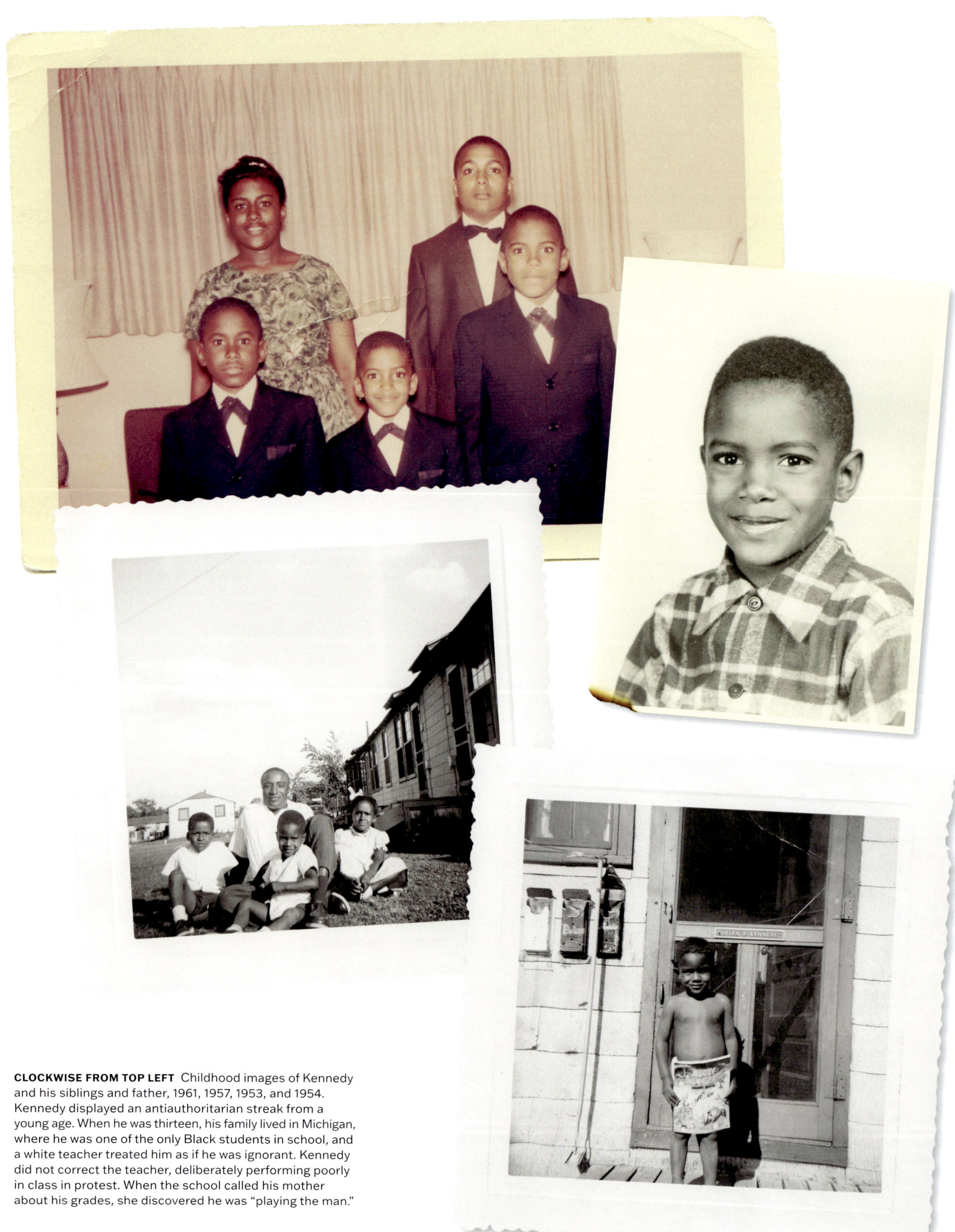

CLOCKWISE FROM TOP LEFT Childhood images of Kennedy and his siblings and father, 1961, 1957, 1953, and 1954. Kennedy displayed an antiauthoritarian streak from a young age. When he was thirteen, his family lived in Michigan, where he was one of the only Black students in school, and a white teacher treated him as if he was ignorant. Kennedy did not correct the teacher, deliberately performing poorly in class in protest. When the school called his mother about his grades, she discovered he was "playing the man."

BELOW, LEFT TO RIGHT
Amos Paul Kennedy, Jr., *Artists Make Lousy Slaves*, after 2012, letterpress on chipboard, 8 × 6 inches (20.25 × 15.25 cm), Detroit. Kennedy presents the sleeve of his custom Kennedy Prints! shirt, which features an antique woodcut of an African playing a drum. With typical Kennedy humor, the sleeve also reads "Established 1949"—the year he was conceived, not born.

In his charge to artists in an essay on the creative practice, Black author and civil rights figure James Baldwin reminds us of the purpose of the artist. The production of art is essentially a record of what it means to be human—in Baldwin's words, it is a revelation of "all that [the artist] can possibly discover concerning the mystery of the human being."[1] Artists are distinguished from other actors in society because they are endowed with the gift of archiving the here and now to guide us into the future.

Amos Paul Kennedy, Jr., accomplished printer and book builder, is an artist of a coming time. Like the prophet Amos of the Hebrew Bible, he uses his rhetorical eloquence and embodied performance to sound the alarm for social justice.[2] The term *performance* here refers to Amos's unique expression of his reflections on everyday life, not an assumed theatricality. Kennedy is like the *griot*, the revered position in many African communities: a keeper of history, a holder of knowledge, and a masterful storyteller. While griots' performances are often wrapped in humor, they are also sharp and even cynical, as griots reveal and speak the truth.[3]

I first met Kennedy in 2007 at the Vespine Gallery on South Halsted in Chicago, where I purchased journals he had crafted by hand, with covers made from cardboard food packaging and pages from Italian straw paper. He had just returned from a seminal trip to Italy, where he met with Alberto Casiraghi, a prolific publisher of artists' books sold at remarkably egalitarian prices.[4] Casiraghi's modest yet prodigious approach affirmed Kennedy's personal philosophy of working swiftly to disseminate information, as expressed in one of his many catchphrases: "Put the message in the hands of the people and move on."

By the time we met in Chicago, Kennedy had begun wearing his now infamous uniform of denim overalls and a pink long-sleeved shirt—garments that pay homage to the civil rights movement, with the denim overalls representing the working class (and, for some, Black sharecroppers of an earlier era) and the pink shirt referencing the dandyism of social justice activists.[5] I recall a reserve and coyness about him, but his work spoke loudly and without apology.

Real performance art is troubling, messy, and significant. Through his printed matter, Kennedy expresses a civil commitment and documents the community in ways that exemplify Baldwin's charge: The artist's role is to disturb the peace.

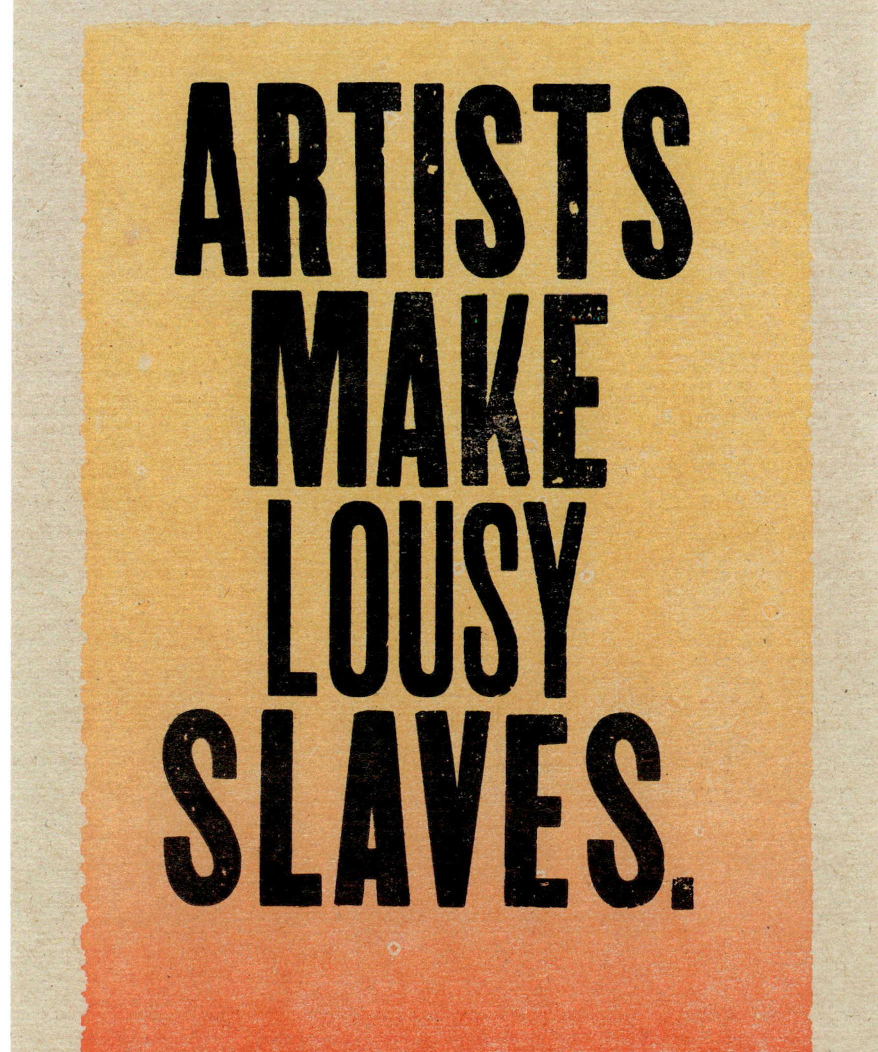

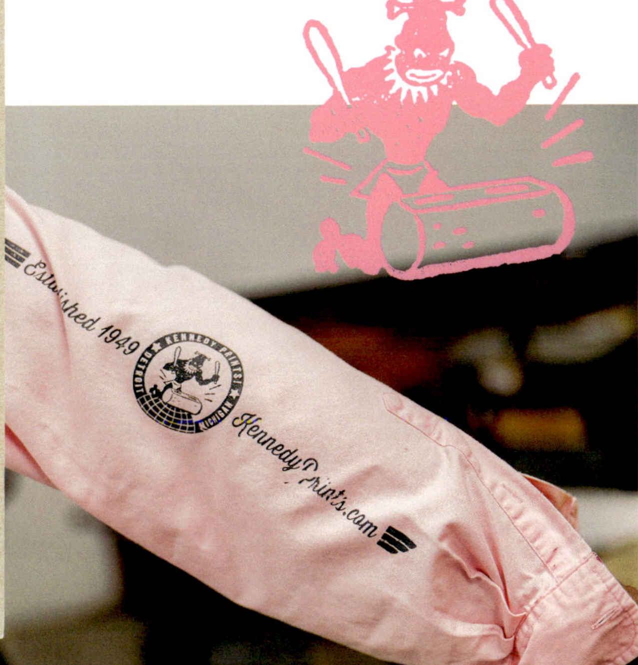

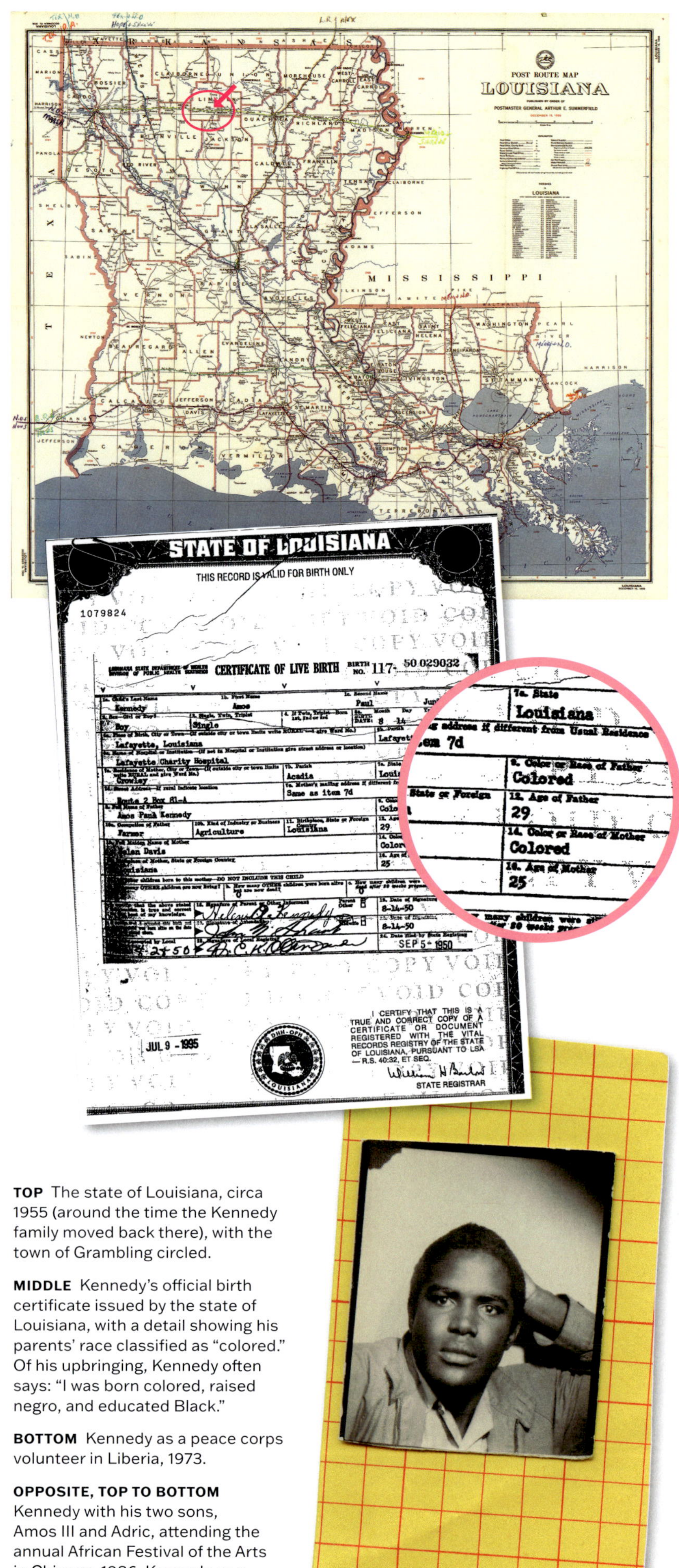

TOP The state of Louisiana, circa 1955 (around the time the Kennedy family moved back there), with the town of Grambling circled.

MIDDLE Kennedy's official birth certificate issued by the state of Louisiana, with a detail showing his parents' race classified as "colored." Of his upbringing, Kennedy often says: "I was born colored, raised negro, and educated Black."

BOTTOM Kennedy as a peace corps volunteer in Liberia, 1973.

OPPOSITE, TOP TO BOTTOM Kennedy with his two sons, Amos III and Adric, attending the annual African Festival of the Arts in Chicago, 1986. Kennedy as a young man in Maryland, 1977.

BORN TO DO THIS WORK

The third child of five, Kennedy was born in 1950 in Lafayette, Louisiana, into what he describes as a nuclear family. After various moves around the eastern United States in his early life, the family returned to Louisiana in 1958, this time resettling upstate in the small town of Grambling. Established in 1901 when Black farmers instituted a Black vocational school there, Grambling's largely Black population provided a uniquely independent and segregated environment for Kennedy to grow up in. The town was led by a Black mayor and was home to Grambling State University, one of the Historically Black Colleges and Universities (HBCUs) established in the late nineteenth and early twentieth centuries, where Kennedy's father taught.

Kennedy's family narrative stands out from the usual perception of Black life in the United States during this time: Both his parents were academics. His father, Amos Paul Kennedy, Sr., was a professor of agriculture and chemistry, and his mother, Helen Augusta Davis Kennedy, was a professor of accounting who pursued her degree after raising their family. Of his mother, Kennedy proudly quips, "By the time I left for college, I had invested the best years of my life into shaping her into a full PhD."[6] She was one of the first women to earn a doctorate in accounting in the United States.

Kennedy's earliest encounter with printing occurred in Louisiana, when his mother took his Cub Scout troop on a field trip to the neighboring town's newspaper. There he was introduced to and fascinated by the Linotype machines and other presses. He reminisces, "You have to realize this was 1959, '60, something of that nature. You've got a troop of little colored boys running around this white newspaper. That's unusual in the South, but for some reason, they let us do it."[7]

Of the town of Grambling, where Kennedy spent close to fifteen years, he remembers: "There was a sense of safety there, and I was protected from the trauma of whiteness that lurked outside the city limits."[8] This sense of security allowed for a spirit of inquiry. Later, as a curious undergraduate student at Grambling State, Kennedy often found himself walking about campus. On one such occasion, he happened upon the school's printshop, run by his family's neighbor Nathaniel Blake, tucked away behind the old dining common. Kennedy describes the shop as a "space with a Linotype machine, an offset press, and a darkroom for offset plates."[9] He helped Blake with odd jobs for a semester, and the elder Black pressman went on to shape Kennedy's interests in a variety of ways.

To hear Kennedy recall the printing that happened in Blake's shop is to be treated to a brief history of the craft in the African American community. Up until the 1960s, it was considered an honorable and essential vocation. Because of segregation, HBCUs were underresourced (as were many nonwhite businesses or institutions in the United

States during this time), so printmaking was not observed as a fine art but rather as a craft of making do.[10] Excellence was not defined as exclusive and limited; instead, it meant producing good work for the community—work that would make its members proud. (This idea has much deeper roots, stretching back across the Atlantic to Africa, where the distinction between the sacred and the secular is infinitesimal in many cosmologies. In this world-view, creative production for the spirit realm is honored in the practice of daily life, and so-called fine objects are made to celebrate everyday existence.[11])

Kennedy's academic life at Grambling, while it included courses on art and photography, ultimately led to a degree in mathematics. Like many young Black people of this era, he was encouraged to focus on a practical course of study that would provide him with a solid middle-class life. After graduation and a tour with the peace corps in Liberia—the influence of which appears in his prints featuring African proverbs (see pages 176–79)—he began a career as a computer programmer, joining IBM in the D.C. area in 1973. He moved to Cleveland, Ohio, in 1978 and soon started a family, with a son born in 1980 and another in 1985.

Despite his career's promise of stability, Kennedy felt coding was unchallenging and boring. He sought solace in the pen's fluid play in the creation of calligraphy. This diversion, which came to preoccupy his time outside work, began when he found a copy of the classic Speedball lettering textbook in a bookstore. "I was good at it," he remembers, and he became "fascinated with how letters moved on the page."[12]

For two years while living in Maryland, he took calligraphy courses, but lettering was an avocation that only hinted at a more passionate undercurrent: Kennedy is fascinated by letters, words, and books. "For some people, it's in their DNA, it's in their blood to be around books," he says. "You can be a printer, a seller, a writer. The desire for words made me want to be a librarian because I wanted to be around books."[13] (In fact, after moving from Maryland to Cleveland, he enrolled briefly in a master of library science program.)

It was through his calligraphy studies that he was introduced to and influenced by Thomas Ingmire, a master calligrapher whose inventive letterforms extend the concept of literacy. For Kennedy, Ingmire foregrounds a highly personal act of writing—one that reflects individual utterances and thus rejects uniformity. Kennedy observed the power of Ingmire's letters and how they performed alone on the page to capture the polysemy of his chosen texts.[14] Creating letters with a life of their own is a generative process that fosters an openness to possibility—a lesson Kennedy pocketed for future endeavors, but ones that engaged with type rather than hand lettering.

Calligraphy may have been the hobby that fulfilled Kennedy outside his professional life, but not until a family trip to Colonial Williamsburg did he reencounter the letterpress enactments that had

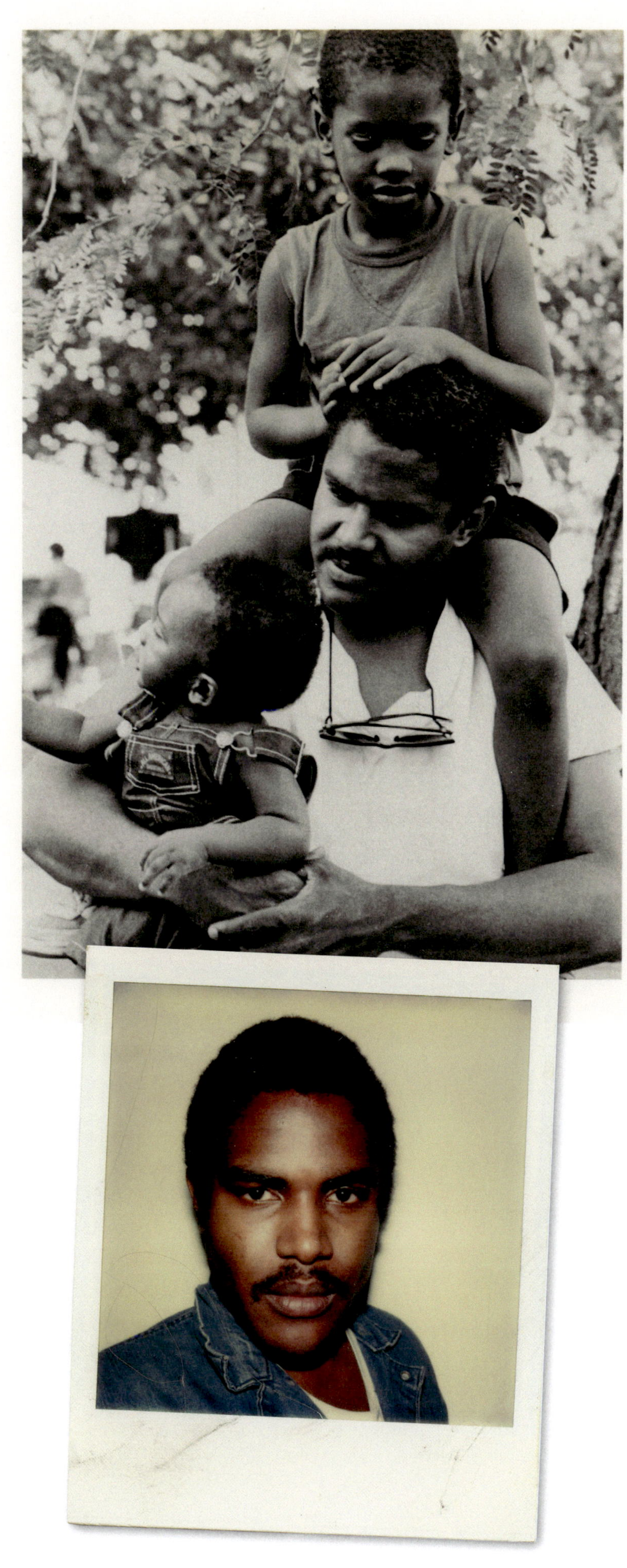

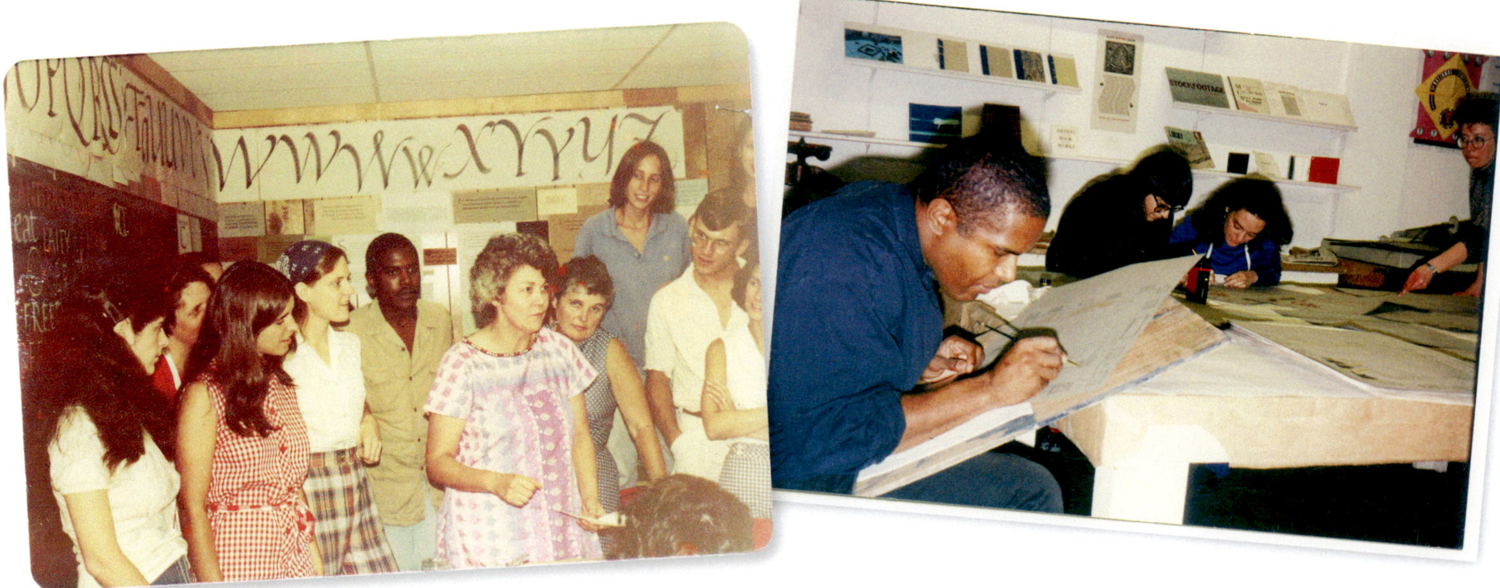

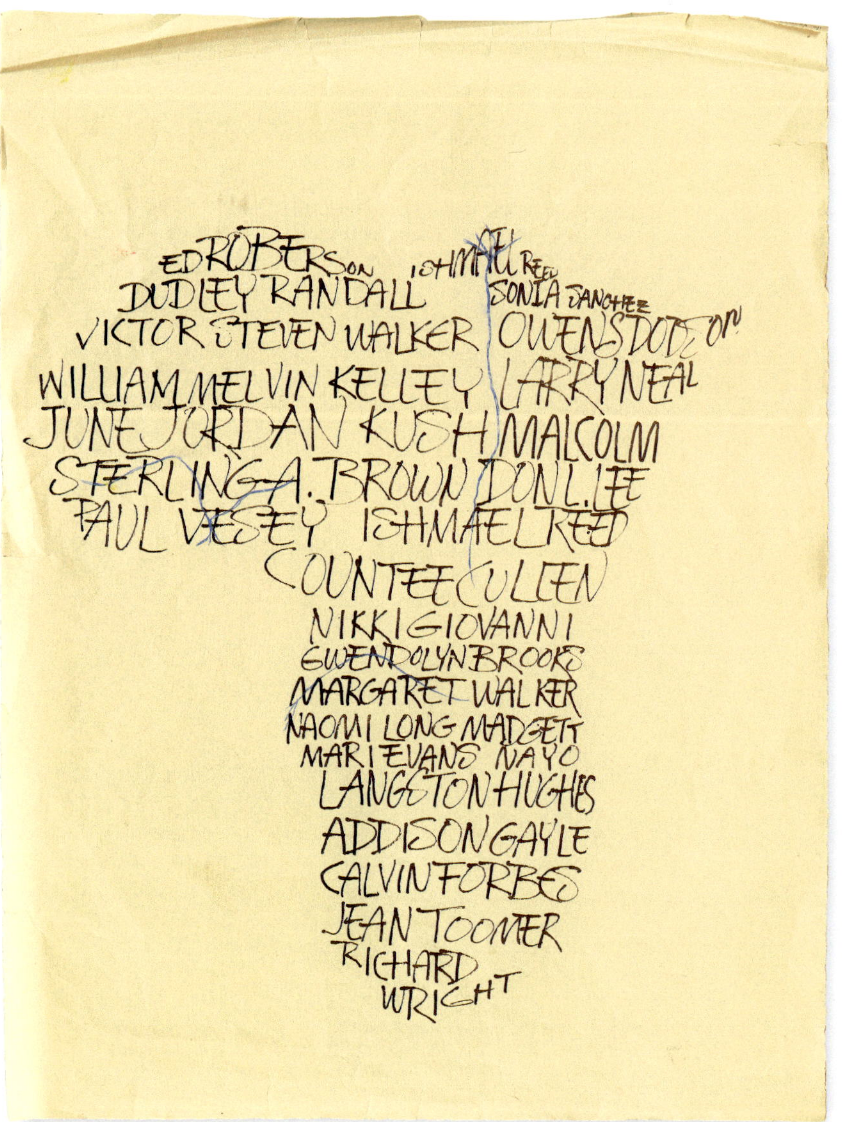

first excited him as a child. "I saw a Black docent printing on an old wooden press," he remembers. "Printing all these multiples. It was amazing."[15] He was so moved by the scene that upon going home to Chicago (where his family had moved in 1980), he enrolled in a letterpress course at Artist Book Works, a community arts center that would later become the esteemed Center for Book and Paper Arts affiliated with Columbia College Chicago. Artist Book Works became a place of education and affirmation for Kennedy. After six months of taking classes, he procured a Vandercook printing press—basically for free, as he only had to pay the cost of moving it—and was gifted four cabinets of type. He felt "the universe had just opened up to say, 'Here is the path that you should travel.'"[16]

Kennedy printed broadsides from his basement for two years and increased his community of professional artists through Artist Book Works, then found himself at a crossroads. A confluence of factors, including his family's move to Milwaukee, brought this on. He saw an opportunity in this relocation: "I had heard from the first day I started taking letterpress printing that there was this [professor] in Madison, Walter Hamady, who made the best books in the world—that he was a genius," Kennedy remembers.[17] So, at thirty-eight, he started to think seriously about graduate school.

THE UNSCHOOLING OF AMOS

We who believe in freedom cannot rest.
—Ella Baker, speech at the Mississippi Freedom Democratic Party convention on August 6, 1964

First heard by Kennedy in a song by the Black women's a cappella group Sweet Honey in the Rock, these words from civil rights activist Ella Baker became a rallying cry for him—one of many. When he was growing up, the segregated though sacred campus of Grambling had schooled him in the words of classic civil rights thinkers such as Baldwin and

Martin Luther King, Jr., as well as some who were further afield, like Martinican Marxist philosopher Frantz Fanon. Of the literature of the negritude movement, Kennedy remembers:

> *In the late '60s, the Black Arts movement introduced me to Nikki Giovanni, Sonia Sanchez, and [Amiri Baraka, formerly known as] LeRoi Jones—all these poets and writers were just out there in the ether. You didn't need to be an English major to know what was going on in Black literature. It was part of that whole Black power, Black pride moment. That's when the Wall of Respect went up in Chicago, and I remember Alvin Ailey's dance troupe coming to perform at Grambling. It was just part of being at any HBCU at that time.*[18]

He also gathered visual inspiration from early Black modernist artists such as painter Jacob Lawrence, muralist John Biggers, and printmaker Charles W. White.

So when at nearly forty he moved forward in the arts of letterpress printing and book building, abandoning the corporate success that had been equated with advancement for Black people, these cultural contributions came with him as references to build on and messages to further.

In 1995, Kennedy matriculated in the MFA program in graphic design at the University of Wisconsin–Madison. His position as a student was unique not solely because of his age, but also because he commuted to Madison from Milwaukee, had his own press, and had already been practicing printmaking for several years. Though his adviser was esteemed graphic designer Philip Hamilton, Kennedy worked primarily with noted book artist Walter Hamady. He describes Hamady as "too inventive to be a traditional fine artist, [with] too much mastery of the message to be a mere book artist."[19] Kennedy's program of study focused singularly on bookmaking—so much so that in his history and theory courses, which required research papers, he would submit his assignments in book form. Hamady expanded the techniques and creative possibilities of bookmaking for Kennedy, as did Bill Bunce, a gregarious and unconventional art librarian at Madison who invited students to disassemble books to better understand their bindings.[20]

Around this time, Kennedy was also exposed to the work of early twentieth-century Dutch printmaker Hendrik Nicolaas (H. N.) Werkman. While not well known in the United States in his time, Werkman was an avant-garde typographer and fine artist who used the press in expressive ways, chronicled in his magazine *The Next Call*. He is recognized for his *druksels* technique: an abstract method of printing in which the press is a formal, not strictly communicative tool. He pioneered the repetitive process of applying the brayer, or hand inking roller, to type or low-relief cutout shapes, then passing the sheet

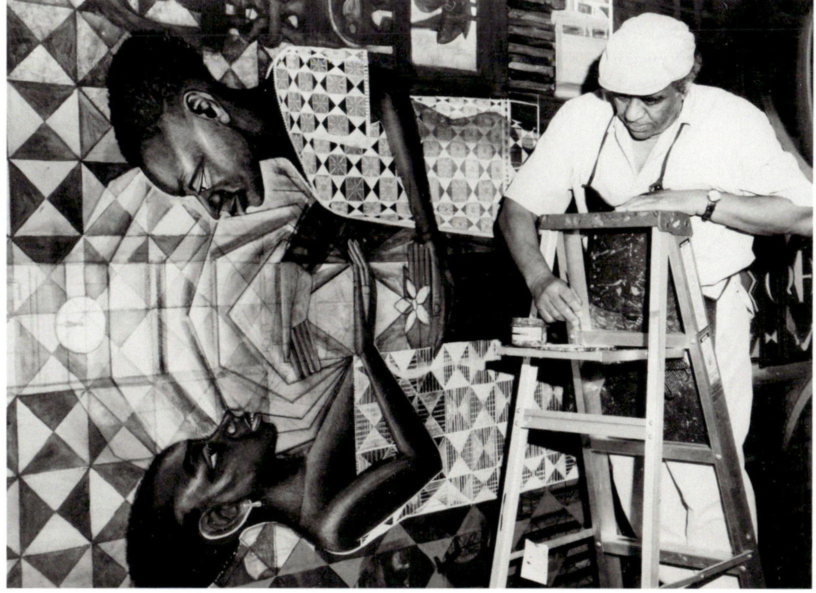

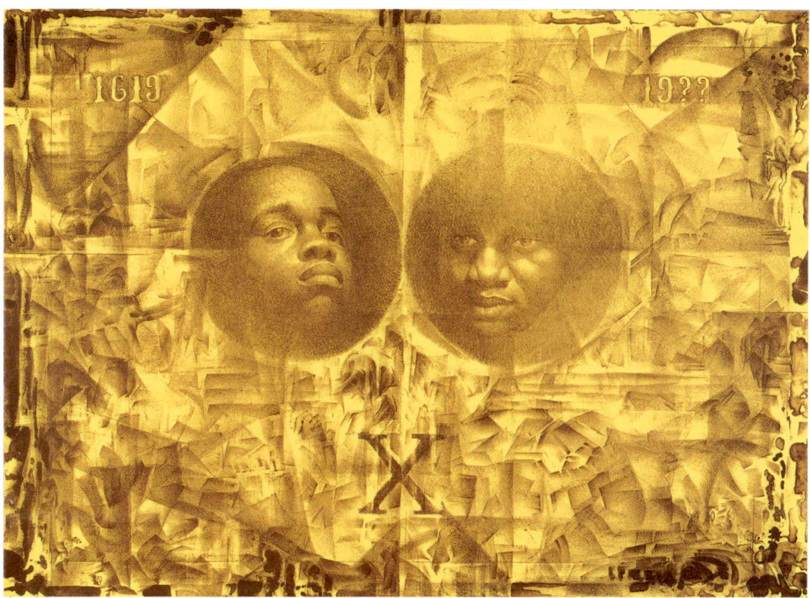

TOP Muralist John Biggers working on *House of the Turtle* at the HBCU Hampton University in Virginia, circa 1990. Biggers's piece incorporates fractal patterns he observed during his travels in West Africa.

BOTTOM Charles W. White, *Wanted Poster Series #14a*, 1970, lithograph, 22 × 30¼ inches (56 × 76.75 cm), Los Angeles. White's portraits of two Black men, one labeled "1619" and the other "19??", expresses the ongoing oppression of Black people since some of the first enslaved Africans were brought to the continent.

OPPOSITE TOP, LEFT TO RIGHT Kennedy in a calligraphy class led by Sheila Waters (in the purple and blue dress), 1976, and hand-painting a broadside at Artist Book Works, 1989, both in Chicago.

OPPOSITE, BOTTOM Amos Paul Kennedy, Jr., calligraphy featuring the names of Black writers in the shape of Africa, with the Nile and Niger Rivers marked in blue, 1979, pen on paper, 25⅜ × 19 inches (64.5 × 48.25 cm), Oak Park, Illinois.

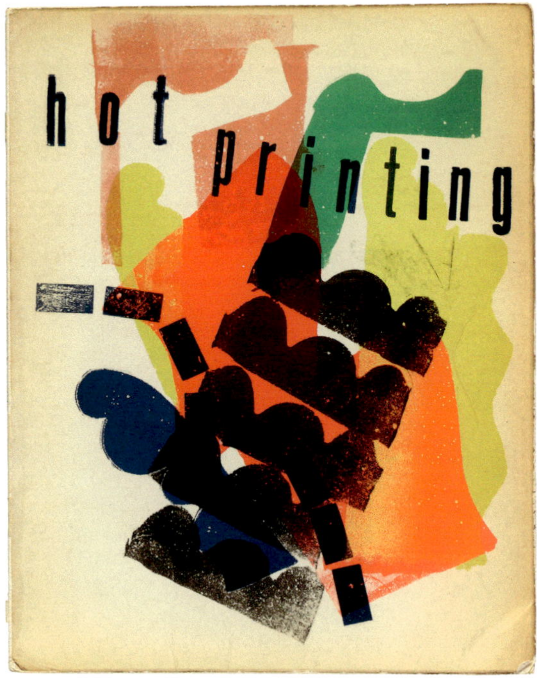

TOP H. N. Werkman, proof for an alternate cover of *Hot Printing*, circa 1935, letterpress, 10¼ × 8 inches (26 × 20.25 cm), Groningen, Netherlands. Werkman called his *druksels* experiments "hot printing," inspired by "hot jazz," Louis Armstrong's phrase for his highly energetic, improvisational music.

BOTTOM AND OPPOSITE, TOP RIGHT Amos Paul Kennedy, Jr., cover and interiors from *An Experiment Combining Bad Printing and Bad Book Binding*, 2022, letterpress on paper, 7¾ × 5⅜ inches (20 × 13.75 cm) folded, 7¾ × 21 inches (20 × 53.5 cm) unfolded, Colorado Springs, Colorado. Here, Kennedy shares his technique of what he calls bad printing, in part inspired by Werkman's hot printing.

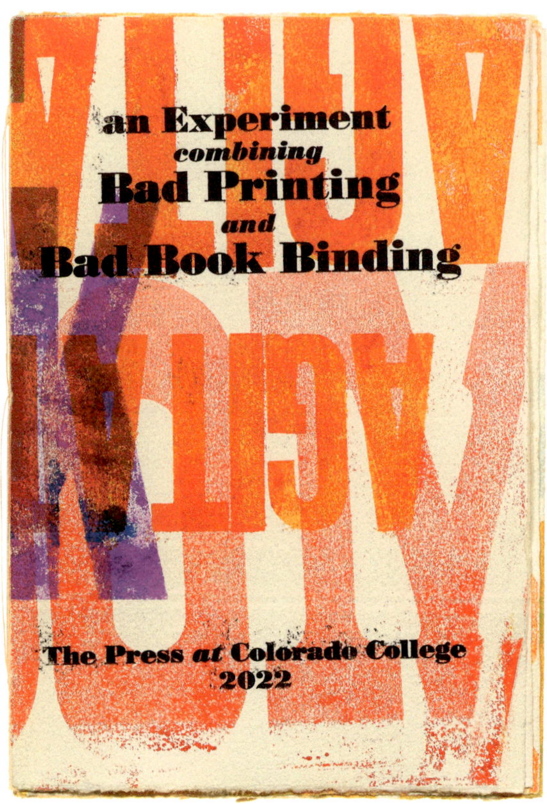

several times through the press to achieve a layered effect with impressions in multiple colors. Werkman also played with the edge of the brayer on the paper to produce ink lines of various thicknesses. Kennedy adapted this idea of overlapping and repeating forms into his own unique style, inking type of different faces in multiple colors to create imbricating backgrounds for his messages of social justice. Perhaps even more significantly, Kennedy was drawn to Werkman because he operated a clandestine press during World War II. Both artists recognized the political power of creative expression and used their craft to counter oppression. (For Werkman, this artistic resistance came at a steep price: He was executed by the Gestapo in 1945.)[21]

During his time in Madison, Kennedy honed his crafts of printing and bookmaking, using his printshop—his own personal laboratory, as Baldwin called for—to experiment and build on the already vast skills he had gained at Artist Book Works in Chicago. He named his first press The Idiot Press of Amos Paul Kennedy, Jr., playfully restoring the word "idiot" to its etymological meaning: that of a private citizen of Athens, independent from the ruling class. Always the logophile, Kennedy here again recalls the art of the griot, reclaiming a word with negative contemporary connotations to acknowledge the intertwined nuances of language and history and his place within them.

But, as Kennedy likes to say, he has "changed the name of [his] press as many times as colored people change their hairstyle."[22] He called his second press Kennedy and Sons Fine Printing, a name that reflected the professional-quality bookmaking and commercial printing he was undertaking as a small business owner. Concurrently, he operated Jubalee Press, an imprint named for the celebration of slavery's end in the United States. "The first was a business venture and the second was to lose all the money I made from the first," he half-kids.[23] Under Jubalee (the name of which Kennedy deliberately misspelled to capture a sense of Black dialect), he published books that affirmed his passion for African and African American storytelling and folklore. In this way, he recouped spoken Black idioms into print as a way of filling a void in Black publishing:

> *One of the things I realized when I took my first course in letterpress printing was that there is a severe shortage of the Black voice in what we call book arts, fine books, and special collections. . . . And I determined that I would spend my life promoting the negro culture. . . . And I would print the works of negro authors. And most of my work until 2000 was exclusively Black authors of the Black experience.*[24]

Notable projects produced for Jubalee include *African Proverbs*, a 1996 book shaped like a snake, with each serpentine page printed with a saying

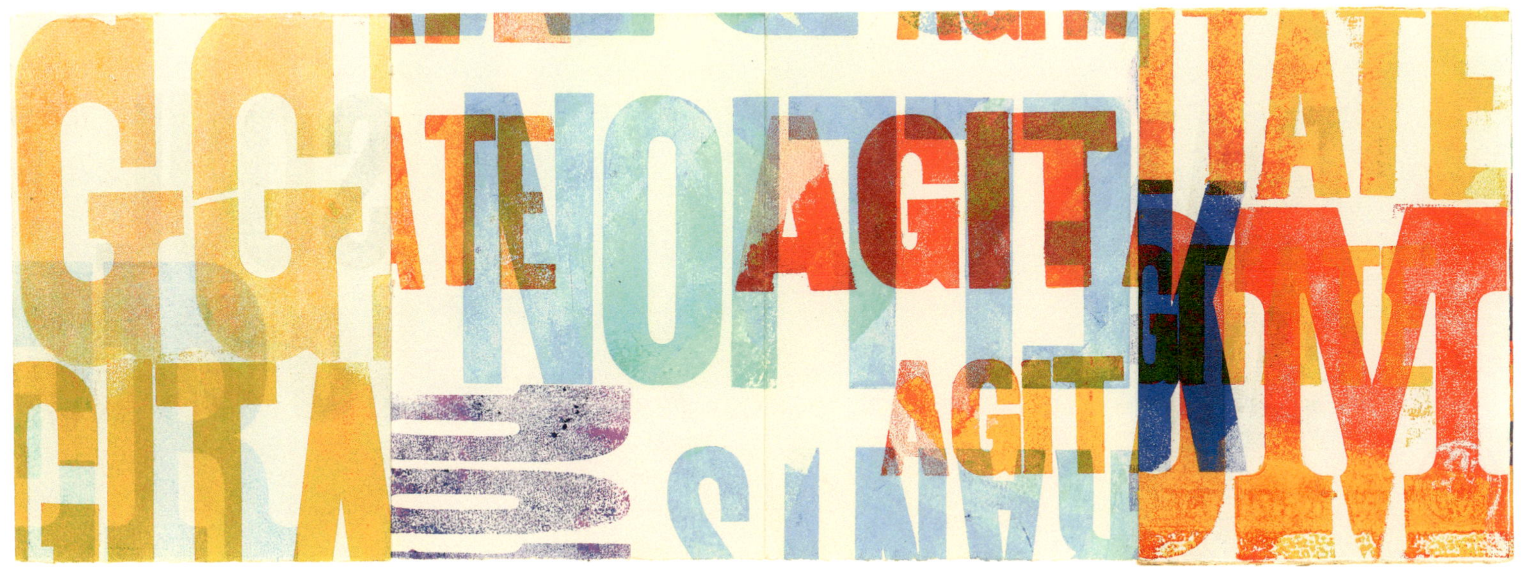

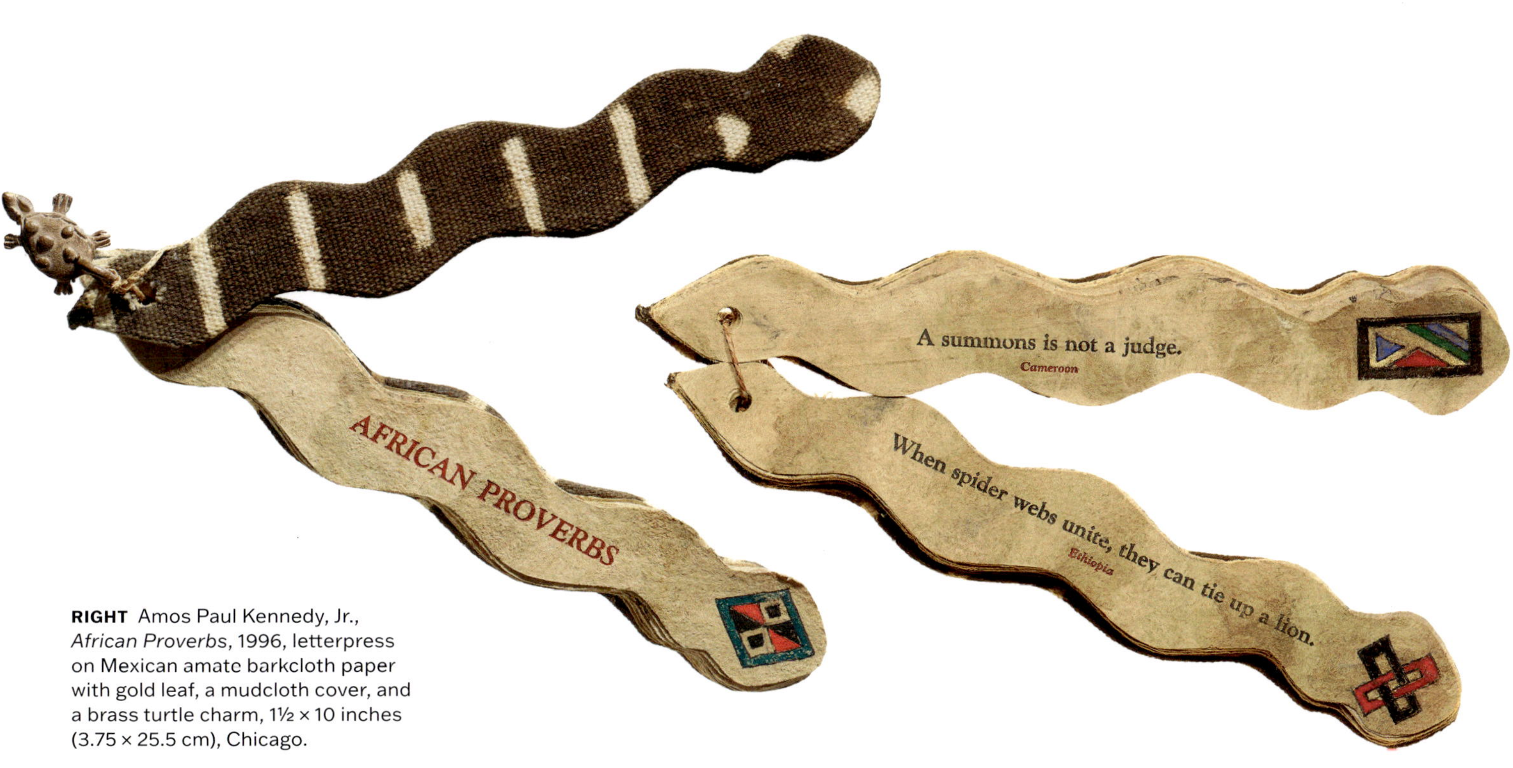

RIGHT Amos Paul Kennedy, Jr., *African Proverbs*, 1996, letterpress on Mexican amate barkcloth paper with gold leaf, a mudcloth cover, and a brass turtle charm, 1½ × 10 inches (3.75 × 25.5 cm), Chicago.

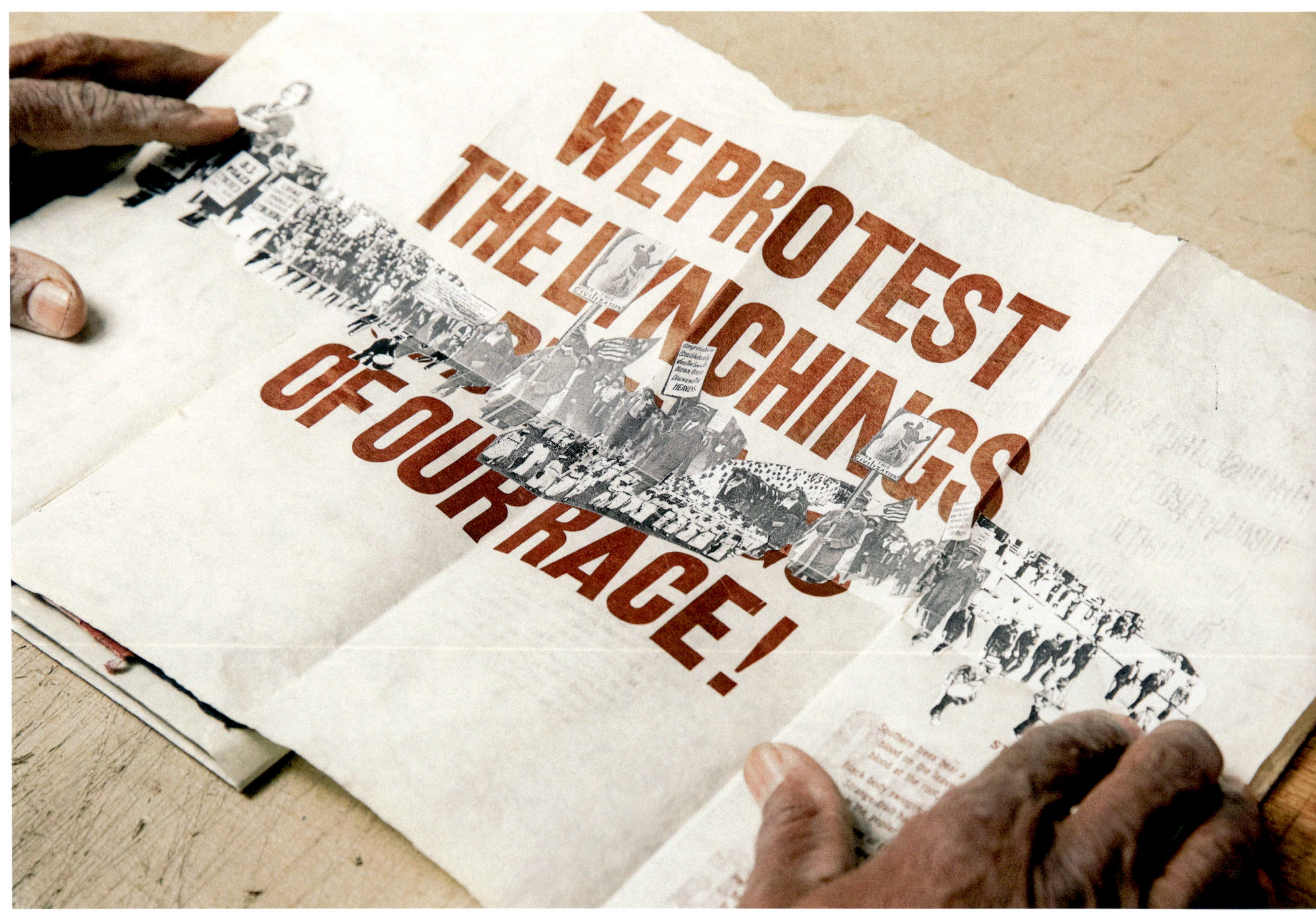

from an African kingdom or country. But perhaps his most significant artist's book is *Strange Fruit*, dedicated to "the 3,513 negroes lynched and burned in American between 1892 and 1927." The 1994 book, which takes its name from the 1937 song penned by communist Lewis Allan and committed to American consciousness by singer Billie Holiday, includes "The Haunted Oak" by Paul Laurence Dunbar and "The Lynching" and "If We Must Die," both by Claude McKay—poems by Black literary figures who had influenced Kennedy's work. A concertina structure made from handmade abaca paper, multilayered and constructed in ways that perform the text, *Strange Fruit* does not sacrifice content over form. Its pages reproduce newspaper clippings and postcards printed with images of lynching victims to call attention to the terror African Americans experienced after the Civil War and well into the next century (see pages 94–97).

Both Kennedy's creative work and his self-presentation reflect a form of performance—of reanimating history. Though clearly intellectually and creatively astute, he puts forward a faux-naïf performance of bygone Black stereotypes, rejecting the label of artist and claiming instead, "I'm just a humble negro printer." While the word *negro* has fallen out of use and is often considered offensive in the United States, its hard-won acceptance in the 1920s (at the urging of Black leader W. E. B. Du Bois) was considered a triumph over the other option in wide use at the time.[25] In his insistence on self-identifying as negro, Kennedy defiantly exercises the power to choose his own name, forcing his audience to confront an uncomfortable history and reconcile it with the purportedly post-racial present.

This supposed color blindness was present in Kennedy's next professional environment: academia. After earning his MFA, he was appointed in 1998 to the Indiana University School of Art (now the Lois Eskenazi School of Art, Architecture, and Design), where he was the first African American art faculty member to hold a tenure-track position. While many of the graduate students revered Kennedy as the only professor who truly engaged them, his stay at Indiana University was brief. There he printed and mailed his *Nappygrams*, a now collectible series of sardonic postcards that responded to social injustices—some of which Kennedy experienced himself while at the university. Invited to give the keynote address at the university's Friends of the Art Library annual gala, he shared with his colleagues what it was like to be a Black professor there, performing once more

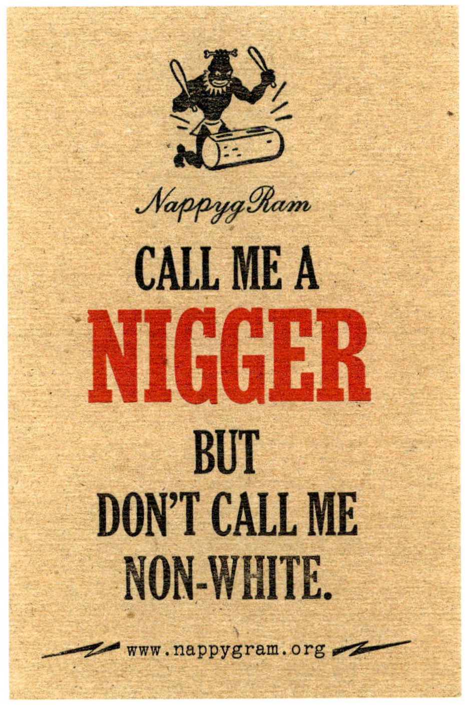

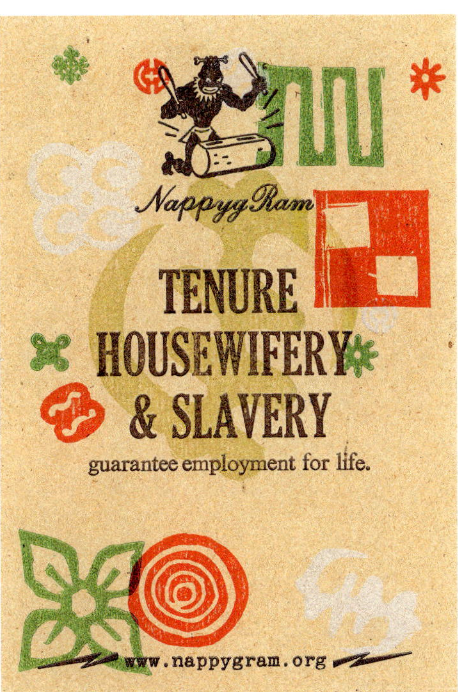

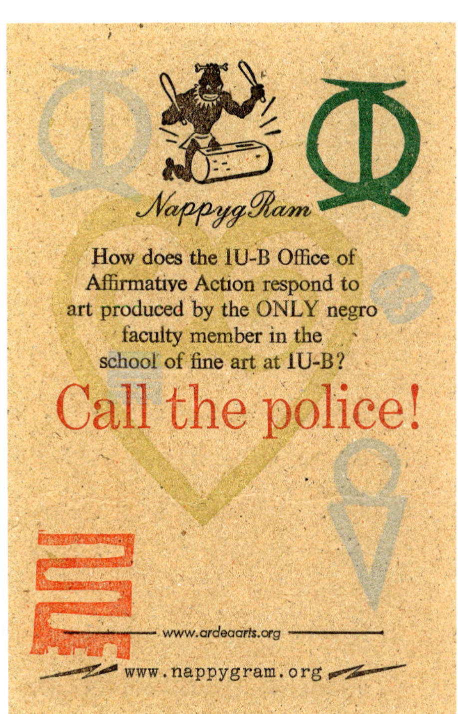

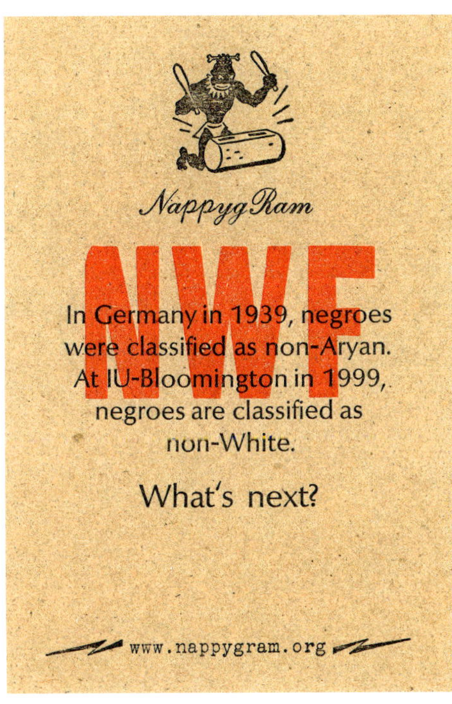

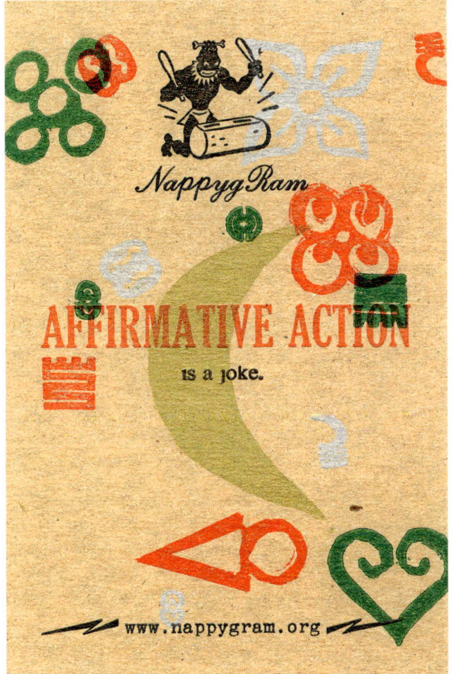

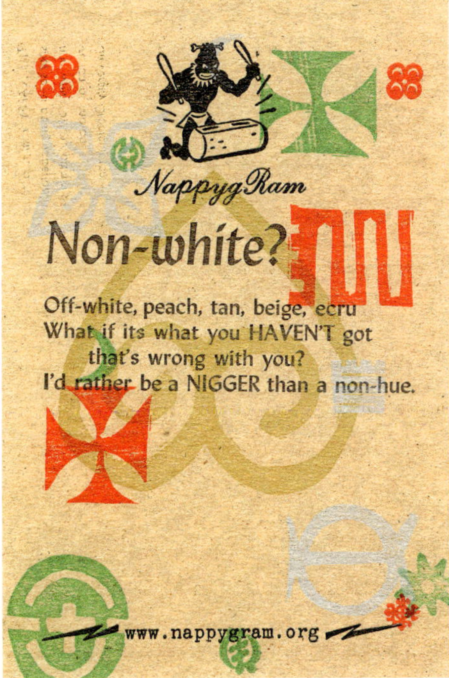

TOP Amos Paul Kennedy, Jr., selections from the *Nappygrams* series, 1998–99, letterpress on chipboard, 6 × 4 inches (15.25 × 10 cm), Bloomington, Indiana. “When something wrong happened, I'd make a *Nappygram* and distribute it in the mail and around the Indiana University campus,” Kennedy explains. When he sent one titled *Affirmative Action Is a Joke* to the school's affirmative action office, its staff called the police.

OPPOSITE Kennedy with the center foldout spread of *Strange Fruit: Words of Protest to the Lynchings and Burnings of My People*, 1994, offset and letterpress on handmade abaca paper, 6 × 5 inches (15.25 × 12.75 cm) folded, 12 × 17¾ inches (30.5 × 45 cm) unfolded, Chicago. The foldout of this edition features collaged imagery of marching protesters.

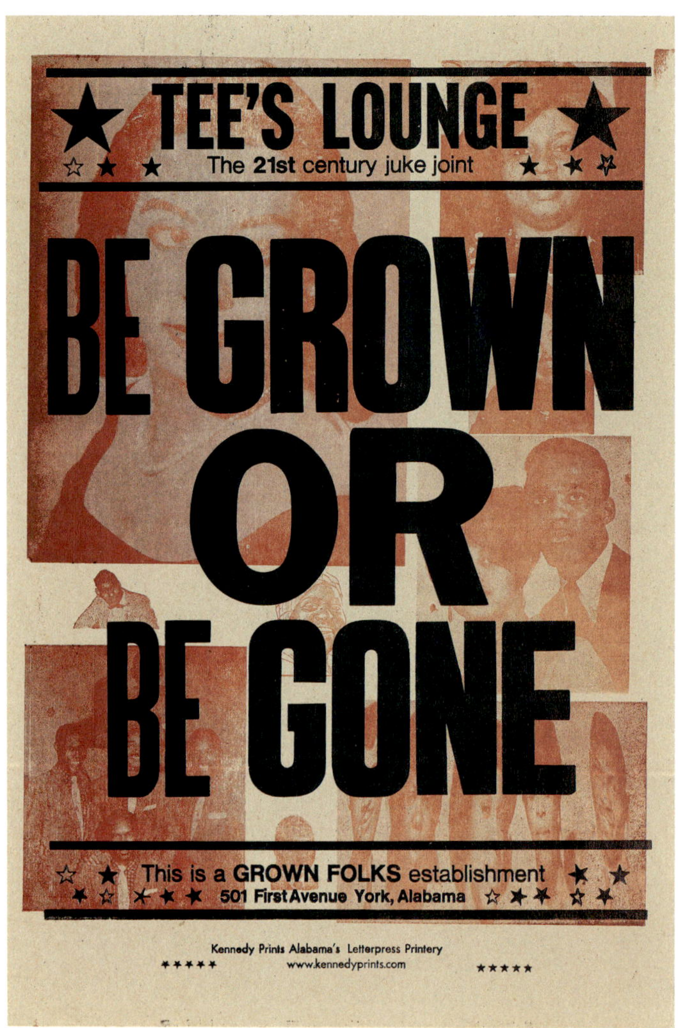

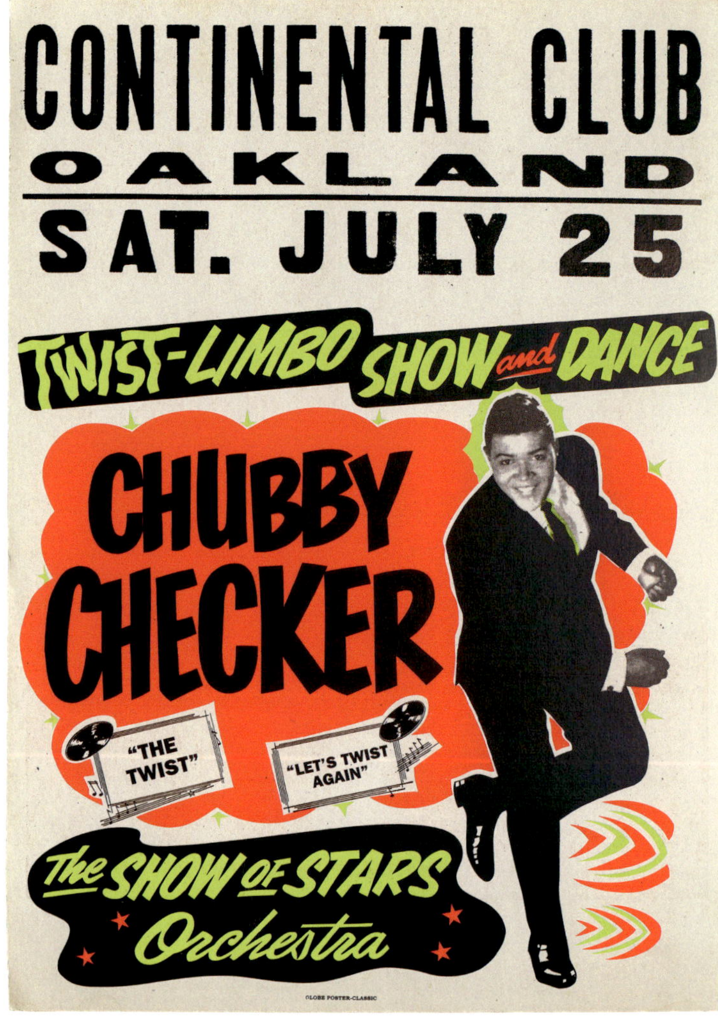

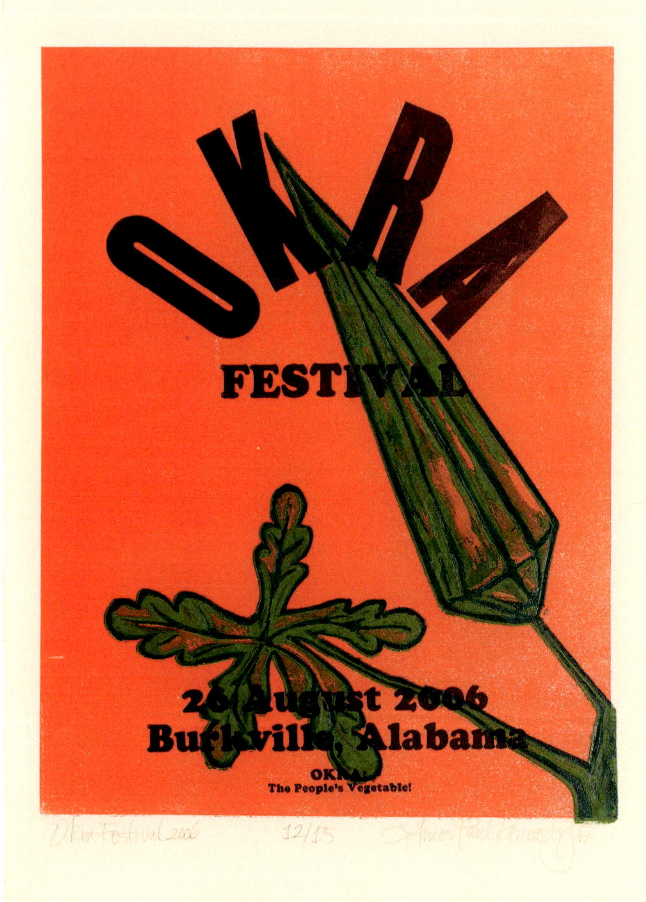

the role of social irritant. "The American university is now a corporate environment," he remembers. "Ultimately, my stay at IU did very little for the development of my craft."[26] His departure from the school marked a precise shift in his career away from the world of fine art. Instead, he would dedicate himself to art for the people.

TO PRINT IS TO SERVE

Perhaps the primary distinction of the artist is that he must actively cultivate that state which most men, necessarily, must avoid: the state of being alone. . . . The precise role of the artist, then, is to illuminate that darkness, blaze roads through that vast forest, so that we will not, in all our doing, lose sight of its purpose, which is, after all, to make the work a more human dwelling place.
—James Baldwin, "The Creative Process," 1962

Kennedy moved to Alabama in 2002 when he was invited to be an artist in residence at the Coleman Center for the Arts in the small town of York. He went on to spend ten years within the state in three rural towns: York, Akron, and Gordo. There he encountered the ideas of architect Samuel "Sambo" Mockbee, who established the Rural Studio at Auburn University in 1993 to teach the social responsibilities of architecture and provide quality student-built housing to poor communities in the state's Black Belt.[27] (A charismatic professor, Mockbee is also the original speaker of one of Kennedy's favorite aphorisms: "Proceed and be bold.") The experience in these places, according to Kennedy, ". . . made me realize that art should be democratized and not something exclusive, but . . . should be inclusive. It should be something available for everybody. And this is what posters allowed me to do. Make something that was affordable and that everybody could get in their house."[28]

Initially, his transition from artists' books to posters was an economic choice: "I first started doing posters because I needed revenue in a hurry," he says. "And a well-crafted book can take up to two years. In order to make a living, I had to be able to create a volume large enough to sustain myself."[29] He soon discovered that the bold immediacy of the poster also helped him connect with—and be of service to—his neighbors. One remarkable and humorous example is *Ladies, No Fighting in the Bathroom*, a poster Kennedy gifted to the owner of Tee's Lounge in York when he was having trouble with his female clientele (see page 260). With its loud type and colloquial messaging, it is a favorite of many, even those outside the state and unfamiliar with the scene at Tee's. (Kennedy finds it amusing that it has proven most popular among mothers with two daughters.) Other early acts of printing in service to his community include Kennedy's long-running poster series for both the Okra Festival in Burkville (see pages 244–45) and the Rooster Day Festival in York.

Trademarks of Kennedy's posters are his use of chipboard—an eco-friendly and affordable substrate with a warm brown color he likens to soil. "It reflects the ruralness of large swaths of the United States," he says. "And I wanted to use materials that I identified with my Southern heritage."[30] Inspired by the legacy of letterpress houses like Indiana's Tribune Showprint, Globe Poster of Baltimore, Maryland, and Hatch Show Print of Nashville, Tennessee, all of which created iconic music posters throughout the twentieth century, Kennedy always makes a statement, mixing metal type and large sans serif wood type—his favorite is Cooper Black—with bright, fearless color. His typesetting also reflects the vernacular of the signage he encountered in Alabama: centered and justified for ease of reading.

Kennedy's ink and type are usually found or inexpensively sourced, and he carves his own linocuts, stencils, and pressure prints (a flexible template with a raised design placed between the paper and the printing cylinder). "My work in the rural South taught me to use what I have to make what I want," he says. "It taught me that the message was more important than the medium."[31] Key to Kennedy's work is just how this message finds its way onto the medium: His provocative quotes and adages float over typographic backgrounds made up of related words, printed so densely—one on top of the other in multiple passes and colors—that they are nearly subliminal.

For Kennedy, Alabama provided the isolation that Baldwin says artists must experience to create critical work. But it was also a carrefour—an intersection

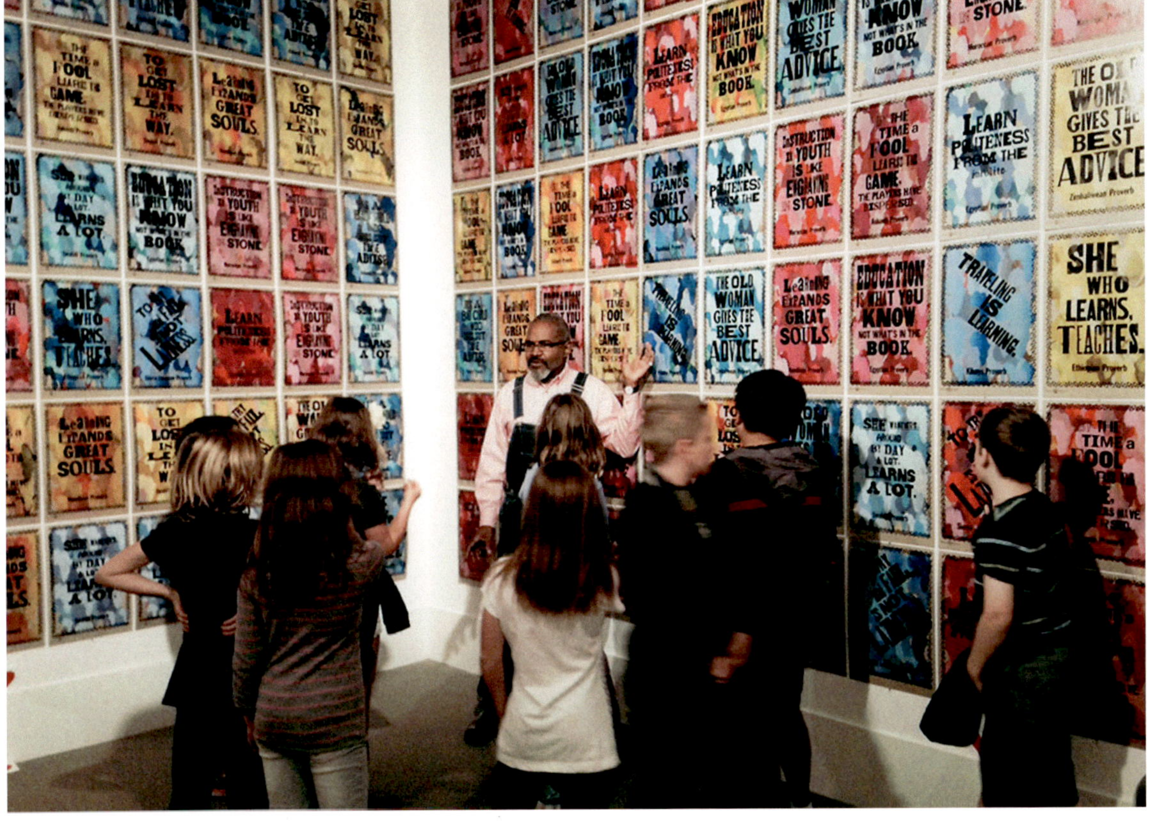

Photo courtesy of Ohio University

OPPOSITE, FAR LEFT, TOP TO BOTTOM Amos Paul Kennedy, Jr., *Be Grown or Be Gone*, circa 2002 (circa 2009 reprint), 19 × 12½ inches (48.25 × 31.75 cm), letterpress on chipboard, York, Alabama, and an Okra Festival event poster, 2006, letterpress on paper, 21⅛ × 15½ inches (54 × 39.5 cm), Akron, Alabama.

OPPOSITE, TOP RIGHT Unknown designer, event poster for a Chubby Checker concert with the Show of Stars Orchestra, circa 1965, 31½ × 22 inches (80 × 56 cm), Baltimore. The music posters of Kennedy's youth had a formative effect on him.

BOTTOM Kennedy with students in front of an installation of his *African Proverbs* poster series at the Kennedy Museum of Art at Ohio University, 2014.

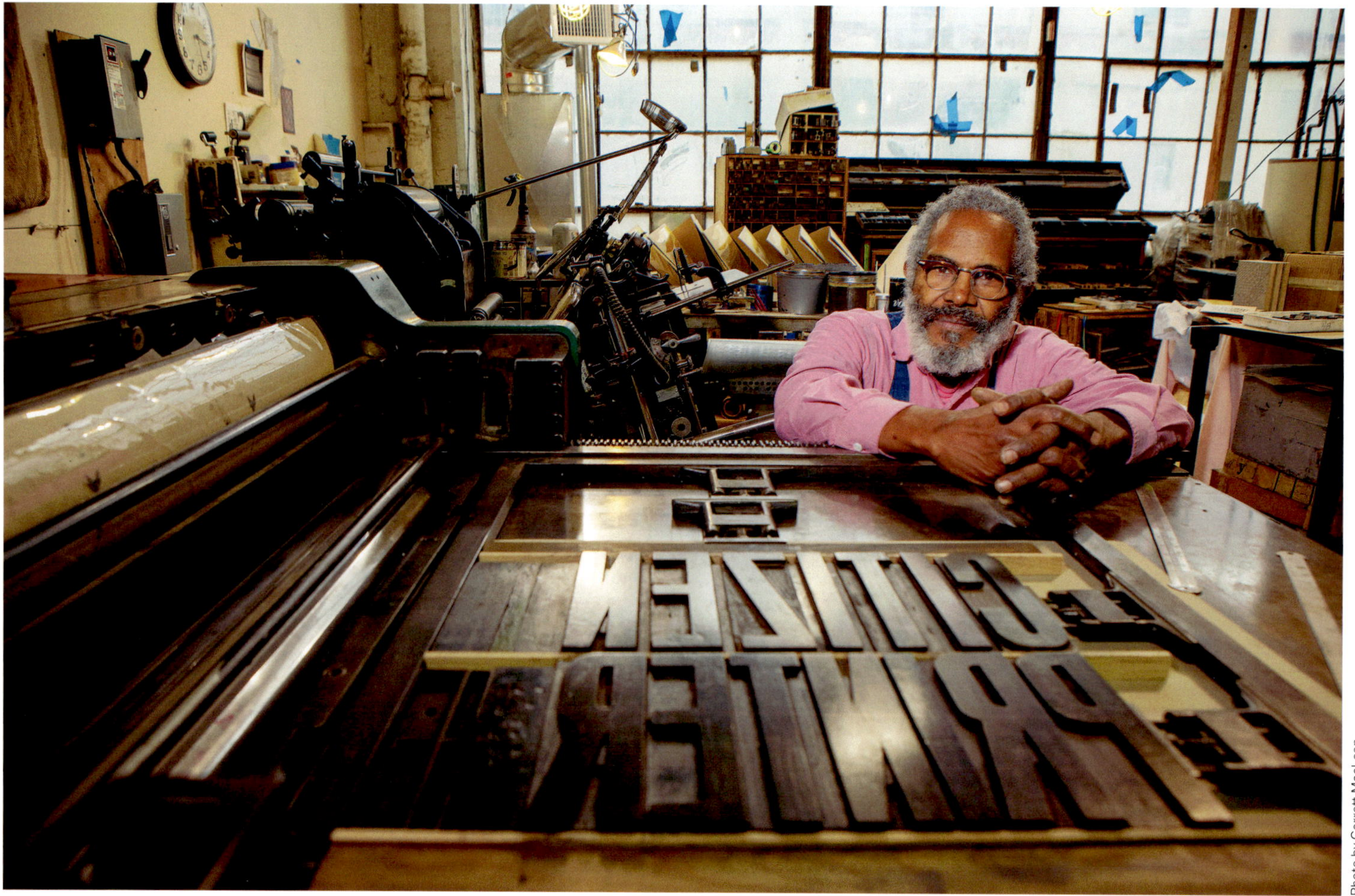

Photo by Garrett MacLean

TOP Kennedy in his Detroit printshop with the words "citizen printer" locked up on the press, 2021.

OPPOSITE Amos Paul Kennedy, Jr., *Proceed and Be Bold!*, circa 2002 (after 2012 reprint), letterpress on chipboard, 19 × 12½ inches (48.25 × 31.75 cm), Detroit.

and transitional space that other makers, scholars, students, and even neighbors passed through to work with him. Alabama was transformative in that Kennedy was able to crystalize and test-drive his philosophy of what it could mean to be "a social printer, a social activist with a press."[32] His posters for Tee's Lounge represent his ability to situate himself in community and make his work accessible, and they also demonstrate his generosity.

Despite Kennedy's insistence on the lowbrow (or maybe because of it), his works can't help but be collectible. Today, they are in the permanent collections of the Library of Congress, the Metropolitan Museum of Art, the University of California at Santa Barbara, the University of North Carolina at Greensboro, and the University of Illinois Urbana–Champaign. He has exhibited far and wide, including at New York City's Poster House and the Museum of Modern Art Library, the Brooklyn Public Library, the Kennedy Museum of Art at Ohio University, the University of Akron, and the Bainbridge Island Museum of Art. He is the subject of the 2008 documentary *Proceed and Be Bold!*, directed by Laura Zinger,[33] and he is the recipient of the individual laureate award from the American Printing Historical Association. Each year, he leads letterpress workshops around the United States. As a traveling instructor, he revives the role of itinerant printer, a generations-old exchange in which tradespeople would journey to offer their services on the road and study with others to achieve mastery. It is no mistake that Kennedy has chosen letterpress, a tool that came into wide use when the fight for Black liberation began. In teaching it, he shares how we can use the tools of our history to access the larger lessons of our past.

In 2013, Kennedy left Alabama for Detroit to live his philosophy full time in an affordable city with working-class roots that offered a new chance of community building. In 2018, he embarked on his Pile of Bricks project, revitalizing a space that will become a place for teaching and preserving the art of printmaking. As he said in an oral history project at the University of Wisconsin in 2018, "People have to know that there are multiple solutions to exercises. And this, I think, is necessary to build strong citizens that in turn will build a strong nation, a strong civilization."[34] In choosing to live in a different way—to enact one of the multiple solutions to the exercise that is existence—he sets a powerful example in life and in craft. He hopes this space will survive him and help others use letterpress to share their voices.

Amos Paul Kennedy, Jr., a creator who is consumed with critically interrogating our unexamined assumptions and using his work as a platform to dismantle injustice, is a CITIZEN PRINTER.

★ Architecture is about shelter for the soul. ★

PROCEED AND BE BOLD!

★ Sambo Mockbee ★

Established 1949 KennedyPrints.com

Amos Paul Kennedy, Jr., & the Legacy of Black Printing in America

by **KELLY WALTERS**

It has long been our anxious wish to see, in this slave-holding, slave-trading, and negro-hating land, a printing press and paper, permanently established, under the complete control and direction of the immediate victims of slavery and oppression . . . that the man who has *suffered the wrong* is the man to *demand redress*—that the man STRUCK is the man to CRY OUT—and that he who has *endured the cruel pangs of Slavery* is the man to *advocate Liberty*.

—FREDERICK DOUGLASS, "Our Paper and Its Prospects," from the first issue of *The North Star*, December 3, 1847

OPPOSITE Amos Paul Kennedy, Jr., *If There Is No Struggle, There Is No Progress*, after 2012, letterpress on paper, 38 × 26 inches (96.5 × 66.5 cm), Detroit. Kennedy created the background for this print with a brayer, rolling excess ink from a previous job onto the paper until the brayer was clean.

I was told years ago that everything you do is political, and so my art is really a political statement. And the story of my art, when someone can actually cipher it out, is a statement of what I envision the world to be.

—AMOS PAUL KENNEDY, JR., quoted in "Words to Live By," *American Craft* magazine, 2011

IF THERE IS NO STRUGGLE, THERE IS NO PROGRESS

FREDERICK DOUGLASS

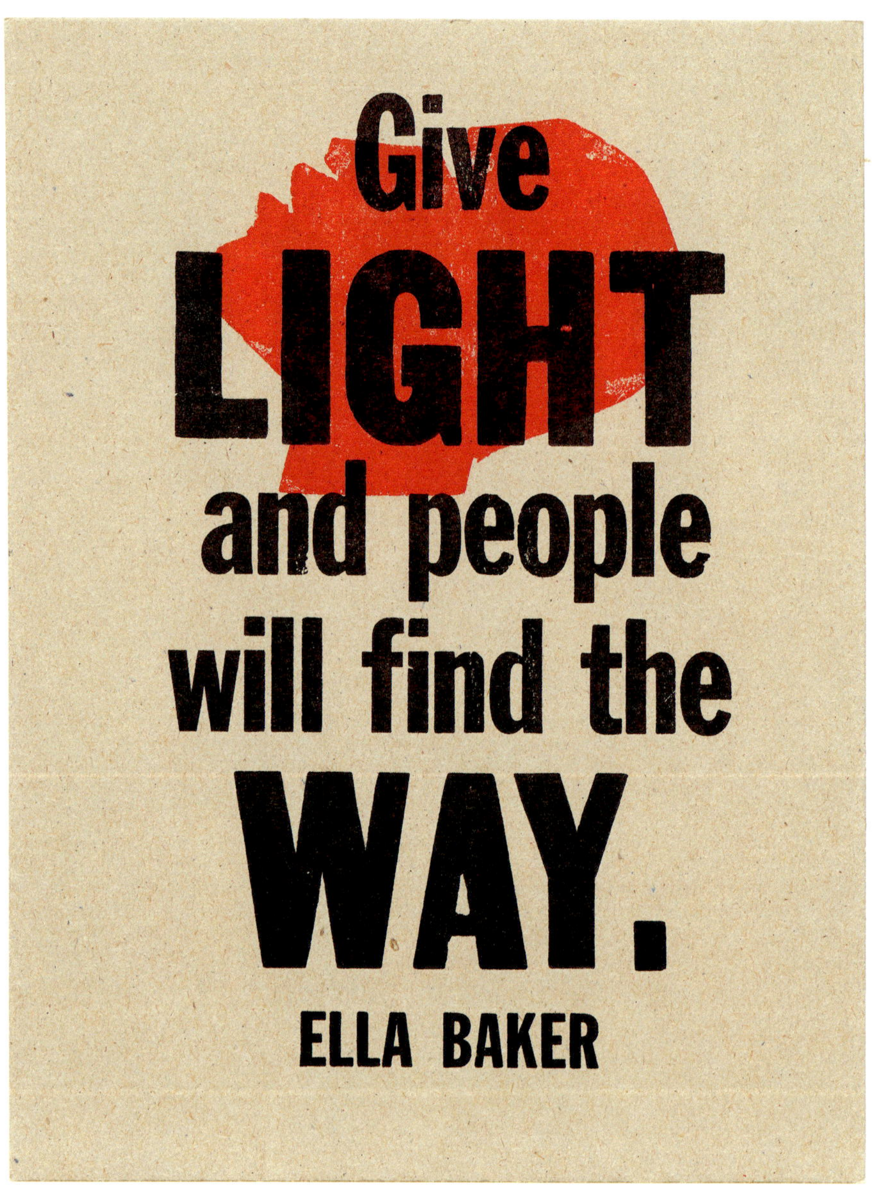

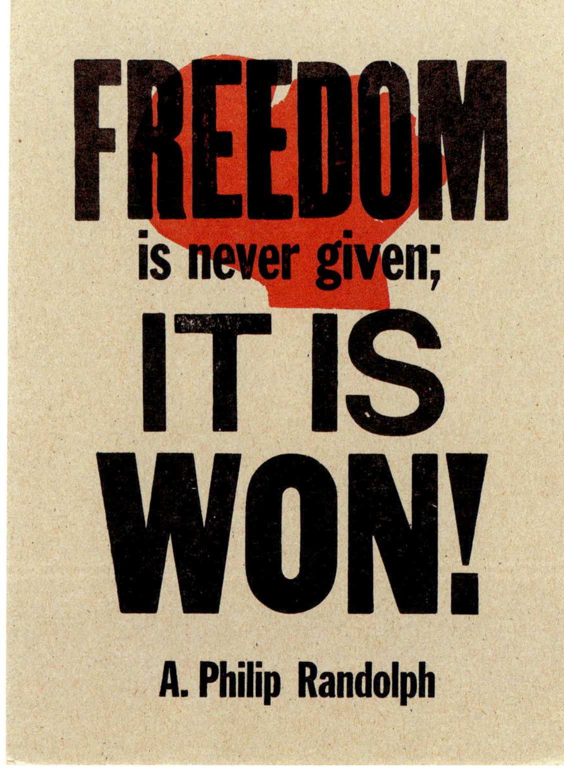

TOP TO BOTTOM Amos Paul Kennedy, Jr., *Give Light and People Will Find the Way* and *Freedom Is Never Given; It is Won!*, 2014, letterpress on chipboard, 8 × 6 inches (20.25 × 15.25 cm), Detroit.

OPPOSITE, TOP TO BOTTOM Unknown designers, *Caution!! Colored People of Boston*, 1851, 12 × 10 inches (30.5 × 25 cm), Boston, and *Outrage, Fellow Citizens*, 1837, 9 × 11⅞ inches (23 × 30 cm), New York, both letterpress.

Amos Paul Kennedy, Jr., is globally celebrated for making bold political posters that tackle issues of race, class, and social justice. In the design community, he is most recognized for his craft—for using letterpress printing as his primary medium in the creation of posters, handbills, artists' books, and other print ephemera. In a field that sometimes feels almost exclusively white, Kennedy stands out as a Black printer ("a humble negro printer," as he calls himself) who is extremely outspoken about the impacts of white supremacy, racism, and social inequality. Through his fearless language, dynamic typography, and loud layers of ink, Kennedy's prints call out proudly, capturing attention and forcing viewers to stop and consider what he has to say.

Born in Louisiana in 1950, Kennedy has witnessed the evolving trajectory of Black liberation in the United States—from growing up in the 1960s during the civil rights era, to encountering the rise of Black nationalism as a young man in the '70s, to experiencing a new wave of activism in the post–civil rights present. Kennedy explains that from his vantage point, "We have lost something in this nation, because we have massive protests, but we have no change. . . . In the '60s, massive protests led to the Civil Rights Act and the Voting Rights Act. Now we can have a march with a million people, and it's just this sort of flash mob."[1] His letterpress prints act as a corrective, reviving language from prominent civil rights figures such as Rosa Parks, Ella Baker, Martin Luther King, Jr., Paul Robeson, and Fannie Lou Hamer, and reconnecting us to the powerful legacy of Black liberation.

While I was familiar with Kennedy's work, the first time I was able to hold his prints in my hands was at the Interference Archive in Brooklyn in 2023. I stumbled across a selection of thirteen handbills, all printed on chipboard. I recognized his striking style and discovered that the prints were part of a larger exhibition of his work entitled *Puttin' Ink on Paper*, held at the Brooklyn Public Library in 2017. At 8 by 6 inches (20.25 by 15.25 cm), the handbills all feature text as their main image, some with hopeful passages such as "Give light and people will find the way," others with strong declarations like "Freedom is never given; it is won!" Kennedy uses condensed letterforms to squeeze together words like "strong," "freedom," "right," and "demand," focusing our attention on their meaning in the context of the present. As a designer, I was drawn to these techniques because I deploy similar tactics when thinking about language and considering its typesetting. In many of his prints, Kennedy combines the literal with the symbolic, adding imagery such as the upturned head in the prints at left to suggest the resilience to persevere.

For Kennedy, the best medium is always the one that guarantees the rapid transmission of content to its viewer. The handbill format allows him to circulate multiple copies of a single layout widely and cheaply, either by hand or via the postal service. This process allows him to literally get the word out, and it is by this act of circulation that his activism is achieved. Kennedy's other most prolific medium is the poster. Historically, posters have also been highly ephemeral and designed to speak to the masses, wheat-pasted on walls to announce upcoming events or to attract attention to important issues. Regardless of format, the urgency of Kennedy's text selection becomes even more apparent when you notice the chipboard's humble quality, as well as the ink splashes and other imperfections that indicate how quickly he works to speak his mind.

Kennedy's use of letterpress technology—despite its reputation as a slow process—also reflects the urgency of his message. In choosing an analog print method from an older time, Kennedy connects the crucial needs of the present to those of the past, when abolitionists first deployed print in the fight for freedom. Along the way, he engages with several forms of narrative and visual arts developed within Black culture over the past 200 years. In doing so, he continues—and calls for the continuation of—the vital tradition of Black intellectual curiosity and authorship through print.

EARLY PRINT PUBLISHING & THE ABOLITIONIST MOVEMENT

When we think about Kennedy's work, it is important to understand how he builds on print publishing technologies developed just as the abolitionist movement was coalescing. After painter and inventor Bass Otis created the first American lithograph in 1819, advances in lithography and chromolithography rapidly expanded, and reduced production and shipping costs made it easier to manufacture and send printed documents across the United States and abroad. Major commercial print centers like Chicago, Philadelphia, New York, and Boston saw an increased demand for print ephemera such as political documents, religious publications, and maps.[2]

This burgeoning publishing industry had a direct impact on countering white supremacy. With the creation of abolitionist books, newspapers, pamphlets, and broadsides, the printing press became a persuasive tool to both spread information and fight disinformation, organize supporters of the cause, and offer serious rebuttals to racist accounts. Particularly important to Kennedy's practice are broadsides, large sheets of cheap paper printed on only one side and plastered to public walls. (Today, these are considered the ancestor of the poster, one of Kennedy's favorite formats.) Broadsides were usually advertisements, but many were proclamations or political announcements, and they provided a critical form of communication for abolitionists.

In Kennedy's posters, we see formal links to broadsides that publicized abolitionist gatherings and sought justice for formerly enslaved people who had been captured and returned to bondage.

CAUTION!!
COLORED PEOPLE
OF BOSTON, ONE & ALL,
You are hereby respectfully CAUTIONED and advised, to avoid conversing with the
Watchmen and Police Officers of Boston,
For since the recent ORDER OF THE MAYOR & ALDERMEN, they are empowered to act as
KIDNAPPERS
AND
Slave Catchers,
And they have already been actually employed in KIDNAPPING, CATCHING, AND KEEPING SLAVES. Therefore, if you value your LIBERTY, and the *Welfare of the Fugitives* among you, *Shun* them in every possible manner, as so many *HOUNDS* on the track of the most unfortunate of your race.
Keep a Sharp Look Out for KIDNAPPERS, and have TOP EYE open.
APRIL 24, 1851.

OUTRAGE.
Fellow Citizens,
AN
ABOLITIONIST,
of the most revolting character is among you, exciting the feelings of the North against the South. A seditious Lecture is to be delivered
THIS EVENING,
at 7 o'clock, at the Presbyterian Church in Cannon-street.
You are requested to attend and unite in putting down and silencing by peaceable means this tool of evil and fanaticism.
Let the rights of the States guaranteed by the Constitution *be protected.*
Feb. 27, 1837. *The Union forever!*

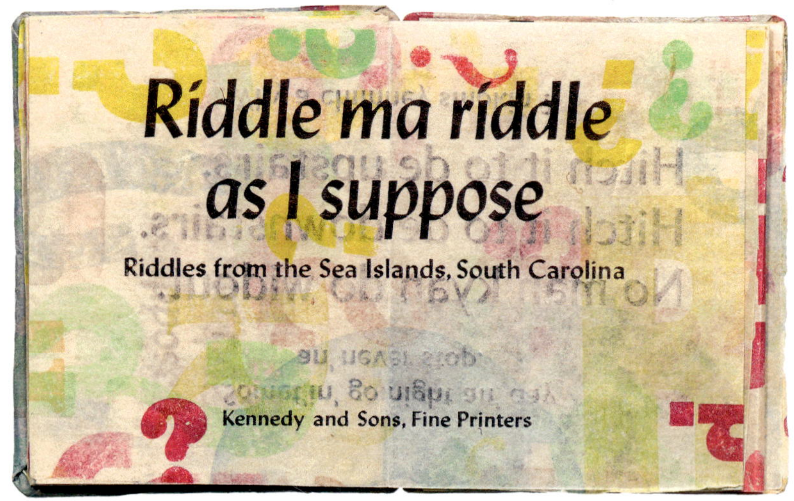

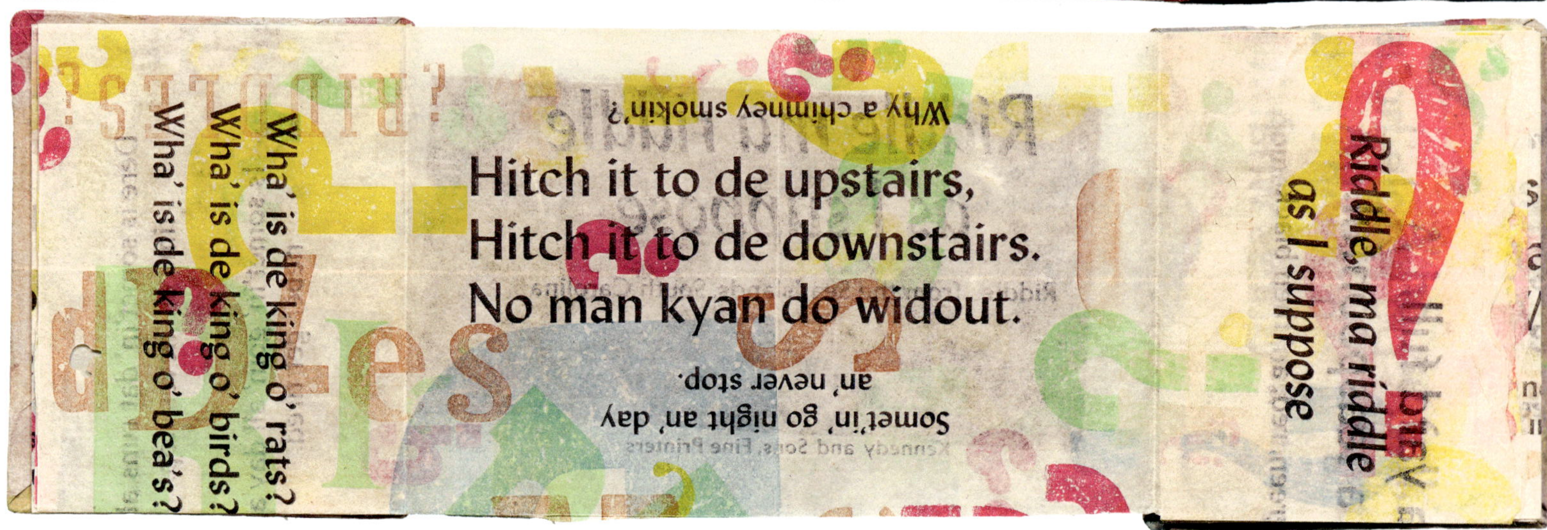

TOP Amos Paul Kennedy, Jr., interiors from *Riddle Ma Riddle*, 1996, letterpress on handmade abaca paper, 3 × 2⅜ inches (7.5 × 6 cm) folded, 3 × 9 inches (7.5 × 23.75 cm) unfolded, Milwaukee, Wisconsin. Kennedy shares, "I set the text in Lydian, which is very humanist—it looks like it was written by hand. I wanted the type to echo the distinct humanity of the Gullah people's words."

OPPOSITE, TOP AND MIDDLE Black students in the printshops of Tuskegee University, circa 1940, and Atlanta University (now Clark Atlanta University), 1904.

OPPOSITE, BOTTOM Frederick Douglass (editor), front page of *The North Star*, vol. 1, no. 38, letterpress, 1848, Rochester, New York.

Kennedy's poster *If There Is No Struggle, There Is No Progress* (see page 59) amplifies orator and activist Frederick Douglass, who—after escaping slavery himself—delivered these words in an 1857 speech on emancipation.[3] Kennedy borrows the typographic strategies of this earlier era by selectively staggering the type in different styles and sizes. The varied type sizes reflect the process used by printers of early broadsides, who often did not have enough letters in a single typeface to complete their print. These characteristics bring a sense of movement to the design. Kennedy, too, lacks complete cases for many of his chosen typefaces, and so he also mismatches his text, but he embraces that irregularity: "I'm not trying to do pristine work," he says. "While you would have to be a real typographer to see the different typefaces in some of my prints, it creates discomfort for the eye even in laypeople, and so you look closer at the words themselves."[4]

Kennedy's first letterpress projects included artists' books, some of which recall slave narratives of the nineteenth century. These pamphlets and books documented the inhumane conditions experienced in slavery by people who became free and went on to write about their experiences.[5] The strong writing demonstrated in these materials expanded the realm of Black authorship, elevating the public perception of Black people.[6]

In his artist's book *Riddle Ma Riddle*, Kennedy also explores the Black linguistic traditions of the enslaved, but instead of concentrating on the written power of slave pamphlets, he focuses on spoken language—specifically, the dialect and riddles of the Gullah people, the descendants of those brought to work the cotton plantations of the Sea Islands, located off the Atlantic coast of the Southern states. The Gullah (also called the Geechee) developed a distinct culture and a creole language rich with loan words and verbal games from Central and West Africa. Of this project, Kennedy says:

> *There's a strong history of riddles in West Africa. It is part of the culture. There is even a riddle without a real answer—the whole point instead was to provoke discussion. In the '20s and '30s, the WPA[7] went out collecting folklore and recorded some of the Geechee riddles brought over from Africa, and later I printed them in* Riddle Ma Riddle, *a book with a folded structure that was supposed to be playful, like a riddle itself. The thing is: I didn't include any of the riddles' answers! [laughs]*
>
> *I am interested in riddles because for so long they were passed down as instruction between adults and children, but now they are disap-*

pearing from the culture. With them, we lose a sense of history, a sense of shared knowledge, and a sense of intergenerational community.[8]

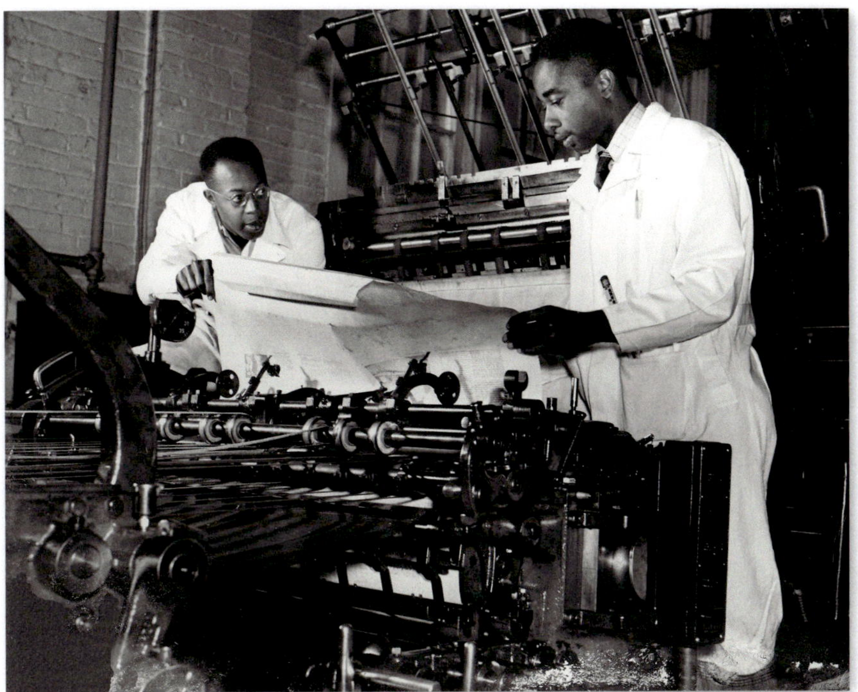

Kennedy's passion for spoken language highlights how communication has continued to evolve within the Black community since Africans were first enslaved in the United States. From the dialect that came about in the Sea Islands to the African American Vernacular English (AAVE) spoken in many Black communities today, these root words and rhythmic patterns all hold traces from our Black ancestors. Black writer and poet Amiri Baraka speaks to this transformation and how white culture has tended to position Black language:

> *What is called now a "Southern accent" or "Negro speech" was once simply the accent of a foreigner trying to speak a new and unfamiliar language, although it was characteristic of the white masters to attribute the slave's "inability" to speak perfect English to the same kind of "childishness" that was used to explain the African's belief in the supernatural. The owners, when they bothered to listen, were impressed that even the songs of their native American slaves were "incomprehensible" or "unintelligible."*[9]

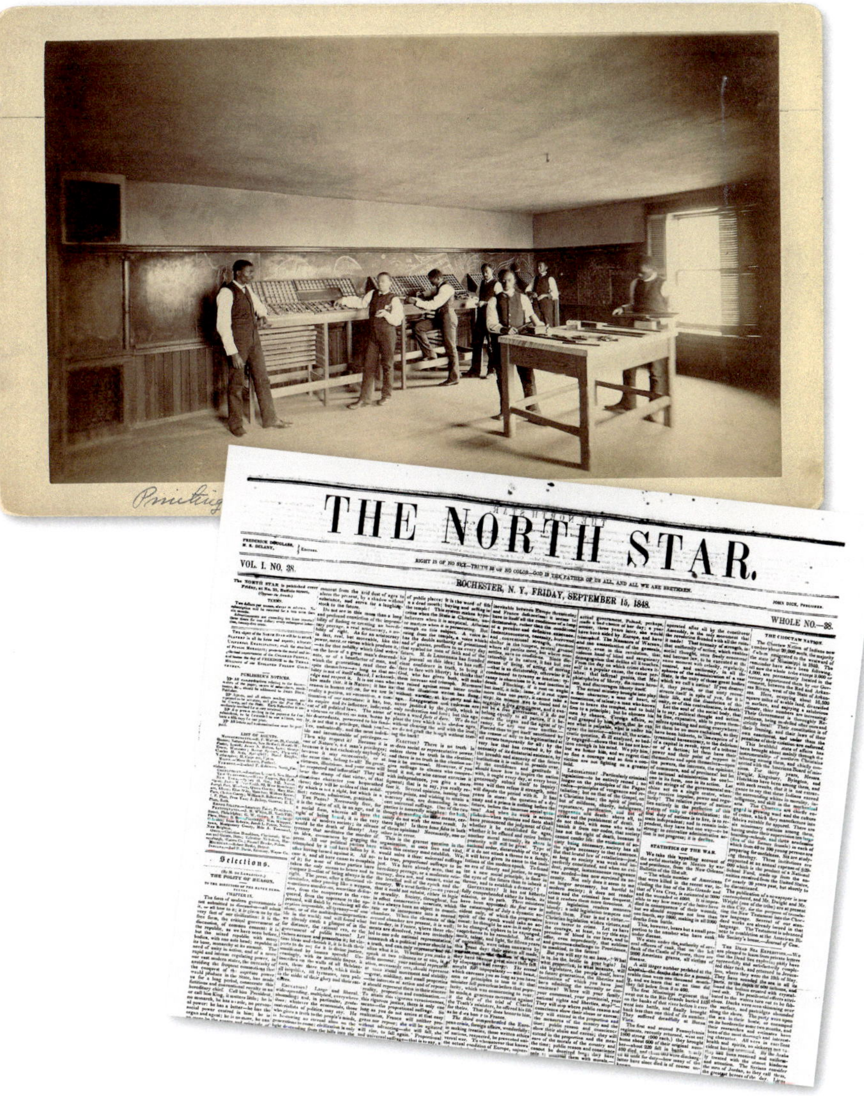

THE NORTH STAR.

VOL. I. NO. 38.

ROCHESTER, N. Y. FRIDAY, SEPTEMBER 15, 1848.

WHOLE NO.—38.

In *Riddle Ma Riddle*, Kennedy activates the unconventional structure of the artist's book and sets text in expressive and nonlinear ways to meaningfully mimic and preserve the historical colloquialisms of the Gullah. In highlighting the poetic "incomprehensibility" of their riddles, he also mobilizes so-called negro speech to evoke histories of oppression and liberation at the same time.

EARLY BLACK NEWSPAPERS & PRINT AT HBCUS

Abolitionist broadsides and pamphlets developed alongside the Black newspaper, which went on to advance the ideas of Black liberation on a larger scale. Reverend John Wilk's *Freedom's Journal* (1827–29), Frederick Douglass's *The North Star* (1847–51), and Mary Ann Shadd's *Provincial Freeman* (1853–57) are important to the legacy of Black print publishing because for the first time African Americans could see themselves fully represented in the press.[10] Mainstream white newspapers did not report the news from Black communities. As a result, it was necessary that Black people form their own news platforms to share information about the social, political, and economic conditions impacting them. Black women made major contributions, with journalists such as Ida B. Wells and Mary Church Terrell writing articles that engaged in racial debates and pushed for civil rights. Wells was also among the first to report on the lynchings and other racist atrocities happening in the South following the Civil War.[11]

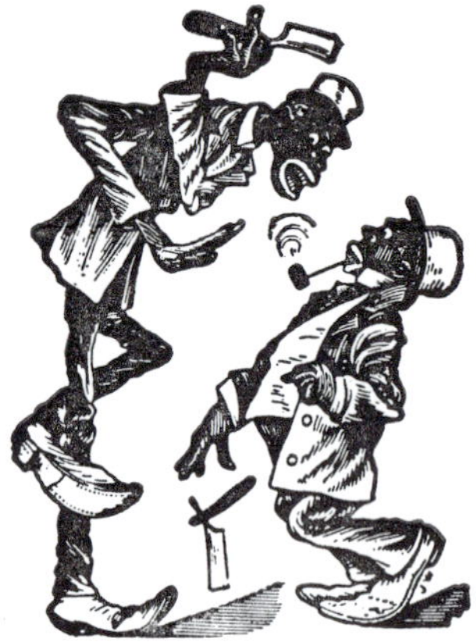

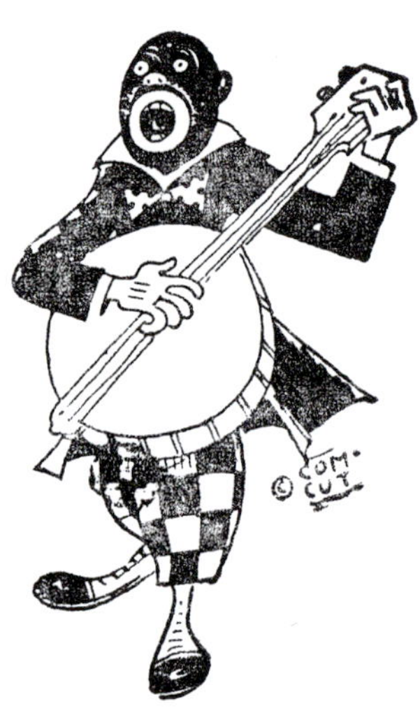

The reach of Black newspapers grew exponentially during this time. According to Kinshasha Holman Conwill, former director of the National Museum of African American History and Culture, "The number of African American newspapers proliferated in the early 1900s. By 1979, more than 350 African American newspapers, magazines, and bulletins were publishing on a weekly, monthly, or quarterly basis."[12] During this period, print publishing also found its way to HBCUs, such as Tuskegee, Howard, Claflin, and Southern Universities. These institutions recognized the importance of having access to print, as well as the field's potential to provide vocational opportunities to students. In addition to creating their own print collateral, HBCUs served their surrounding communities by producing printed matter for local businesses, organizations, and events.

Kennedy himself attended Grambling State University, an HBCU in northern Louisiana, and he often remarks on the lasting value of these schools to Black people:

> *There were more than 100 HBCUs founded after the Civil War to educate the formerly enslaved peoples. And for the longest time, that was the only place Black people could go for an education beyond high school. Here is where teachers introduced Black people to art and math. So these institutions fostered a lot of the visual culture that made Black America, and they were and still are extremely important. Printing was also taught at many of these universities.*[13]

Throughout his printing career, Kennedy has embodied the early HBCUs' spirit of printing for the local community, producing event posters for neighbors, friends, and organizations with which he felt an affinity. For Kennedy, printing is how he shows up.

ART & POLITICS DURING THE HARLEM RENAISSANCE

By the early 1920s, it was not only reportage taking up column inches in Black publications: An abundance of Black cultural expression was finding its way into print production, and several literary publications were beginning to reshape Black consciousness in the United States. Scholar of African American literature Melissa Barton highlights that "the period from about 1917 to about 1939 saw unprecedented achievements in African American publication, performance, and visual arts. In the near century since that time, this period has captured the American popular imagination with its style, music, and dance, and elicited hundreds of scholarly monographs and articles, exhibitions, and revivals."[14]

One notable publication from this time that inspired Kennedy is *Fire!!: Devoted to Younger Negro Artists*, a short-lived literary journal cofounded in 1926 by Wallace Thurman, Langston Hughes, Aaron Douglas, Countee Cullen, Zora Neale Hurston, Gwendolyn Bennett, and Richard Bruce Nugent. Their contributions, which included narratives of Black queerness, interracial love, and sex work, actively challenged the mainstream, seeking to disrupt the respectability politics put forth as a way to equality by Black leaders like W. E. B. Du Bois. In *Propaganda and Aesthetics: The Literary Politics of Afro-American Magazines in the Twentieth Century*, Abby Arthur Johnson and Ronald Maberry Johnson describe the outlook of the editorial team: "They selected *Fire!!* as a title because, in Hughes's words, they desired to 'épater le bourgeois,' to burn up a lot of the old stereotyped Uncle Tom ideas of the past."[15]

Kennedy's letterpress prints also continually push against respectability politics, with ideas and language that intentionally stir the pot. He responded to *Fire!!* directly with his own 2003 pamphlet by the

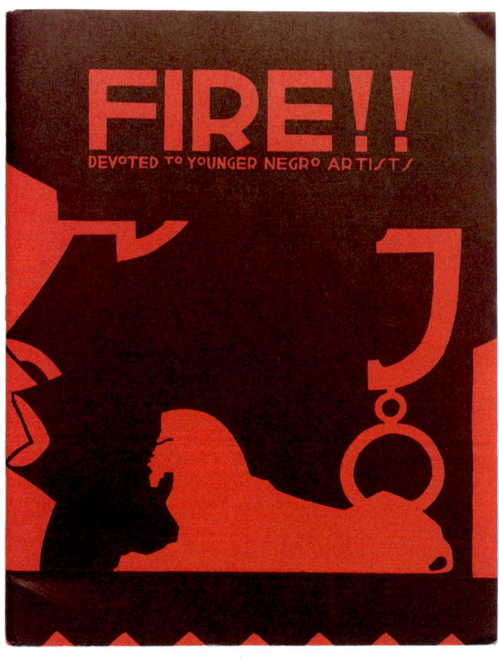

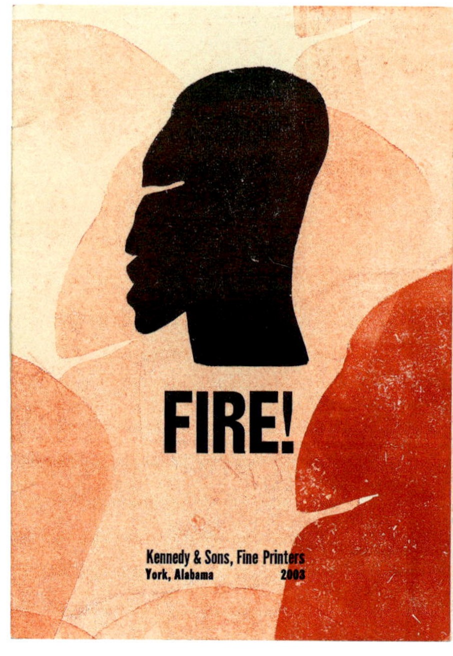

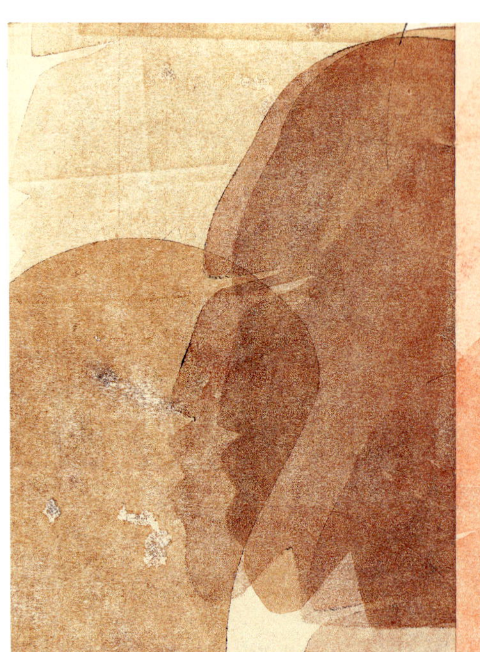

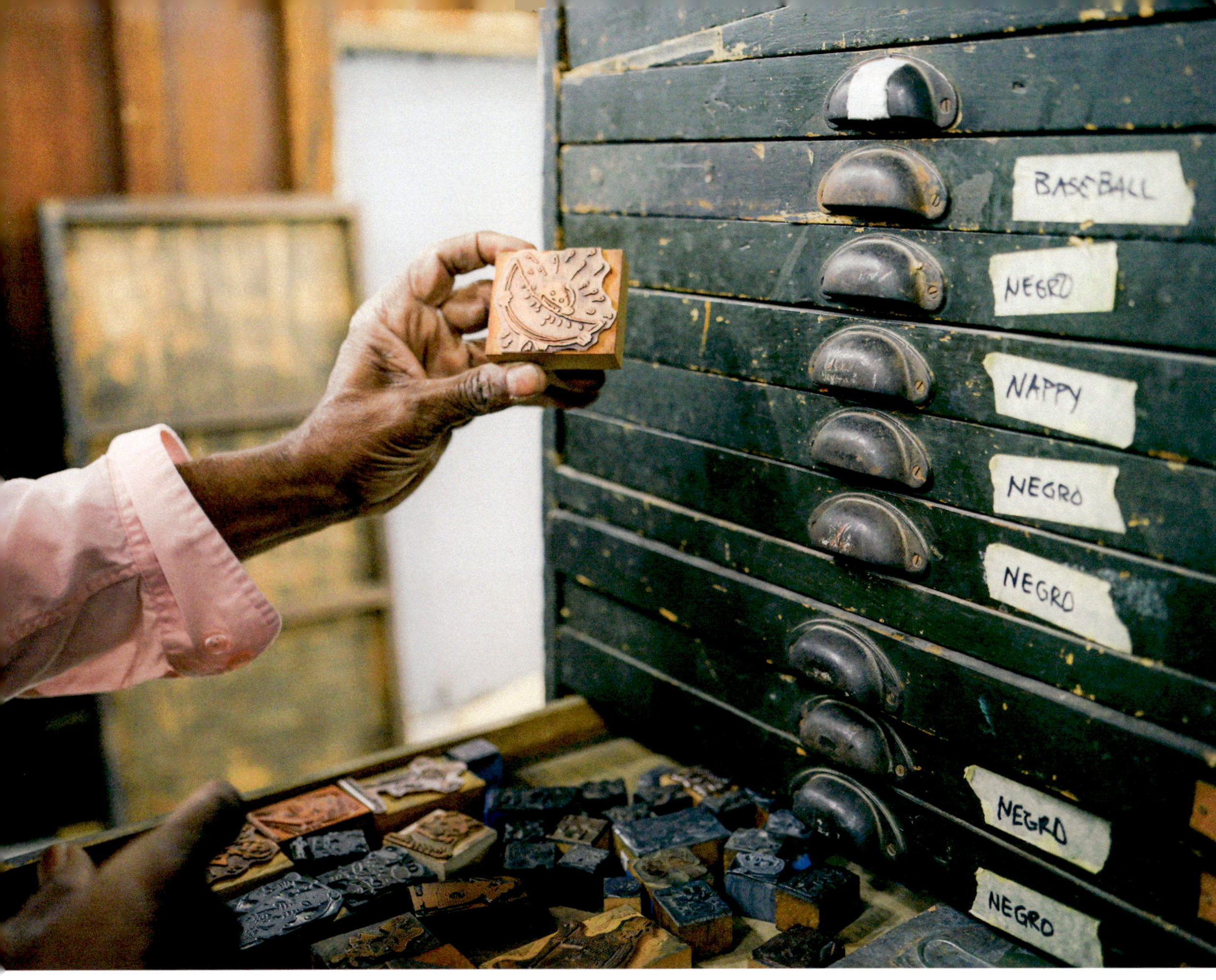

same name, which features a recurring motif of a Black man in profile created with a hand-carved Masonite cut. This image pays tribute to artist Aaron Douglas, who sought out inspiration from African art, including geometric patterns and angular figures with stylized features, and who contributed the cover to the first and only issue of *Fire!!* Kennedy's appropriation of this figure speaks to his respect for the era. "The Harlem Renaissance defined a huge swath of my education," he recounts. "I was inspired by the concerted efforts to create such a profound development in the arts by Black people."[16]

Historically, not all representations of the Black body had been as positive. Minstrel spectacles first emerged in the 1830s, popularized in part by T. D. Rice, a white performer in blackface who used the stage name Jim Crow. These racist caricatures swiftly made their way into print in the form of lithographs and woodcuts. Even while the new Black press and Black artistic and literary movements of the nineteenth and early twentieth centuries flourished, such racist publishing and entertainment continued to proliferate, as Jim Crow laws and racial cruelty gripped the South and the American

TOP Kennedy selects a cut featuring a Black figure with a watermelon slice from his typecase. Such imagery frequently appeared on "coon cards" of the nineteenth century: anti-Black postcards distributed after the Civil War as a means of disparaging newly emancipated Black citizens.

OPPOSITE, TOP Two examples from Kennedy's personal collection of antique woodcuts featuring minstrel and otherwise stereotypical Black imagery. Kennedy also collects cuts of Black heroes, such as Malcolm X (see page 273).

OPPOSITE, BOTTOM FAR LEFT Aaron Douglas, cover of *Fire!!: Devoted to Younger Negro Artists*, issue 1, 1926 (1985 facsimile printing), offset, 10⅞ × 8½ inches (27.5 × 21.5 cm), New York.

BOTTOM, OPPOSITE MIDDLE TO RIGHT Amos Paul Kennedy, Jr., cover and interiors of *Fire!*, 2003, letterpress on paper, 11½ × 8 inches (29.25 × 20.25 cm), York, Alabama.

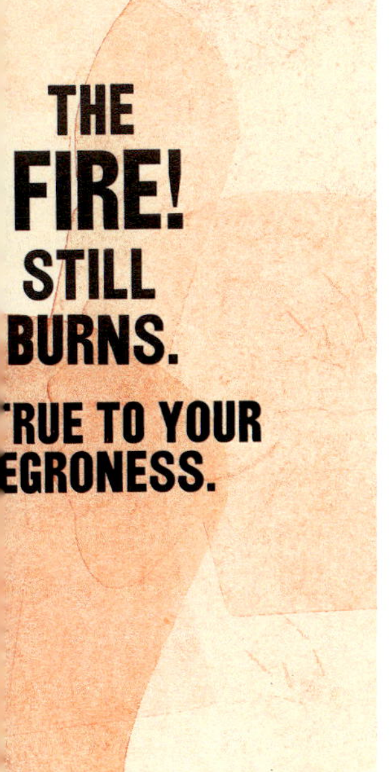

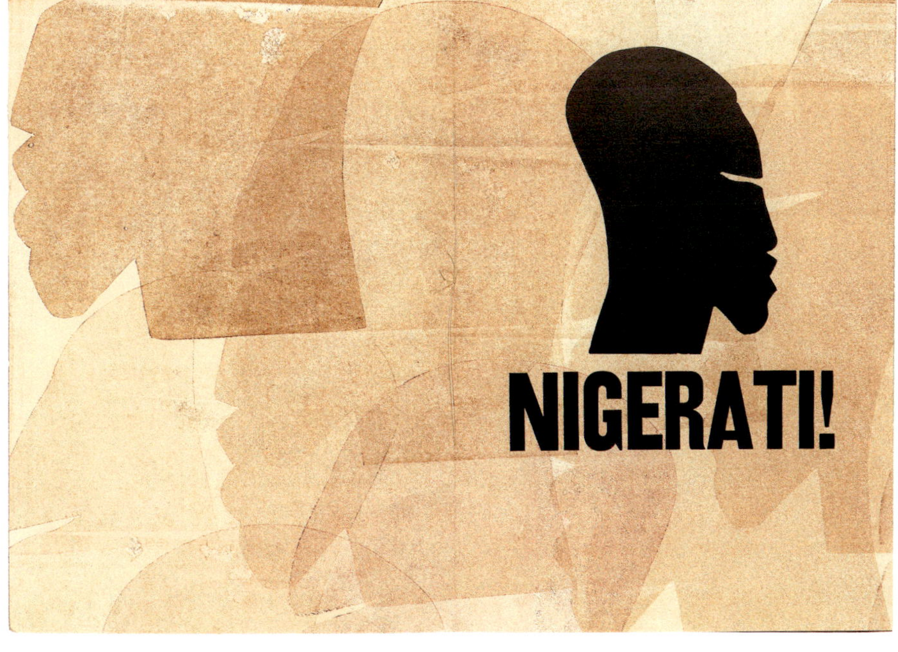

consciousness. These images strategically positioned Blacks as inferior beings, and they remain embedded in the foundation of the United States today.[17]

The New Negro movement emerged in the 1920s specifically to counter these racist ideas from the first 300 years of Black existence in America. The philosophical underpinning of the Harlem Renaissance's artistic accomplishments, this movement presented a reconstructed identity of Black people as educated, economically stable, and sophisticated. The cultural works associated with the New Negro shared the complexities of Black life and gave more dimension and depth to Black people's existence as individuals. In "The Trope of a New Negro and the Reconstruction of the Image of the Black," Henry Louis Gates, Jr., acknowledges the complicated semiotics of Black representation through his comparisons of early racialized graphics and the self-determination of the New Negro:

> *It is the several definitions of the "New Negro" as the sign of a new racial self, the Public Negro Self, after 1895 that apply most directly to the New Negro Renaissance of the Jazz Age. This black and racial self, as we define it here, does not exist as an entity or group of entities but "only" as a coded system of signs, complete with masks and mythology. At least since its usages after 1895, the name has implied a tension between strictly political concerns and strictly artistic concerns.*[18]

Gates references both political and artistic motivations that reshaped the Black image in this era, highlighting the ways Black artists were reinventing themselves, creating masks or leaning into mythological conceptions of Blackness.

Kennedy also draws upon this difficult history and incorporates the visual vernacular of blackface and minstrel graphics into his own work as part reclamation and part reinvention. He has amassed a collection of around three dozen woodcuts bearing such minstrel imagery—some original antiques, some newly commissioned using photocopies of old books and advertisements. As with his activation of the word *negro* in several of his prints, he takes back these racist relics for his own satirical purposes, shocking contemporary audiences and making us reconsider the meaning of these images.

INFLUENCES FROM SOUTHERN CULTURE & CRAFT

In the transition from the Harlem Renaissance to the civil rights era, abolitionist print publishing began to find a home in Black religious contexts as well. Since the enslavement of Africans began in the United States, Black churches had been safe havens for runaways seeking their freedom. With the formation of the African Methodist Episcopal and Black Baptist churches in the eighteenth century, religious spaces provided early meeting places for abolitionists advocating for Black liberation. Then, after the Civil War, during the era of Reconstruction and Jim Crow, these same churches helped birth the civil rights movement.[19]

Print publishing in the Black church came in the form of religious signage, illustrated biblical scenes, church bulletins, and periodicals. Congregants also used printed fans to cool down in overheated Southern churches before the invention of air-conditioning. These fans acted as promotional tools for local businesses and provided visual mementos from life events such as weddings and funerals. Southern studies professor Charles Reagan Wilson explains their prominence:

> *The original hand-held fans that worshippers used to move the air in Southern churches were palm fans, common in hot climates and used in residences and businesses as well as sacred spaces. In the early twentieth century, printers began producing inexpensive cardboard fans on wood handles for businesses to purchase and distribute with information on the back. . . . Church fans embody a pronounced traditionalism that has long characterized the Southern religious culture.*[20]

Representing a departure from his usual media of posters and handbills, church fans form a recurrent substrate in Kennedy's work. Sometimes he wields them in a traditional way, printing them with typographic patterns that celebrate events and birthdays. But he can also employ them to stun. In a series of 134 fans, each printed with the name of a civil rights activist killed between 1946 and 1968, Kennedy forces the viewer to contend with the deaths of the many who gave their lives for the cause of equality. In addition to including the year and state in which each activist was killed, he prints "Murdered" in red ink across all the designs. His angled text placement suggests the spilling of blood, subverting the perception of the church as a safe space, and challenges the viewer to remember the violence of the Jim Crow era. His use of the fan asks us to contemplate how the rites of funereal memorialization can serve as a tool for historical remembrance as well.

Kennedy's fluency in Southern culture shows up in his work in many ways, including in his posters for craft events like a 2005 quilting workshop led by Mozell Benson (see page 253), in which he prints with scrap wood to mimic fabric-strip quilts. The hand-carved linocut blocks he creates to use as backgrounds in his letterpress prints are also in direct conversation with the asymmetrical grids of the Gee's Bend quilters, a group of Black women in rural

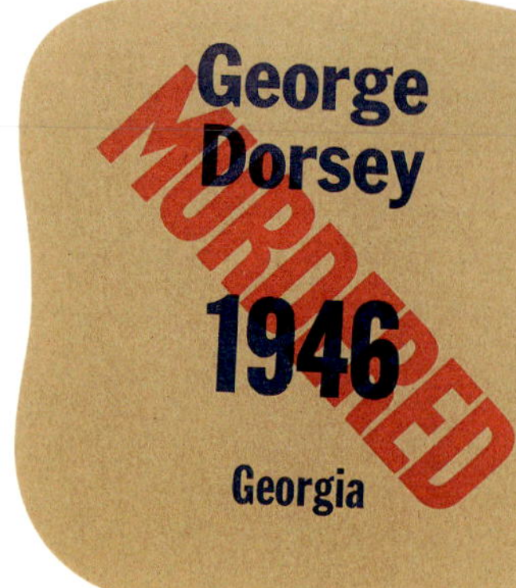

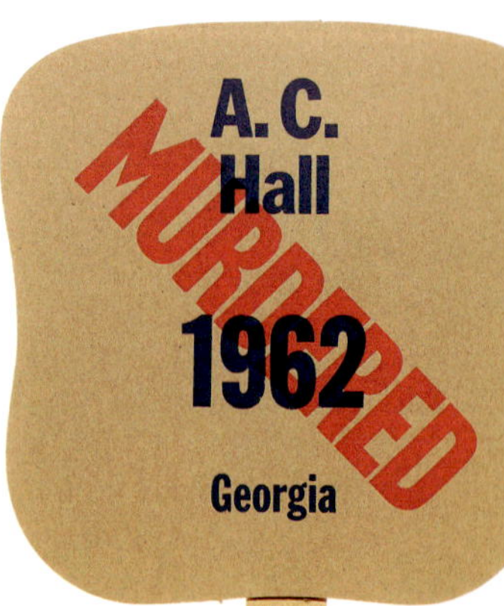

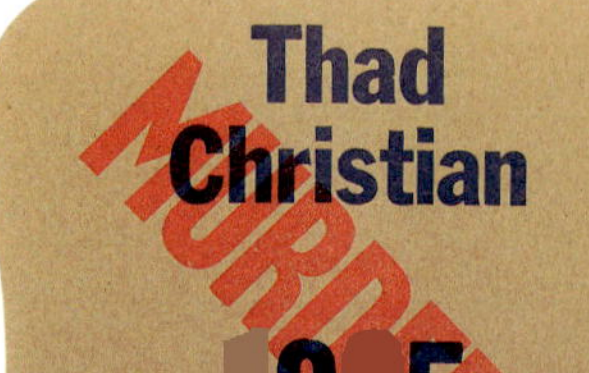

RIGHT Amos Paul Kennedy, Jr., fans for the martyrs of the civil rights movement, 2013, letterpress on chipboard fans, 7⅞ × 7⅞ inches (20 × 20 cm), Detroit.

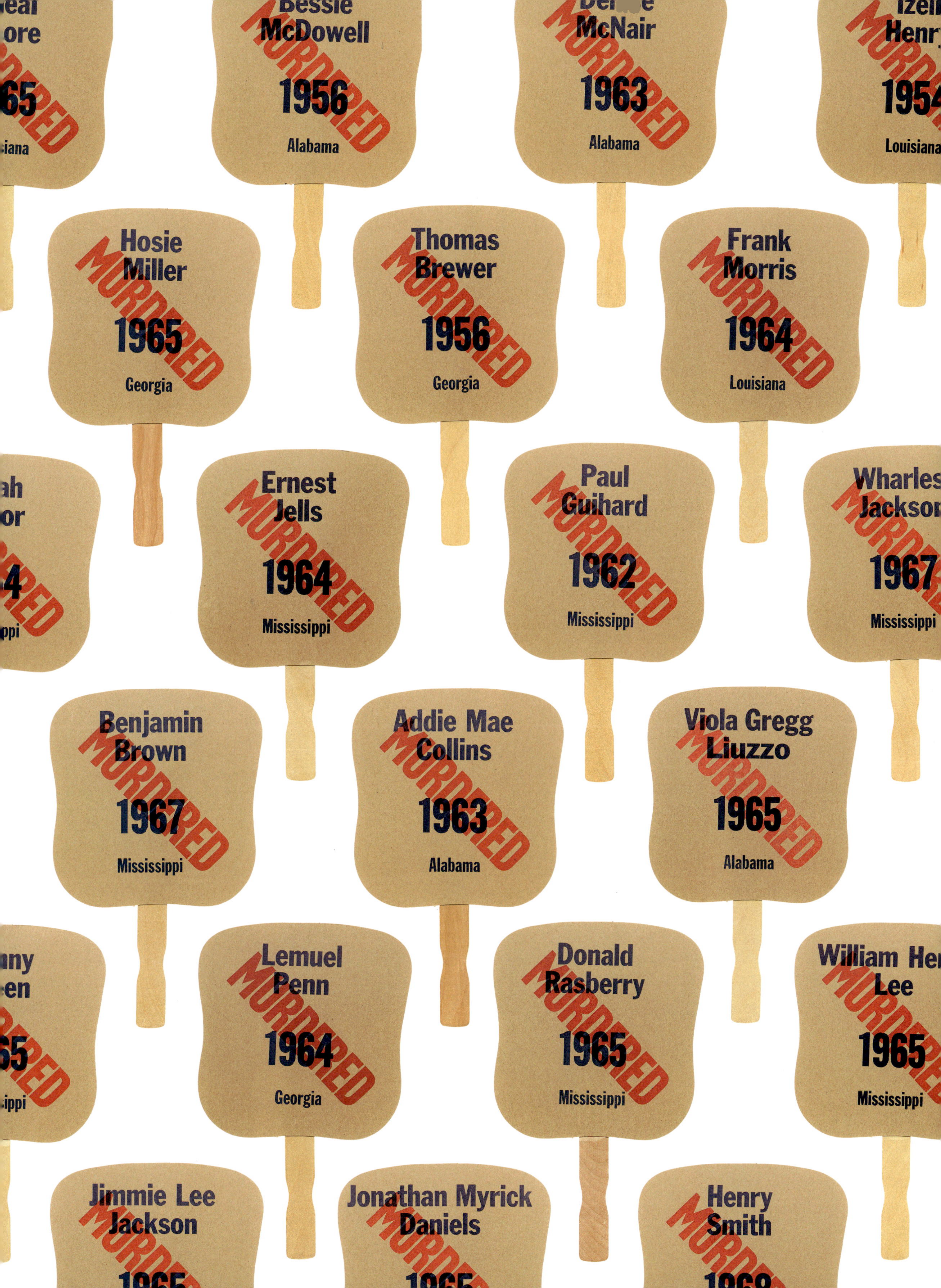

Bessie
McDowell
MURDERED
1956
Alabama
McNair
MURDERED
1963
Alabama
Louisiana
Hosie
Miller
MURDERED
1965
Georgia
Thomas
Brewer
MURDERED
1956
Georgia
Frank
Morris
MURDERED
1964
Louisiana
Ernest
Jells
MURDERED
1964
Mississippi
Paul
Guihard
MURDERED
1962
Mississippi
1967
Mississippi
Benjamin
Brown
MURDERED
1967
Mississippi
Addie Mae
Collins
MURDERED
1963
Alabama
Viola Gregg
Liuzzo
MURDERED
1965
Alabama
Lemuel
Penn
MURDERED
1964
Georgia
Donald
Rasberry
MURDERED
1965
Mississippi
Lee
1965
Mississippi
Jimmie Lee
Jackson
Jonathan Myrick
Daniels
Henry
Smith

Alabama who in the early twentieth century made irregular geometric quilts using fabric remnants. (In 1966, after the quilts were recognized by the art world, the women's work took on an economic and political dimension with the formation of the Freedom Quilting Bee, a cooperative that supported Black female artisans and protected their right to earn fair wages, as well as fundraised for the civil rights movement.)[21]

Holding space for the imperfections and inconsistencies exhibited in the Gee's Bend quilts and in other Southern folk art and craft traditions is what separates Kennedy from other printers. Instead of displaying machine-made perfection, his prints show the signs of the human touch, and the visual experience of his humanity offers viewers a way into larger conversations about social justice.

PRINT PROTEST IN THE CIVIL RIGHTS ERA

The visual language of protest signage from the Montgomery Bus Boycott (1955–56), the March on Washington for Jobs and Freedom (1963), the Selma to Montgomery "Bloody Sunday" march (1965), and the Memphis Sanitation Workers' Strike (1968) brought new typographic aesthetics into the civil rights era. The protest placards produced for these

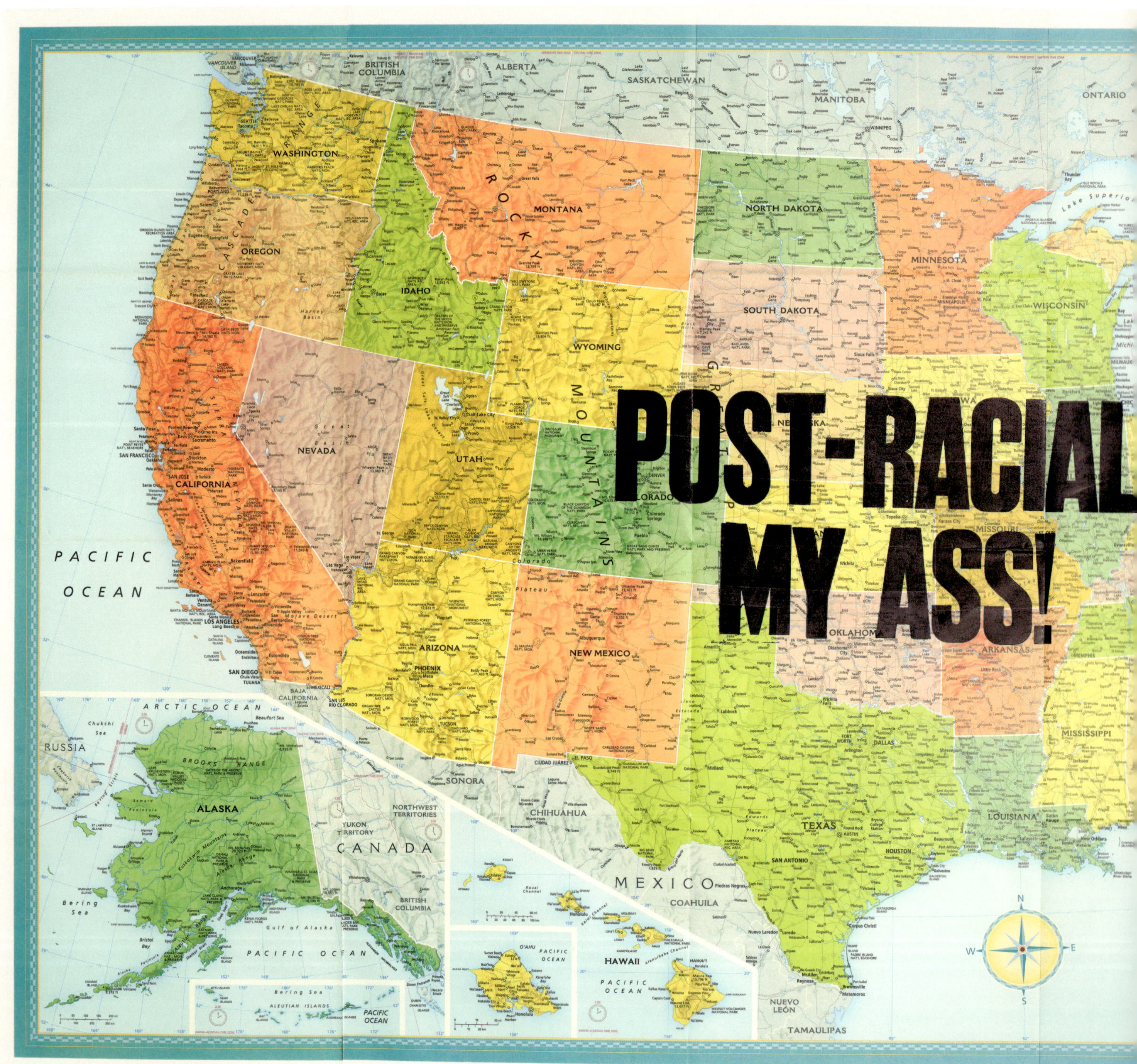

marches defined the 1960s, and more than half a century later, they still echo in Kennedy's prints, with his use of declarative sans serif text in all caps.

In one of his most important undertakings to date, Kennedy documents the first-person story of civil rights icon Rosa Parks, who in 1955 refused to vacate her seat for white passengers on a bus in Montgomery, Alabama (see pages 106–11). While Kennedy uses the type styling of the protest placards of Parks's era, he applies the primary statements over colorful typographic layers that overlap to create spatial density in the background, with each layer of text representing aspects of her life. Metaphorically, one can read these layers as the recurring efforts of Parks and others fed up with the long history of racism. Kennedy reflects on this visual approach:

> *When you look at something like the Rosa Parks portfolio, you'll see that there's one layer that has dates that are significant to her life. Then there's another layer that has places that are significant to her life. This continues for about four layers, because one of the things I like to do is envision people having that aha moment—when that poster has been on the wall for a considerable amount of time, and they see it every day, but suddenly, they turn their head a certain way, and they say, "Oh, the word Montgomery's behind there. I never noticed that before." And that will draw them in to look and study it more.*[22]

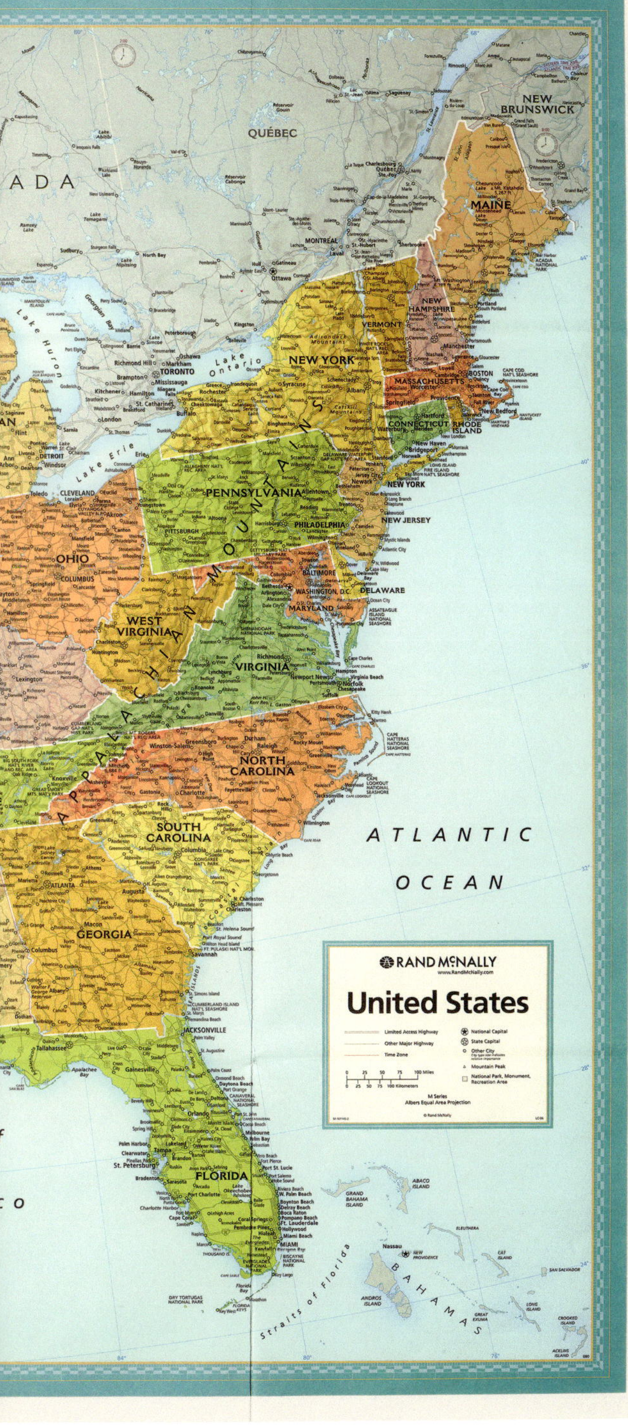

OPPOSITE Amos Paul Kennedy, Jr., *Post-Racial, My Ass!*, circa 2009, letterpress on a highway map of the United States, 32 × 50 inches (81 × 127 cm), Gordo, Alabama. Kennedy's map prints also remind readers that for the first half of the twentieth century, Black motorists could not safely travel throughout the country, and were often denied food and lodging along major routes.

Many in the Jim Crow era fled the South, either due to the lack of economic opportunity resulting from legalized segregation or to escape racist violence. Referred to as the Great Migration, the period between 1910 and 1970 saw six million Black people leave their homes for cities in the North or the West.[23] Kennedy's family made many moves in the early 1950s, with some relatives settling as far away from the South as Oakland, California. The maternal side of my own family was one of the many Black families who left Alabama and Georgia during the Great Migration's second wave. Kennedy speaks to this Black exodus and the site-specific acts of violence perpetrated against Black people through his printed maps:

> *When I print on a map, I am introducing or reinforcing information about a geographical area. Sometimes, like with the* People Died for Your Right to Vote *series* [see pages 120–21], *I print stories specific to a place over a map of it—in that case, Alabama, where four civil rights workers were murdered. But for* Post-Racial, My Ass!, *which I made when President [Barack] Obama was elected in 2008, I used a whole map of the United States. Because there's not a single state where Black people have not encountered racism, no matter how much folks want to congratulate themselves for putting a Black man at the head of all fifty-two of them.*[24]

In addition to the ability of maps to visually represent the stories of physical terrain, they are manufactured with foldability and portability in mind. These features allow Kennedy to send large letterpress prints through the mail (sometimes without an envelope), and recipients can easily unfold and refold the work, unlike a poster mailed in a tube. Again, Kennedy is always thinking about the most economical and efficient way to communicate while inviting viewer participation.

Black printing continued to challenge the mainstream as the 1970s approached. In 1967,

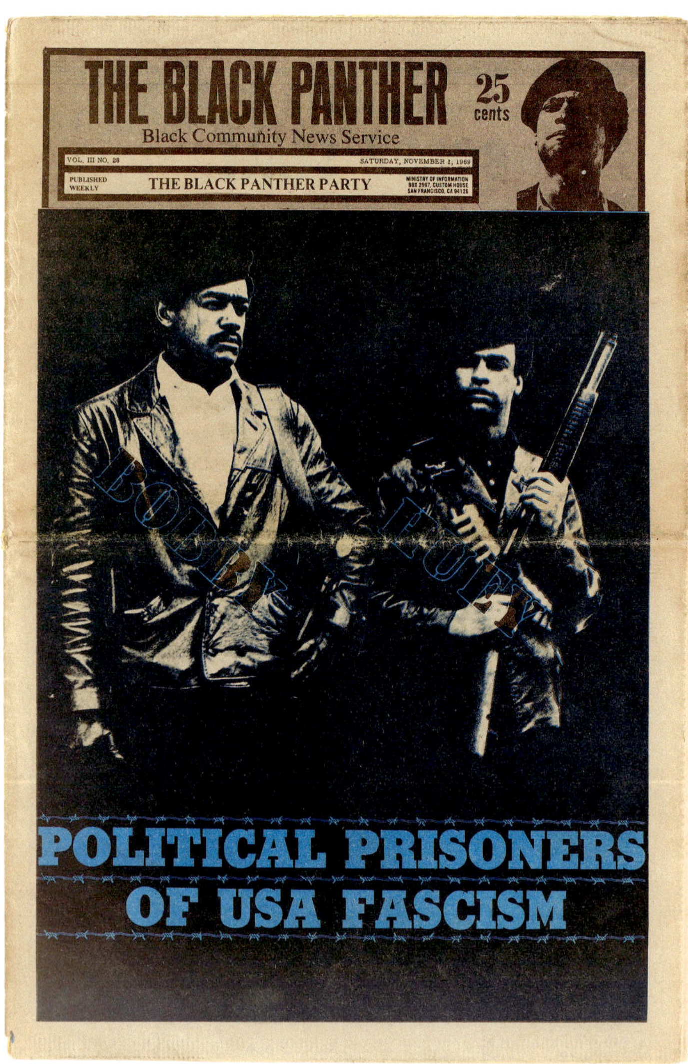

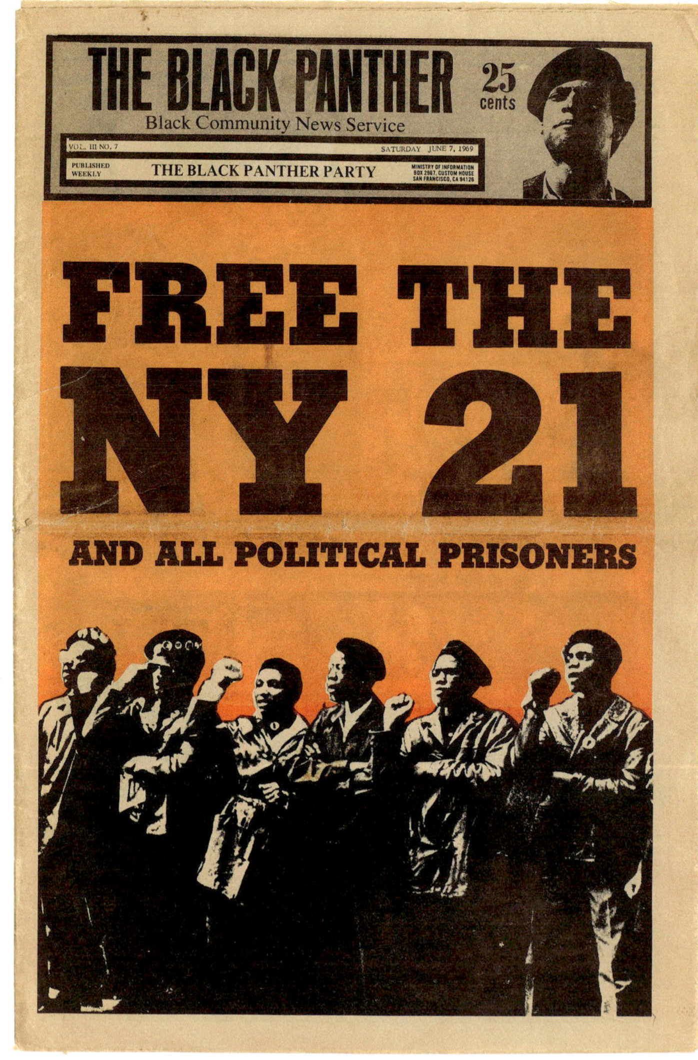

TOP, LEFT TO RIGHT Emory Douglas (designer), front covers of *The Black Panther*, vol. 3, no. 28 (left) and no. 7 (right), 1969, offset, 17 × 11½ inches (43 × 29.5 cm), Oakland, California.

OPPOSITE, TOP LEFT Emory Douglas (designer and illustrator), back cover of *The Black Panther*, vol. 6, no. 30, 1971, offset, 17 × 11½ inches (43 × 29.5 cm), Oakland, California. The speckled pattern was created using Letratone, a dry-transfer screentone.

OPPOSITE, TOP RIGHT Protesters hold typeset signs in a rally of the American Federation of State, County, and Municipal Employees union in Tennessee, 1976.

OPPOSITE, BOTTOM Amos Paul Kennedy, Jr., *Free Health Care for All*, 2023, letterpress on chipboard, 19 × 12½ inches (48.25 × 31.75 cm), Detroit.

Bobby Seale and Huey P. Newton founded the Black Panther Party and established its newspaper to advance their progressive ideas and further the cause of Black liberation. From the first issue, the boldness with which the typographic and illustrative components conveyed their message set the publication apart from Black newspapers of the past. Designer Emory Douglas created numerous issues criticizing the police and depicting officers as pigs, and he identified various forms of oppression faced by Black Americans in his editorial illustrations on poverty, housing, health care, and capitalistic greed. On the issues' front covers, he often featured photographs of incarcerated Panthers, while the back covers functioned as illustrated posters, with heroic portraits of everyday community members. His look and feel for the publication during the height of the Black Power movement reflected the party's attitude of agitation, with young Black men shown in revolutionary attire, complete with guns.

Kennedy has admired Douglas's work since he first encountered the party's newspaper on the Grambling campus in the late 1960s. "It was more radical than anything else going on in Black publishing," he remembers. "But it was more than that. The way he used Letratone patterns to give the work texture and depth, and the way he outlined his portraits with thick lines, making them look like woodcuts. He had limited resources but knew how to work within the perimeters of print."[25] Working with limited resources is something Kennedy also embraces. Much as Douglas made printing on especially cheap newsprint emblematic of the publication, Kennedy has made printing on humble chipboard a key part of his work. Douglas printed using only two colors in each issue, while Kennedy makes do with ink discarded by other printshops, and Douglas's reusable type transfer patterns echo in Kennedy's linocuts, which he uses over and over again. I find this aspect fascinating as it relates to access for both artists and audience: Both Kennedy's and Douglas's material choices result in less cost for the makers, a greater volume of printed material, and more affordable prices for consumers. All these factors enable them to reach a wider public.

When we view Kennedy's work in the context of the protest signs and Black counterculture publishing of the 1960s, we begin to see the larger story that has shaped his design practice. Kennedy even reprinted an excerpt from the Black Panthers' Ten-Point Program, emphasizing "Free Health Care for All"—amplifying an immediate need that is perhaps felt even more today than it was fifty years ago.

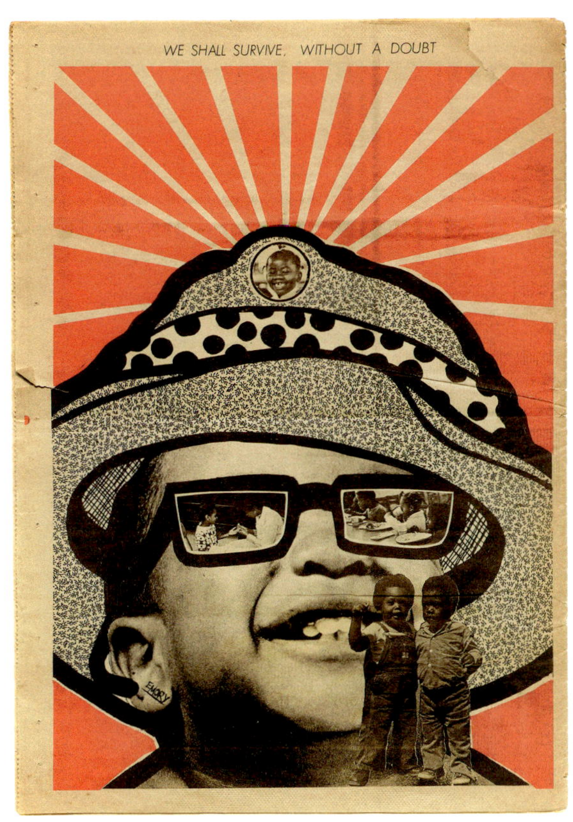

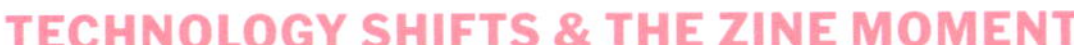

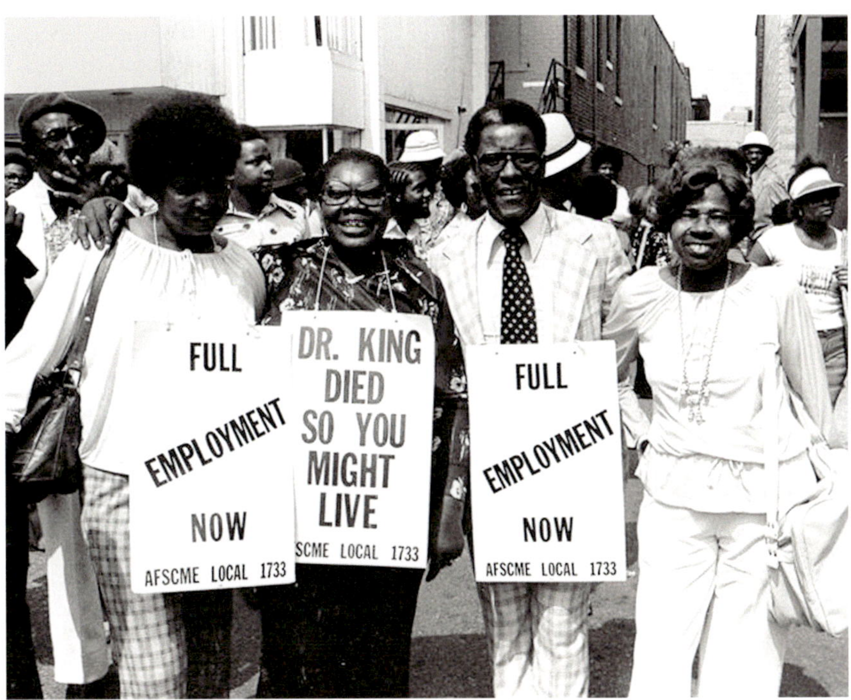

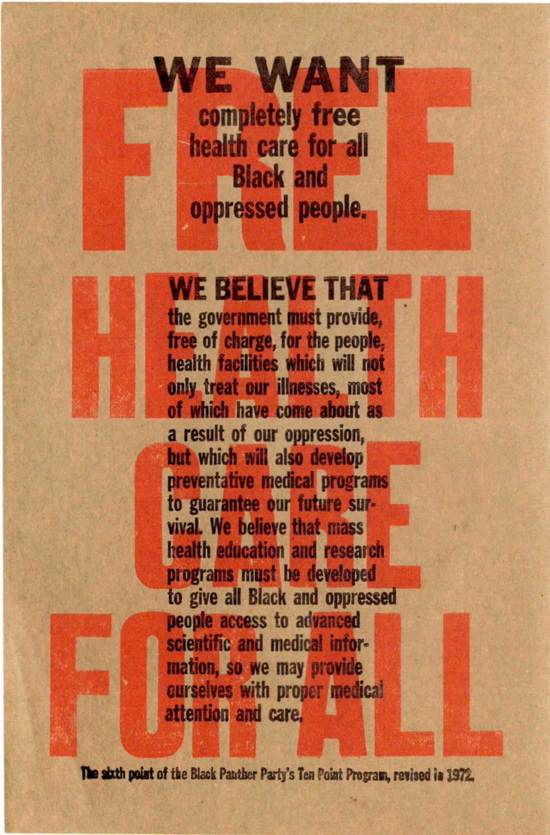

TECHNOLOGY SHIFTS & THE ZINE MOMENT

In the 1960s, photocopying took off as a widespread method of making quick and affordable reproductions. The inherently capitalist need for speed and efficiency in the printing process drove this technology, but it went on to enable a myriad of anti-institutional print trends in the 1970s and beyond, including protest posters, event flyers, and political zines. Art educators Kristin G. Congdon and Doug Blandy explain:

> *Zines have continued to flourish since the 1970s. . . . During the 1990s, the political orientation of zines expanded to include feminist perspectives through the impetus of groups like the riot grrrls. At the same time, cyberpunk zines emerged along with zines created with desktop publishing programs.*[26]

Along with flyers, these small independent publications began to democratize and disseminate a wider mix of sociopolitical views on race, LGBTQIA+ rights, feminist thought, and class conflict.[27] These examples of print ephemera can be seen as descendants of the abolitionist pamphlet, yet their makers took more design liberties, combining cut-and-pasted letterforms, photographs, and graphics with rudimentary typesetting using typewriters or early word processors. With the move away from traditional forms of type composition and layout, altering the placement of letterforms became a political act.

Photocopied flyers also gave groups the ability to advertise their own events with their newly improvised aesthetics. For example, in the 1980s, graphic artist Buddy Esquire (Lemoin Thompson) produced hundreds of hip-hop flyers in the Bronx for rap artists

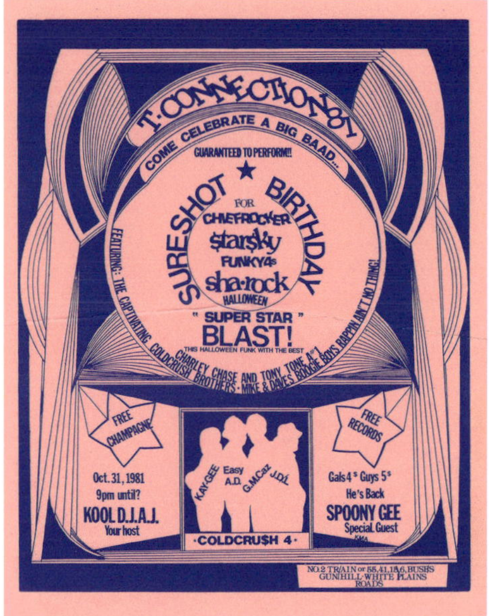

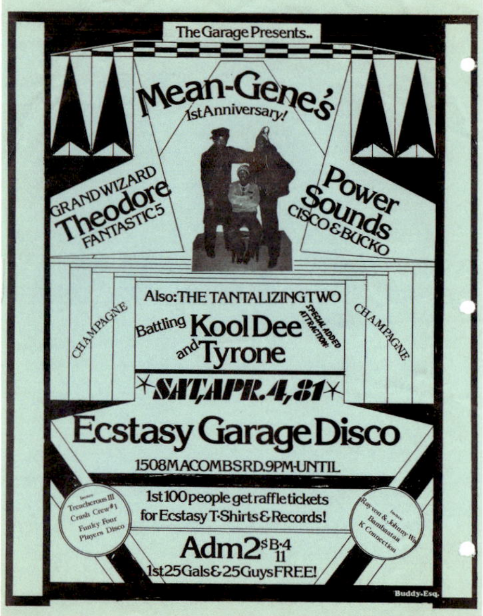

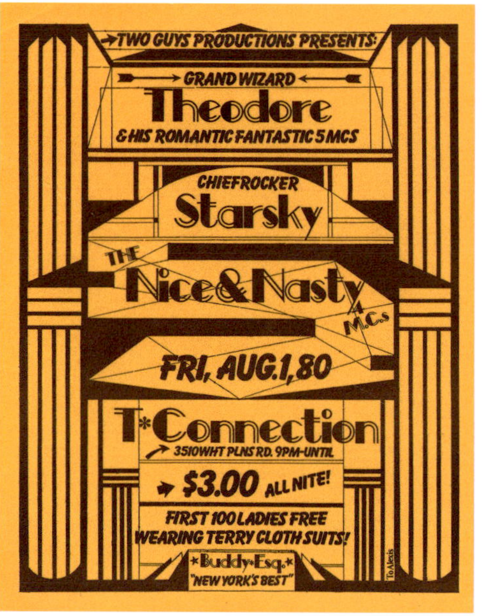

TOP, LEFT TO RIGHT Buddy Esquire (Lemoin Thompson), party flyers for T-Connection, 1981 and 1980, and Ecstasy Garage Disco, 1981, photocopy on colored paper, 8½ × 6½ inches (21.5 × 16.5 cm), New York.

OPPOSITE, TOP Like Esquire's use of Harlem Renaissance–inspired geometric grids, Kennedy explores graphic patterns associated with Black art by printing with patterned linocut blocks. "The circle, the square, the triangle—I've studied these in African beading and masks," he says. "It is so easy to carve them into wood and make multiples into a more complex and modular design."

OPPOSITE, BOTTOM LEFT TO RIGHT Amos Paul Kennedy, Jr., *Gay Pride*, 2005, 19 × 12½ inches (48.25 × 31.75 cm), Akron, Alabama, and *You Have to Risk It to Get That Biscuit*, 2017, from the *Parlor* series, 8 × 6 inches (20.25 × 15.25 cm), Detroit, both letterpress on chipboard. Kennedy's work demonstrates his commitment to community—whether he is printing in support of LGBTQIA+ rights or to document the Black vernacular (and wisdom) of barbershop workers in Richmond, Virginia.

such as Afrika Bambaataa, Jazzy Jay, and Grandmaster Flash. His designs were experimental, combining art deco influences with hand lettering as well as type and graphics styles from early desktop publishing. Kennedy remembers, "All this was in the ether. The underground was redefining graphic design and mass communications—you could not avoid it. It made it into album covers. It made it into magazines. And a book artist like me could see those albums and magazines and flyers and know that change was happening."[28]

In light of these and other technological innovations, such as the development of offset printing, letterpress printing became an antiquated art form. However, while his work may feel like a far cry from that of the zine and flyer makers of the 1980s and '90s, Kennedy redeploys letterpress printing in a similarly countercultural spirit. While more involved than photocopying, letterpress allows him to craft rapid-fire responses to the mainstream or quickly pull a print in support of a cause or event. Like the punk or hip-hop zine makers of the recent past, he uses a mixture of letterforms in different scales and faces, typographically re-creating their loud, bold, and brash aesthetics.

BLACK LIVES MATTER & PRINTING IN THE DIGITAL AGE

In the era of Black Lives Matter and the ongoing fights for LGBTQIA+ and women's rights, it is more important than ever for designers to lend their skills to the fight. The world we live in is on fire, and it is very easy to grow apathetic. It is not enough for a designer to work in a silo, disengaged from politics.

Of the summer of 2020, in which people took to the streets to protest the police murders of George Floyd and Breonna Taylor, Kennedy says: "All of this is nothing new."[29] In the violence against Black Americans, captured on mobile phones and posted online as evidence, he sees the past: the 1968 Selma to Montgomery marchers, whose brutal beatings by state troopers appeared in photographs across the world, and the mutilated face of young Emmett Till, bravely shared by his mother in the pages of *Jet* after a white mob tortured and murdered him in 1955. For Kennedy, the real difference is that in the age of the internet, printed matter has become the second choice for getting out information, and most protest signage—once printed by hand in the basements of churches and unions—is now produced digitally, which feels a step removed from the humanity it seeks to protect.

While circulation in the digital sphere does not hold the same tactile quality as print, it can have an even broader reach, Kennedy concedes, and so he prints and posts new graphics online to add his voice to the groundswell of a younger generation clamoring for change. In *Know Justice, Know Peace*, he subverts the expected "No Justice, No Peace" chant and weakens its transactional demand, wisely emphasizing instead that we must understand the conditions of justice before we can hope to achieve it (see page 168). And he does not stop at issues of race, extending his generous attention to all marginalized peoples, as in his prints defending the rights of LGBTQIA+ individuals. As he explains, "I'm always on the side of whoever's still bleeding."[30]

Using letterpress printing as an anchor to the past, Kennedy's work presents us with questions about the United States' claims to liberty and justice for all, which are fraught with contradiction and have never been fully realized. While he says that he prints spontaneously, his process is methodical: Letterpress printing, as a medium, requires the maker to think in steps—from considering the design of the text, to finding and arranging the specific letters, to inking the letters, to running a piece of paper through the press. You must be aware of your body—your arms, your hands, and your fingers. You must move both with and against the machine. Whether Kennedy is printing one of his populist proverbs or a more confrontational call for justice, he is channeling the power of 200 years of abolitionist craft.

We still need this power in print.

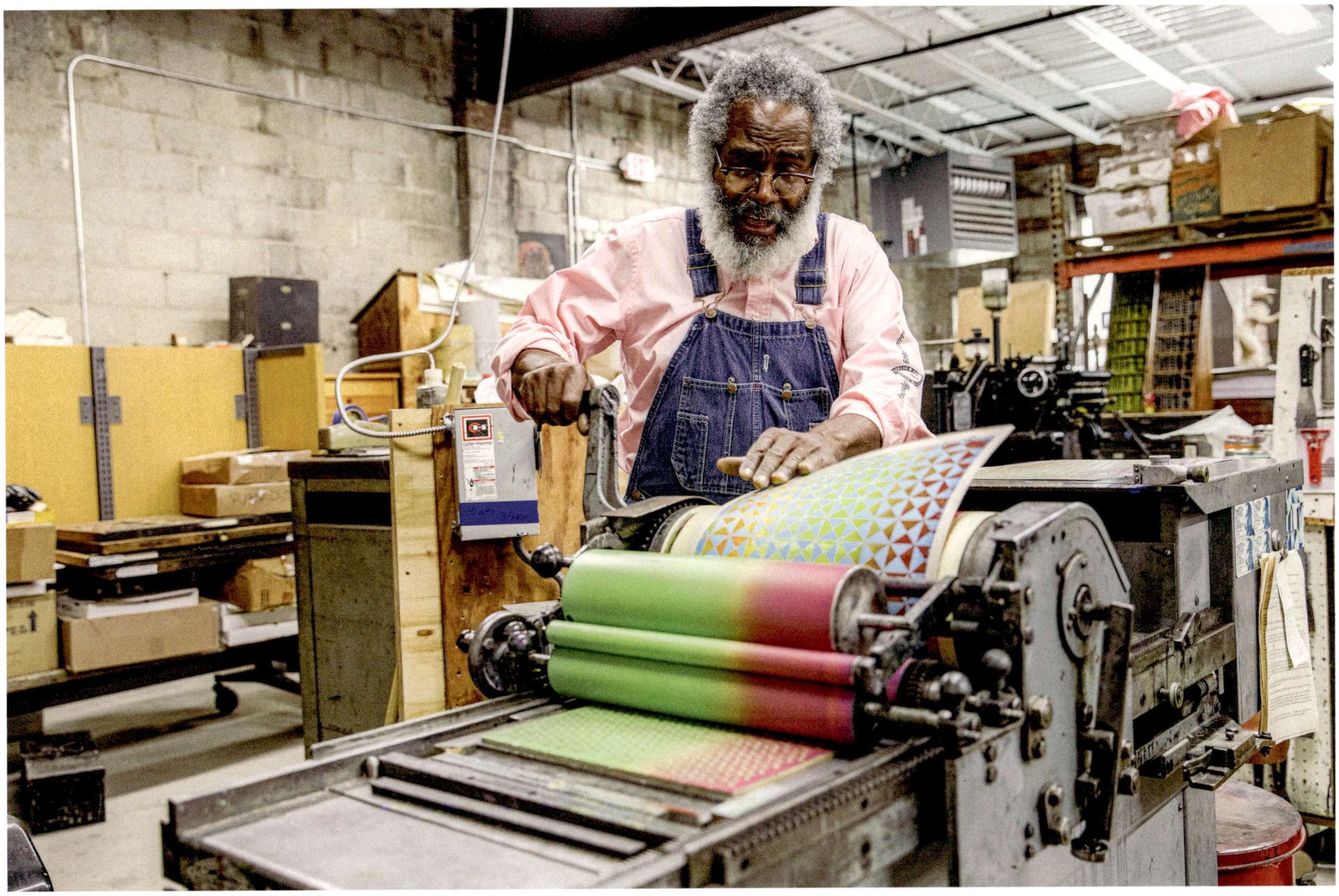

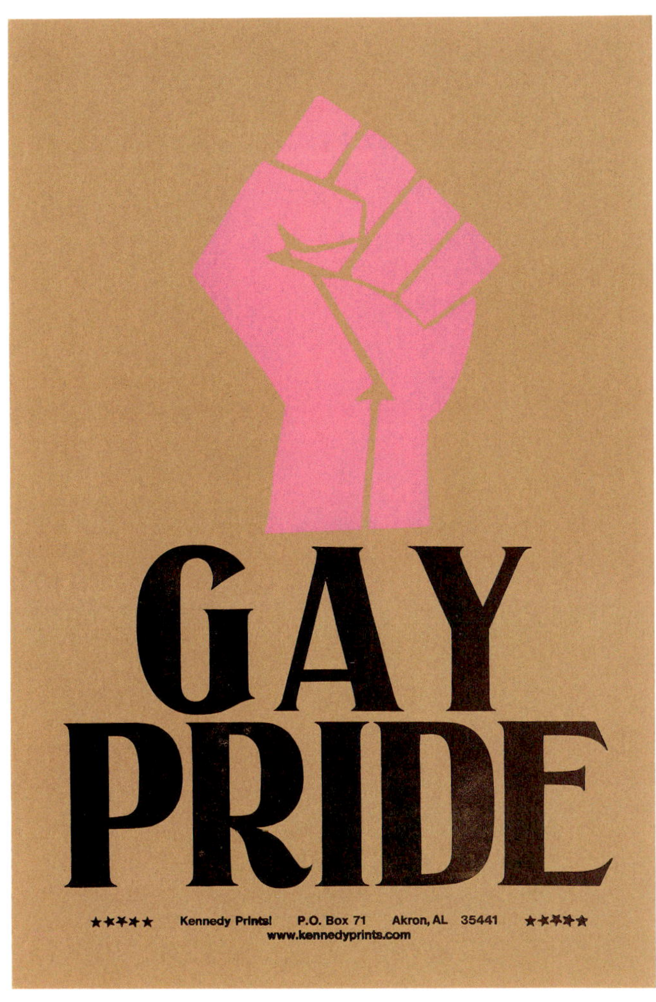
GAY
PRIDE
★★★★★ Kennedy Prints! P.O. Box 71 Akron, AL 35441 ★★★★★
www.kennedyprints.com

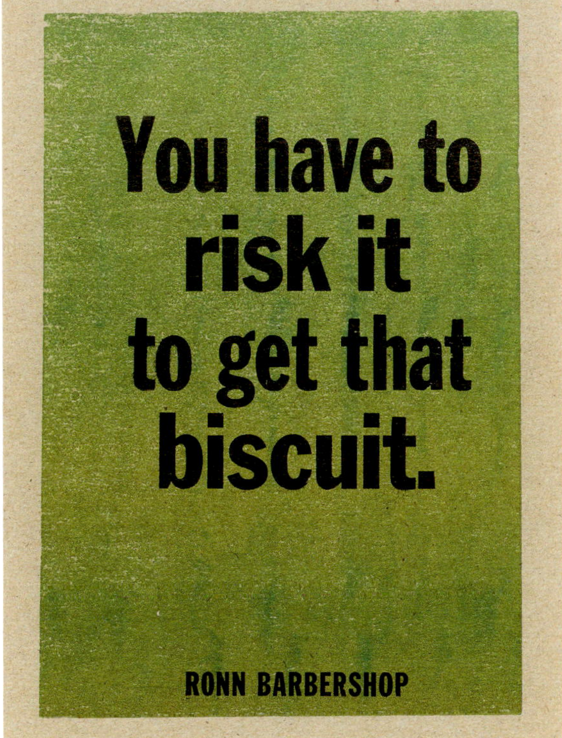
You have to
risk it
to get that
biscuit.
RONN BARBERSHOP

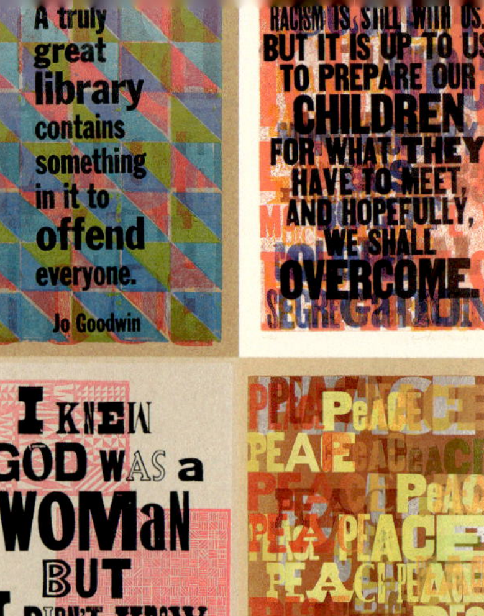
A truly great library contains something in it to offend everyone.
Jo Goodwin
RACISM IS STILL WITH US BUT IT IS UP TO US TO PREPARE OUR CHILDREN FOR WHAT THEY HAVE TO MEET, AND HOPEFULLY, WE SHALL OVERCOME.

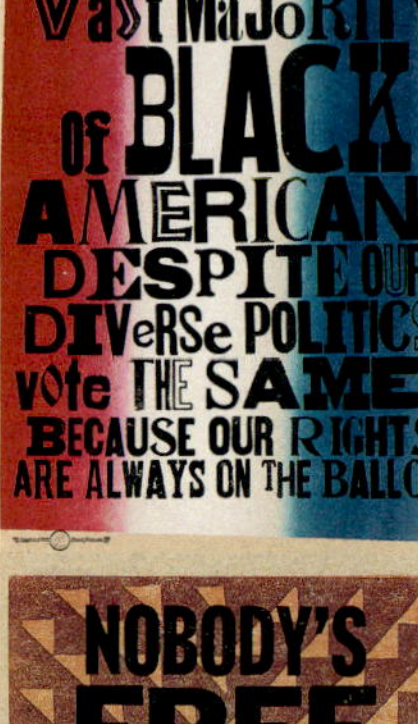
Vast MaJoRITY of BLACK AMERICANS, DESPITE OUR DIVERSE POLITICS, vote THE SAME? BECAUSE OUR RIGHTS ARE ALWAYS ON THE BALLOT.

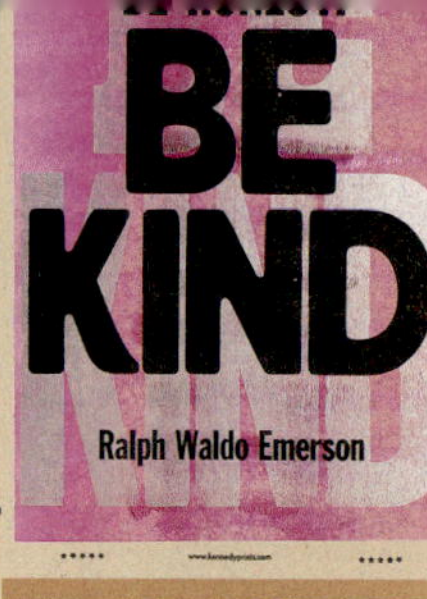
BE KIND
Ralph Waldo Emerson

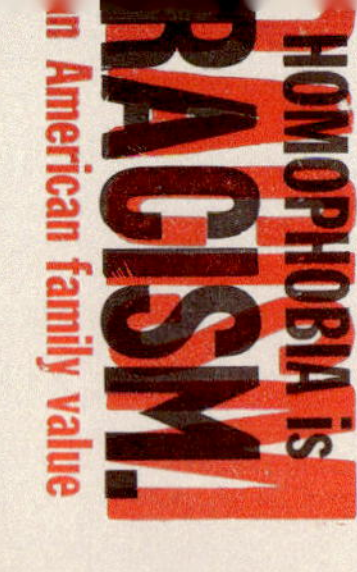
HOMOPHOBIA is RACISM!
an American family value

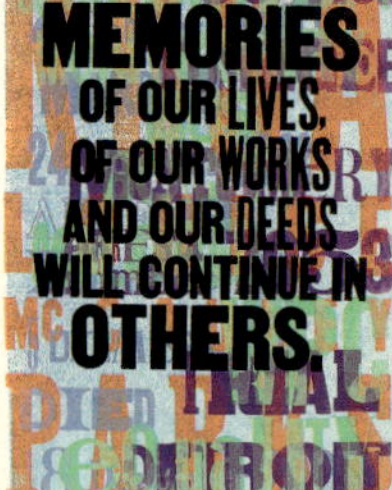
MEMORIES OF OUR LIVES, OF OUR WORKS AND OUR DEEDS WILL CONTINUE IN OTHERS.

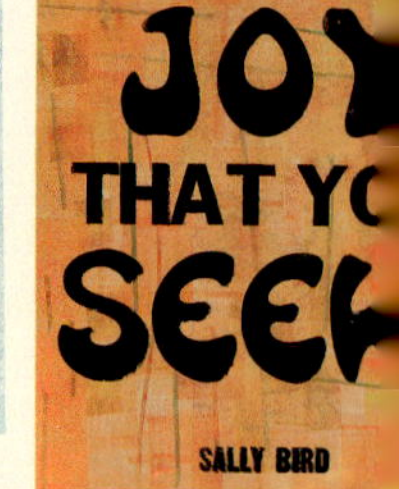
SALLY BIRD

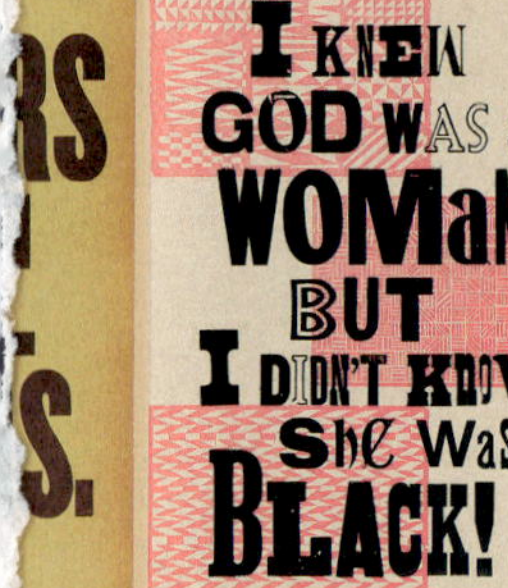
I KNEW GOD WAS a WOMaN BUT I DIDN'T KNOW ShE WaS BLACK!

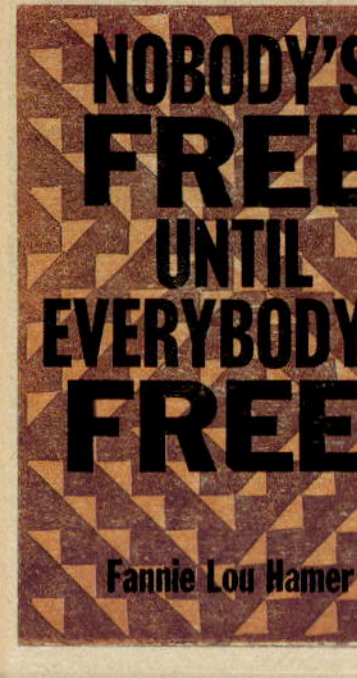
NOBODY'S FREE UNTIL EVERYBODY'S FREE.
Fannie Lou Hamer

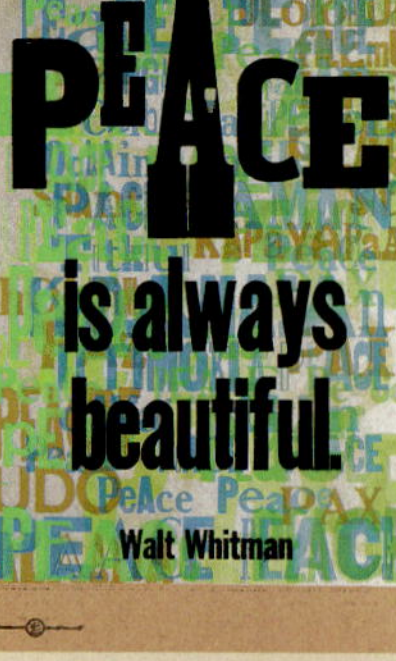
PEACE is always beautiful
Walt Whitman

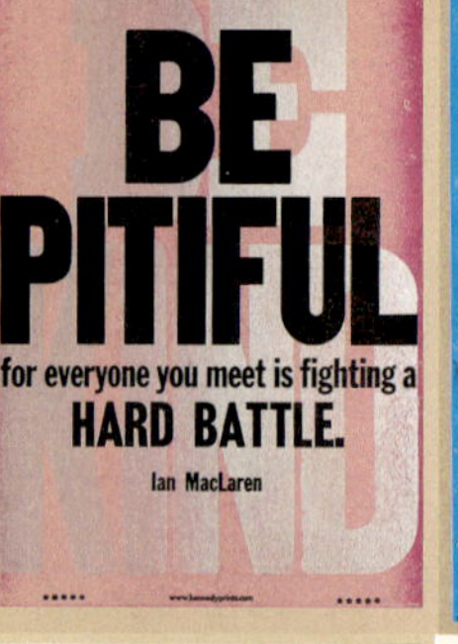
BE PITIFUL
for everyone you meet is fighting a HARD BATTLE.
Ian MacLaren

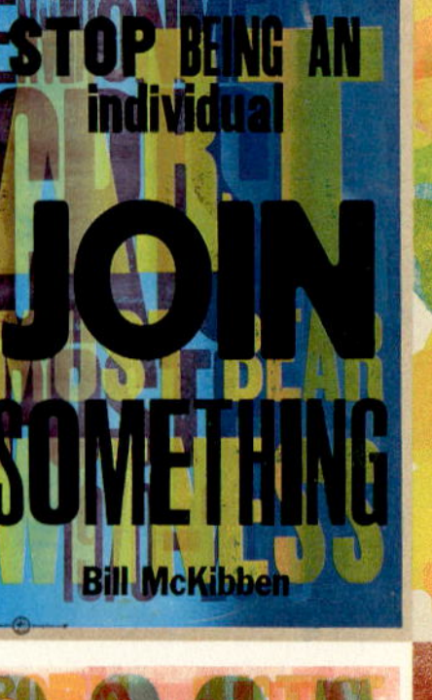
STOP BEING AN individual
JOIN SOMETHING
Bill McKibben

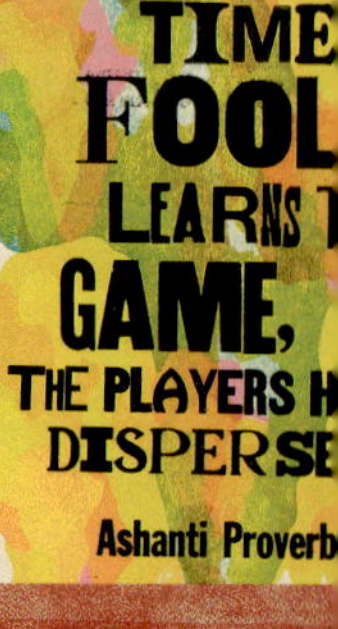
Ashanti Proverb

ARTISTS ARE THE GATEKEEPERS OF TRUTH.
WE ARE CIVILIZATION'S RADICAL VOICE.
Paul Robeson

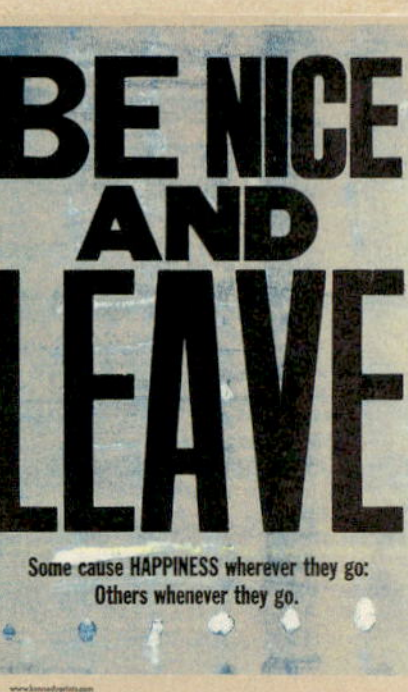
BE NICE AND LEAVE
Some cause HAPPINESS wherever they go; Others whenever they go.

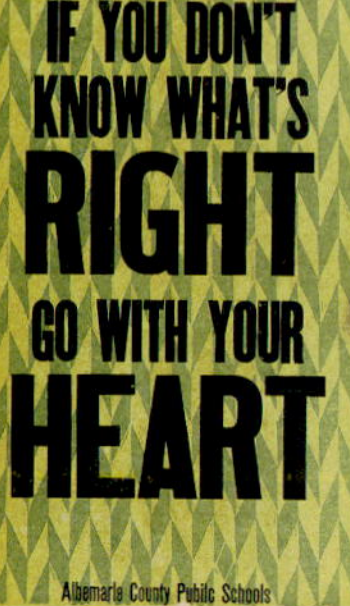
IF YOU DON'T KNOW WHAT'S RIGHT GO WITH YOUR HEART

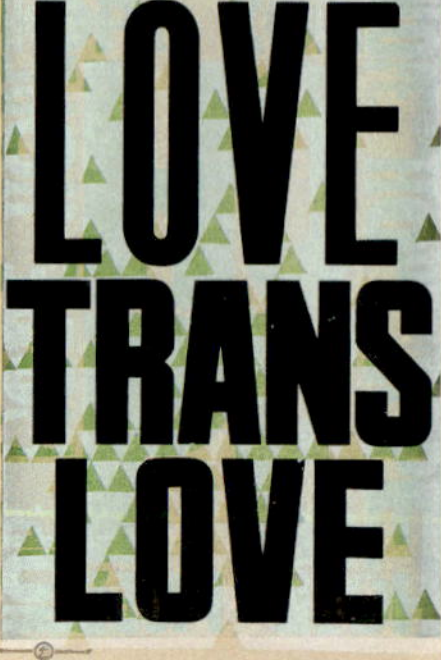
LOVE TRANS LOVE

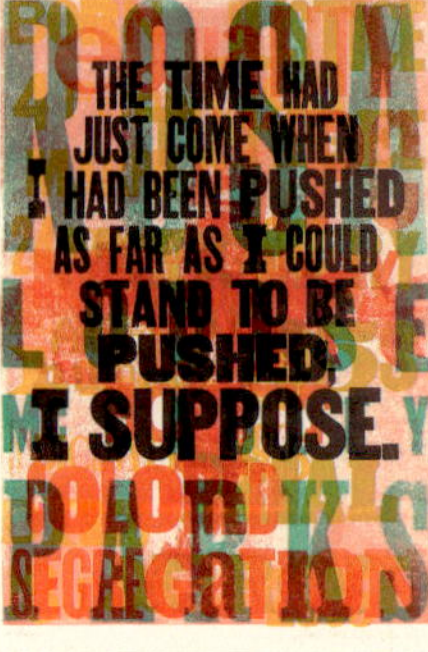
THE TIME HAD JUST COME WHEN I HAD BEEN PUSHED AS FAR AS I COULD STAND TO BE PUSHED I SUPPOSE.

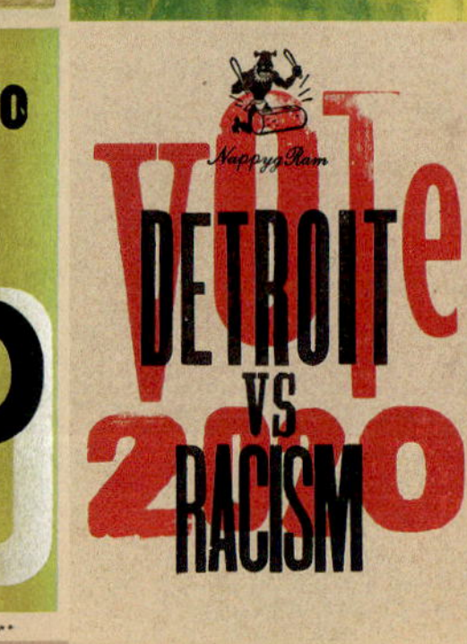
DETROIT VS RACISM

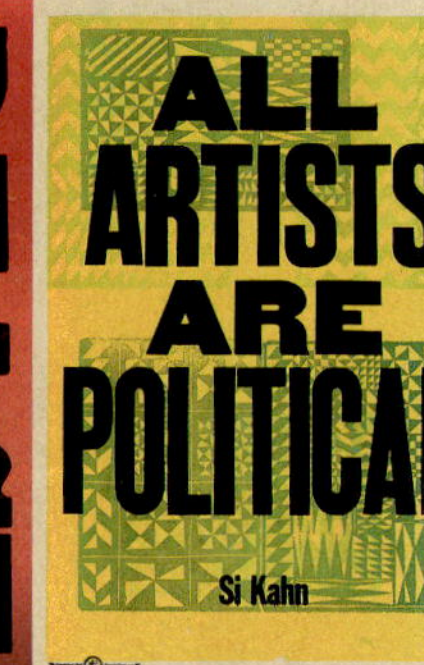
ALL ARTISTS ARE POLITICAL
Si Kahn

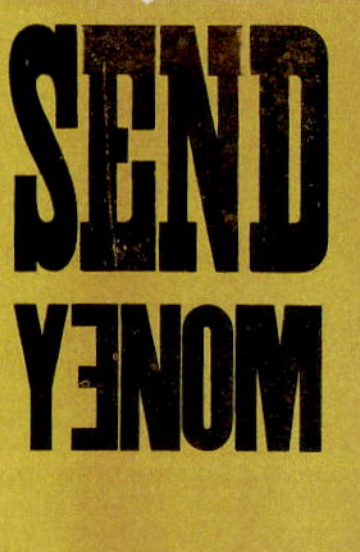
SEND MONEY

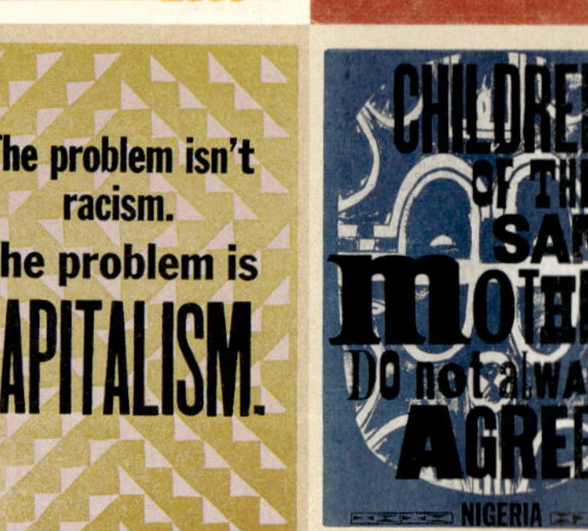
The problem isn't racism. The problem is CAPITALISM.

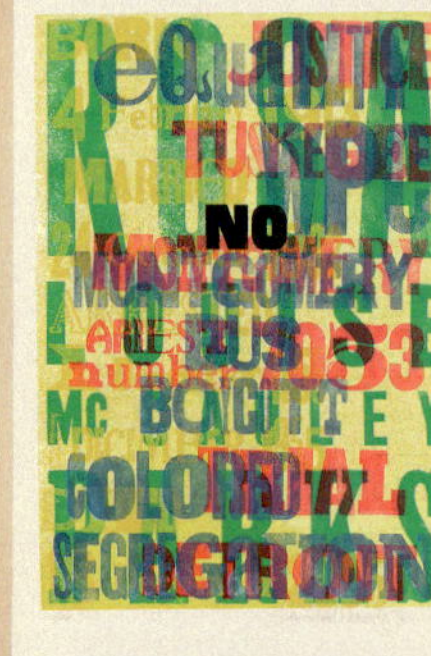

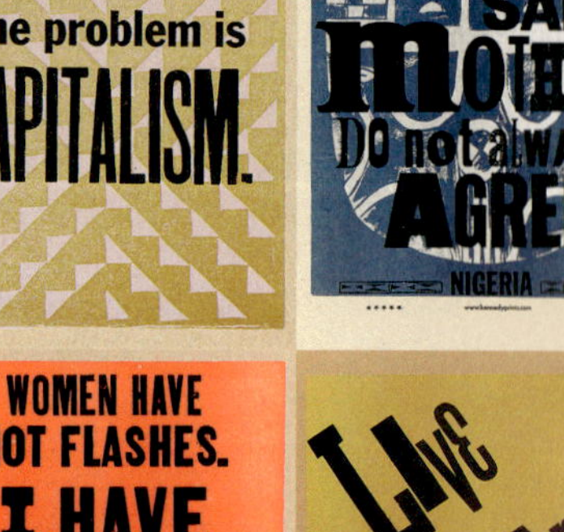
NIGERIA

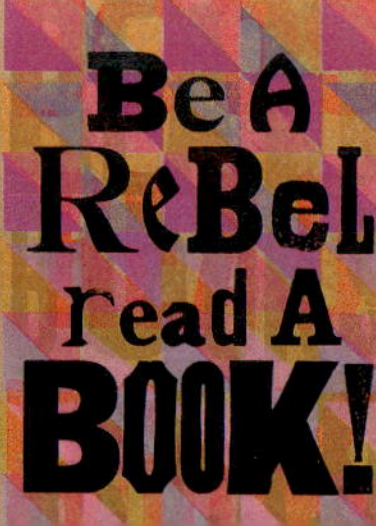
YOU CAN'T OPEN THE GATES OF HELL JUST TO TAKE A

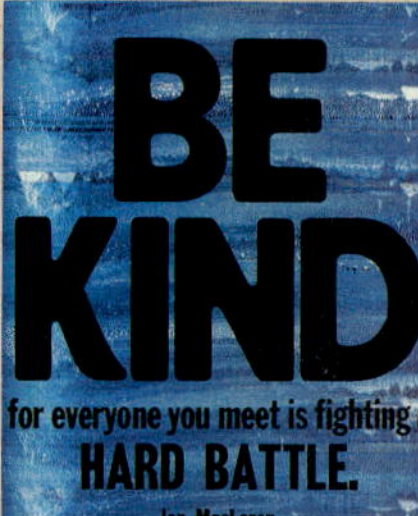
BE KIND
for everyone you meet is fighting a HARD BATTLE.
Ian MacLaren

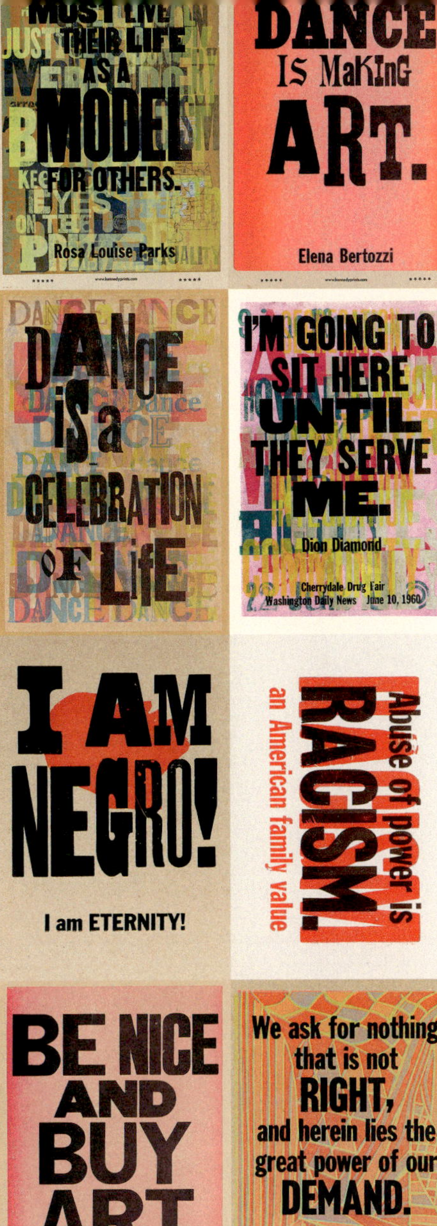
MUST LIVE THEIR LIFE AS A MODEL FOR OTHERS.
Rosa Louise Parks
DANCE IS MAKING ART.
Elena Bertozzi
DANCE IS A CELEBRATION OF LIFE
I'M GOING TO SIT HERE UNTIL THEY SERVE ME.
Dion Diamond
I AM NEGRO!
I am ETERNITY!
Abuse of power is RACISM.
an American family value
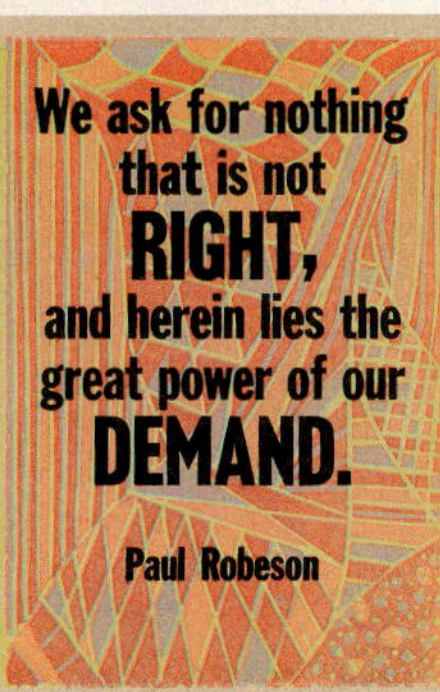
We ask for nothing that is not RIGHT, and herein lies the great power of our DEMAND.
Paul Robeson
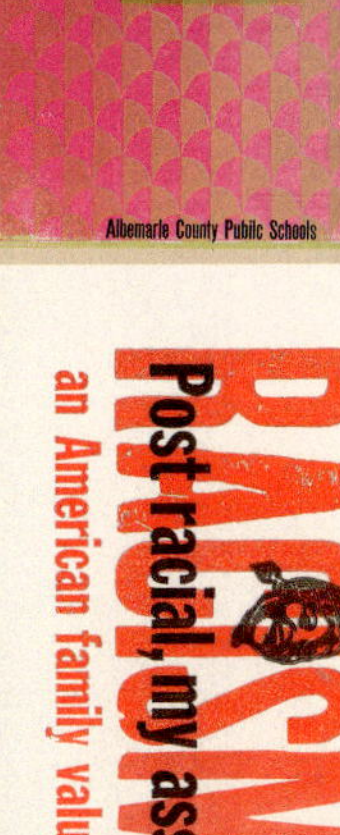
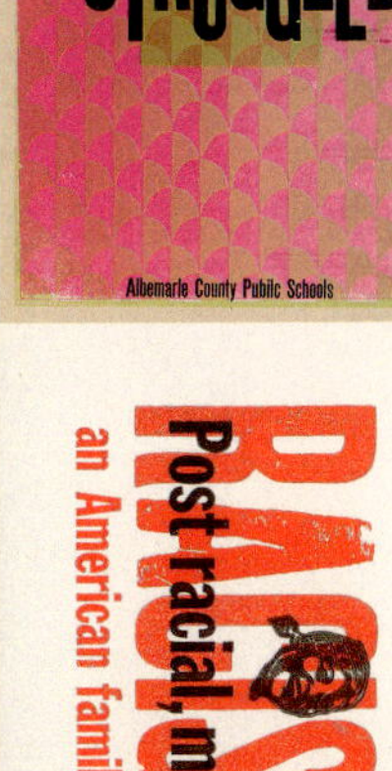
I HAVE STRUGGLED
Albemarle County Public Schools
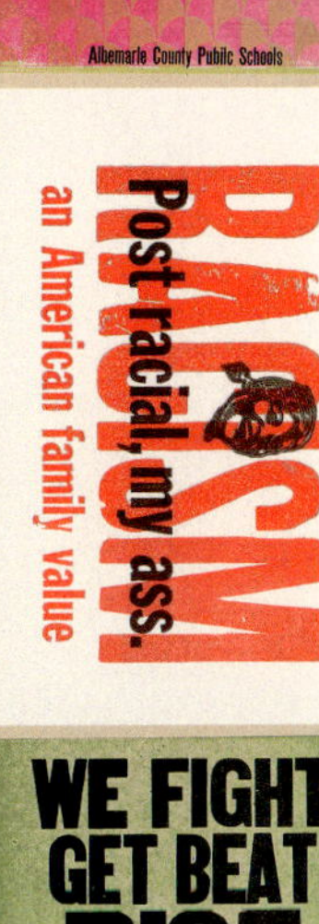
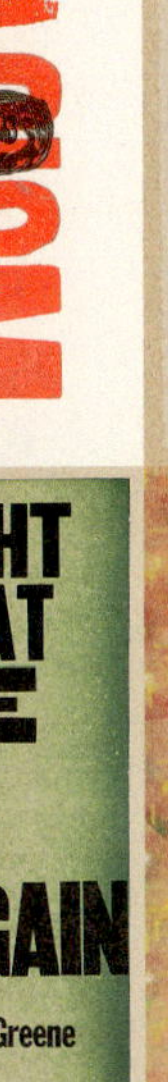
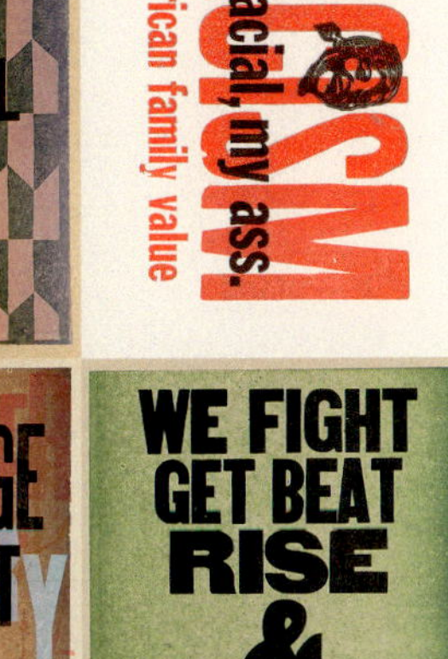
RACISM
Post-racial, my ass.
an American family value
WE FIGHT GET BEAT RISE & FIGHT AGAIN
General Nathanael Greene

IF THERE IS NO STRUGGLE THERE IS NO PROGRESS
FREDERICK DOUGLASS
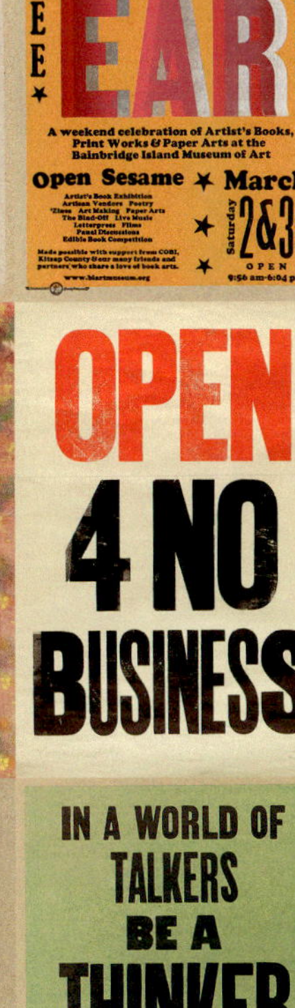
OPEN 4 NO BUSINESS
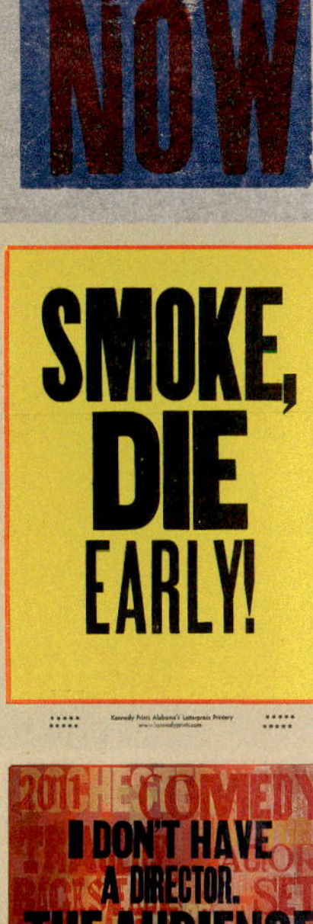
SMOKE, DIE EARLY!
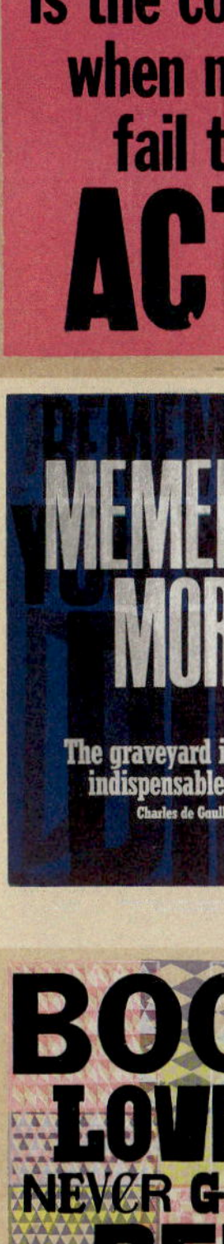
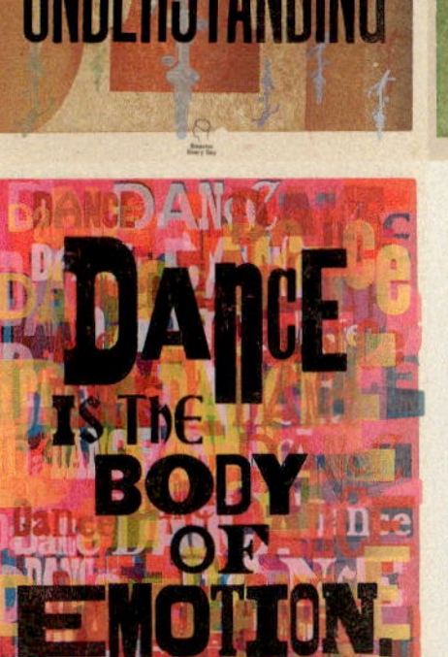
DANCE IS THE BODY OF EMOTION.
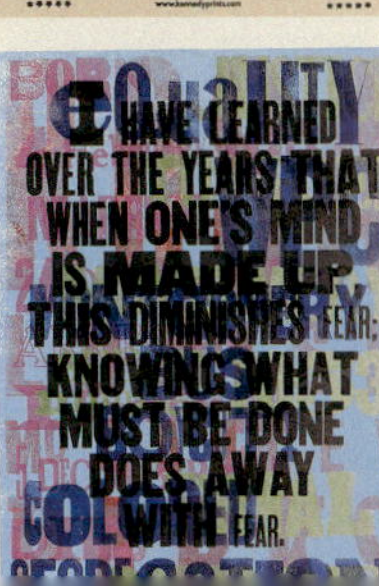
I HAVE LEARNED OVER THE YEARS THAT WHEN ONE'S MIND IS MADE UP, THIS DIMINISHES FEAR; KNOWING WHAT MUST BE DONE DOES AWAY WITH FEAR.
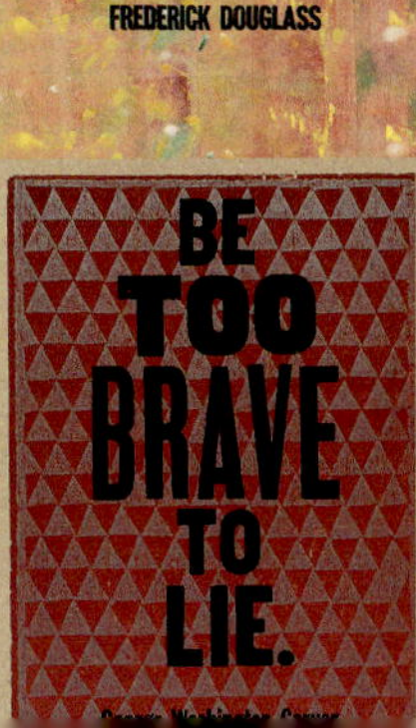
BE TOO BRAVE TO LIE.
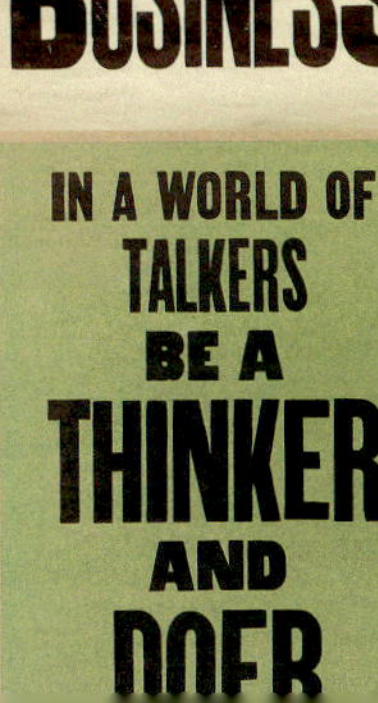
IN A WORLD OF TALKERS BE A THINKER AND DOER
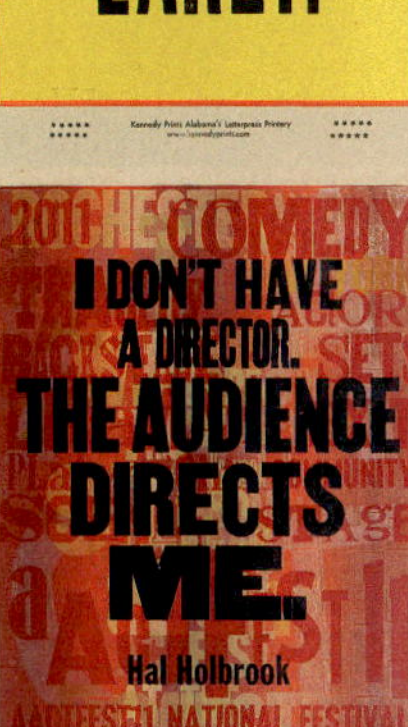
I DON'T HAVE A DIRECTOR. THE AUDIENCE DIRECTS ME.
Hal Holbrook

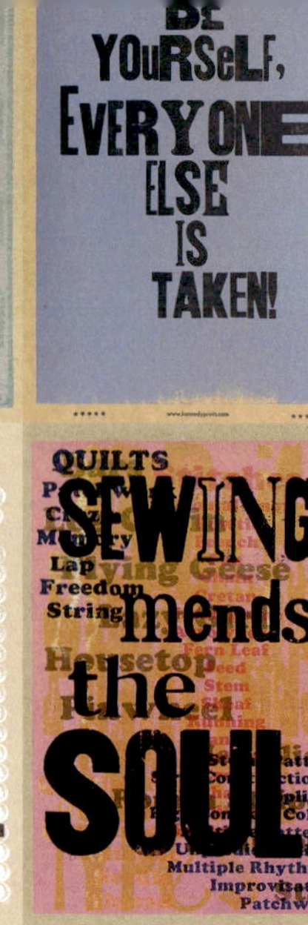

BE YOURSELF, EVERYONE ELSE IS TAKEN!
QUILTS
SEWING mends the SOUL

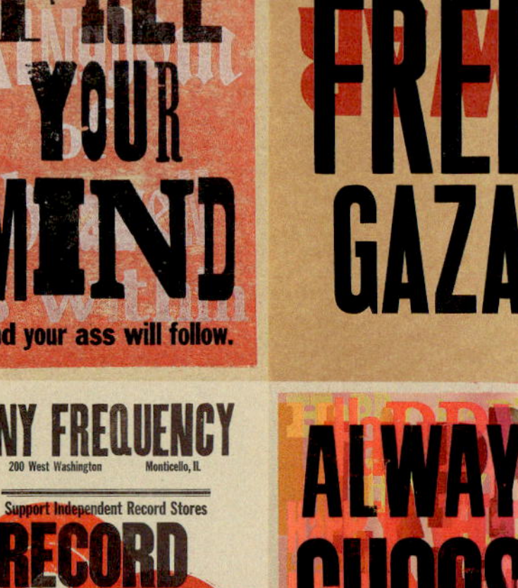

FREE YOUR MIND
and your ass will follow.
FREE GAZA

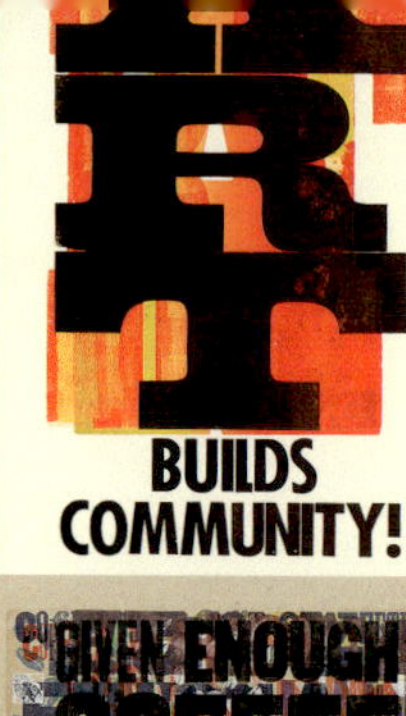

BUILDS COMMUNITY!

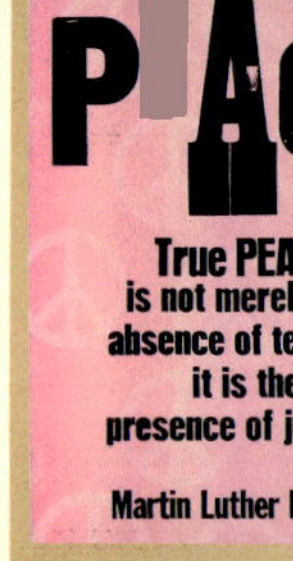

PEACE
True PEACE is not merely the absence of tension; it is the presence of justice.
Martin Luther King, Jr.

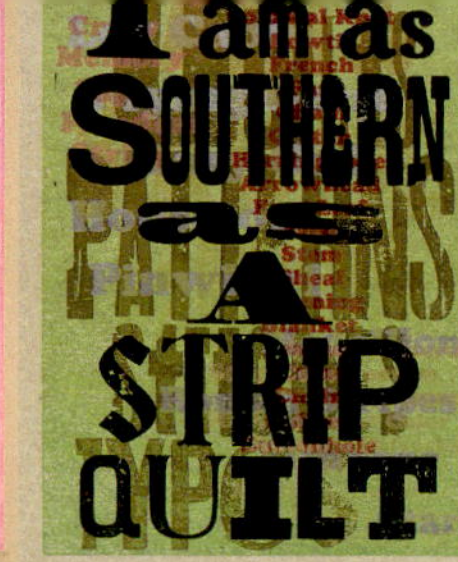

I am as SOUTHERN as A STRIP QUILT

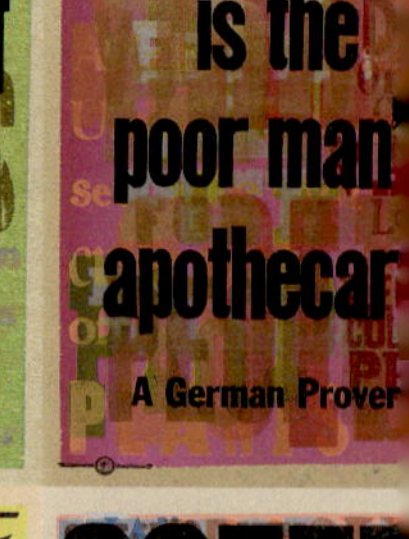

is the poor man's apothecar
A German Prover

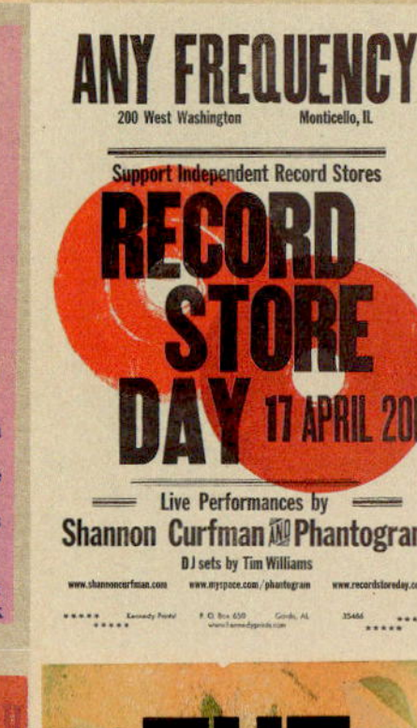

ANY FREQUENCY
290 West Washington
Monticello, IL
Support Independent Record Stores
RECORD STORE DAY
17 APRIL 2010
Live Performances by
Shannon Curfman
Phantogram
DJ sets by Tim Williams

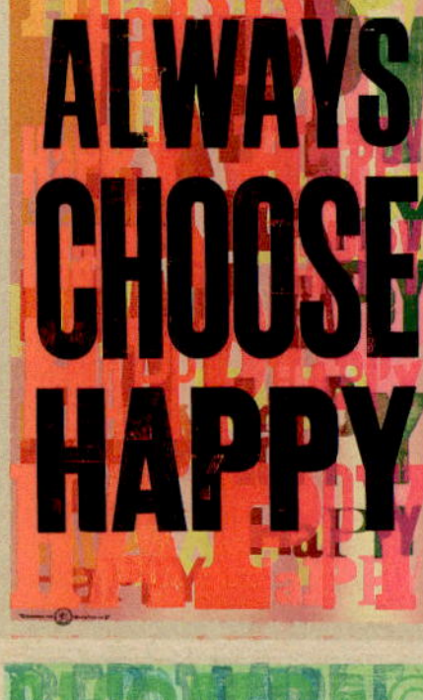

ALWAYS CHOOSE HAPPY

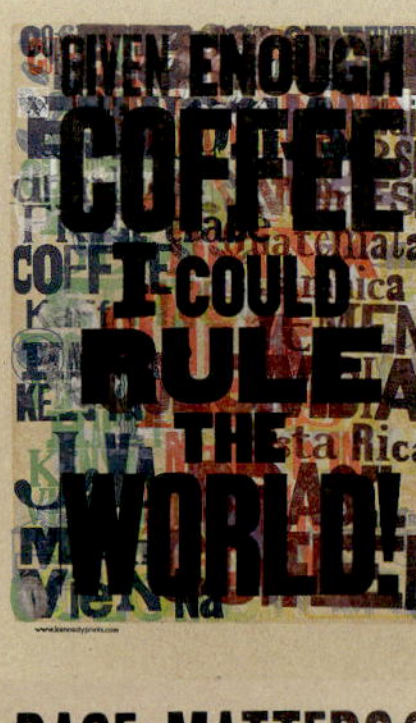

GIVEN ENOUGH COFFEE I COULD RULE THE WORLD!

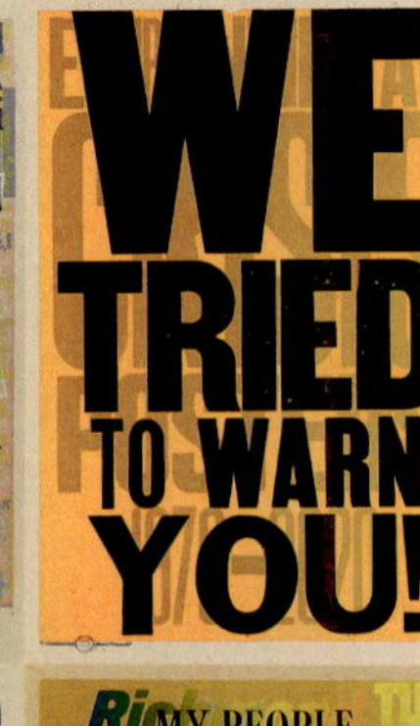

WE TRIED TO WARN YOU!

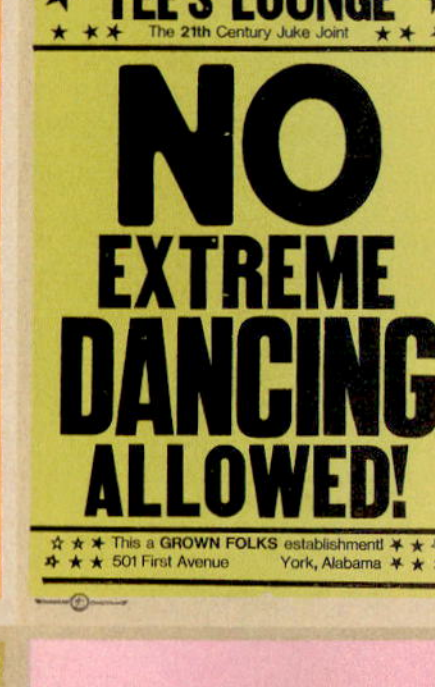

TEE'S LOUNGE
The 21th Century Juke Joint
NO EXTREME DANCING ALLOWED!
This a GROWN FOLKS establishment
501 First Avenue
York, Alabama

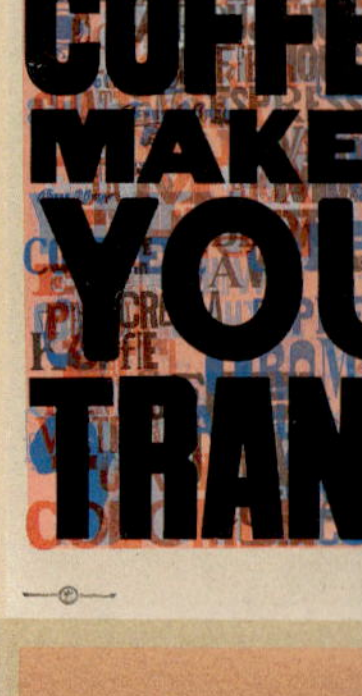

COFFE MAKE YOU TRAN

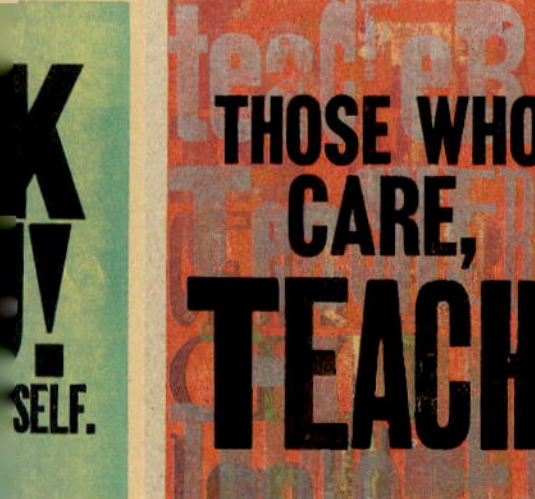

THOSE WHO CARE, TEACH.

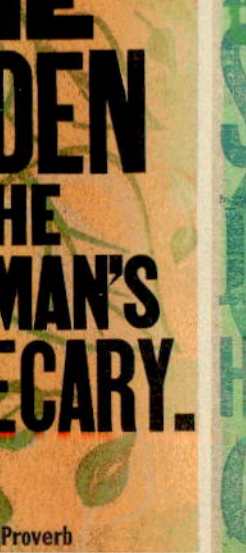

THE GARDEN IS THE POOR MAN'S APOTHECARY.
A German Proverb

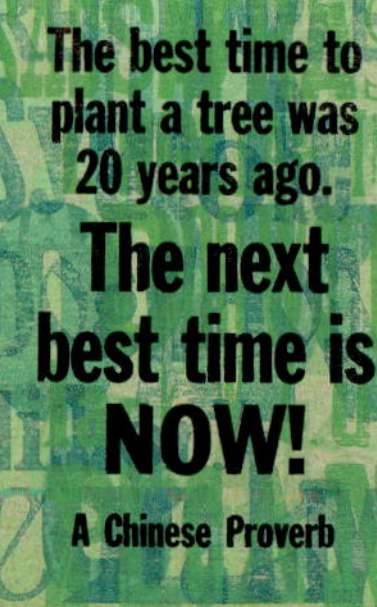

The best time to plant a tree was 20 years ago.
The next best time is NOW!
A Chinese Proverb

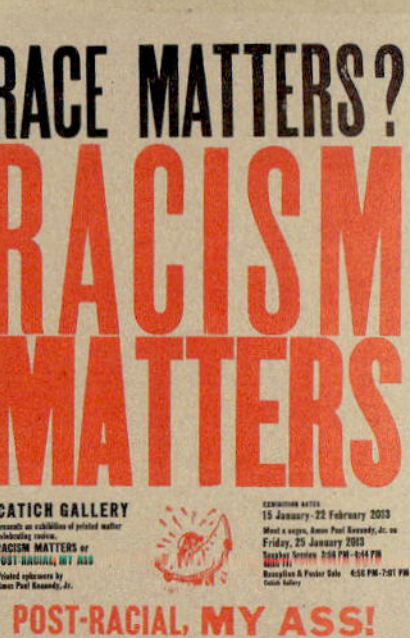

RACE MATTERS?
RACISM MATTERS
CATICH GALLERY
POST-RACIAL MY ASS!

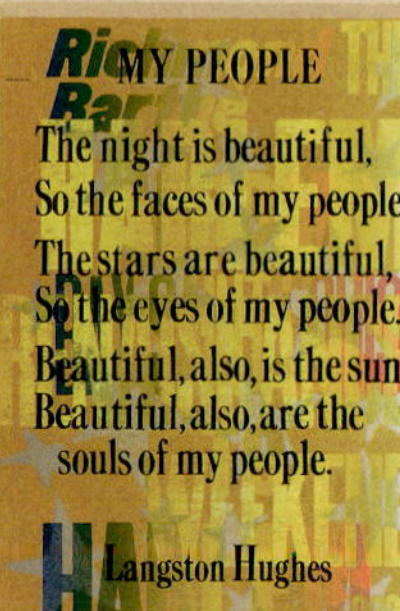

MY PEOPLE
The night is beautiful,
So the faces of my people.
The stars are beautiful,
So the eyes of my people.
Beautiful, also, is the sun.
Beautiful, also, are the souls of my people.
Langston Hughes
Celebrating black brilliance and creativity in the Bay.
Sponsored by the 100 Men DBA

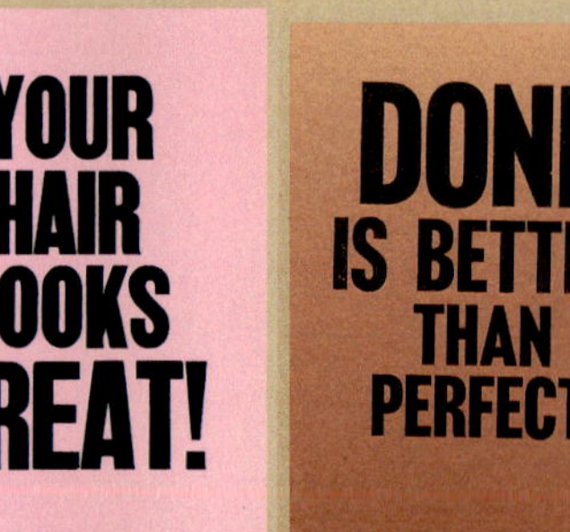

YOUR HAIR LOOKS GREAT!
DONE IS BETTER THAN PERFECT.
Canvas the Salon

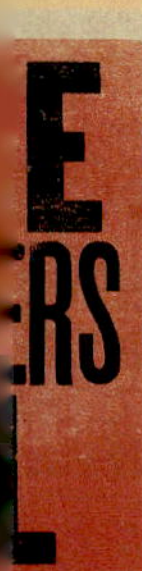

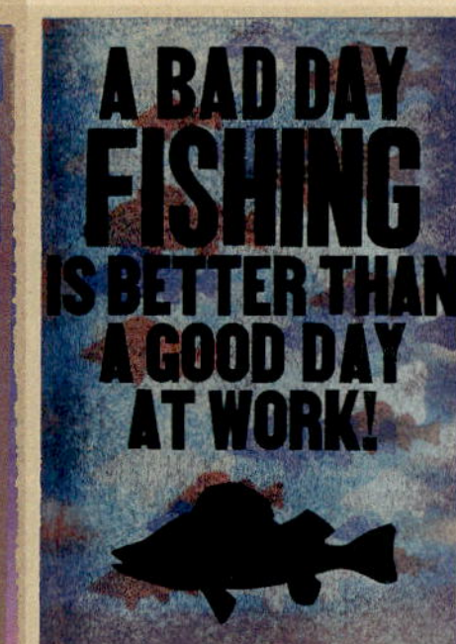

COMMON SENSE IS NOT COMMON.
A BAD DAY FISHING IS BETTER THAN A GOOD DAY AT WORK!

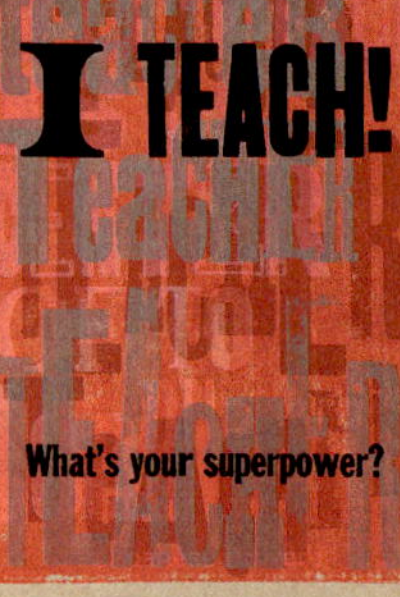

I TEACH!
What's your superpower?

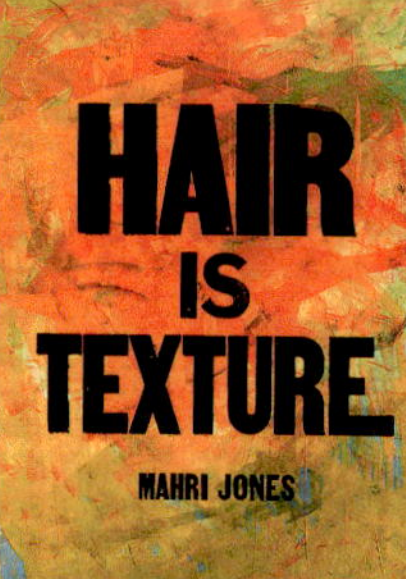

HAIR IS TEXTURE.
MAHRI JONES

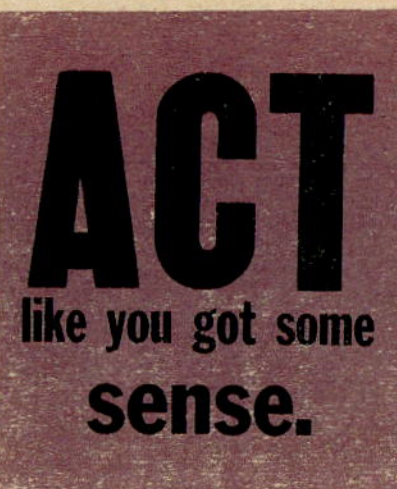

ACT like you got some sense.
HAYWOOD'S

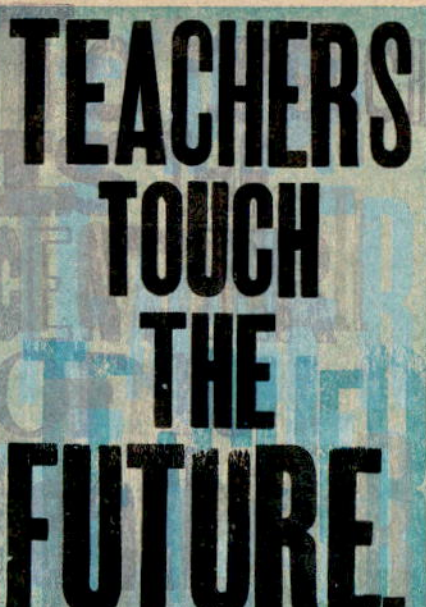

TEACHERS TOUCH THE FUTURE.

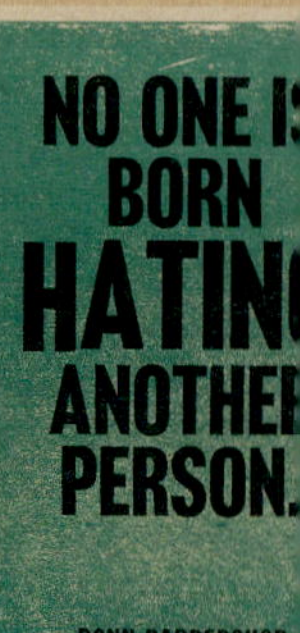

NO ONE IS BORN HATING ANOTHER PERSON.
RONN BARBERSHOP

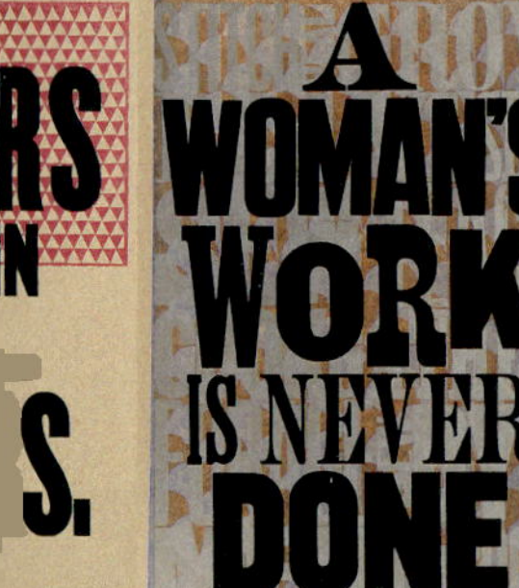

A WOMAN'S WORK IS NEVER DONE
SHE WHO PLANTS A GARDEN PLANTS HAPPINESS.

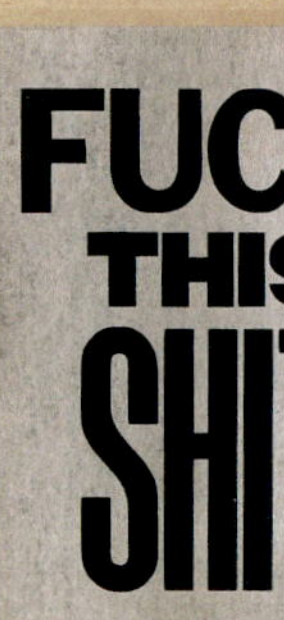

FUCK THIS SHIT

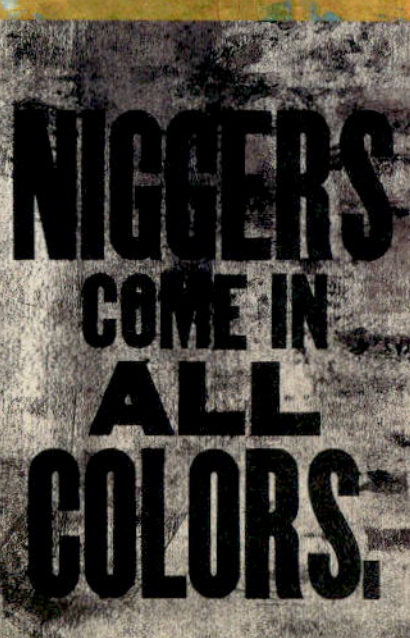

NIGGERS COME IN ALL COLORS.

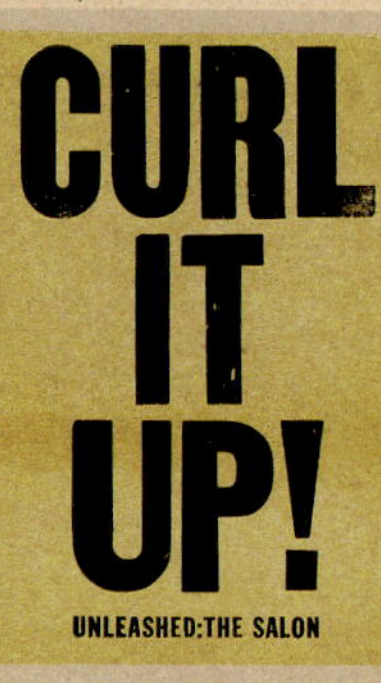

CURL IT UP!
UNLEASHED: THE SALON

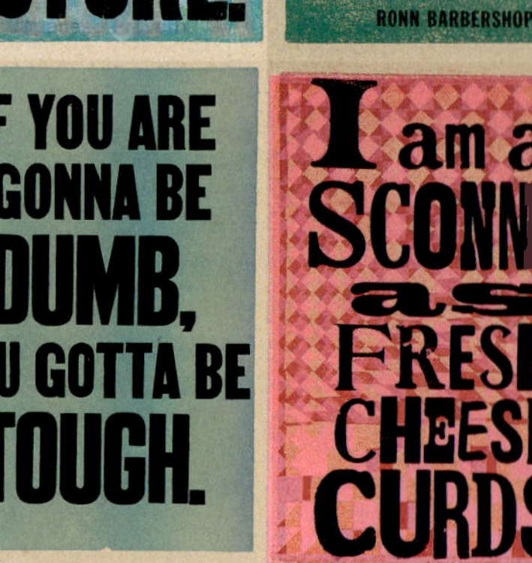

IF YOU ARE GONNA BE DUMB, YOU GOTTA BE TOUGH.
I am a SCONN as FRESH CHEESE CURDS

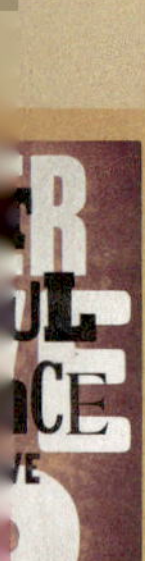

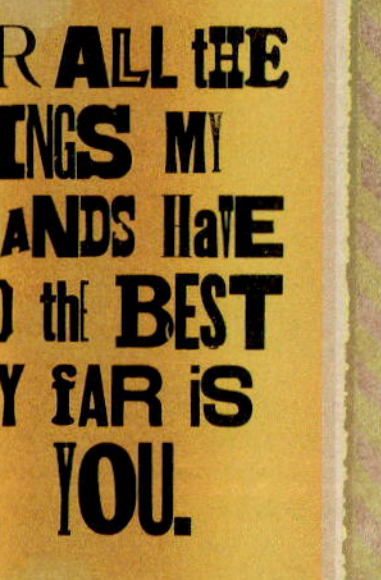

FOR ALL THE THINGS MY HANDS HAVE HELD THE BEST BY FAR IS YOU.
Andrew McMahon

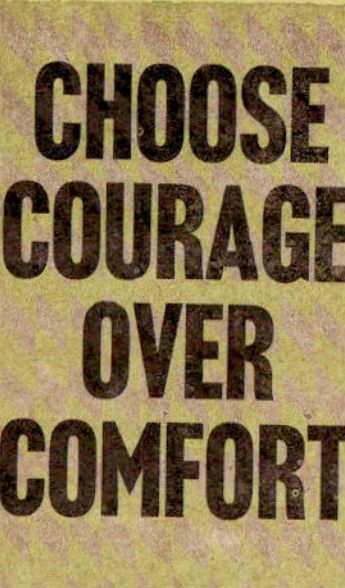

CHOOSE COURAGE OVER COMFORT

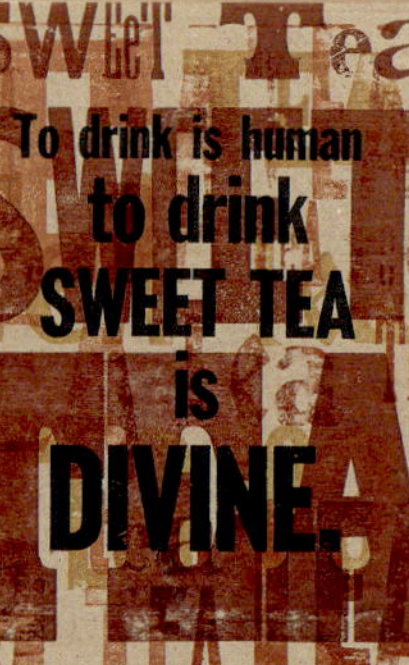

Sweet Tea
To drink is human
to drink SWEET TEA is DIVINE.

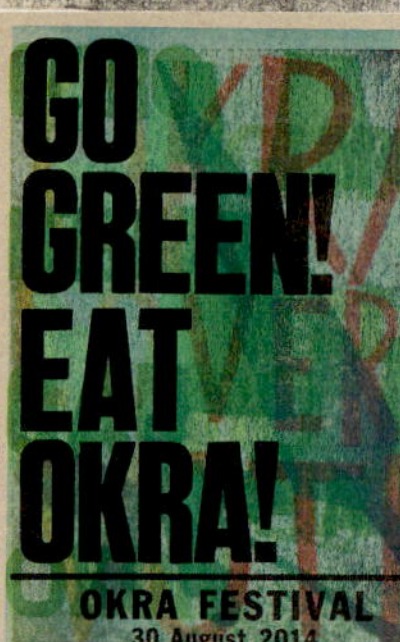

GO GREEN! EAT OKRA!
OKRA FESTIVAL
30 August 2014
Burkville, Alabama

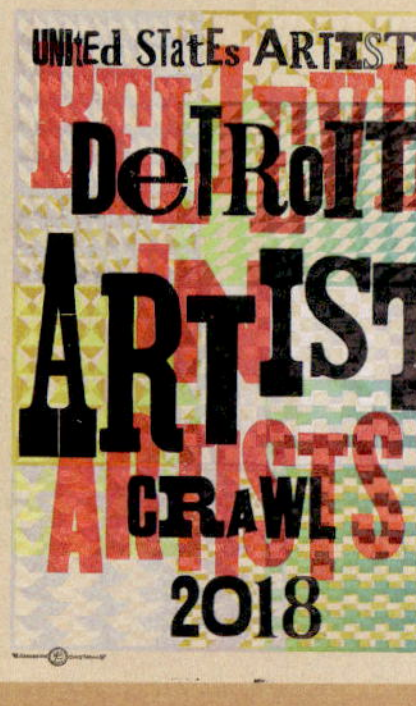

United States ARTISTS
DETROIT ARTIST CRAWL
2018

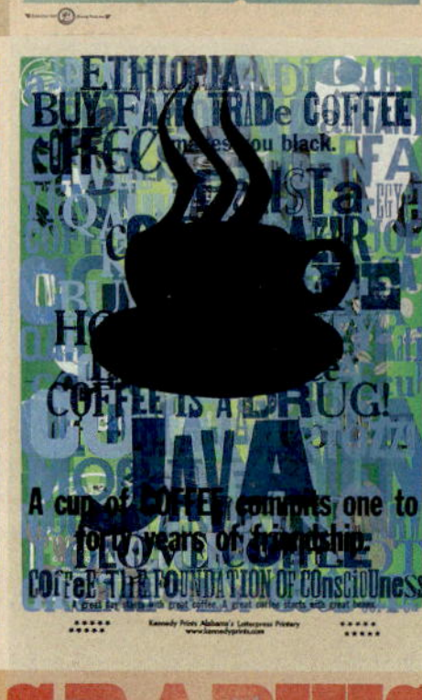

ETHIOPIA
BUY FAIR TRADE COFFEE
COFFEE IS A DRUG!
JAVA

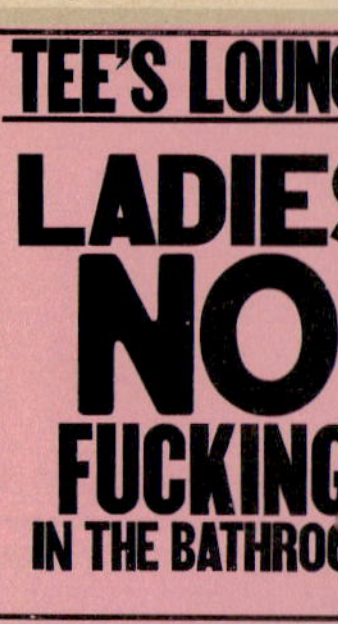

TEE'S LOUN
LADIES NO FUCKING IN THE BATHROO
This is a GROWN FOLKS establishment
501 First Avenue
York, Alabama

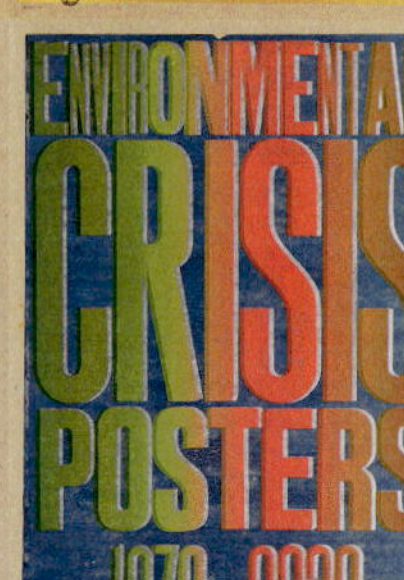

ENVIRONMENTAL CRISIS POSTERS

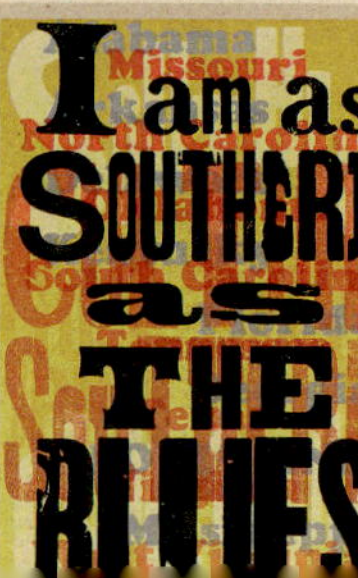

I am as SOUTHERN as THE BLUES

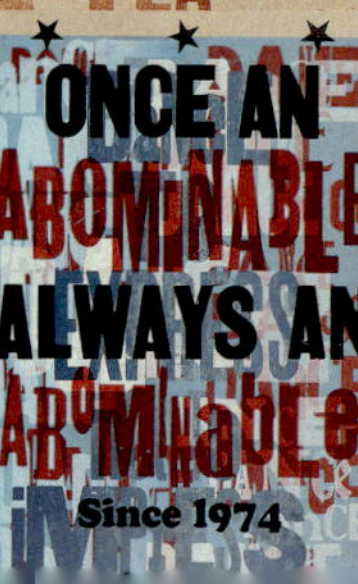

ONCE AN ABOMINABLE ALWAYS AN ABOMINABLE
Since 1974

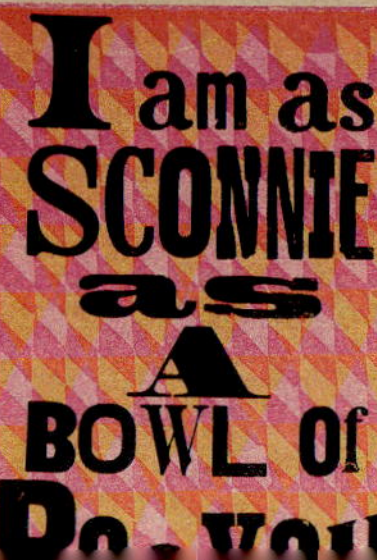

I am as SCONNIE as A BOWL OF

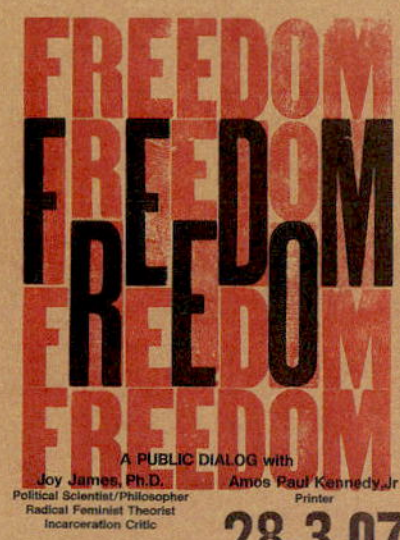

FREEDOM

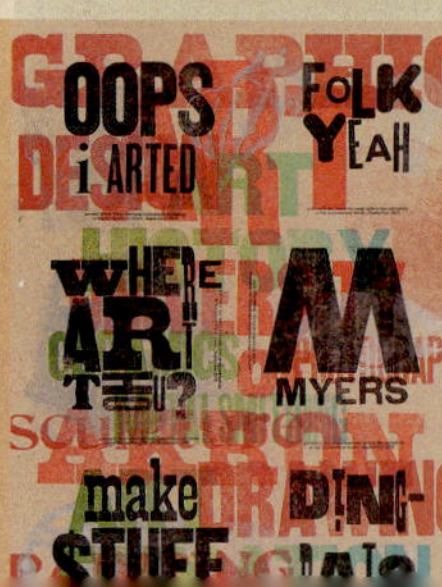

OOPS I ARTED
FOLK YEAH
MYERS
make STUFF

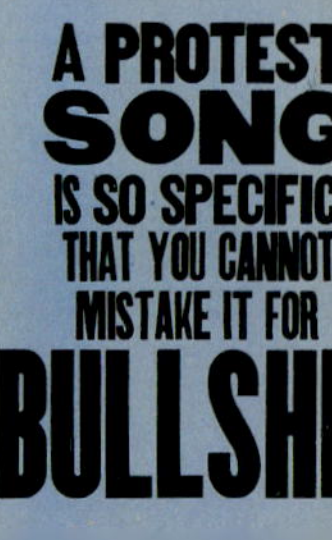

A PROTEST SONG IS SO SPECIFIC THAT YOU CANNOT MISTAKE IT FOR BULLSH

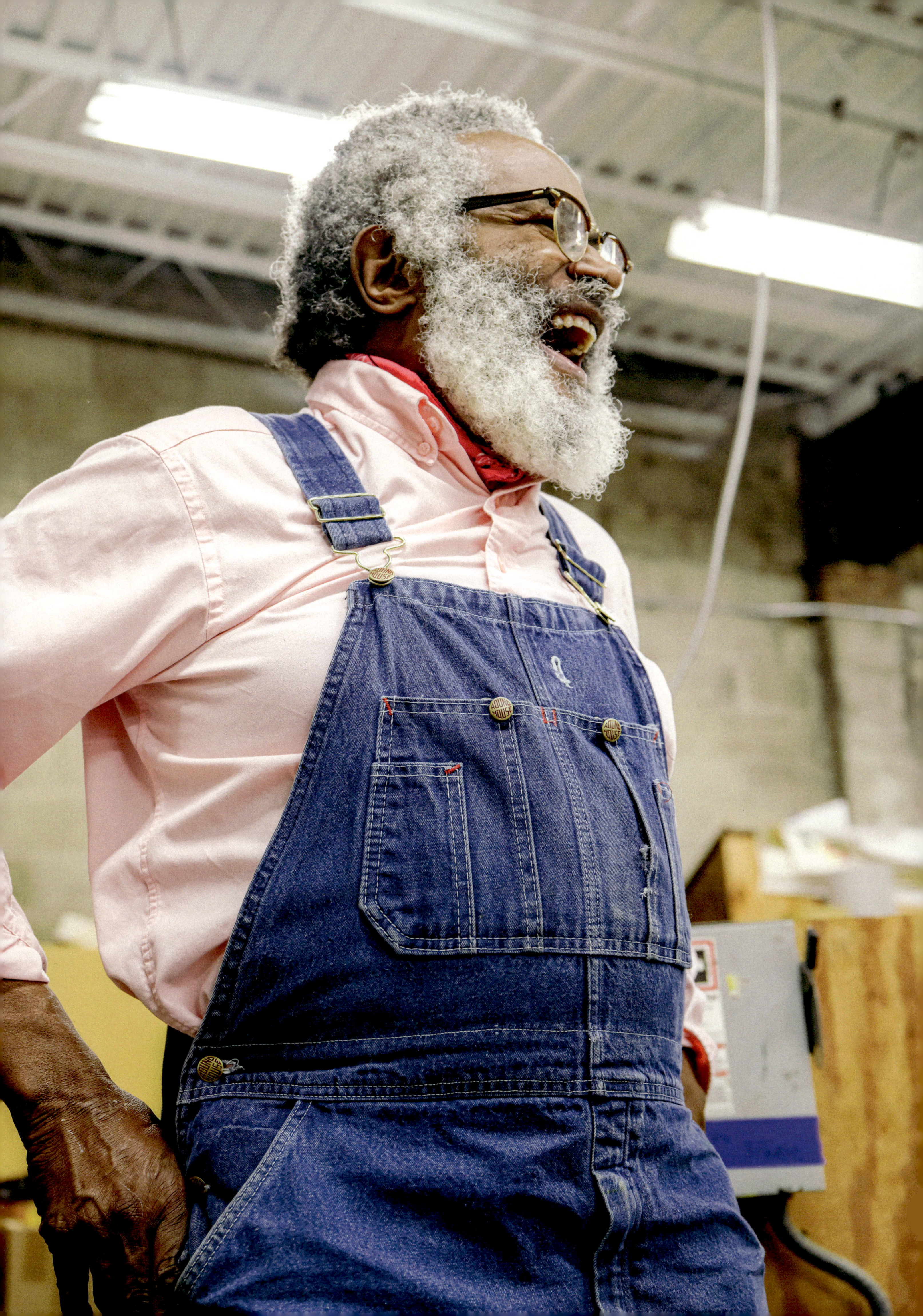

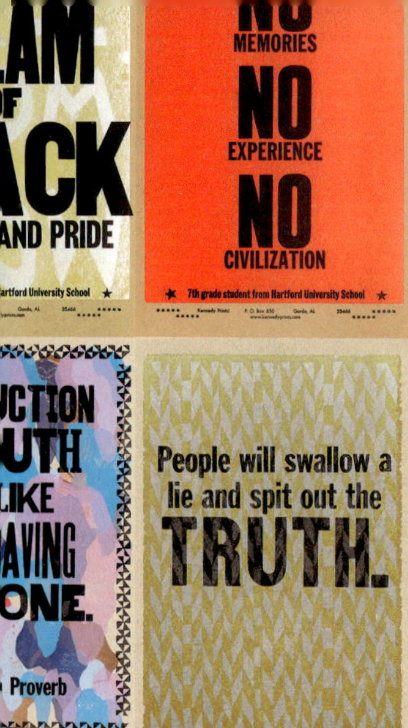
NO EXPERIENCE
NO CIVILIZATION
7th grade student from Hartford University School
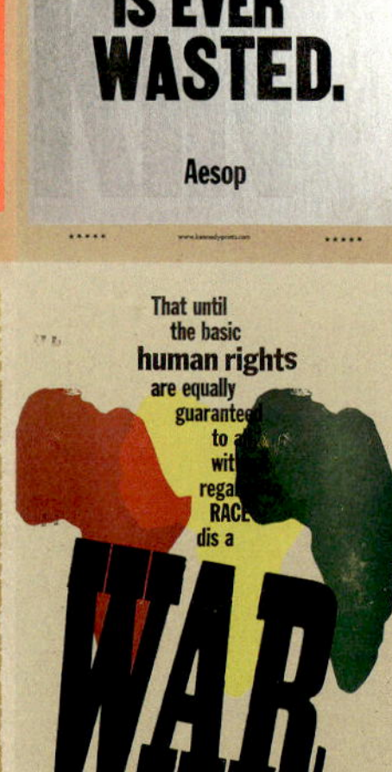
NO MATTER HOW SMALL, IS EVER WASTED.
Aesop
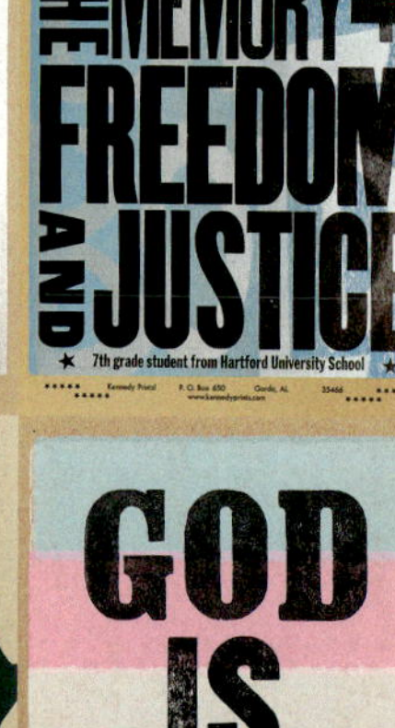
FREEDOM AND JUSTICE
7th grade student from Hartford University School
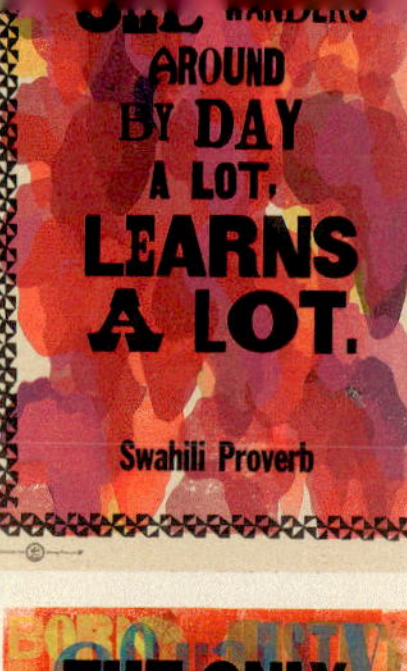
BY DAY A LOT, LEARNS A LOT.
Swahili Proverb
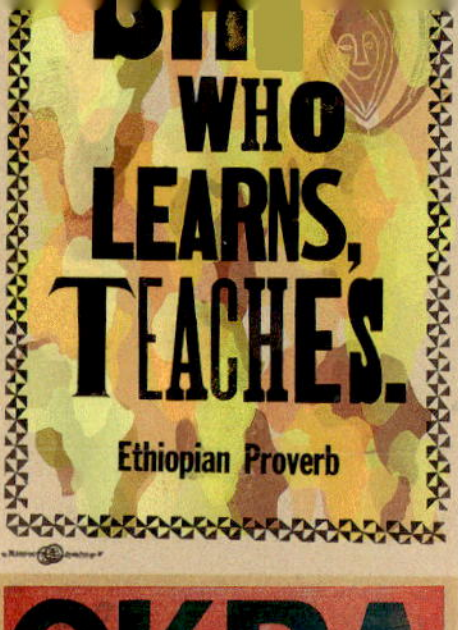
WHO LEARNS, TEACHES.
Ethiopian Proverb
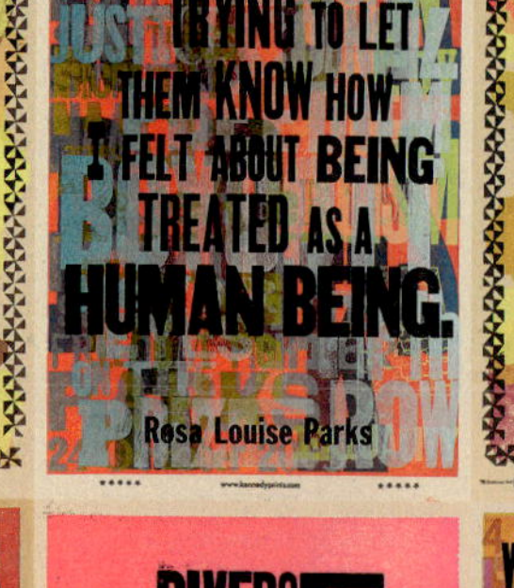
HUMAN BEING.
Rosa Louise Parks
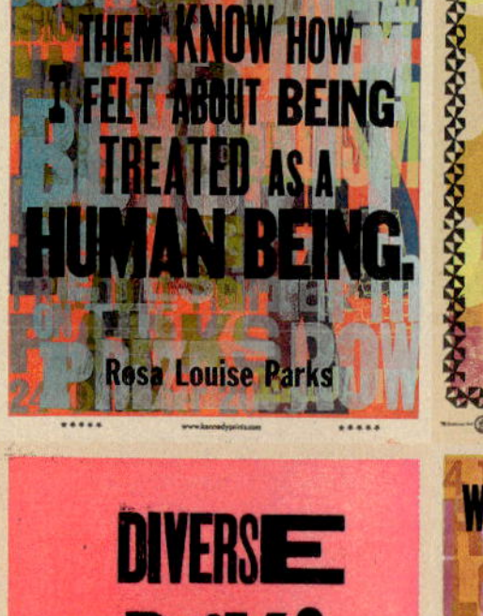
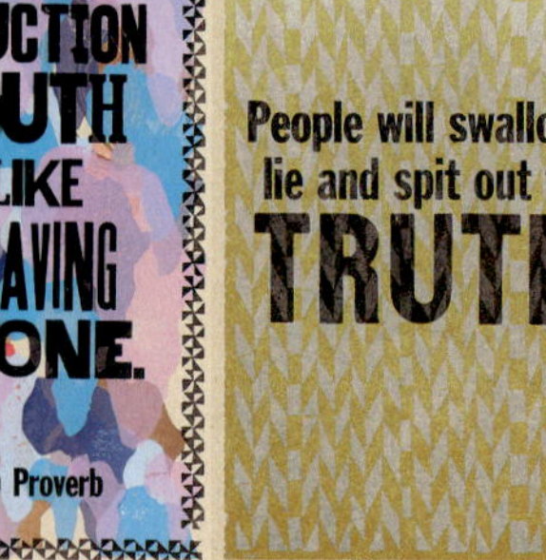
People will swallow a lie and spit out the TRUTH.
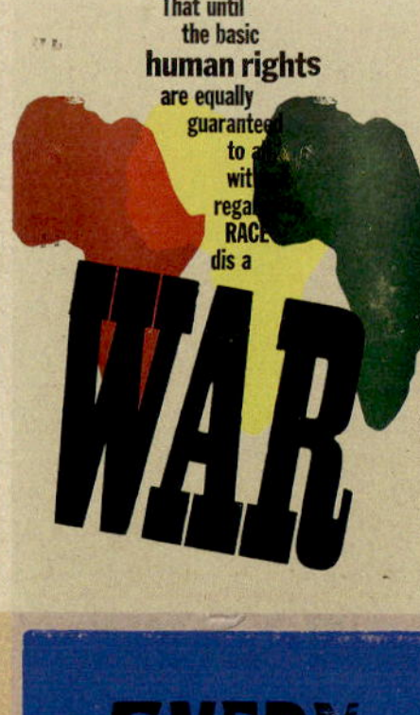
WAR
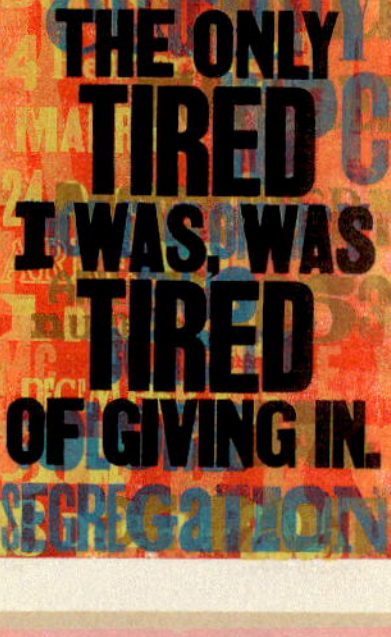
THE ONLY TIRED I WAS, WAS TIRED OF GIVING IN.
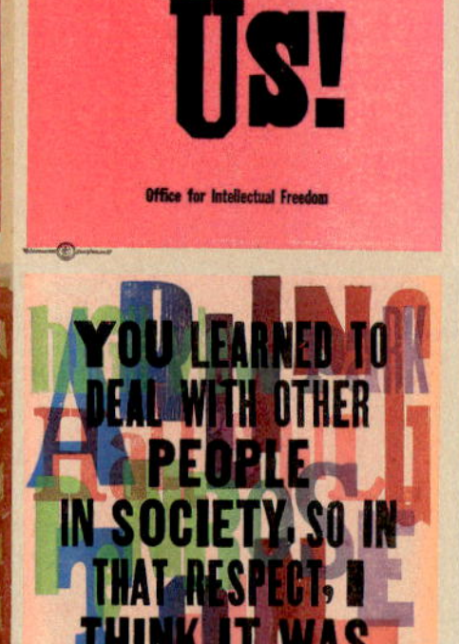
DIVERSE BOOKS NEED US!
Office for Intellectual Freedom
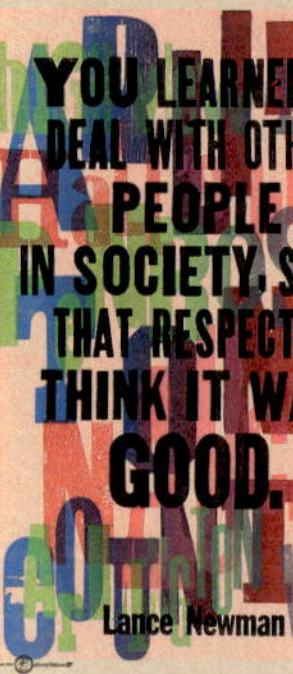
YOU LEARNED TO DEAL WITH OTHER PEOPLE IN SOCIETY, SO IN THAT RESPECT, I THINK IT WAS GOOD.
Lance Newman
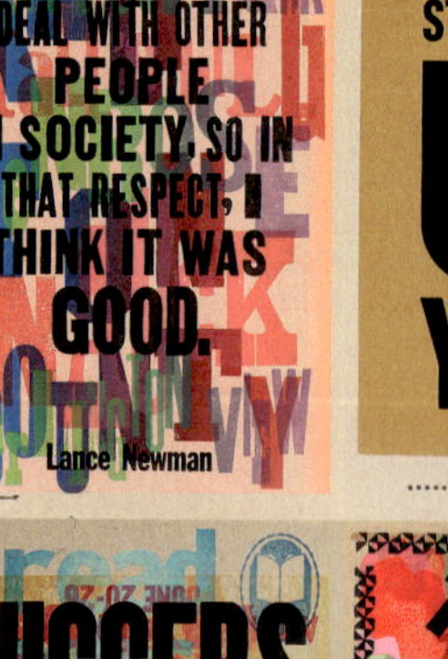
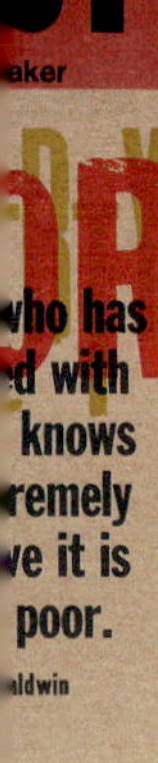
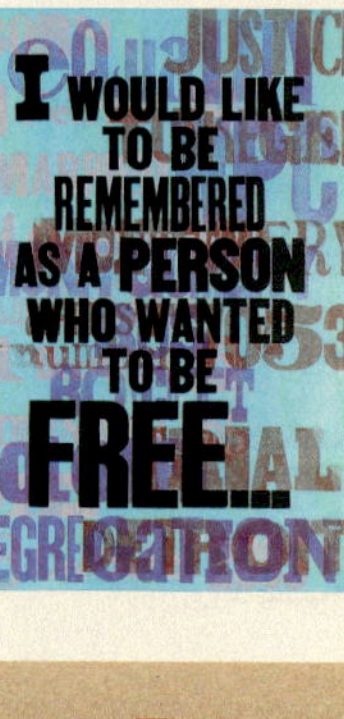
I WOULD LIKE TO BE REMEMBERED AS A PERSON WHO WANTED TO BE FREE...
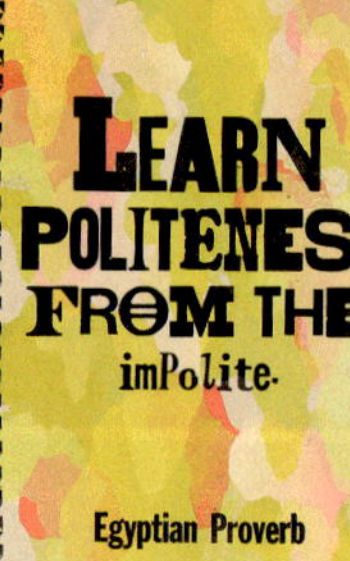
LEARN POLITENESS FROM THE imPolite.
Egyptian Proverb
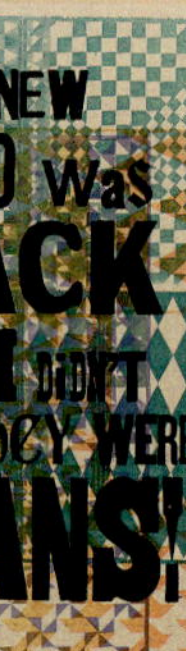
I KNEW GOD WAS BLACK
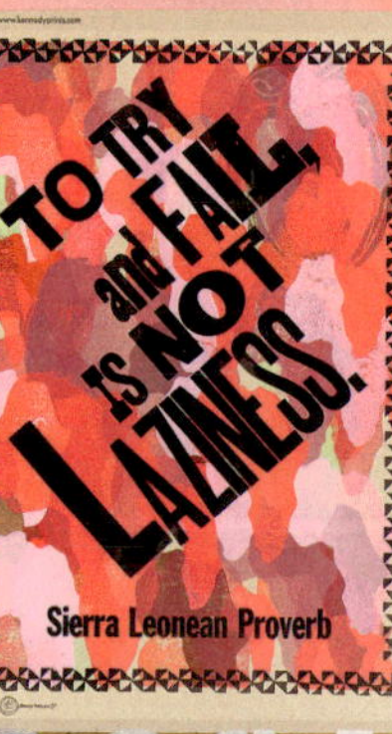
TO TRY and FAIL IS NOT LAZINESS.
Sierra Leonean Proverb
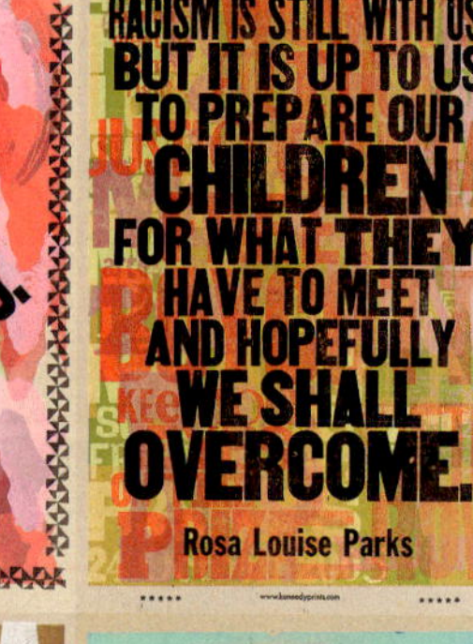
RACISM IS STILL WITH US, BUT IT IS UP TO US TO PREPARE OUR CHILDREN FOR WHAT THEY HAVE TO MEET AND HOPEFULLY WE SHALL OVERCOME.
Rosa Louise Parks
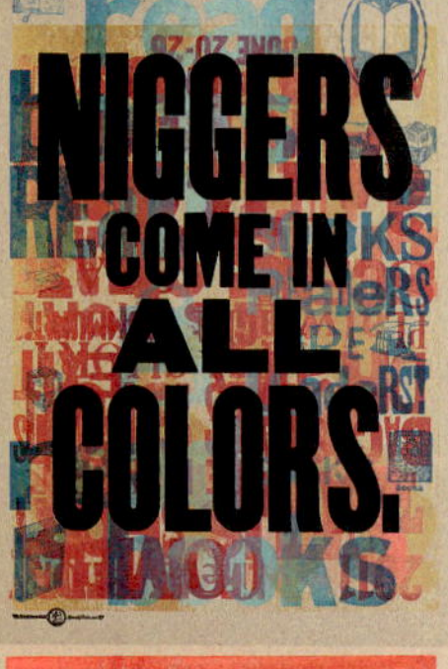
NIGGERS COME IN ALL COLORS.
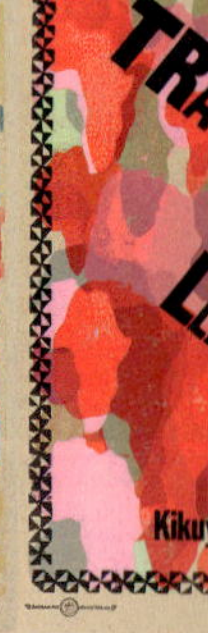
Kikuyu
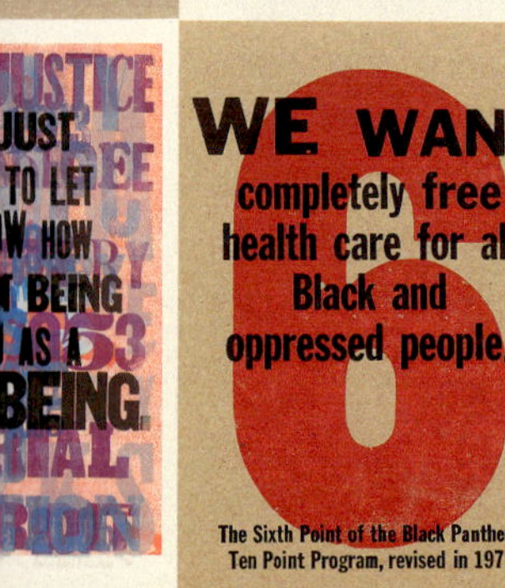
WE WANT completely free health care for all Black and oppressed people.
The Sixth Point of the Black Panther's Ten Point Program, revised in 1972
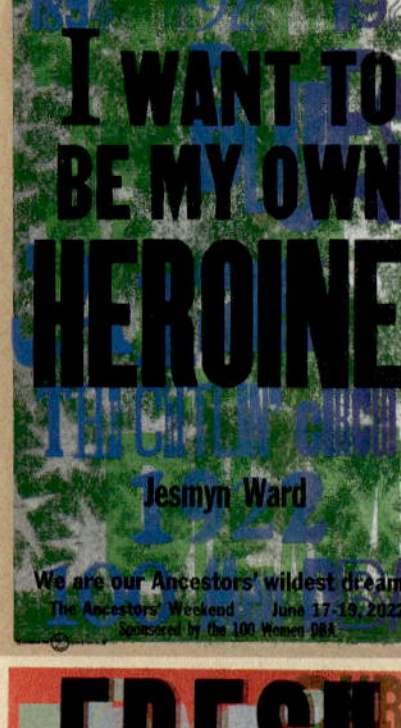
I WANT TO BE MY OWN HEROINE.
Jesmyn Ward
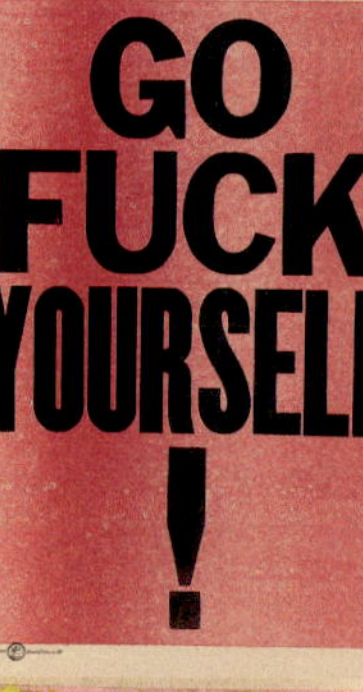
GO FUCK YOURSELF !
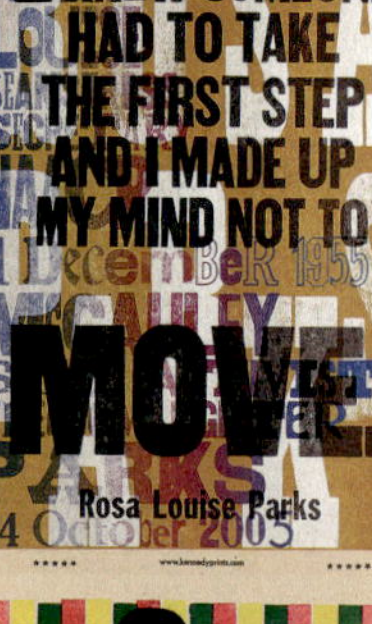
I KNEW SOMEONE HAD TO TAKE THE FIRST STEP AND I MADE UP MY MIND NOT TO MOVE.
Rosa Louise Parks
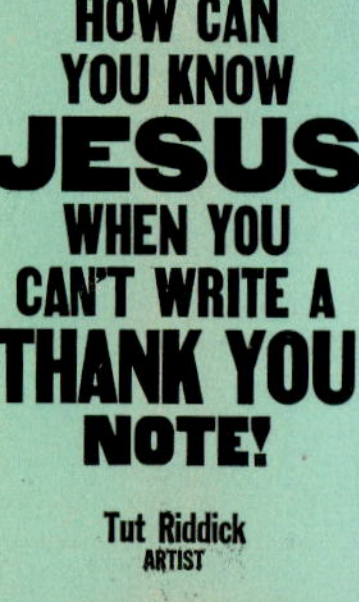
HOW CAN YOU KNOW JESUS WHEN YOU CAN'T WRITE A THANK YOU NOTE!
Tut Riddick
ARTIST
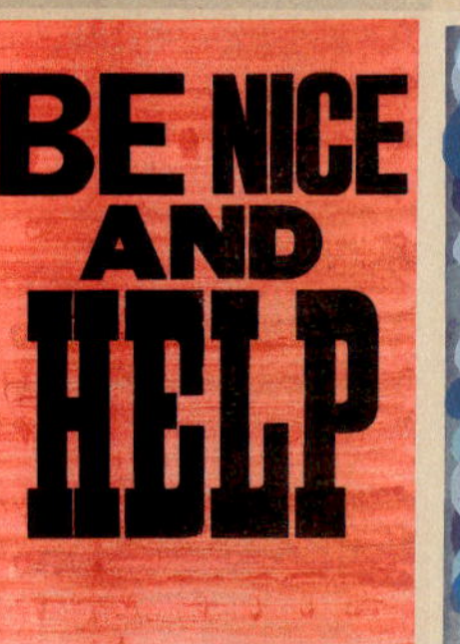
BE NICE AND HELP
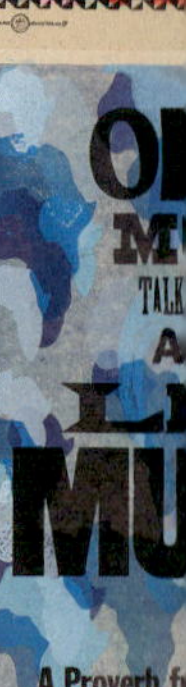
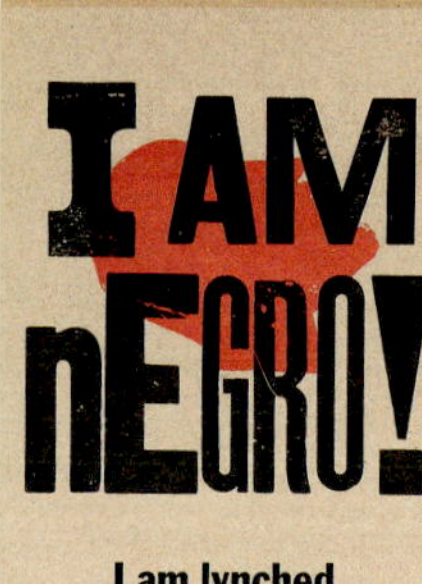
I AM nEGRO!
I am lynched.
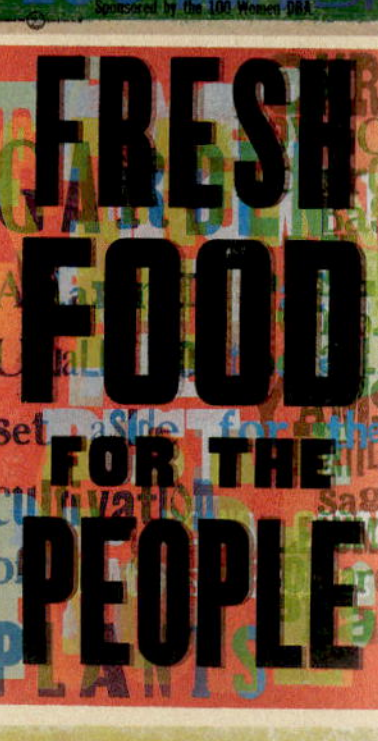
FRESH FOOD FOR THE PEOPLE
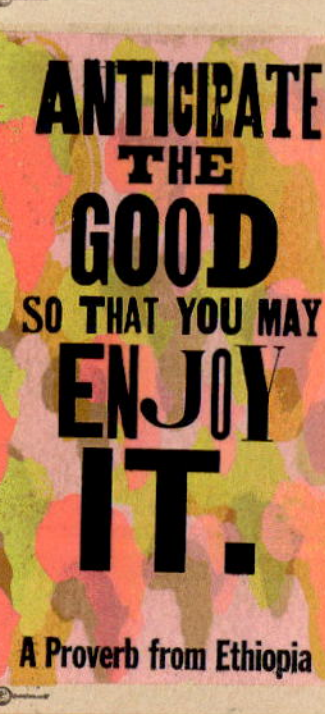
ANTICIPATE THE GOOD SO THAT YOU MAY ENJOY IT.
A Proverb from Ethiopia
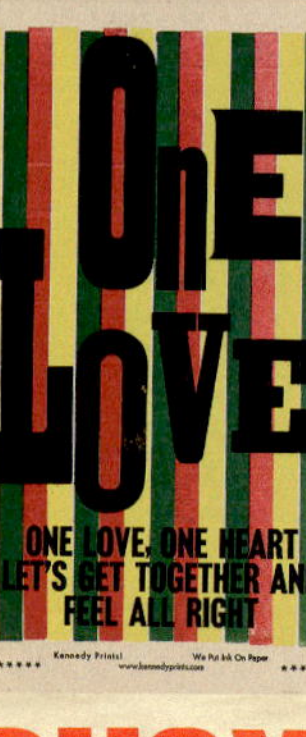
OnE LOVE
ONE LOVE, ONE HEART LET'S GET TOGETHER AND FEEL ALL RIGHT
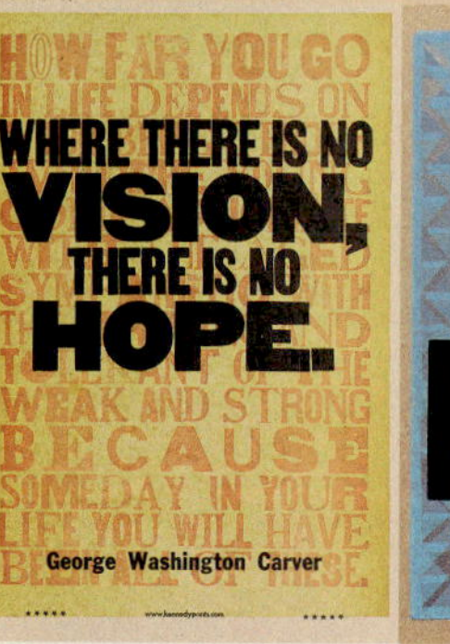
WHERE THERE IS NO VISION, THERE IS NO HOPE.
George Washington Carver
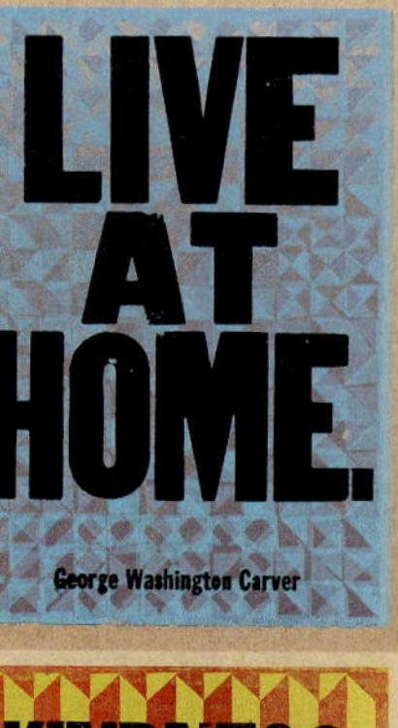
LIVE AT HOME.
George Washington Carver
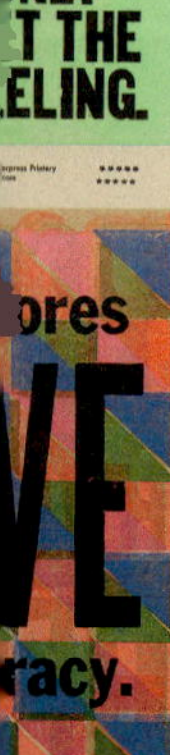
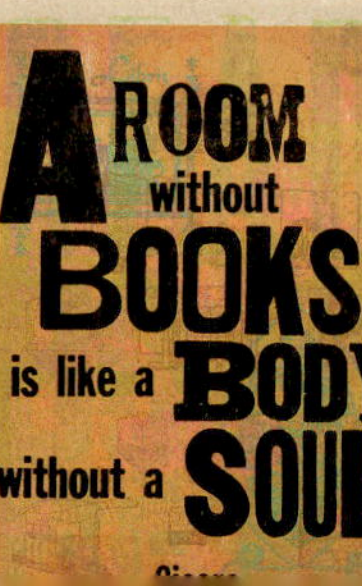
A ROOM without BOOKS is like a BODY without a SOUL.
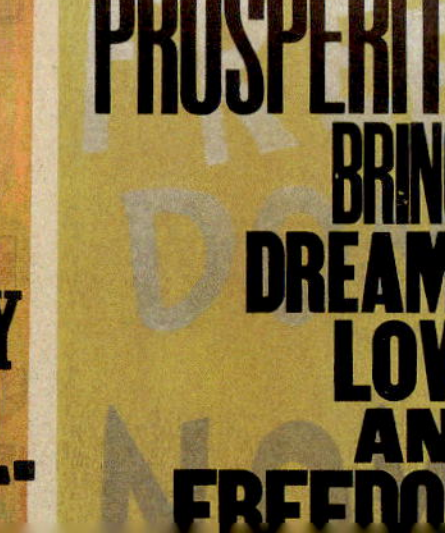
PROSPERITY BRINGS DREAMS LOVE AND FREEDOM
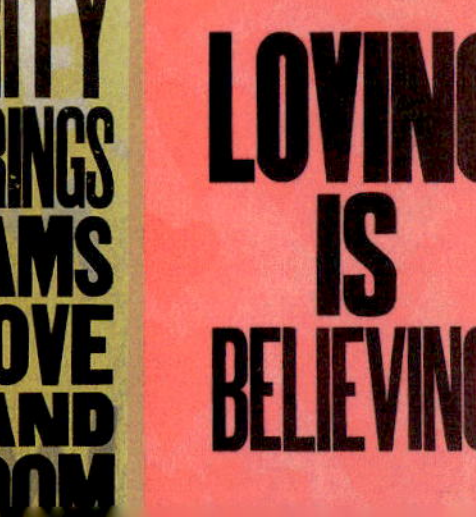
LOVING IS BELIEVING
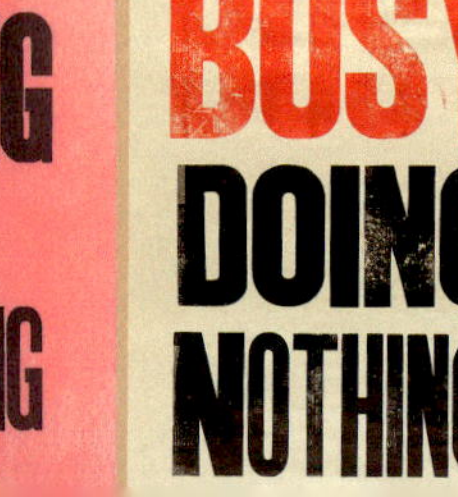
BUSY DOING NOTHING
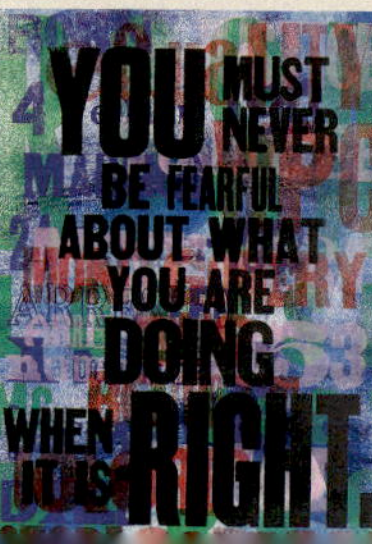
YOU MUST NEVER BE FEARFUL ABOUT WHAT YOU ARE DOING WHEN IT IS RIGHT.
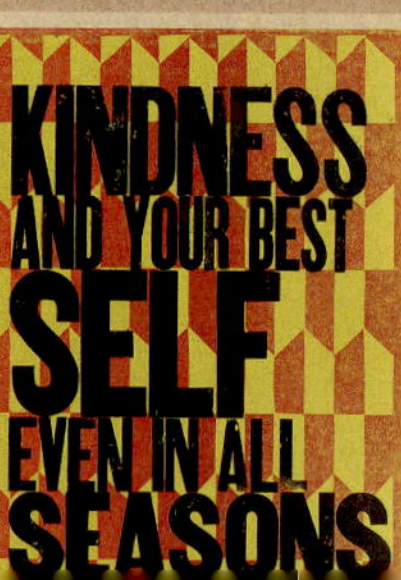
KINDNESS AND YOUR BEST SELF EVEN IN ALL SEASONS
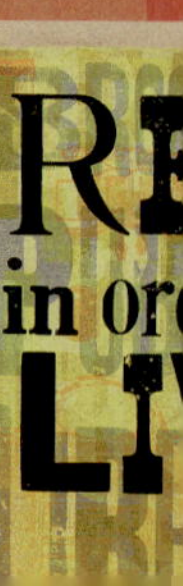

AM
EGRO!
I am bi.

I DON'T WANT TO GO TO HEAVEN, NONE OF MY FRIENDS ARE THERE.
Oscar Wilde

PEACE ON EARTH

GET UP STAND UP
GET UP, STAND UP
STAND UP FOR YOUR RIGHTS!
GET UP, STAND UP
DON'T GIVE UP THE FIGHT!

SCIENCE IS ABOUT TO HAPPEN

NO FREEDOM BOYCOTT
Rosa Louise Parks

YOUR LIBRARY IS YOUR PARADISE.
Desiderius Erasmus

WOULD LIKE
O BE KNOWN
A PERSON WHO
CONCERNED
UT FREEDOM &
LITY & JUSTICE &
PROSPERITY
ALL PEOPLE.
Rosa Louise Parks

MEMENTO MORI
Call no man happy till he is dead.
Aeschylus

COFFEE MADE ME BLACK

IF BAD PRINTING IS WRONG WE DON'T WANNA BE RIGHT!

I WAS JUST TRYING TO LET THEM KNOW HOW I FELT ABOUT BEING TREATED AS A HUMAN BEING.

LIFE
You ain't gonna get rich, so you might as well get HAPPY!

It is difficult to get a man to understand something when his salary depends upon his not understanding it.
UPTON SINCLAIR

A WISE WOMAN WHO KNOWS PROVERBS RECONCILES DIFFICULTIES
A Yoruba Proverb

JUSTICE IS A SPECIAL PRIVILEGE FOR BLACKS
IN THE UNITED STATES OF AMERICA.

A NATION MAY LOSE ITS LIBERTIES AND BE A CENTURY IN FINDING IT OUT.
John M. Langston

STOP GIVING US HOMEWORK
Albemarle County Public Schools

I KNEW GOD WAS BLACK BUT I DIDN'T KNOW THEY WERE FEMME!

I KNEW SOMEONE HAD TO TAKE THE FIRST STEP AND I MADE UP MY MIND NOT TO MOVE.

REMEMBER STONEWALL 1969

LL I WAS
ING WAS
RYING TO
T HOME
OM WORK.
Rosa Louise Parks

I'M TOO OLD FOR THIS SHIT

PACE IN TERRA

I ain't afraid to live in a world with Trans people.
I am afraid to live in a world without them.

I CAN'T BREATHE!

NIGGERS COME IN ALL COLORS.

THE EARTH WILLINGLY TEACHES RIGHTEOUSNESS TO THOSE WHO CAN LEARN
Xenophon

OWN THE MEANS OF PRODUCTION

STAY OUT of the Drama
Albemarle County Public Schools

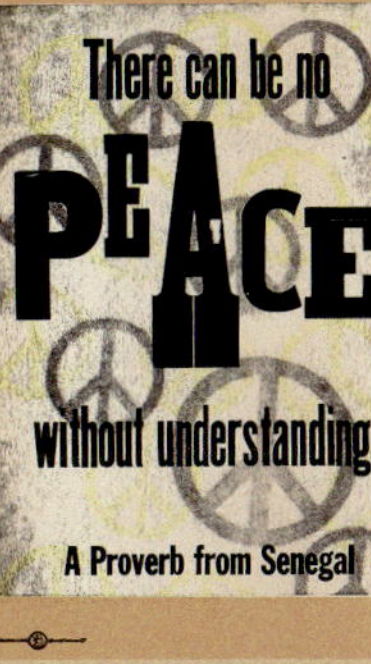

There can be no PEACE without understanding.
A Proverb from Senegal

I don't want a job. I want MONEY.

WHICH SIDE ARE YOU ON?

CRAFT.
Handmade by Humans

NOW
JUSTICE
NOW
PEACE

GREAT ARTISTS NEVER RETIRE
They just quit their day job.
Celebrating Bryant's retirement on 29 May 2023

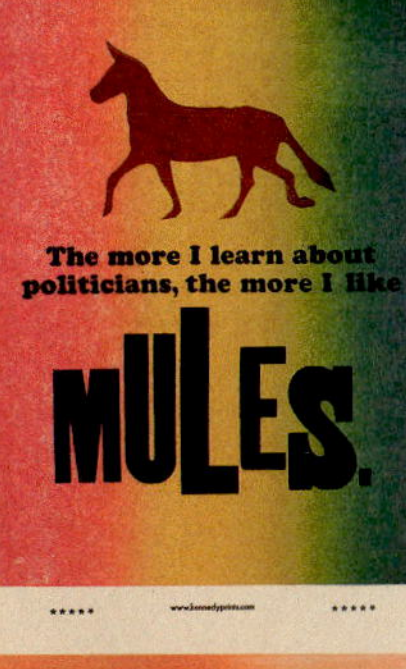

PEACE ON EARTH

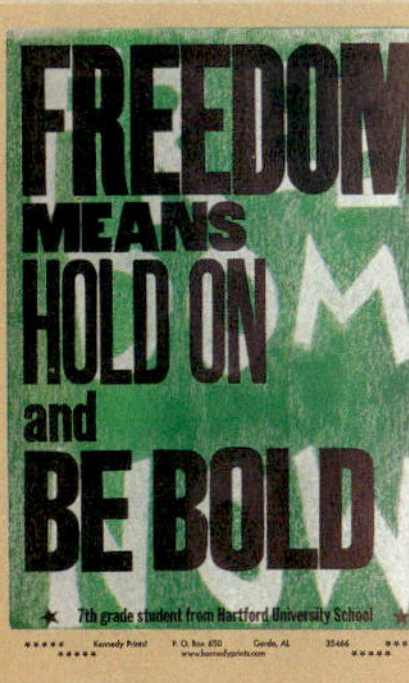

Since 1998 empowering our LGBTQ community
Grand Rapids Pride Center

I WOULD LIKE TO BE REMEMBERED AS A PERSON WHO WANTED TO BE FREE AND WANTED OTHER PEOPLE TO BE ALSO FREE.
Rosa Louise Parks

E BOLD
ND HAVE
REEDOM
EN YOU ARE
ROWN

EDUCATION IS WHAT YOU KNOW NOT WHAT'S IN THE BOOK.

WHAT MAKES PRIDE?

VOTE CLIMATE, JOBS JUSTICE
THIS NOVEMBER
Sign the pledge at www.peoplesclimate.org

Principles of American $ Capitalism
PRIVATIZE PROFITS SOCIALIZE RISKS

Take your share of the WORLD and let other people take theirs.
George Washington Carver

I WOULD TELL YOU TO GO TO HELL BUT I WORK THERE AND I DON'T WANT TO SEE YOU

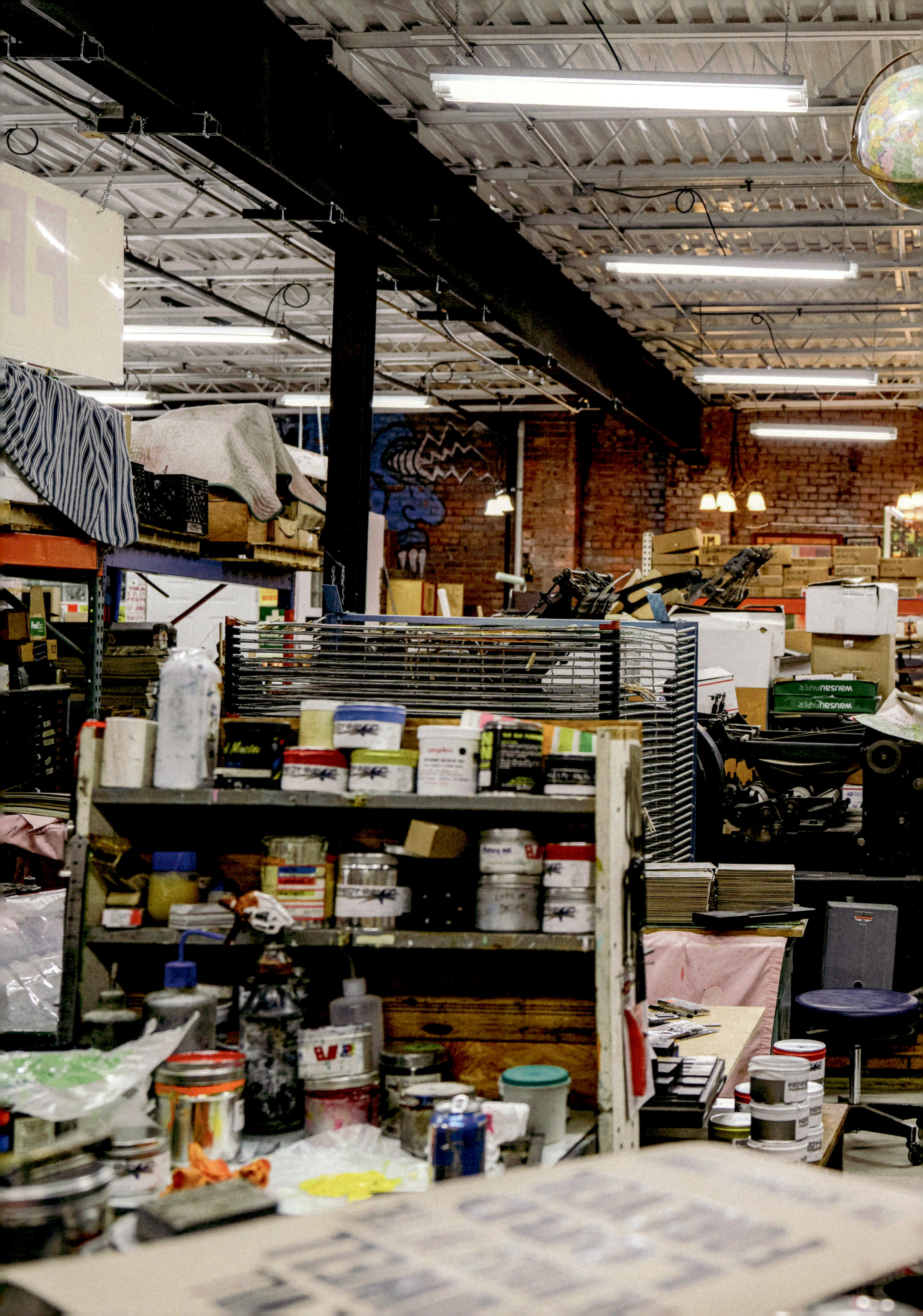

wausau PAPER

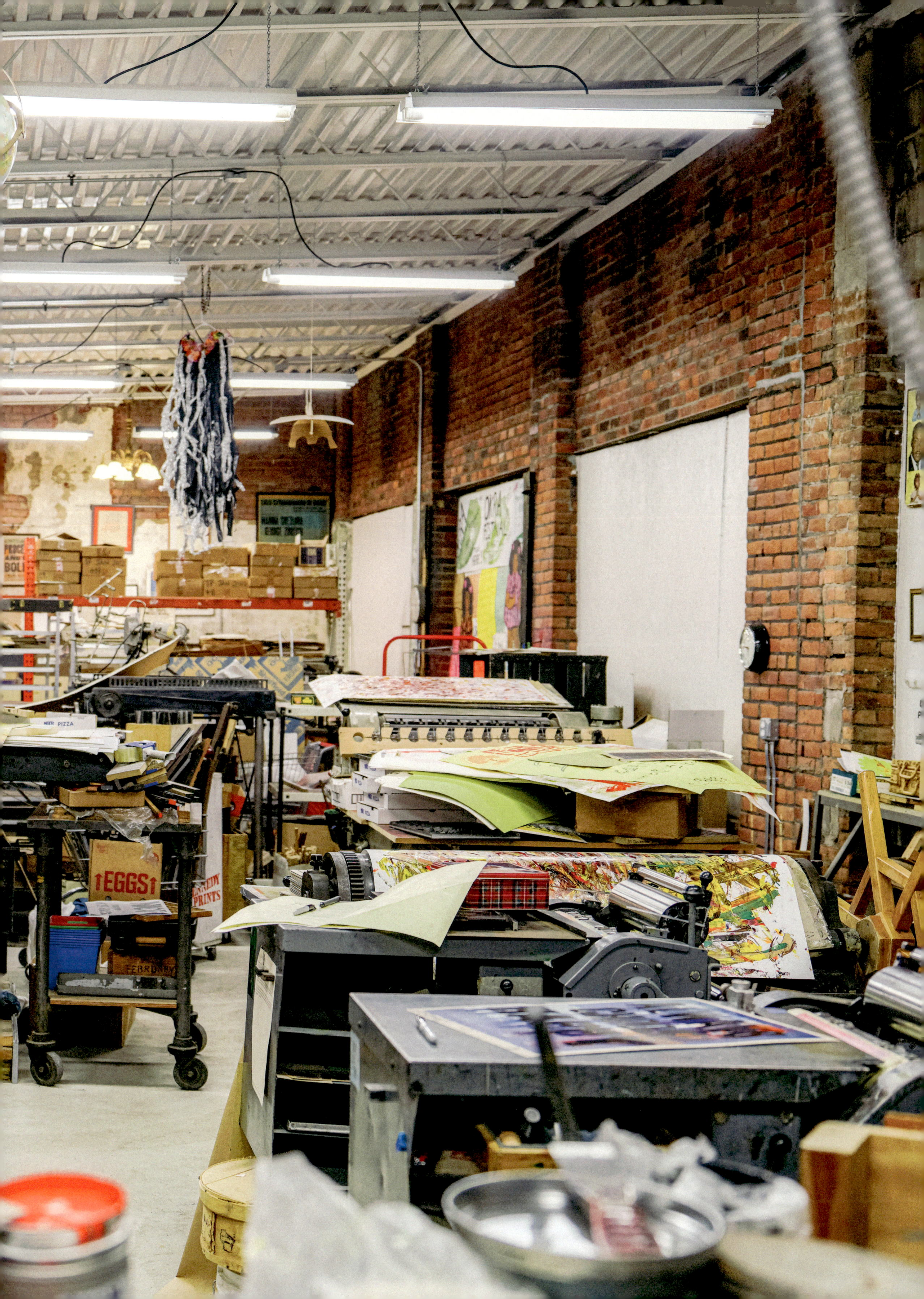
↑EGGS↑

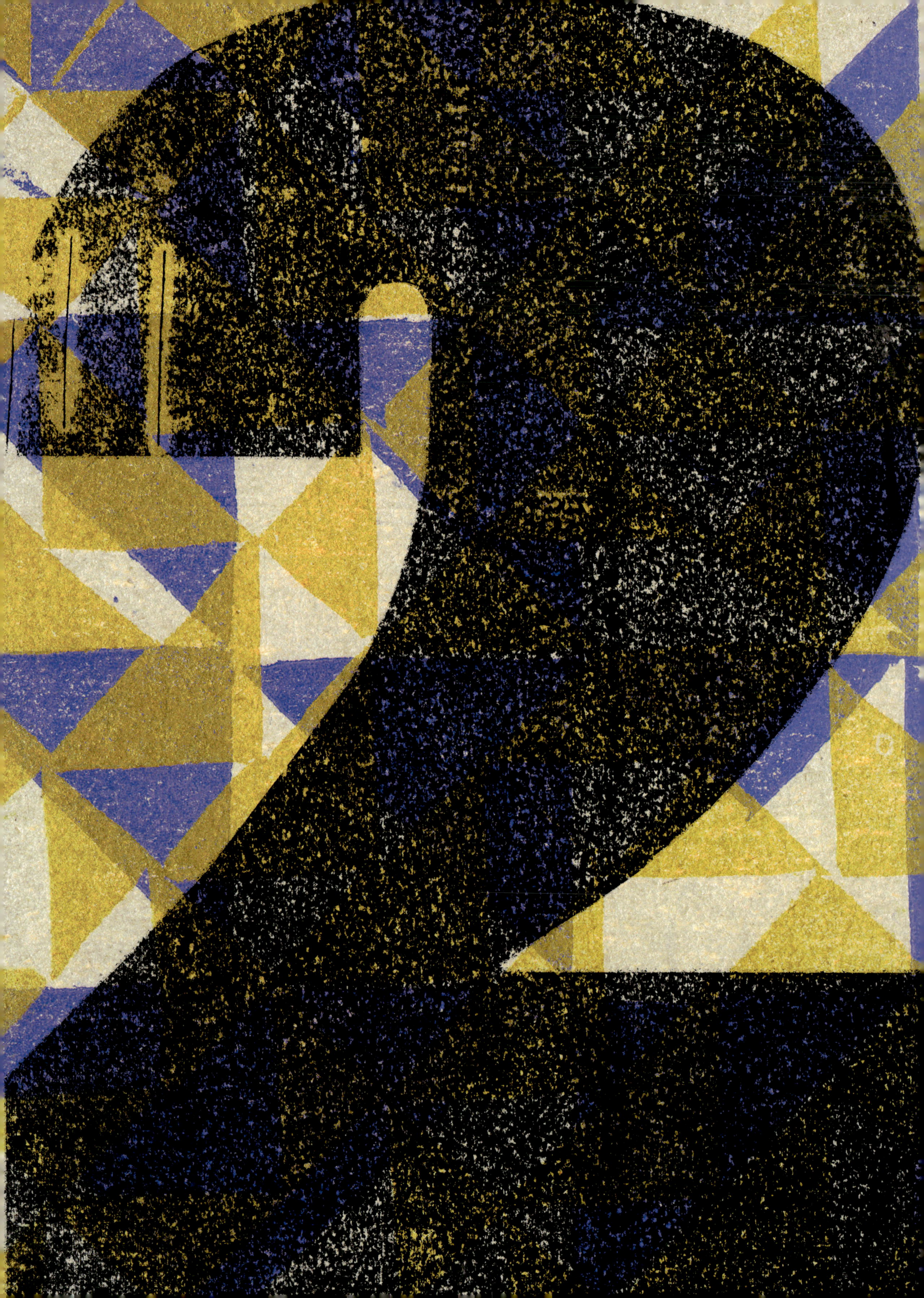

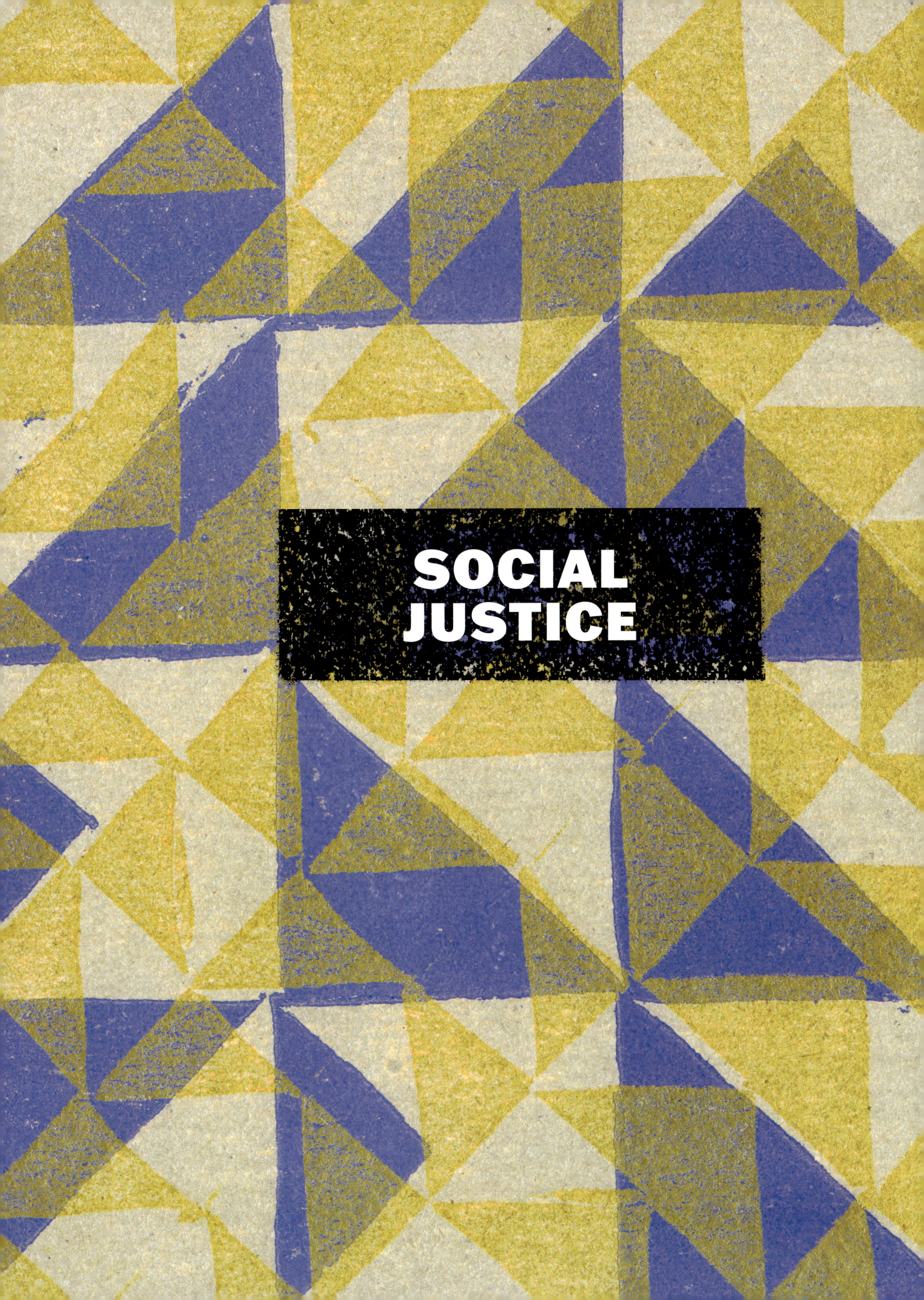
SOCIAL
JUSTICE

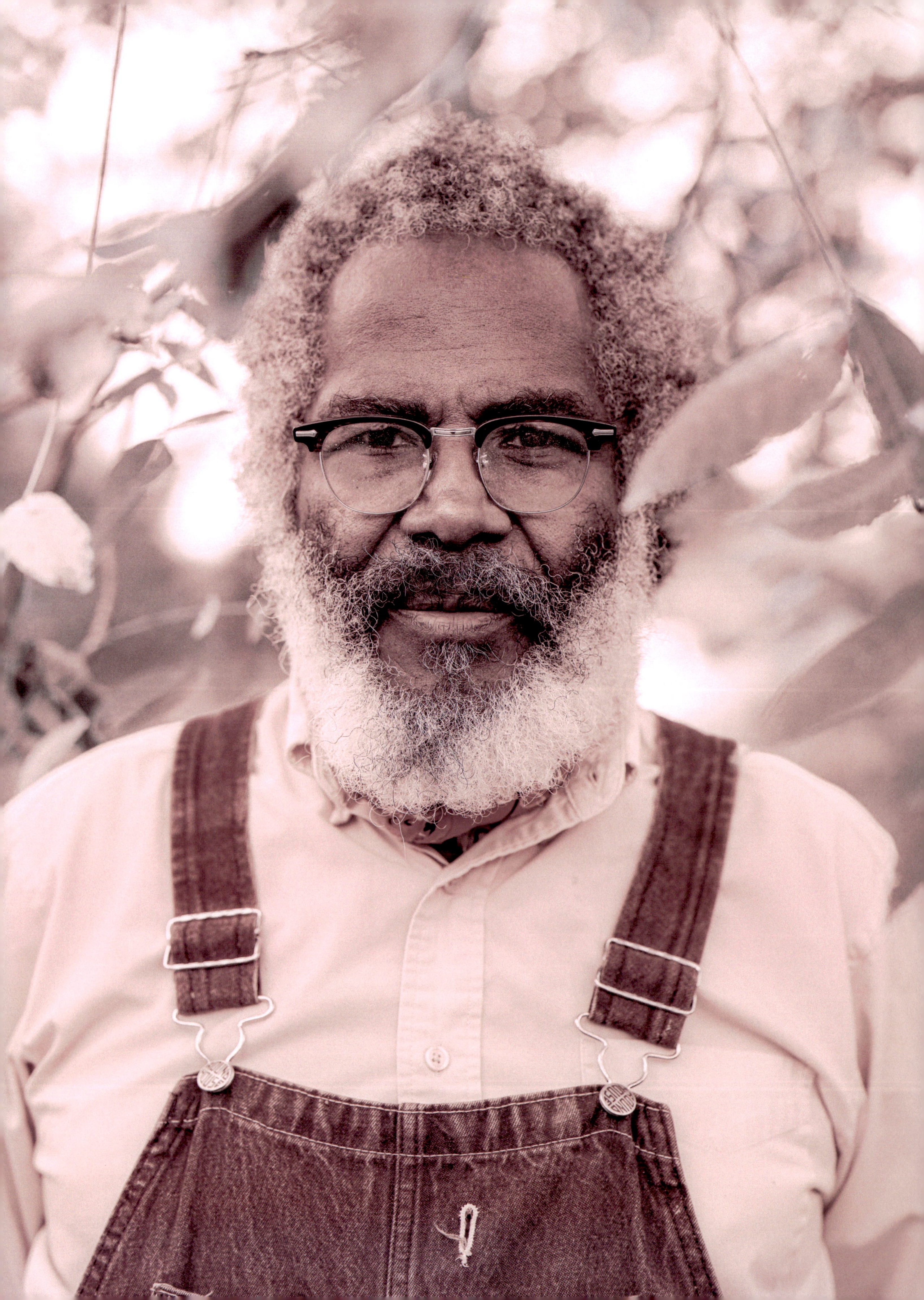

"People ask me when I got into social justice. I tell them August 14, 1950: the day I was born colored in these United States of America."

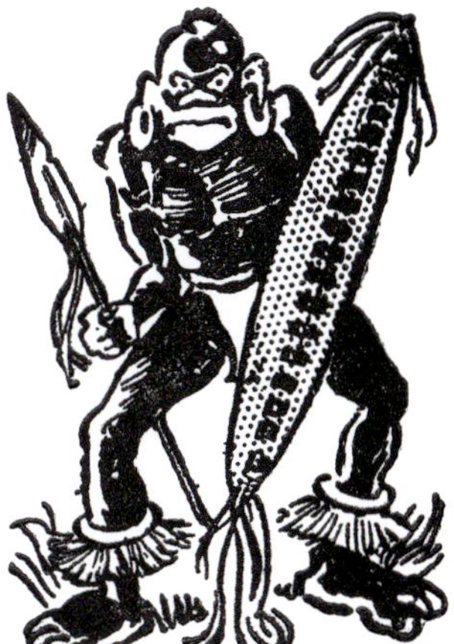

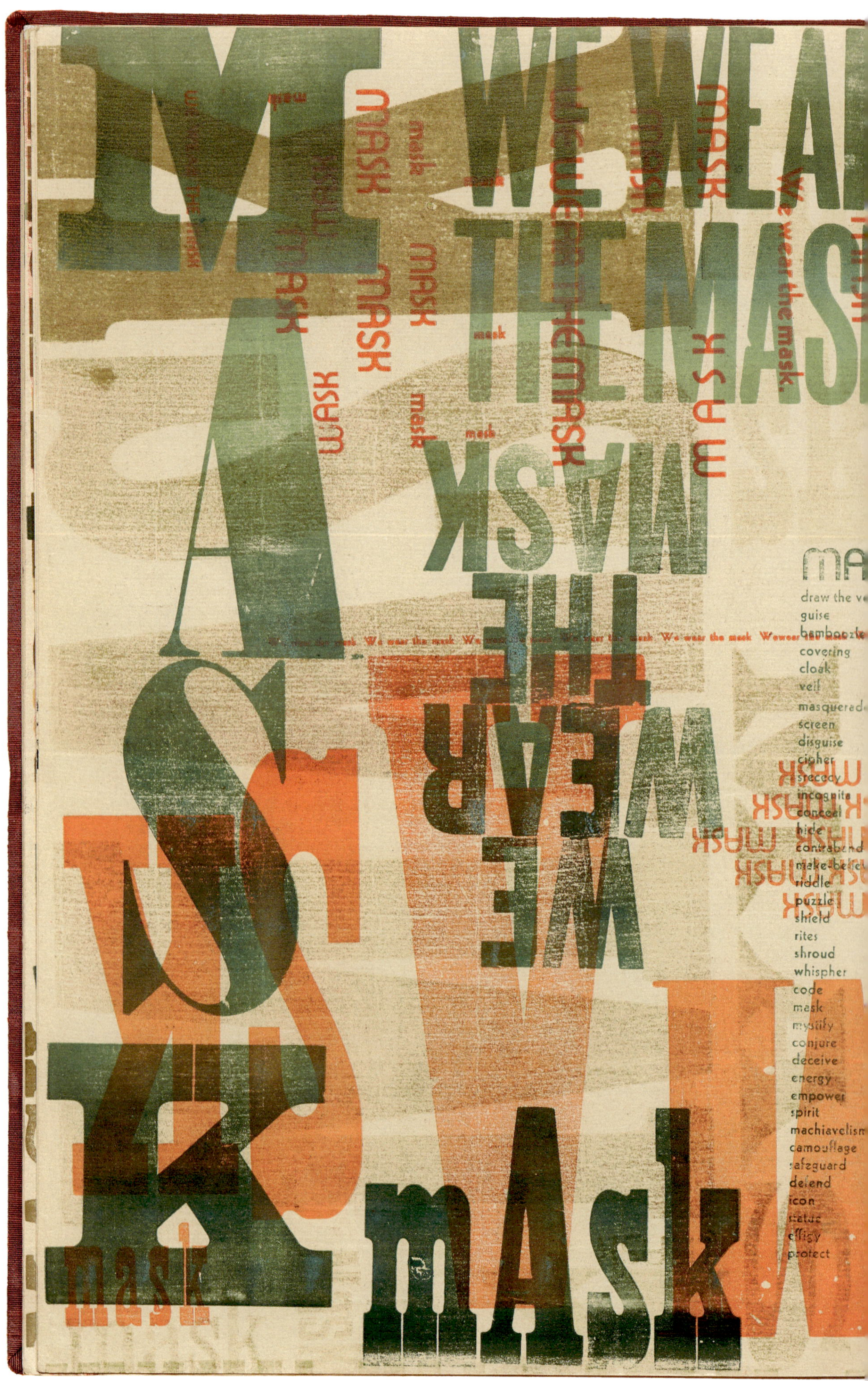
WE WEAR
THE MASK
We wear the mask.
WE WEAR THE MASK
mask
guise
covering
cloak
veil
screen
disguise
cipher
incognito
conceal
hide
riddle
puzzle
shield
rites
shroud
whispher
code
mask
mystify
conjure
deceive
energy
spirit
machiavelism
camouflage
safeguard
defend
icon
status
protect
mAsk

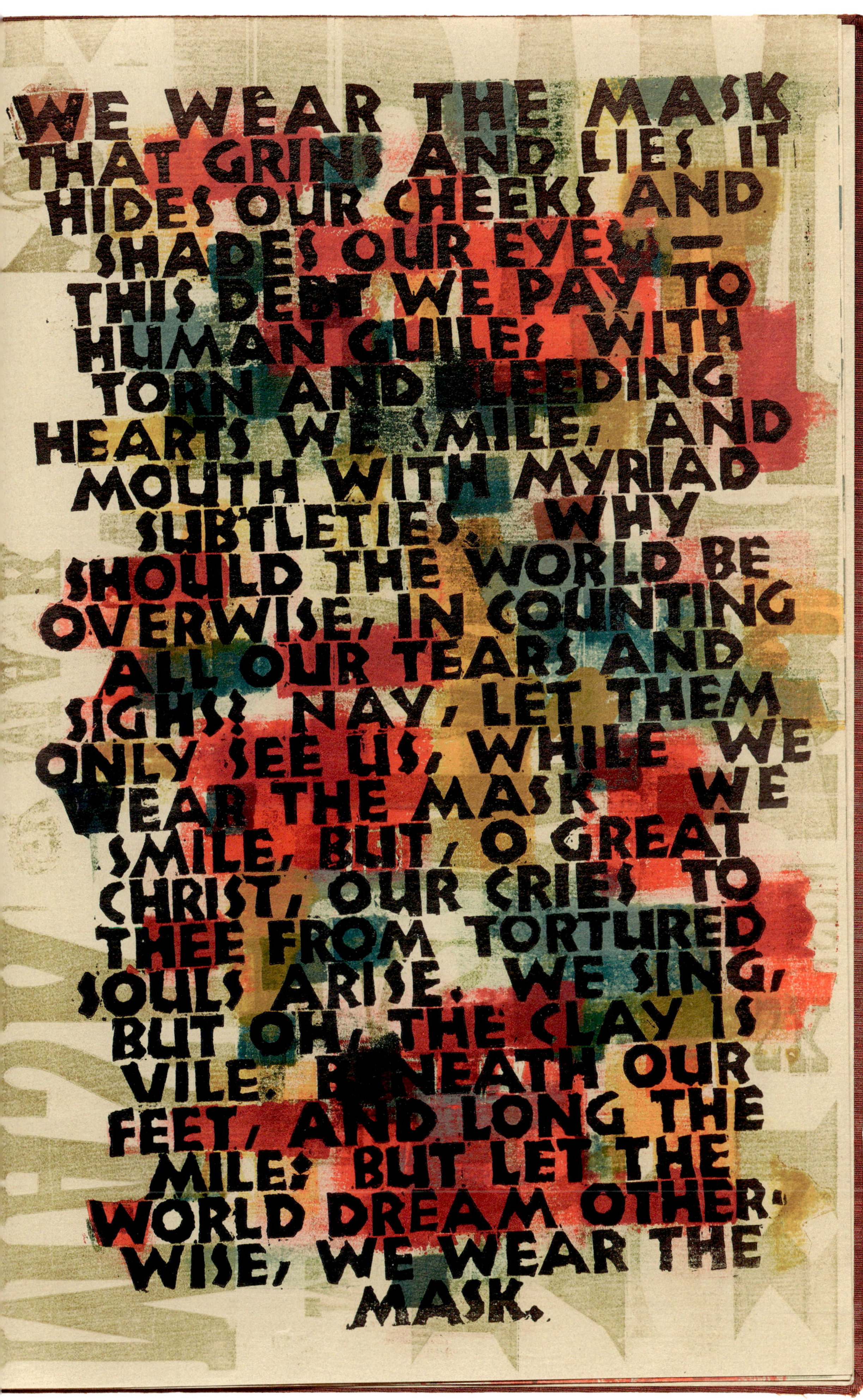
WE WEAR THE MASK
THAT GRINS AND LIES IT
HIDES OUR CHEEKS AND
SHADES OUR EYES —
THIS DEBT WE PAY TO
HUMAN GUILE; WITH
TORN AND BLEEDING
HEARTS WE SMILE, AND
MOUTH WITH MYRIAD
SUBTLETIES. WHY
SHOULD THE WORLD BE
OVERWISE, IN COUNTING
ALL OUR TEARS AND
SIGHS? NAY, LET THEM
ONLY SEE US, WHILE WE
WEAR THE MASK. WE
SMILE, BUT, O GREAT
CHRIST, OUR CRIES TO
THEE FROM TORTURED
SOULS ARISE. WE SING,
BUT OH, THE CLAY IS
VILE. BENEATH OUR
FEET, AND LONG THE
MILE; BUT LET THE
WORLD DREAM OTHER-
WISE, WE WEAR THE
MASK.

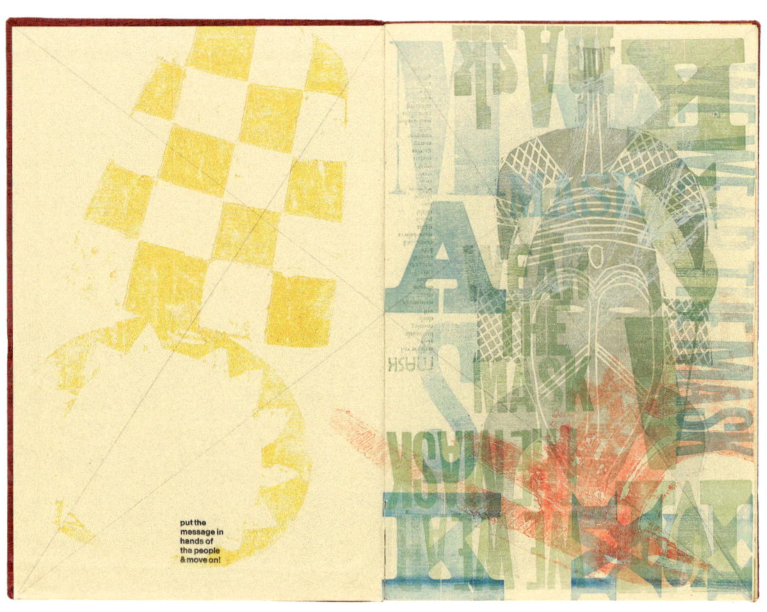
put the
message in
hands of
the people
& move on!

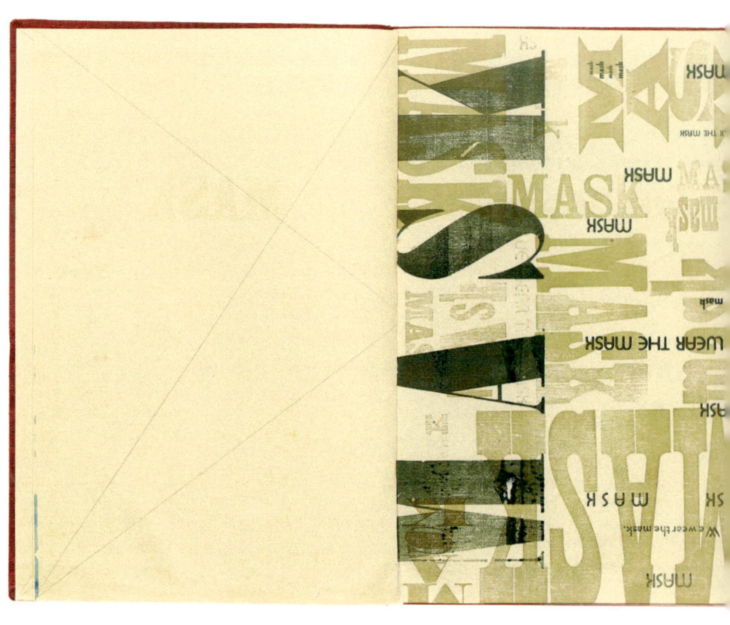

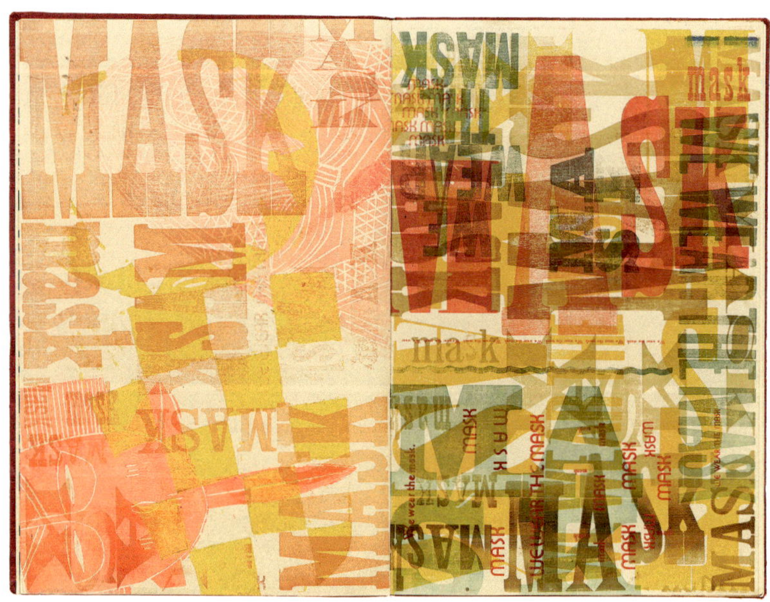

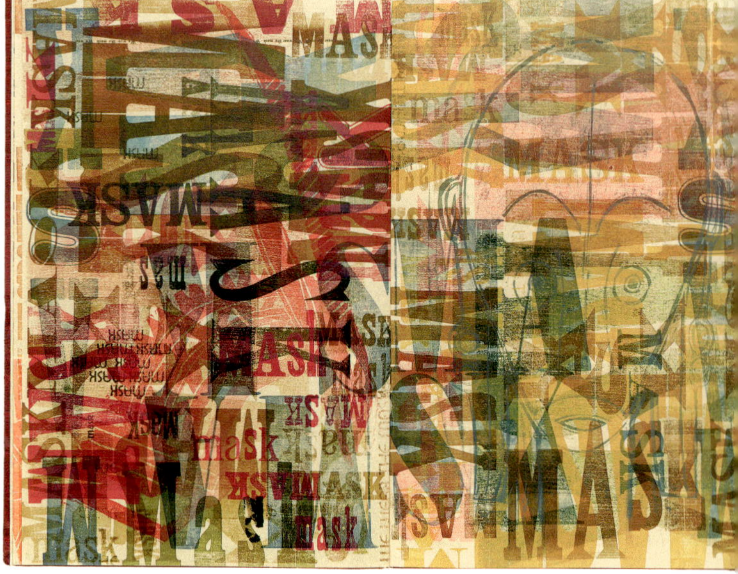

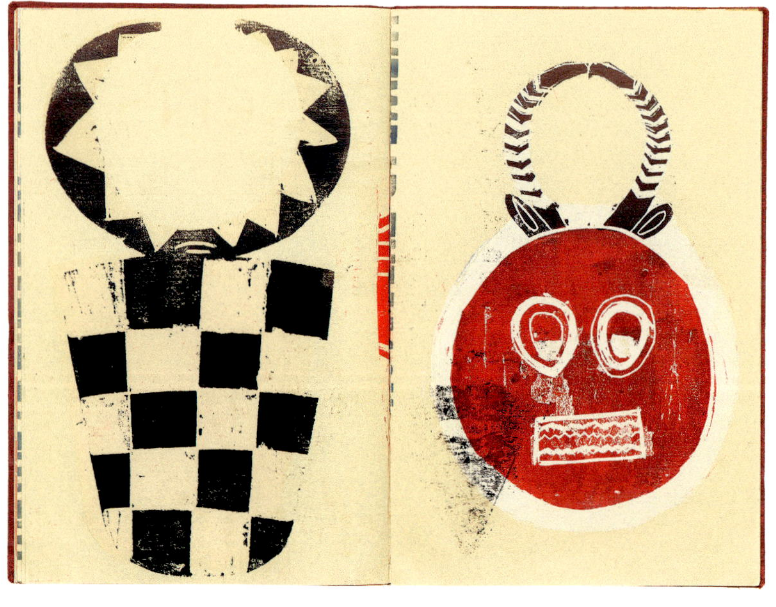

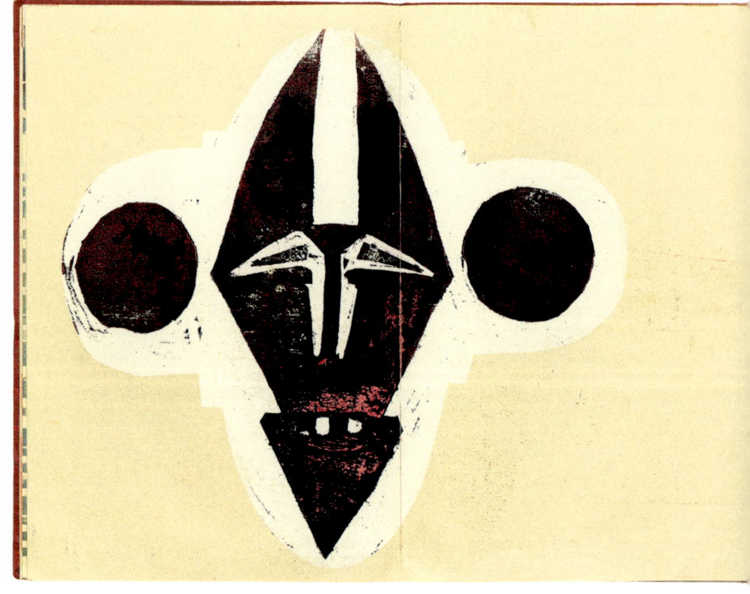

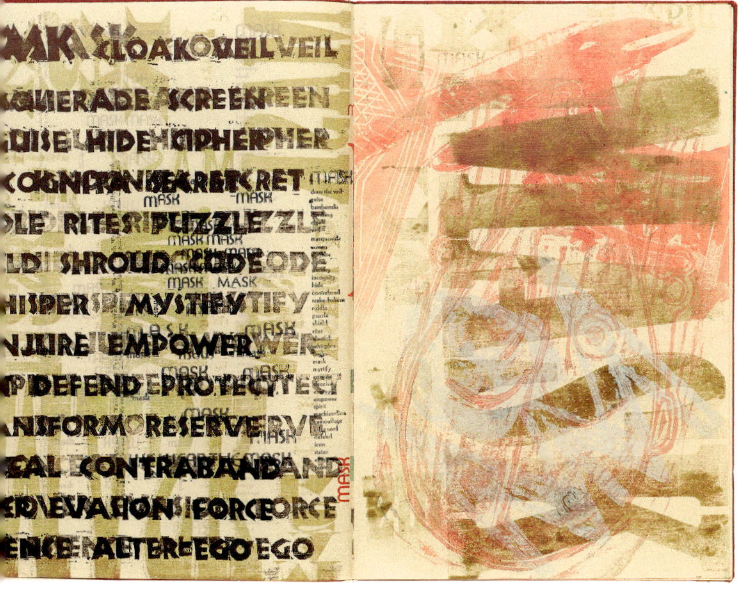
CLOAK VEIL
SCREEN
HIDE CIPHER
SECRET
RITES PUZZLE
SHROUD CODE
MYSTIFY
EMPOWER
DEFEND PROTECT
RESERVE
CONTRABAND
FORCE
ALTER-EGO

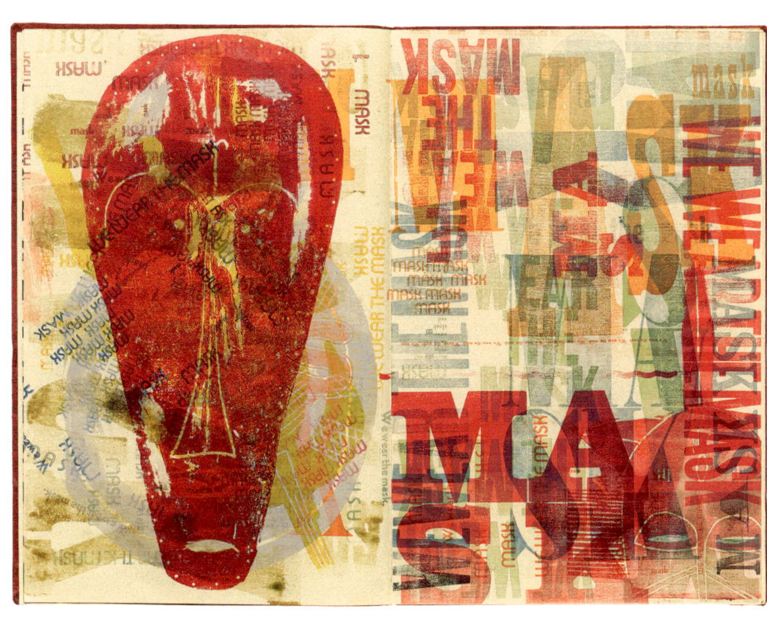
MASK
THE MASK
WEAR THE MASK

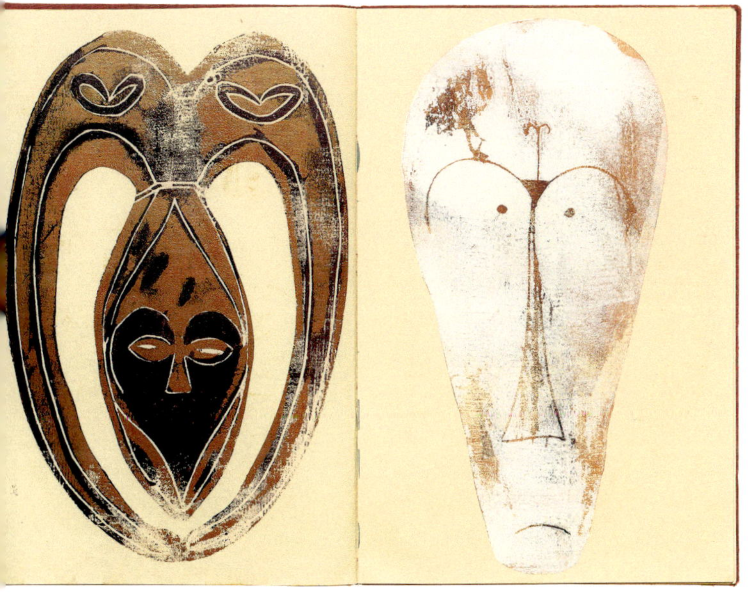

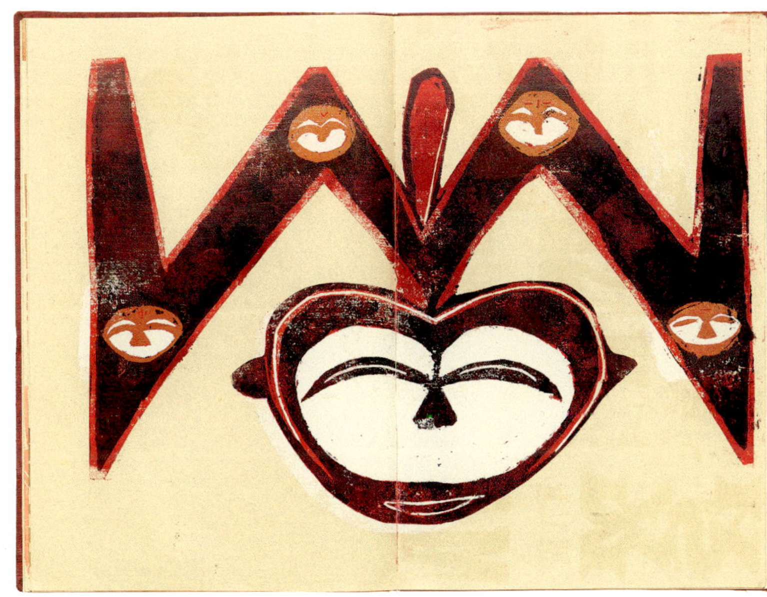

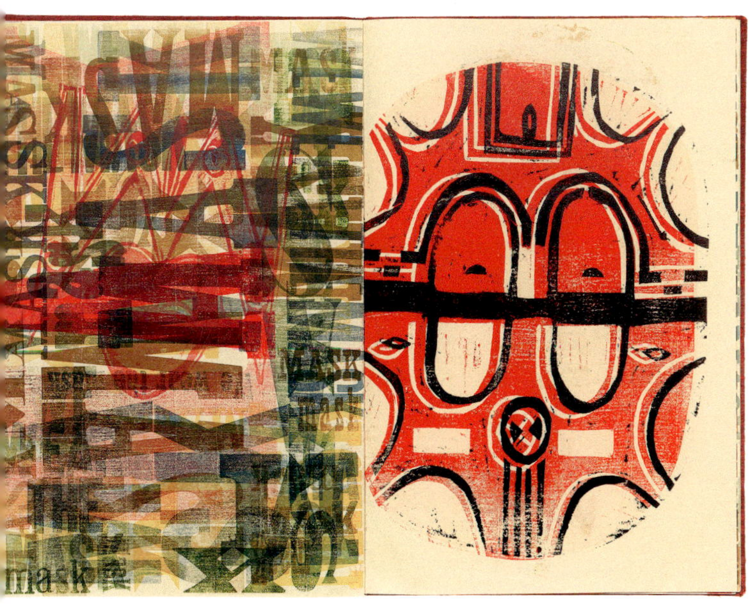
mask

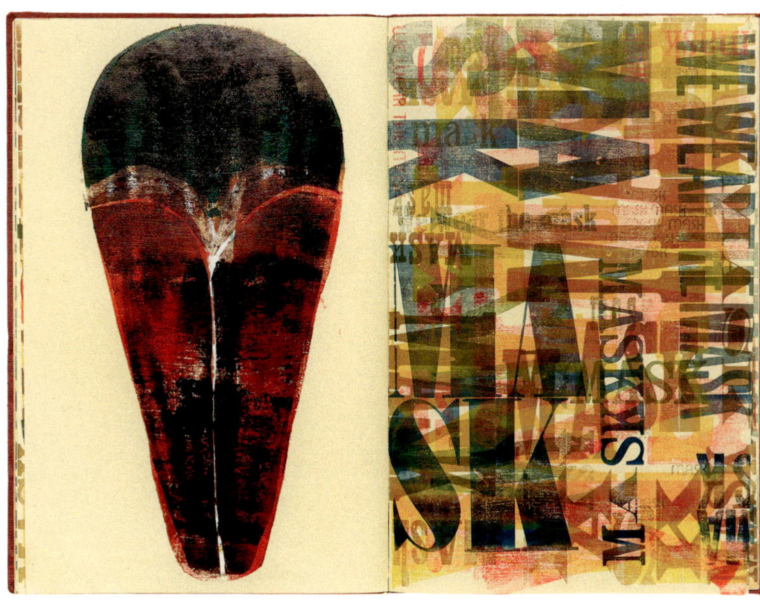
mask

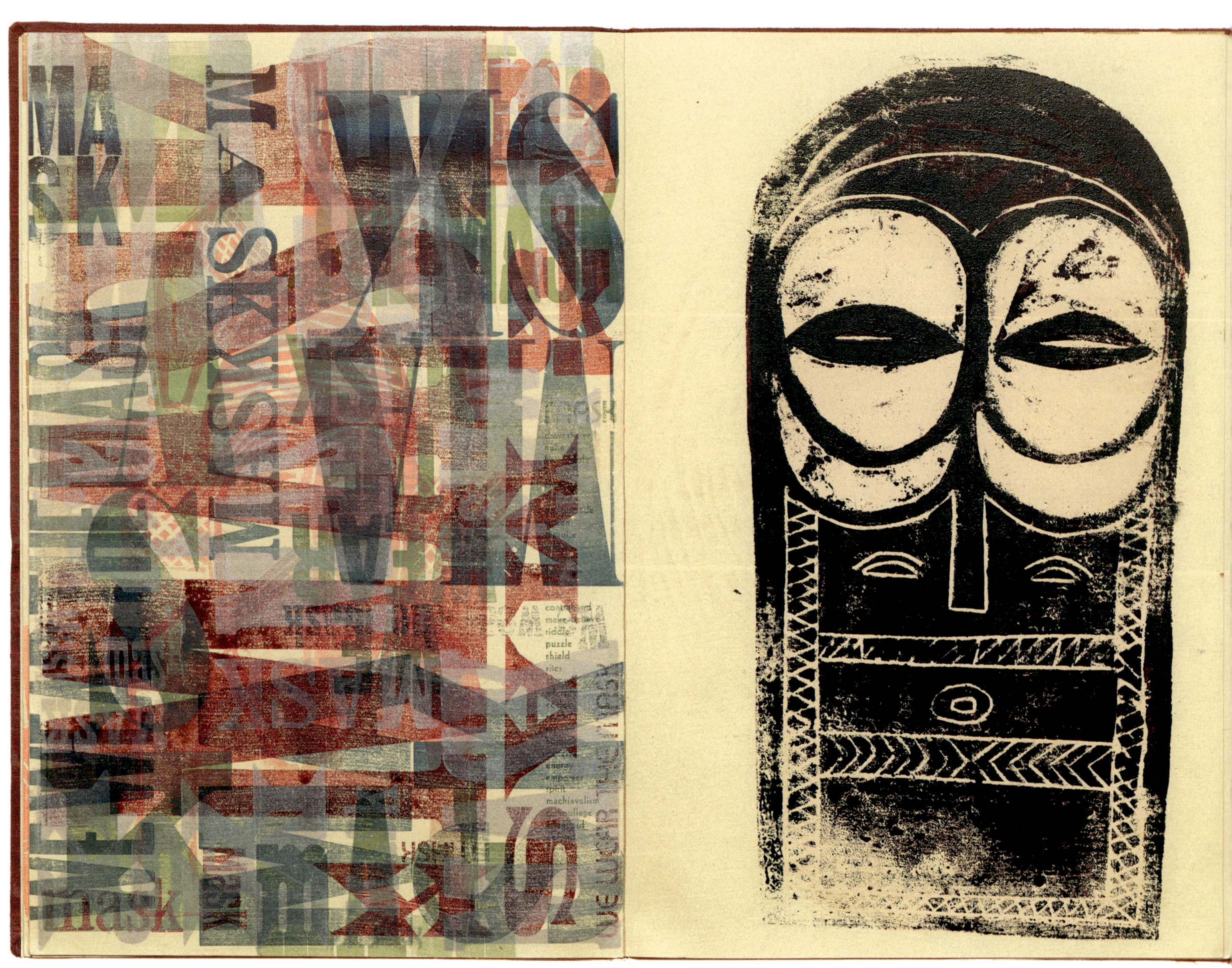

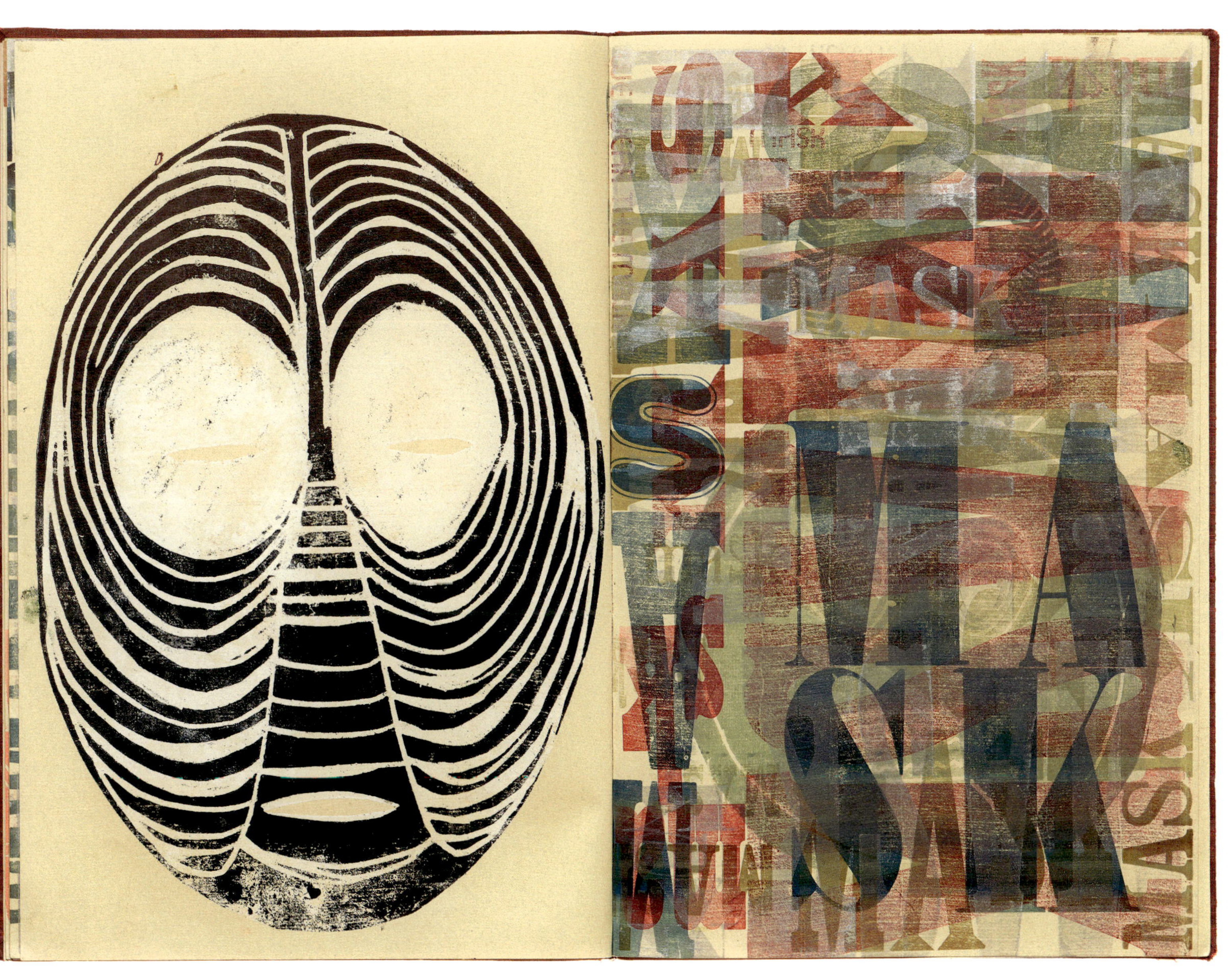
MASK

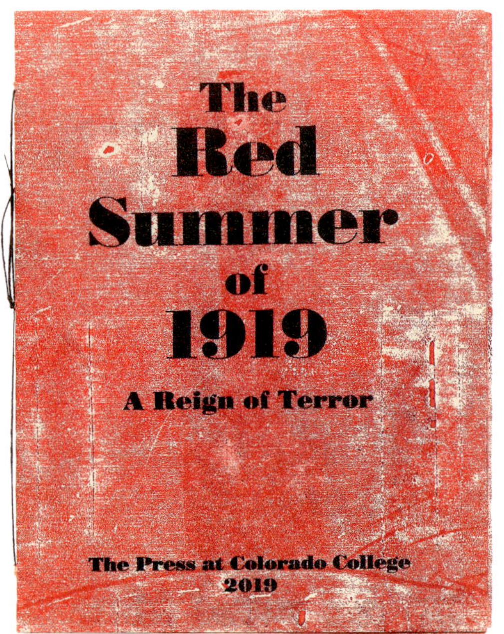
The
Red
Summer
of
1919
A Reign of Terror
The Press at Colorado College
2019

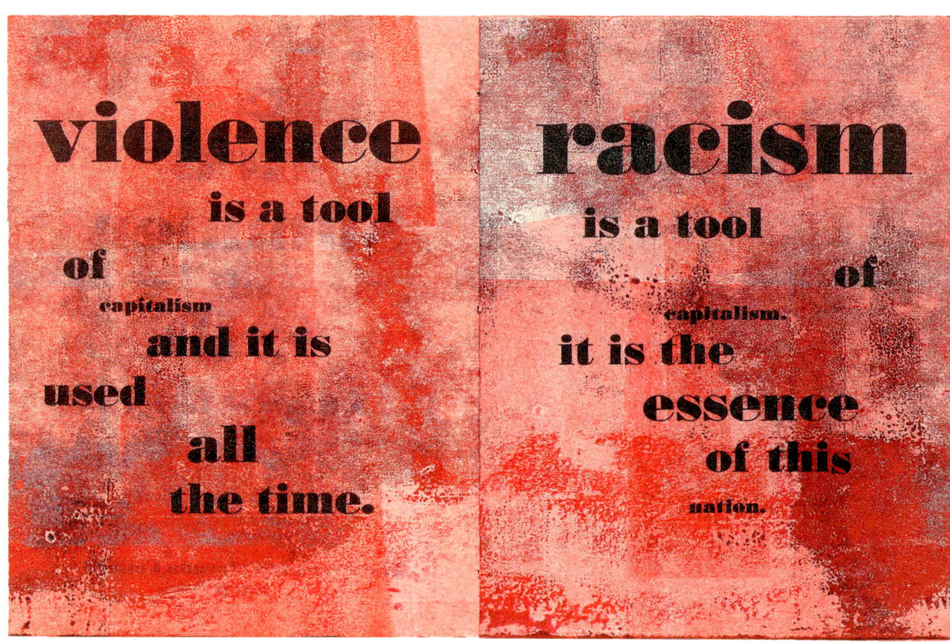
violence
is a tool
of
capitalism
and it is
used
all
the time.
racism
is a tool
of
capitalism.
it is the
essence
of this
nation.

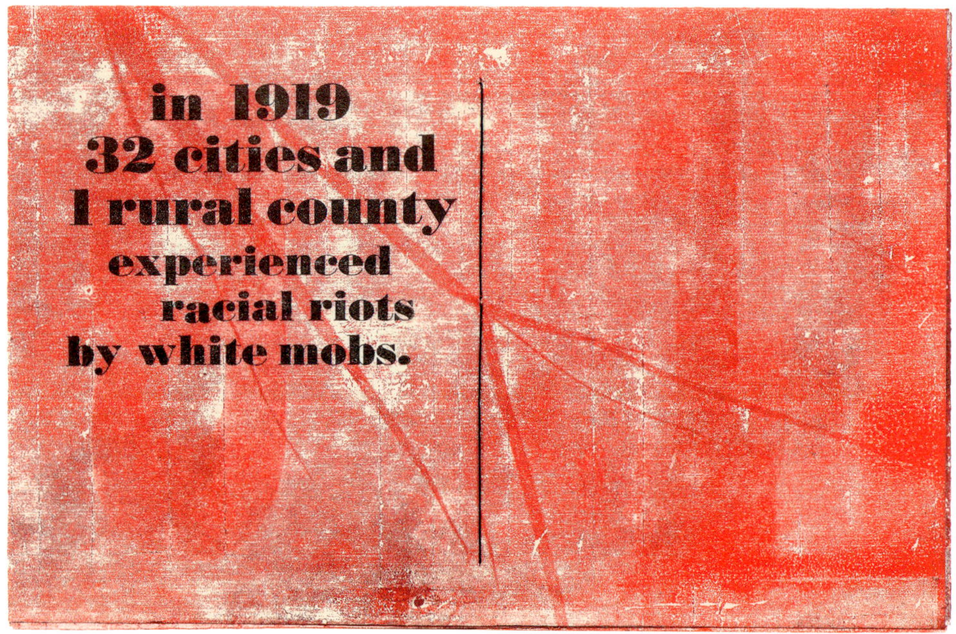
in 1919
32 cities and
1 rural county
experienced
racial riots
by white mobs.

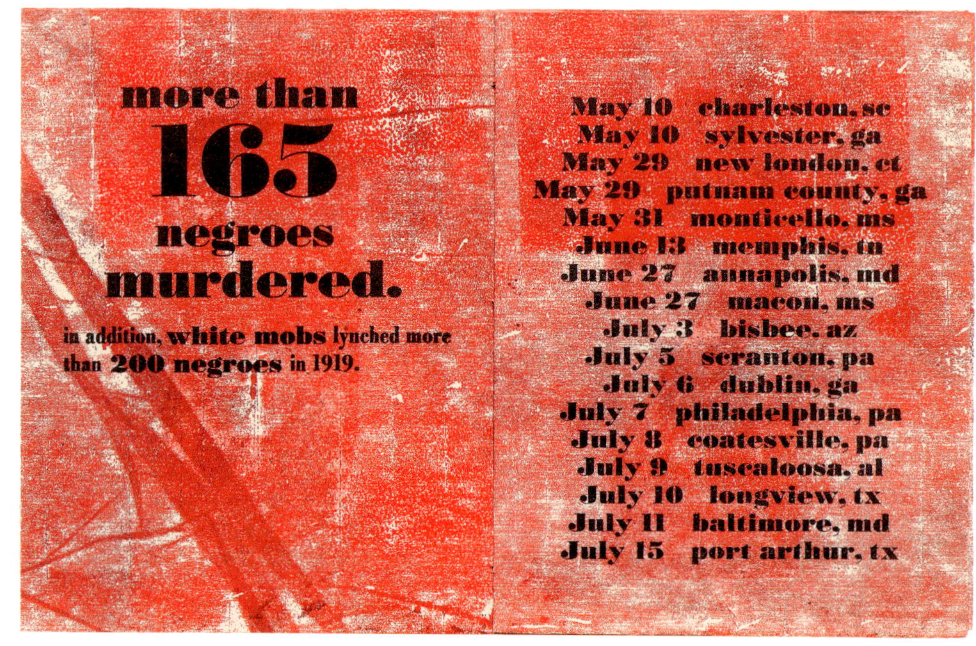
more than
165
negroes
murdered.
in addition, white mobs lynched more
than 200 negroes in 1919.
May 10 charleston, sc
May 10 sylvester, ga
May 29 new london, ct
May 29 putnam county, ga
May 31 monticello, ms
June 13 memphis, tn
June 27 annapolis, md
June 27 macon, ms
July 3 bisbee, az
July 5 scranton, pa
July 6 dublin, ga
July 7 philadelphia, pa
July 8 coatesville, pa
July 9 tuscaloosa, al
July 10 longview, tx
July 11 baltimore, md
July 15 port arthur, tx

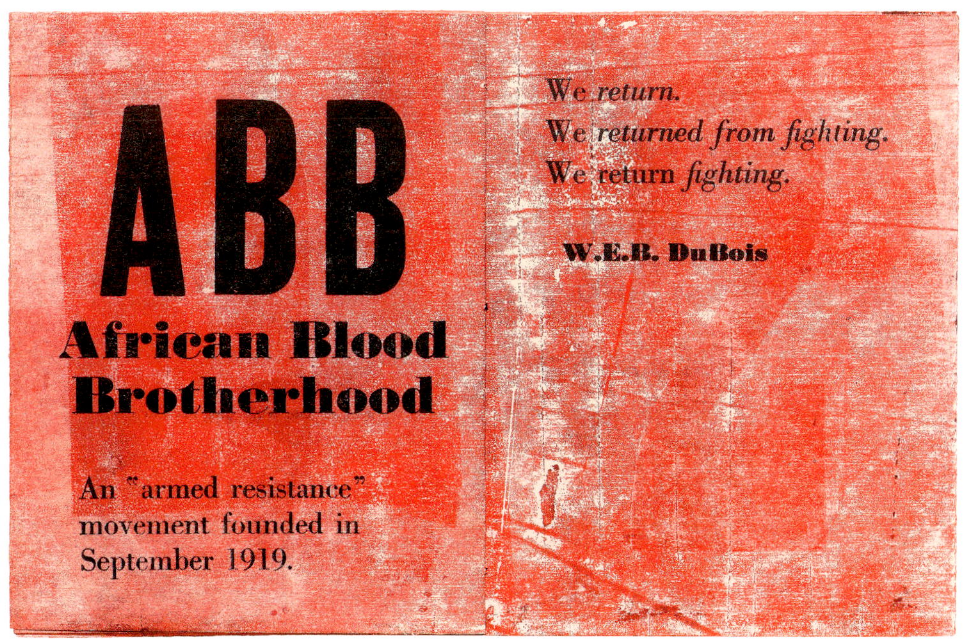

July 19 washington, dc
July 21 norfolk, va
July 23 new orleans, la
July 23 darby, pa
July 26 hobson city, al
July 27 chicago, il
July 28 newberry, sc
July 31 bloomington, il
July 31 syracuse, ny
July 31 philadelphia, pa
August 4 hattiesburg, ms
August 6 texarkana, tx
August 21 new york city, ny
August 30 knoxville, tn
September 28 omaha, ne
October 1 elaine, ar

237

negroes were murdered in Elaine, AR.

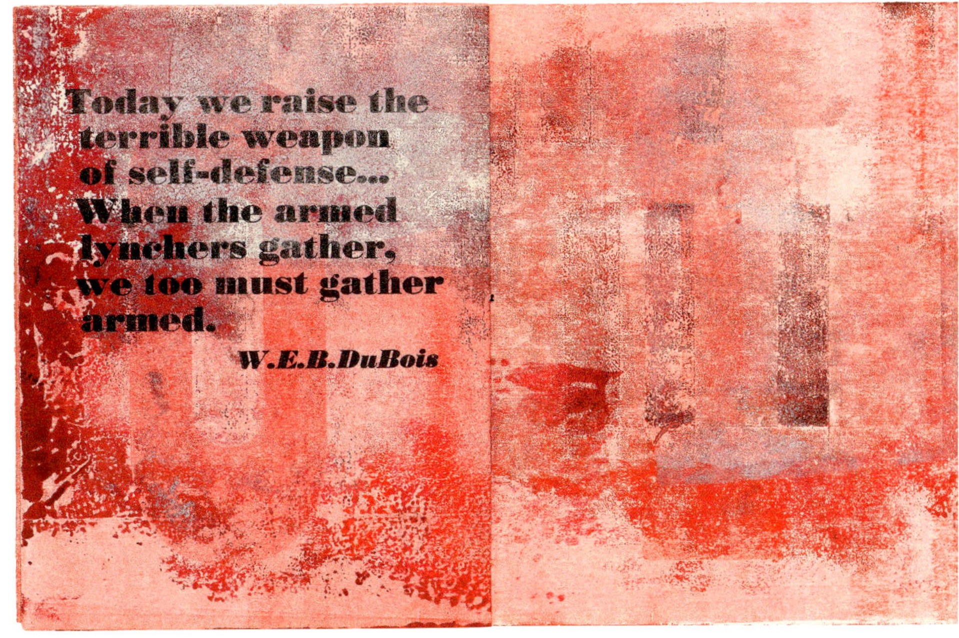

LYNCH
ING BU
RNING

CHARRED BONES RIDDLING 3513 VIOLENCE RAPE MO
swingingbodies
B BARBARISM STAKE ROPE KU KULX KLAN SHOOTI
burningflesh
NG 3513 NIGGER H.R.11279 POPLARTREE GASOLINE
riddlings
BURNINGFLESH CHIVALRY LYNCHING JIMCROW 3513
mobviolence
DEATH AT THE HANDS OF PARTIES UNKNOWN. VIOLEN
southernfears
CE BODIESSWINGING 3513 ASHES BLOOD LYNCHING
kukulxklan
MOB SOUVENIERS STRANGEFRUIT SPORTING 3513
3513

LYNCH
ING BU
RNING
3513

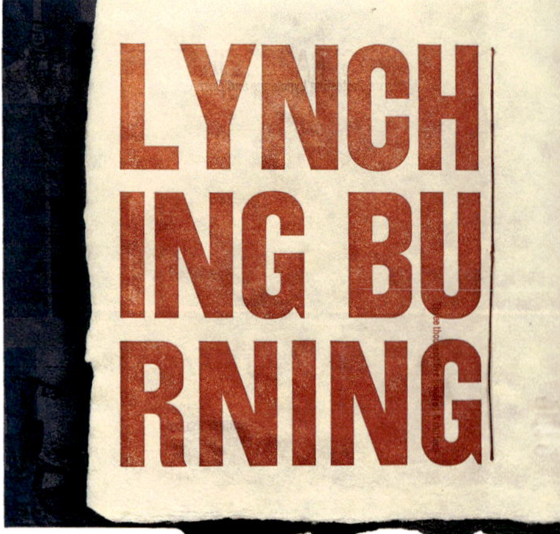

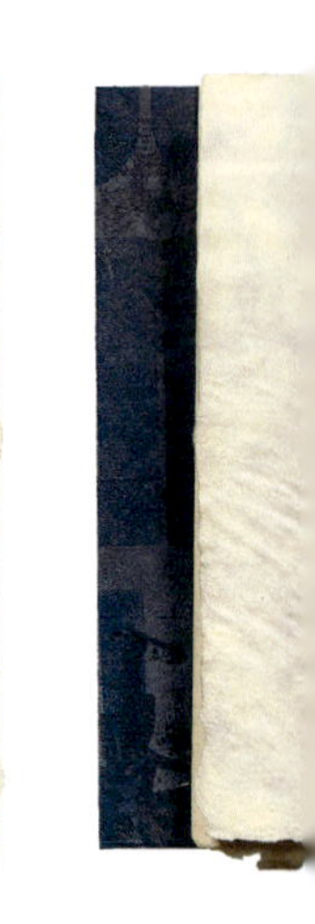

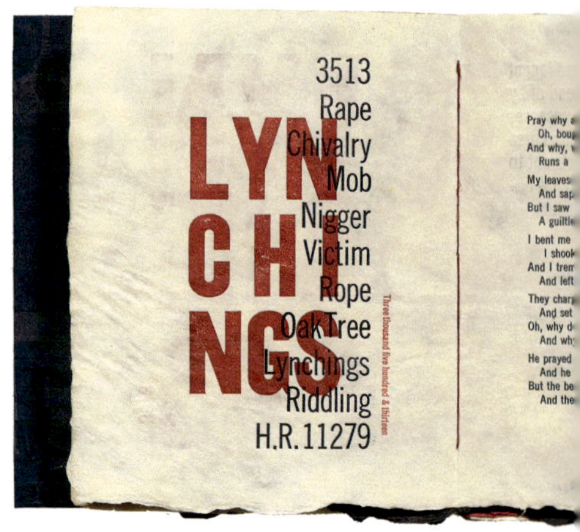

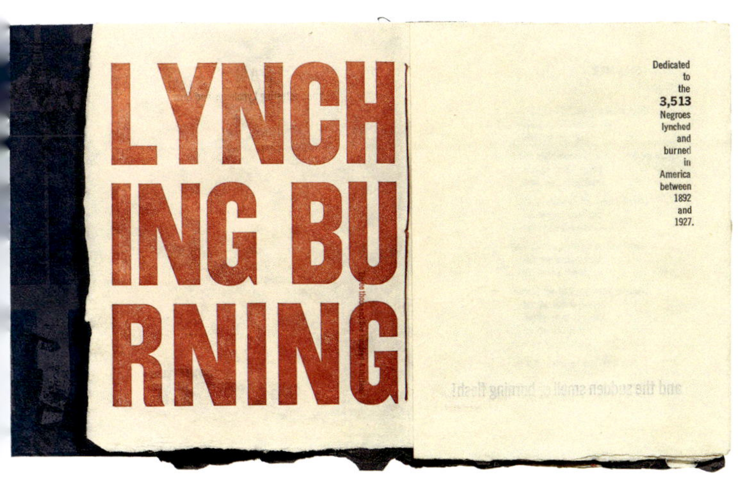
LYNCH
ING BU
RNING
Dedicated to the 3,513 Negroes lynched and burned in America between 1892 and 1927.

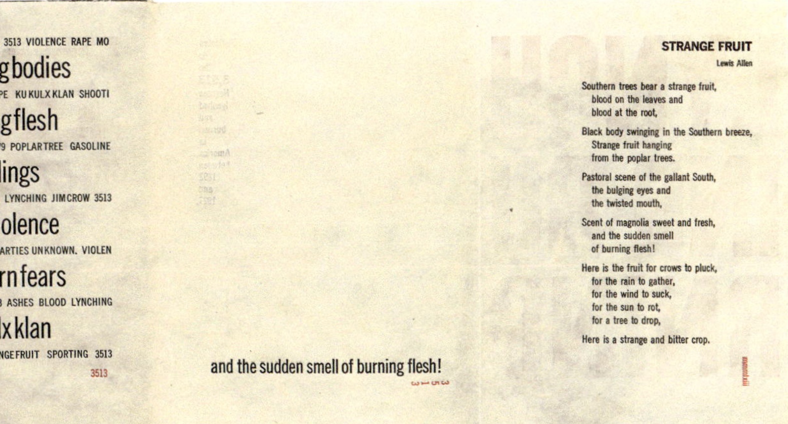
and the sudden smell of burning flesh!
STRANGE FRUIT
Lewis Allen
Southern trees bear a strange fruit,
blood on the leaves and
blood at the root,
Black body swinging in the Southern breeze,
Strange fruit hanging
from the poplar trees.
Pastoral scene of the gallant South,
the bulging eyes and
the twisted mouth,
Scent of magnolia sweet and fresh,
and the sudden smell
of burning flesh!
Here is the fruit for crows to pluck,
for the rain to gather,
for the wind to suck,
for the sun to rot,
for a tree to drop,
Here is a strange and bitter crop.

76
Negro women were lynched between 1892 and 1927.
3513

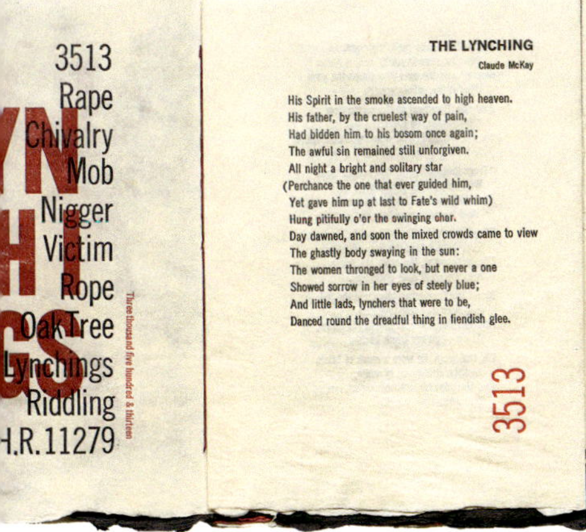
3513
Rape
Chivalry
Mob
Nigger
Victim
Rope
OakTree
Lynchings
Riddling
H.R.11279
THE LYNCHING
Claude McKay
His Spirit in the smoke ascended to high heaven.
His father, by the cruelest way of pain,
Had bidden him to his bosom once again;
The awful sin remained still unforgiven.
All night a bright and solitary star
(Perchance the one that ever guided him,
Yet gave him up at last to Fate's wild whim)
Hung pitifully o'er the swinging char.
Day dawned, and soon the mixed crowds came to view
The ghastly body swaying in the sun:
The women thronged to look, but never a one
Showed sorrow in her eyes of steely blue;
And little lads, lynchers that were to be,
Danced round the dreadful thing in fiendish glee.
3513

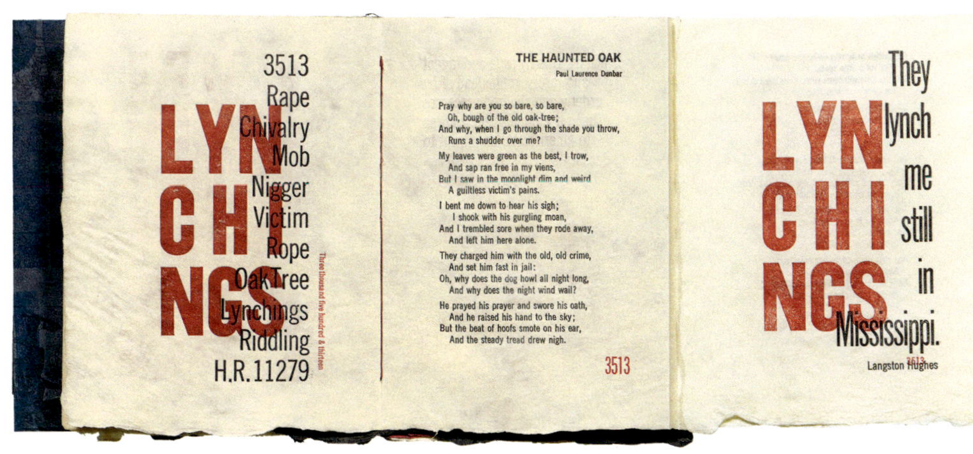
3513
Rape
Chivalry
Mob
Nigger
Victim
Rope
OakTree
Lynchings
Riddling
H.R.11279
LYN
CHI
NGS
THE HAUNTED OAK
Paul Laurence Dunbar
Pray why are you so bare, so bare,
Oh, bough of the old oak-tree;
And why, when I go through the shade you throw,
Runs a shudder over me?
My leaves were green as the best, I trow,
And sap ran free in my viens,
But I saw in the moonlight dim and weird
A guiltless victim's pains.
I bent me down to hear his sigh;
I shook with his gurgling moan,
And I trembled sore when they rode away,
And left him here alone.
They charged him with the old, old crime,
And set him fast in jail:
Oh, why does the dog howl all night long,
And why does the night wind wail?
He prayed his prayer and swore his oath,
And he raised his hand to the sky;
But the beat of hoofs smote on his ear,
And the steady tread drew nigh.
3513
They
lynch
me
still
in
Mississippi.
Langston Hughes
LYN
CHI
NGS

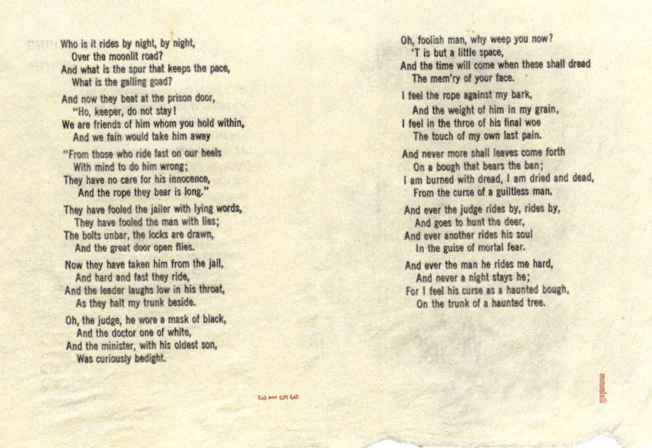
Who is it rides by night, by night,
Over the moonlit road?
And what is the spur that keeps the pace,
What is the galling goad?
And now they beat at the prison door,
"Ho, keeper, do not stay!
We are friends of him whom you hold within,
And we fain would take him away
"From those who ride fast on our heels
With mind to do him wrong;
They have no care for his innocence,
And the rope they bear is long."
They have fooled the jailer with lying words,
They have fooled the man with lies;
The bolts unbar, the locks are drawn,
And the great door open flies.
Now they have taken him from the jail,
And hard and fast they ride,
And the leader laughs low in his throat,
As they halt my trunk beside.
Oh, the judge, he wore a mask of black,
And the doctor one of white,
And the minister, with his oldest son,
Was curiously bedight.
Oh, foolish man, why weep you now?
'T is but a little space,
And the time will come when these shall dread
The mem'ry of your face.
I feel the rope against my bark,
And the weight of him in my grain,
I feel in the throe of his final woe
The touch of my own last pain.
And never more shall leaves come forth
On a bough that bears the ban;
I am burned with dread, I am dried and dead,
From the curse of a guiltless man.
And ever the judge rides by, rides by,
And goes to hunt the deer,
And ever another rides his soul
In the guise of mortal fear.
And ever the man he rides me hard,
And never a night stays he;
For I feel his curse as a haunted bough,
On the trunk of a haunted tree.
3513

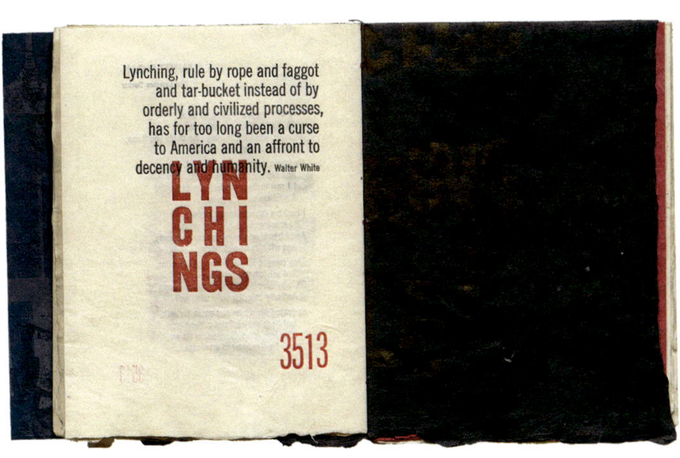
Lynching, rule by rope and faggot and tar-bucket instead of by orderly and civilized processes, has for too long been a curse to America and an affront to decency and humanity. Walter White
LYN
CHI
NGS
3513

BUR
NIN
G S

and the sudden smell
of burning flesh!

3513

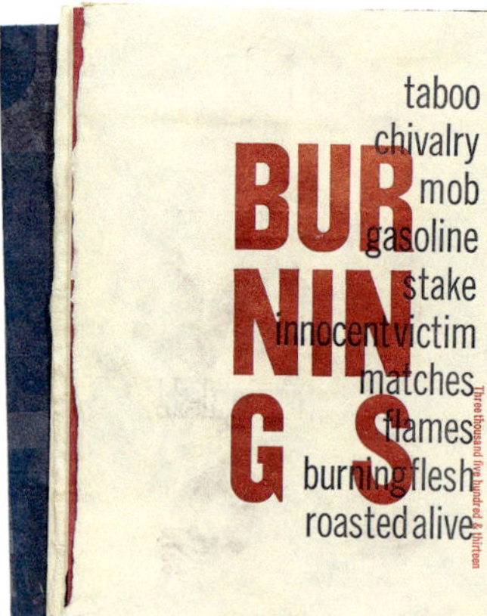

These burning without trail are in the senses deepest unjust to my race. But it is not this injustice alone which stirs my heart. These barbarous scenes are more disgraceful and degarding to the people who inflict the punishment than those who receive it.

Booker T. Washington Letter to the New York Tribune 1904

3513

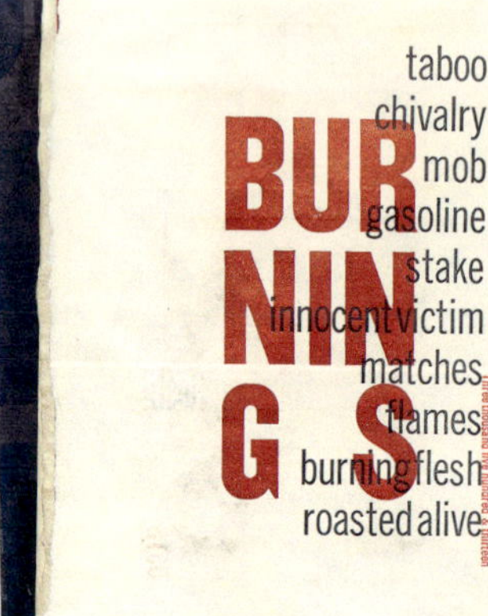

BURN
THE
NIGGER

3513

BURN THE NIGGER, reiterated McBane. We seem to have the right nigger, but whether we have or not, burn a nigger. It is an assault upon the white race, in the person of old Mrs. Ochiltree, committed by the black race, in the person of some nigger. It would justify the white people in burning **any** nigger. The example would be all the more powerful if we got the wrong one. It would serve notice on the niggers that we shall hold the whole race responsible for the misdeeds of of each individual.

Charles W. Chesnutt, THE MARROW OF TRADITION (1901)

The Silent Protest Parade, July 28, 1917, in New York City organized by the N.A.A.C.P.

We return.
We return from fighting. We return fighting.
Make way for Democracy!
We saved it in France, and by the Great Jehovah,
we will save it in the U.S.A., or know the reason why!

Three thousand five hundred & thirteen

3513

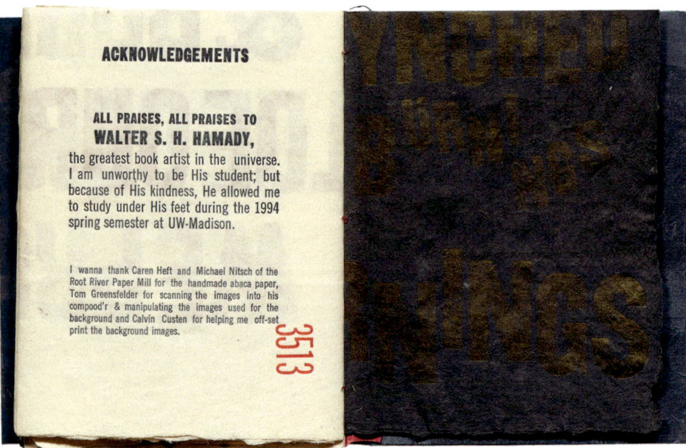

ACKNOWLEDGEMENTS

ALL PRAISES, ALL PRAISES TO
WALTER S. H. HAMADY,
the greatest book artist in the universe. I am unworthy to be His student; but because of His kindness, He allowed me to study under His feet during the 1994 spring semester at UW-Madison.

I wanna thank Caren Heft and Michael Nitsch of the Root River Paper Mill for the handmade abaca paper, Tom Greenstelder for scanning the images into his compood'r & manipulating the images used for the background and Calvin Custen for helping me off-set print the background images.

3513

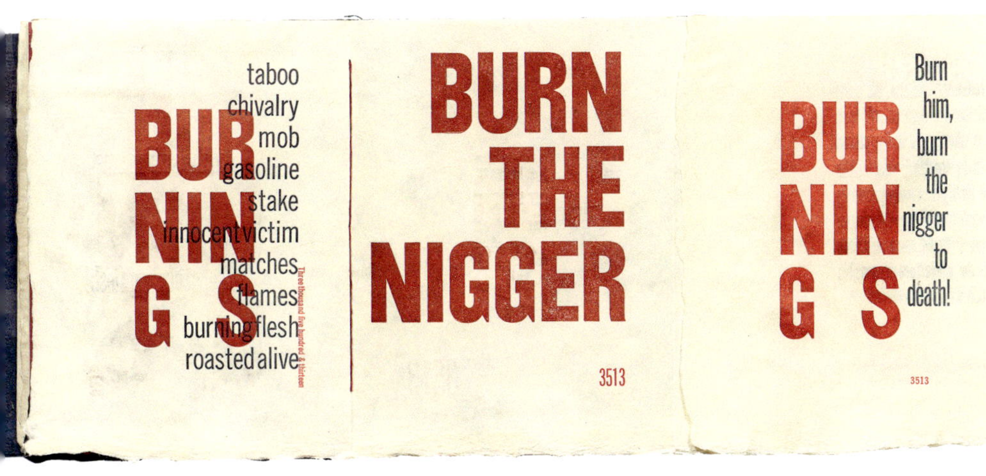
BURNINGS
taboo
chivalry
mob
gasoline
stake
innocent victim
matches
flames
burning flesh
roasted alive
BURN
THE
NIGGER
3513
BURNINGS
Burn
him,
burn
the
nigger
to
death!
3513

BURNINGS
rightnigger
burnanigger
somenigger
anynigger
theniggers
3513

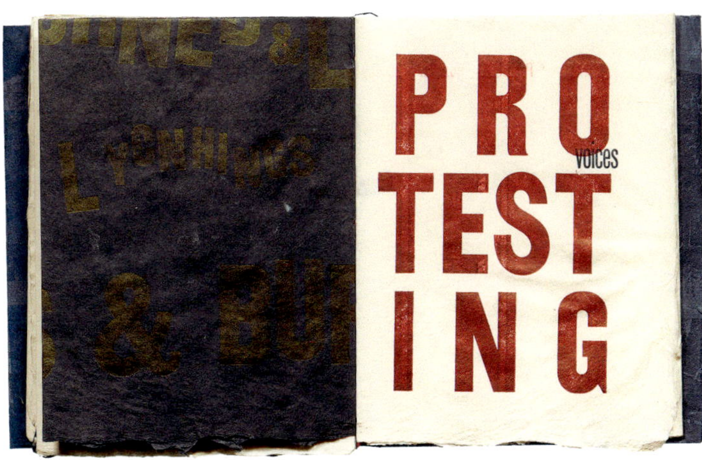
PRO
voices
TEST
ING

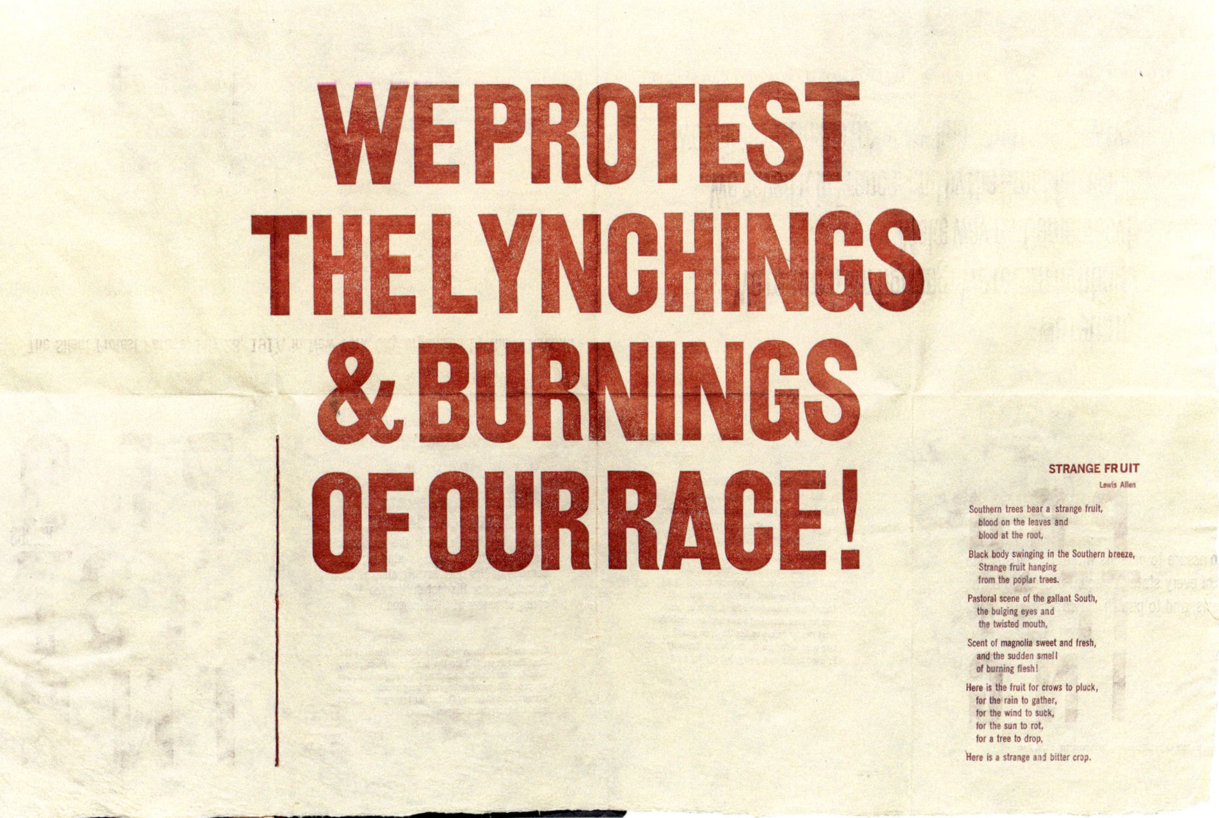
WE PROTEST
THE LYNCHINGS
& BURNINGS
OF OUR RACE!
STRANGE FRUIT
Lewis Allen
Southern trees bear a strange fruit,
blood on the leaves and
blood at the root,
Black body swinging in the Southern breeze,
Strange fruit hanging
from the poplar trees.
Pastoral scene of the gallant South,
the bulging eyes and
the twisted mouth,
Scent of magnolia sweet and fresh,
and the sudden smell
of burning flesh!
Here is the fruit for crows to pluck,
for the rain to gather,
for the wind to suck,
for the sun to rot,
for a tree to drop,
Here is a strange and bitter crop.

THE
CONFEDERATE
STATES OF
AMERICA
WAS A
CRIME
A GAINST
HUMANITY.

“This is one of the first Confederate flags—it is a sacred symbol to backers of the Lost Cause, who believe that enslavement was a social good. I printed things like ‘Robert E. Lee was a traitor’ on a bunch of cheap reproductions for an exhibition in Virginia—and the gallery shipped them right back! Getting censored means you’ve found the nerve.”

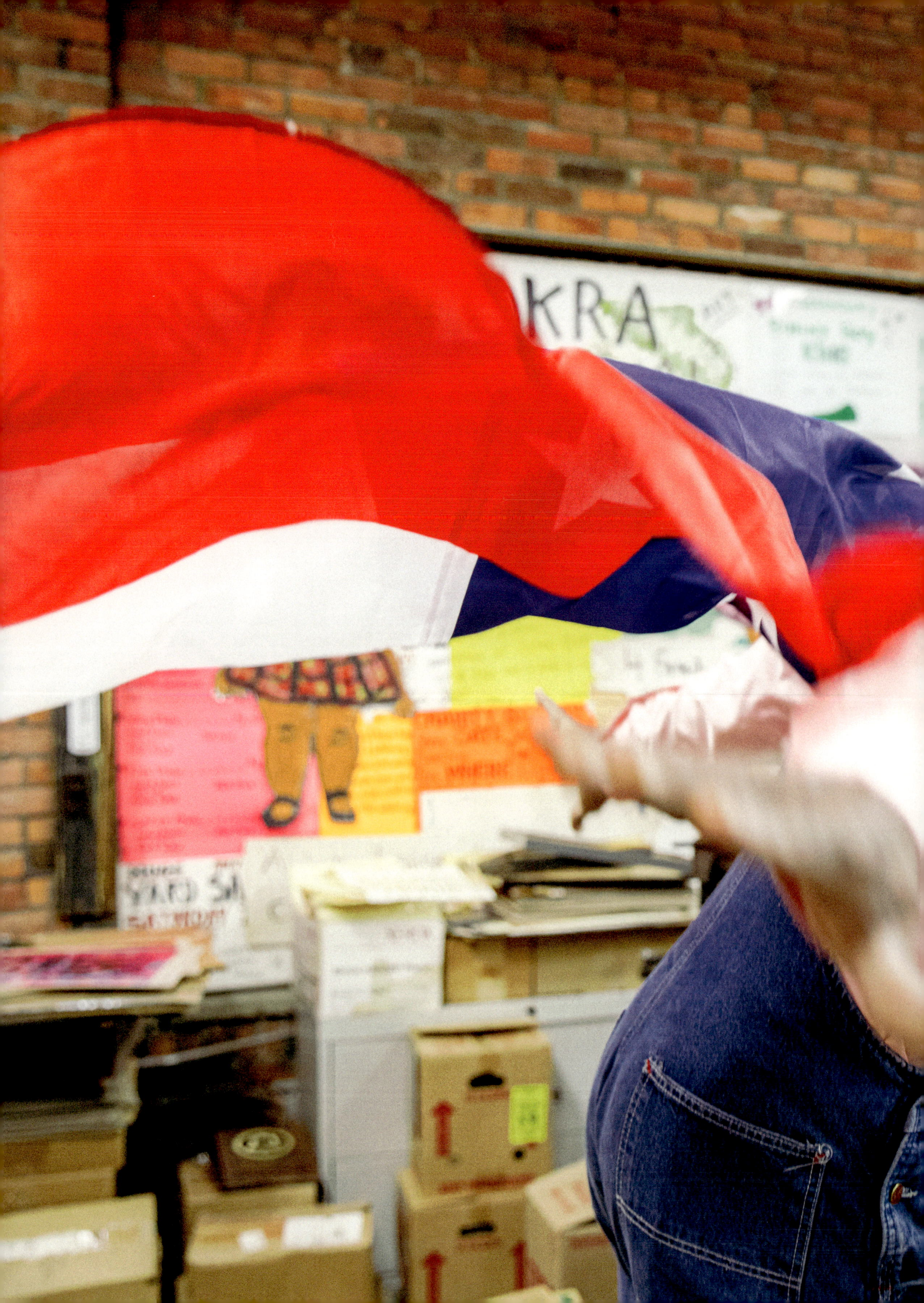
KRA

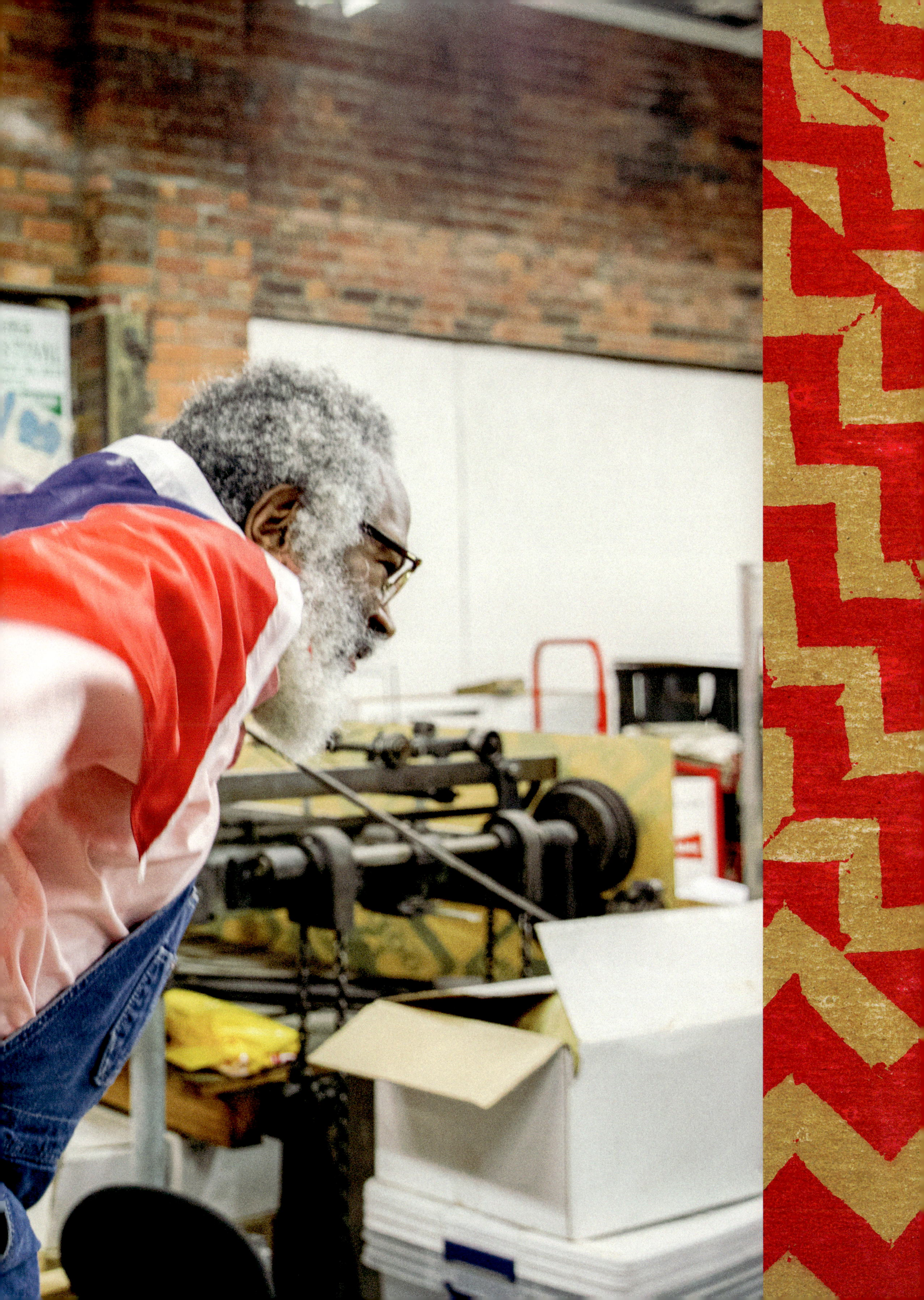

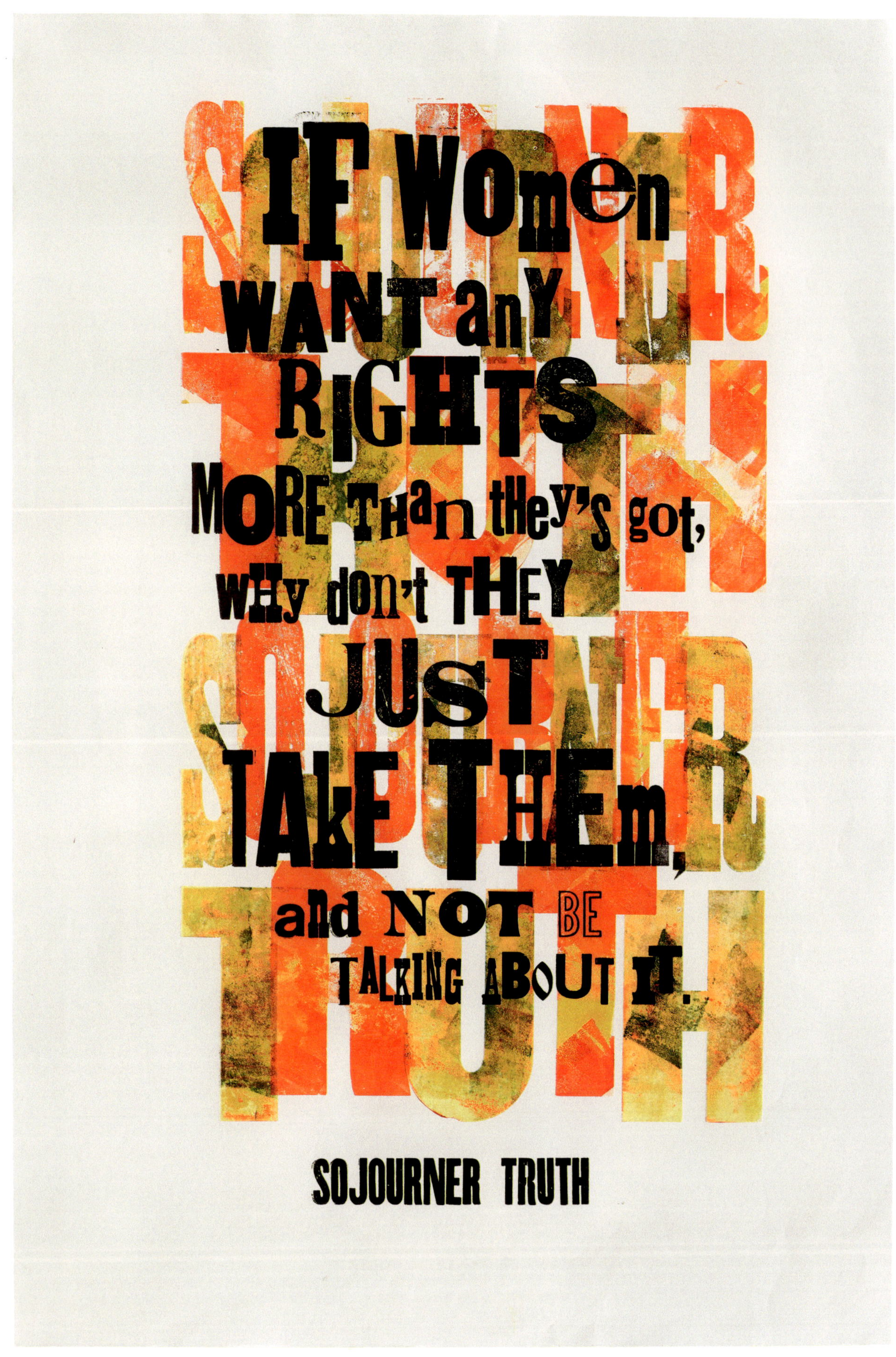
IF Women
WANT anY
RIGHTS
MORE THan tHey's got,
wHy don't THEY
JUST
TAkE THEm,
and NOT BE
TALKING ABOUT IT.
SOJOURNER TRUTH
SOJOURNER TRUTH

POWER

CONCEDES

NOTHING

WITHOUT A

DEMAND.

IT NEVER DID AND

IT NEVER WILL.

FREDERICK DOUGLASS

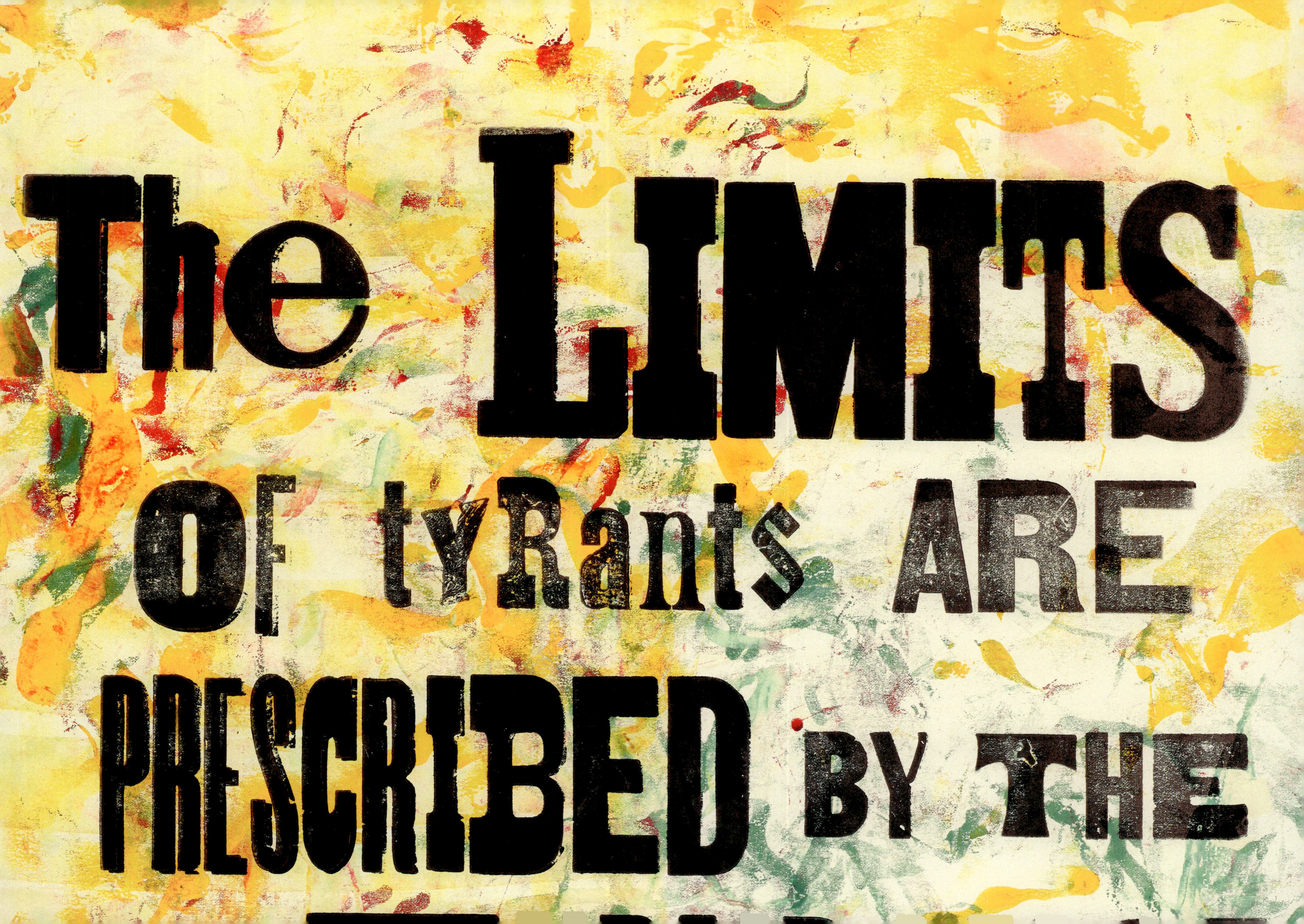
The LIMITS
OF tyRants ARE
PRESCRIBED BY THE

ENDURANCE

OF THOSE WHOM

THEY OPPRESS.

FREDERICK DOUGLASS

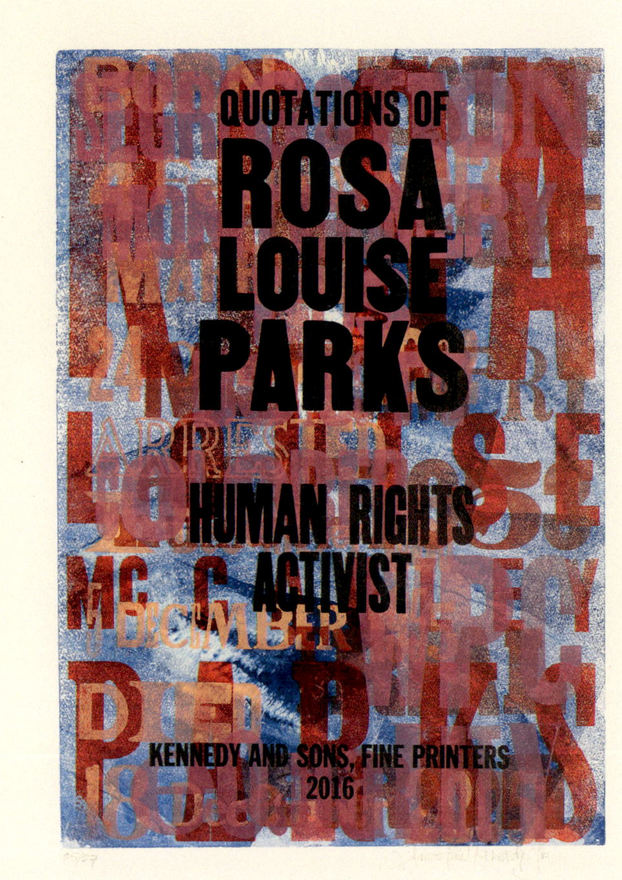
QUOTATIONS OF
ROSA
LOUISE
PARKS
HUMAN RIGHTS
ACTIVIST
KENNEDY AND SONS, FINE PRINTERS
2016

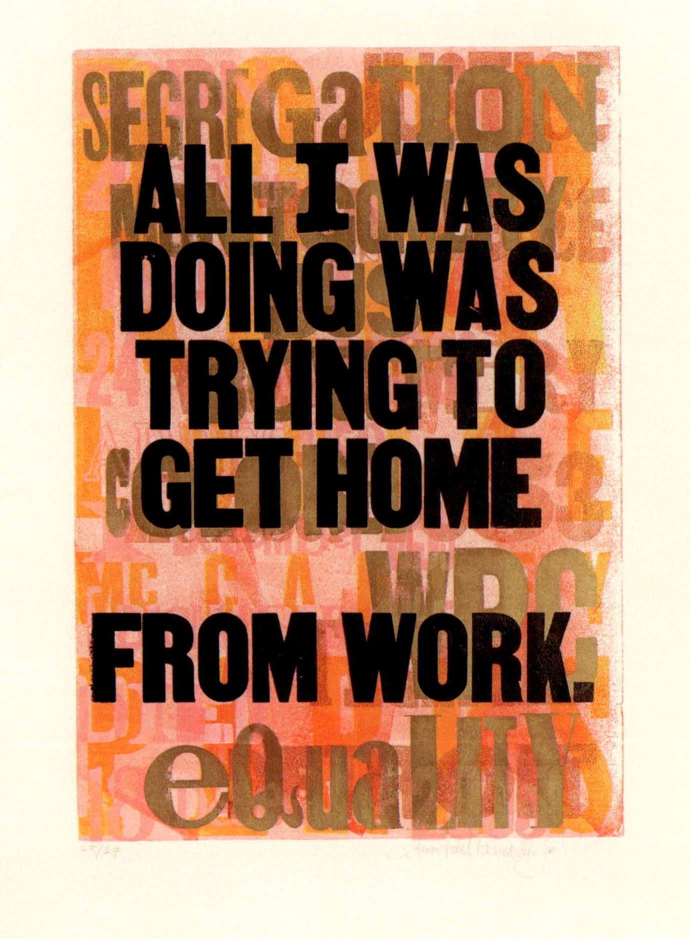
ALL I WAS
DOING WAS
TRYING TO
GET HOME
FROM WORK.

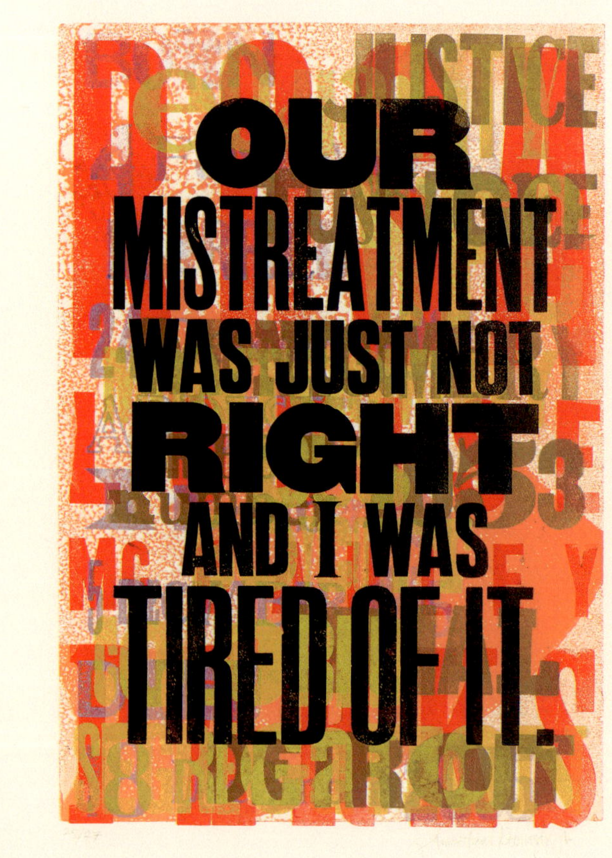
OUR
MISTREATMENT
WAS JUST NOT
RIGHT
AND I WAS
TIRED OF IT.

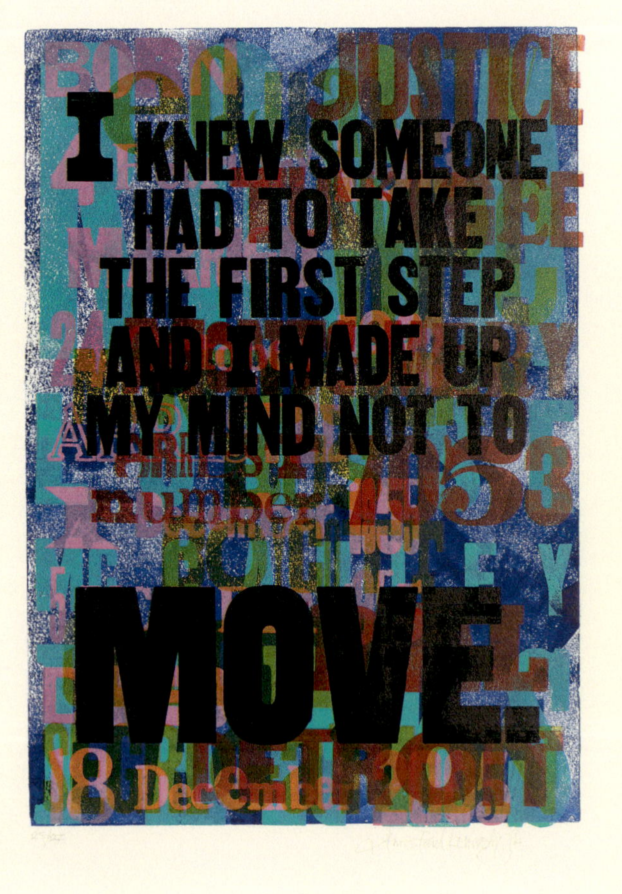
I KNEW SOMEONE
HAD TO TAKE
THE FIRST STEP
AND I MADE UP
MY MIND NOT TO
MOVE.

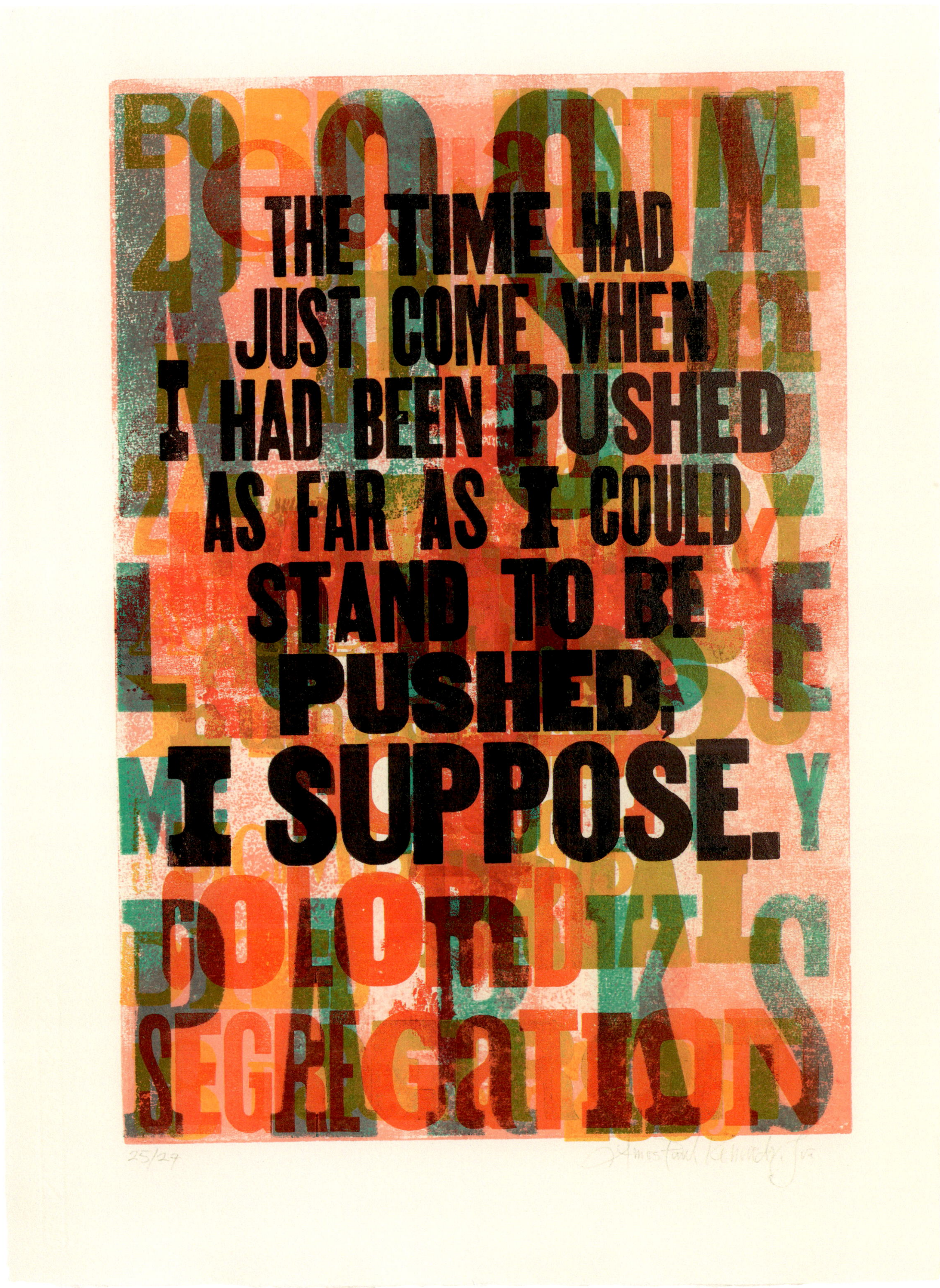
THE TIME HAD
JUST COME WHEN
I HAD BEEN PUSHED
AS FAR AS I COULD
STAND TO BE
PUSHED,
I SUPPOSE.
COLORED
SEGREGATION
25/27

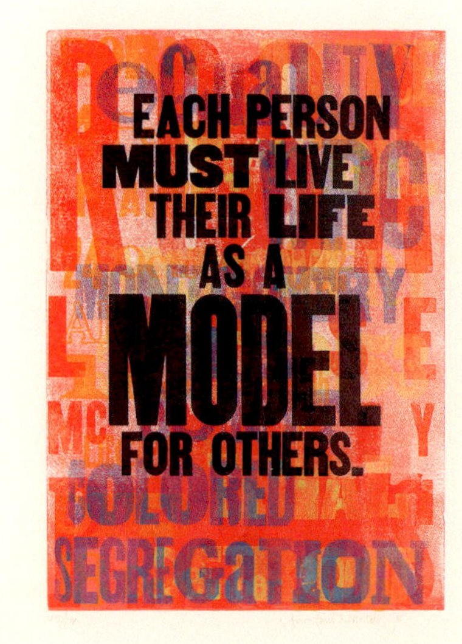
EACH PERSON
MUST LIVE
THEIR LIFE
AS A
MODEL
FOR OTHERS.

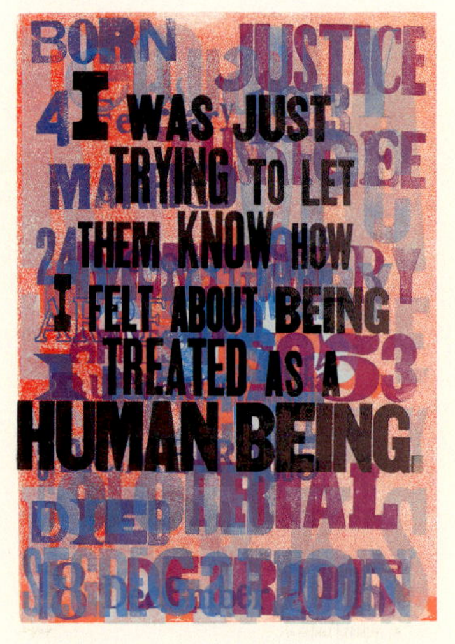
I WAS JUST
TRYING TO LET
THEM KNOW HOW
I FELT ABOUT BEING
TREATED AS A
HUMAN BEING.

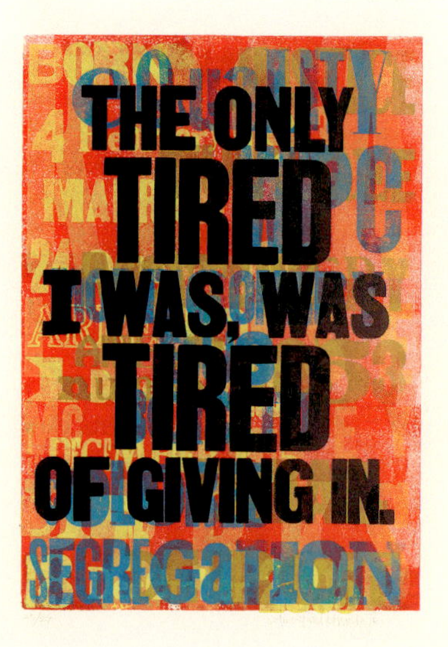
THE ONLY
TIRED
I WAS, WAS
TIRED
OF GIVING IN.

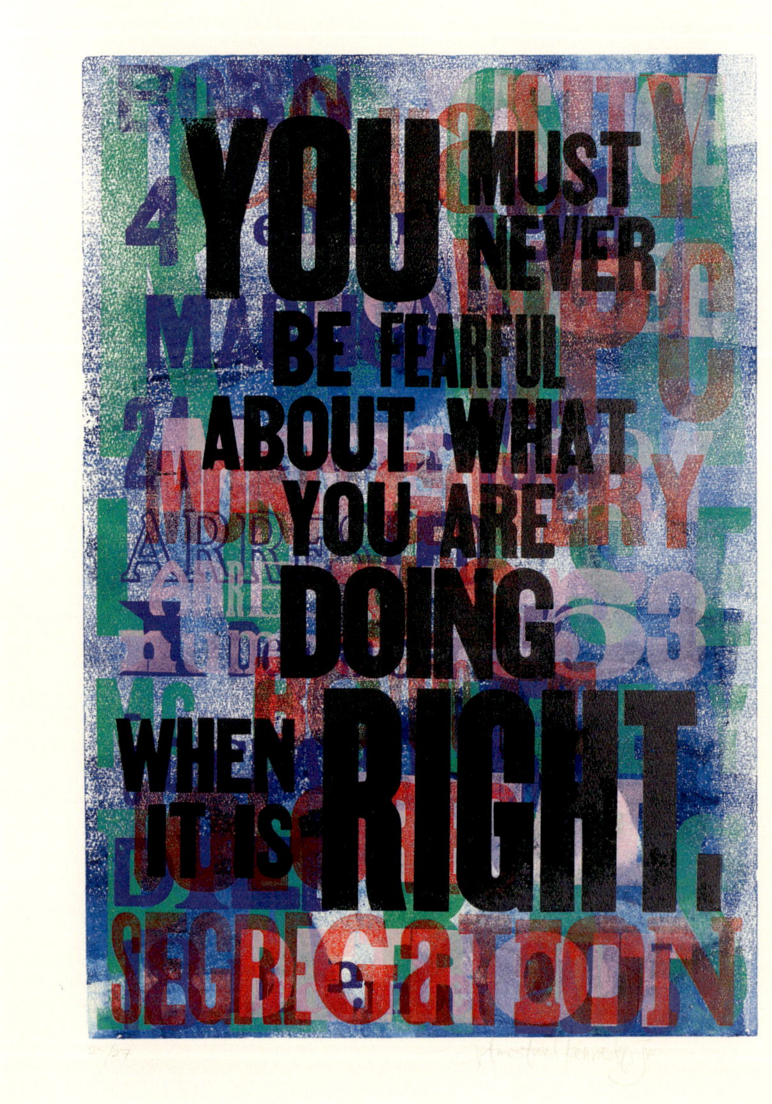
YOU MUST
NEVER
BE FEARFUL
ABOUT WHAT
YOU ARE
DOING
WHEN
IT IS RIGHT.
SEGREGATION

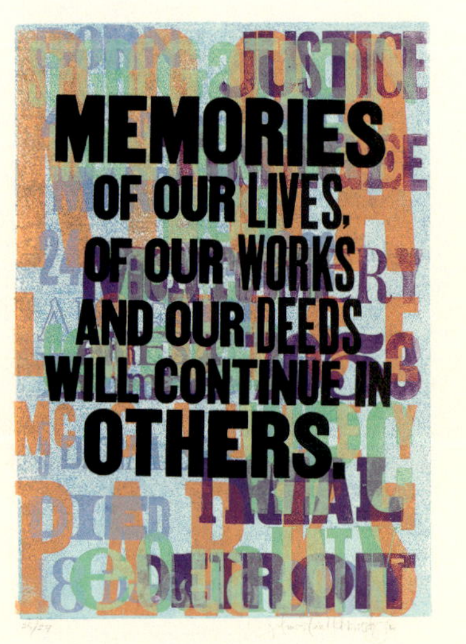
MEMORIES
OF OUR LIVES,
OF OUR WORKS
AND OUR DEEDS
WILL CONTINUE IN
OTHERS.

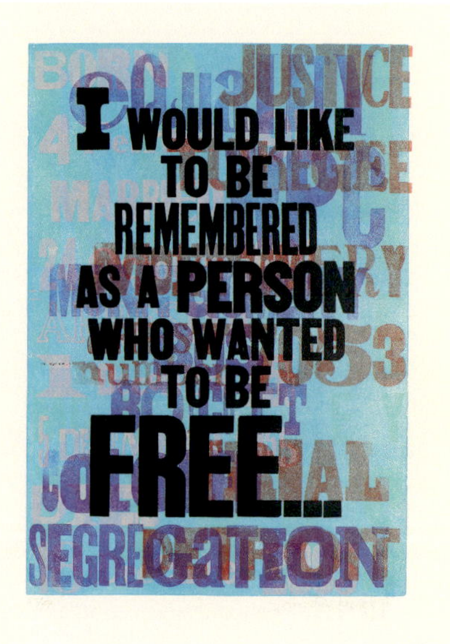
I WOULD LIKE
TO BE
REMEMBERED
AS A PERSON
WHO WANTED
TO BE
FREE...
SEGREGATION

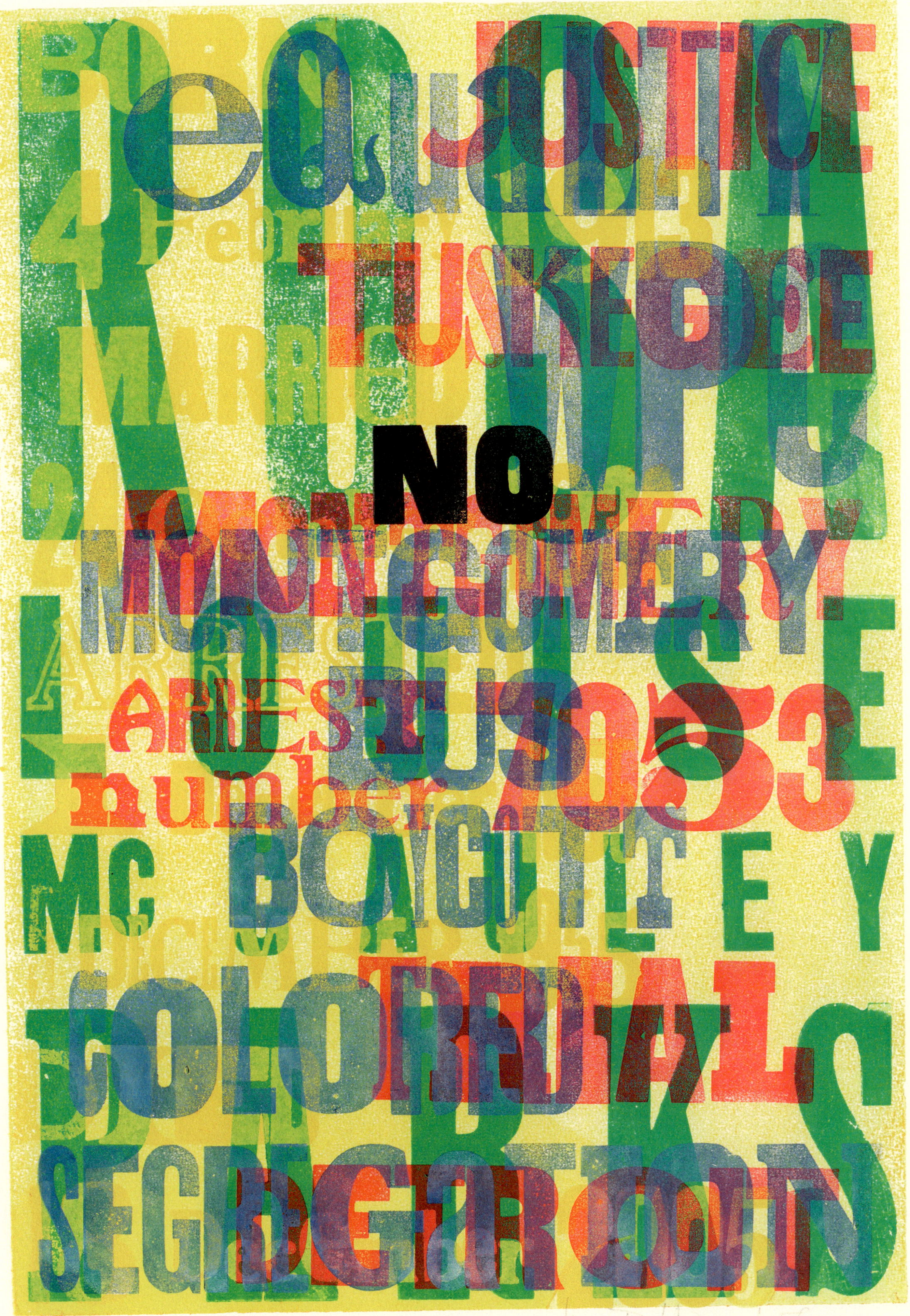

25/27

Amos Paul Kennedy Jr

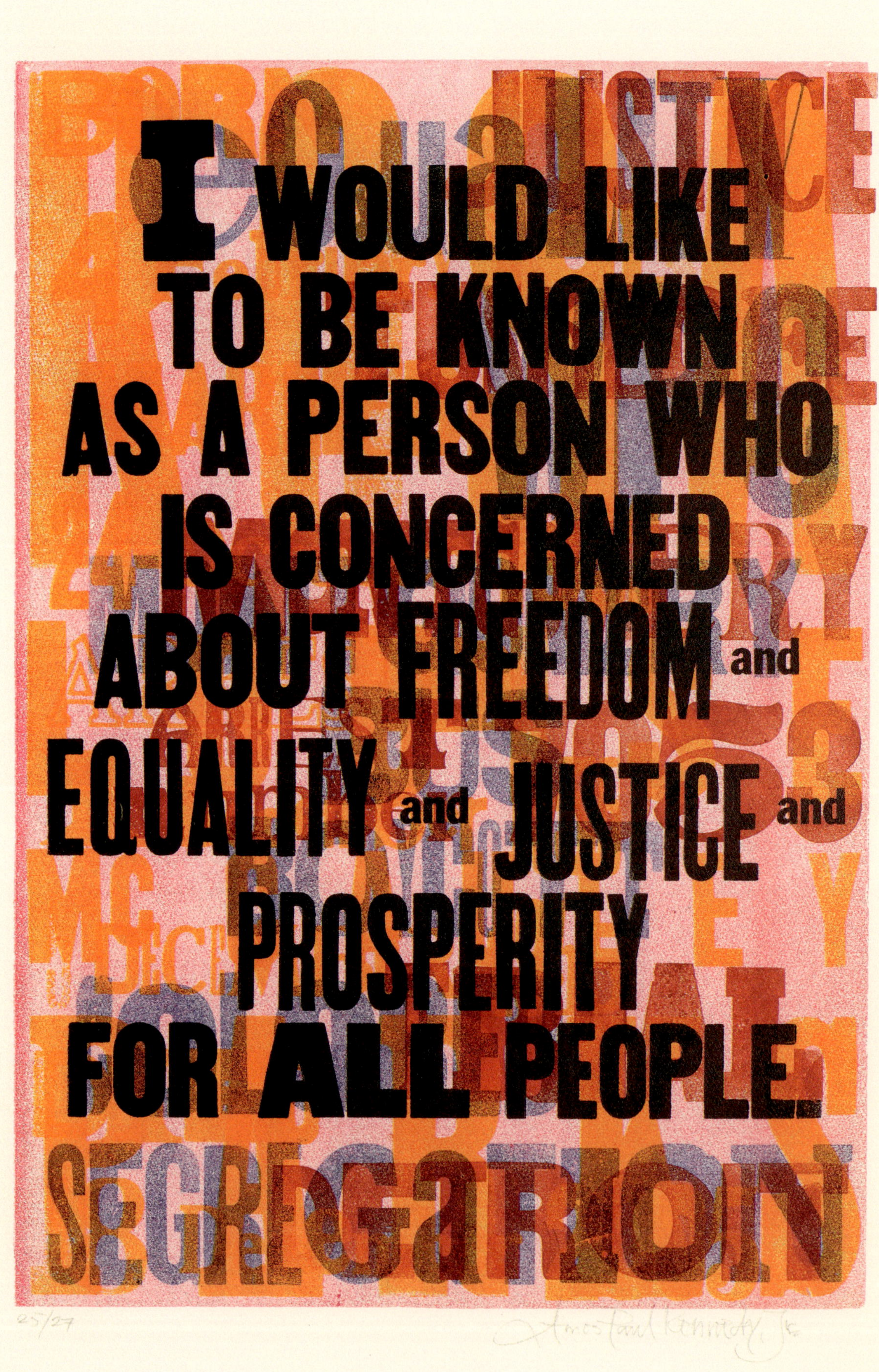
I WOULD LIKE
TO BE KNOWN
AS A PERSON WHO
IS CONCERNED
ABOUT FREEDOM and
EQUALITY and JUSTICE and
PROSPERITY
FOR ALL PEOPLE.

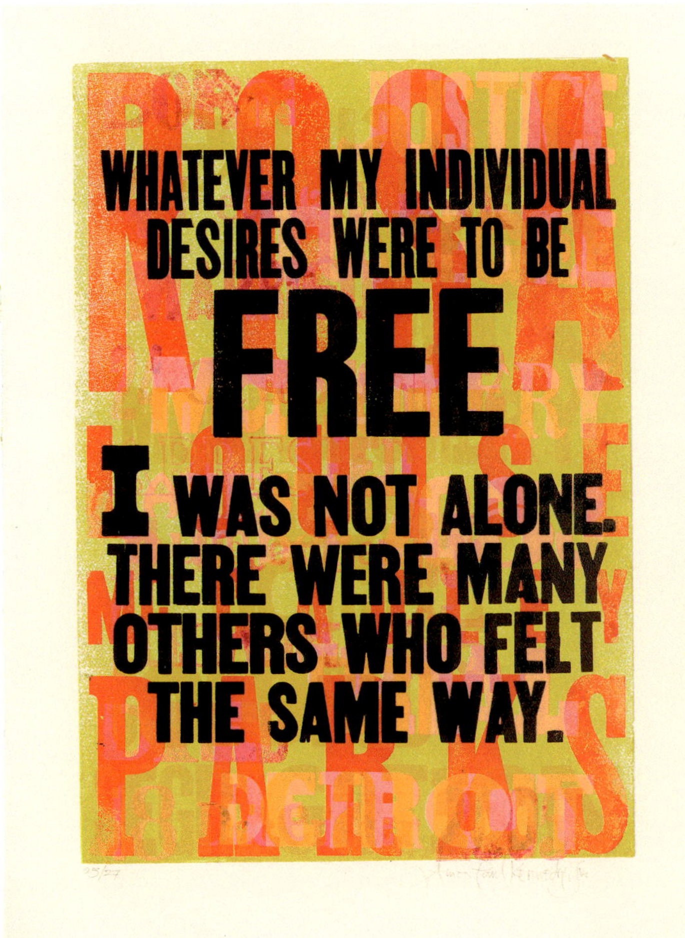

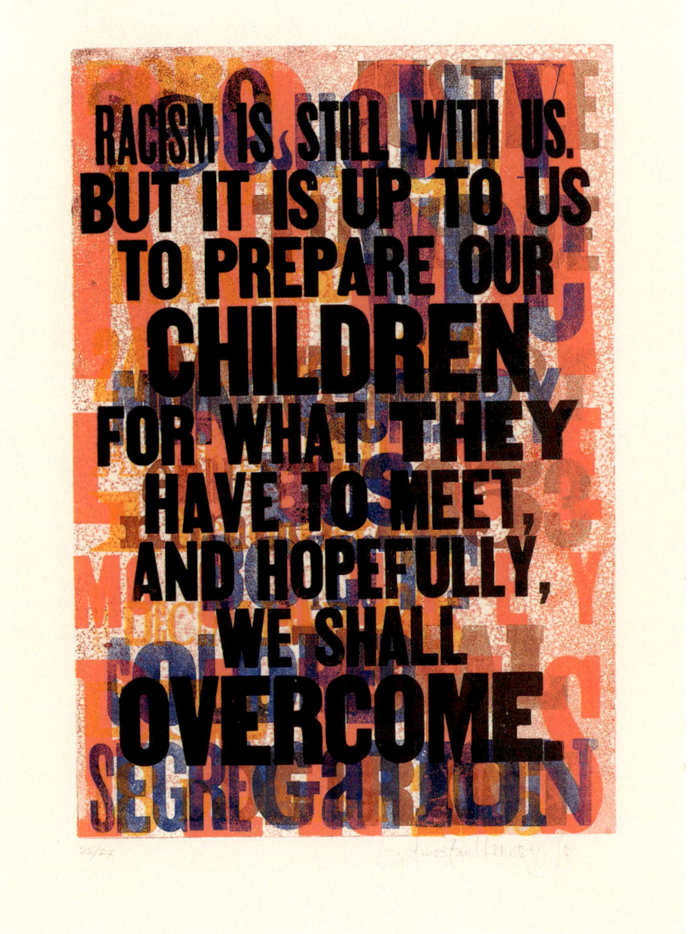

> “I created a portfolio of prints to commemorate the activism of Rosa Parks, using her own words to tell her story. Most people know a sanitized anecdote about her. They think she was an elderly woman who was too tired to give up her bus seat. But she was forty-two and well versed in resistance. She knew exactly what she was doing.”

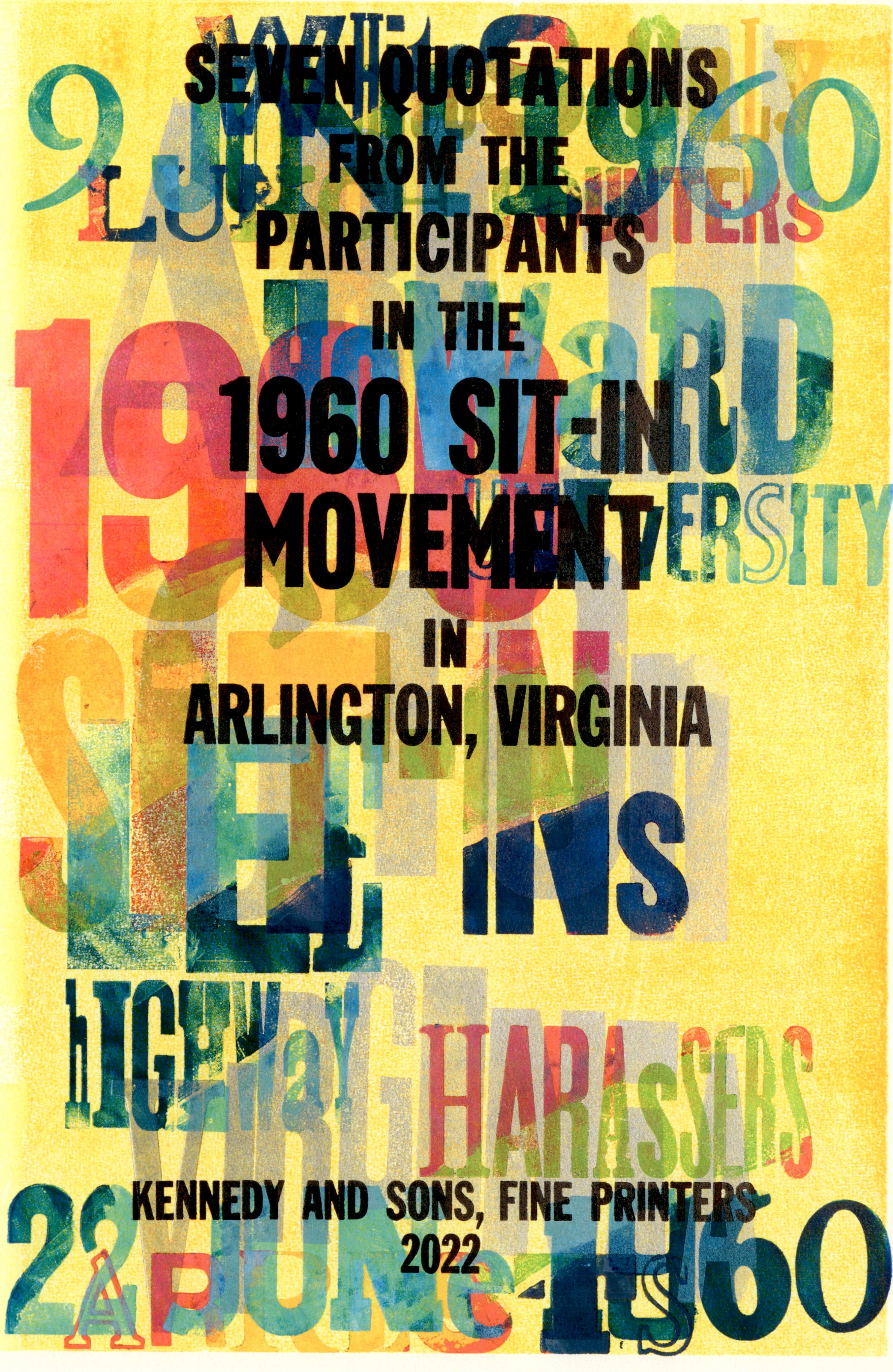

SEVEN QUOTATIONS
FROM THE
PARTICIPANTS
IN THE
1960 SIT-IN
MOVEMENT
IN
ARLINGTON, VIRGINIA
KENNEDY AND SONS, FINE PRINTERS
2022

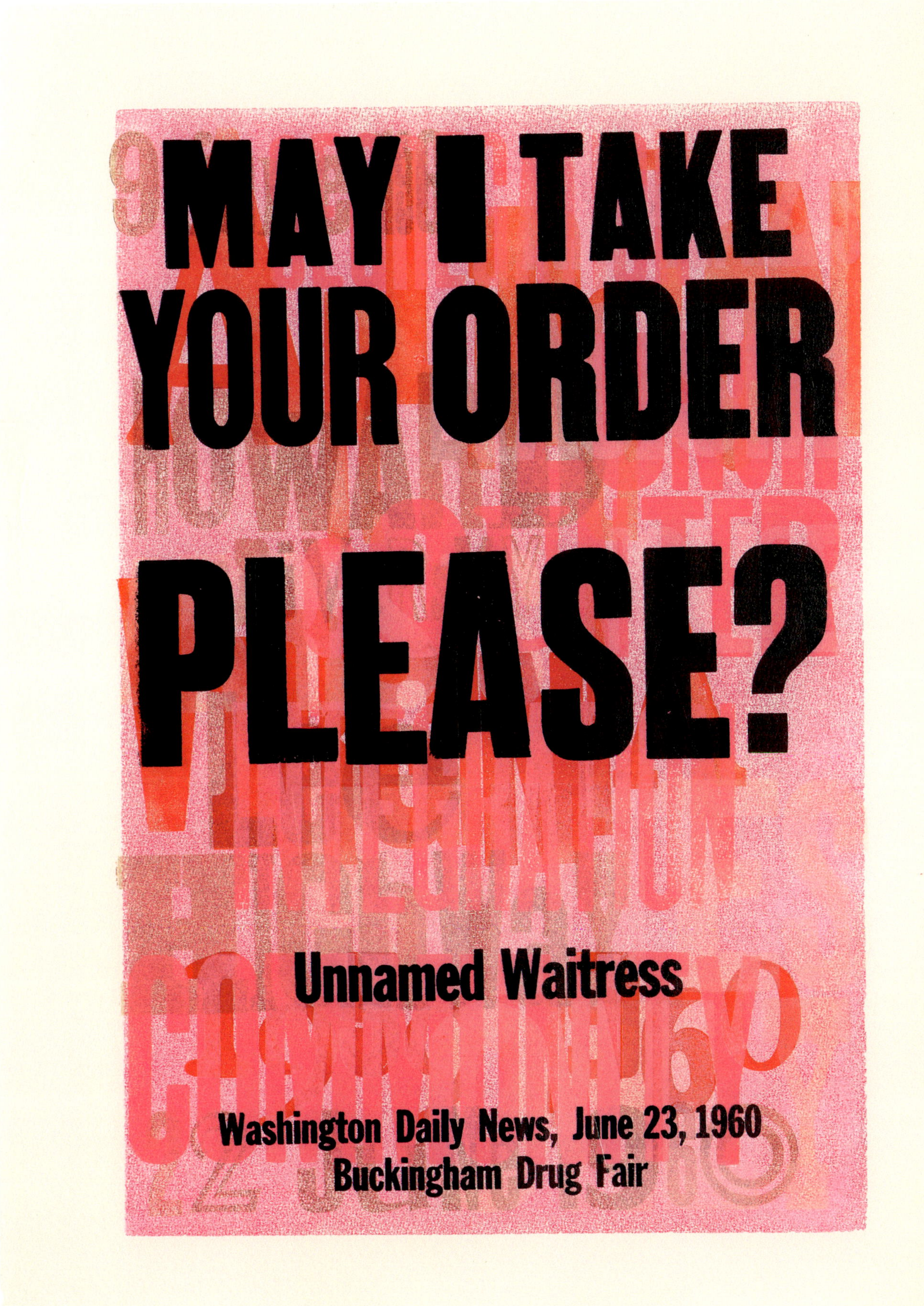
MAY I TAKE
YOUR ORDER
PLEASE?
Unnamed Waitress
Washington Daily News, June 23, 1960
Buckingham Drug Fair

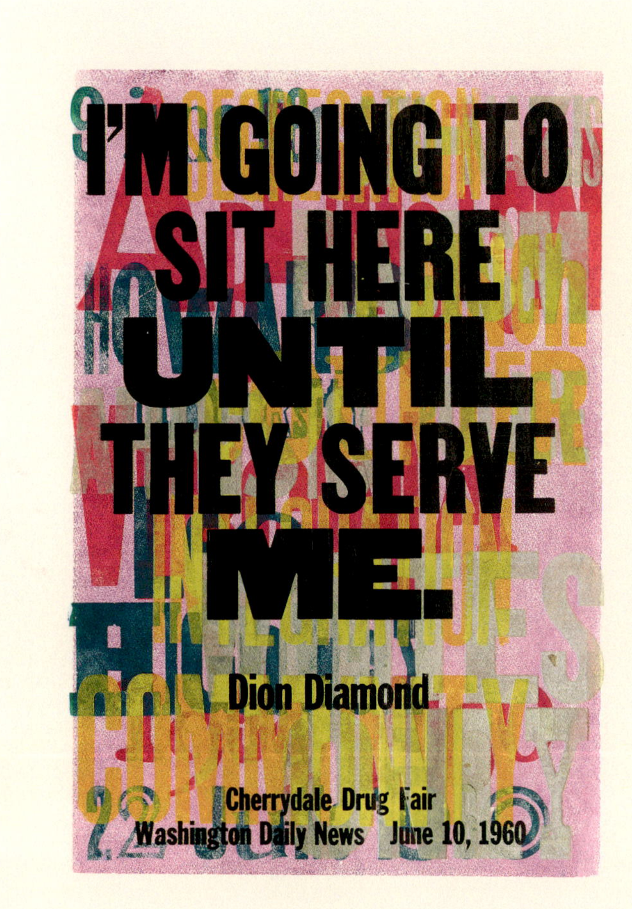

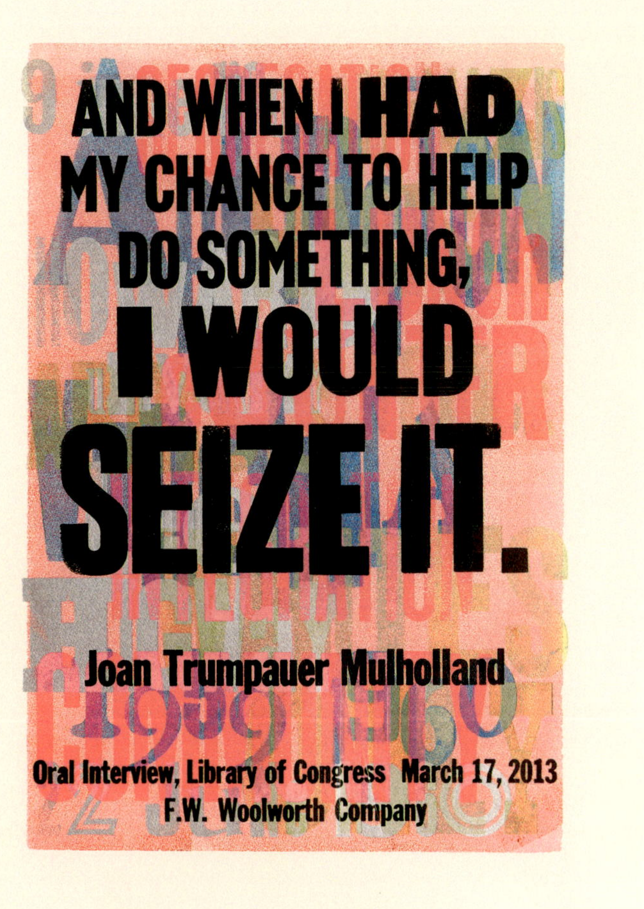

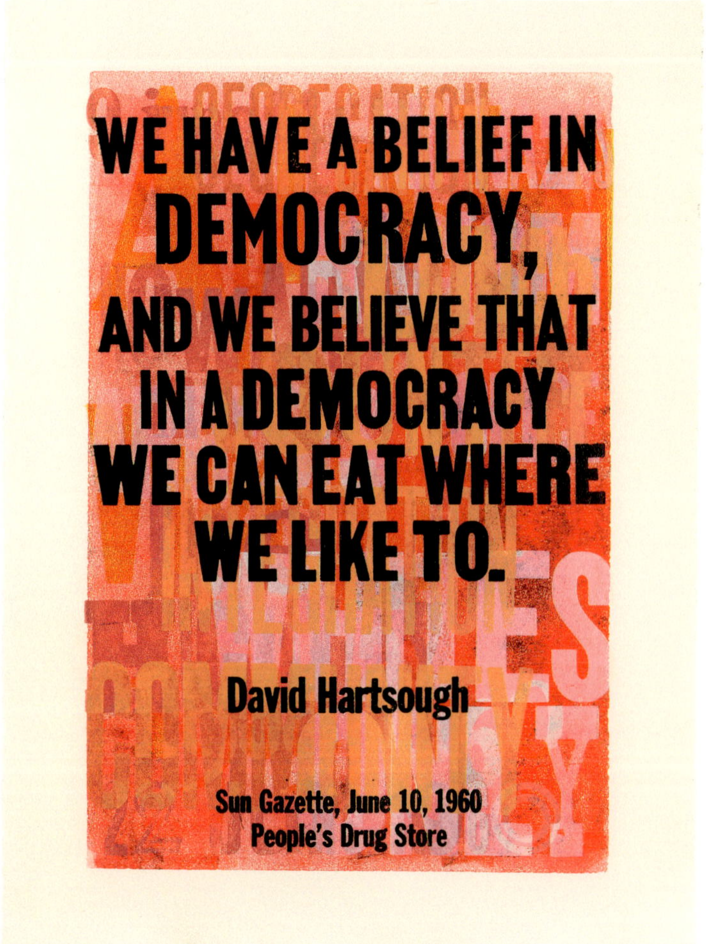

WE HAVE A BELIEF IN
DEMOCRACY,
AND WE BELIEVE THAT
IN A DEMOCRACY
WE CAN EAT WHERE
WE LIKE TO.

David Hartsough

Sun Gazette, June 10, 1960
People's Drug Store

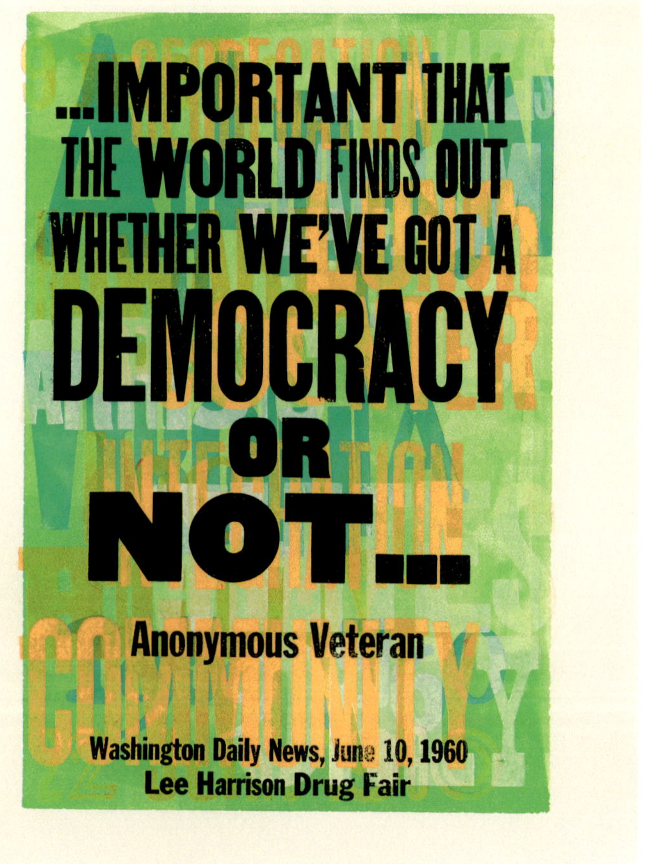

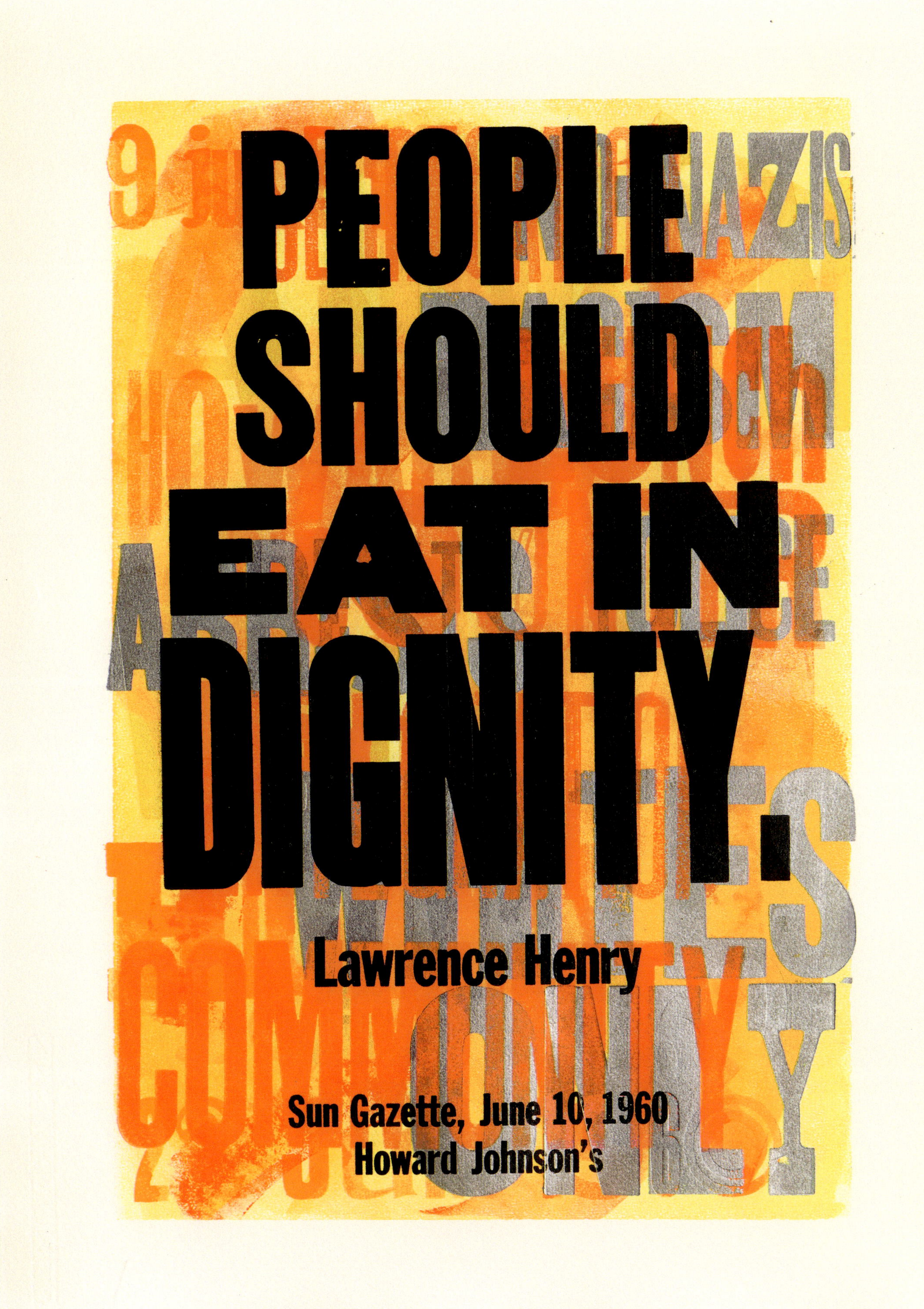
PEOPLE
SHOULD
EAT IN
DIGNITY.
Lawrence Henry
Sun Gazette, June 10, 1960
Howard Johnson's

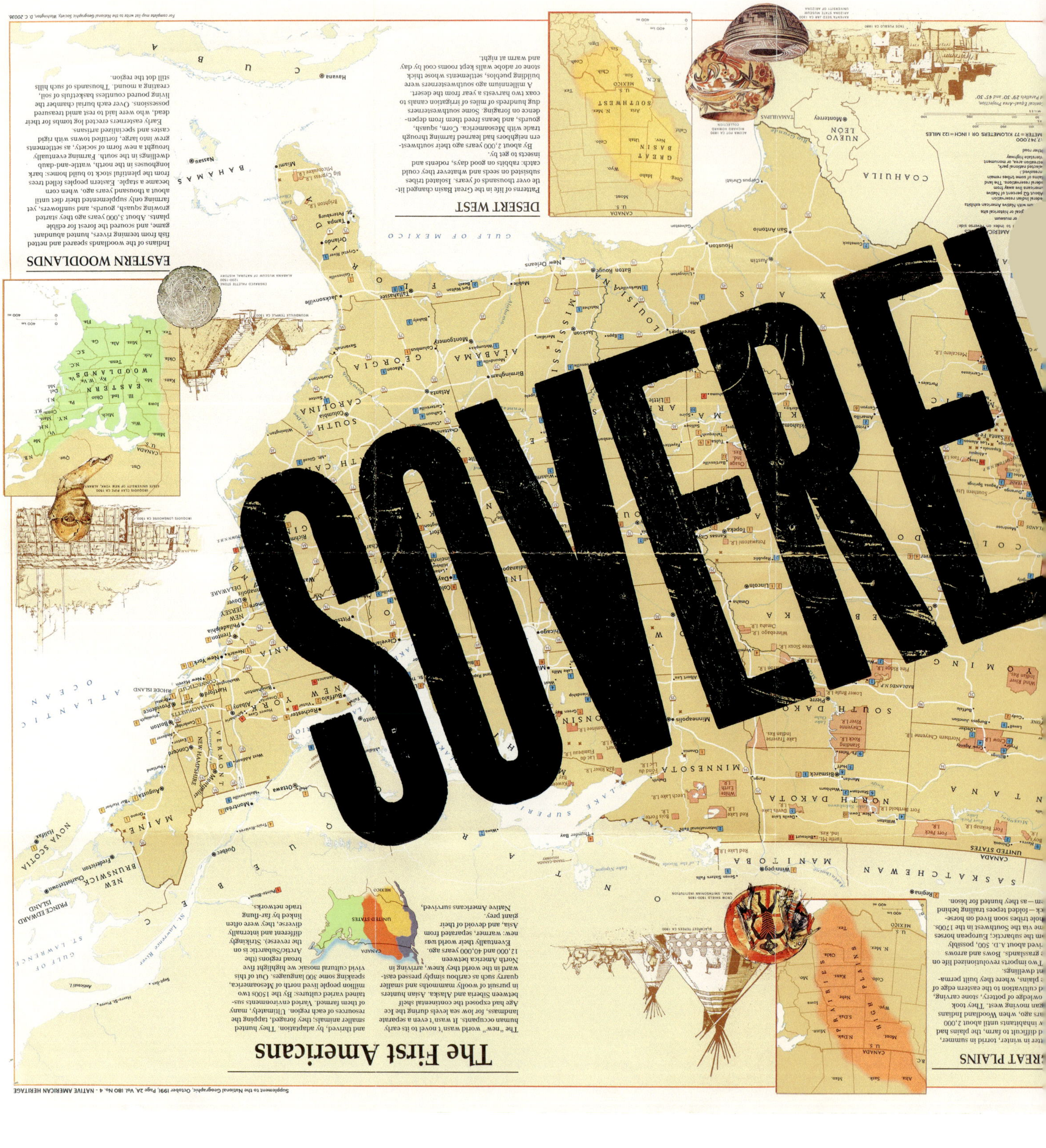

SOVEREI

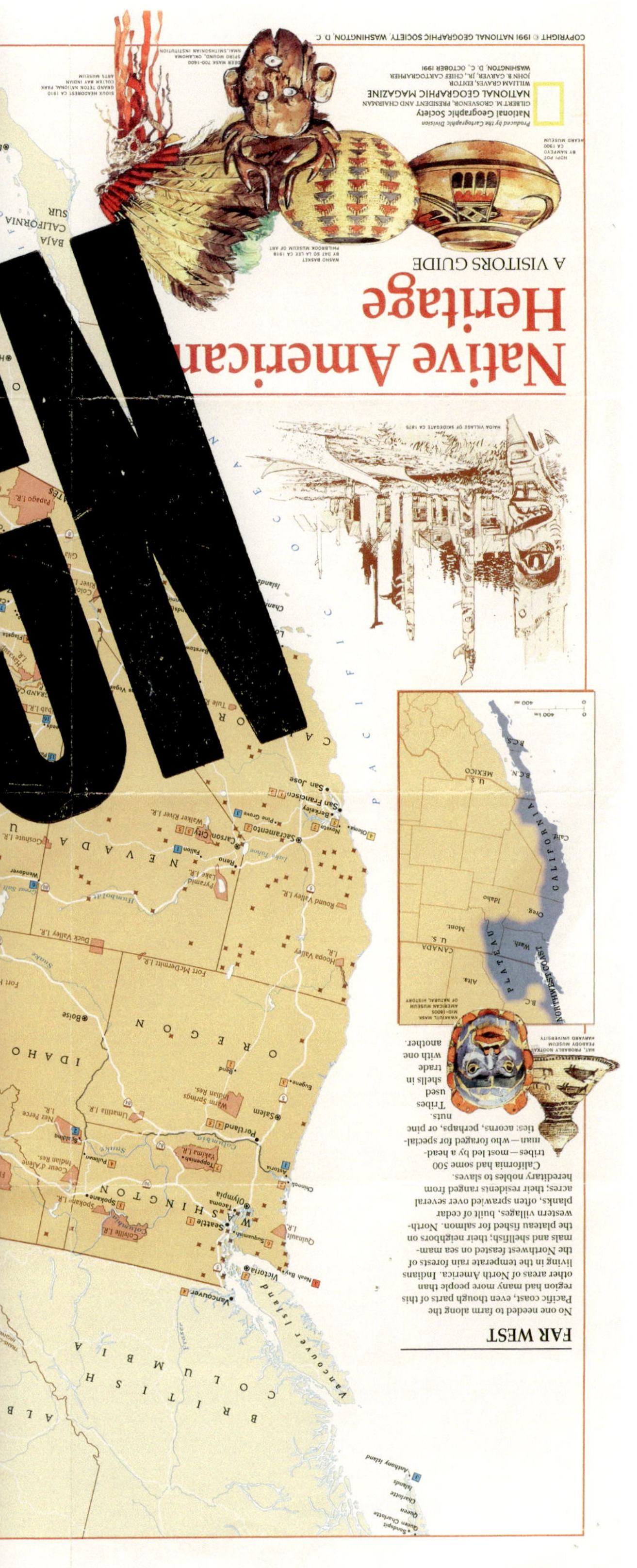

> **“Some say chattel slavery is this country’s original sin, but you can’t look away from the simultaneous genocide of those who lived here first. The government was stealing Black bodies and Indigenous lands at the same time.**
>
> **Now, when I print on a U.S. map, I turn it upside down as a fuck you to the orientation we’re taught of the world.”**

negroes:
stolen peoples
living on
stolen lands.

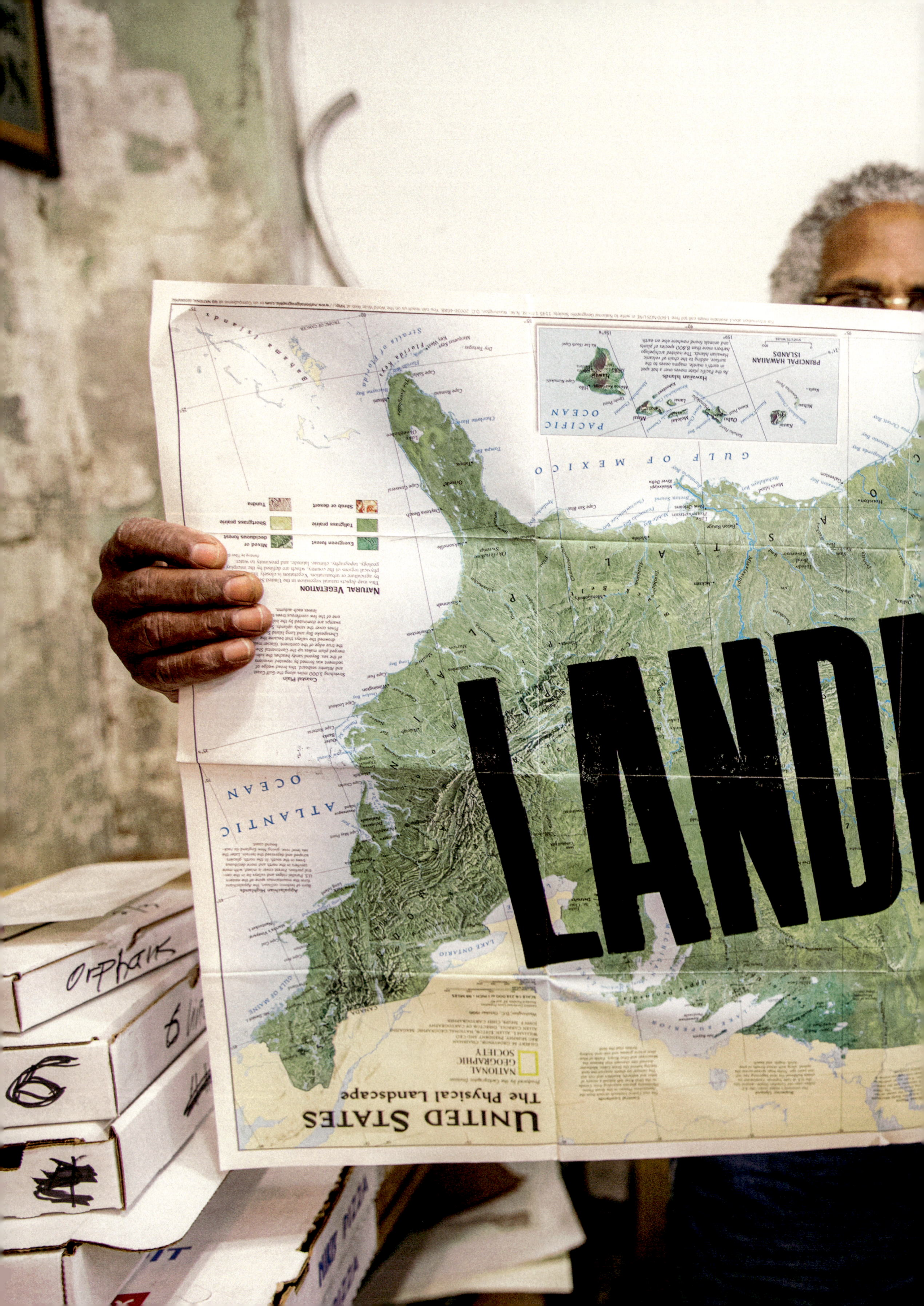
LAND
UNITED STATES
The Physical Landscape
NATIONAL GEOGRAPHIC SOCIETY
GULF OF MEXICO
ATLANTIC OCEAN
PACIFIC OCEAN
Orphan

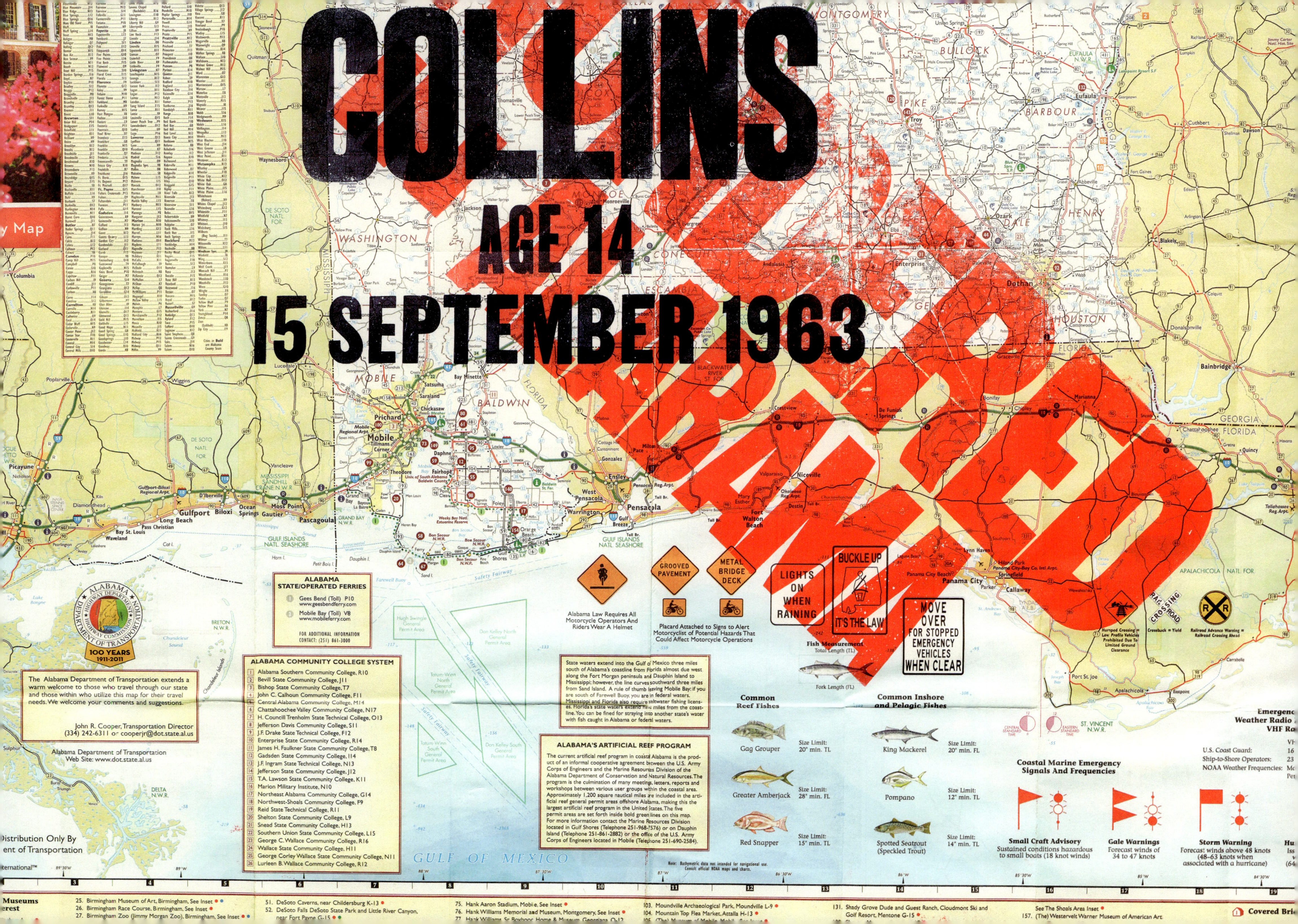
COLLINS
AGE 14
15 SEPTEMBER 1963
LIGHTS ON WHEN RAINING
BUCKLE UP IT'S THE LAW
MOVE OVER FOR STOPPED EMERGENCY VEHICLES WHEN CLEAR
GULF OF MEXICO

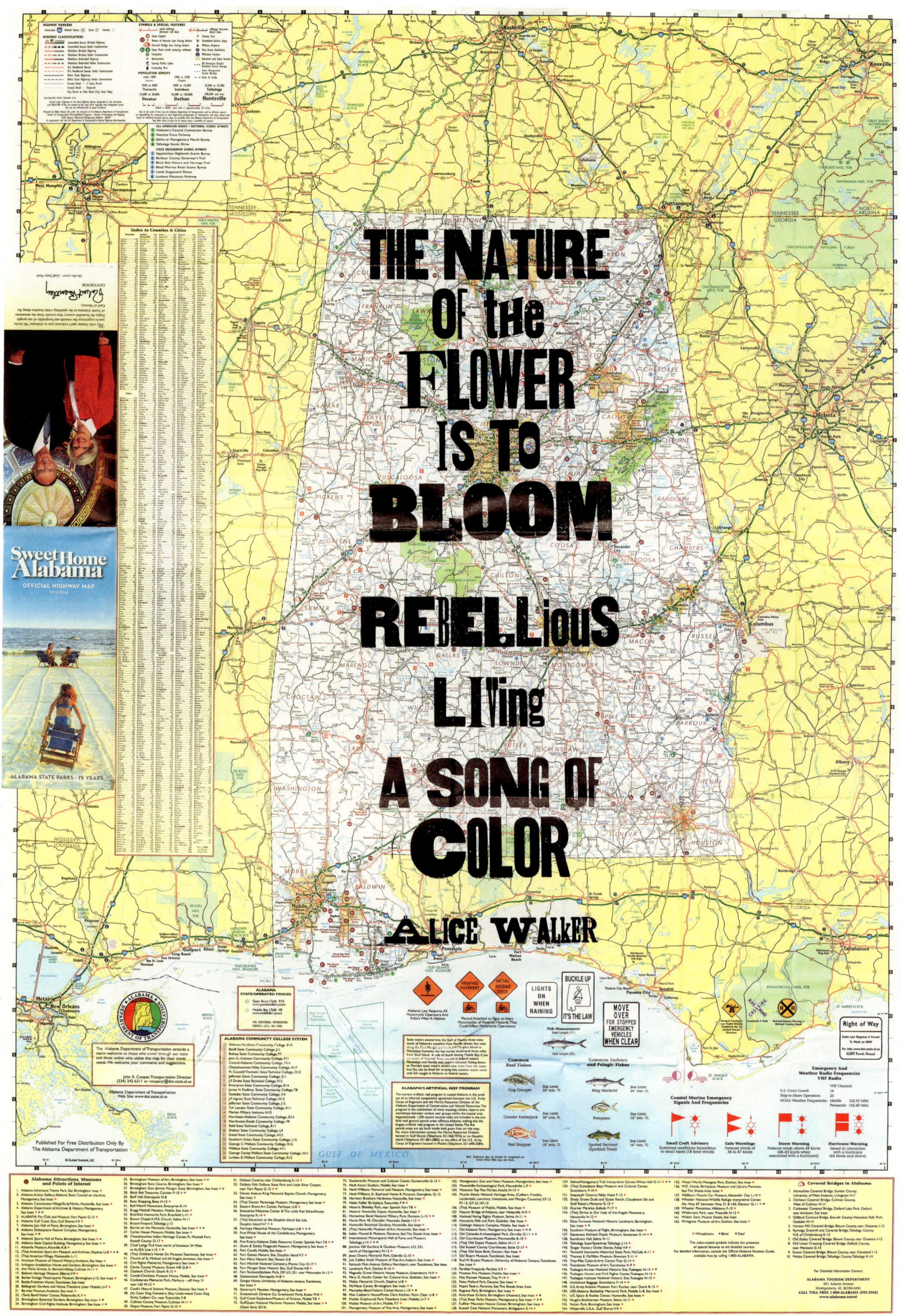
THE NATURE
OF the
FLOWER
IS TO
BLOOM
REBELLious
LIVing
A SONG OF
COLOR
ALICE WALKER
Sweet Home Alabama
OFFICIAL HIGHWAY MAP

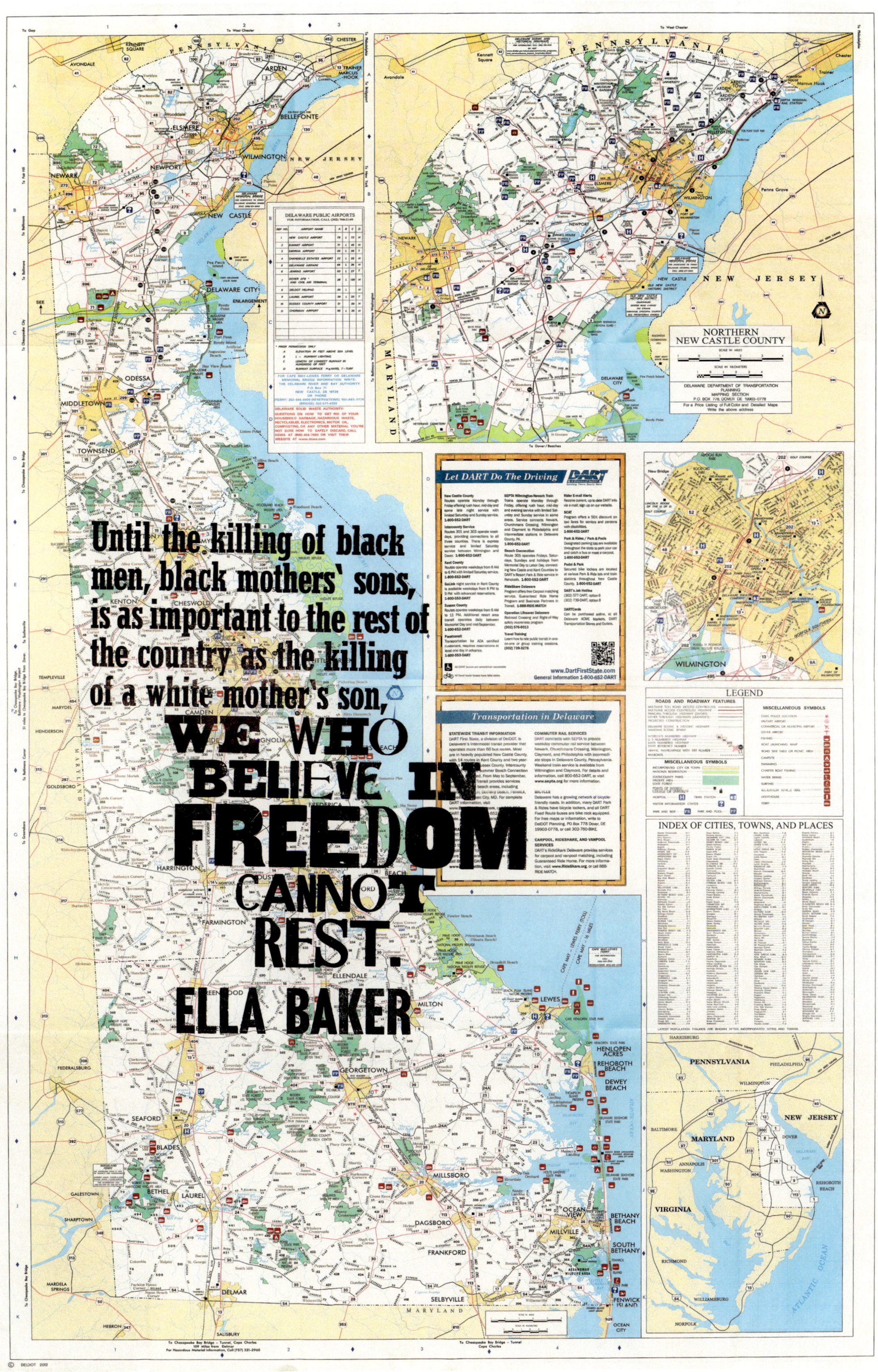
Until the killing of black men, black mothers' sons, is as important to the rest of the country as the killing of a white mother's son,
WE WHO BELIEVE IN FREEDOM CANNOT REST.
ELLA BAKER
NORTHERN NEW CASTLE COUNTY
DELAWARE PUBLIC AIRPORTS
Let DART Do The Driving
Transportation in Delaware
LEGEND
INDEX OF CITIES, TOWNS, AND PLACES

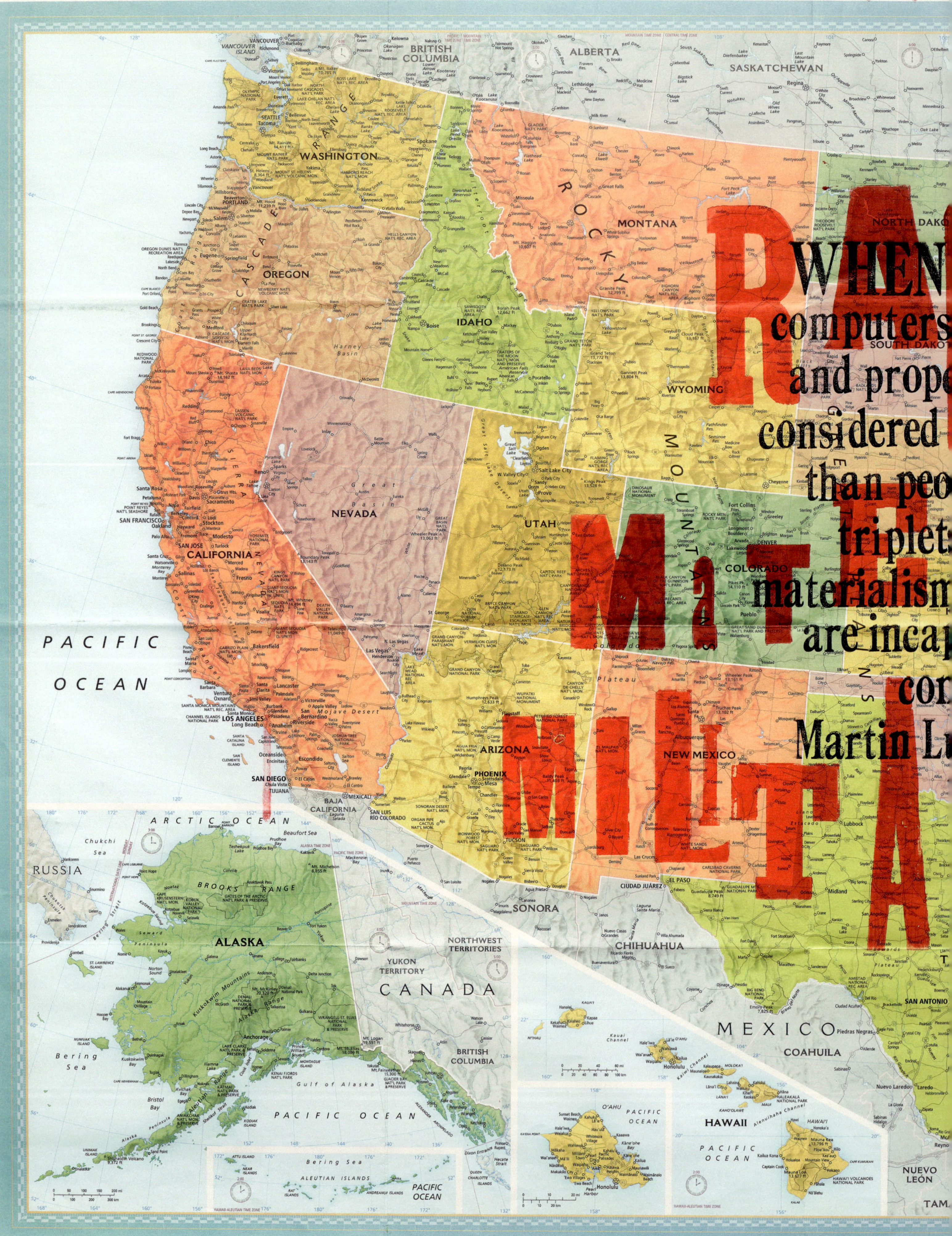
WHEN
computers
and prope
considered
than peo
triplets
materialism
are incap
con
Martin L
PACIFIC OCEAN
WASHINGTON
OREGON
CALIFORNIA
NEVADA
IDAHO
MONTANA
WYOMING
UTAH
COLORADO
ARIZONA
NEW MEXICO
ALASKA
HAWAII
CANADA
MEXICO
RUSSIA
BRITISH COLUMBIA
ALBERTA
SASKATCHEWAN

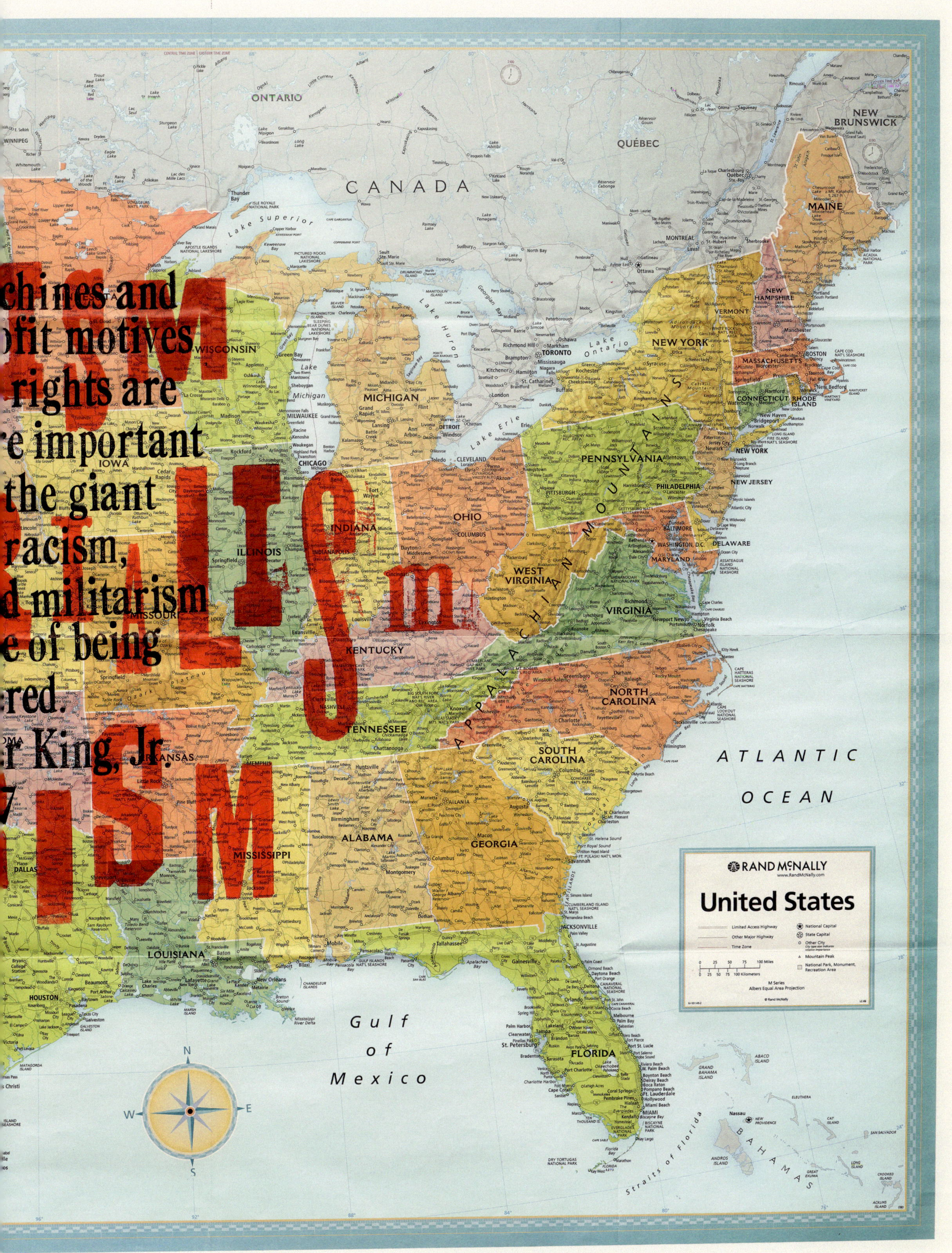

chines and
ofit motives
rights are
re important
the giant
racism,
d militarism
e of being
red.
r King, Jr.
7
ISM
ALISm
ISM
CANADA
ONTARIO
QUÉBEC
NEW BRUNSWICK
MAINE
NEW HAMPSHIRE
VERMONT
MASSACHUSETTS
CONNECTICUT
RHODE ISLAND
NEW YORK
NEW JERSEY
PENNSYLVANIA
DELAWARE
MARYLAND
WEST VIRGINIA
VIRGINIA
NORTH CAROLINA
SOUTH CAROLINA
GEORGIA
FLORIDA
ALABAMA
MISSISSIPPI
LOUISIANA
TENNESSEE
KENTUCKY
OHIO
INDIANA
ILLINOIS
MICHIGAN
WISCONSIN
IOWA
MISSOURI
ARKANSAS
APPALACHIAN MOUNTAINS
Lake Superior
Lake Huron
Lake Michigan
Lake Erie
Lake Ontario
ATLANTIC OCEAN
Gulf of Mexico
BAHAMAS
Straits of Florida
N
S
E
W
RAND McNALLY
www.RandMcNally.com
United States
Limited Access Highway
Other Major Highway
Time Zone
National Capital
State Capital
Other City
Mountain Peak
National Park, Monument, Recreation Area
M Series
Albers Equal Area Projection

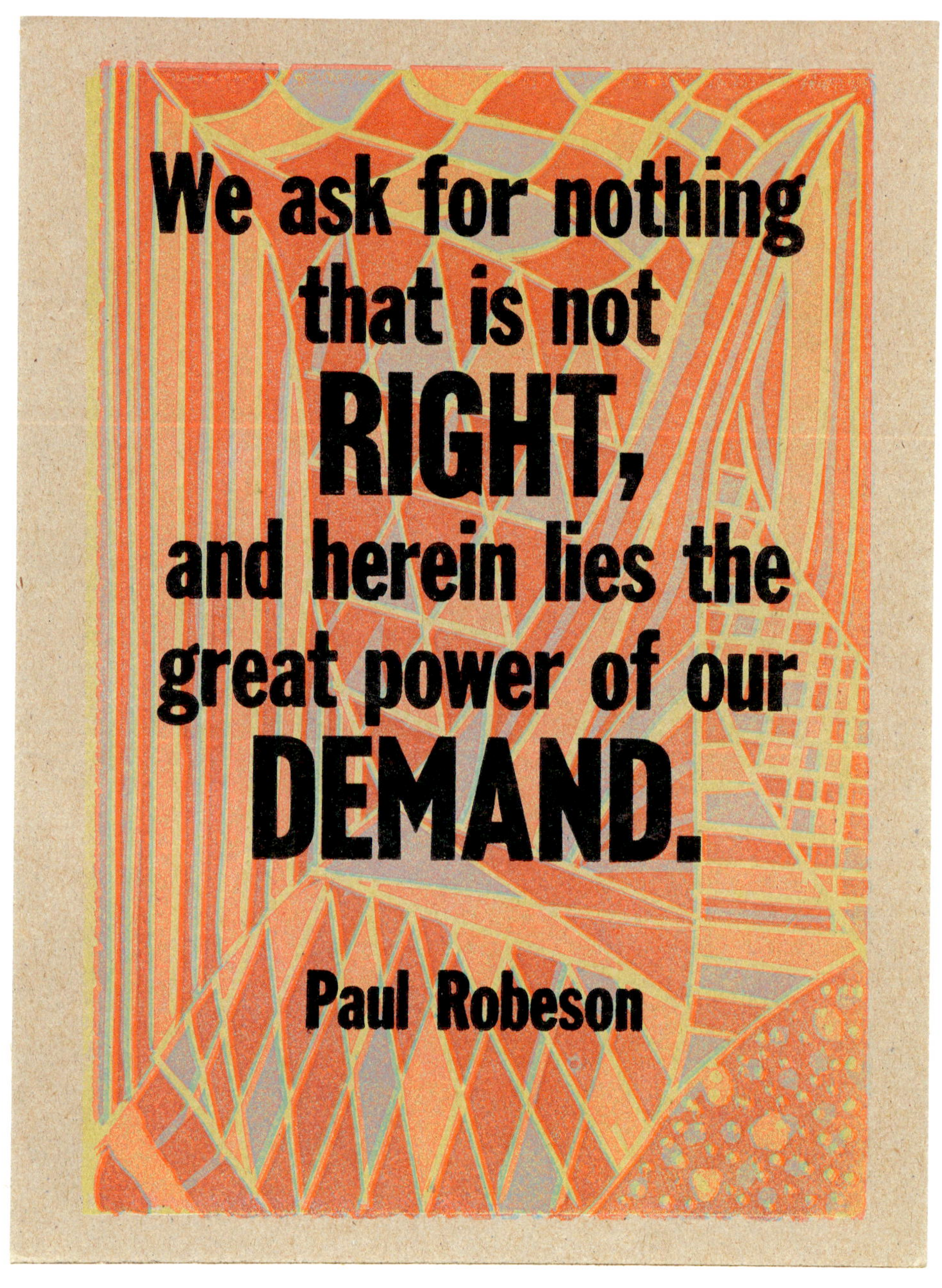
We ask for nothing
that is not
RIGHT,
and herein lies the
great power of our
DEMAND.
Paul Robeson

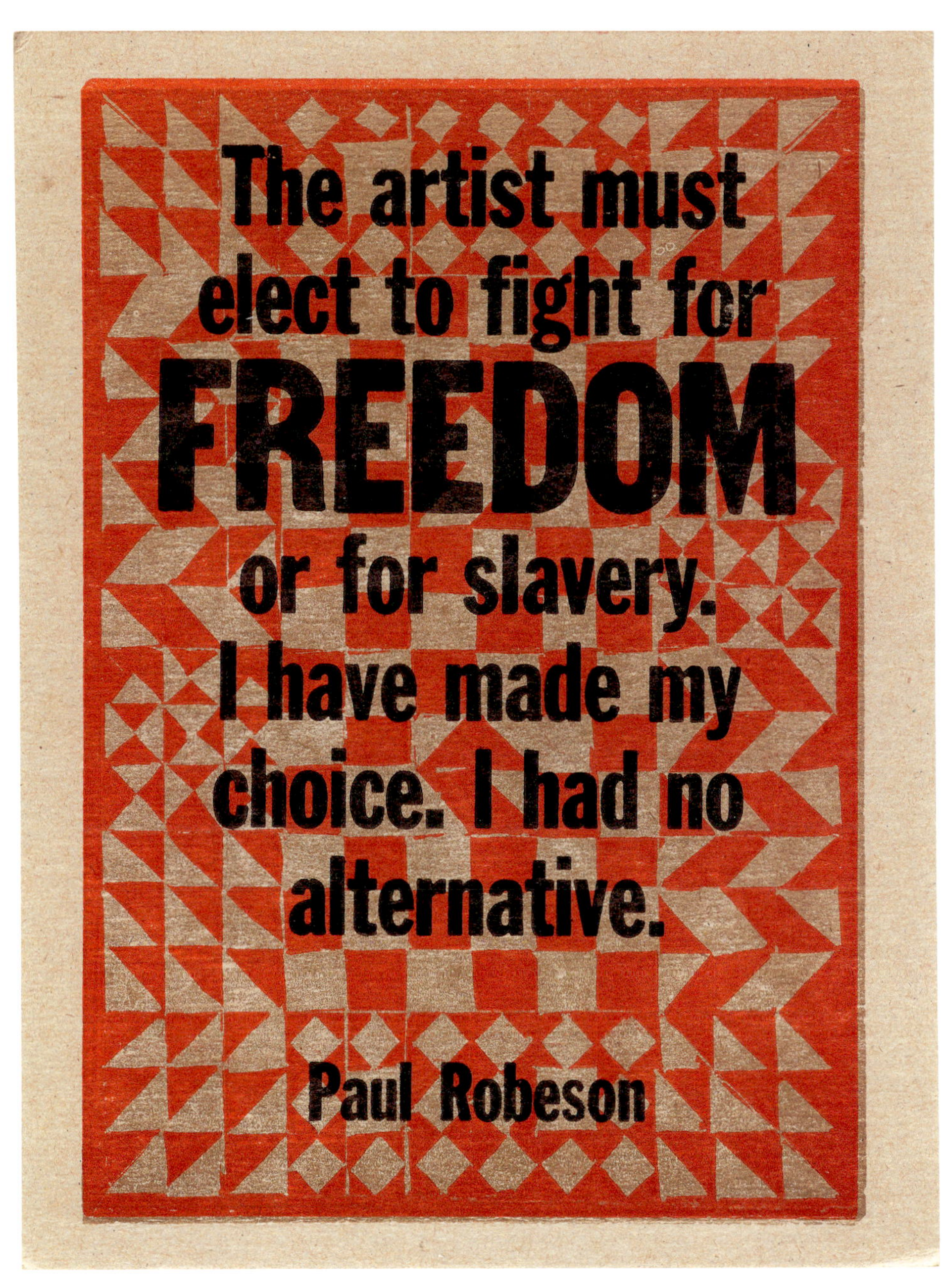
The artist must
elect to fight for
FREEDOM
or for slavery.
I have made my
choice. I had no
alternative.
Paul Robeson

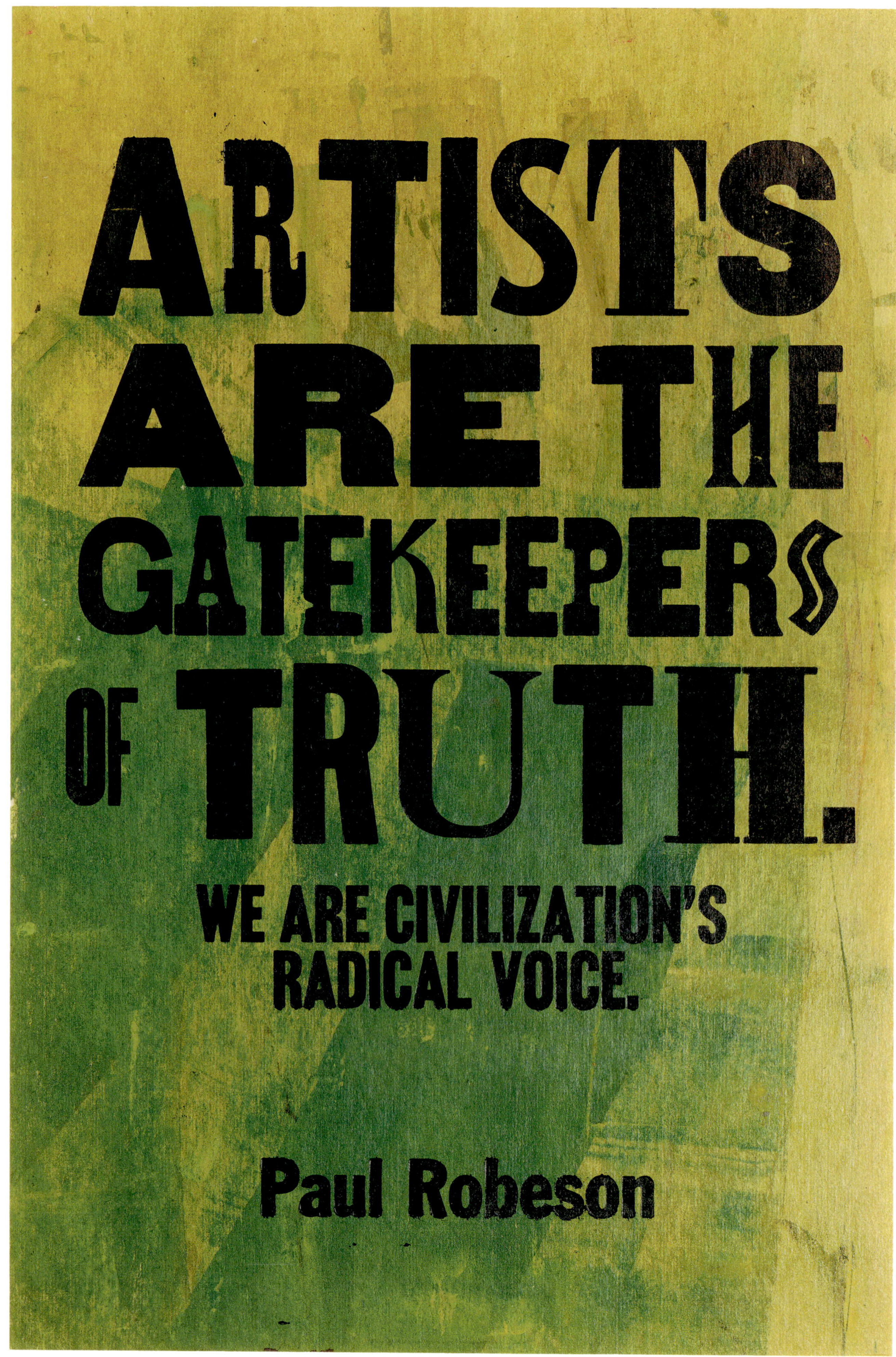
ARTISTS
ARE THE
GATEKEEPERS
OF TRUTH.
WE ARE CIVILIZATION'S
RADICAL VOICE.
Paul Robeson

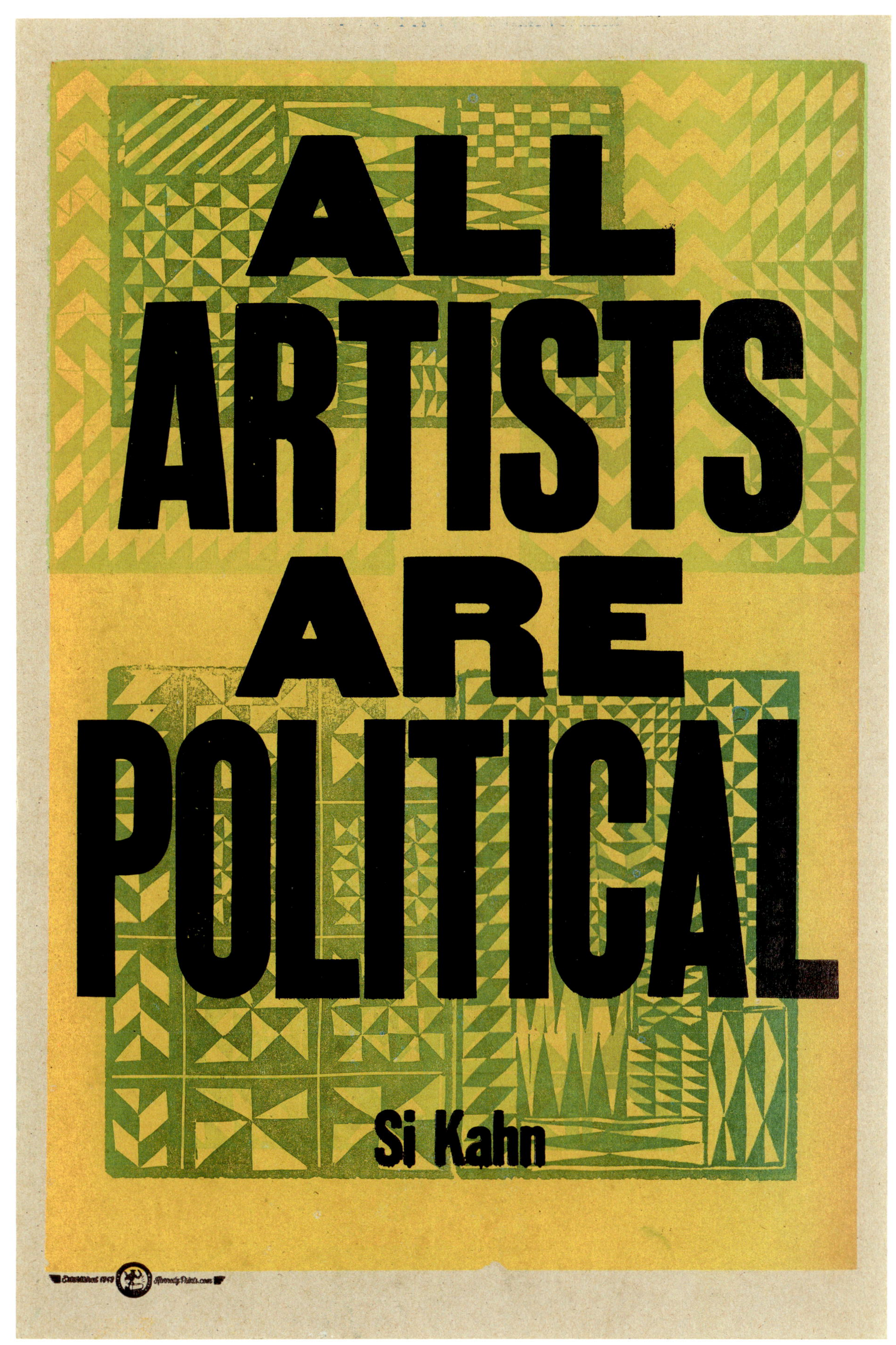
ALL
ARTISTS
ARE
POLITICAL
Si Kahn

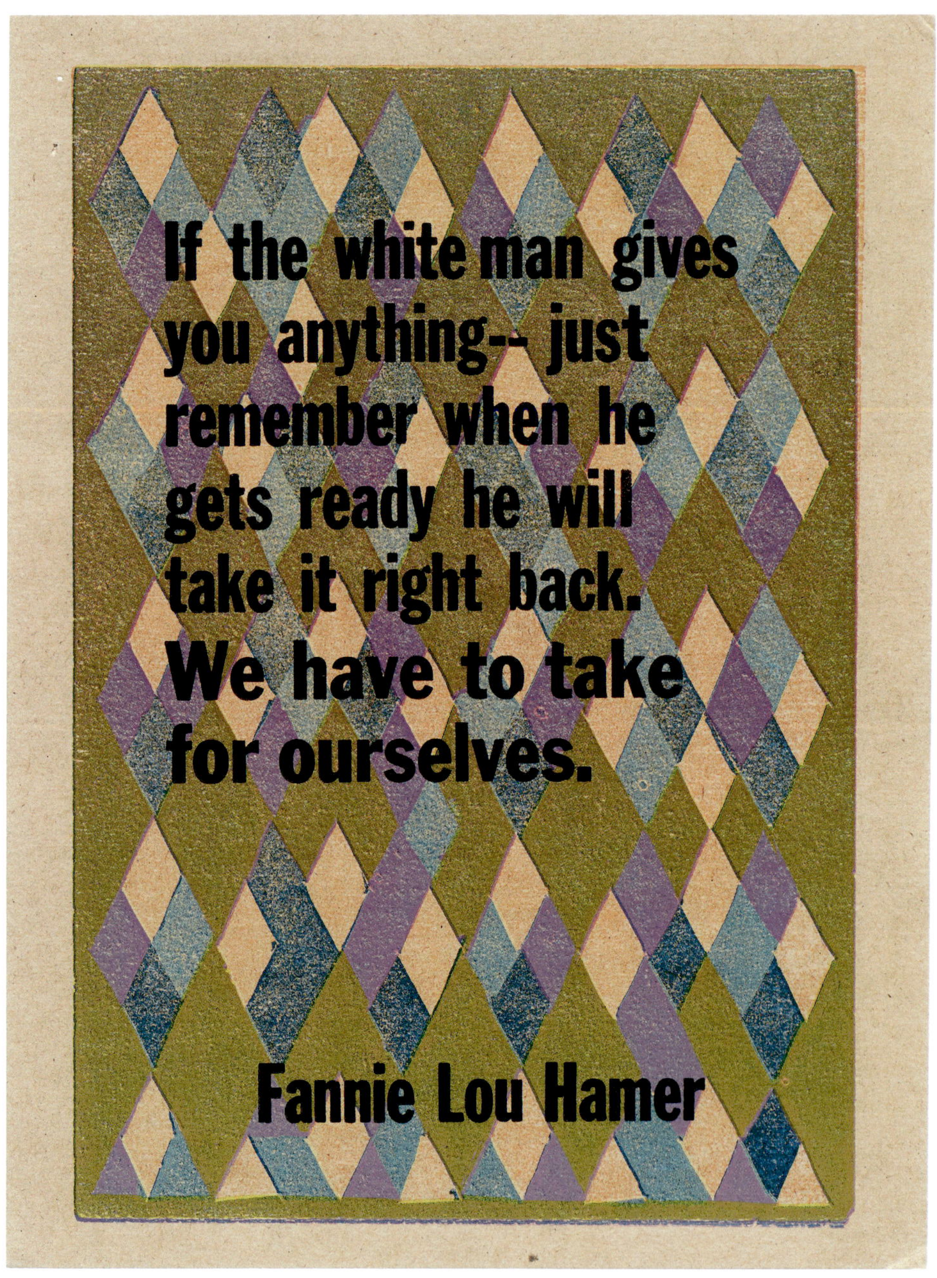
If the white man gives
you anything-- just
remember when he
gets ready he will
take it right back.
We have to take
for ourselves.
Fannie Lou Hamer

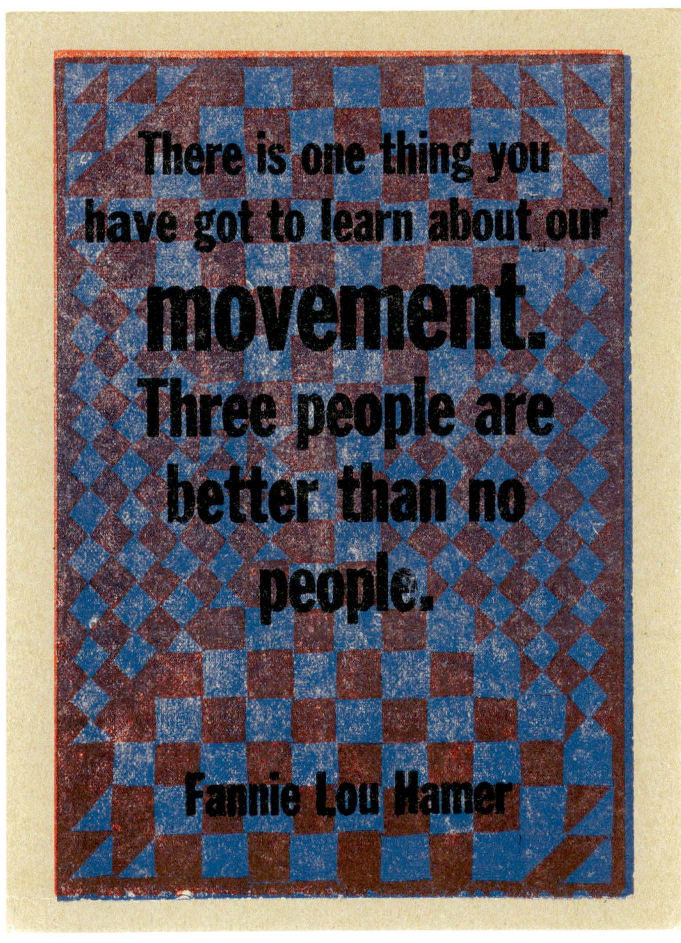
There is one thing you
have got to learn about our
movement.
Three people are
better than no
people.
Fannie Lou Hamer

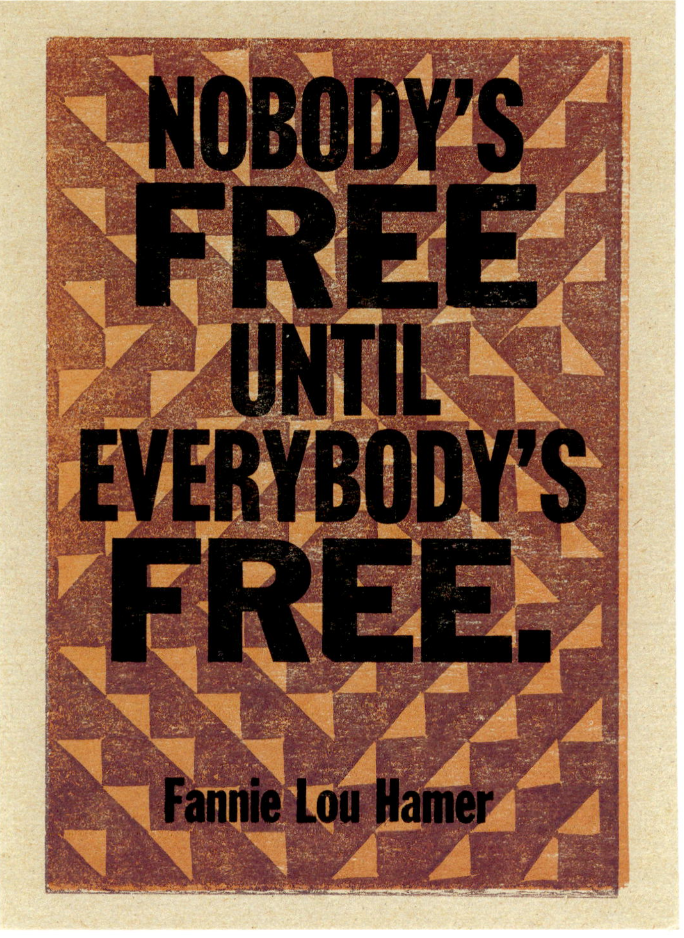
NOBODY'S
FREE
UNTIL
EVERYBODY'S
FREE.
Fannie Lou Hamer

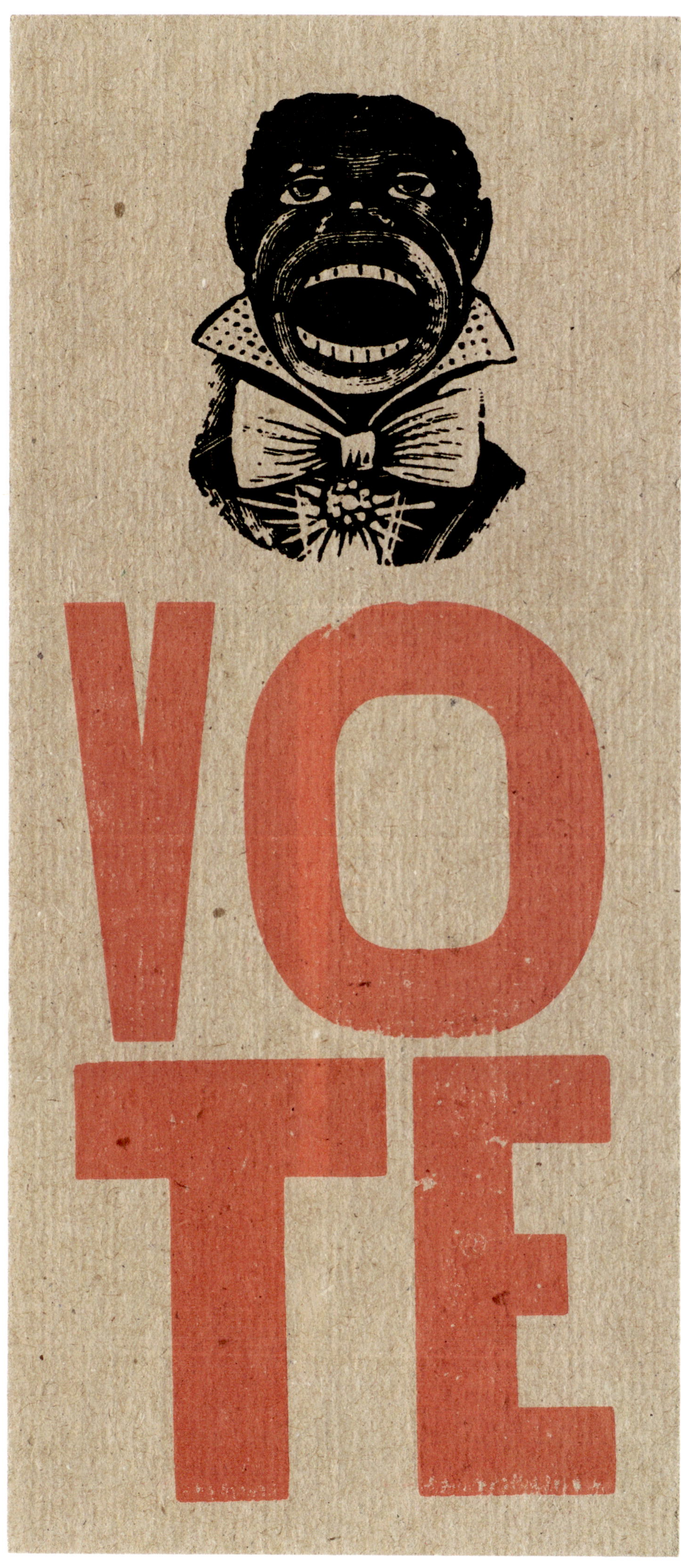
VOTE

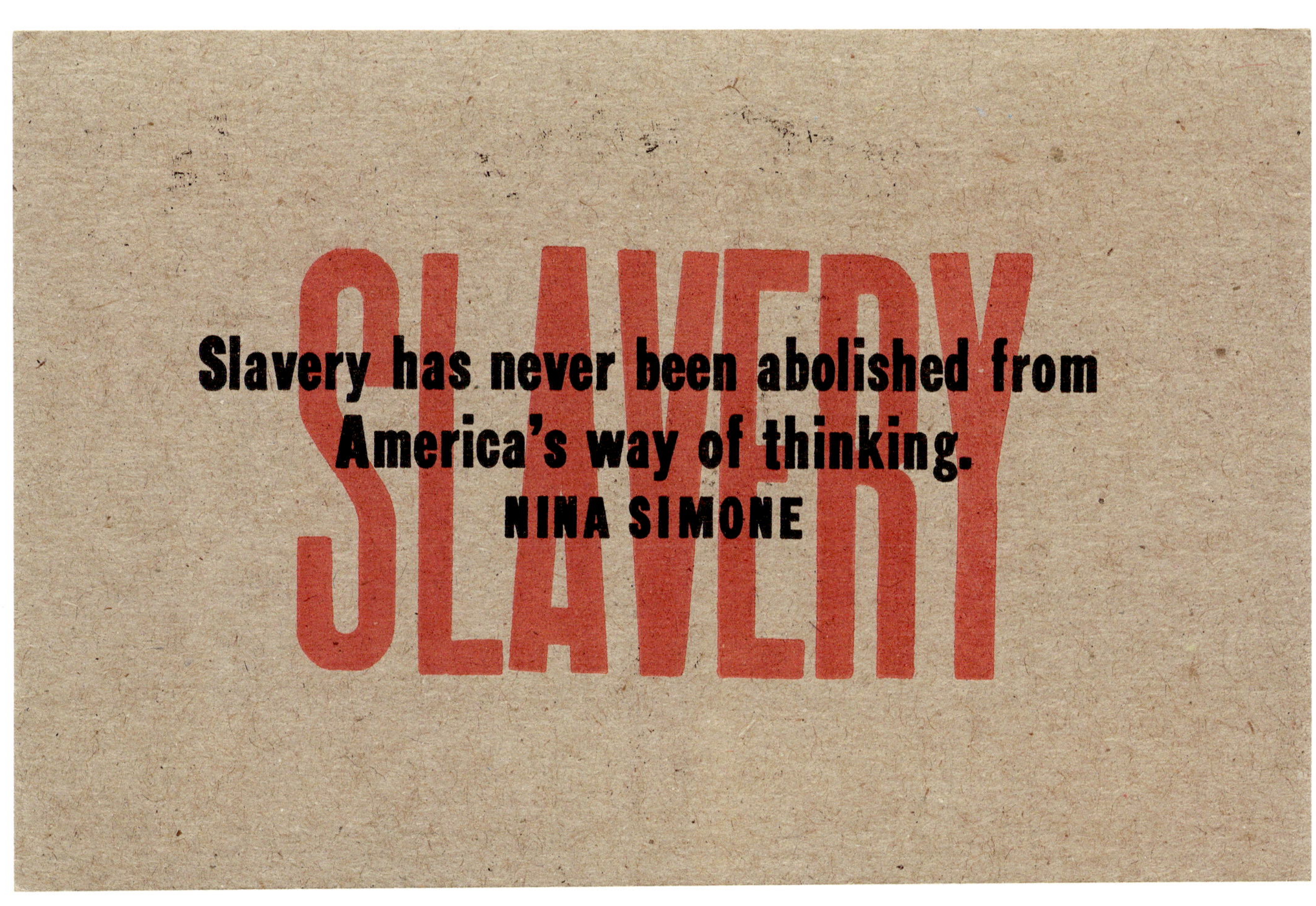
SLAVERY
Slavery has never been abolished from America's way of thinking.
NINA SIMONE

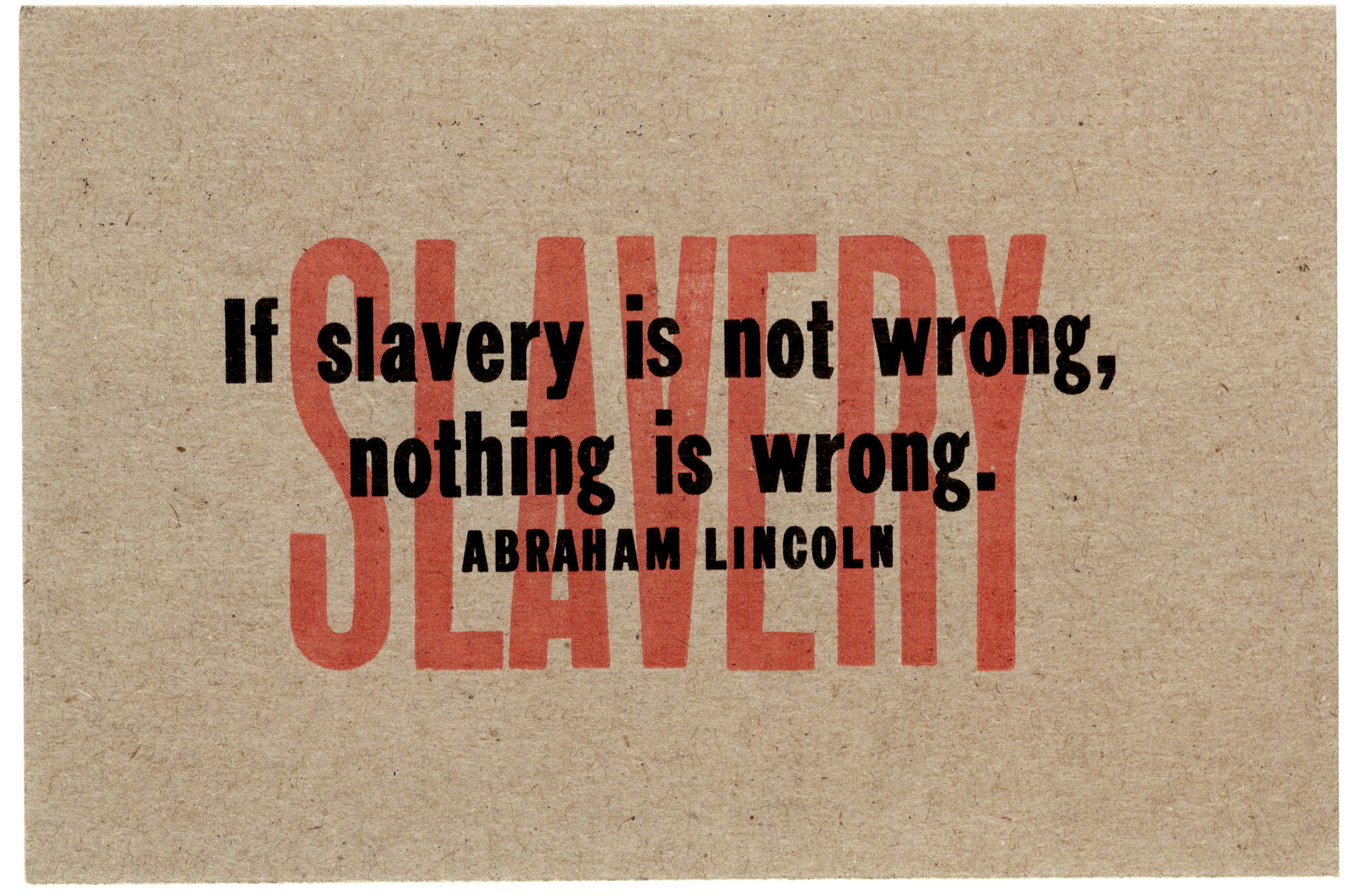
SLAVERY
If slavery is not wrong, nothing is wrong.
ABRAHAM LINCOLN

The Constitution of the United States

We the People of the United States, in Order to form a more perfect Union, establish Justice, insure domestic Tranquility, provide for the common defence, promote the general Welfare, and secure the Blessings of Liberty to ourselves and our Posterity, do ordain and establish this *Constitution* for the United States of America.

Article. I.

Section 1. All legislative Powers herein granted shall be vested in a Congress of the United States, which shall consist of a Senate and House of Representatives.

Section. 2. The House of Representatives shall be composed of Members chosen every second Year by the People of the several States, and the Electors in each State shall have the Qualifications requisite for Electors of the most numerous Branch of the State Legislature.

No person shall be a Representative who shall not have attained to the Age of twenty five Years, and been seven Years a Citizen of the United States, and who shall not, when elected, be an Inhabitant of that State in which he shall be chosen.

[Representatives and direct Taxes shall be apportioned among the several States which may be included within this Union, according to their respective Numbers, which shall be determined by adding to the whole Number of free Persons, including those bound to Service for a Term of Years, and excluding Indians not taxed, three fifths of all other Persons.][1] The actual Enumeration shall be made within three Years after the first Meeting of the Congress of the United States, and within every subsequent Term of ten Years, in such Manner as they shall by Law direct. The Number of Representatives shall not exceed one for every thirty Thousand, but each State shall have at Least one Representative; and until such enumeration shall be made, the State of New Hampshire shall be entitled to chuse three, Massachusetts eight, Rhode-Island and Providence Plantations one, Connecticut five, New-York six, New Jersey four, Pennsylvania eight, Delaware one, Maryland six, Virginia ten, North Carolina five, South Carolina five, and Georgia three.

When vacancies happen in the Representation from any State, the Executive Authority thereof shall issue Writs of Election to fill such Vacancies.

convicted shall nevertheless be liable and subject to Indictment, Trial, Judgment and Punishment, according to Law.

Section. 4. The Times, Places and Manner of holding Elections for Senators and Representatives, shall be prescribed in each State by the Legislature thereof; but the Congress may at any time by Law make or alter such Regulations, except as to the Places of chusing Senators.

The Congress shall assemble at least once in every Year, and such Meeting shall be on the first Monday in December,][4] unless they shall by Law appoint a different Day.

Section. 5. Each House shall be the Judge of the Elections, Returns and Qualifications of its own Members, and a Majority of each shall constitute a Quorum to do Business; but a smaller Number may adjourn from day to day, and may be authorized to compel the Attendance of absent Members, in such Manner, and under such Penalties as each House may provide.

Each House may determine the Rules of its Proceedings, punish its Members for disorderly Behavior, and, with the Concurrence of two thirds, expel a Member.

Each House shall keep a Journal of its Proceedings, and from time to time publish the same, excepting such Parts as may in their Judgment require Secrecy; and the Yeas and Nays of the Members of either House on any question shall, at the Desire of one fifth of those Present, be entered on the Journal.

Neither House, during the Session of Congress, shall, without the Consent of the other, adjourn for more than three days, nor to any other Place than that in which the two Houses shall be sitting.

Section. 6. The Senators and Representatives shall receive a Compensation for their Services, to be ascertained by Law, and paid out of the Treasury of the United States. They shall in all Cases, except

tives may be necessary (except on a question of Adjournment) shall be presented to the President of the United States; and before the Same shall take Effect, shall be approved by him, or being disapproved by him, shall be repassed by two thirds of the Senate and House of Representatives, according to the Rules and Limitations prescribed in the Case of a Bill.

Section. 8. The Congress shall have Power To lay and collect Taxes, Duties, Imposts and Excises, to pay the Debts and provide for the common Defence and general Welfare of the United States; but all Duties, Imposts and Excises shall be uniform throughout the United States;

To borrow Money on the credit of the United States;

To regulate Commerce with foreign Nations, and among the several States, and with the Indian Tribes;

To establish an uniform Rule of Naturalization, and uniform Laws on the subject of Bankruptcies throughout the United States;

To coin Money, regulate the Value thereof, and of foreign Coin, and fix the Standard of Weights and Measures;

To provide for the Punishment of counterfeiting the Securities and current Coin of the United States;

To establish Post Offices and post Roads;

To promote the Progress of Science and useful Arts, by securing for limited Times to Authors and Inventors the exclusive Right to their respective Writings and Discoveries;

To constitute Tribunals inferior to the supreme Court;

To define and punish Piracies and Felonies committed on the high Seas, and Offences against the Law of Nations;

To declare War, grant Letters of Marque and Reprisal, and make Rules concerning Captures on Land and Water;

To raise and support Armies, but no Appropriation of Money to that Use shall be for a longer Term than two Years;

To provide and maintain a Navy;

To make Rules for the Government and Regulation of the land and naval Forces;

To provide for calling forth the Militia to execute

Section. 3. The Senate of the United States shall be composed of two Senators from each state, [chosen by the Legislature thereof,][2] for six Years; and each Senator shall have one Vote.

Immediately after they shall be assembled in Consequence of the first Election, they shall be divided as equally as may be into three Classes. The Seats of the Senators of the first Class shall be vacated at the Expiration of the second Year, of the second Class at the Expiration of the fourth Year, and of the third Class at the Expiration of the sixth Year, so that one third may be chosen every second Year; [and if Vacancies happen by Resignation, or otherwise, during the Recess of the Legislature of any State, the Executive thereof may make temporary Appointments until the next Meeting of the Legislature, which shall then fill such Vacancies].[3]

No Person shall be a Senator who shall not have attained to the Age of thirty Years, and been nine Years a Citizen of the United States, and who shall not, when elected, be an Inhabitant of that State for which he shall be chosen.

The Vice President of the United States shall be President of the Senate, but shall have no Vote, unless they be equally divided.

The Senate shall chuse their other Officers, and also a President pro tempore, in the Absence of the Vice President, or when he shall exercise the Office of President of the United States.

The Senate shall have the sole Power to try all Impeachments. When sitting for that Purpose, they shall be on Oath or Affirmation. When the President of the United States is tried, the Chief Justice shall preside: And no Person shall be convicted without the Concurrence of two thirds of the Members present.

Judgment in Cases of Impeachment shall not extend further than to removal from Office, and disqualification to hold and enjoy any Office of honor, Trust or Profit under the United States: but the Party

Debate in either House, they shall not be questioned in any other Place.

No Senator or Representative shall, during the Time for which he was elected, be appointed to any civil Office under the Authority of the United States, which shall have been created, or the Emoluments whereof shall have been increased during such time; and no Person holding any Office under the United States, shall be a Member of either House during his Continuance in Office.

Section. 7. All Bills for raising Revenue shall originate in the House of Representatives; but the Senate may propose or concur with Amendments as on other Bills.

Every Bill which shall have passed the House of Representatives and the Senate, shall, before it become a Law, be presented to the President of the United States; If he approve he shall sign it, but if not he shall return it, with his Objections to that House in which it shall have originated, who shall enter the Objections at large on their Journal, and proceed to reconsider it. If after such Reconsideration two thirds of that House shall agree to pass the Bill, it shall be sent, together with the Objections, to the other House, by which it shall likewise be reconsidered, and if approved by two thirds of that House, it shall become a Law. But in all such Cases the Votes of both Houses shall be determined by yeas and Nays, and the Names of the Persons voting for and against the Bill shall be entered on the Journal of each House respectively. If any Bill shall not be returned by the President within ten days (Sundays excepted) after it shall have been presented to him, the Same shall be a Law, in like Manner as if he had signed it, unless the Congress by their Adjournment prevent its Return, in which Case it shall not be a Law.

Every Order, Resolution, or Vote to which the Concurrence of the Senate and House of Representa-

may be employed in the Service of the United States, reserving to the States respectively, the Appointment of the Officers, and the Authority of training the Militia according to the discipline prescribed by Congress;

To exercise exclusive Legislation in all Cases whatsoever, over such District (not exceeding ten Miles square) as may, by Cession of particular States, and the Acceptance of Congress, become the Seat of the Government of the United States, and to exercise like Authority over all Places purchased by the Consent of the Legislature of the State in which the Same shall be, for the Erection of Forts, Magazines, Arsenals, dock-Yards, and other needful Buildings;—And

To make all Laws which shall be necessary and proper for carrying into Execution the foregoing Powers, and all other Powers vested by this Constitution in the Government of the United States, or in any Department or Office thereof.

Section. 9. The Migration or Importation of such Persons as any of the States now existing shall think proper to admit, shall not be prohibited by the Congress prior to the Year one thousand eight hundred and eight, but a Tax or duty may be imposed on such Importation, not exceeding ten dollars for each Person.

The Privilege of the Writ of Habeas Corpus shall not be suspended, unless when in Cases of Rebellion or Invasion the public Safety may require it.

No Bill of Attainder or ex post facto Law shall be passed.

[5]No Capitation, or other direct, Tax shall be laid, unless in Proportion to the Census or Enumeration herein before directed to be taken.

No Tax or Duty shall be laid on Articles exported from any State.

No Preference shall be given by any Regulation of Commerce or Revenue to the Ports of one State over those of another: nor shall Vessels bound to, or from, one State be obliged to enter, clear, or pay Duties in another.

No Money shall be drawn from the Treasury, but in Consequence of Appropriations made by Law; and a regular Statement and Account of the Receipts and

1. The part in brackets was changed by section 2 of the fourteenth amendment.
2. The part in brackets was changed by section 1 of the seventeenth amendment.
3. The part in brackets was changed by clause 2 of the seventeenth amendment.
4. The part in brackets was changed by section 2, of the twentieth amendment.
5. See also the sixteenth amendment.

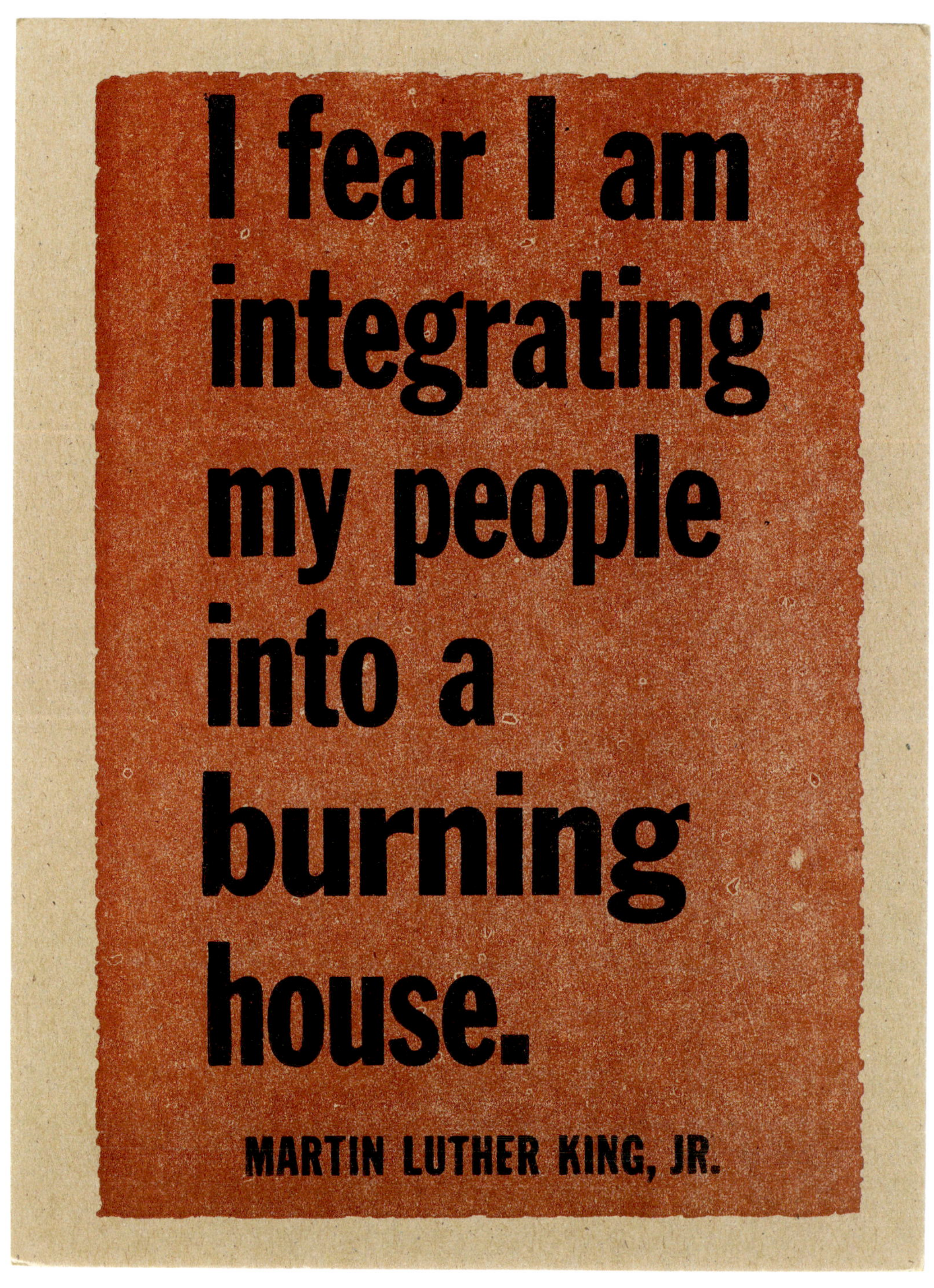
I fear I am
integrating
my people
into a
burning
house.
MARTIN LUTHER KING, JR.

LIFE'S MOST PERSISTENT AND URGENT QUESTION IS WHAT ARE YOU DOING FOR OTHERS?

DR. MARTIN LUTHER KING, JR.

END
SLAVERY
NOW

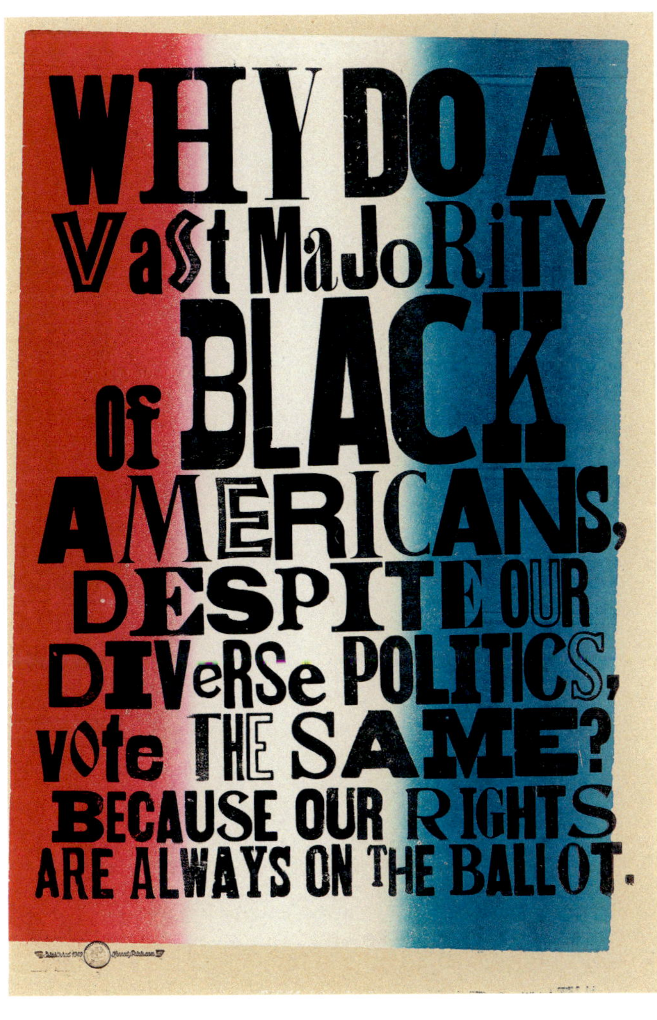
WHY DO A
VAST MAJORITY
OF BLACK
AMERICANS,
DESPITE OUR
DIVERSE POLITICS,
VOTE THE SAME?
BECAUSE OUR RIGHTS
ARE ALWAYS ON THE BALLOT.

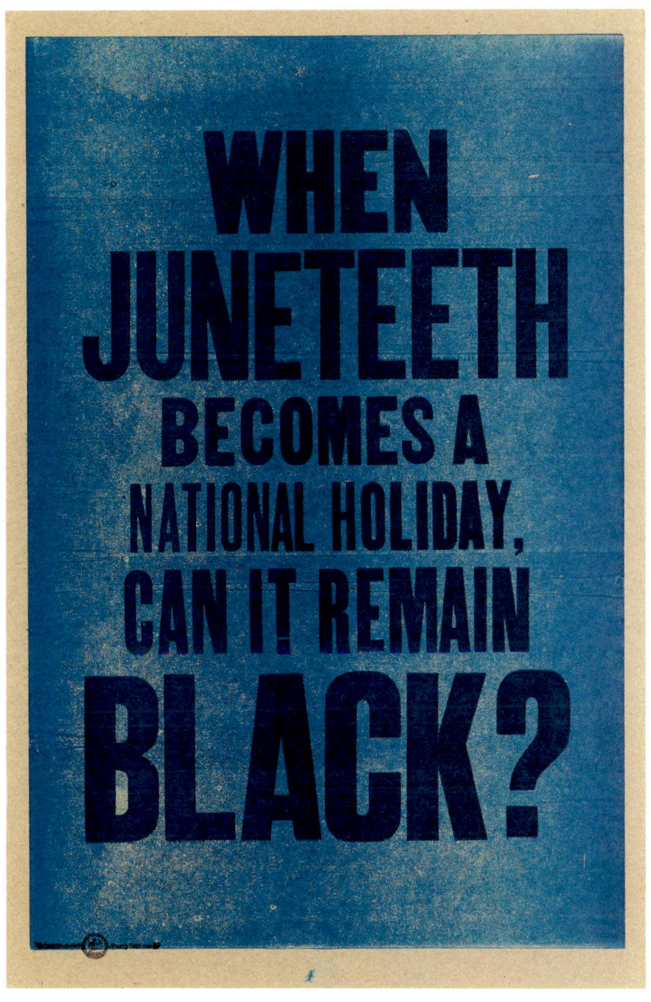
WHEN
JUNETEETH
BECOMES A
NATIONAL HOLIDAY,
CAN IT REMAIN
BLACK?

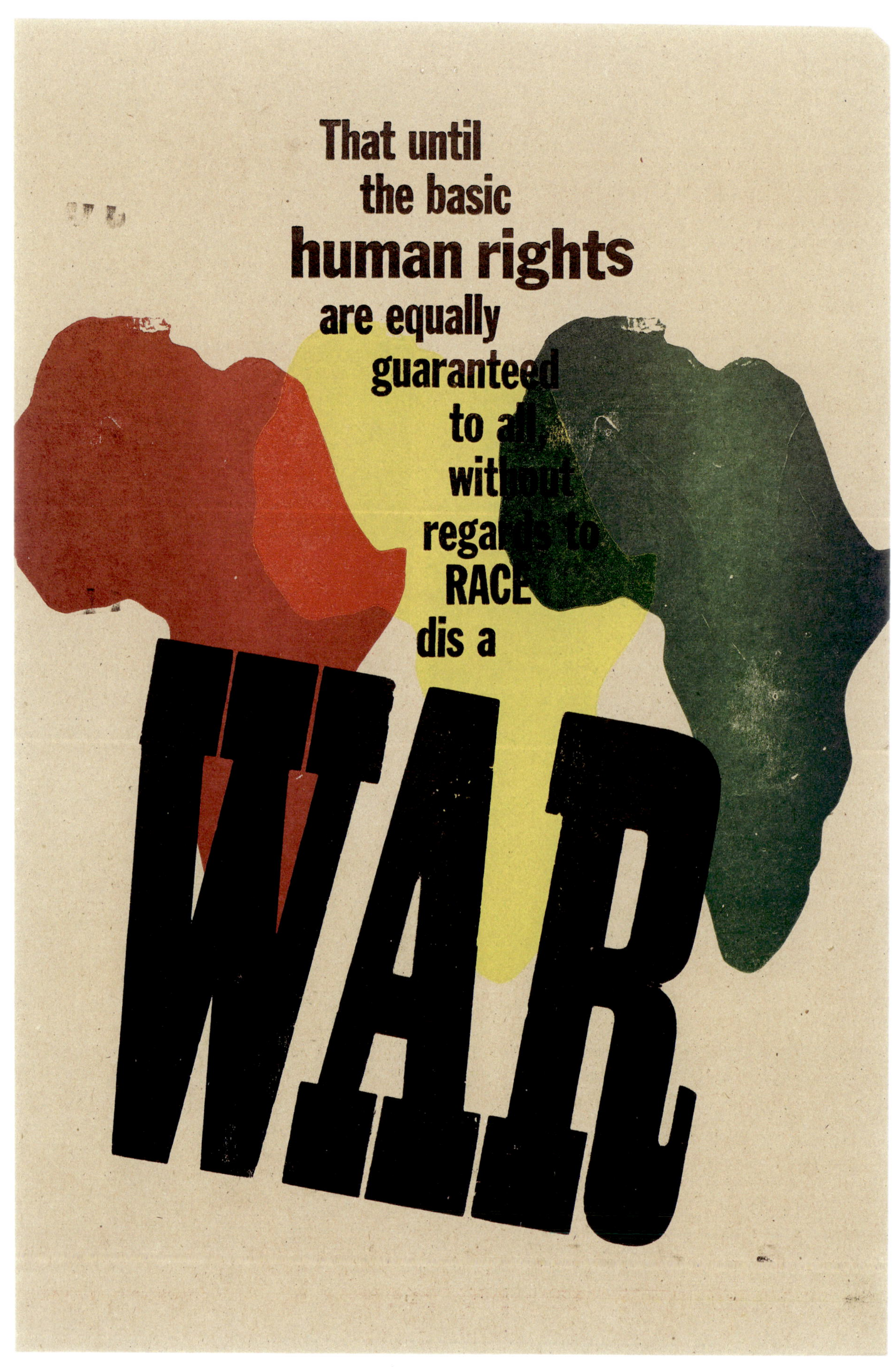
That until
the basic
human rights
are equally
guaranteed
to all,
without
regards to
RACE
dis a
WAR

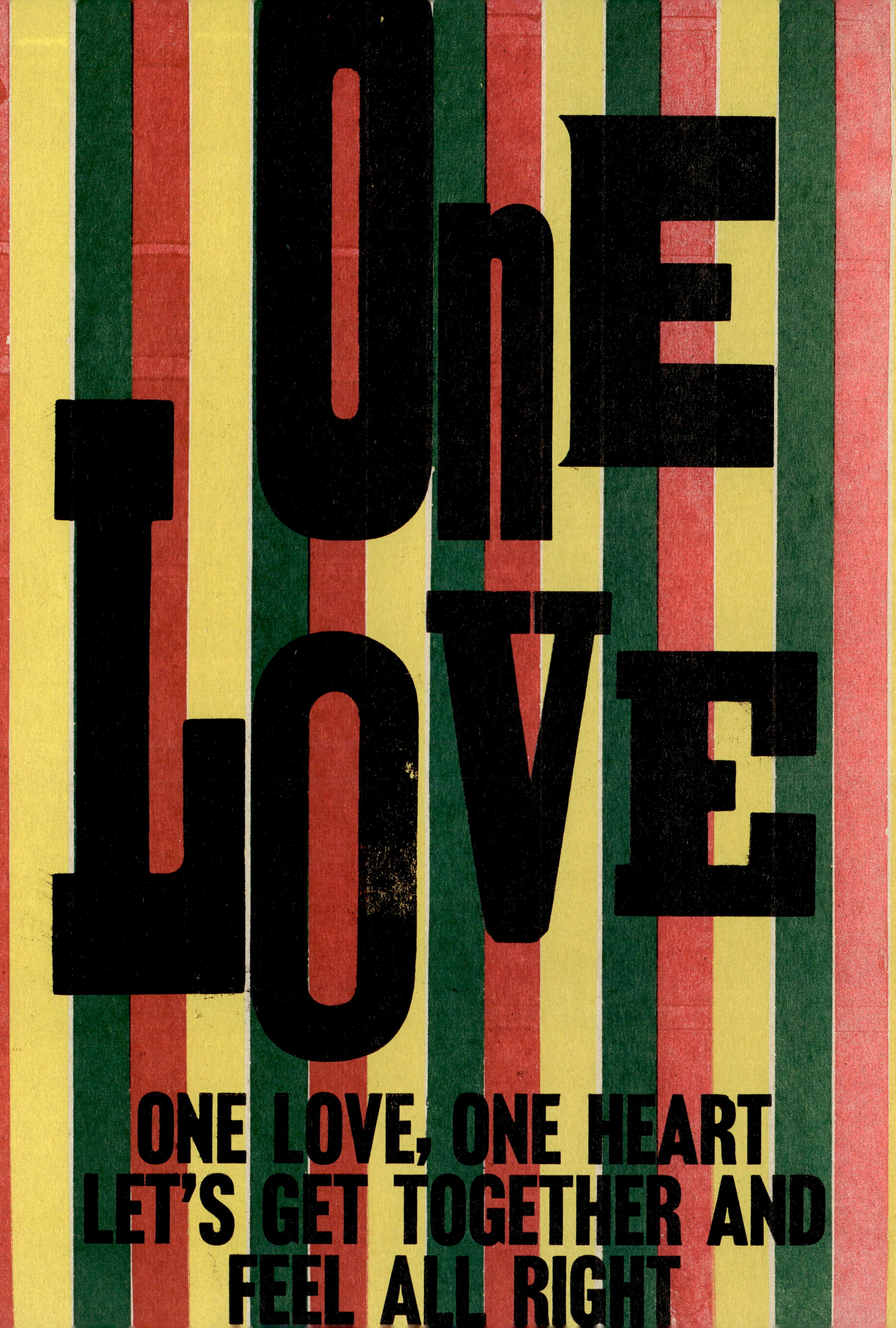
ONE
LOVE
ONE LOVE, ONE HEART
LET'S GET TOGETHER AND
FEEL ALL RIGHT

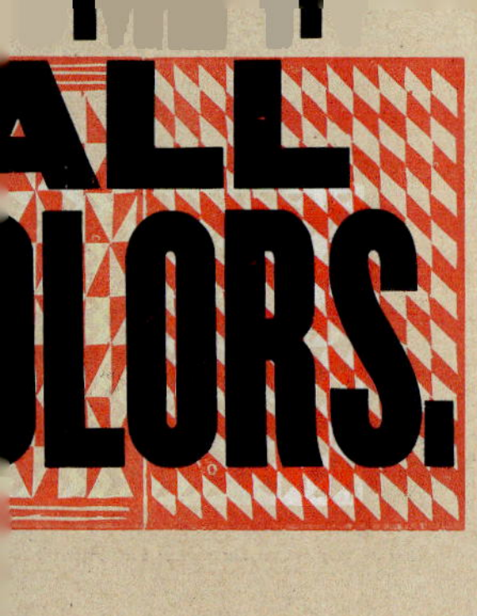

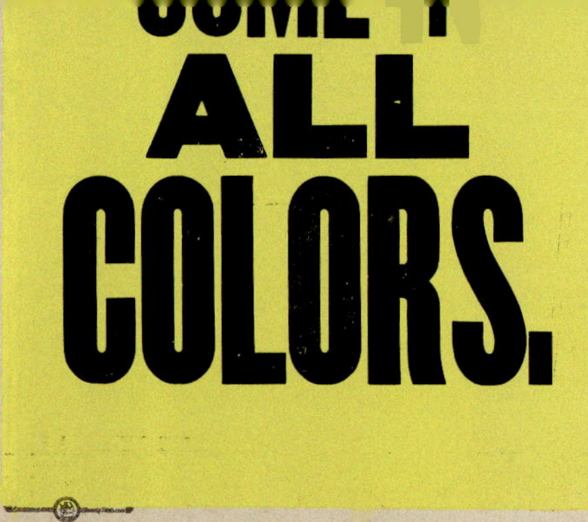
ALL
COLORS.

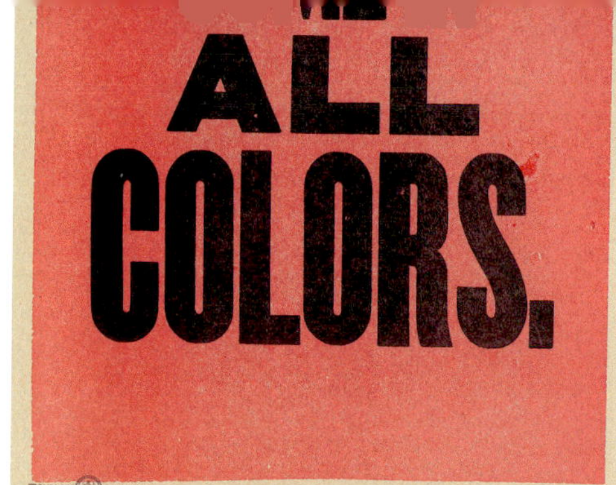
ALL
COLORS.

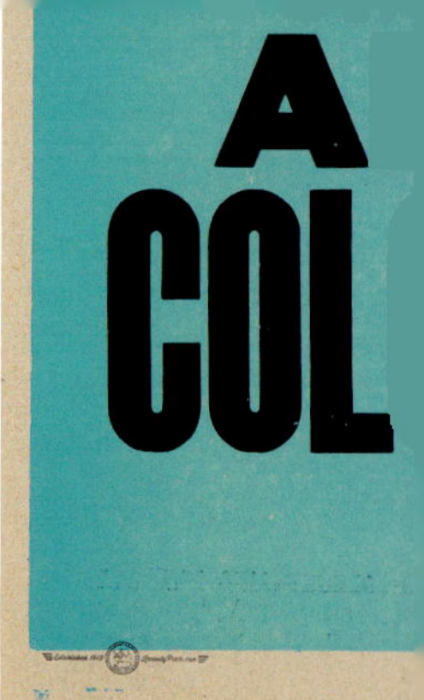

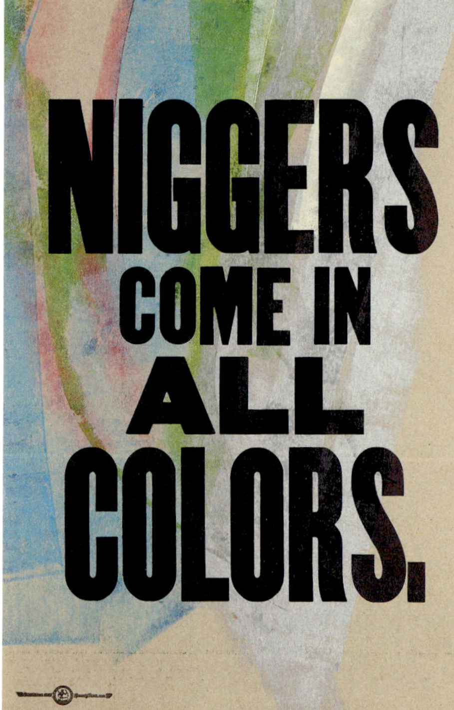
NIGGERS
COME IN
ALL
COLORS.

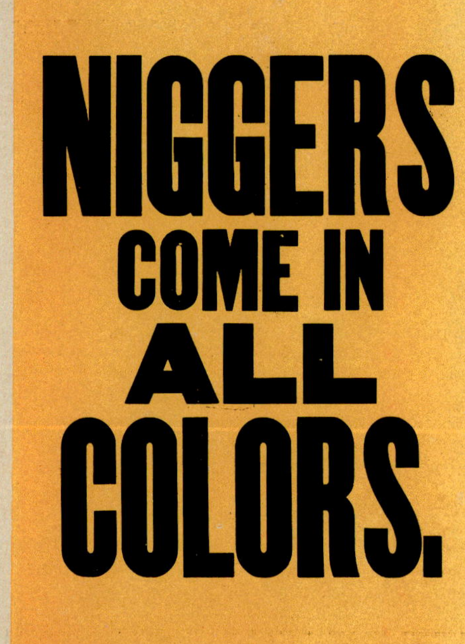
NIGGERS
COME IN
ALL
COLORS.

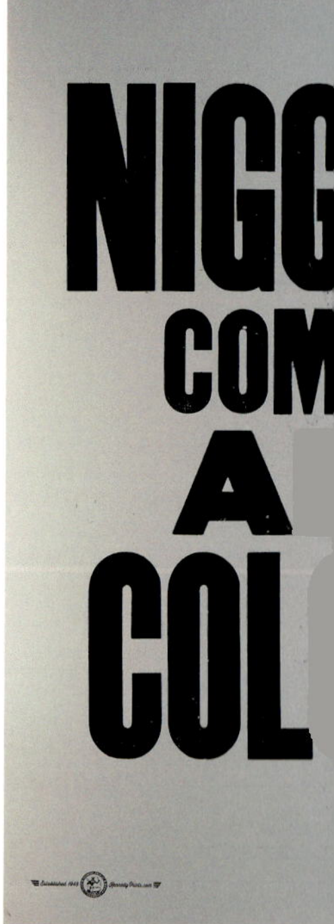

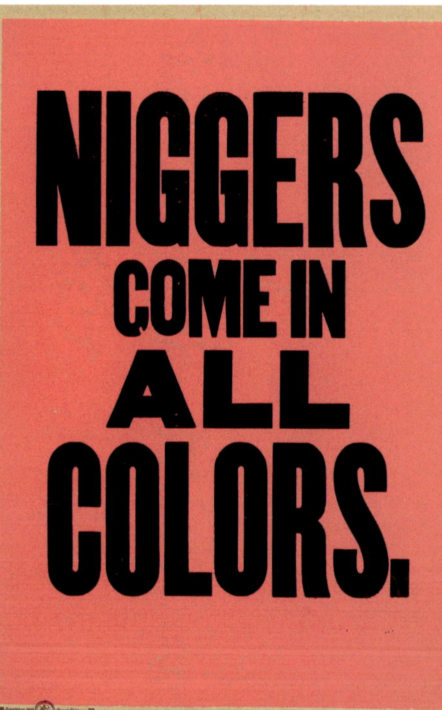
NIGGERS
COME IN
ALL
COLORS.

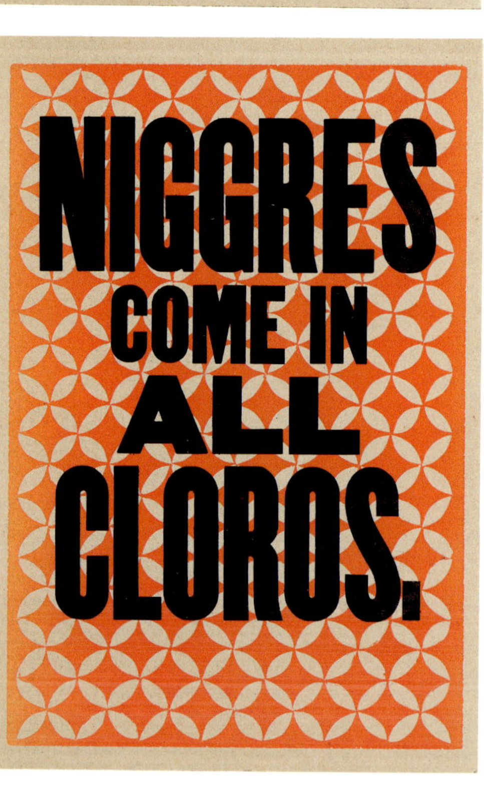
NIGGRES
COME IN
ALL
CLOROS.

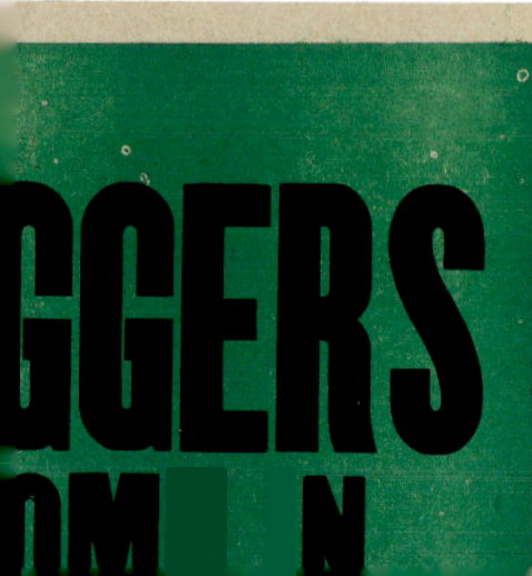

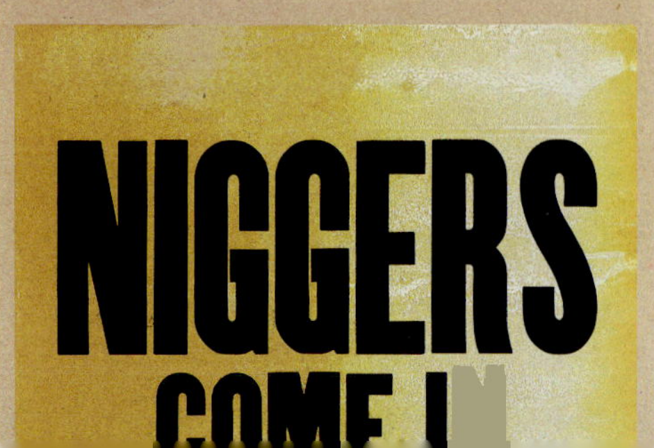
NIGGERS

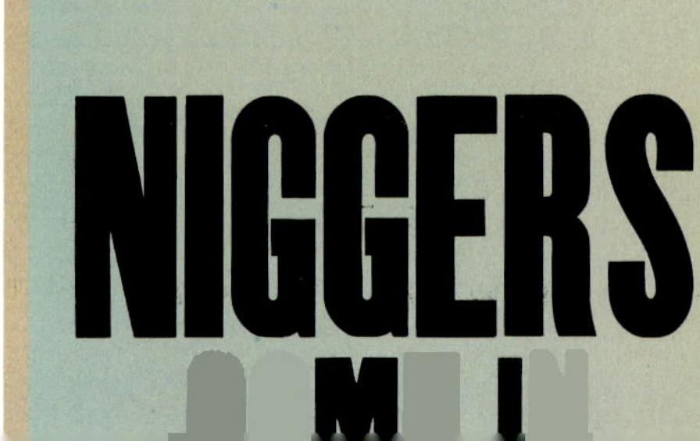
NIGGERS

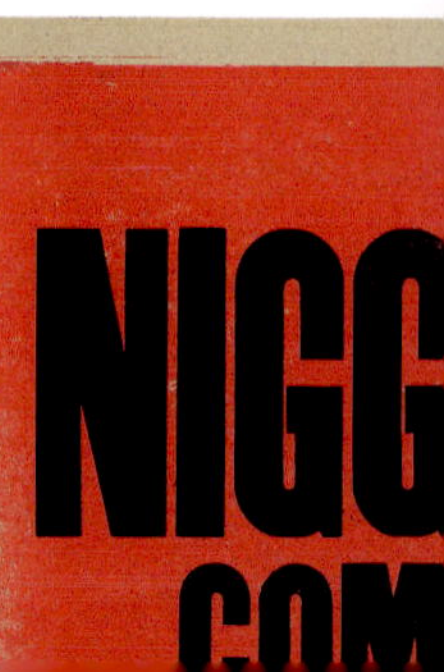

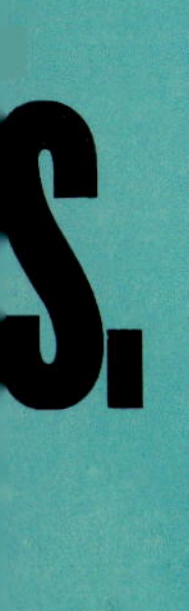

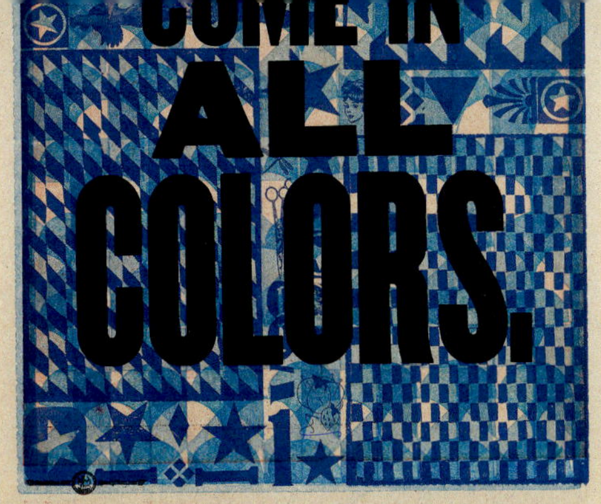

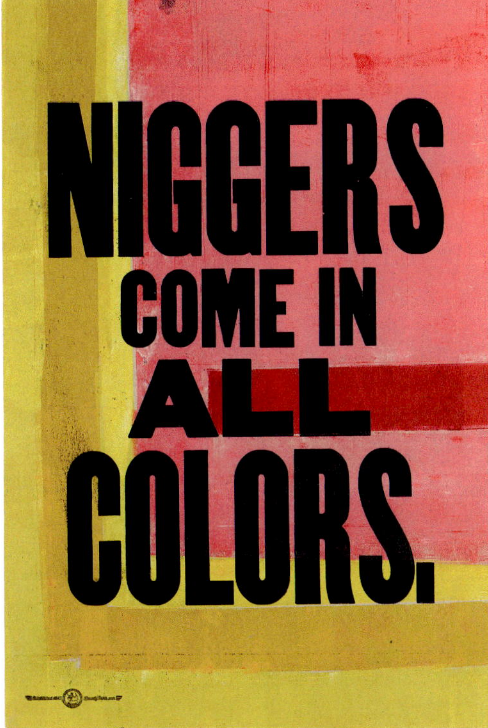

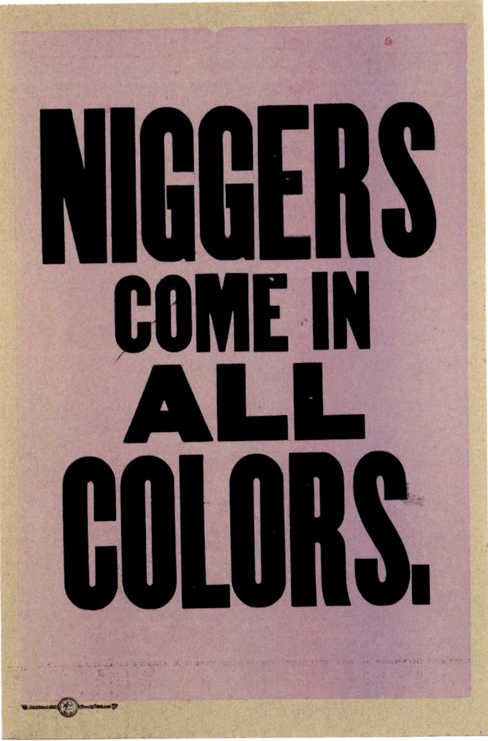

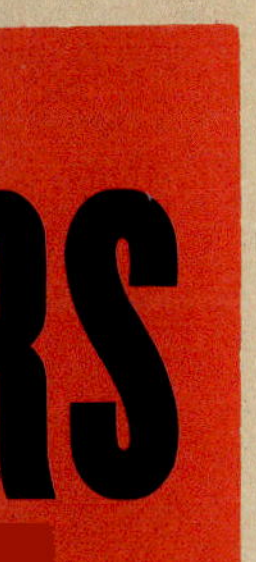

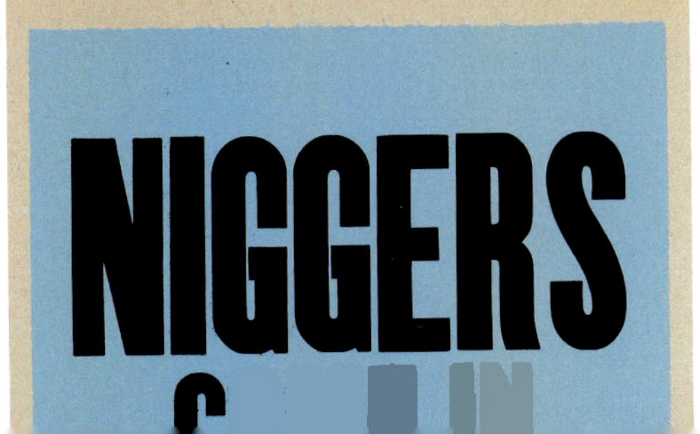

“For some, this saying means that stereotypical things said about Black people—lazy, stupid, poor—can be used against folks of other races and ethnicities, too. But for me, it is positive: It means that niggers are people, and that people, with all their attributes, good and bad, come in all colors.

Like it or not, this word is more American than apple pie.”

EVERYDAY I
DREAM
OF
BLACK
FREEDOM AND PRIDE

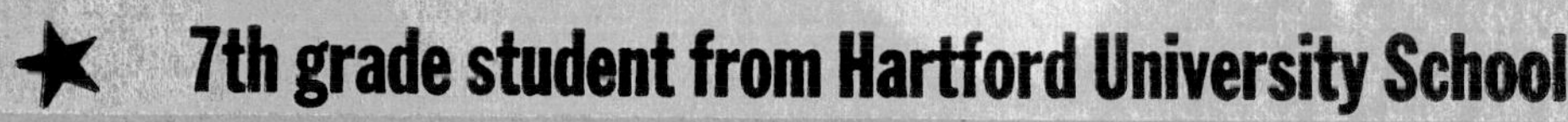

★★★★★ Kennedy Prints! P. O. Box 650 Gordo, AL 35466 ★★★★★
★★★★★ www.kennedyprints.com ★★★★★

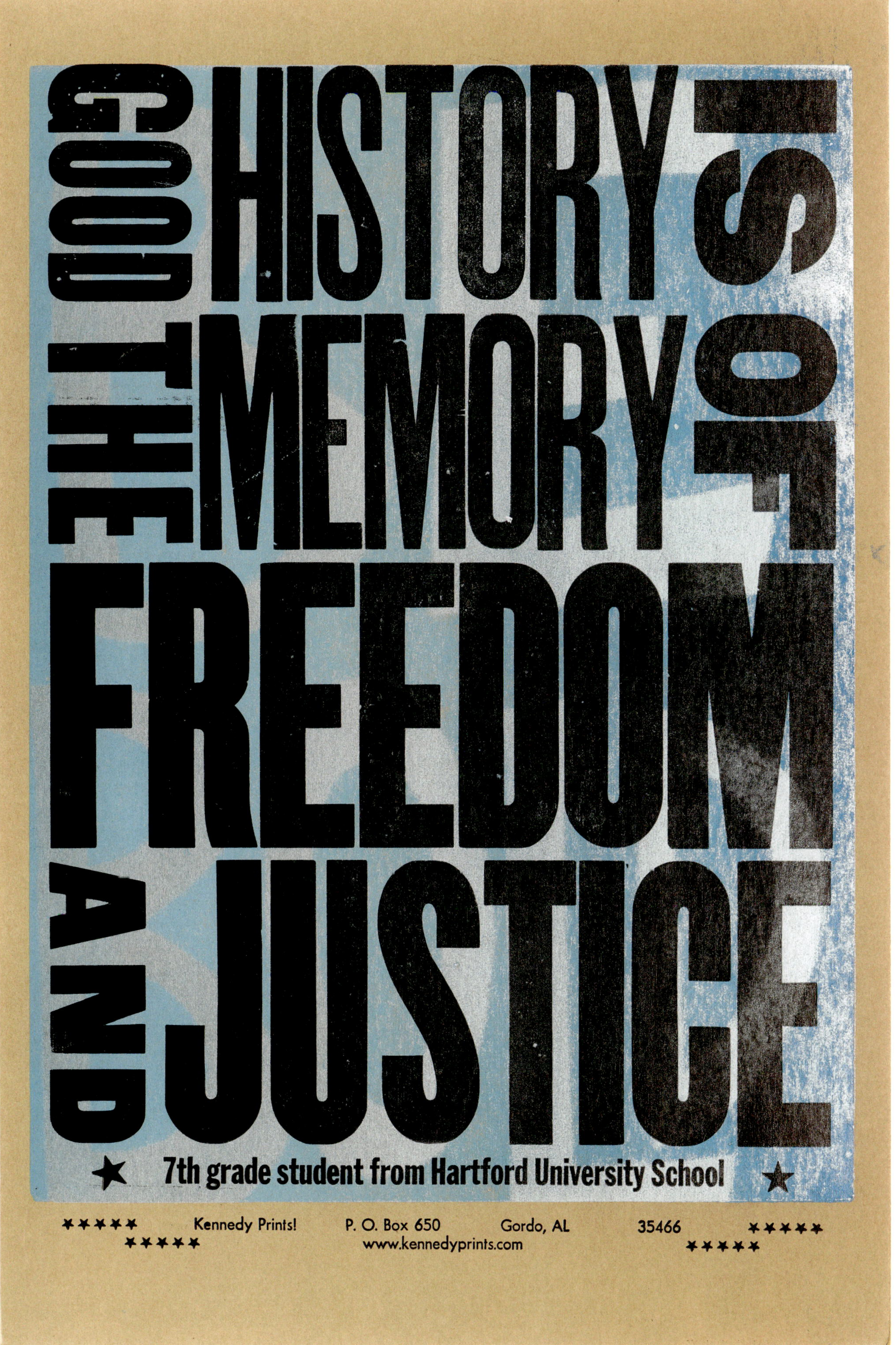
GOOD HISTORY IS
THE MEMORY OF
FREEDOM
AND JUSTICE
★ 7th grade student from Hartford University School ★
Kennedy Prints! P. O. Box 650 Gordo, AL 35466
www.kennedyprints.com

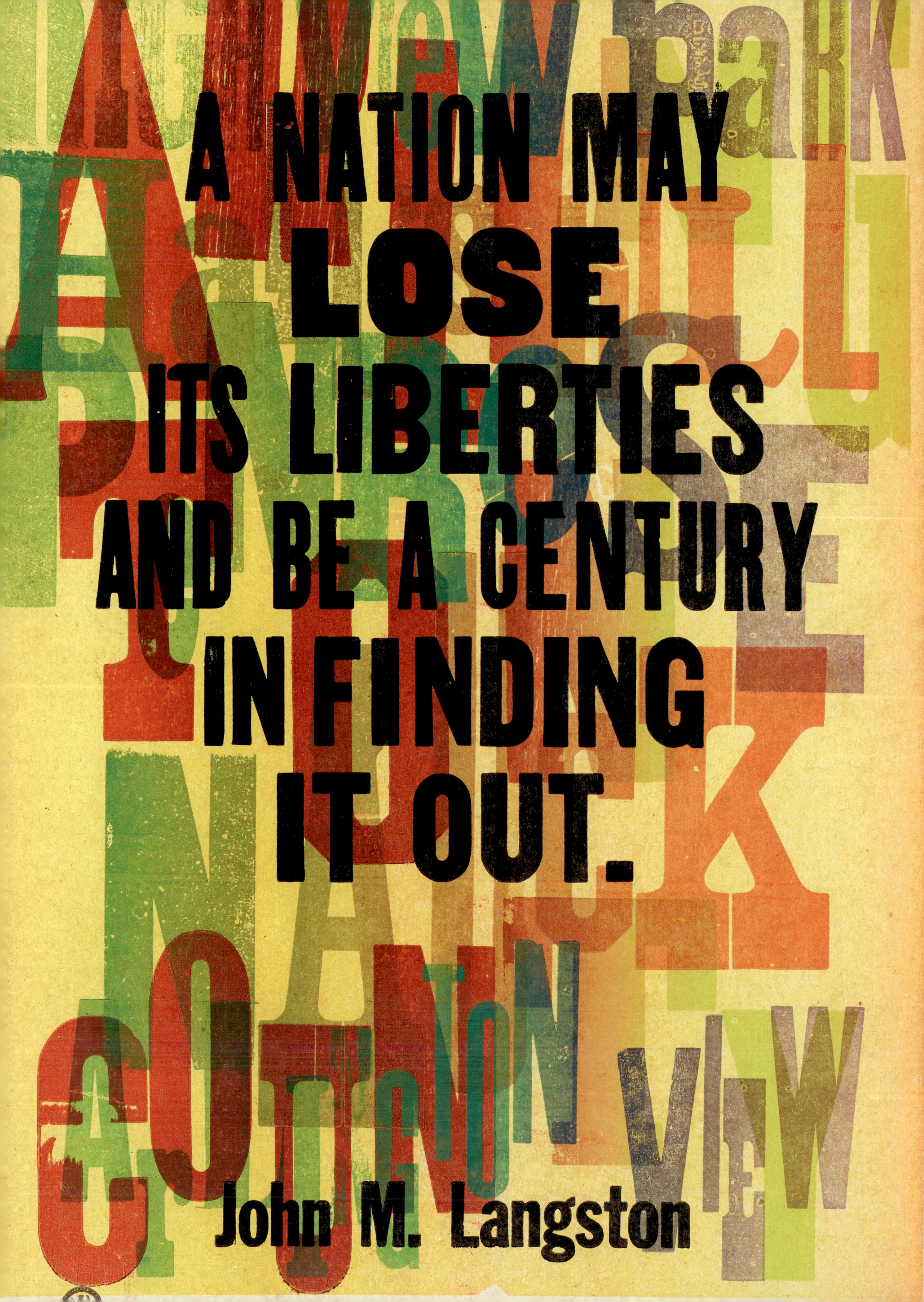
A NATION MAY
LOSE
ITS LIBERTIES
AND BE A CENTURY
IN FINDING
IT OUT.
John M. Langston

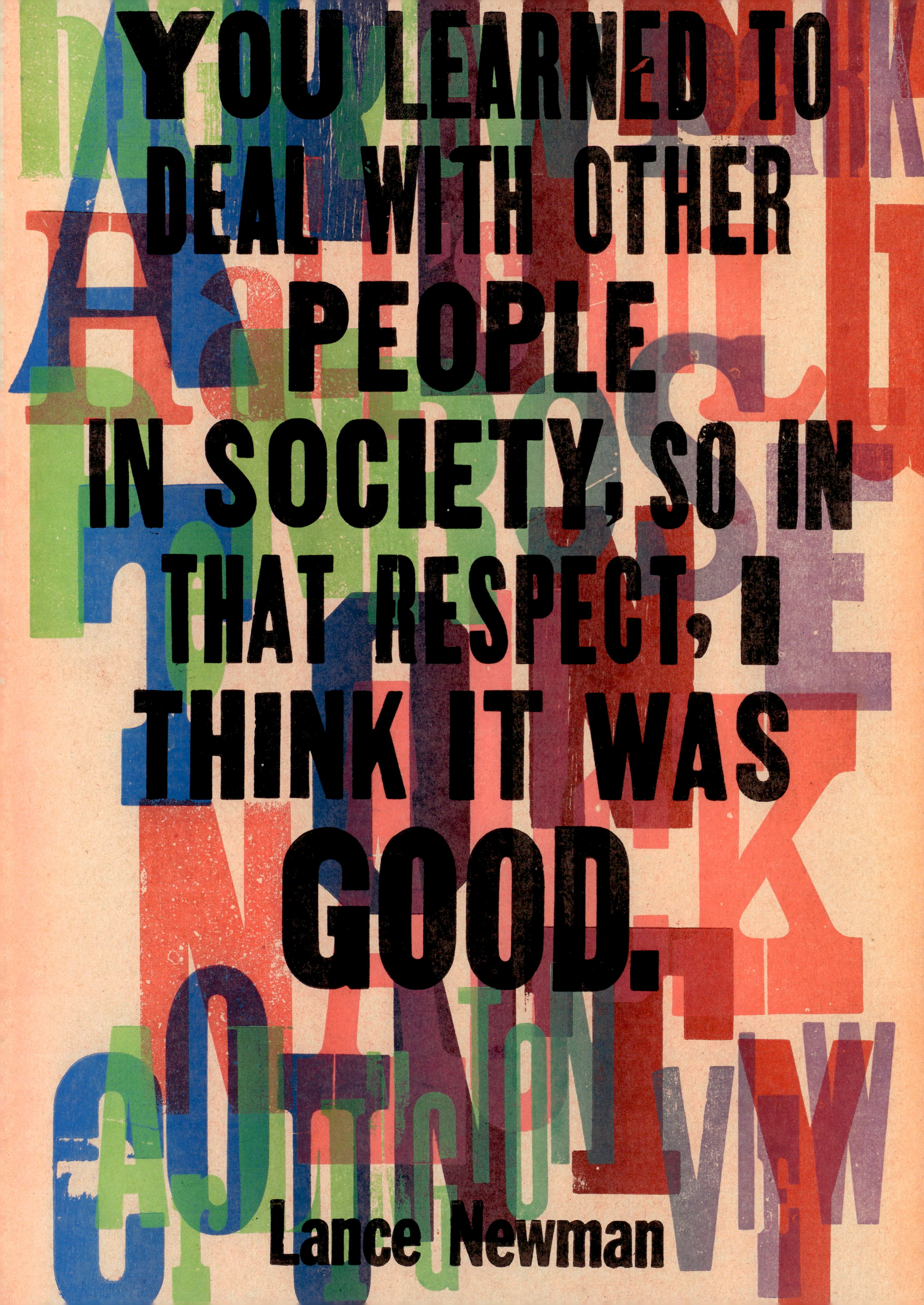
YOU LEARNED TO
DEAL WITH OTHER
PEOPLE
IN SOCIETY, SO IN
THAT RESPECT, I
THINK IT WAS
GOOD.
Lance Newman

If you are rich, money works for you. If you are poor, you work for money.

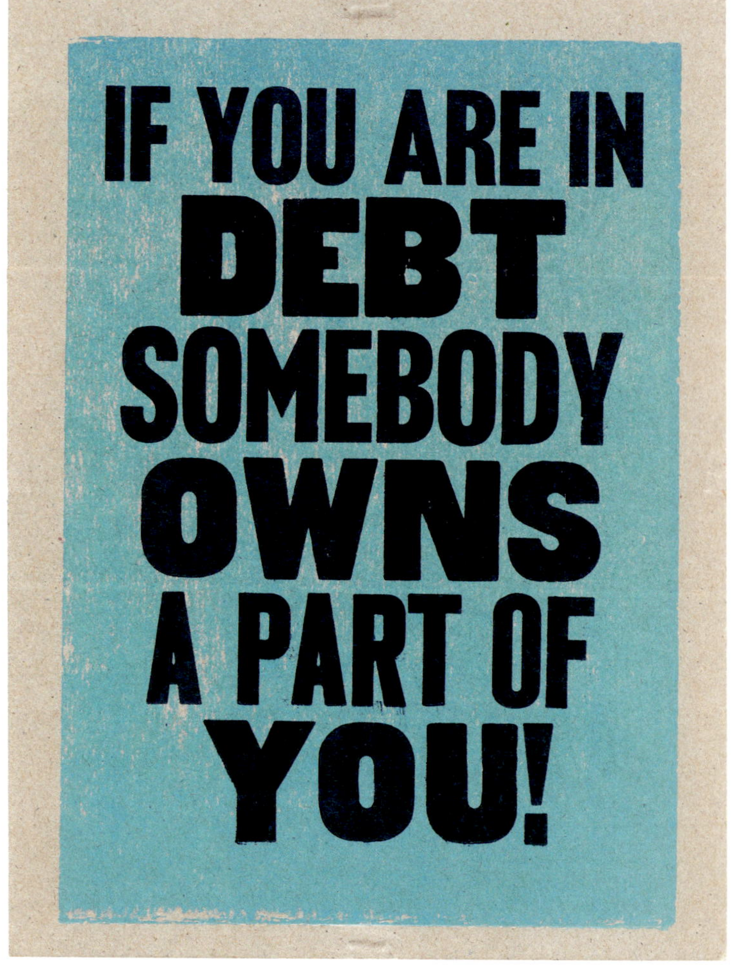

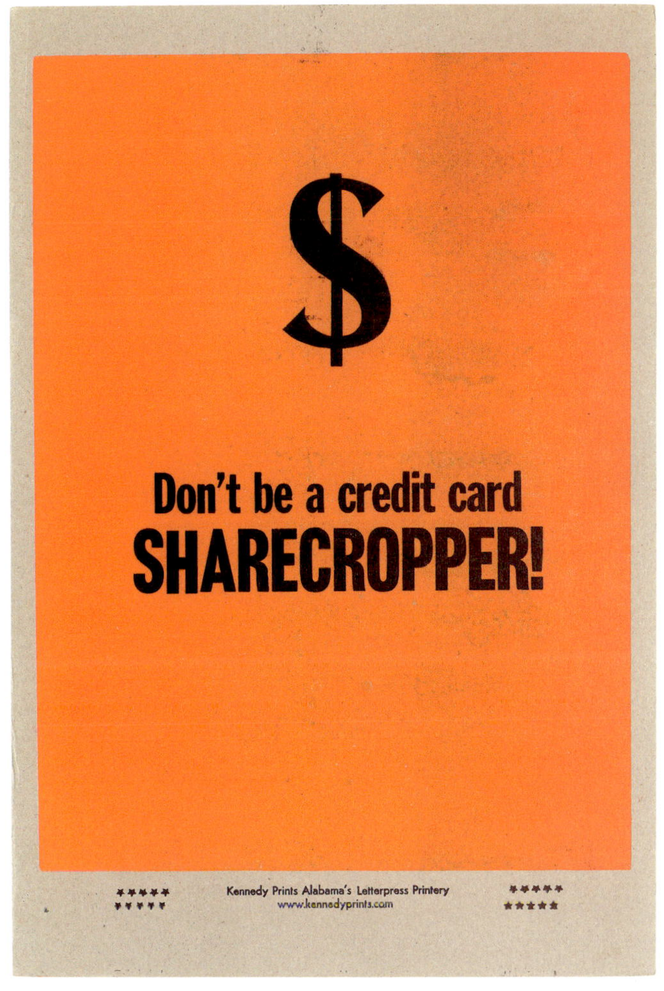
$
Don't be a credit card
SHARECROPPER!
Kennedy Prints Alabama's Letterpress Printery
www.kennedyprints.com

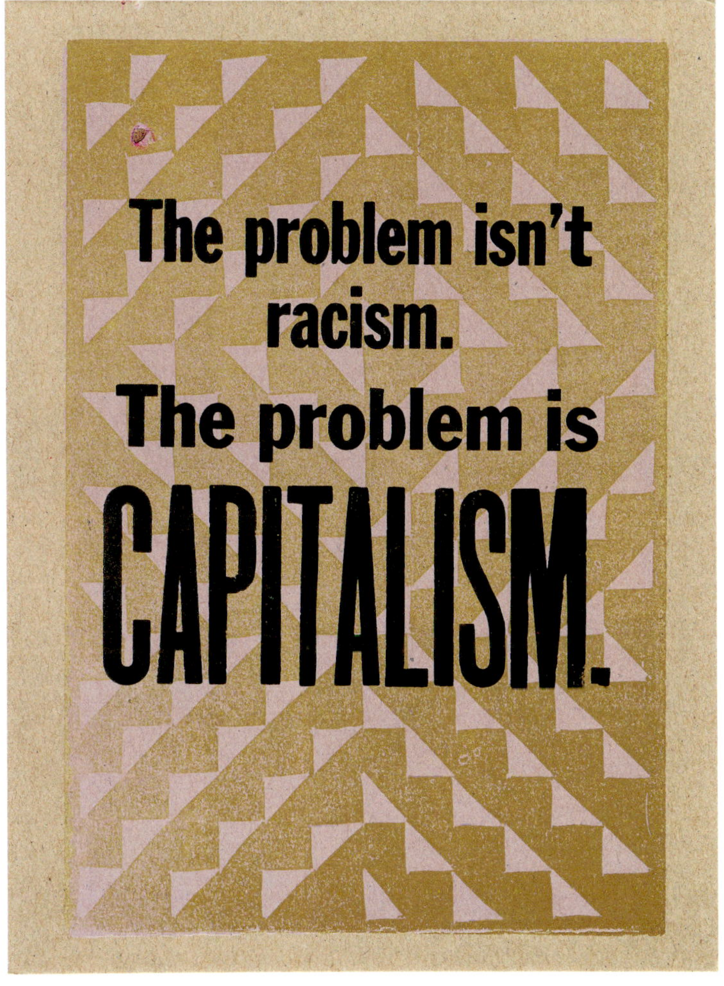
The problem isn't
racism.
The problem is
CAPITALISM.

SEND

MONEY

I don't want a job.

I want MONEY.

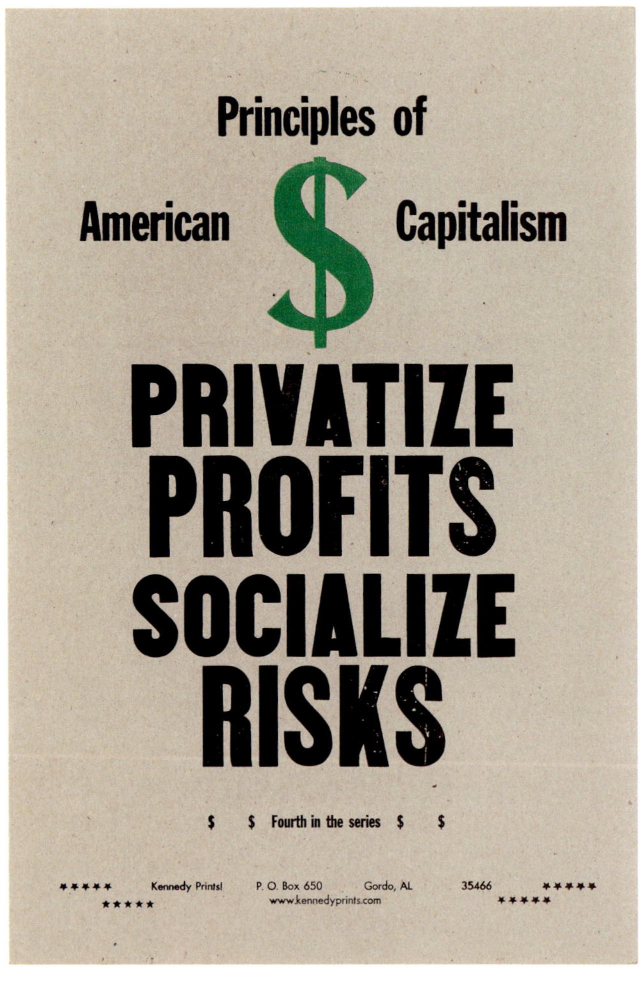
Principles of
American $ Capitalism
PRIVATIZE
PROFITS
SOCIALIZE
RISKS
$ $ Fourth in the series $ $
Kennedy Prints! P. O. Box 650 Gordo, AL 35466
www.kennedyprints.com

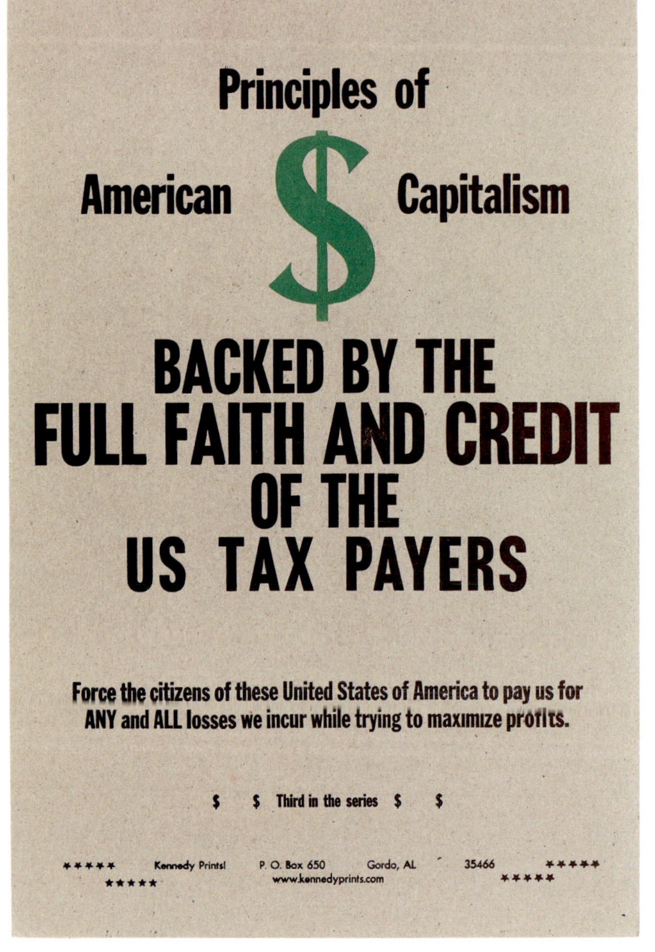
Principles of
American $ Capitalism
BACKED BY THE
FULL FAITH AND CREDIT
OF THE
US TAX PAYERS
Force the citizens of these United States of America to pay us for
ANY and ALL losses we incur while trying to maximize profits.
$ $ Third in the series $ $
Kennedy Prints! P. O. Box 650 Gordo, AL 35466
www.kennedyprints.com

Principles of

American $ Capitalism

TOO BIG TO FAIL

The citizens of these United States of America will pay the BAIL.

$ $ Second in the series $ $

Greed is so destructive. It destroys everything.

Eartha Kitt

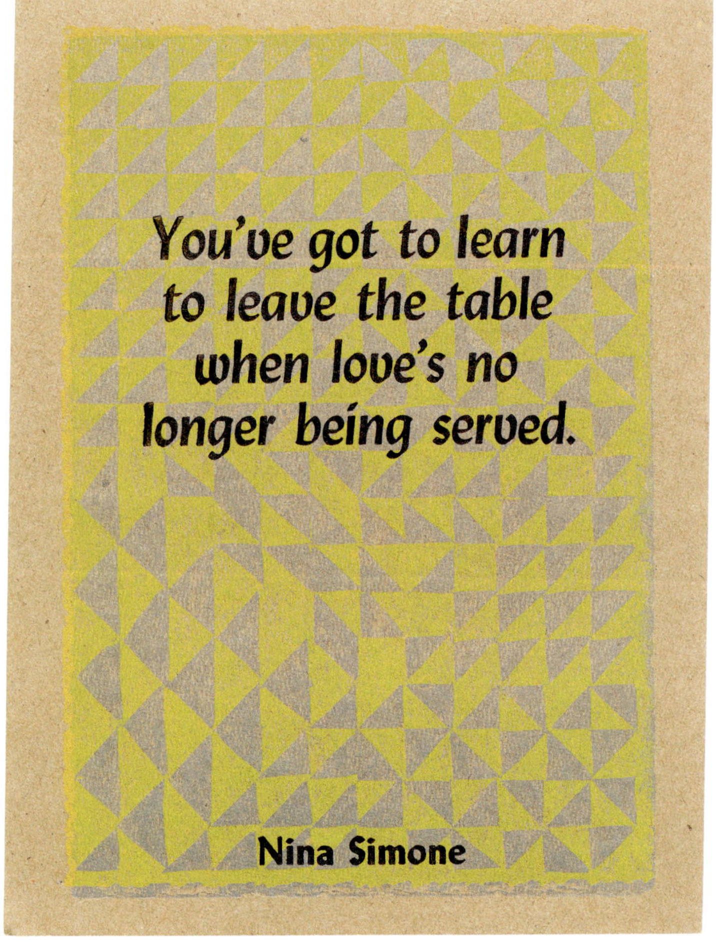

CARING
for myself,
is not
self-indulgence,
it is
self-preservation,
and that
is an act of
political warfare.

Audre Lorde

WOMEN HAVE
HOT FLASHES.

I HAVE
POWER
SURGES.

A Sista Said

Established 1949 KennedyPrints.com

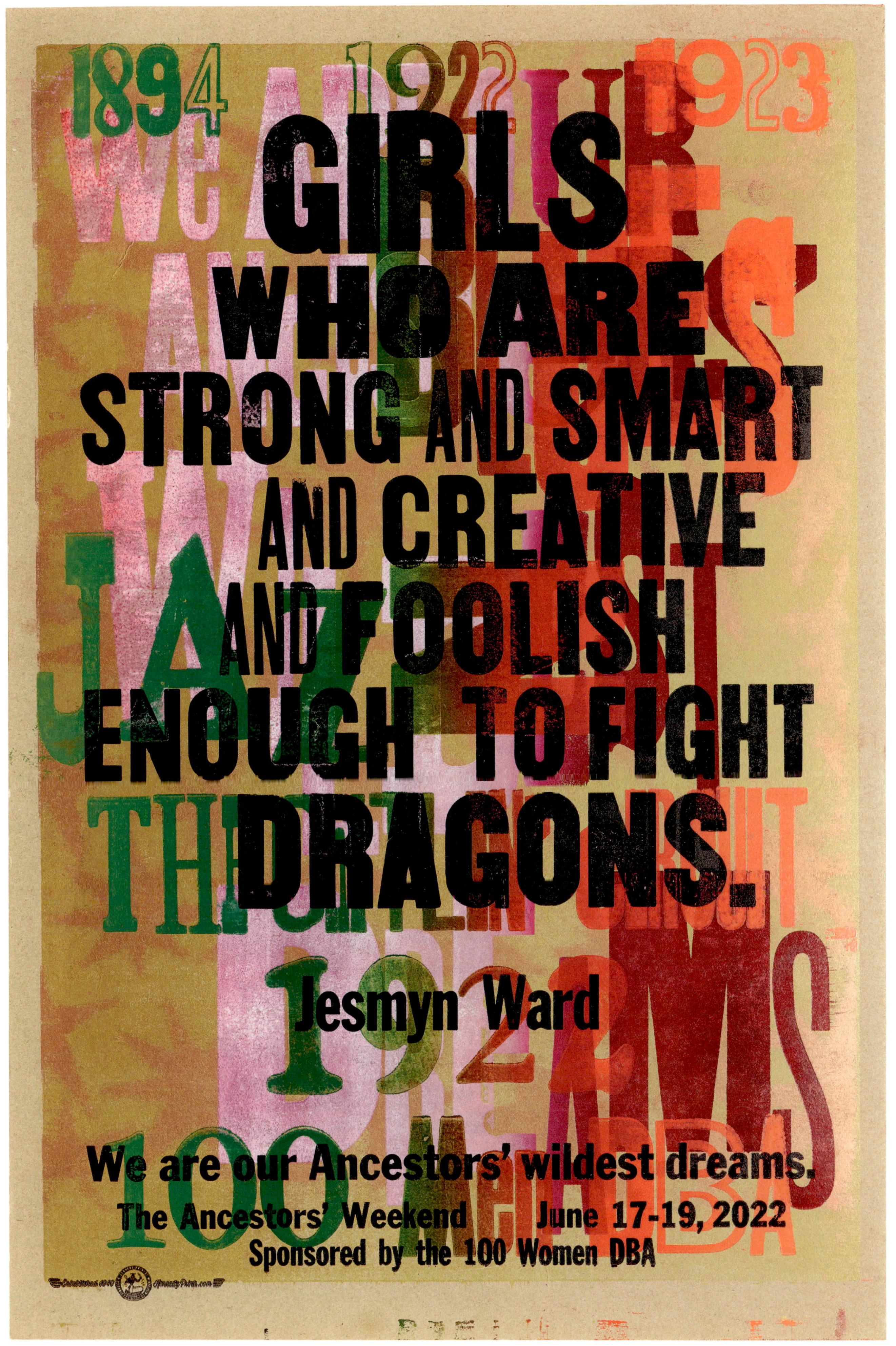
GIRLS
WHO ARE
STRONG AND SMART
AND CREATIVE
AND FOOLISH
ENOUGH TO FIGHT
DRAGONS.
Jesmyn Ward
We are our Ancestors' wildest dreams.
The Ancestors' Weekend June 17-19, 2022
Sponsored by the 100 Women DBA

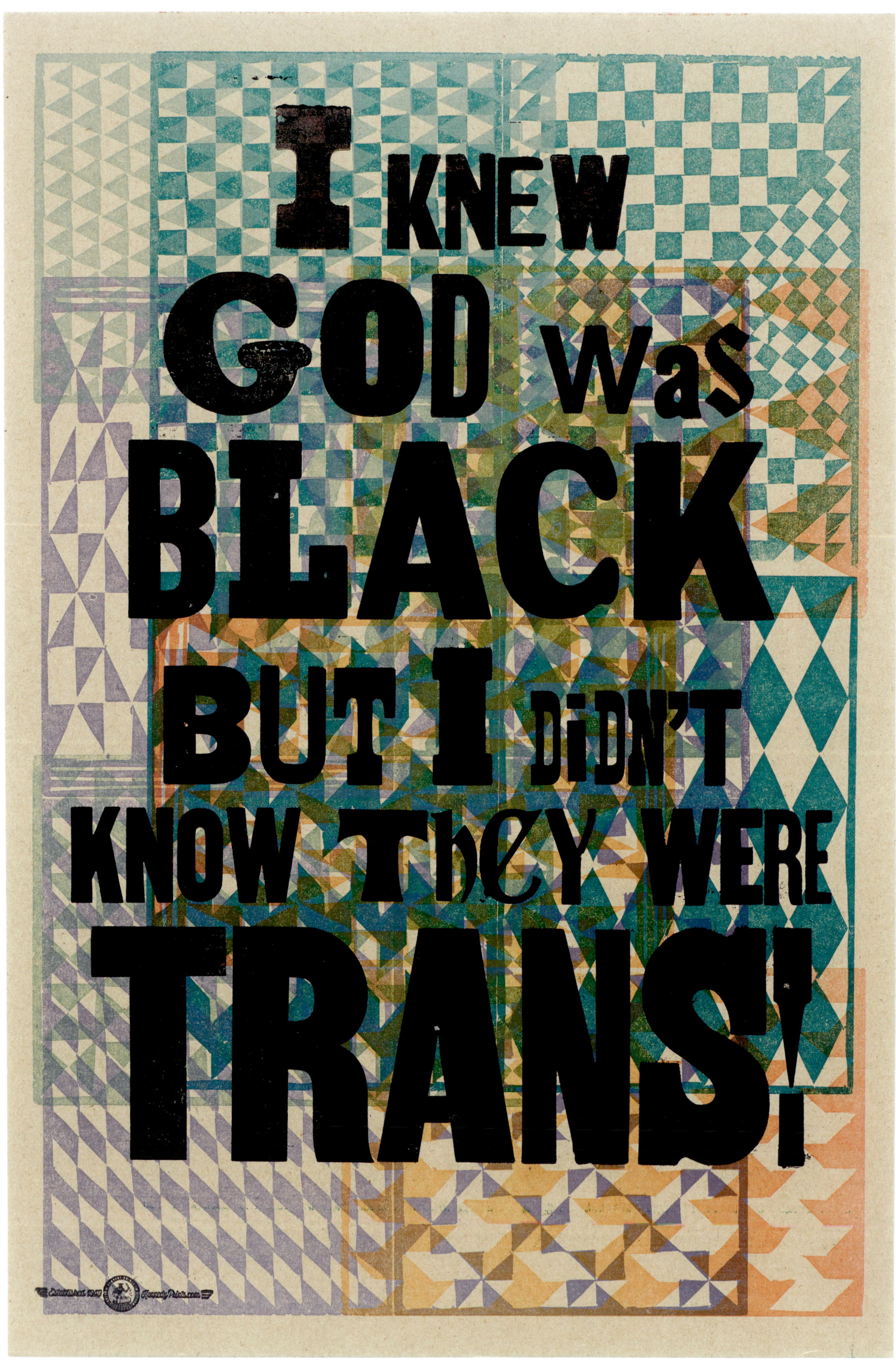
I KNEW
GOD WAS
BLACK
BUT I DIDN'T
KNOW THEY WERE
TRANS!
Established 1949
KennedyPrints.com

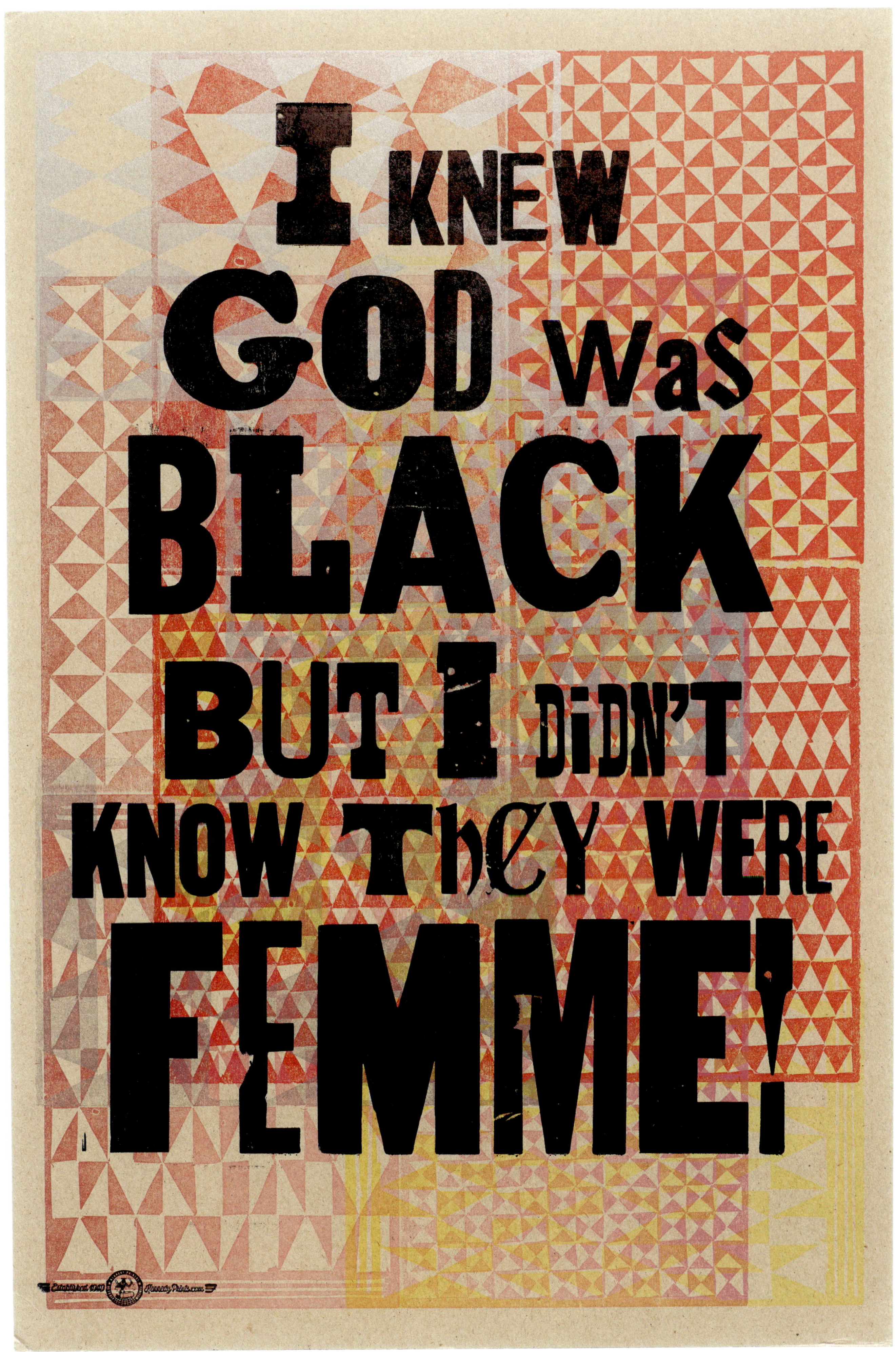
I KNEW
GOD WAS
BLACK
BUT I DIDN'T
KNOW THEY WERE
FEMME!
KennedyPrints.com

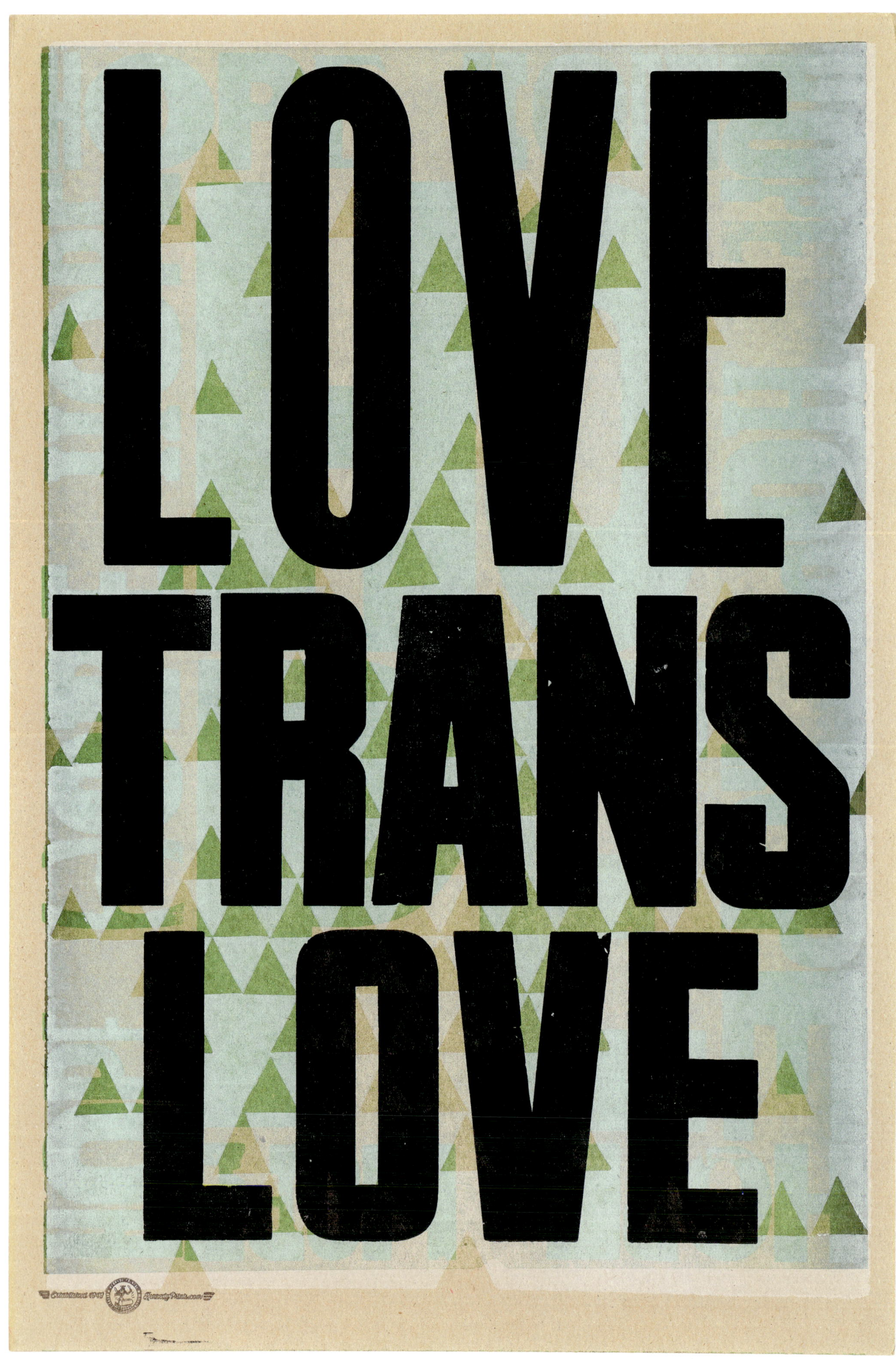
LOVE
TRANS
LOVE

I ain't afraid to live in a world with Trans people.

I am afraid to live in a world without them.

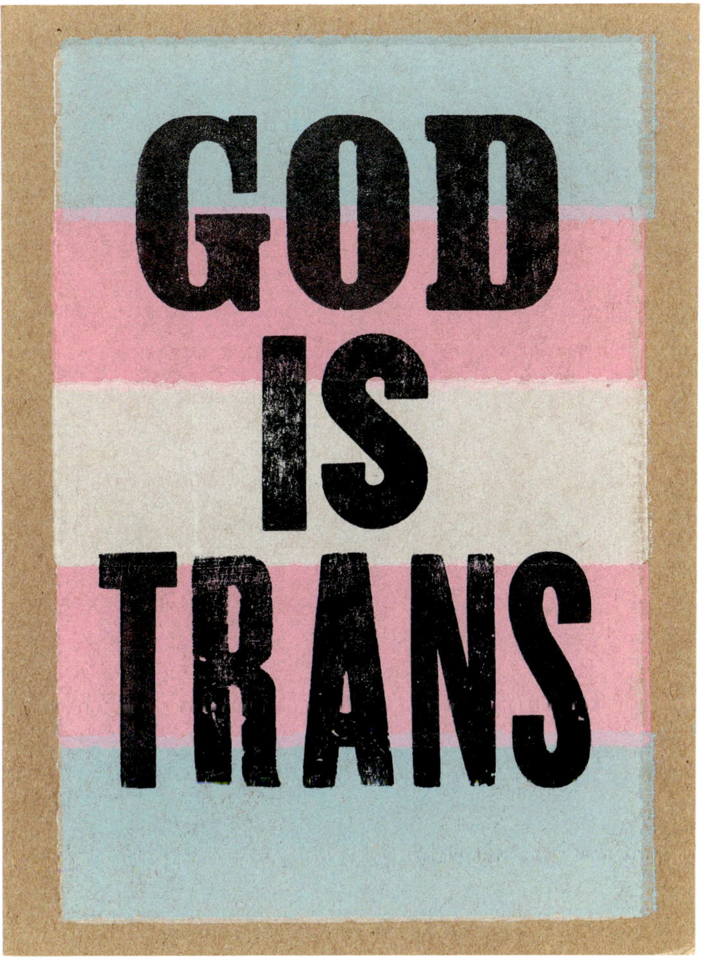

We are Black men
who are proudly gay.
What we offer is our
lives, our love, our
visions. We are risin'
to the love we all need.
We are coming home
with our heads
held up high.

Joseph F. Beam

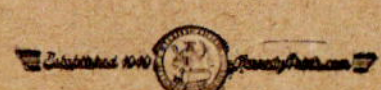

REMEMBER
STONEWALL
1969

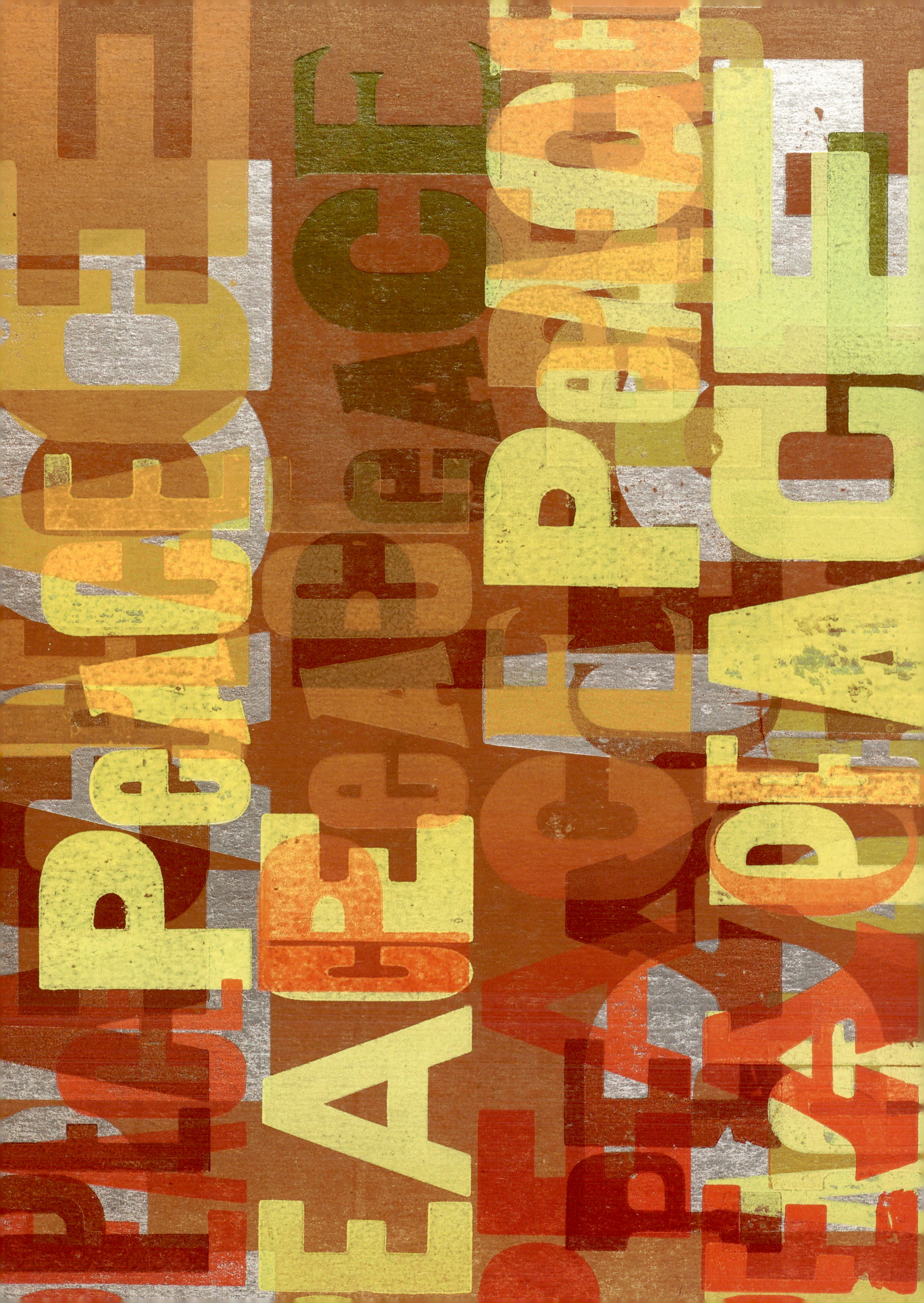

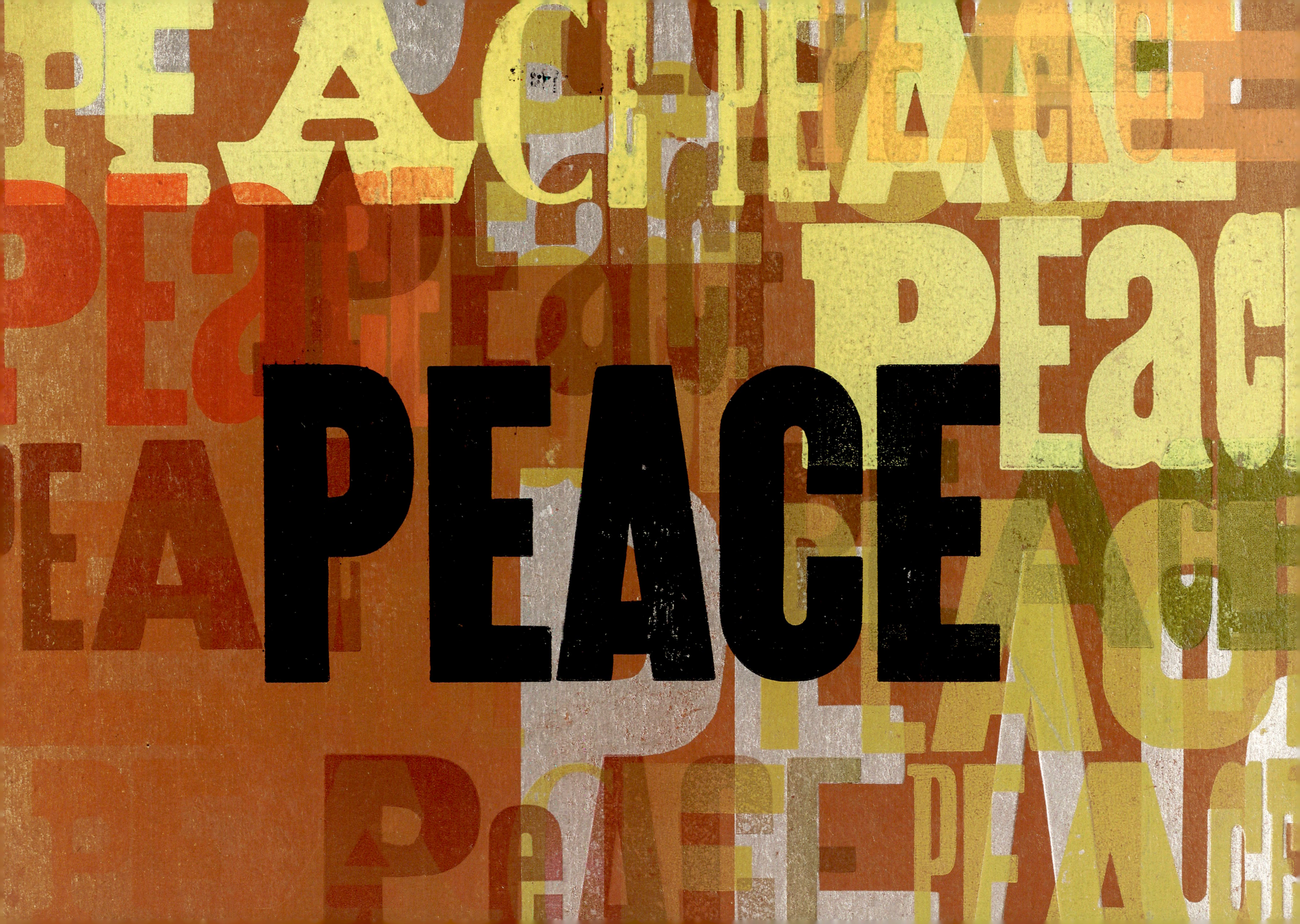
PEACE

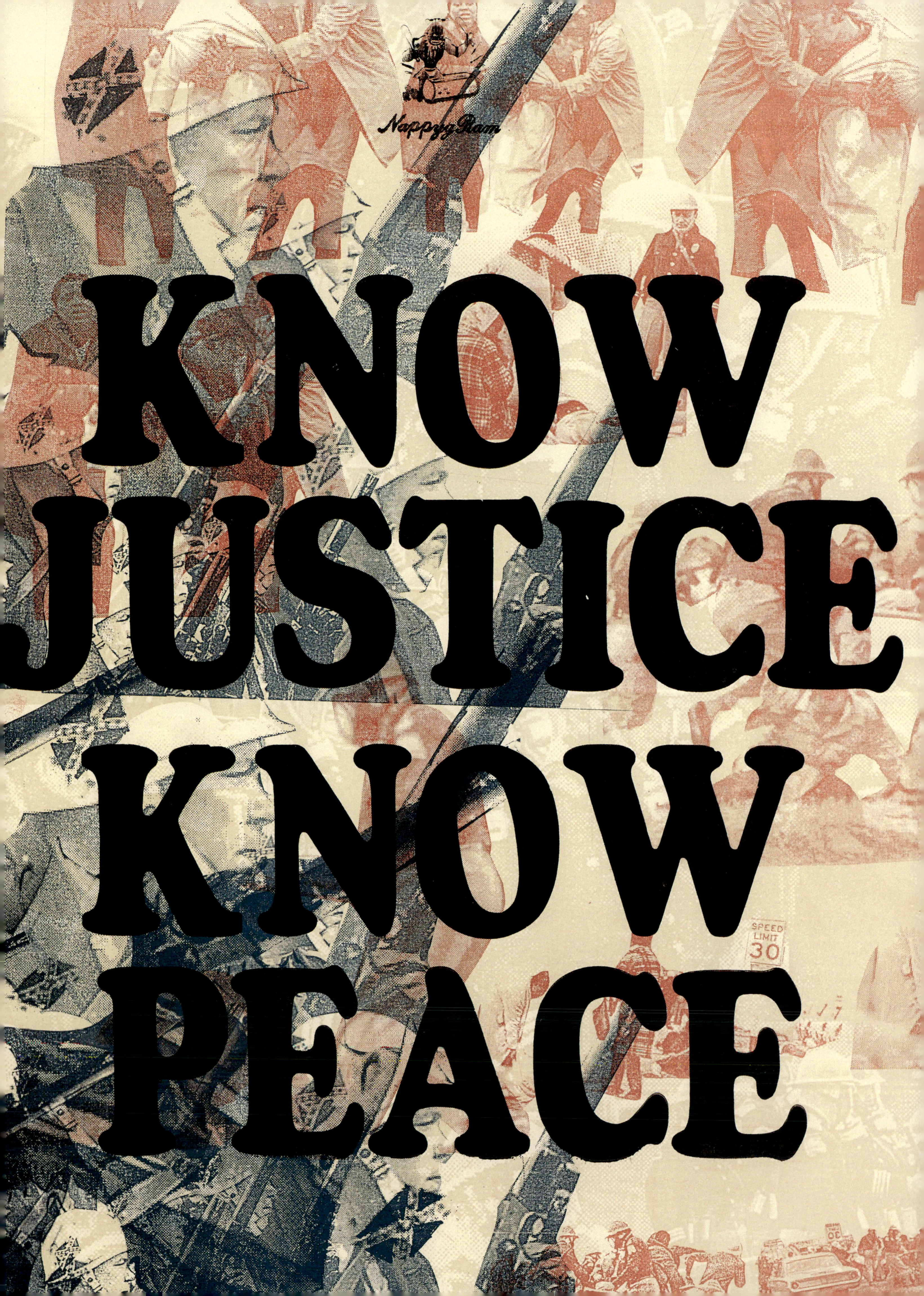
KNOW
JUSTICE
KNOW
PEACE
SPEED LIMIT 30

“During Jim Crow, oppression seemed like just a personal limitation for Black folks—you can't go there, you can't sit here. Now it's clear that injustice is a larger, institutionalized force that harms people of many backgrounds and identities. It penalizes the masses and privileges the few—just like it was designed to do.”

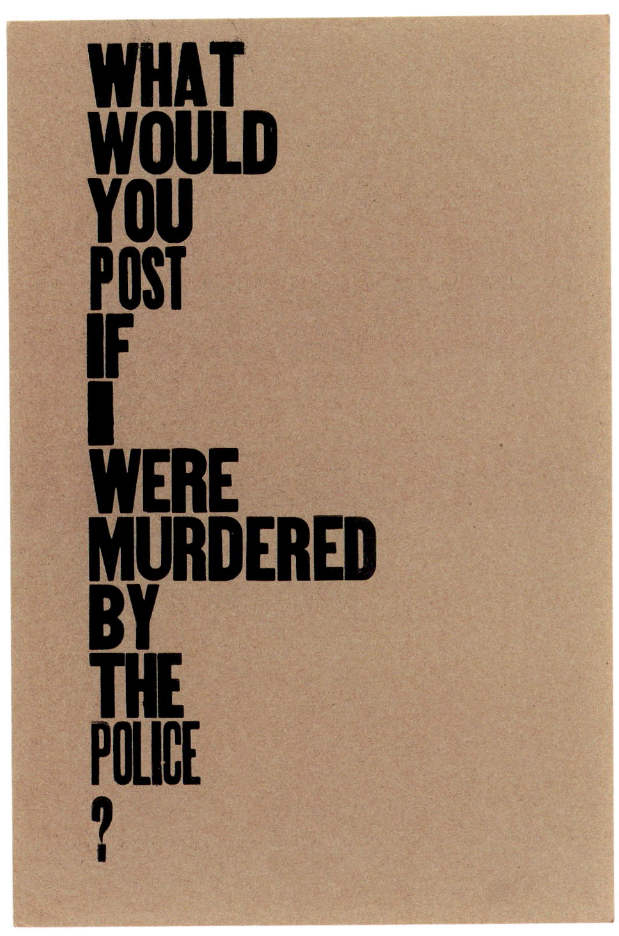

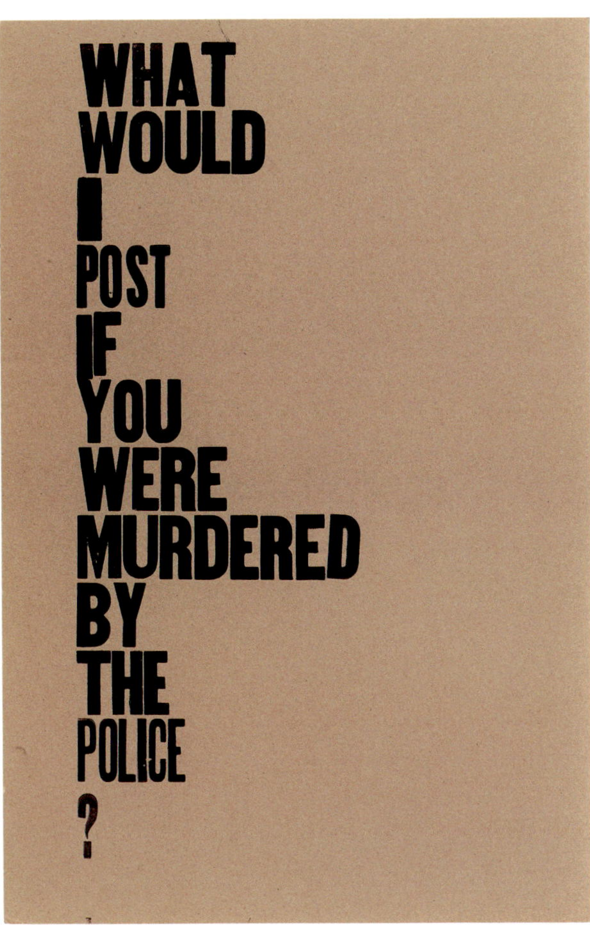

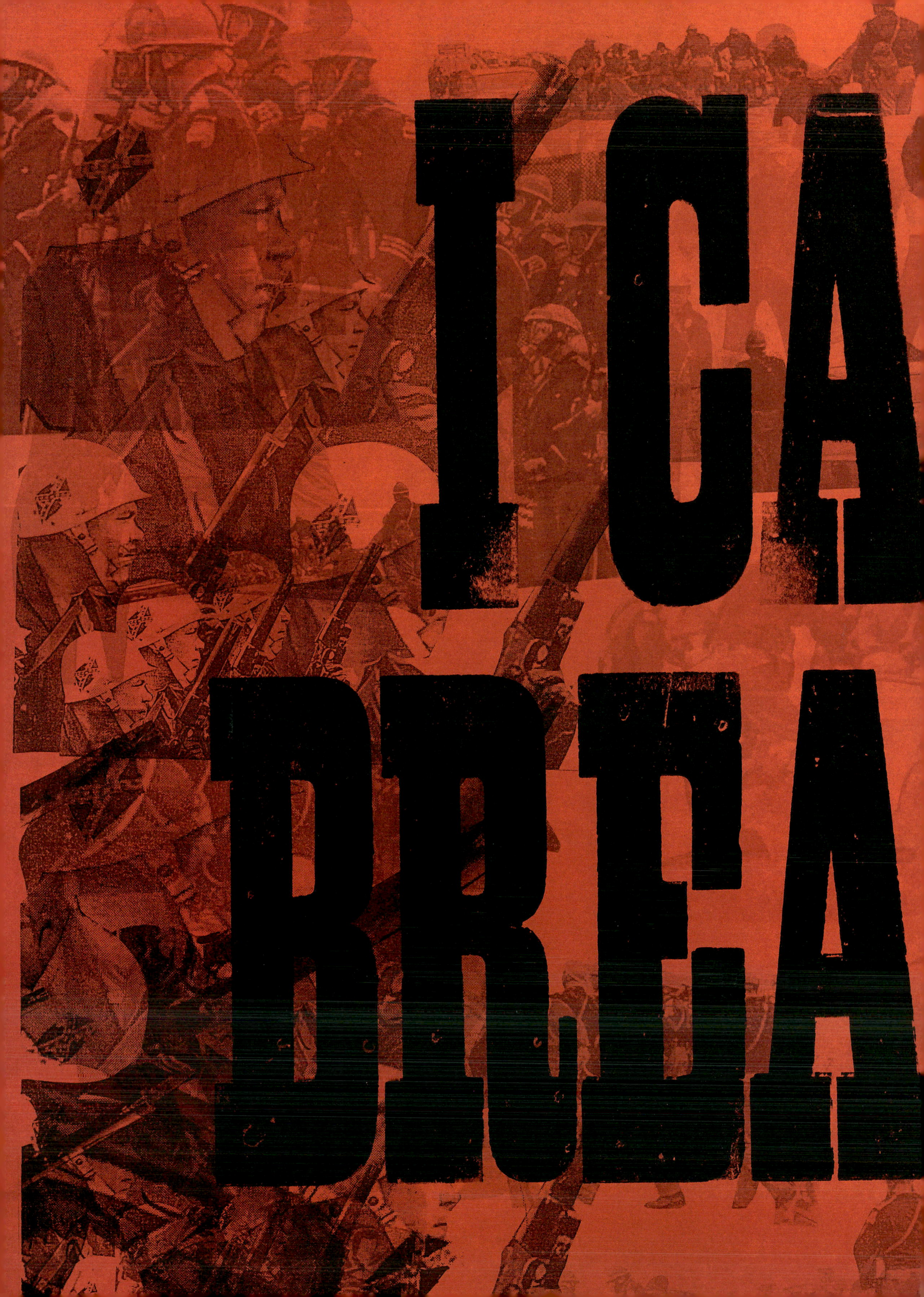
ICA
BREA

N'T
THE!

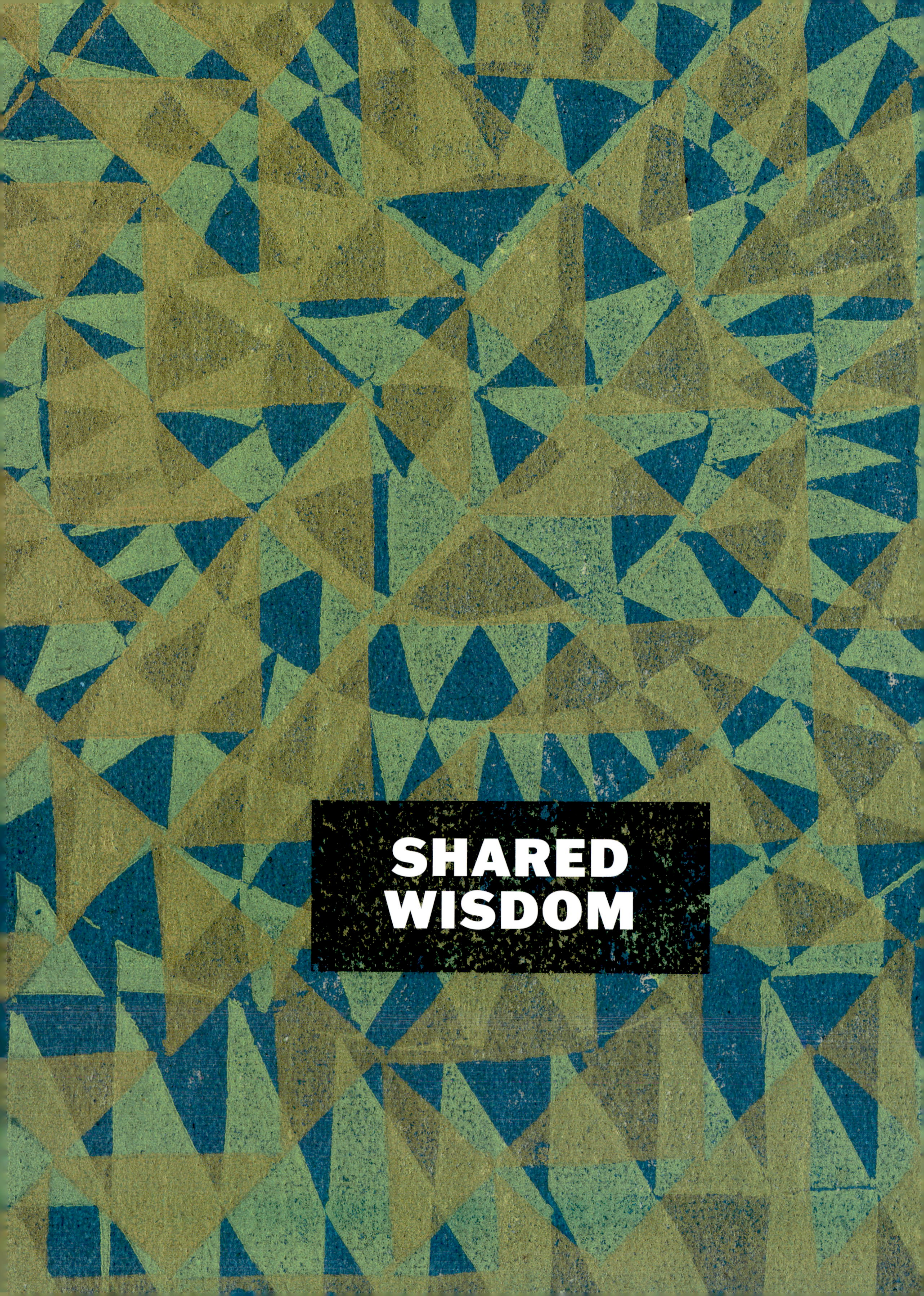
SHARED
WISDOM

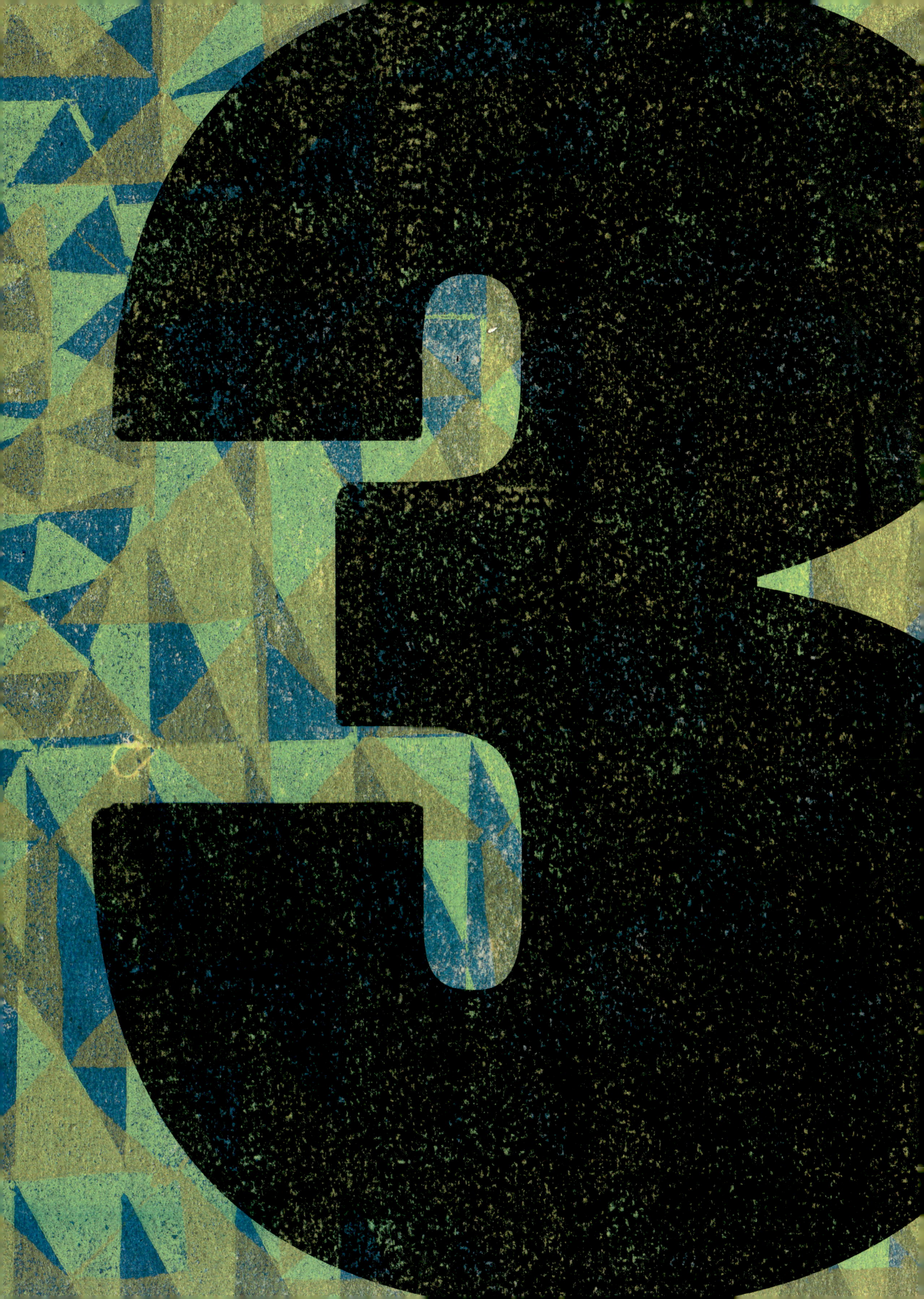

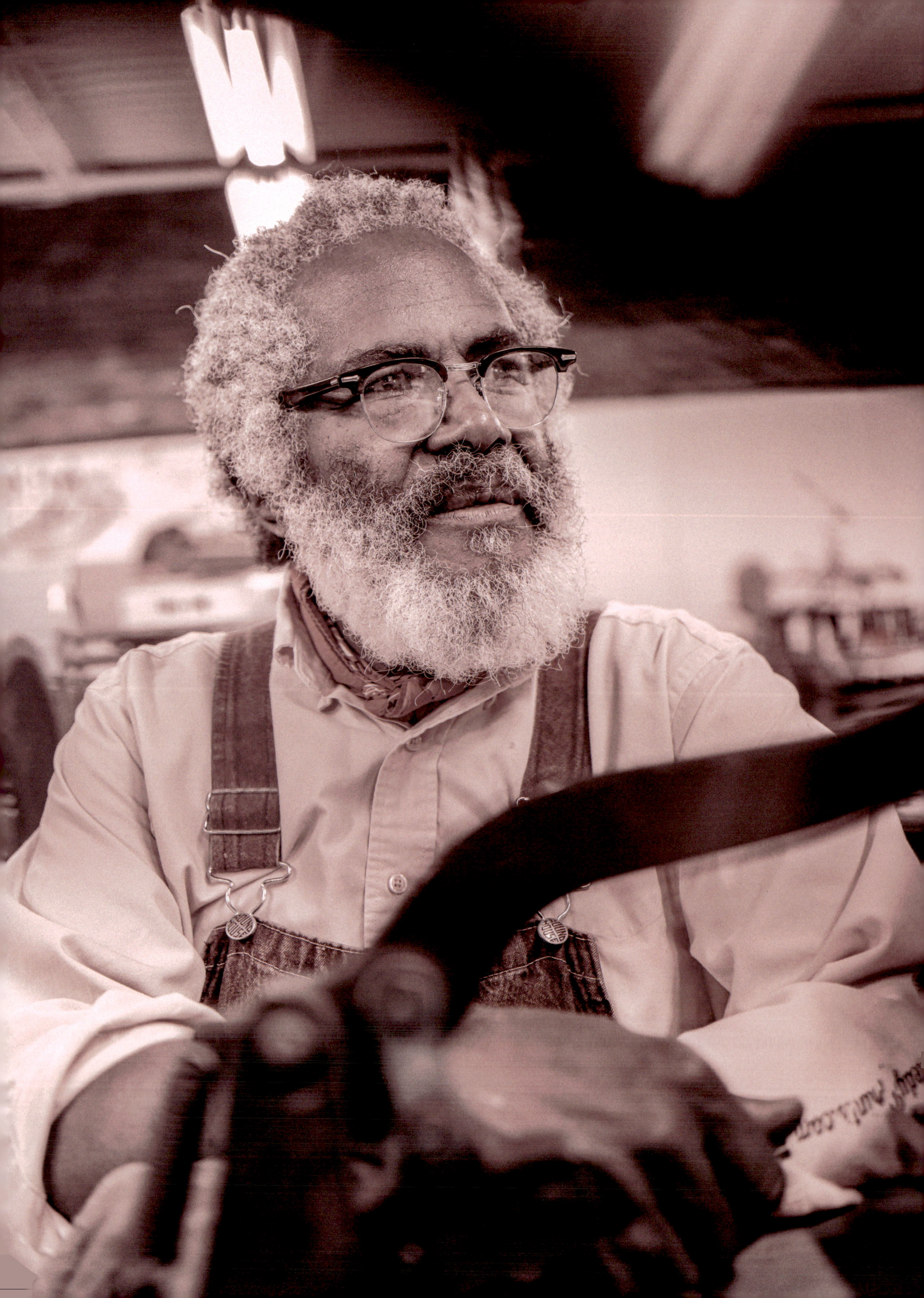

“I have always been fascinated with proverbs, riddles, and aphorisms—these little gems of **shared wisdom**, normally ten words or less, that teach universal lessons. If you listen, you will hear them everywhere.”

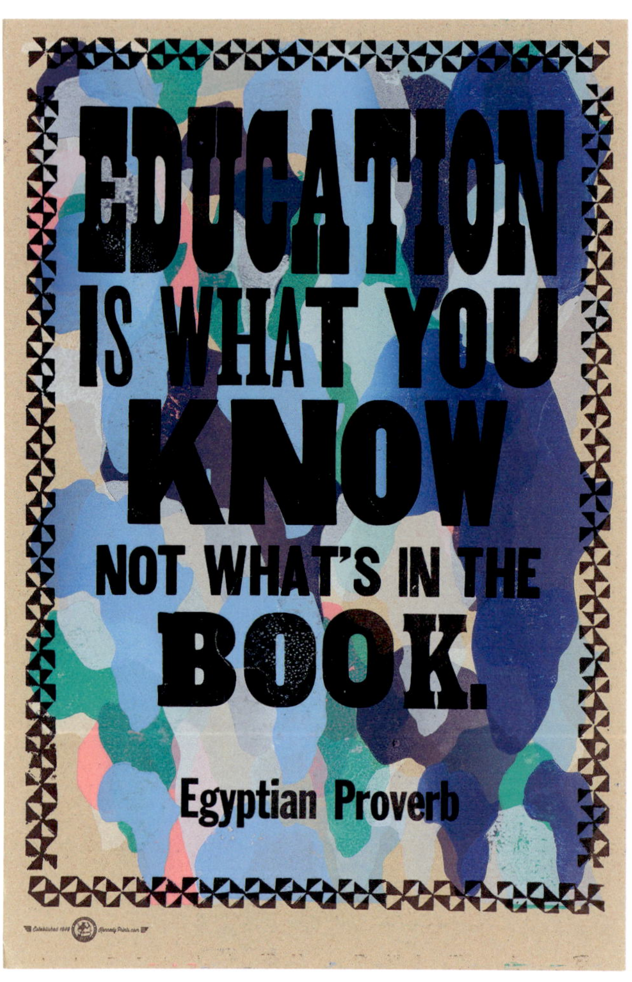
EDUCATION
IS WHAT YOU
KNOW
NOT WHAT'S IN THE
BOOK.
Egyptian Proverb

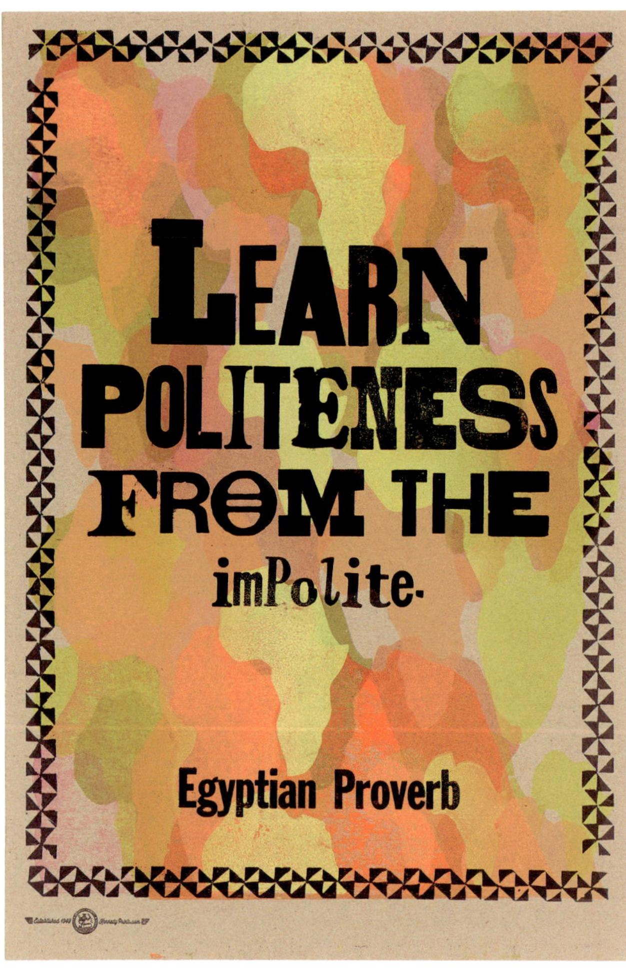
LEARN
POLITENESS
FROM THE
imPolite.
Egyptian Proverb

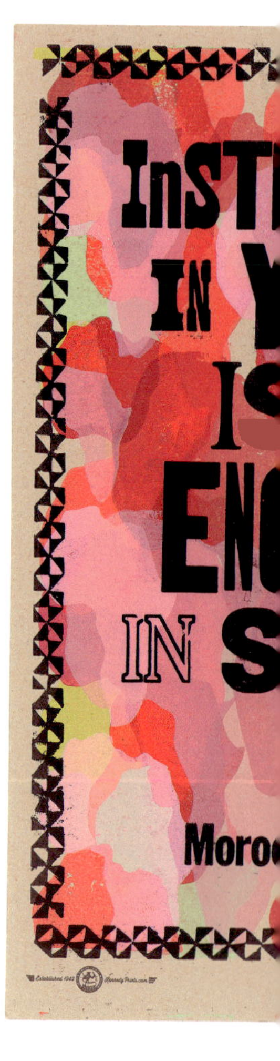

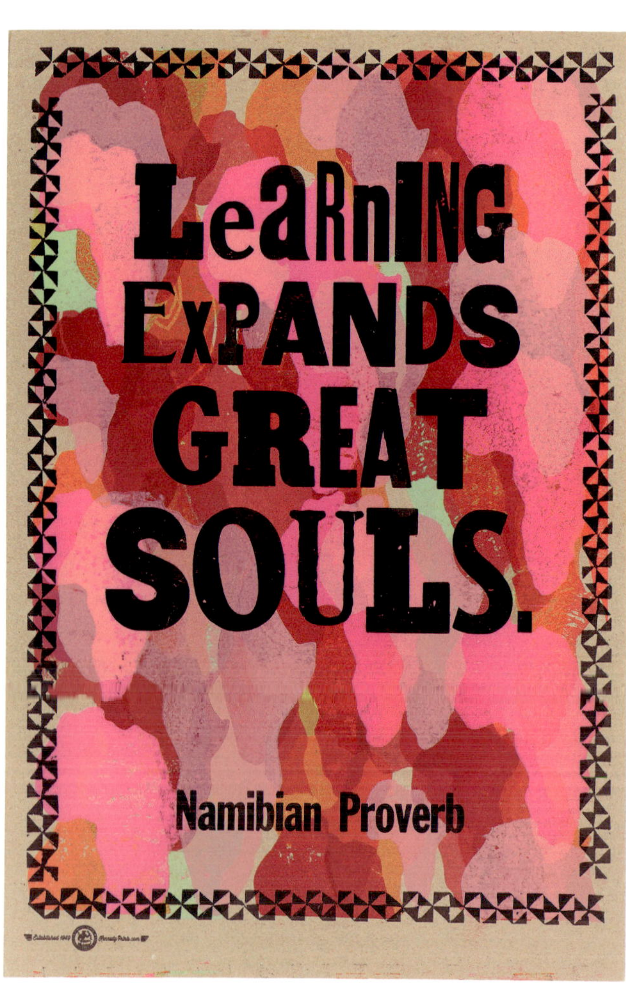
LeaRnING
ExPANDS
GREAT
SOULS.
Namibian Proverb

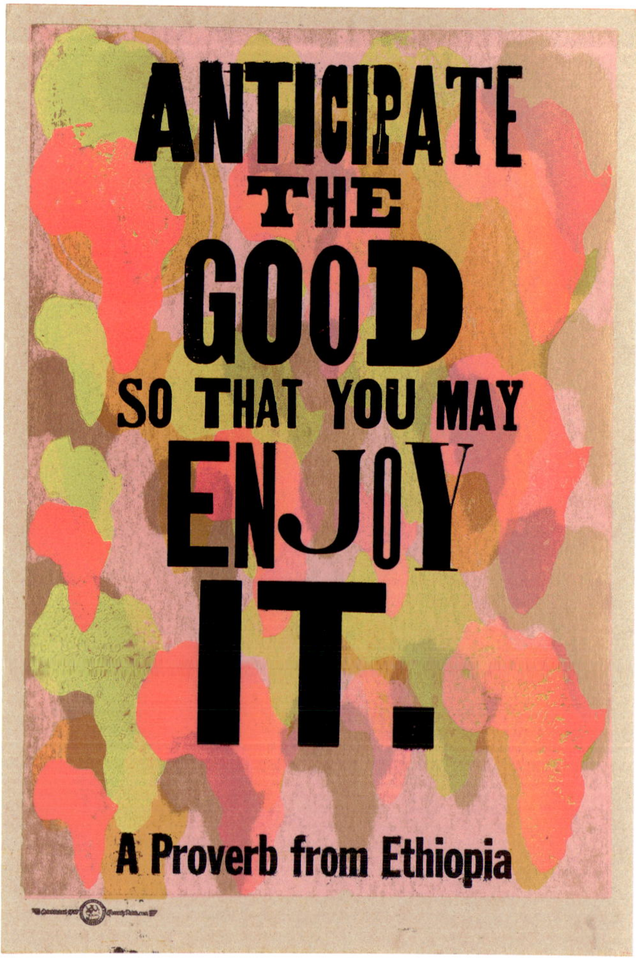
ANTICIPATE
THE
GOOD
SO THAT YOU MAY
ENJOY
IT.
A Proverb from Ethiopia

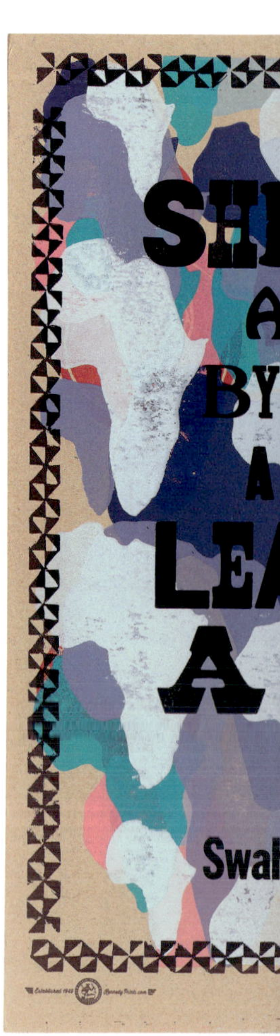

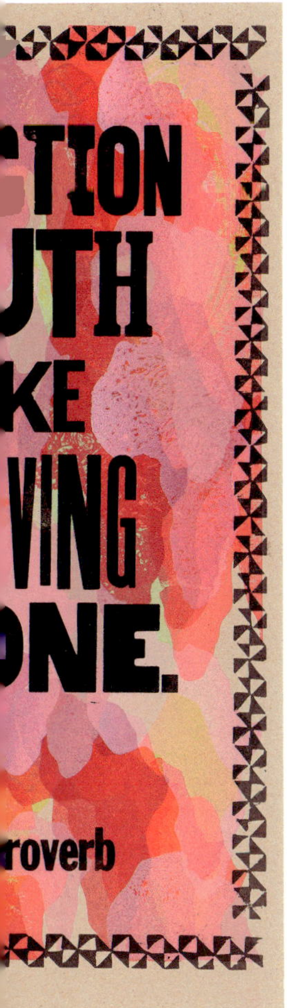

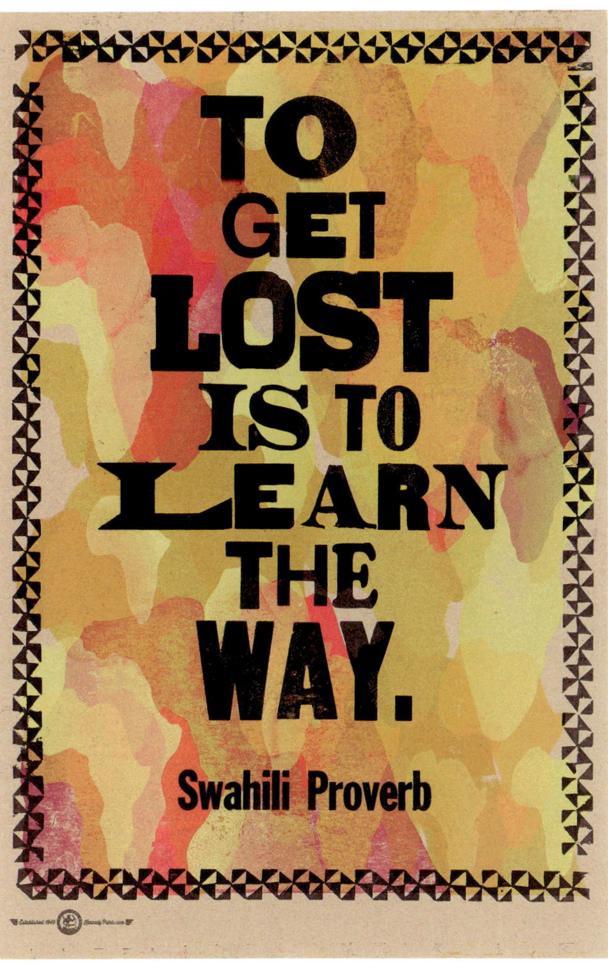
TO
GET
LOST
IS TO
LEARN
THE
WAY.
Swahili Proverb

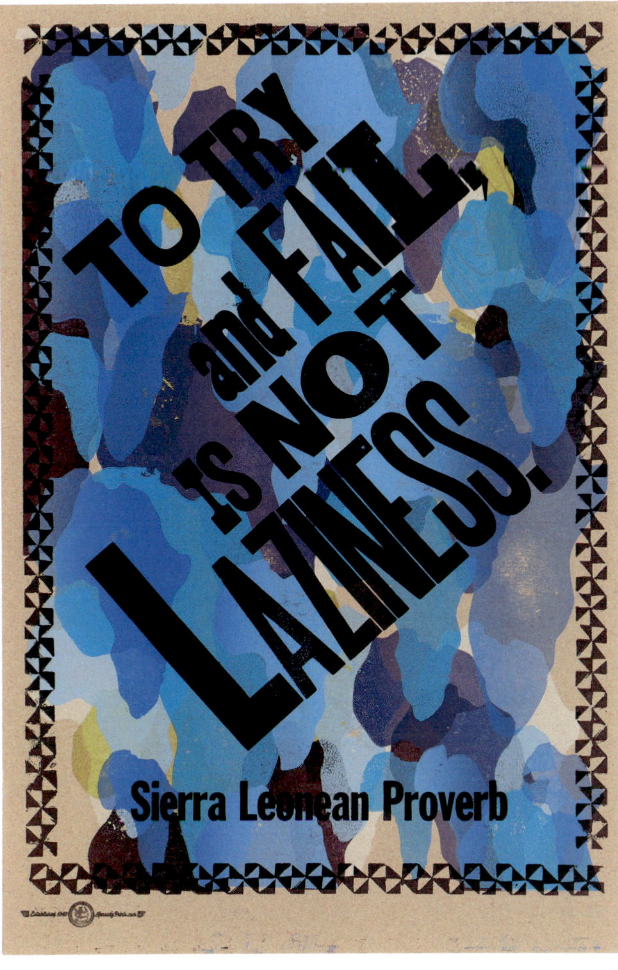
TO TRY
and FAIL,
IS NOT
LAZINESS.
Sierra Leonean Proverb

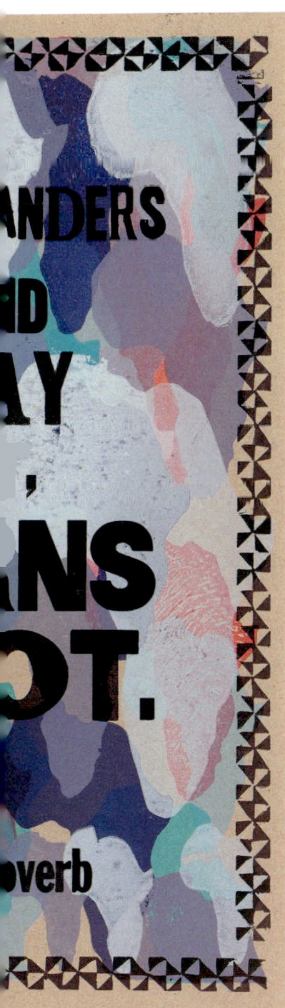

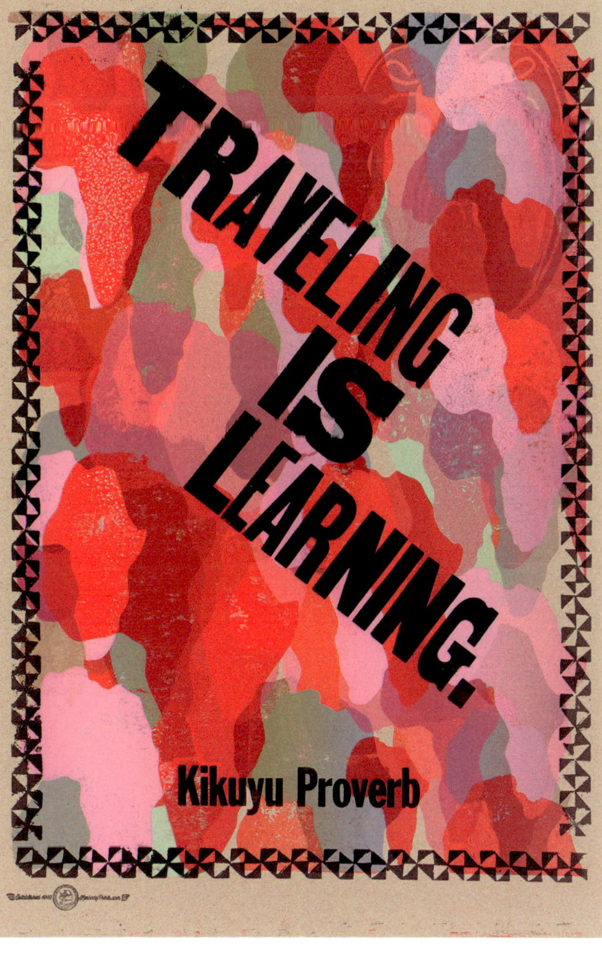
TRAVELING
IS
LEARNING.
Kikuyu Proverb

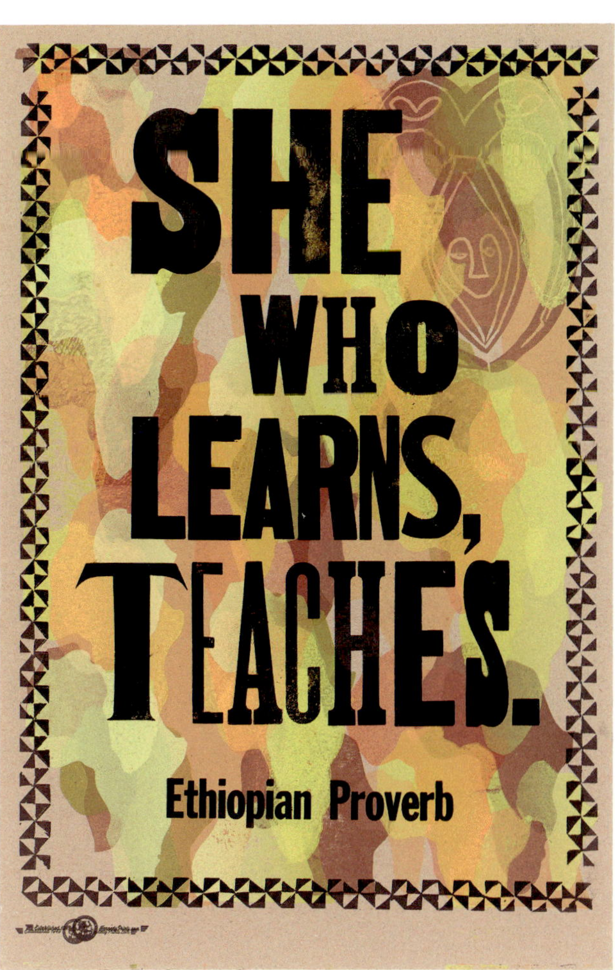
SHE
WHO
LEARNS,
TEACHES.
Ethiopian Proverb

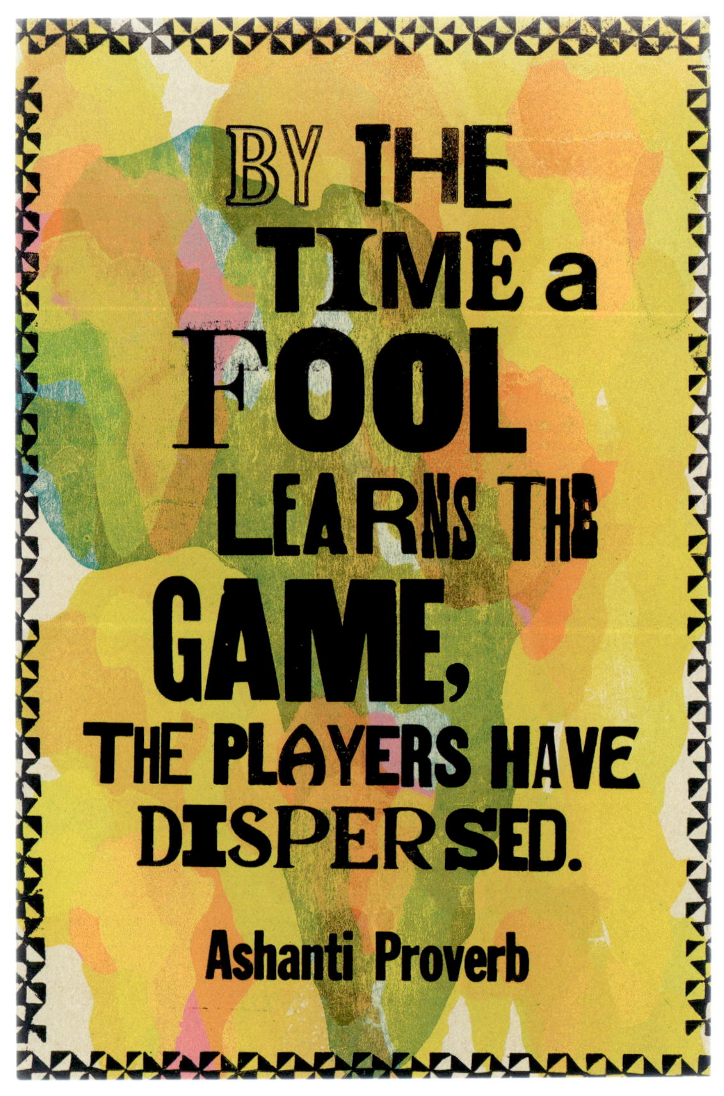
BY THE
TIME a
FOOL
LEARNS THE
GAME,
THE PLAYERS HAVE
DISPERSED.
Ashanti Proverb

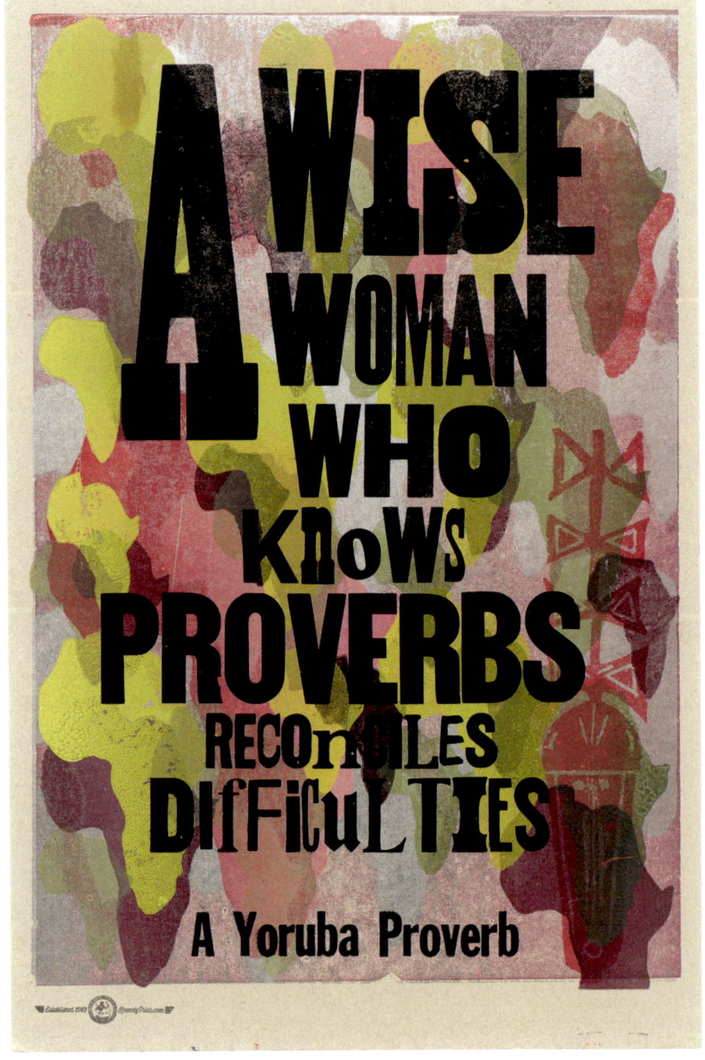
A WISE
WOMAN
WHO
KNOWS
PROVERBS
RECONCILES
DIFFICULTIES
A Yoruba Proverb

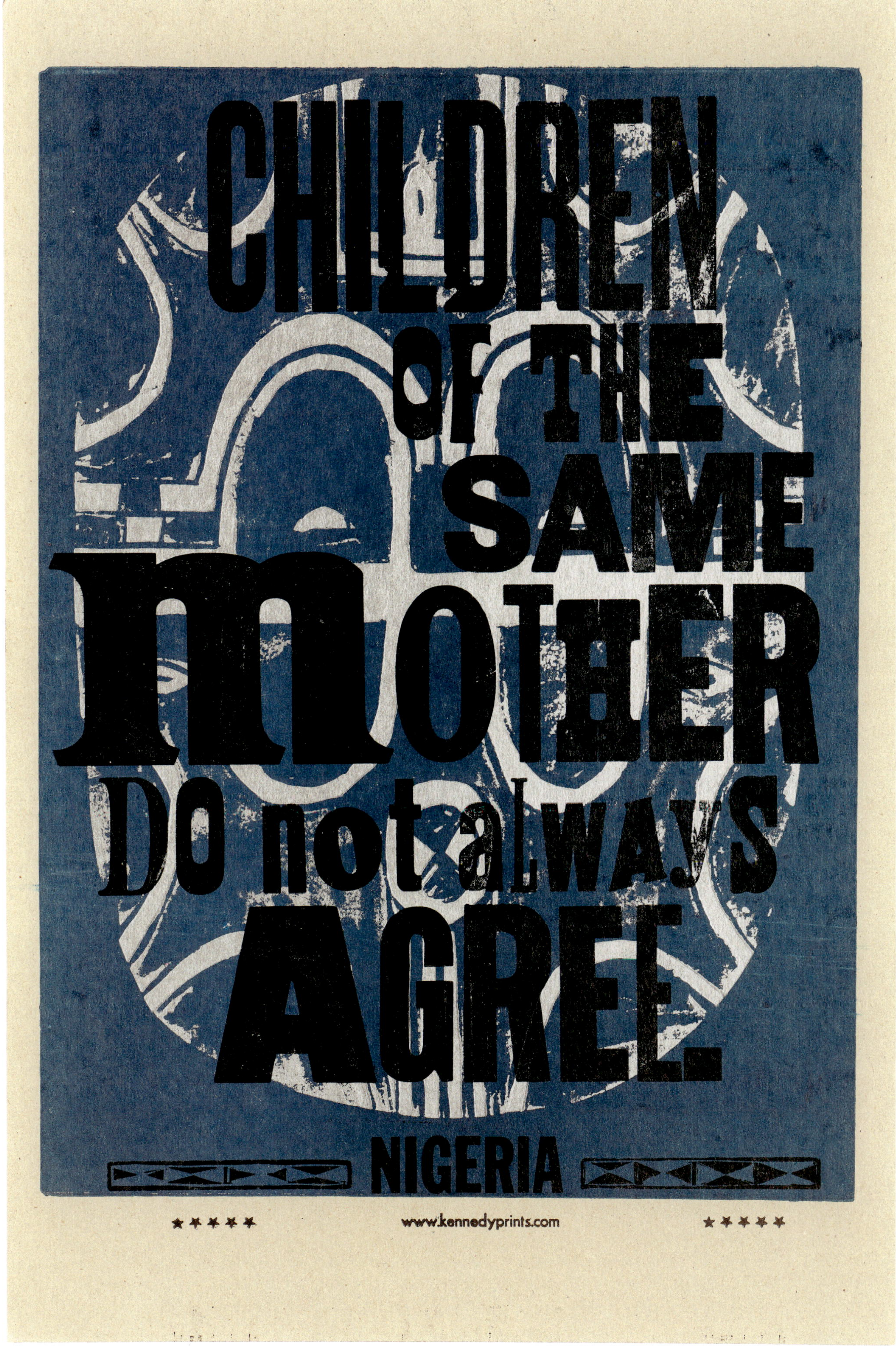
CHILDREN
OF THE
SAME
MOTHER
DO NOT ALWAYS
AGREE.
NIGERIA
www.kennedyprints.com

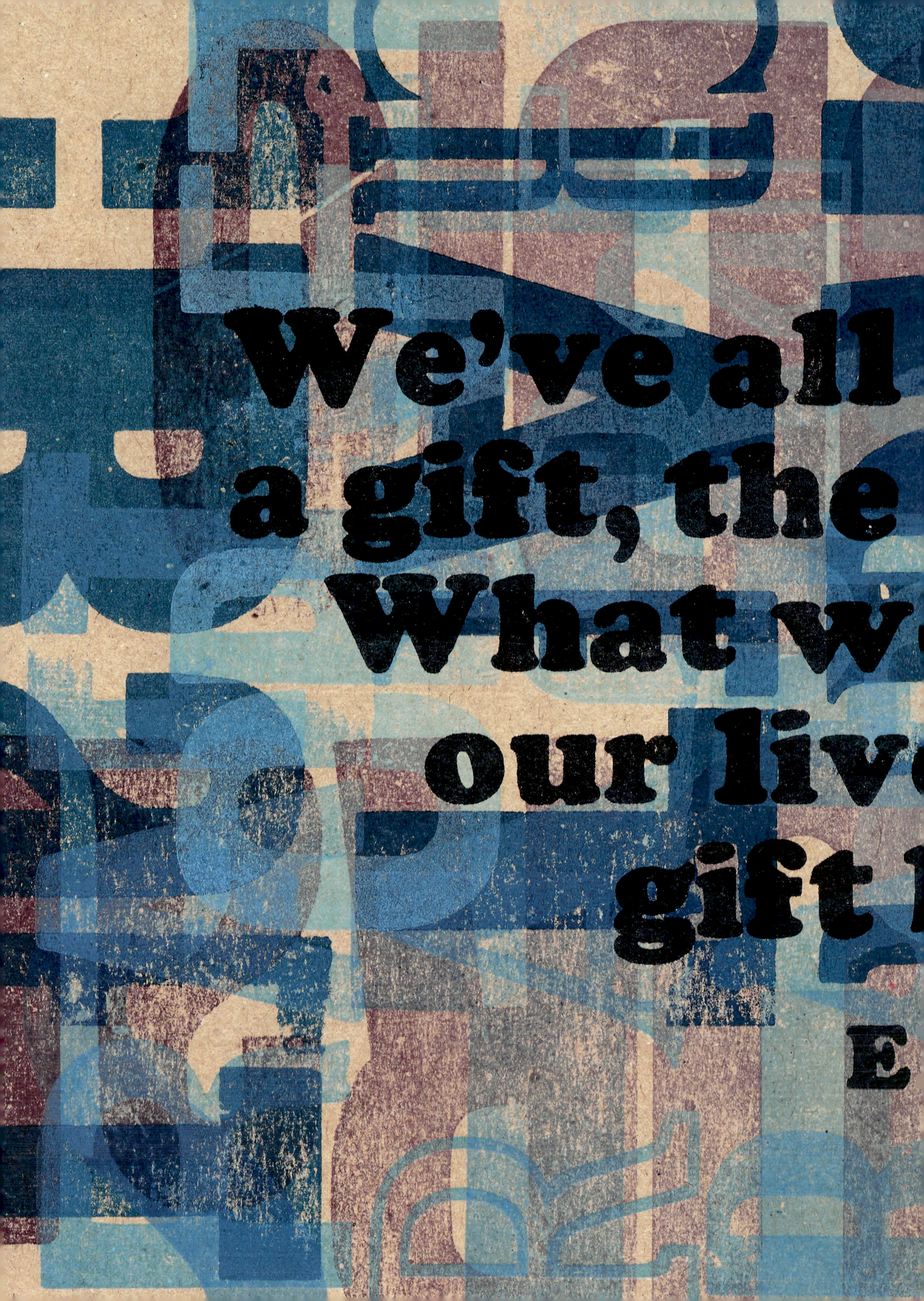
We've all
a gift, the
What w
our liv
gift
E

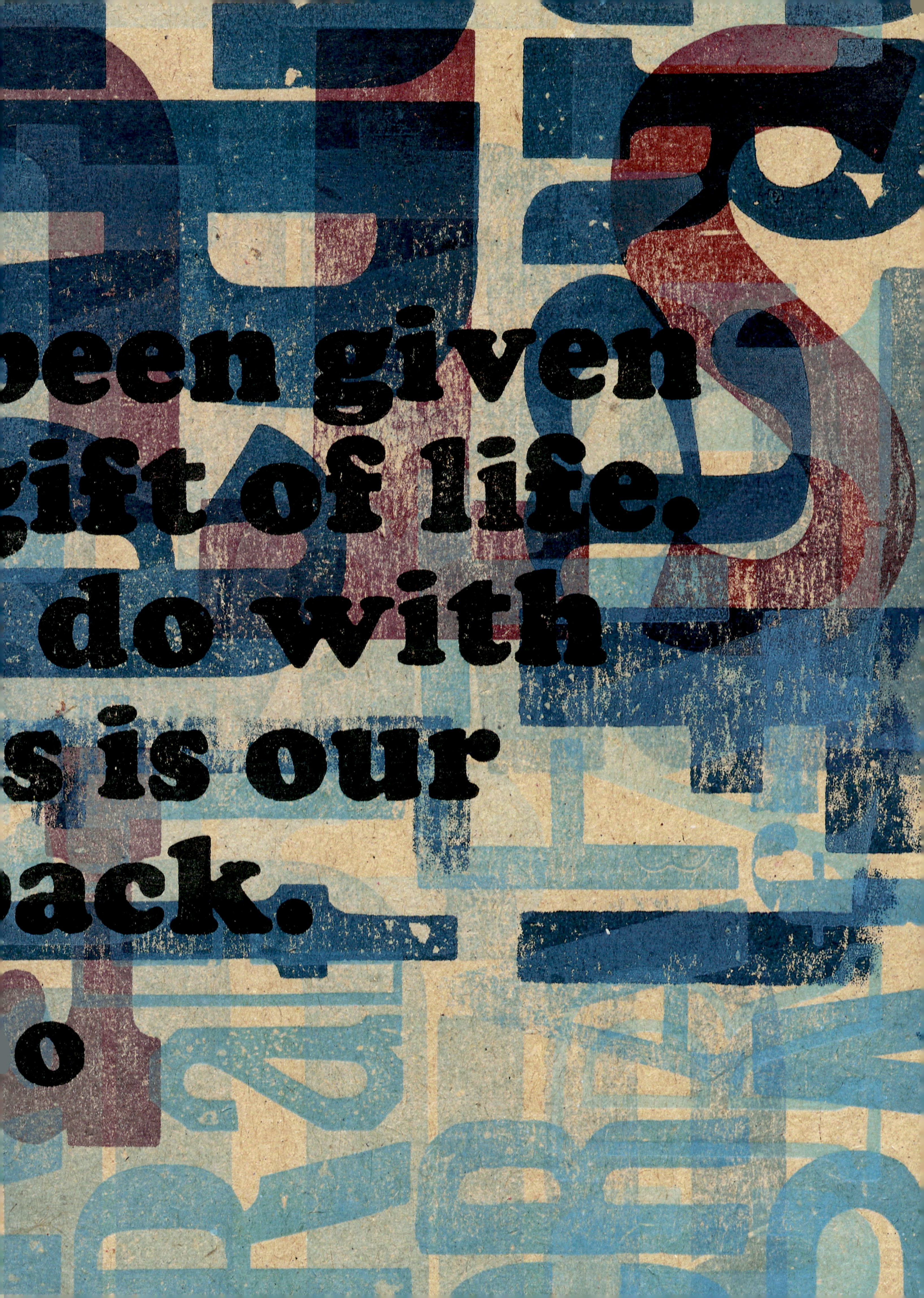
been given
gift of life.
do with
s is our
back.
o

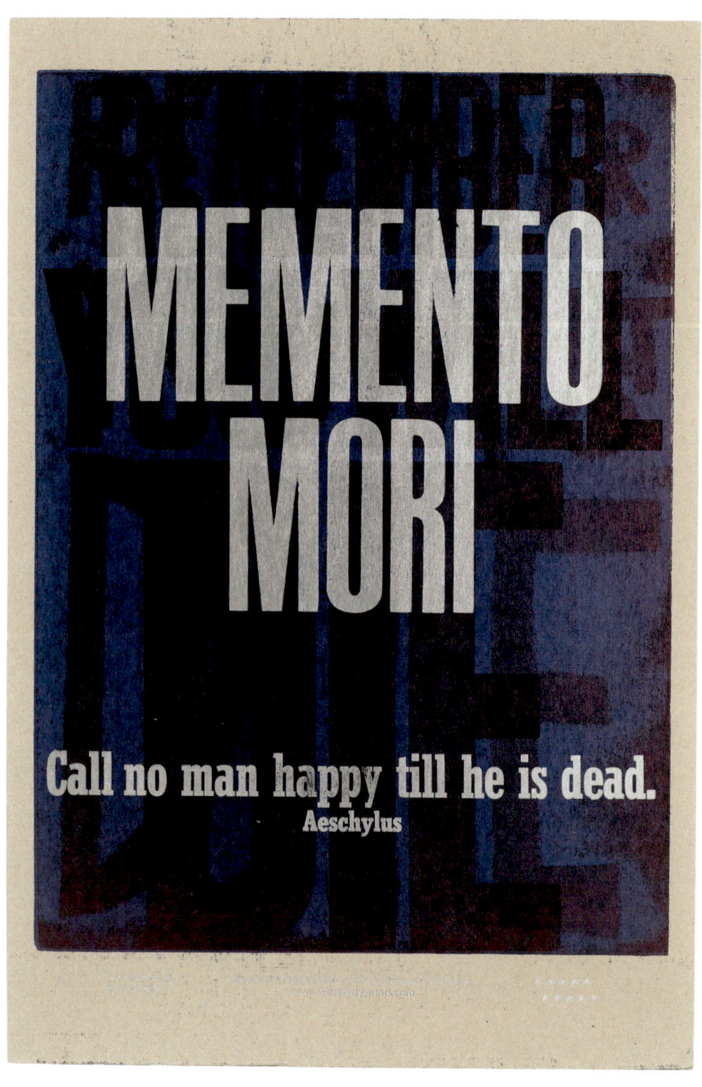
MEMENTO
MORI
Call no man happy till he is dead.
Aeschylus

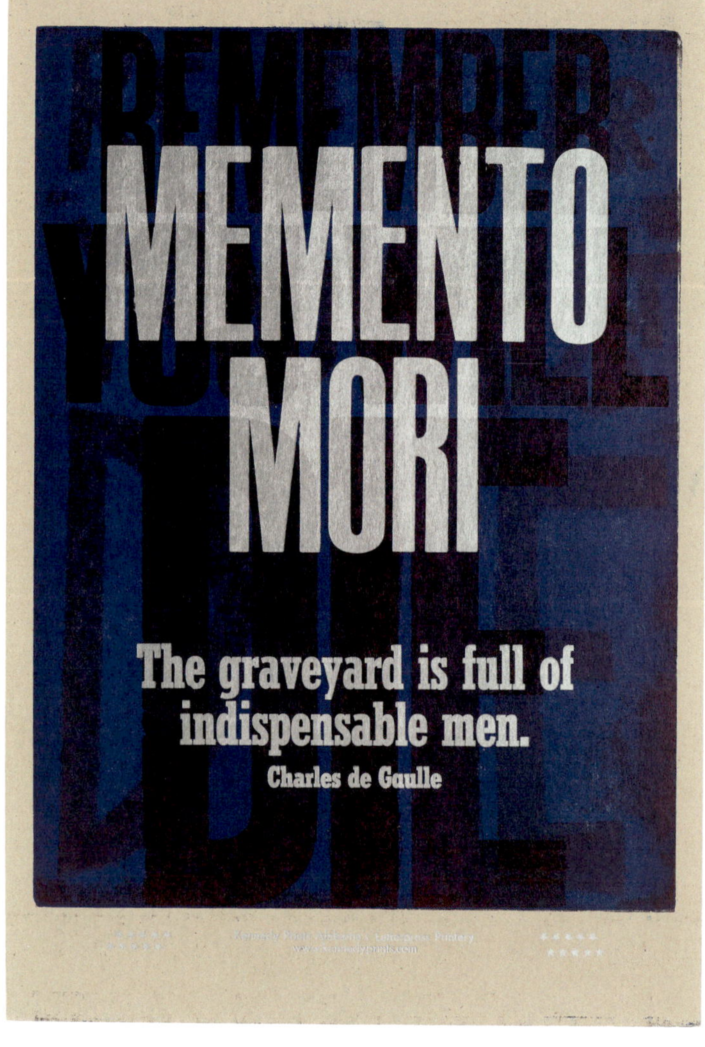
MEMENTO
MORI
The graveyard is full of
indispensable men.
Charles de Gaulle

MEMENTO MORI

You will not die because you are sick but because you are alive.

BE THE
JOY
THAT YOU
SEEK!

SALLY BIRD

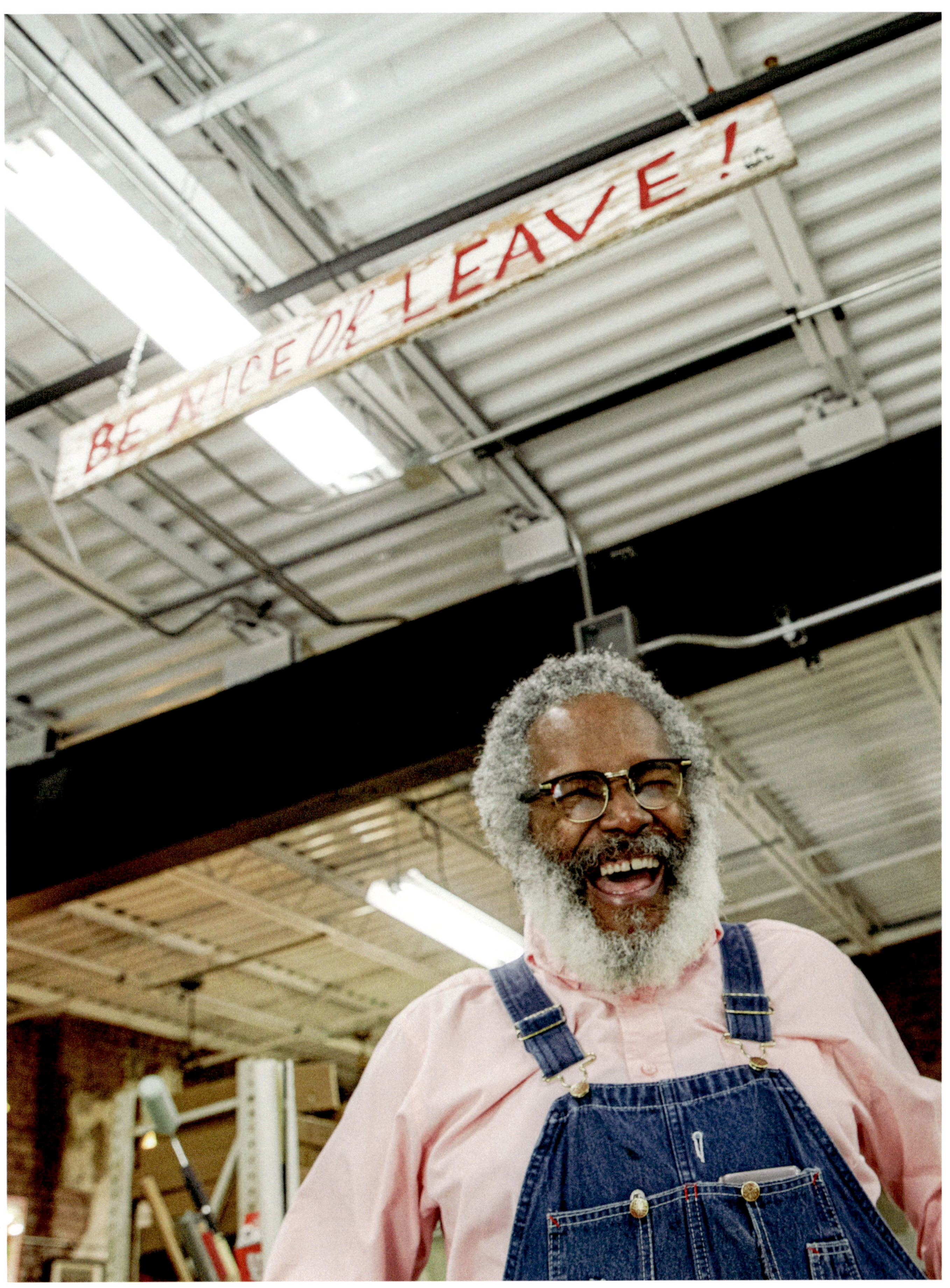
BE NICE OR LEAVE!

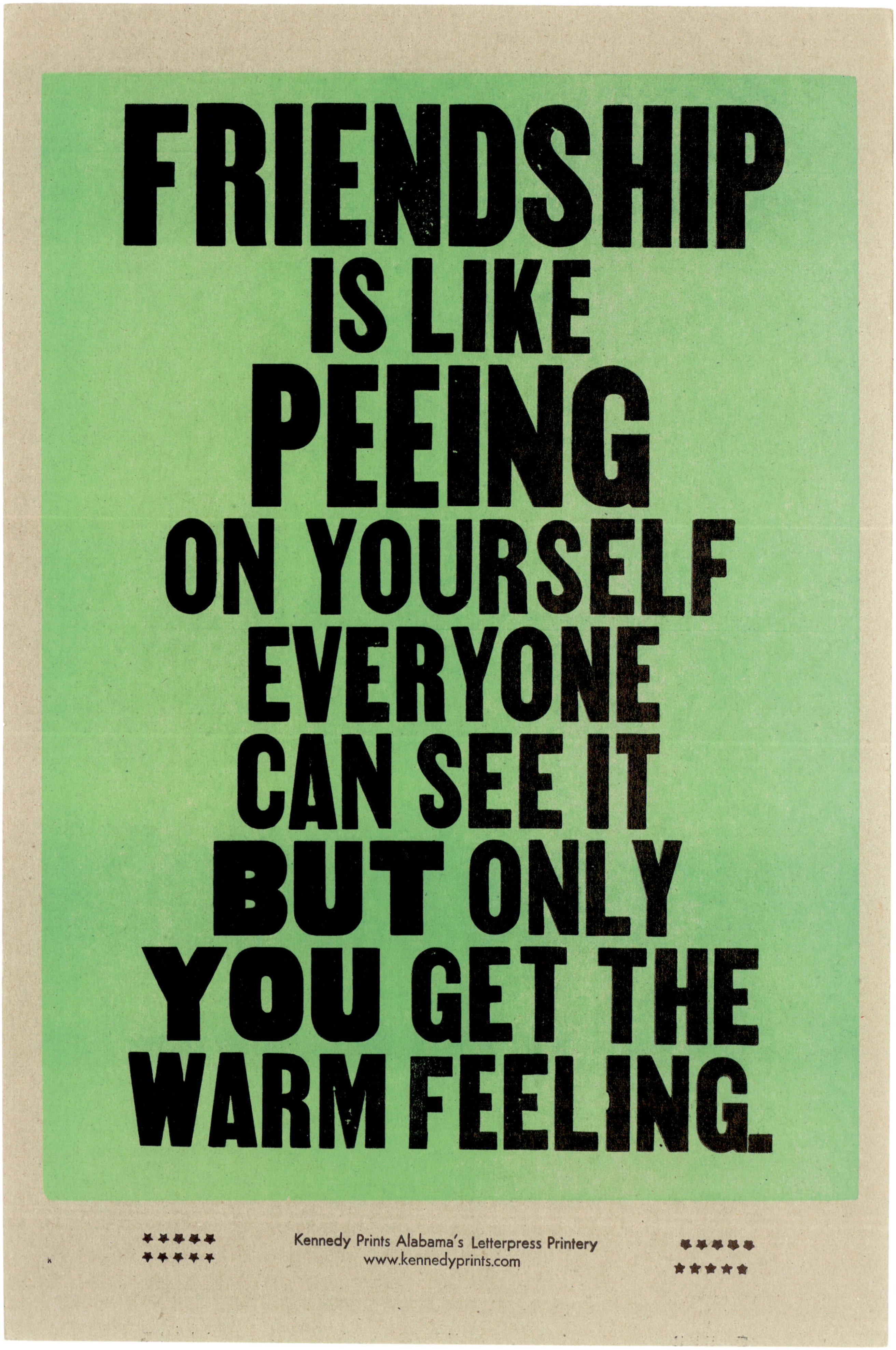

FRIENDSHIP
IS LIKE
PEEING
ON YOURSELF
EVERYONE
CAN SEE IT
BUT ONLY
YOU GET THE
WARM FEELING.

Kennedy Prints Alabama's Letterpress Printery
www.kennedyprints.com

HOW CAN
YOU KNOW
JESUS
WHEN YOU
CAN'T WRITE A
THANK YOU
NOTE!

Tut Riddick
ARTIST

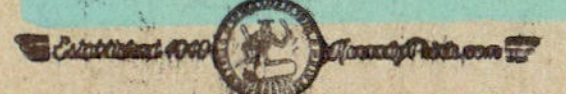

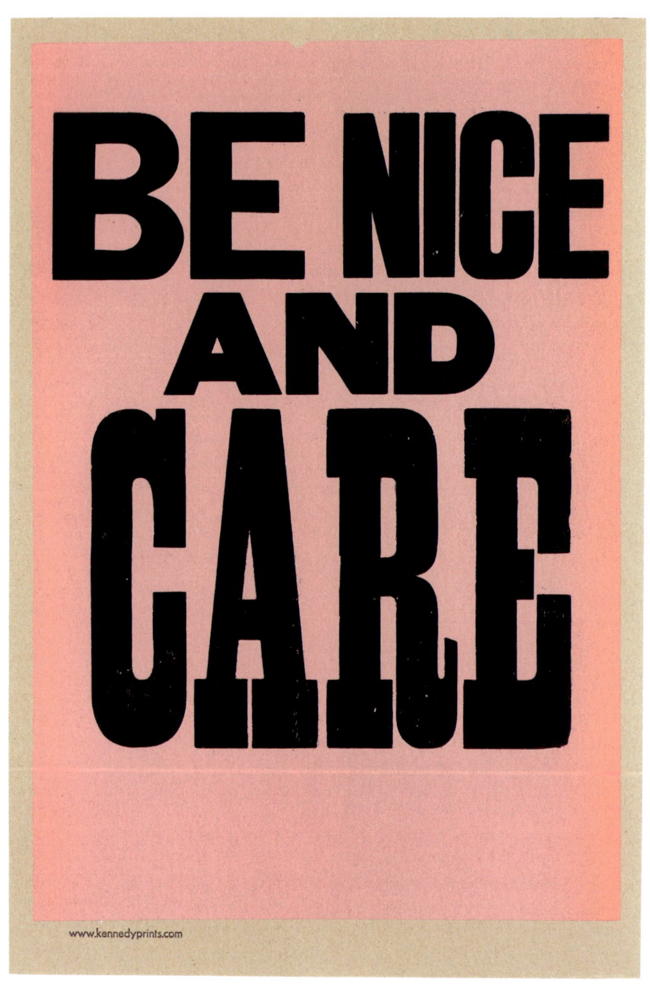
BE NICE
AND
CARE
www.kennedyprints.com

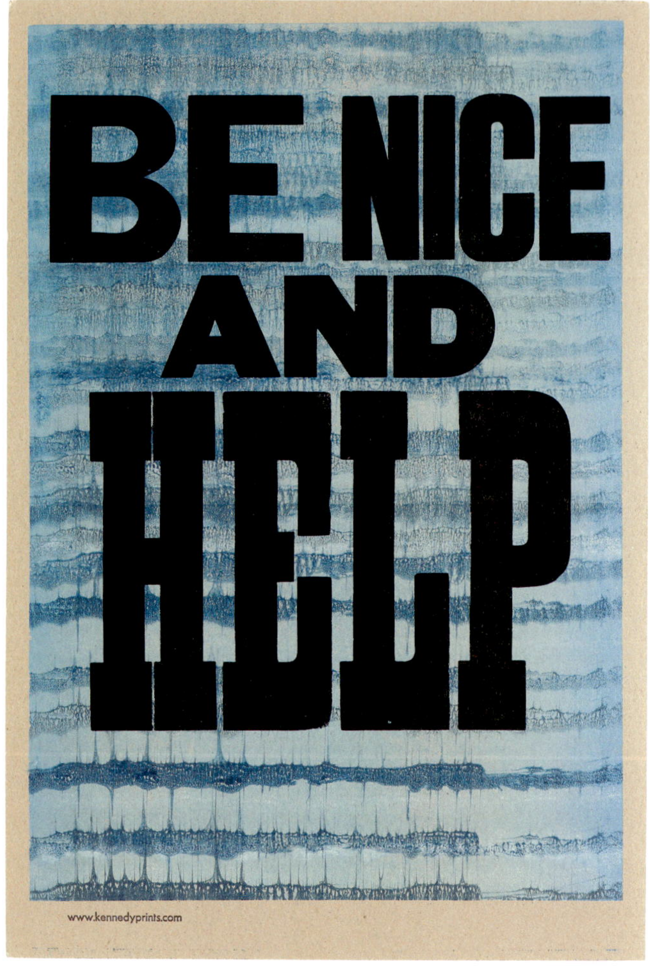
BE NICE
AND
HELP
www.kennedyprints.com

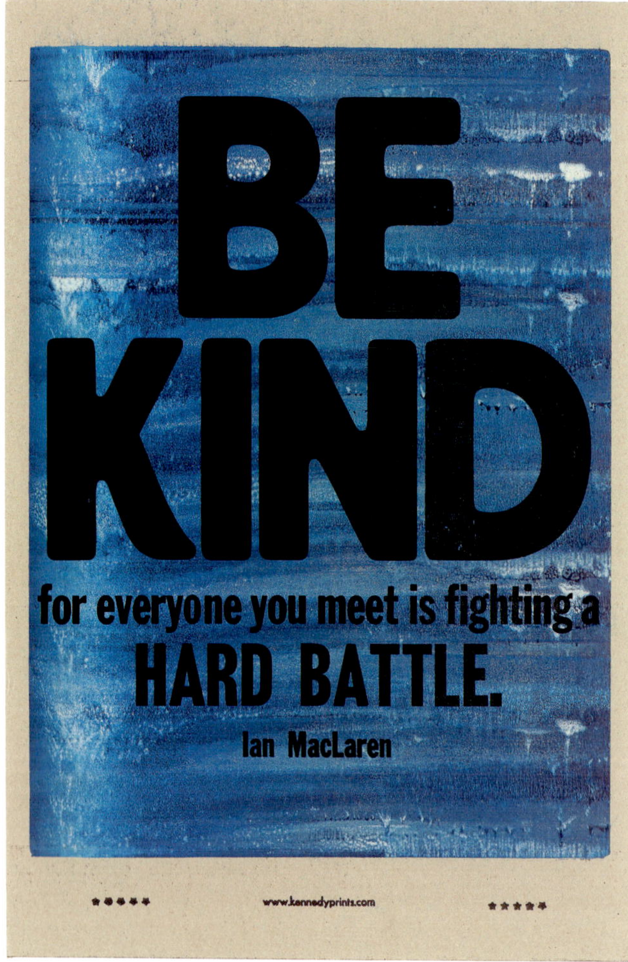
BE
KIND
for everyone you meet is fighting a
HARD BATTLE.
Ian MacLaren
www.kennedyprints.com

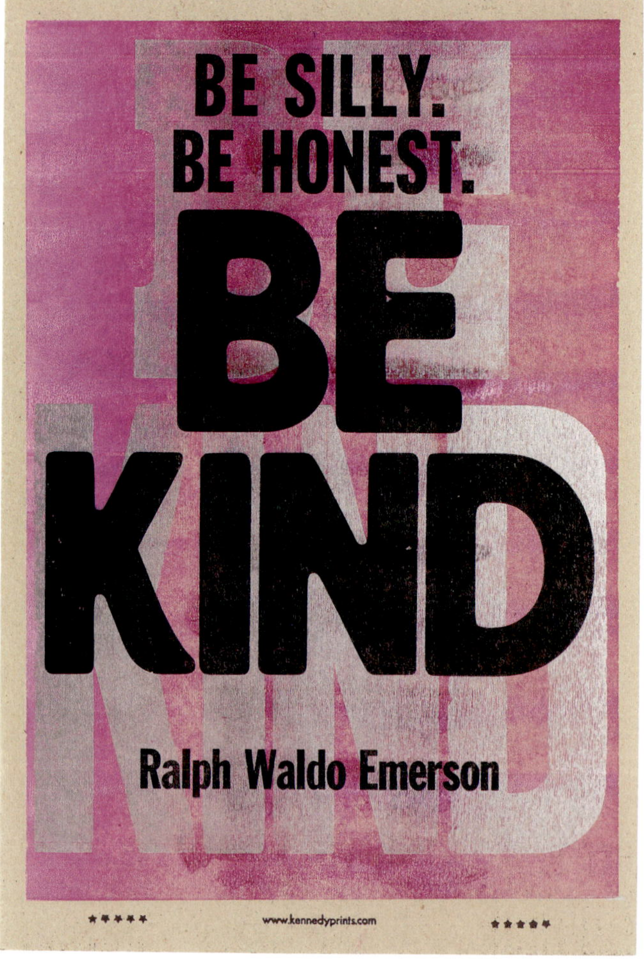
BE SILLY.
BE HONEST.
BE
KIND
Ralph Waldo Emerson
www.kennedyprints.com

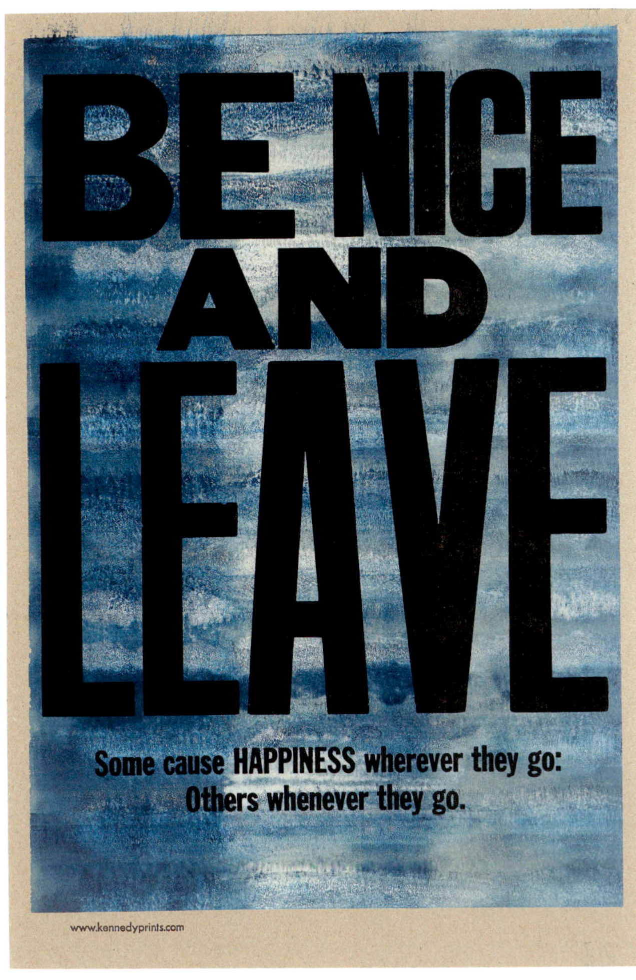
BE NICE
AND
LEAVE
Some cause HAPPINESS wherever they go:
Others whenever they go.
www.kennedyprints.com

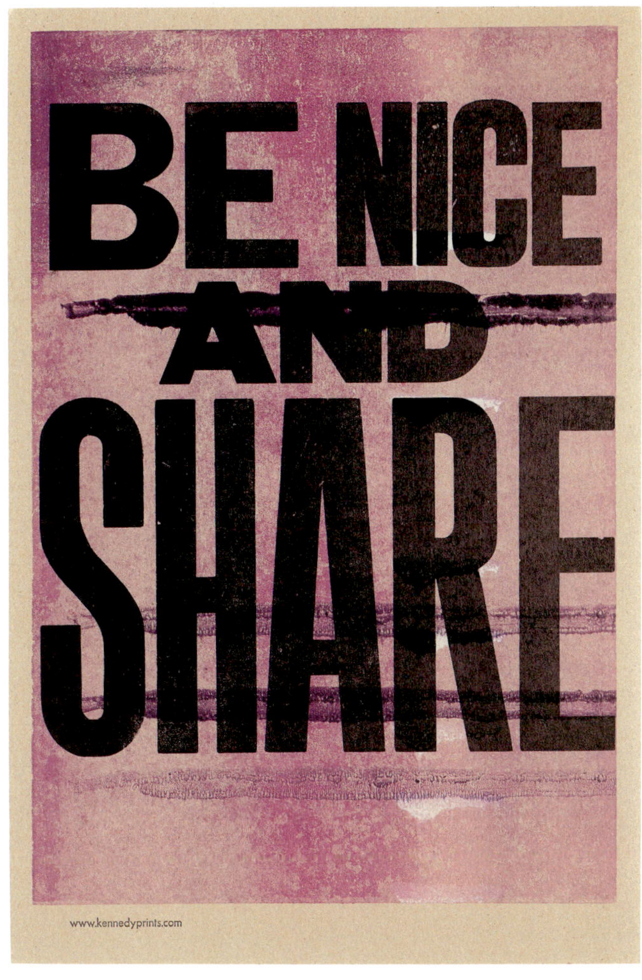
BE NICE
AND
SHARE
www.kennedyprints.com

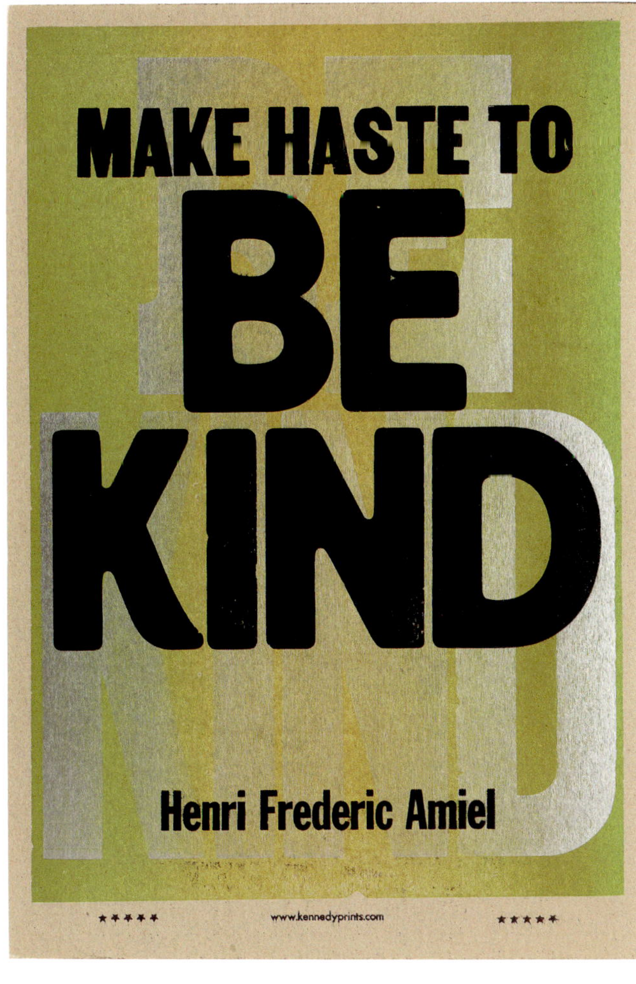
MAKE HASTE TO
BE
KIND
Henri Frederic Amiel
★★★★★ www.kennedyprints.com ★★★★★

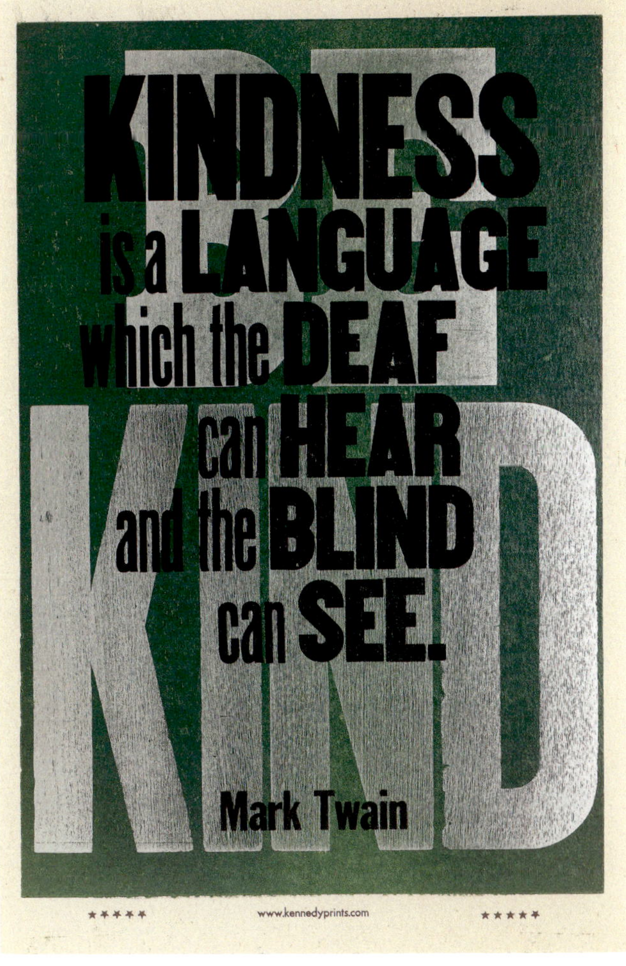
KINDNESS
is a LANGUAGE
which the DEAF
can HEAR
and the BLIND
can SEE.
Mark Twain
★★★★★ www.kennedyprints.com ★★★★★

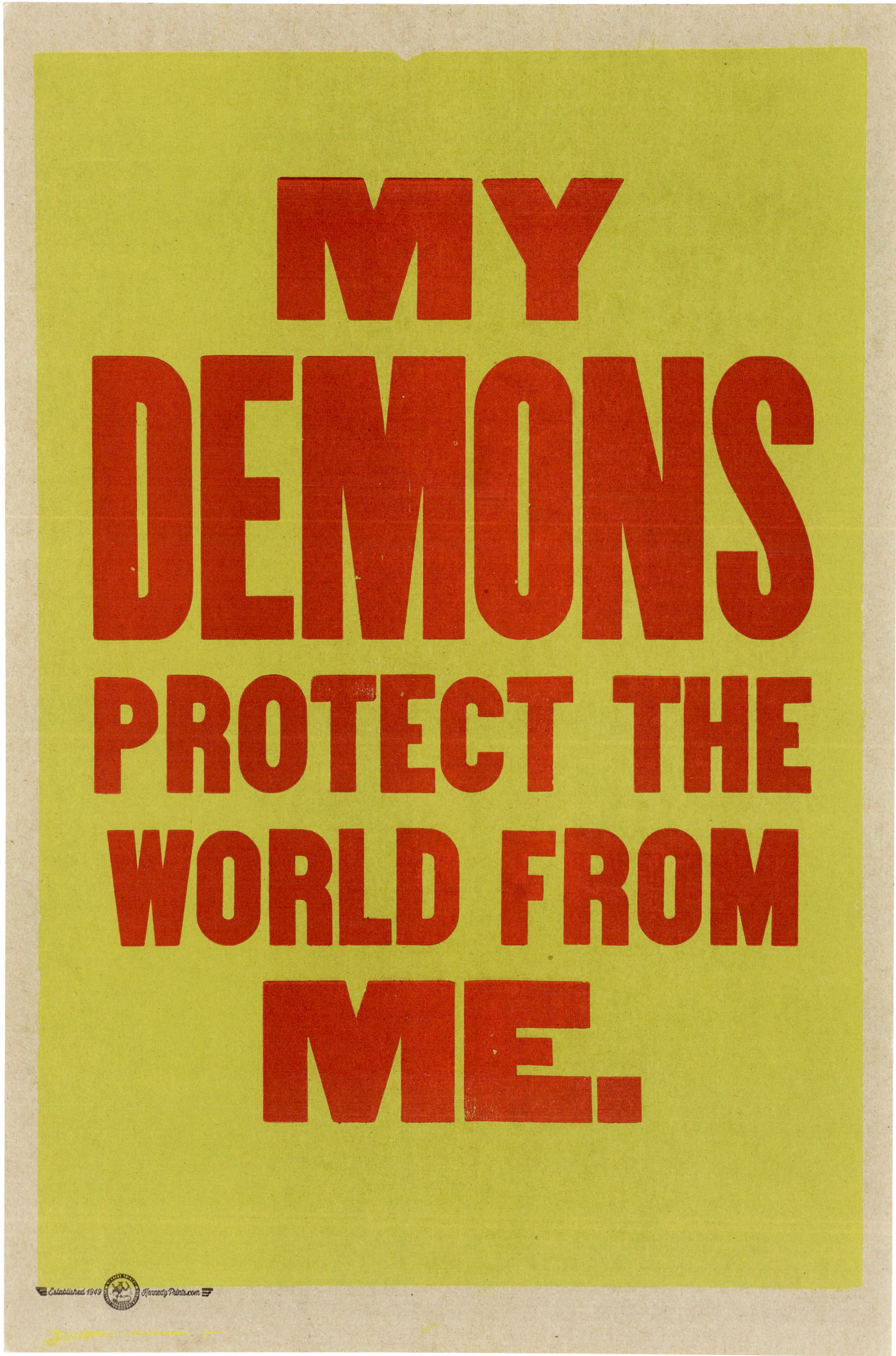
MY
DEMONS
PROTECT THE
WORLD FROM
ME.
Established 1949
KennedyPrints.com

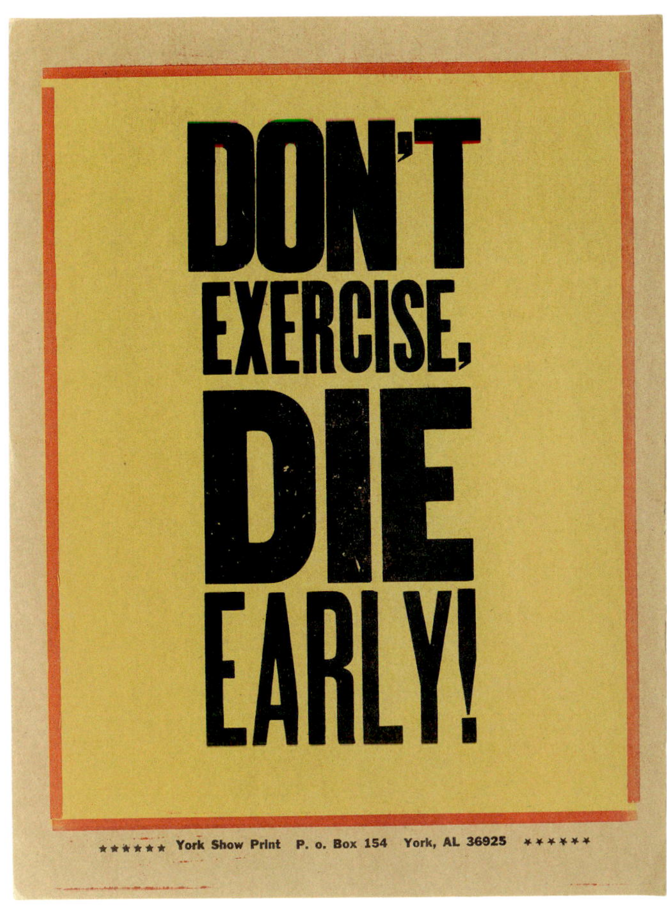
DON'T
EXERCISE,
DIE
EARLY!
****** York Show Print P. o. Box 154 York, AL 36925 ******

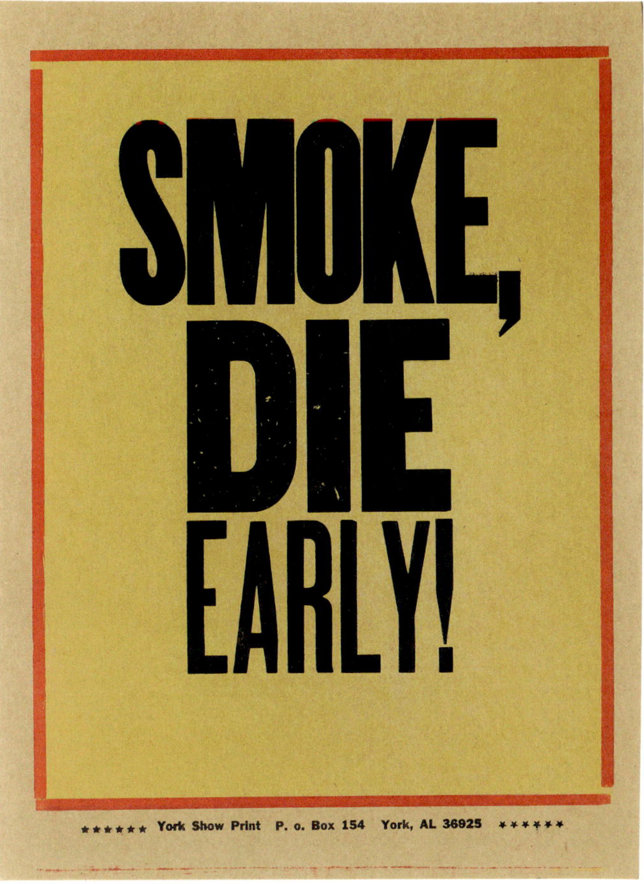
SMOKE,
DIE
EARLY!
****** York Show Print P. o. Box 154 York, AL 36925 ******

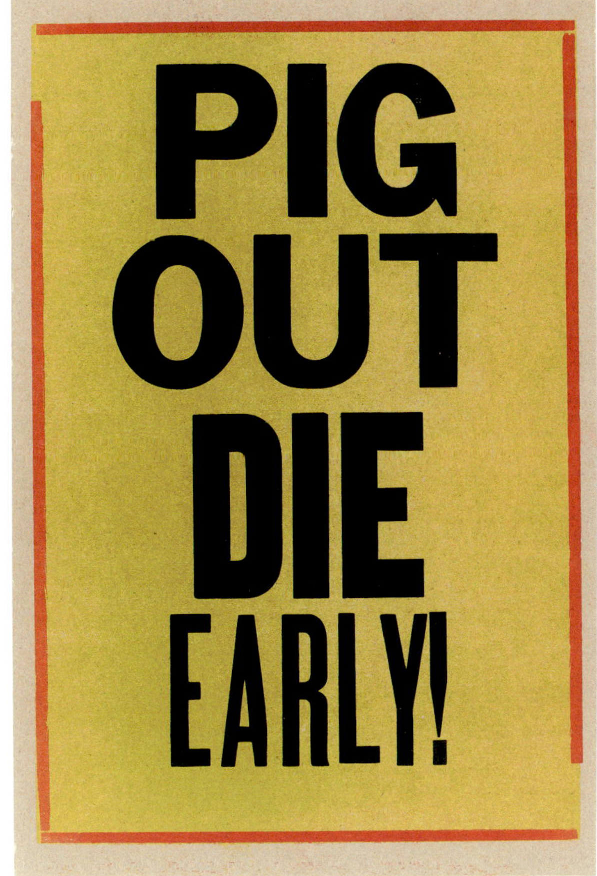
PIG
OUT
DIE
EARLY!

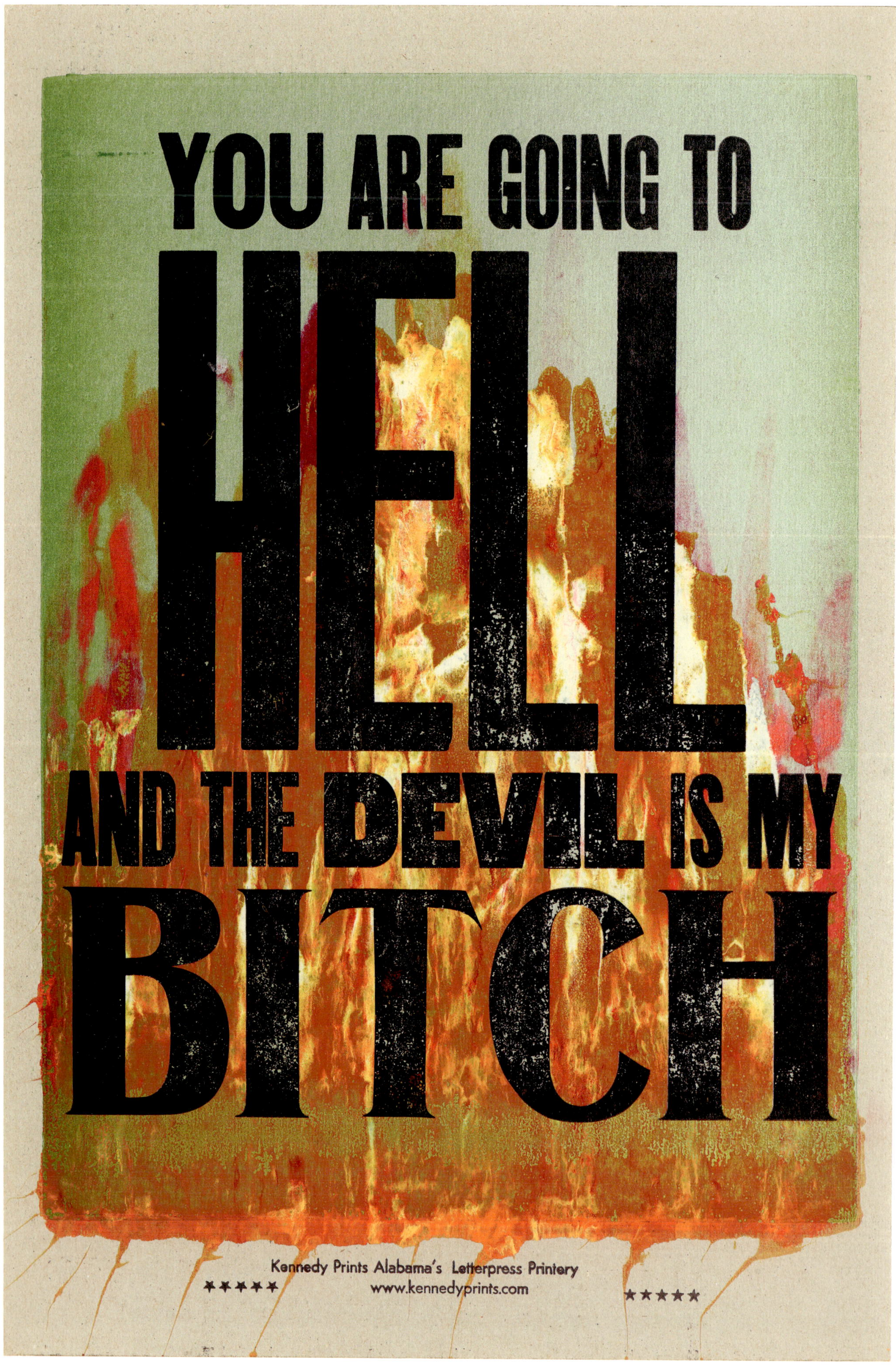
YOU ARE GOING TO
HELL
AND THE DEVIL IS MY
BITCH
Kennedy Prints Alabama's Letterpress Printery
www.kennedyprints.com

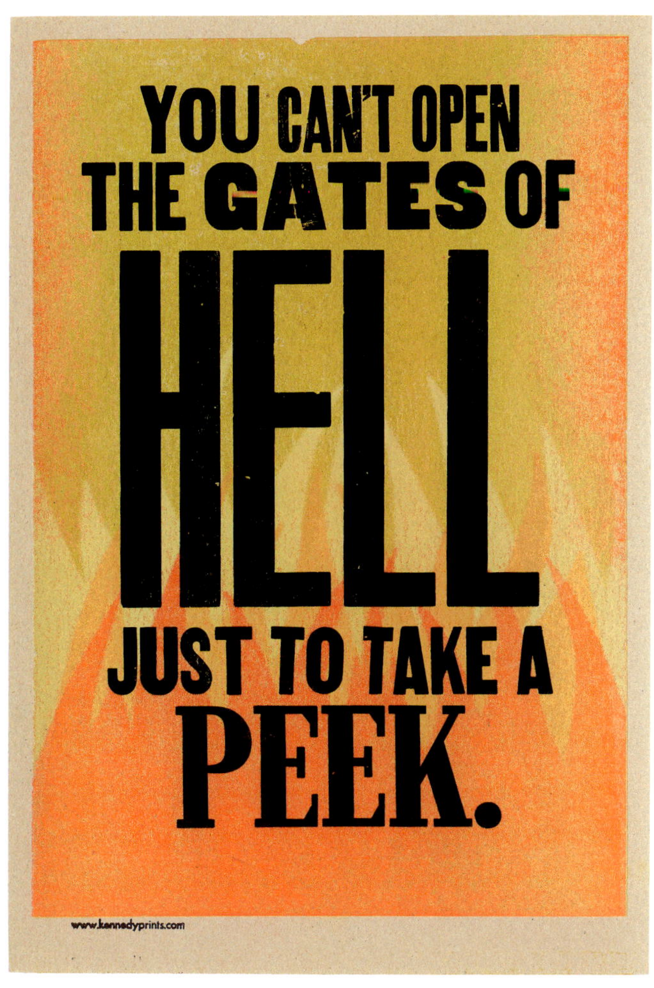
YOU CAN'T OPEN
THE GATES OF
HELL
JUST TO TAKE A
PEEK.
www.kennedyprints.com

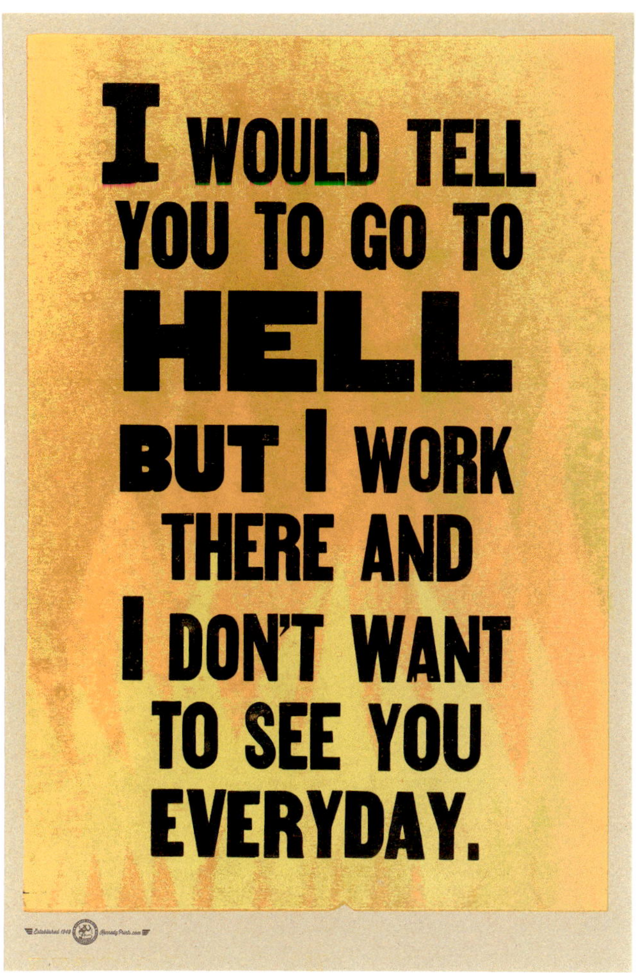
I WOULD TELL
YOU TO GO TO
HELL
BUT I WORK
THERE AND
I DON'T WANT
TO SEE YOU
EVERYDAY.

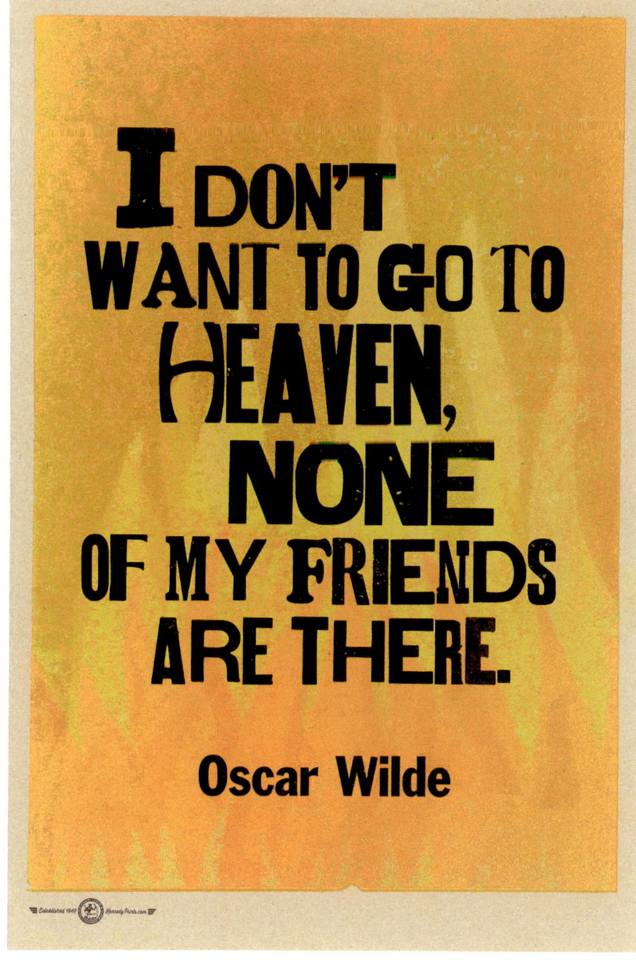
I DON'T
WANT TO GO TO
HEAVEN,
NONE
OF MY FRIENDS
ARE THERE.
Oscar Wilde

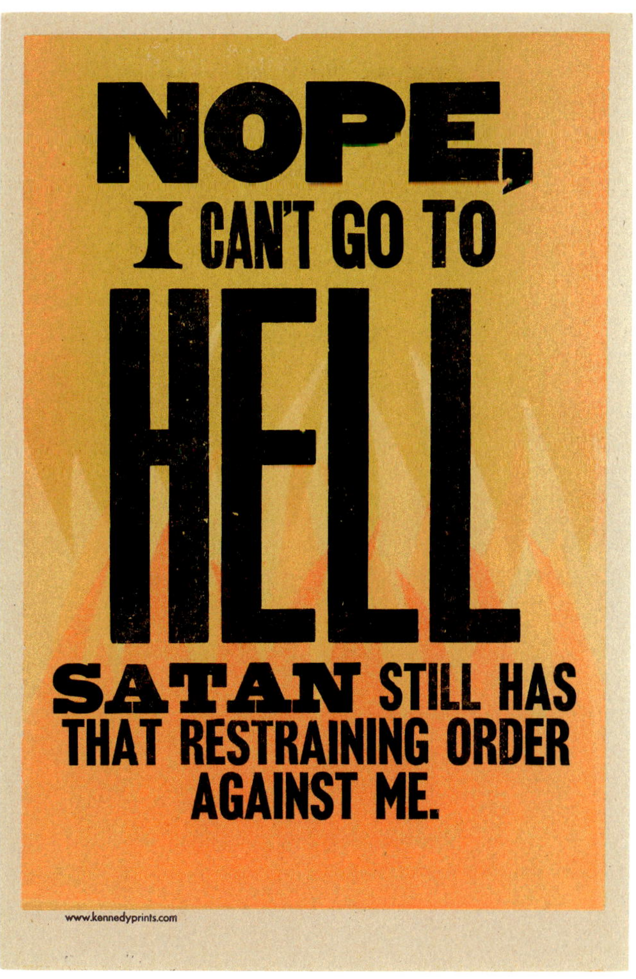
NOPE,
I CAN'T GO TO
HELL
SATAN STILL HAS
THAT RESTRAINING ORDER
AGAINST ME.
www.kennedyprints.com

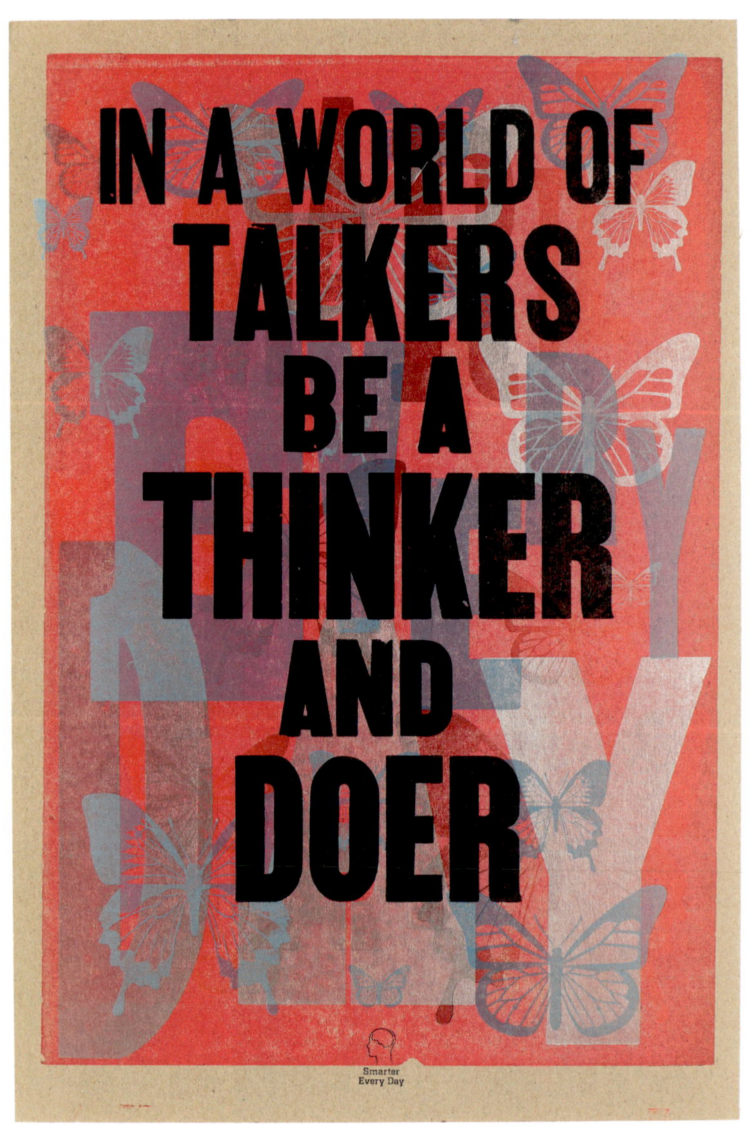
IN A WORLD OF
TALKERS
BE A
THINKER
AND
DOER
Smarter
Every Day

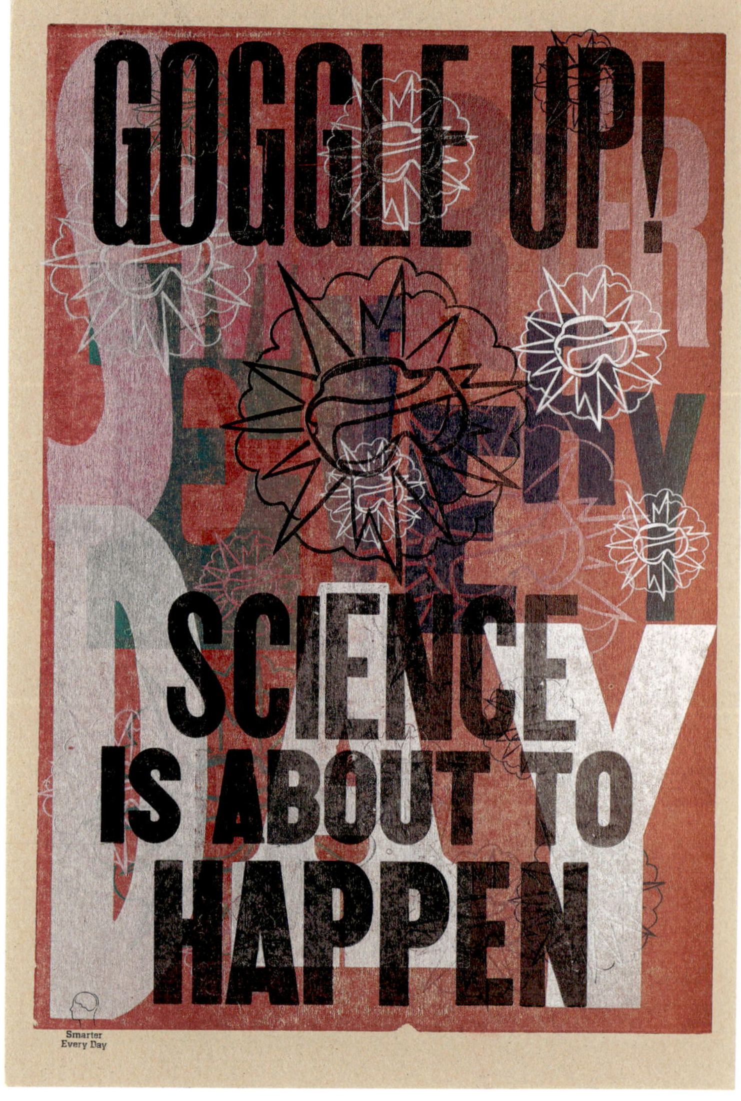
GOGGLE UP!
SCIENCE
IS ABOUT TO
HAPPEN
Smarter
Every Day

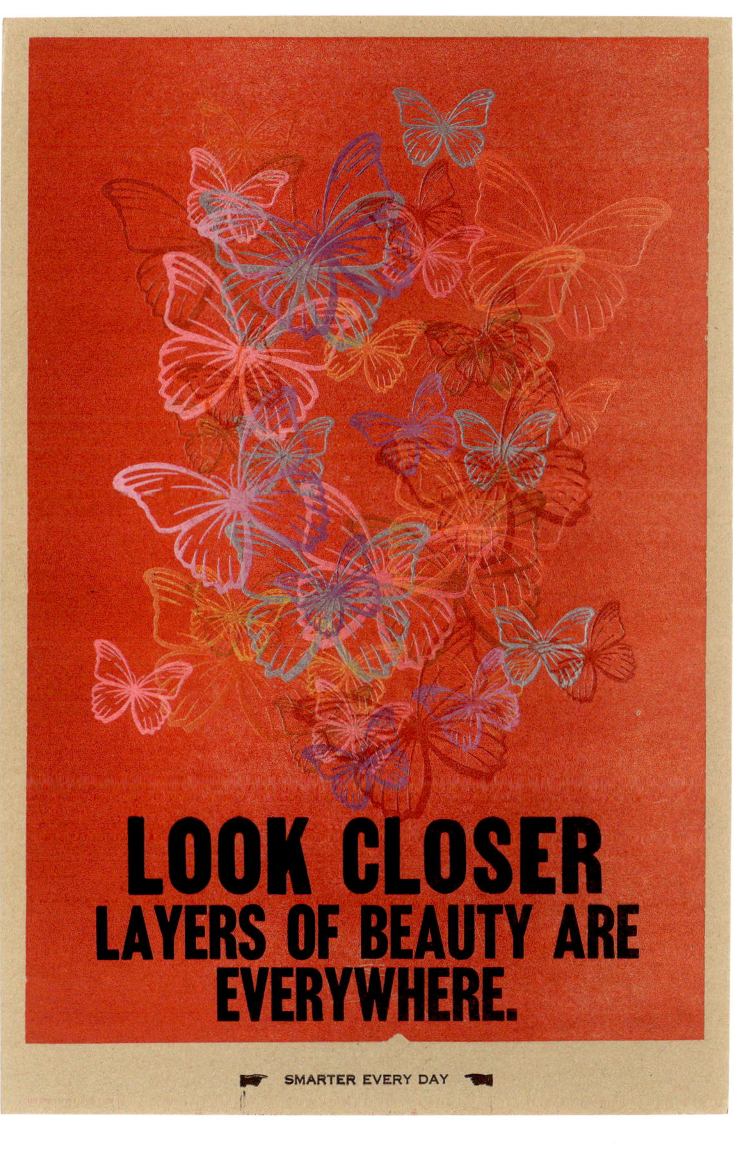
LOOK CLOSER
LAYERS OF BEAUTY ARE
EVERYWHERE.
SMARTER EVERY DAY

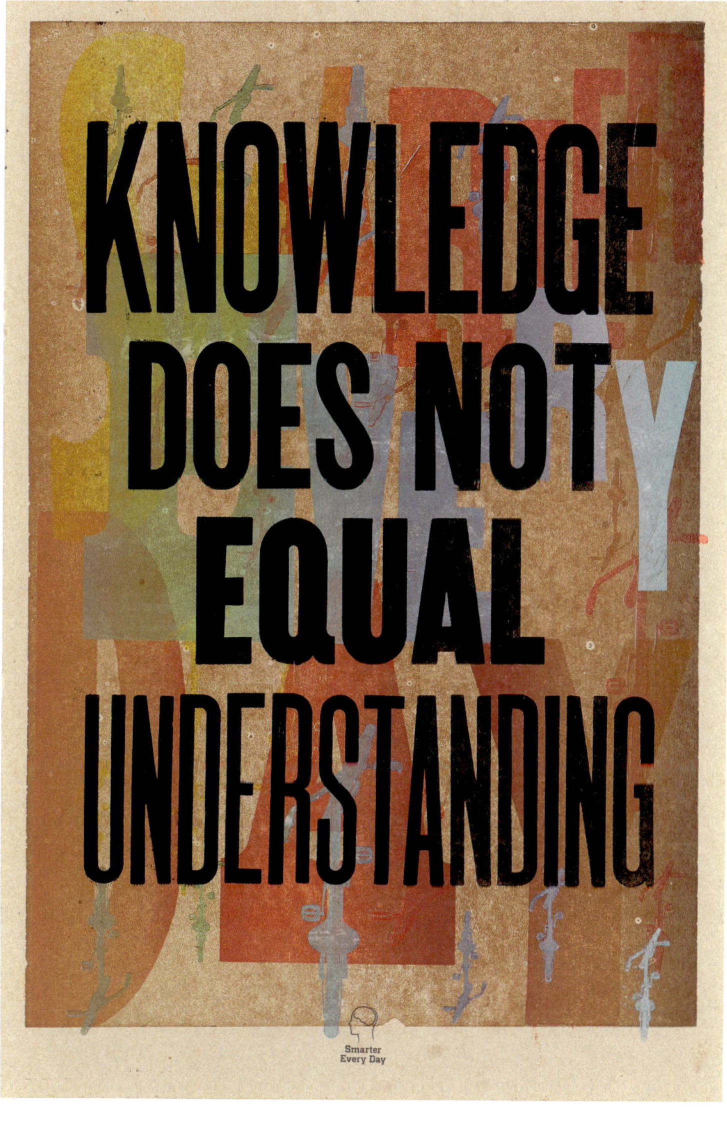
KNOWLEDGE
DOES NOT
EQUAL
UNDERSTANDING
Smarter
Every Day

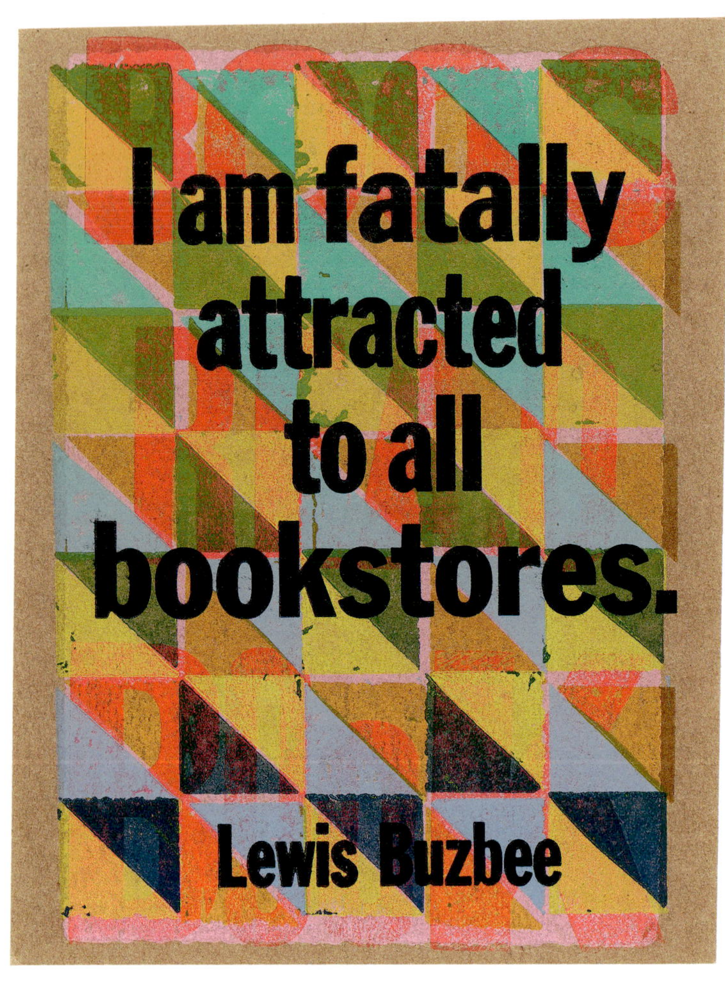
I am fatally
attracted
to all
bookstores.
Lewis Buzbee

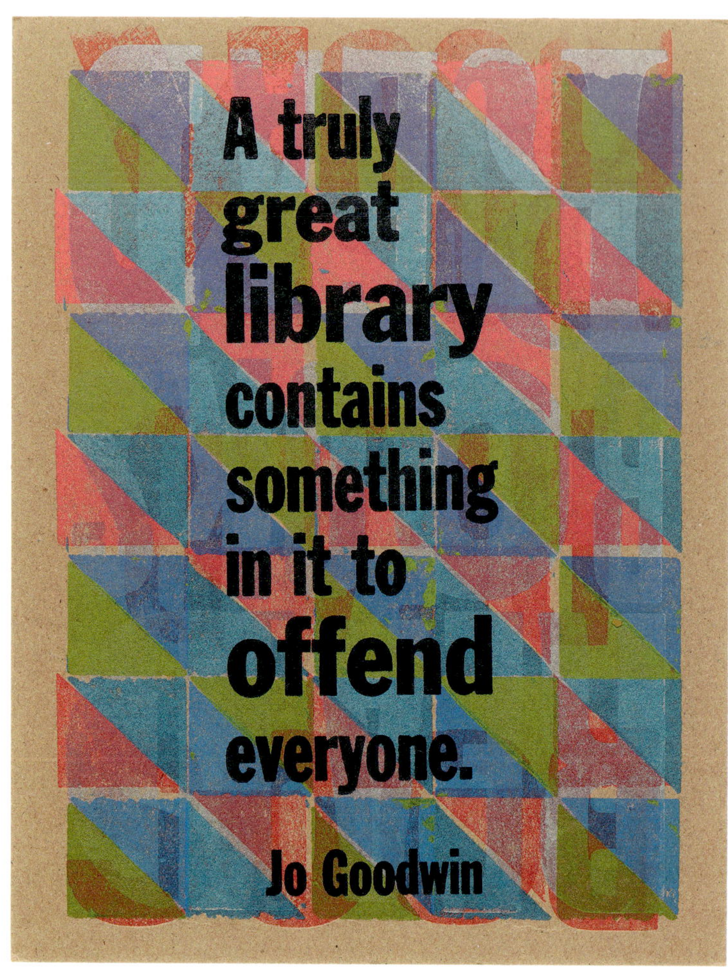
A truly
great
library
contains
something
in it to
offend
everyone.
Jo Goodwin

Bookstores
SAVE
Democracy.

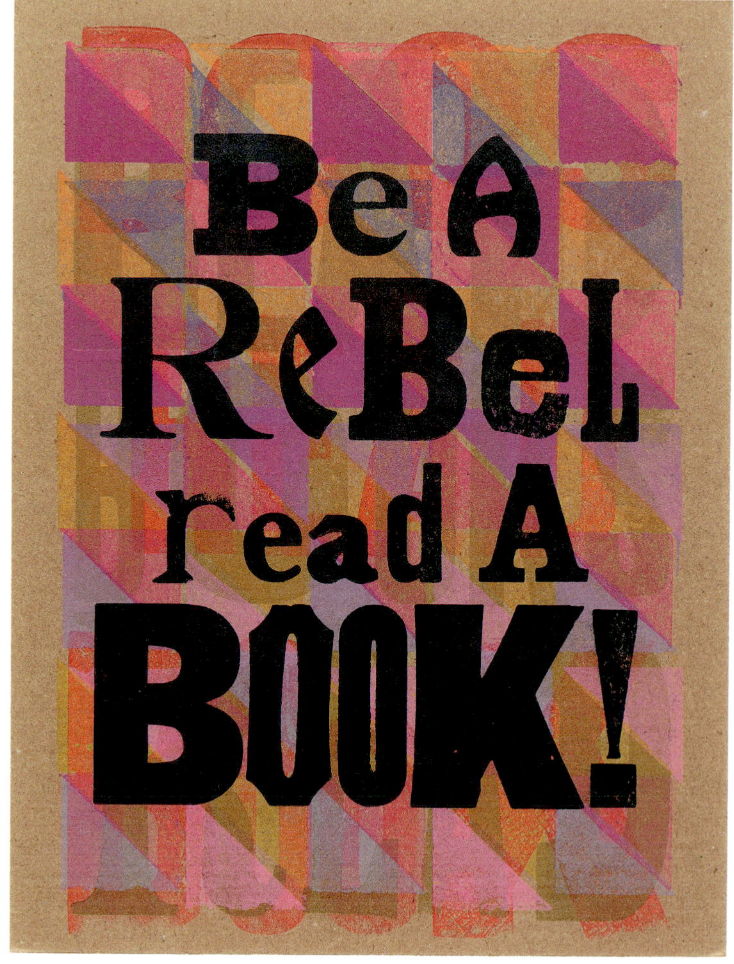
Be A
ReBeL
read A
BOOK!

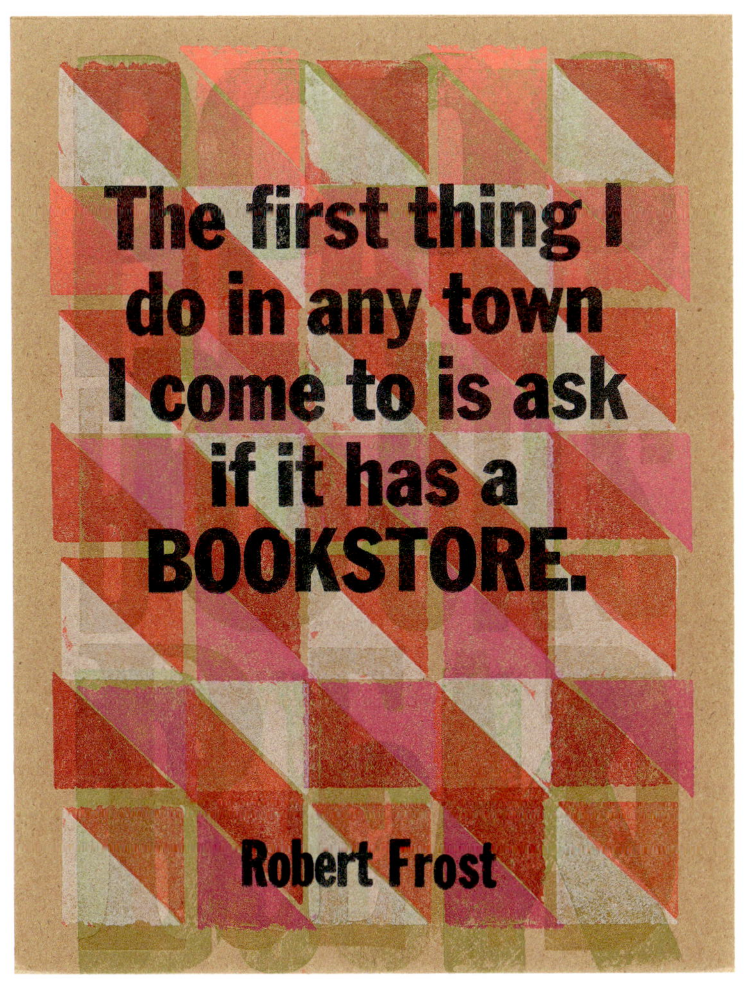
The first thing I do in any town I come to is ask if it has a BOOKSTORE.
Robert Frost

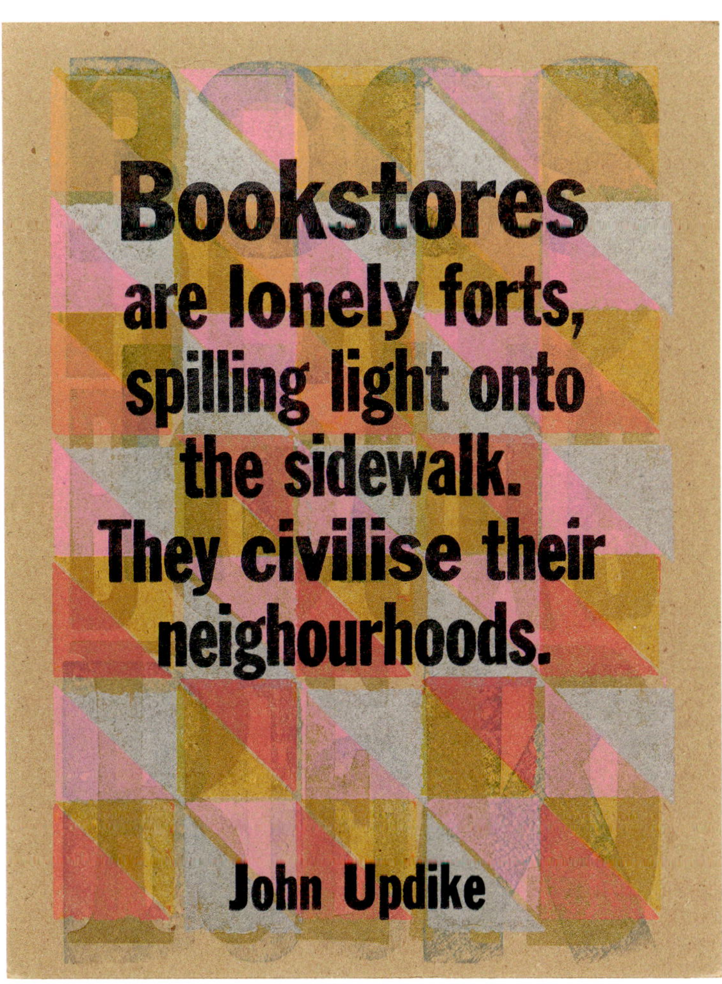
Bookstores are lonely forts, spilling light onto the sidewalk. They civilise their neighourhoods.
John Updike

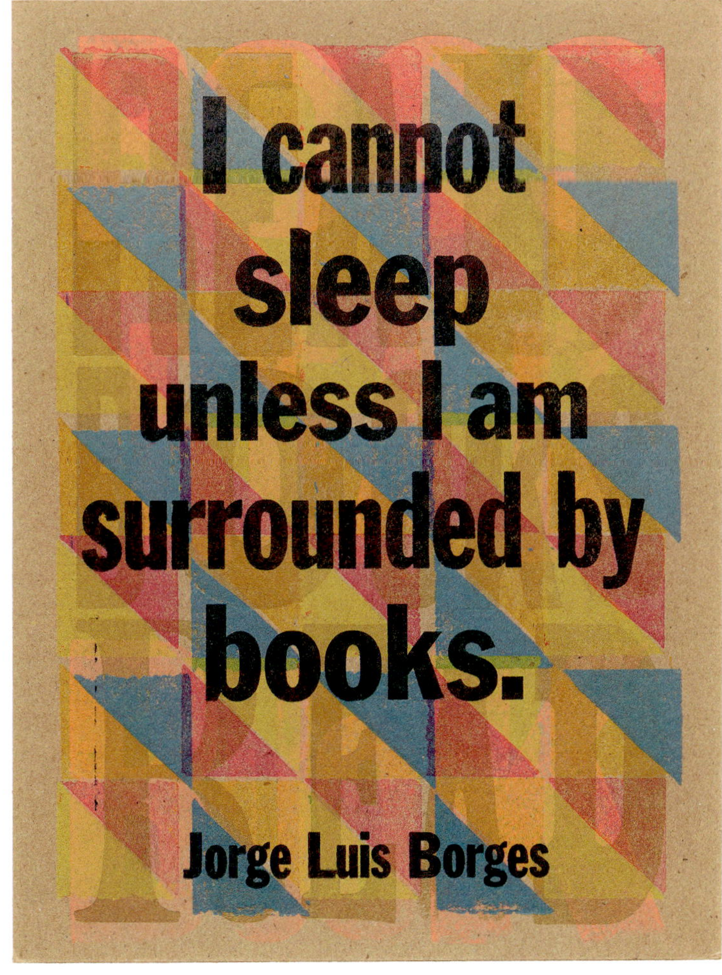
I cannot sleep unless I am surrounded by books.
Jorge Luis Borges

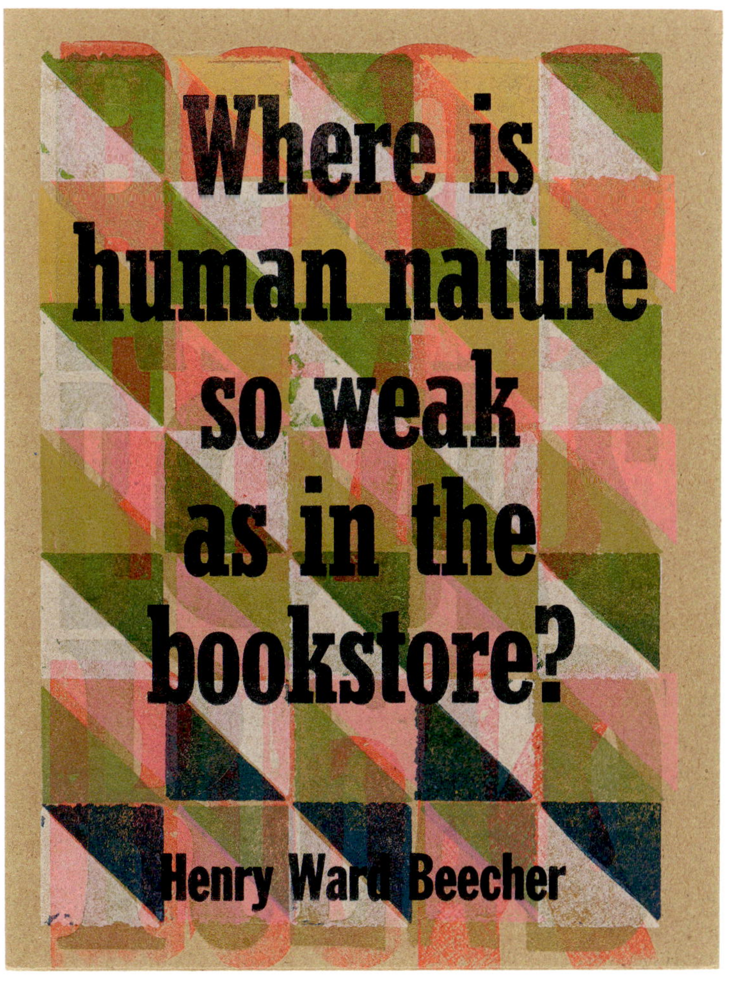
Where is human nature so weak as in the bookstore?
Henry Ward Beecher

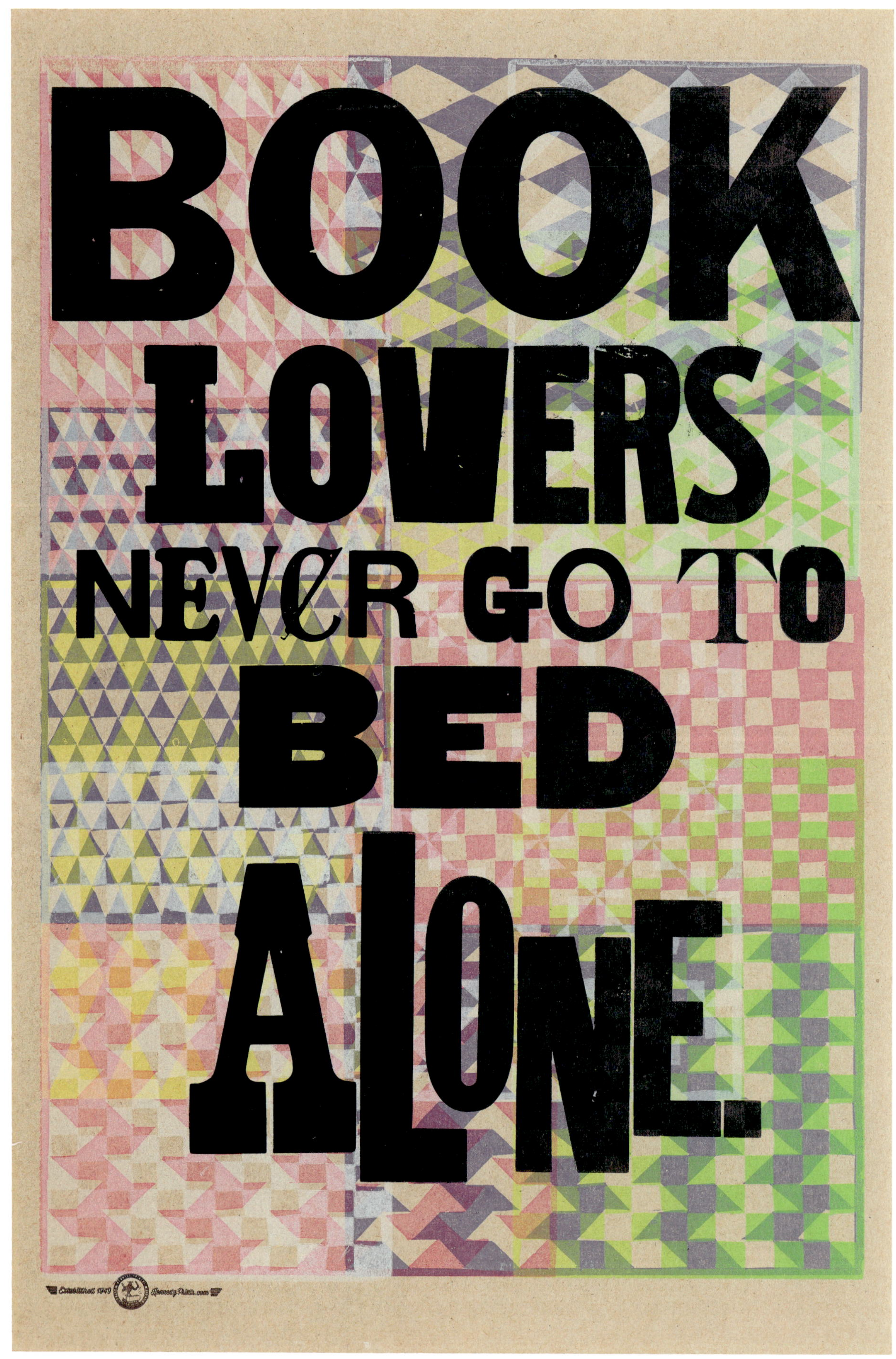
BOOK
LOVERS
NEVER GO TO
BED
ALONE.

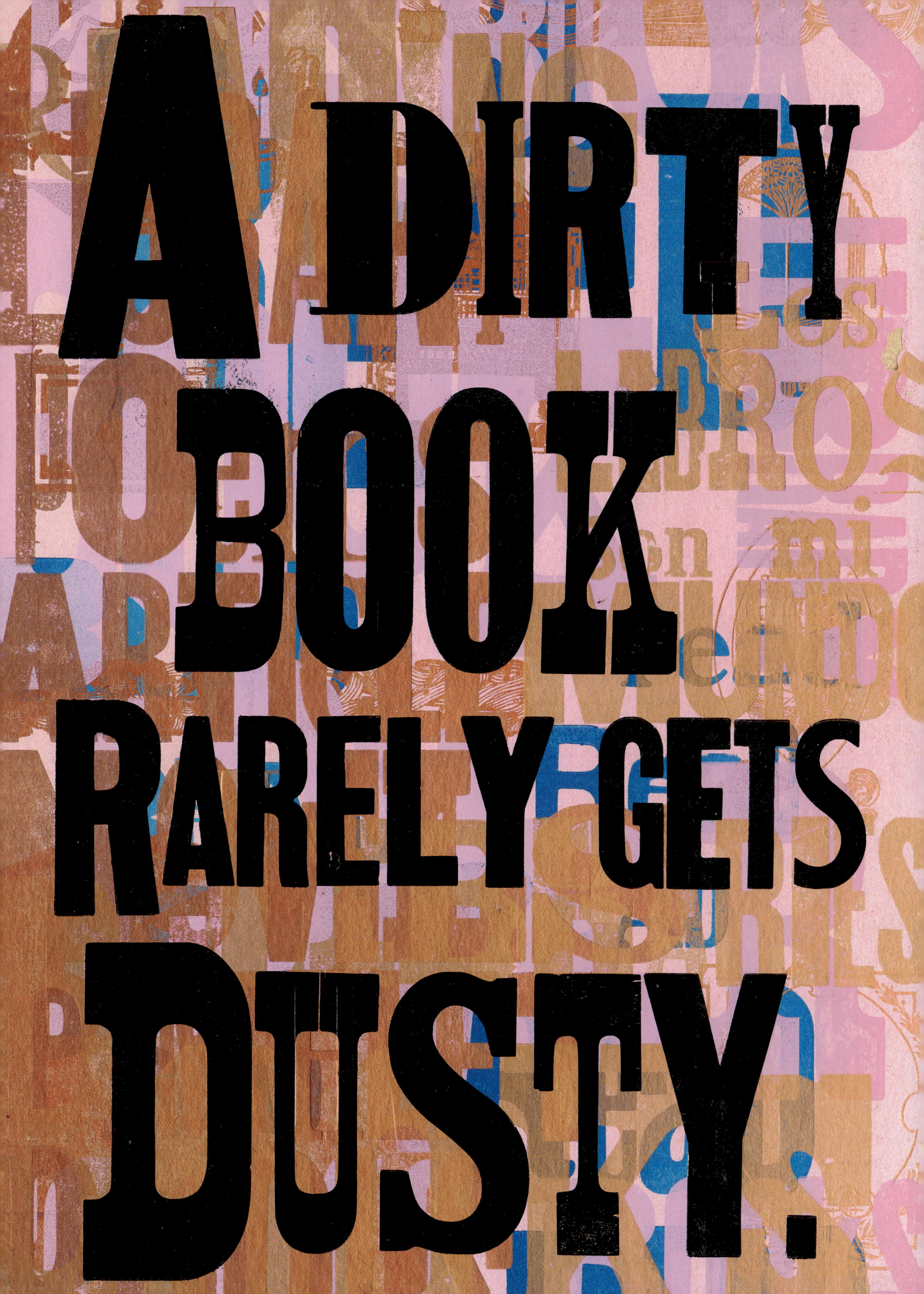
A DIRTY
BOOK
RARELY GETS
DUSTY.

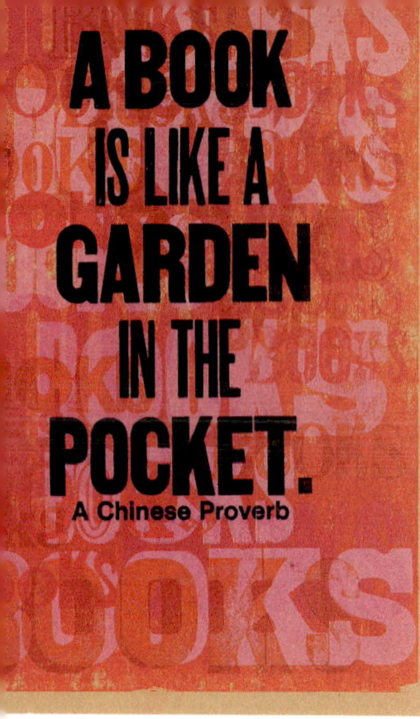
A BOOK
IS LIKE A
GARDEN
IN THE
POCKET.
A Chinese Proverb

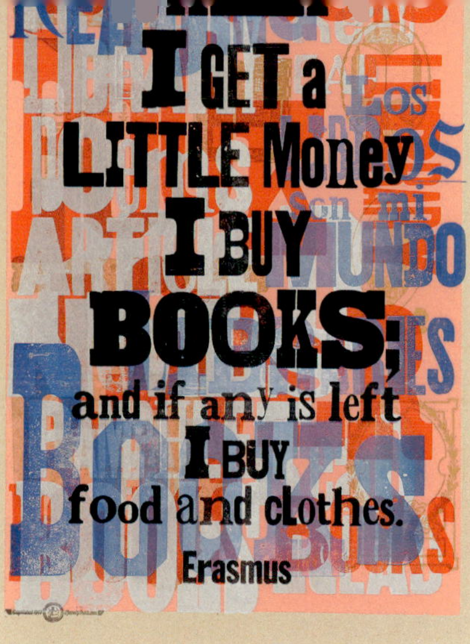
I GET a
LITTLE Money
I BUY
BOOKS;
and if any is left
I BUY
food and clothes.
Erasmus

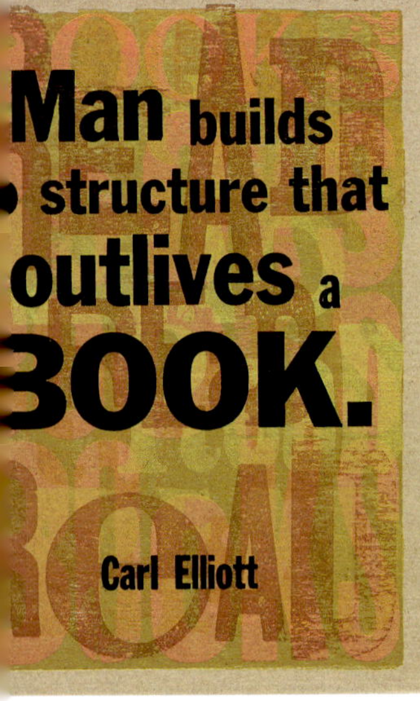
Man builds
structure that
outlives a
OOK.
Carl Elliott

PUBLIC
LIBRARIES
BUILD
COMMUNITY

YOUR
LIBRARY
IS YOUR
PARADISE.
Desiderius Erasmus

EAR THE
LD COAT
and
UY THE
EW BOOK.
Austin Phelps

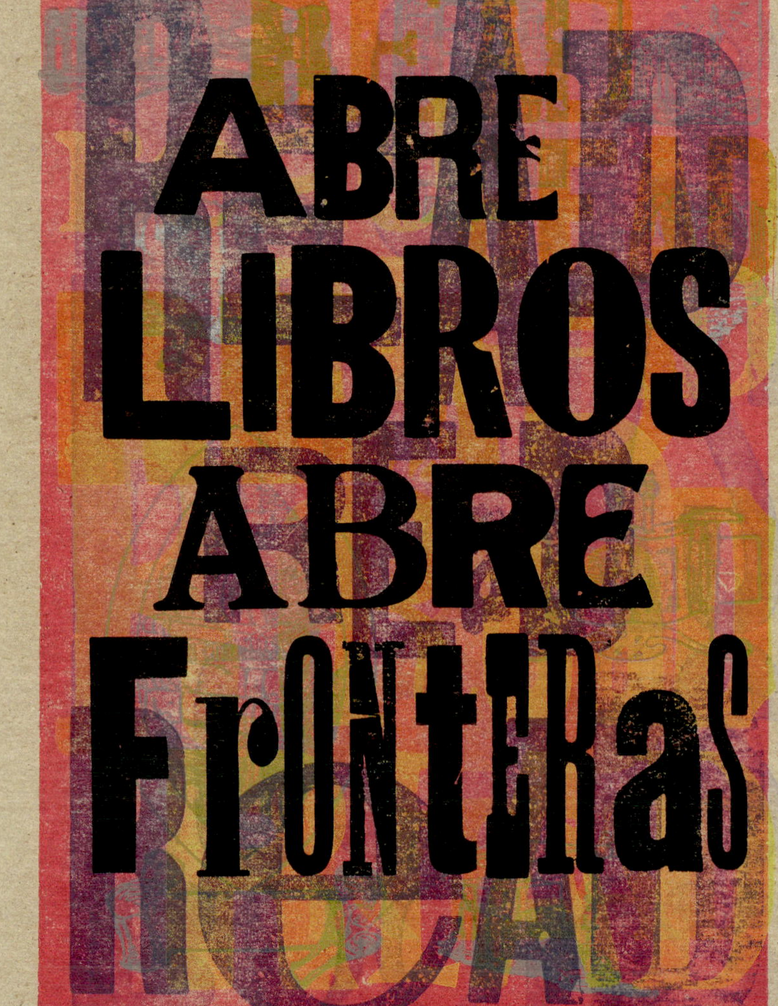
ABRE
LIBROS
ABRE
FrONtERas

A library is not a
luxury
but one of the
necessities
of life.

READ
in order t
LIVE.
Gustave Flaubert

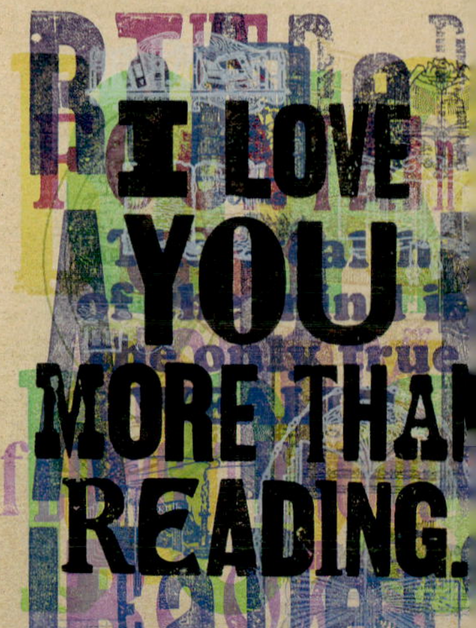
I LOVE
YOU
MORE THA
READING.

A ROOM without BOOKS is like a BODY without a SOUL.
Cicero

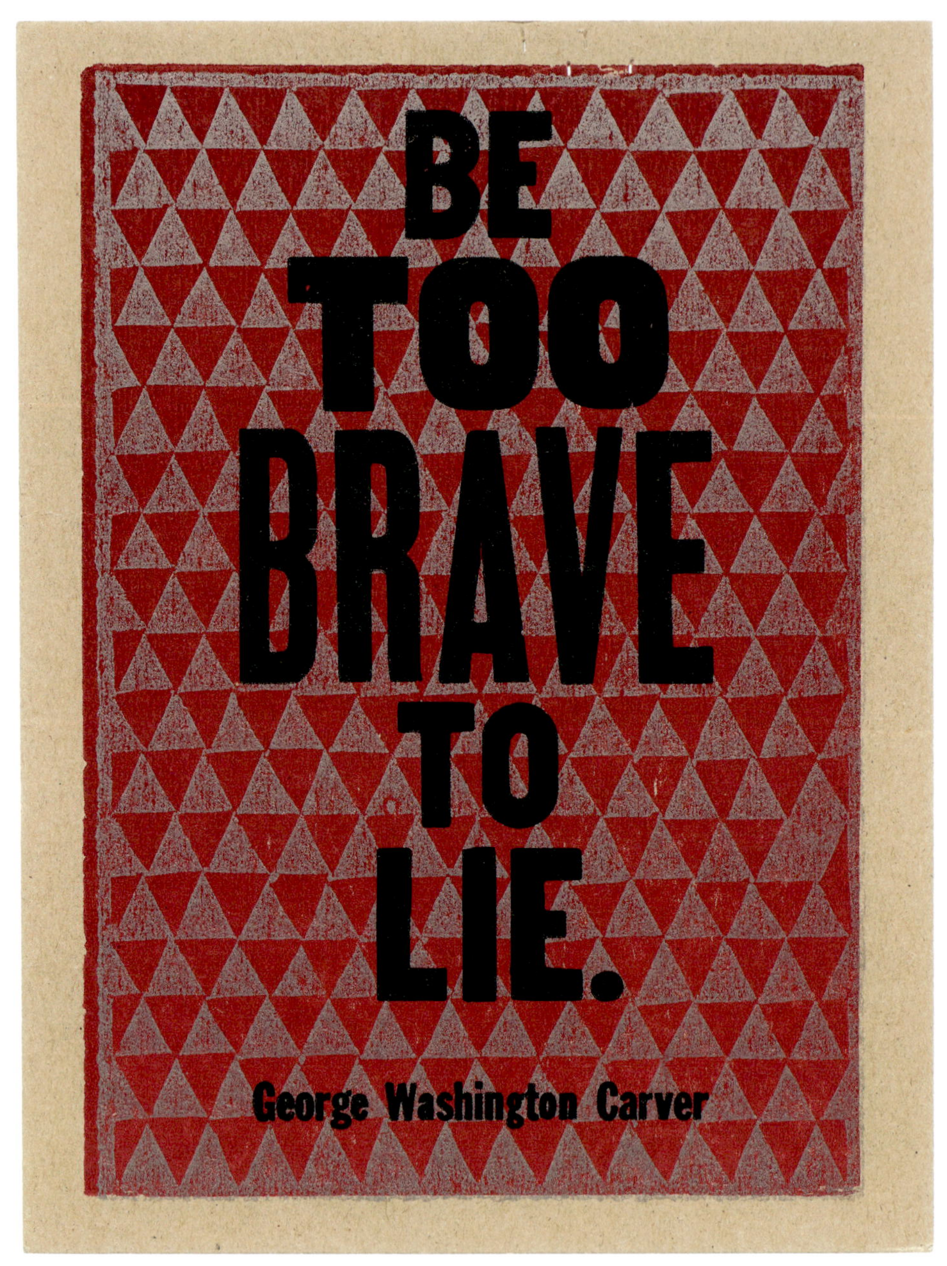
BE
TOO
BRAVE
TO
LIE.
George Washington Carver

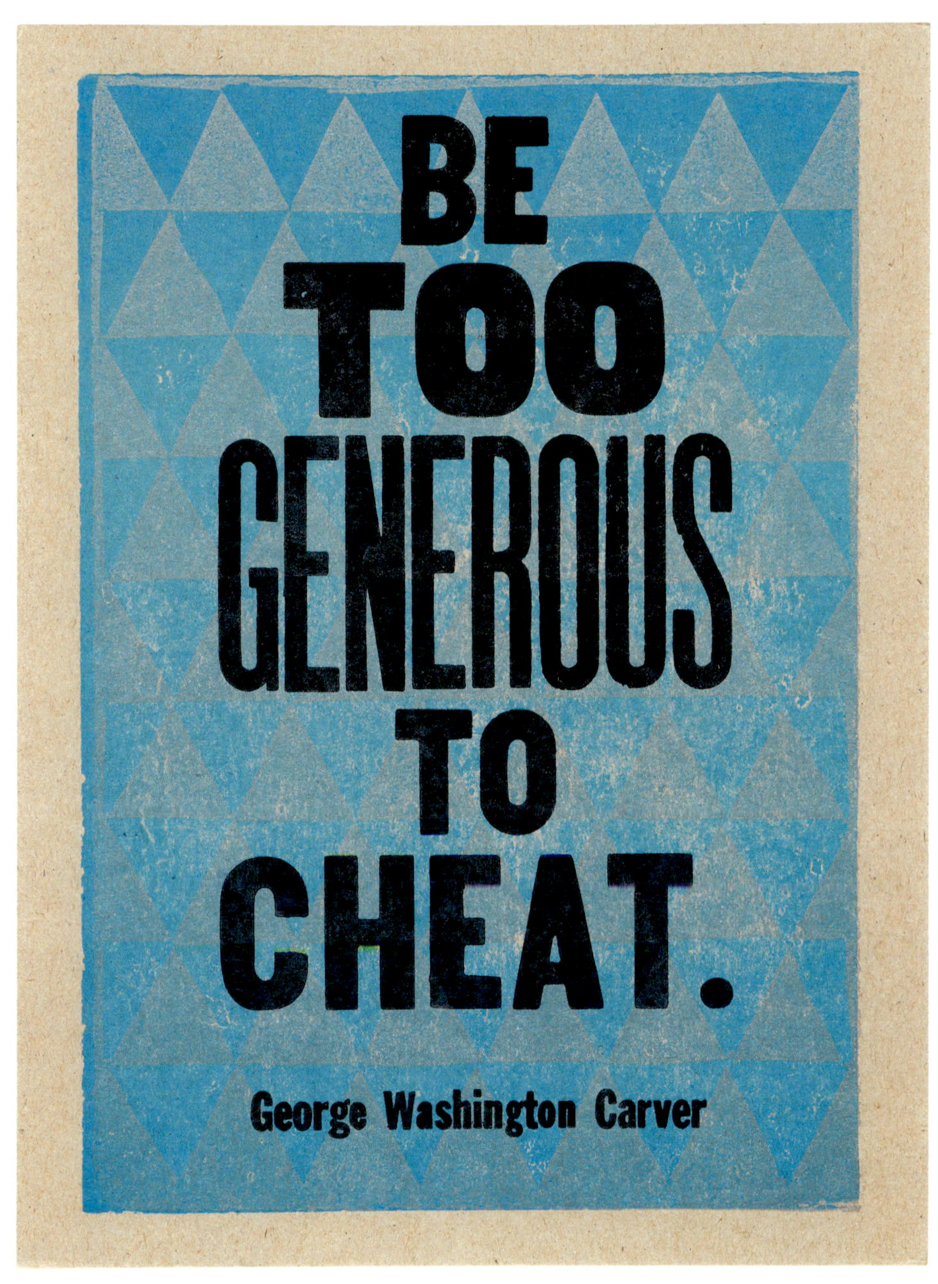
BE
TOO
GENEROUS
TO
CHEAT.
George Washington Carver

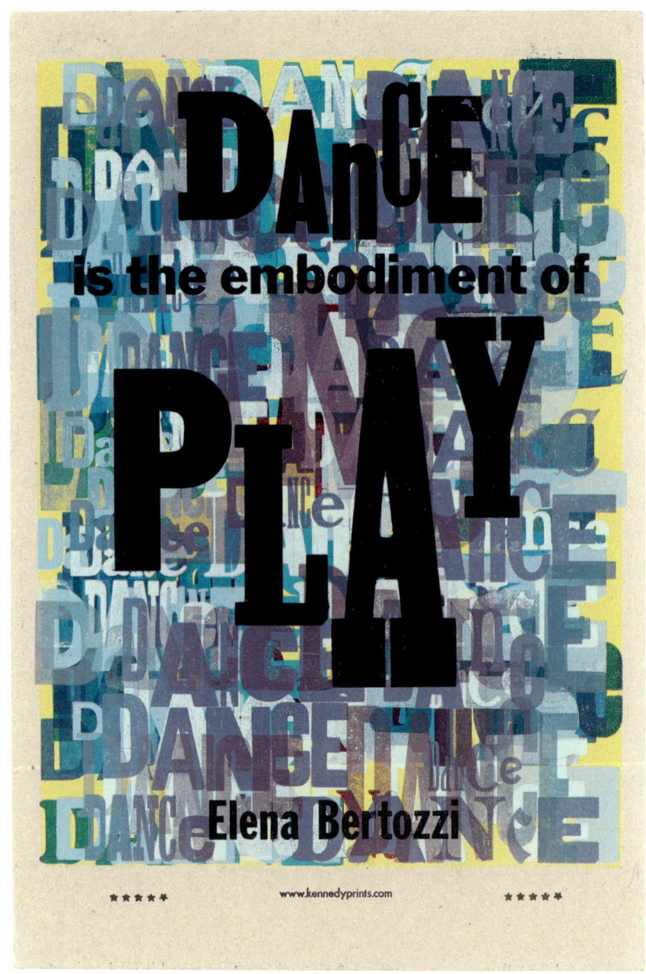
DANCE
is the embodiment of
PLAY
Elena Bertozzi
www.kennedyprints.com

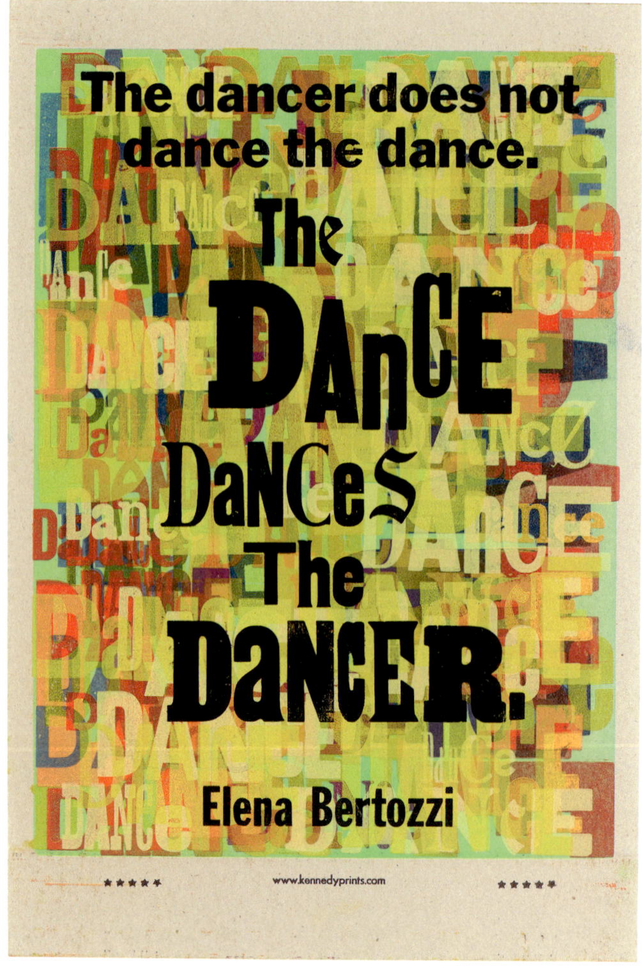
The dancer does not
dance the dance.
The
DANCE
DANCES
The
DANCER.
Elena Bertozzi
www.kennedyprints.com

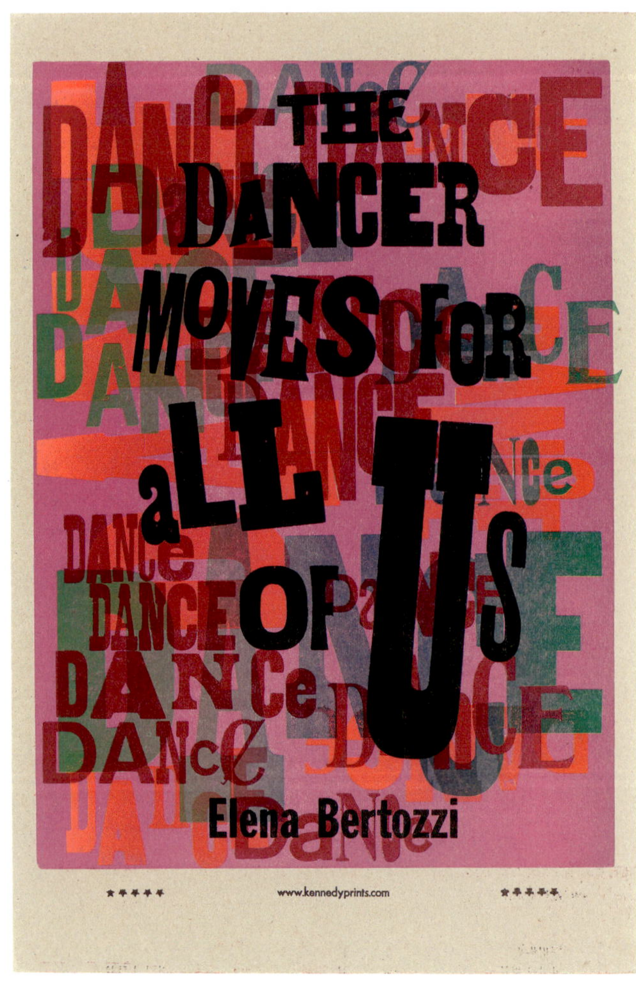
THE
DANCER
MOVES FOR
all
OF
US
Elena Bertozzi
www.kennedyprints.com

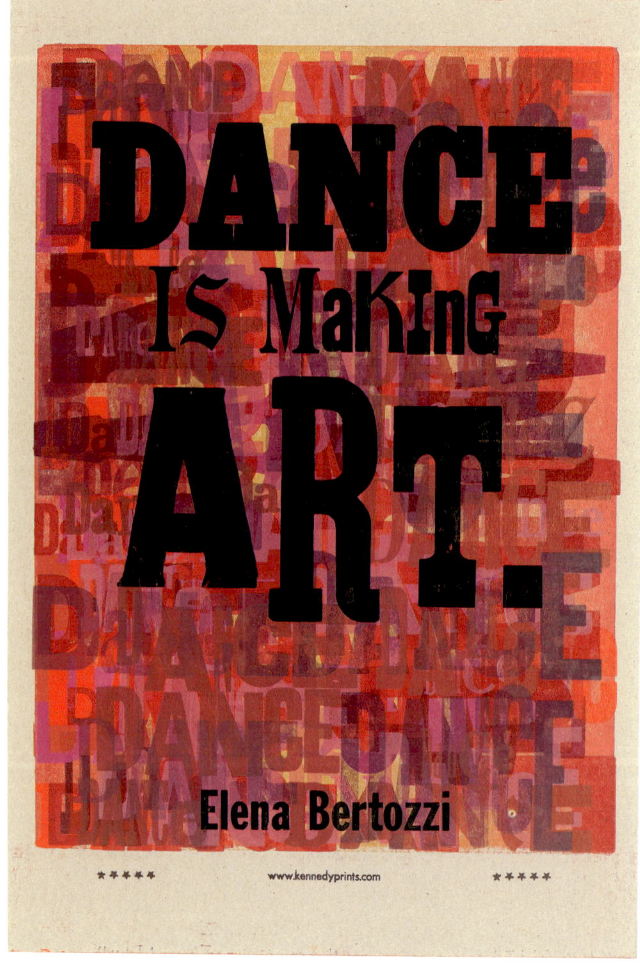
DANCE
IS MAKING
ART.
Elena Bertozzi
www.kennedyprints.com

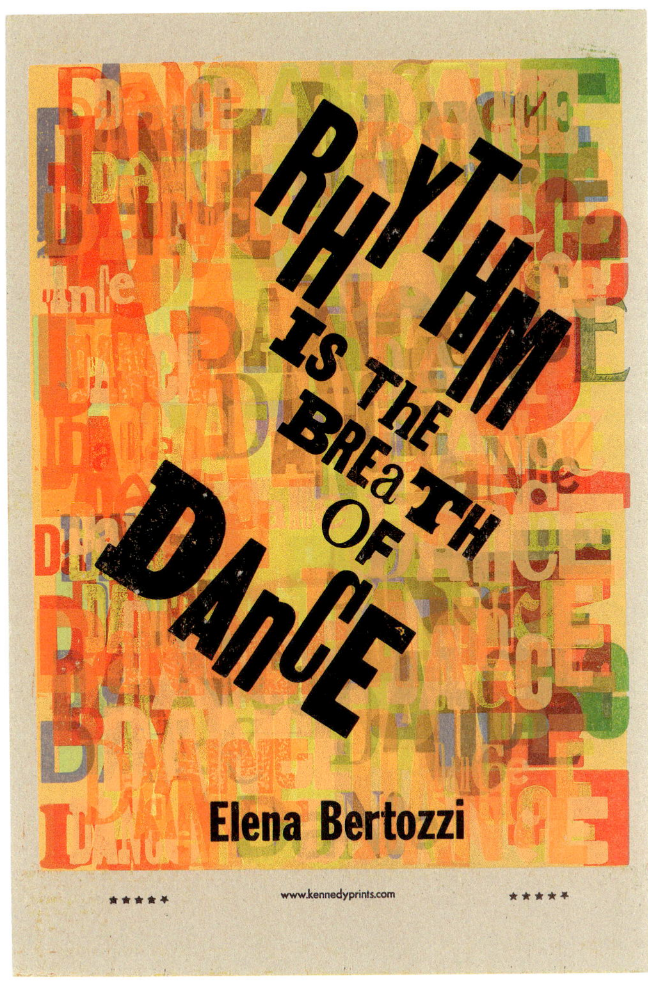
RHYTHM
IS THE
BREATH
OF
DANCE
Elena Bertozzi
www.kennedyprints.com

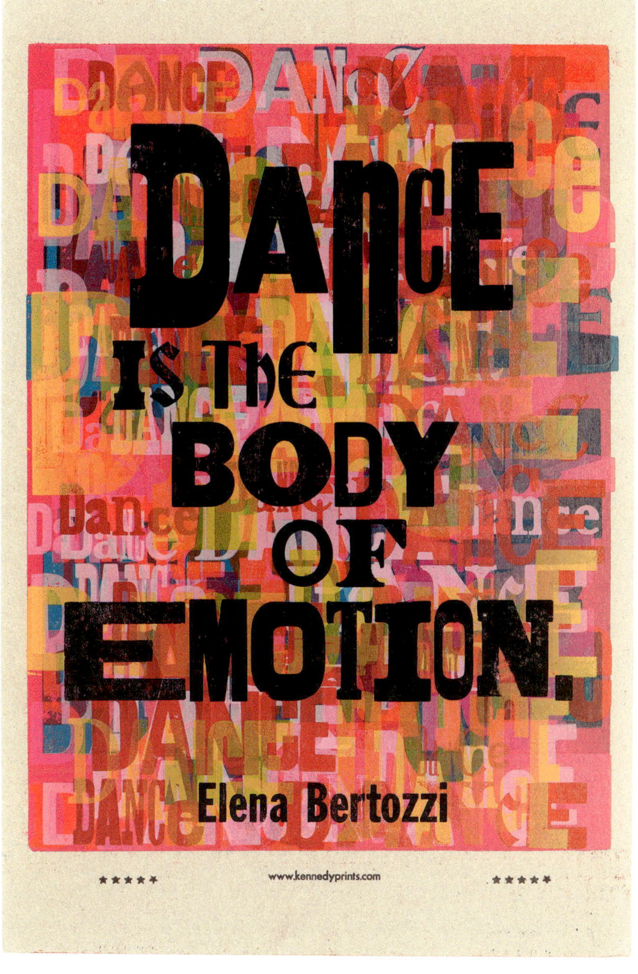
DANCE
IS THE
BODY
OF
EMOTION.
Elena Bertozzi
www.kennedyprints.com

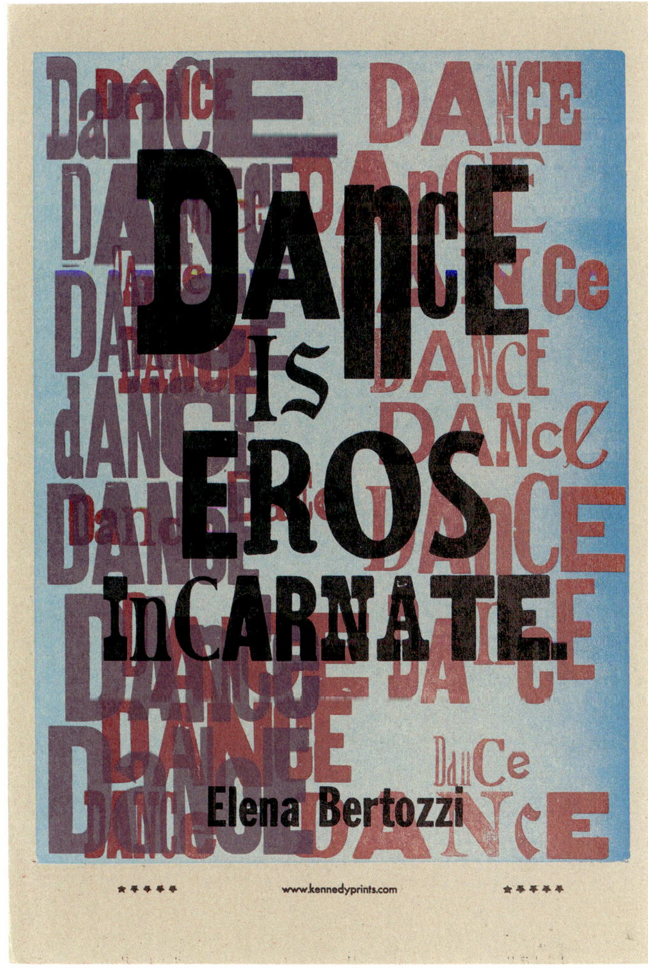
DANCE
IS
EROS
INCARNATE.
Elena Bertozzi
www.kennedyprints.com

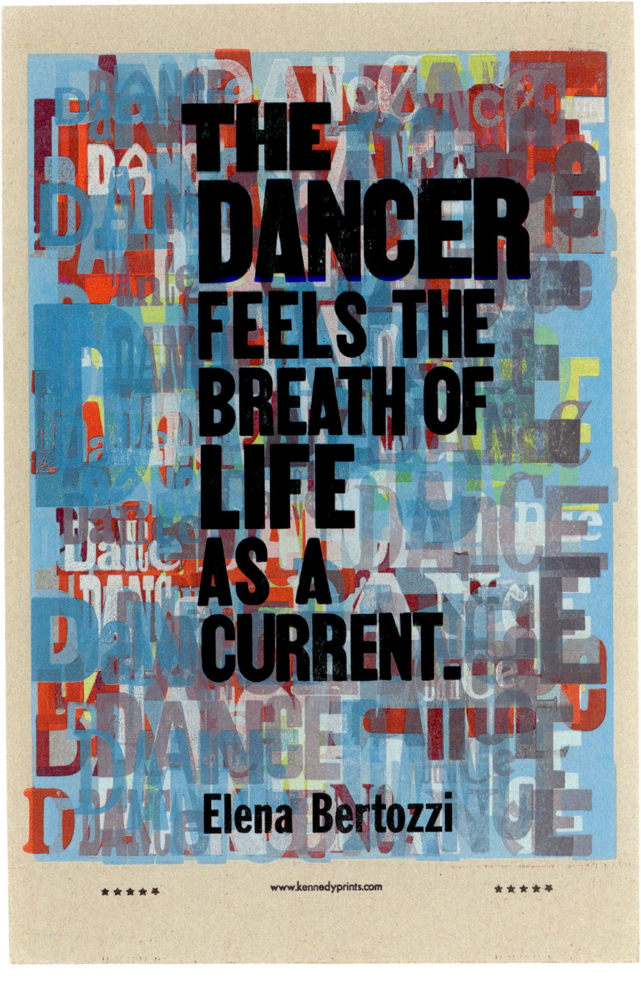
THE
DANCER
FEELS THE
BREATH OF
LIFE
AS A
CURRENT.
Elena Bertozzi
www.kennedyprints.com

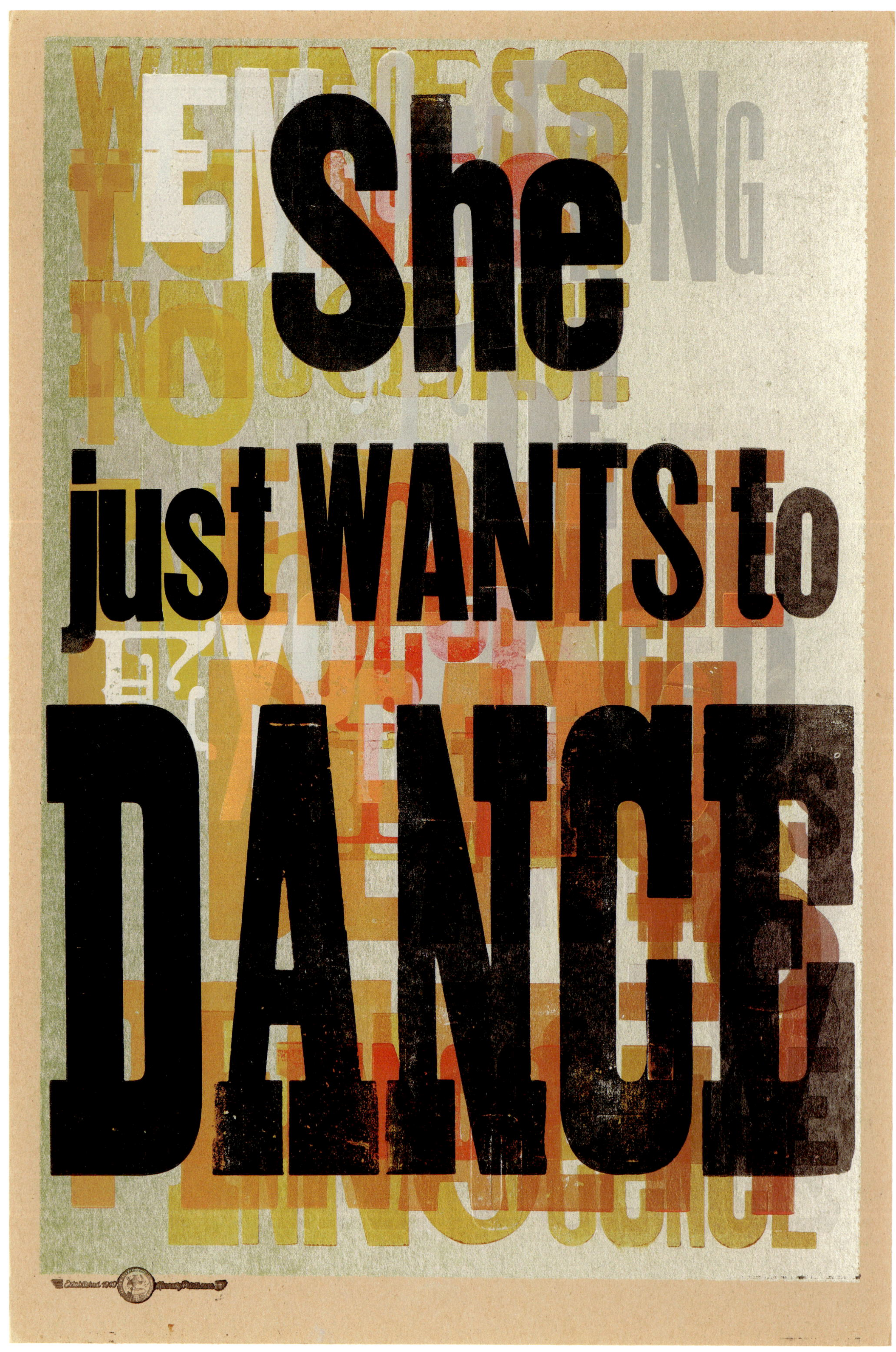
She
just WANTS to
DANCE

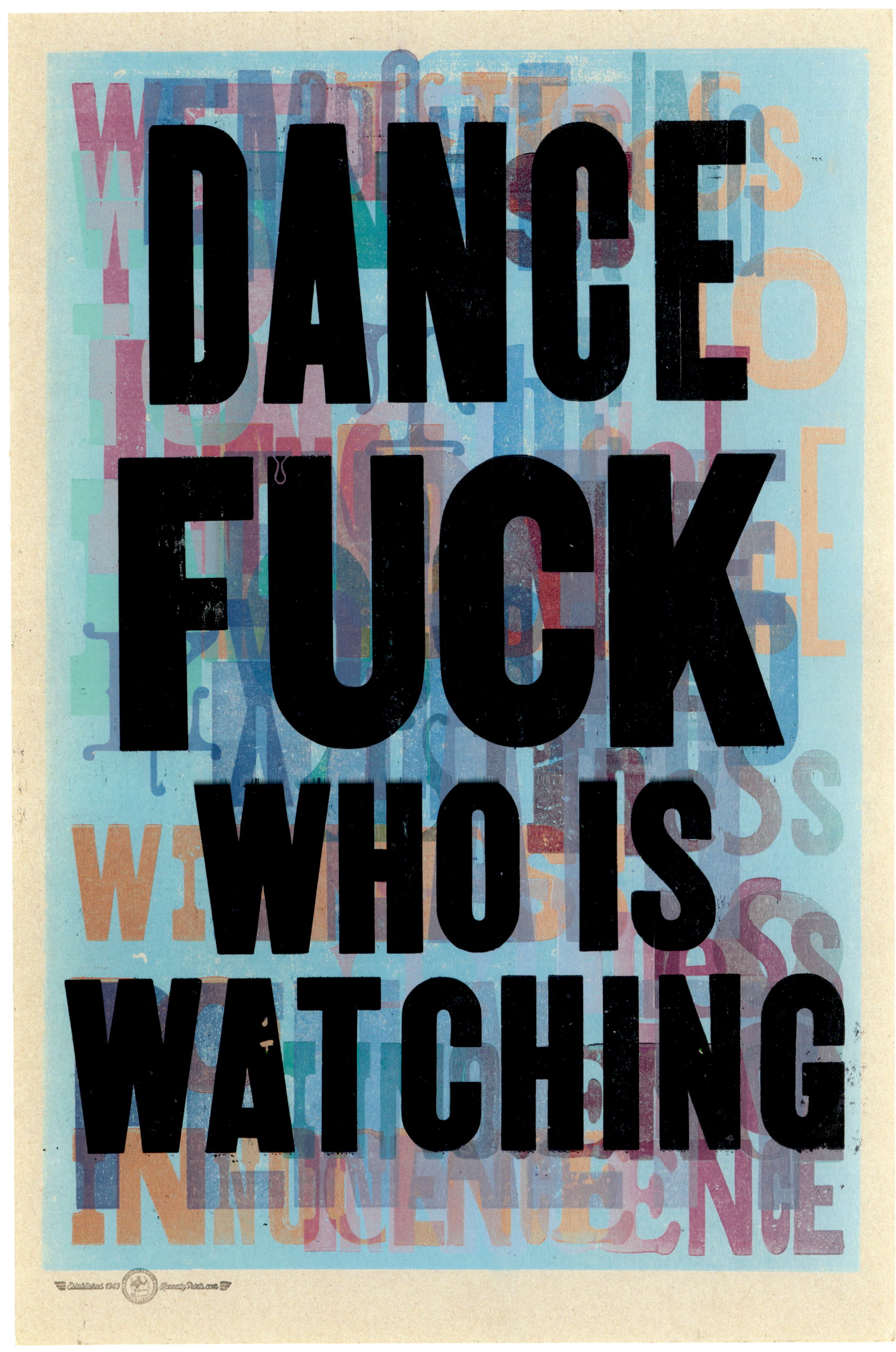
DANCE
FUCK
WHO IS
WATCHING

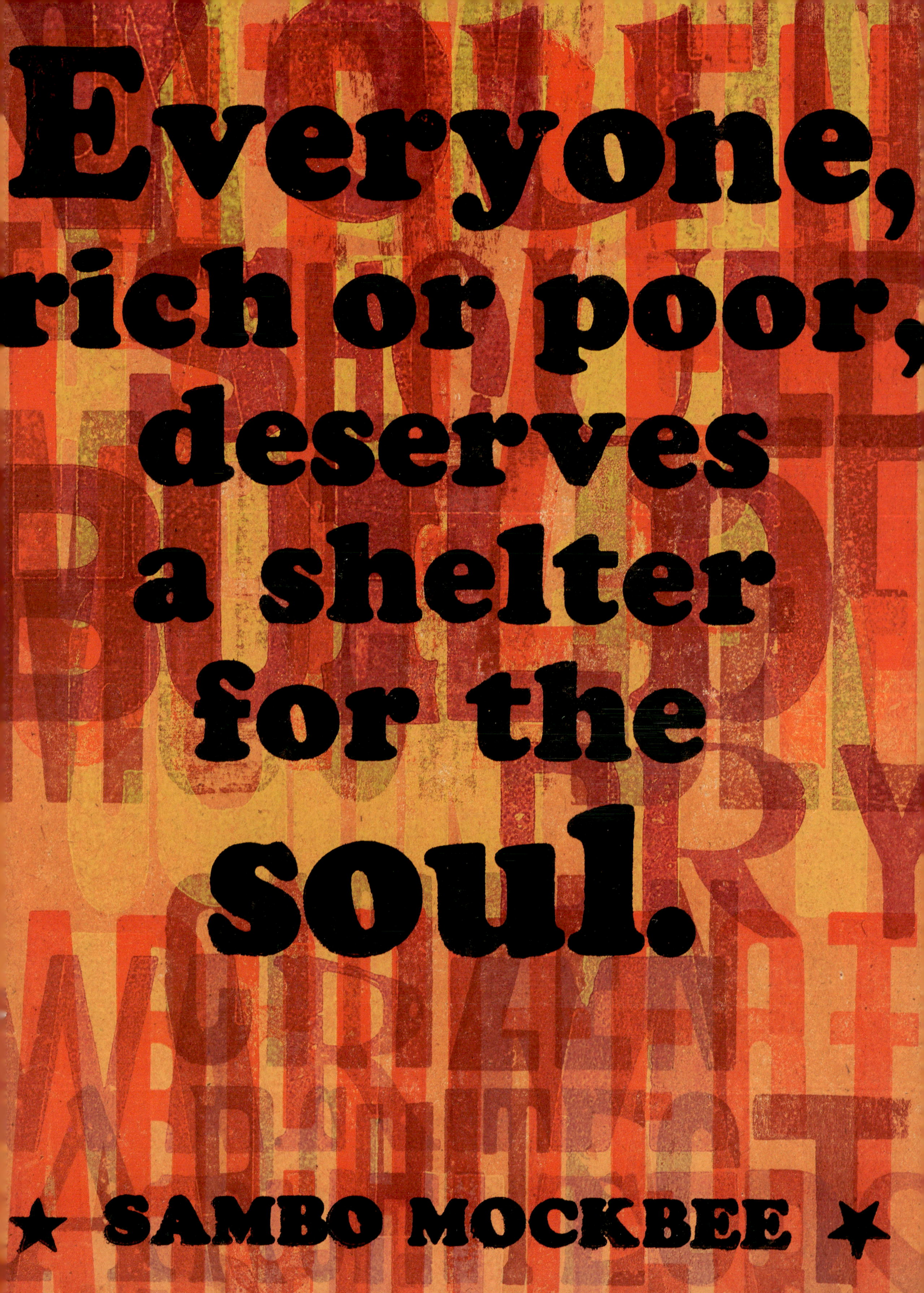
Everyone,
rich or poor,
deserves
a shelter
for the
soul.
★ SAMBO MOCKBEE ★

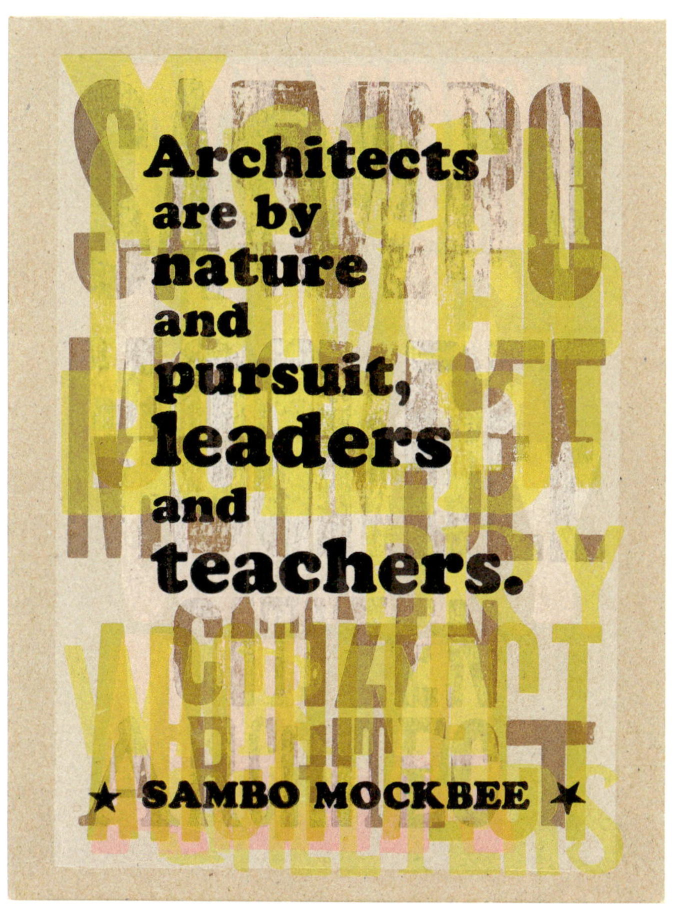
Architects
are by
nature
and
pursuit,
leaders
and
teachers.
★ SAMBO MOCKBEE ★

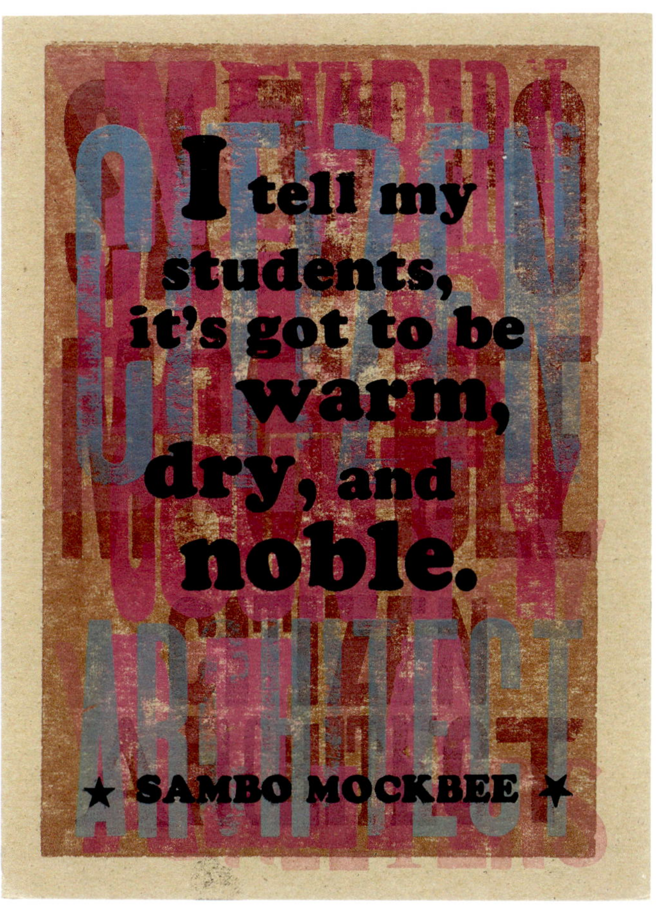
I tell my
students,
it's got to be
warm,
dry, and
noble.
★ SAMBO MOCKBEE ★

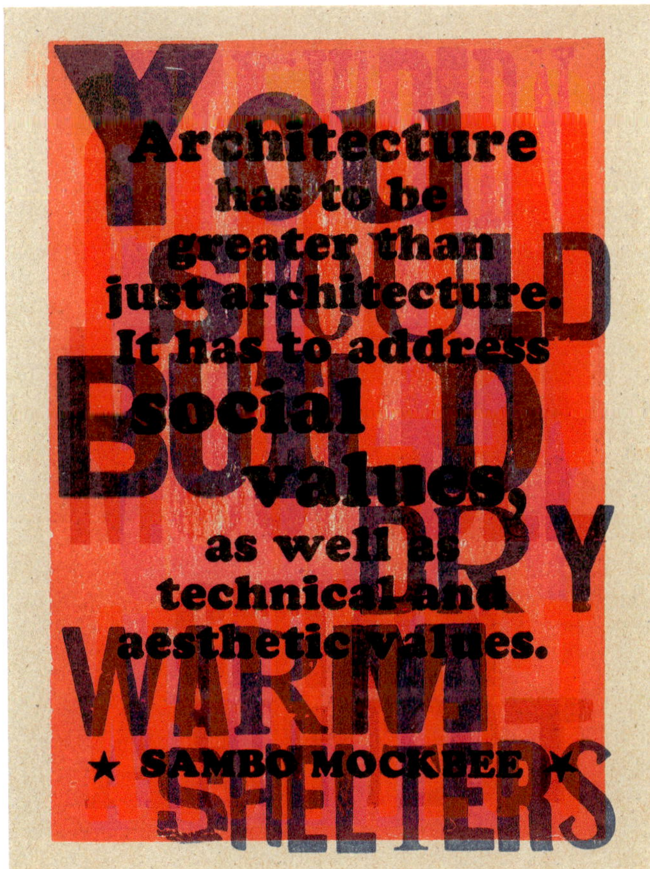
Architecture
has to be
greater than
just architecture.
It has to address
social
values,
as well as
technical and
aesthetic values.
★ SAMBO MOCKBEE ★

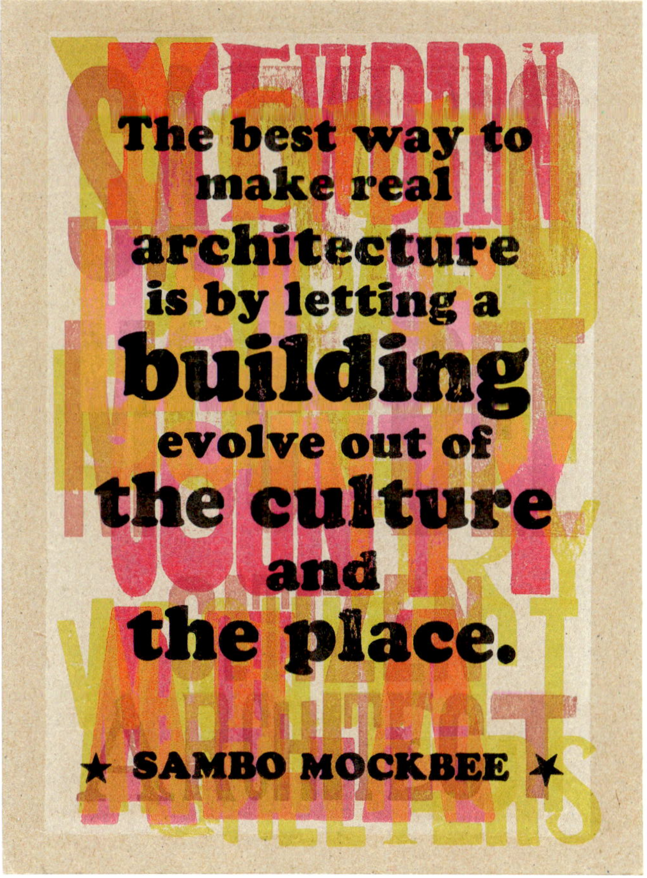
The best way to
make real
architecture
is by letting a
building
evolve out of
the culture
and
the place.
★ SAMBO MOCKBEE ★

“These words were spoken by Sambo Mockbee, a citizen architect who built housing and community spaces for rural folk in Alabama. I did not get to meet him, but we were both drawn to the Black Belt for the same reason: to explore the development of our crafts in service of our communities. We both grew. It was fertile ground.”

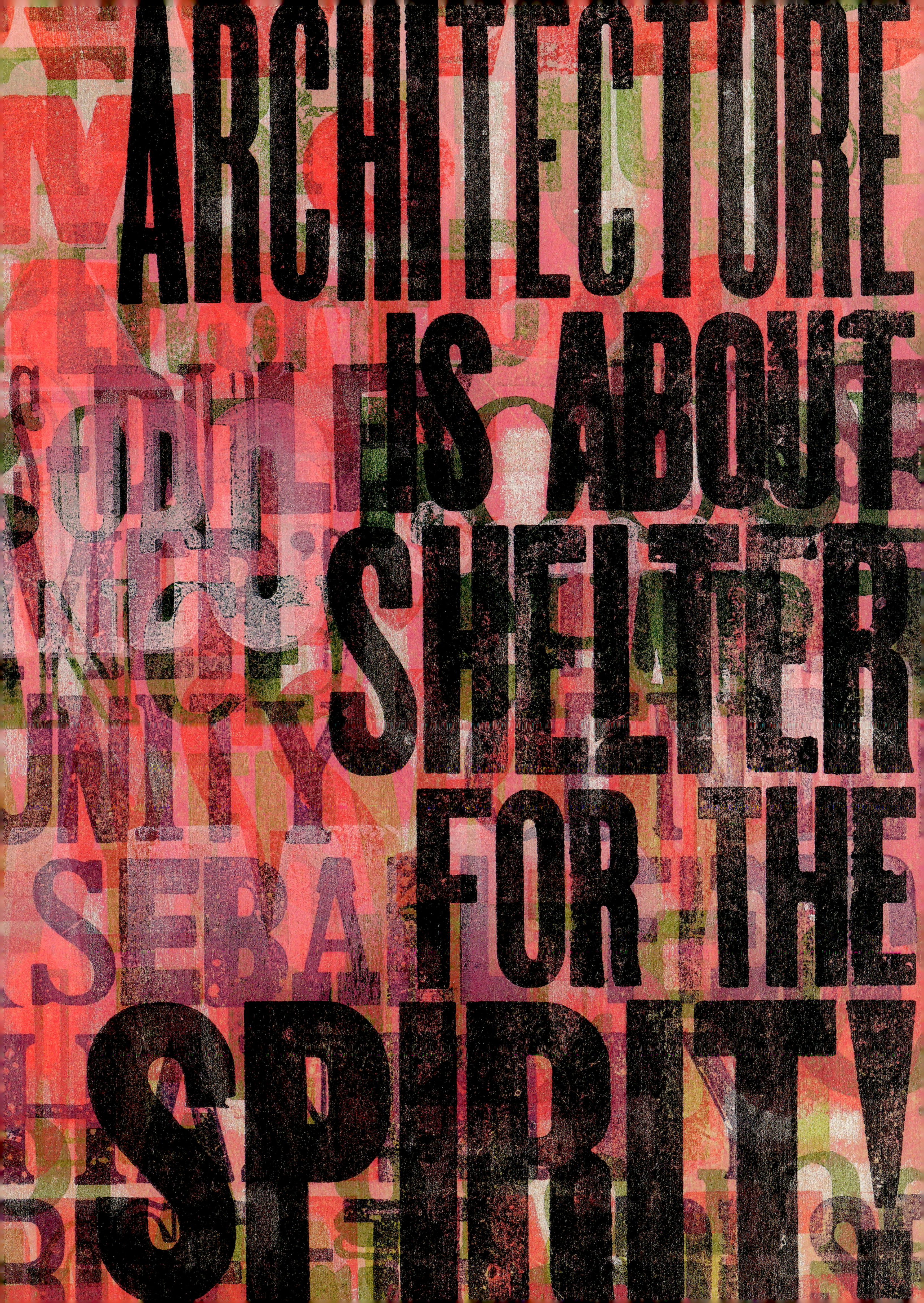
ARCHITECTURE
IS ABOUT
SHELTER
FOR THE
SPIRIT!

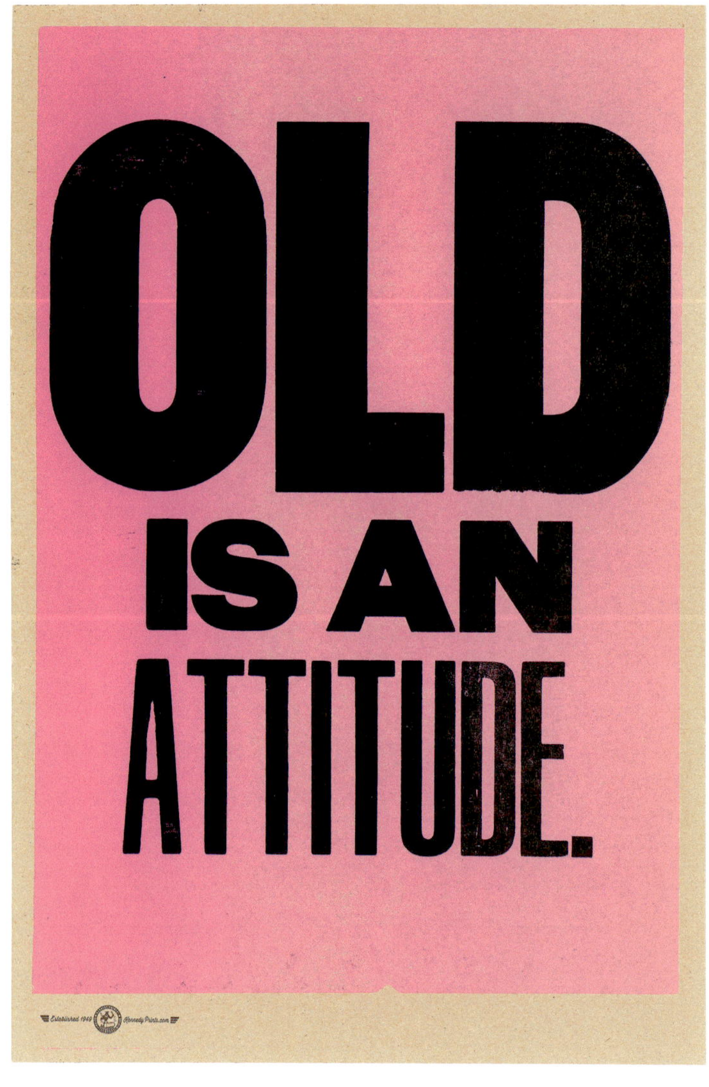
OLD
IS AN
ATTITUDE.

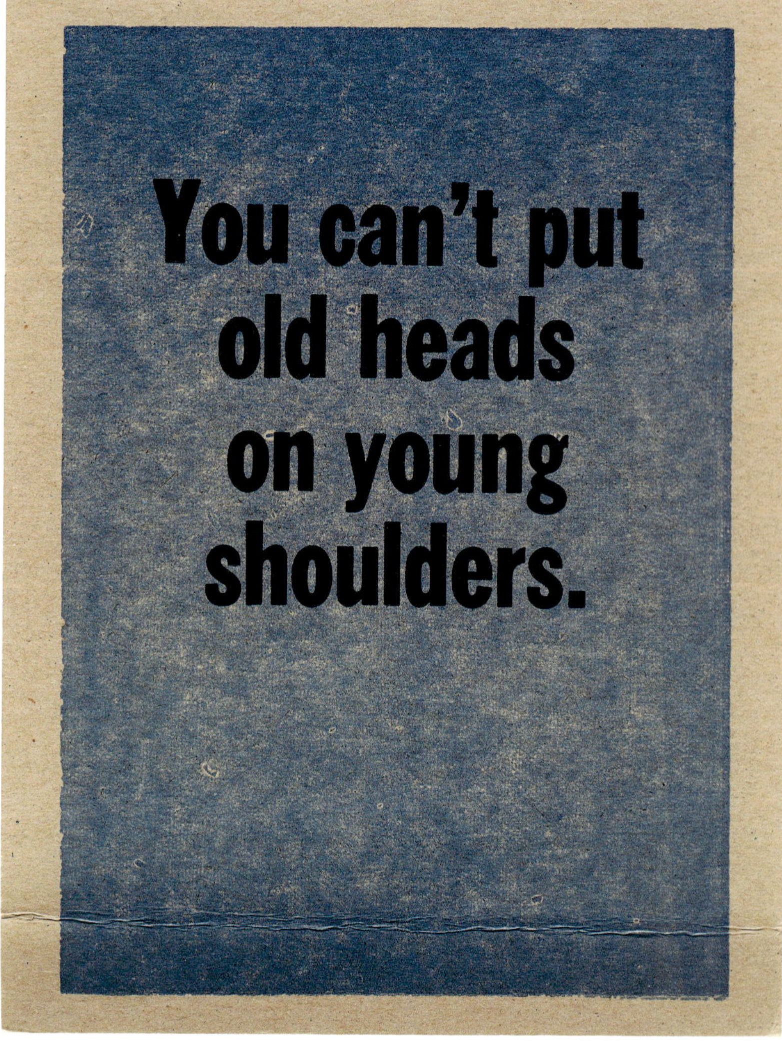
You can't put
old heads
on young
shoulders.

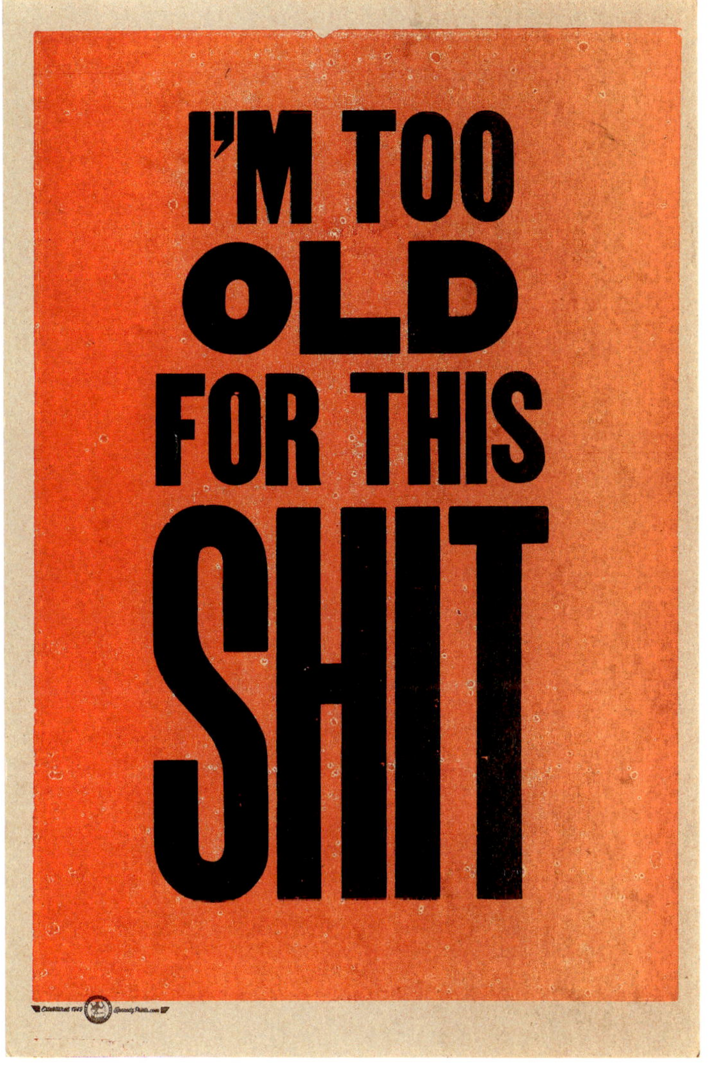
I'M TOO
OLD
FOR THIS
SHIT

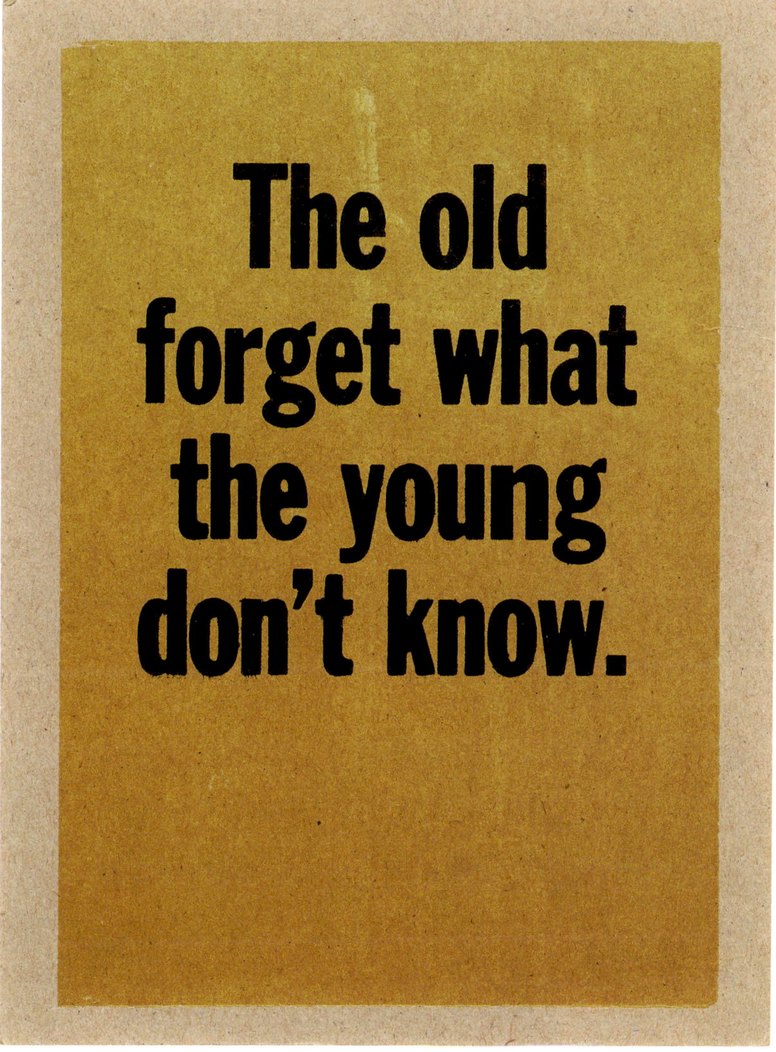
The old
forget what
the young
don't know.

CHILDREN

TIRED OF BEING HARRASSED
BY YOUR STUPID PARENTS?

ACT NOW!

MOVE OUT, GET A JOB,
PAY YOUR OWN BILLS,
WHILE **YOU** STILL
KNOW EVERYTHING.

www.kennedyprints.com

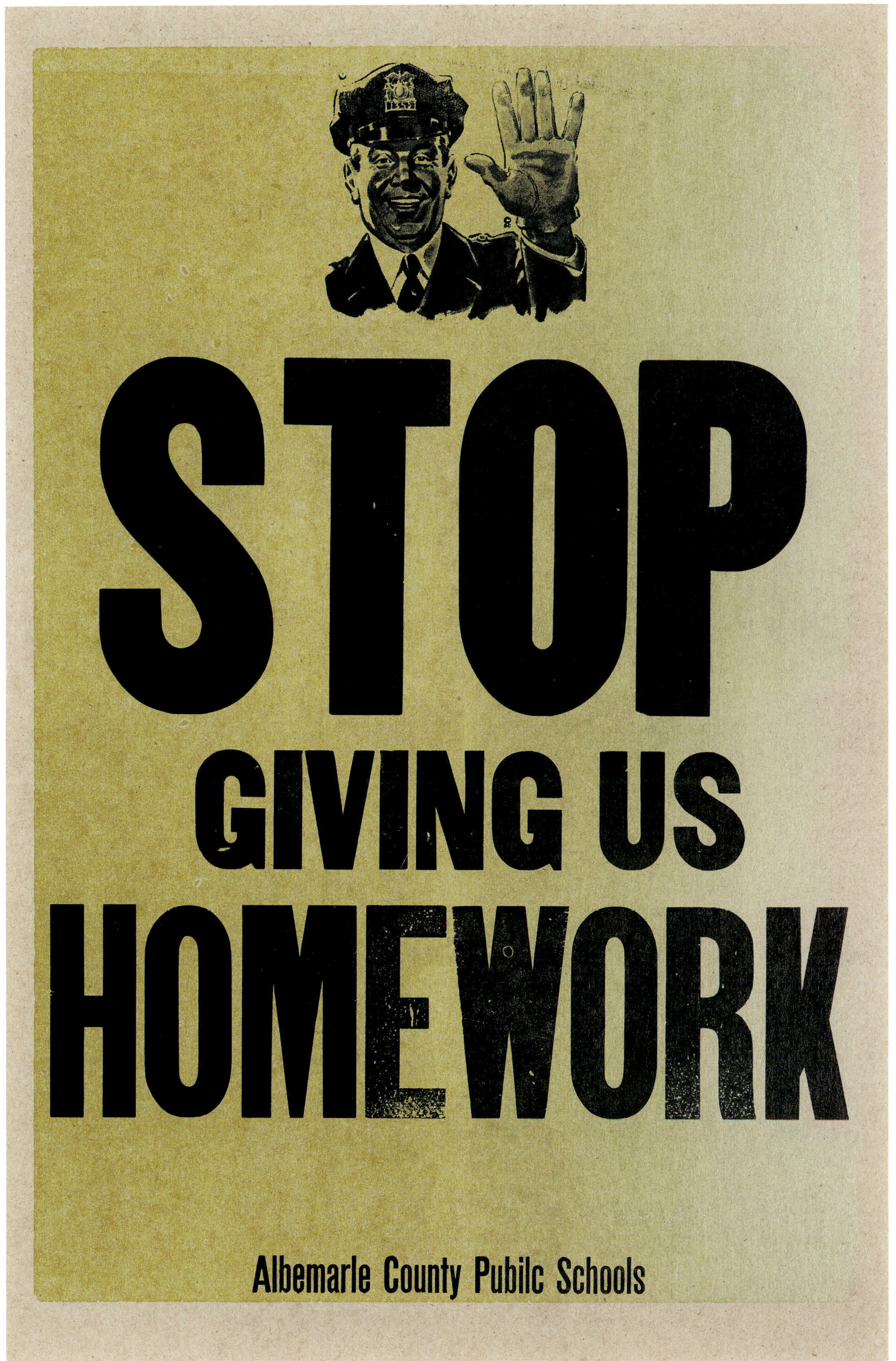
STOP
GIVING US
HOMEWORK
Albemarle County Pubilc Schools

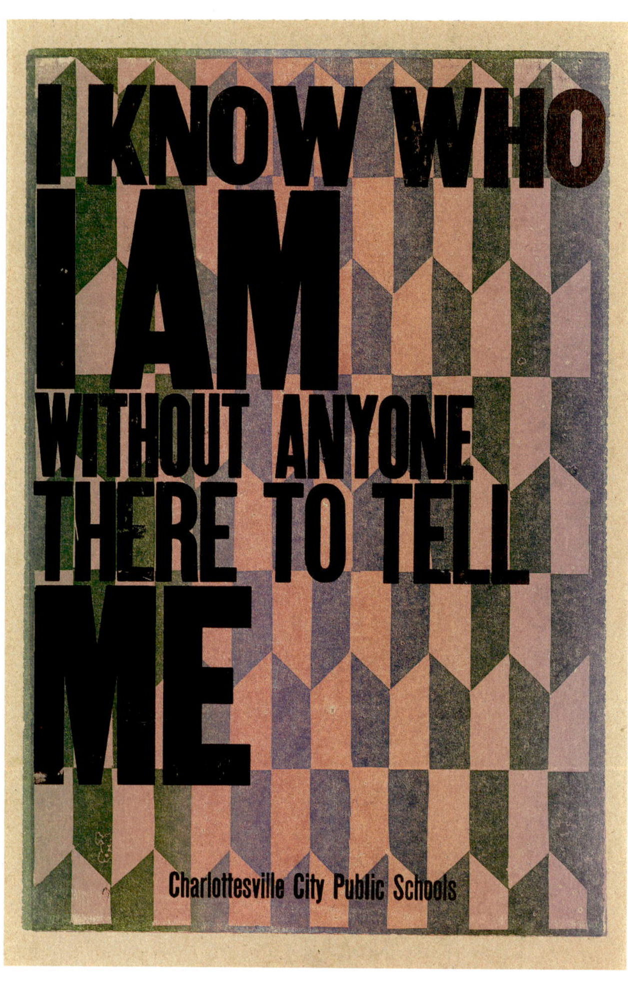
I KNOW WHO
I AM
WITHOUT ANYONE
THERE TO TELL
ME
Charlottesville City Public Schools

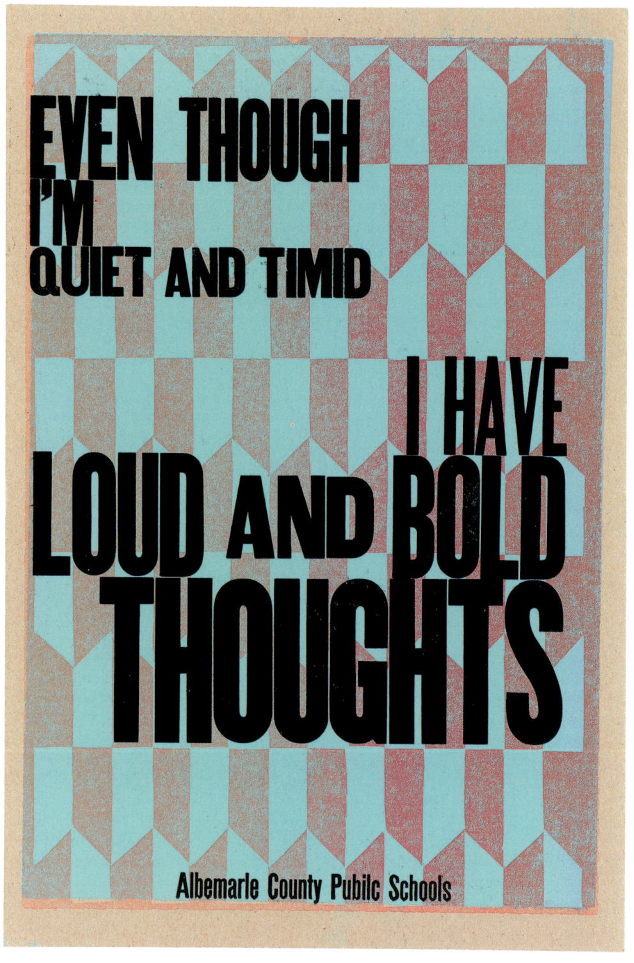
EVEN THOUGH
I'M
QUIET AND TIMID
I HAVE
LOUD AND BOLD
THOUGHTS
Albemarle County Pubilc Schools

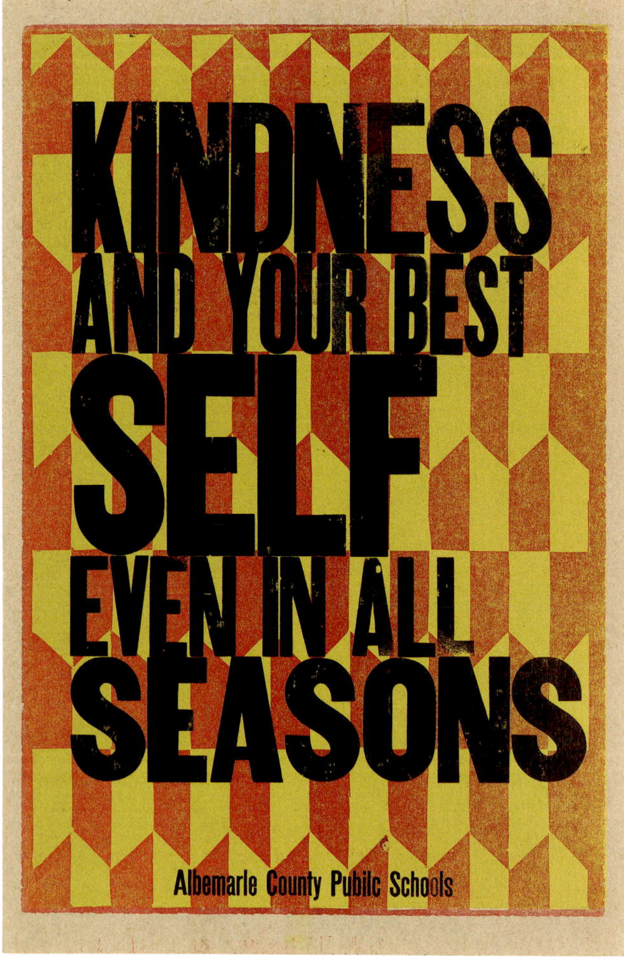
KINDNESS
AND YOUR BEST
SELF
EVEN IN ALL
SEASONS
Albemarle County Pubilc Schools

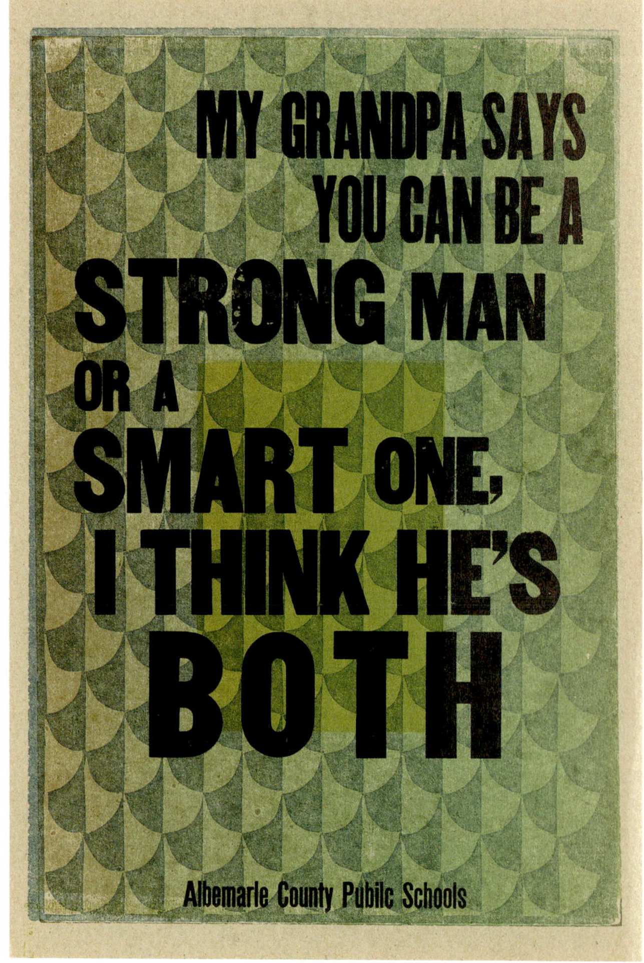
MY GRANDPA SAYS
YOU CAN BE A
STRONG MAN
OR A
SMART ONE,
I THINK HE'S
BOTH
Albemarle County Pubilc Schools

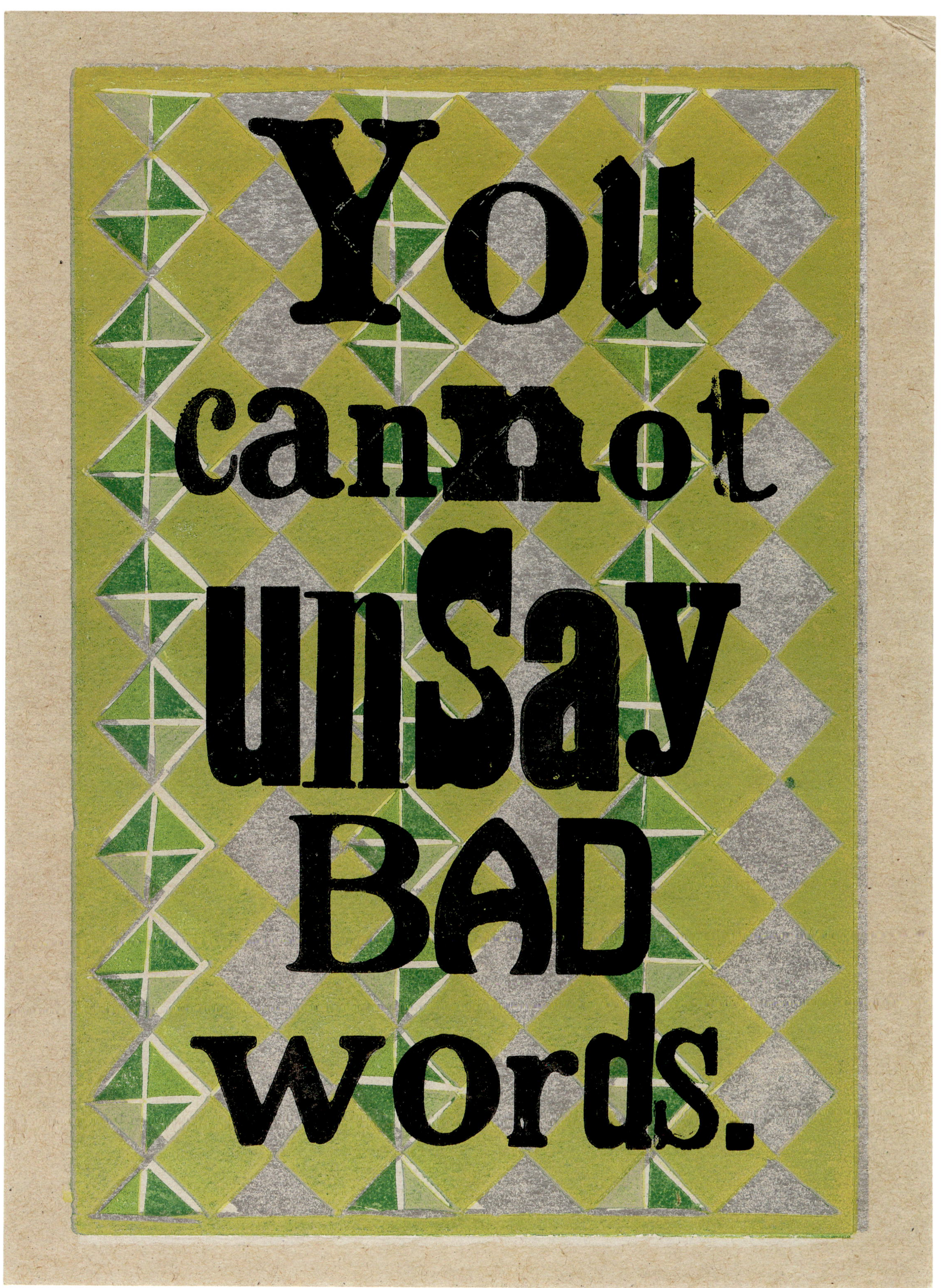
You
cannot
unSay
BAD
words.

It's fun to be

WEIRD!

Oak Johns

> “When I do workshops with young people, I use quotes from the kids themselves. It amplifies their voices to see their own words in print.”

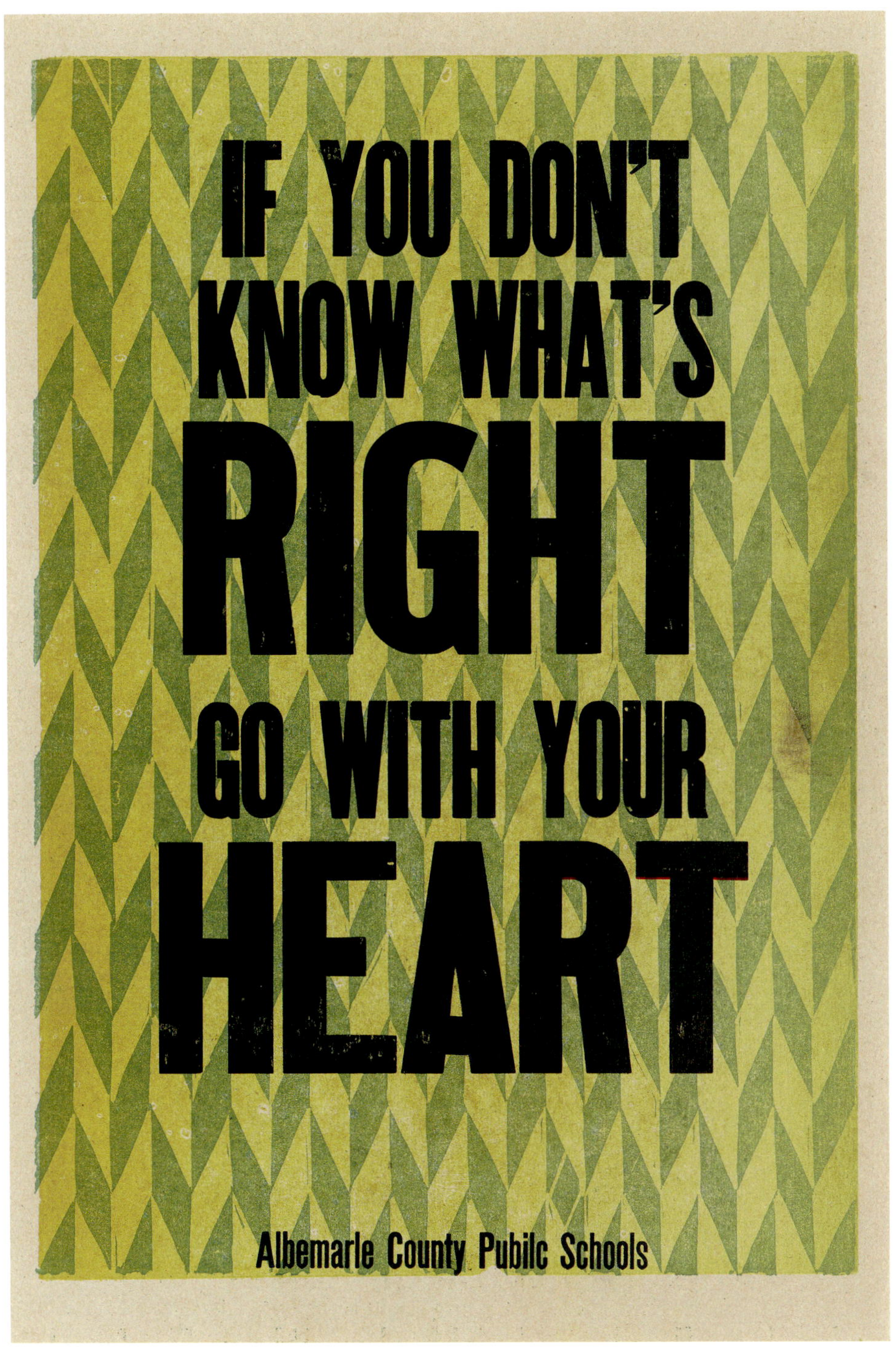

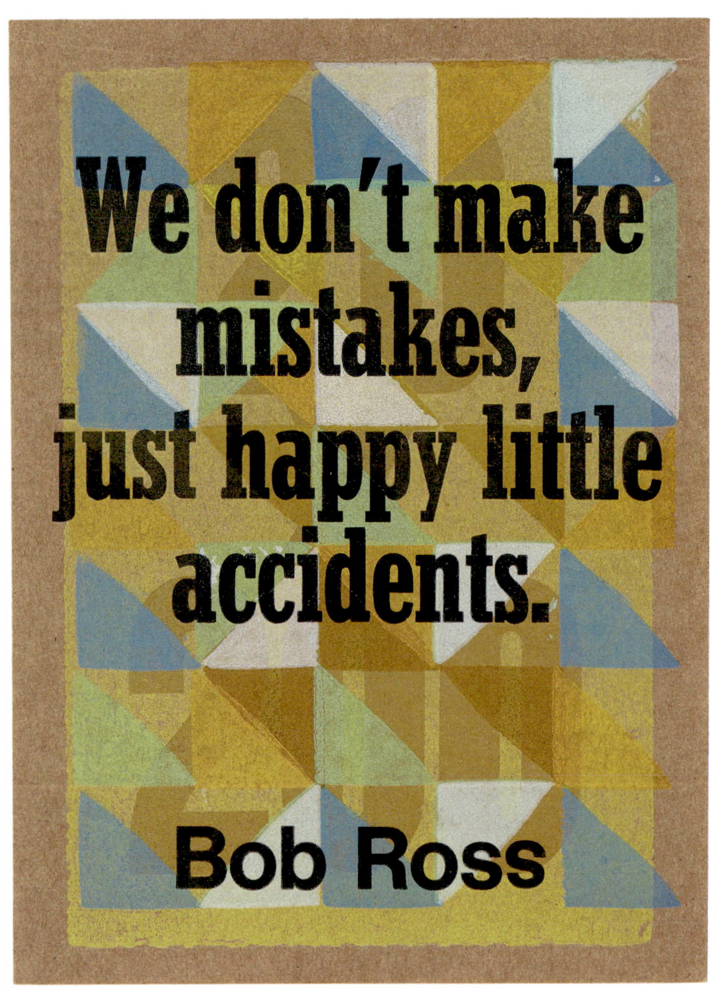
We don't make mistakes, just happy little accidents.
Bob Ross

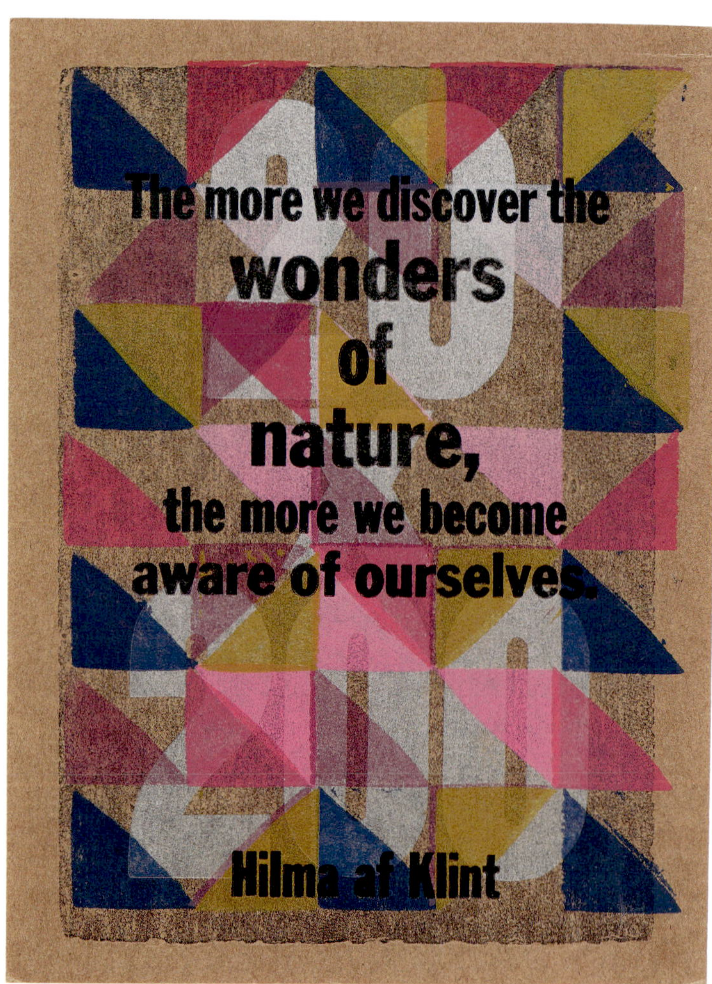
The more we discover the wonders of nature, the more we become aware of ourselves.
Hilma af Klint

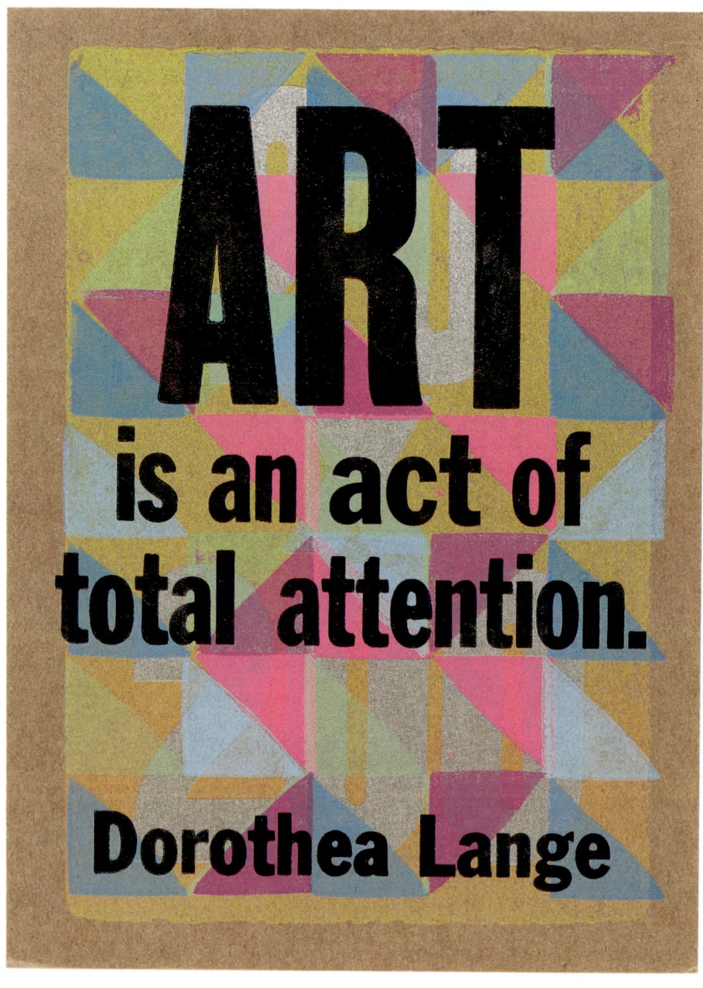
ART is an act of total attention.
Dorothea Lange

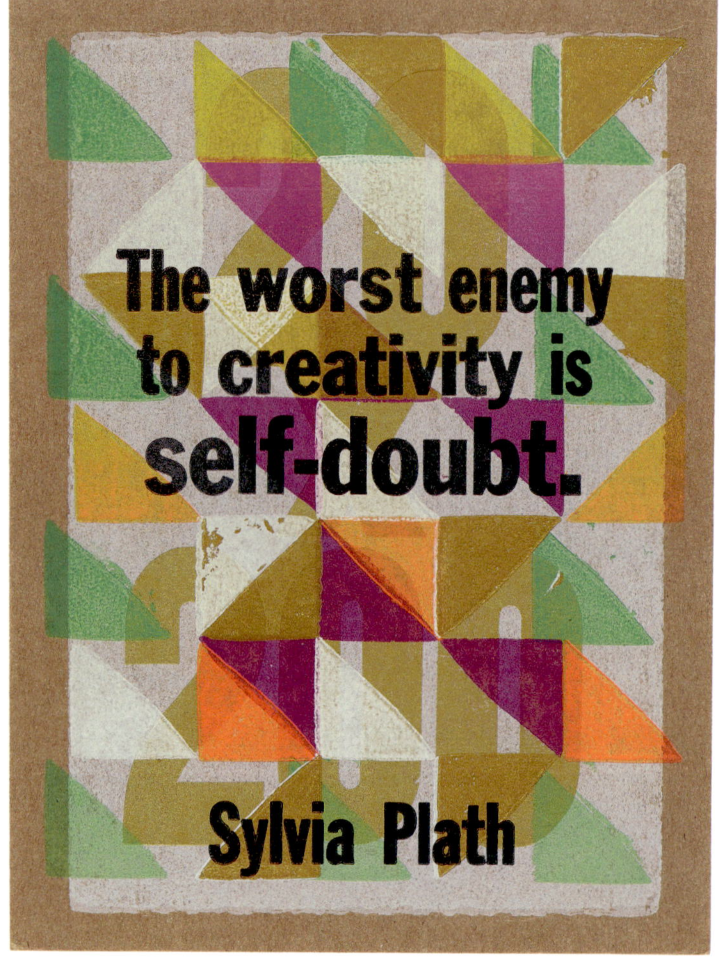
The worst enemy to creativity is self-doubt.
Sylvia Plath

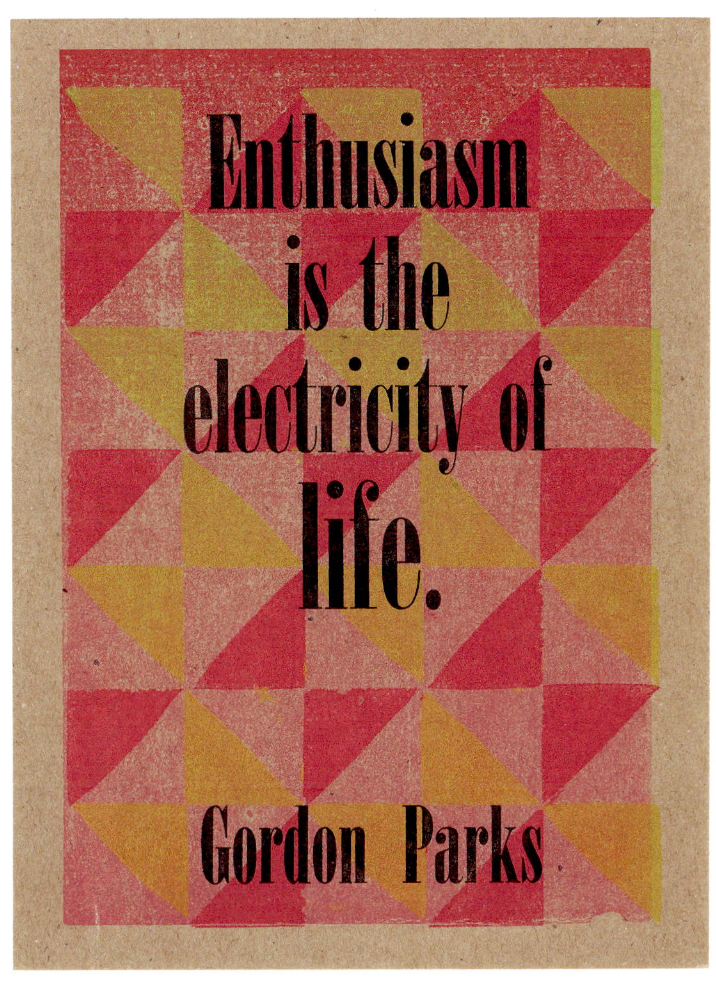
Enthusiasm
is the
electricity of
life.
Gordon Parks

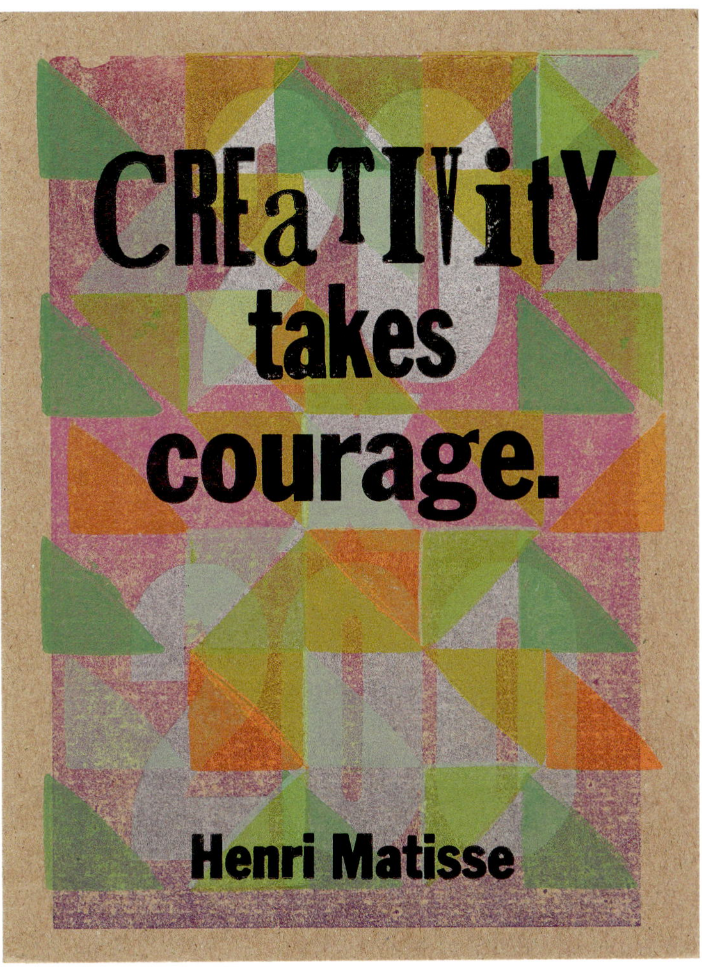
CREaTIVitY
takes
courage.
Henri Matisse

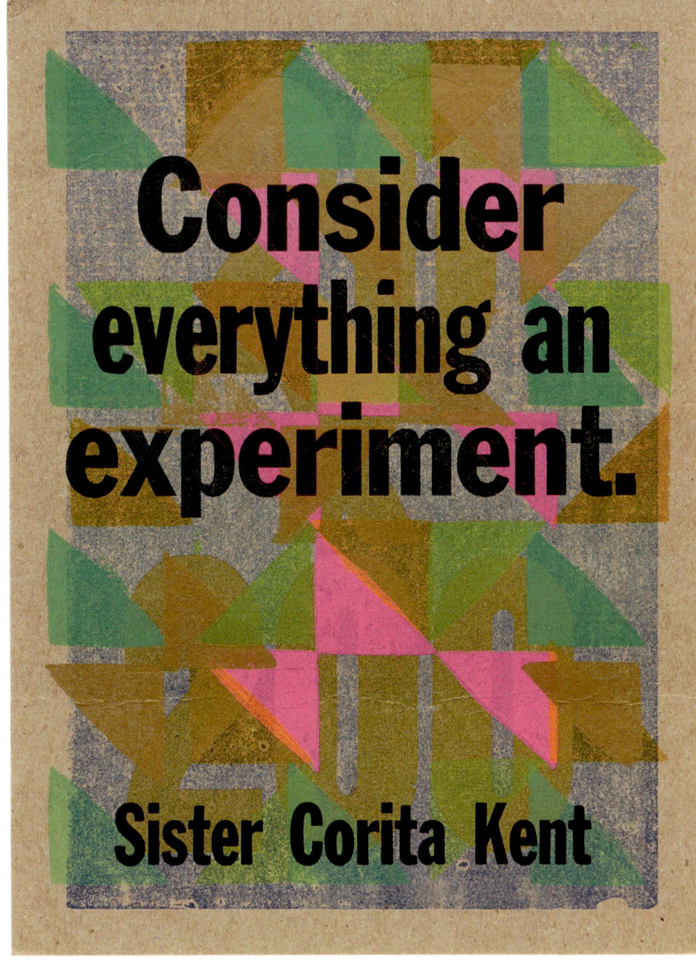
Consider
everything an
experiment.
Sister Corita Kent

I don't paint
dreams or
nightmares.
I paint
my own
reality.
Frida Kahlo

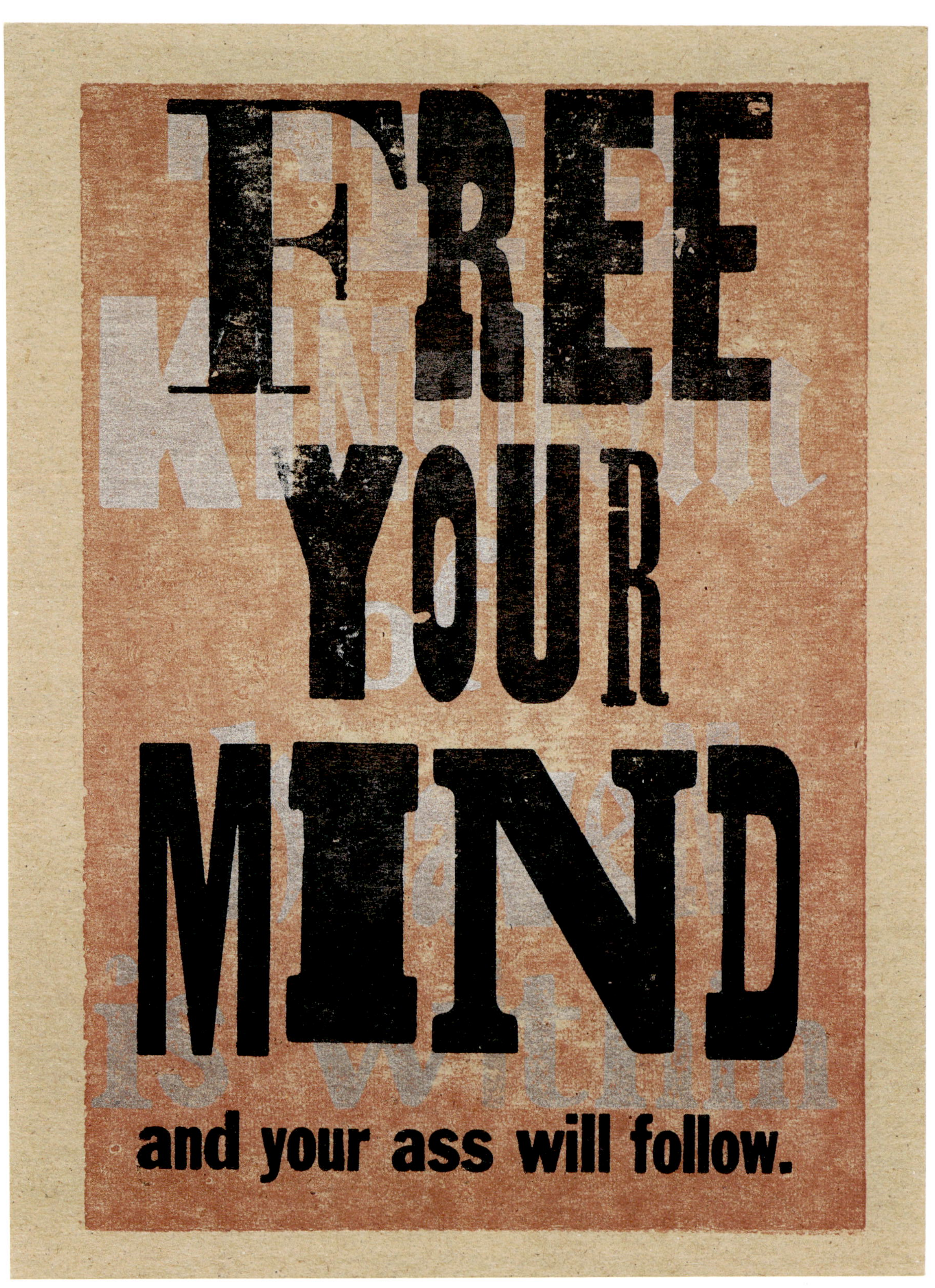
FREE
YOUR
MIND
and your ass will follow.

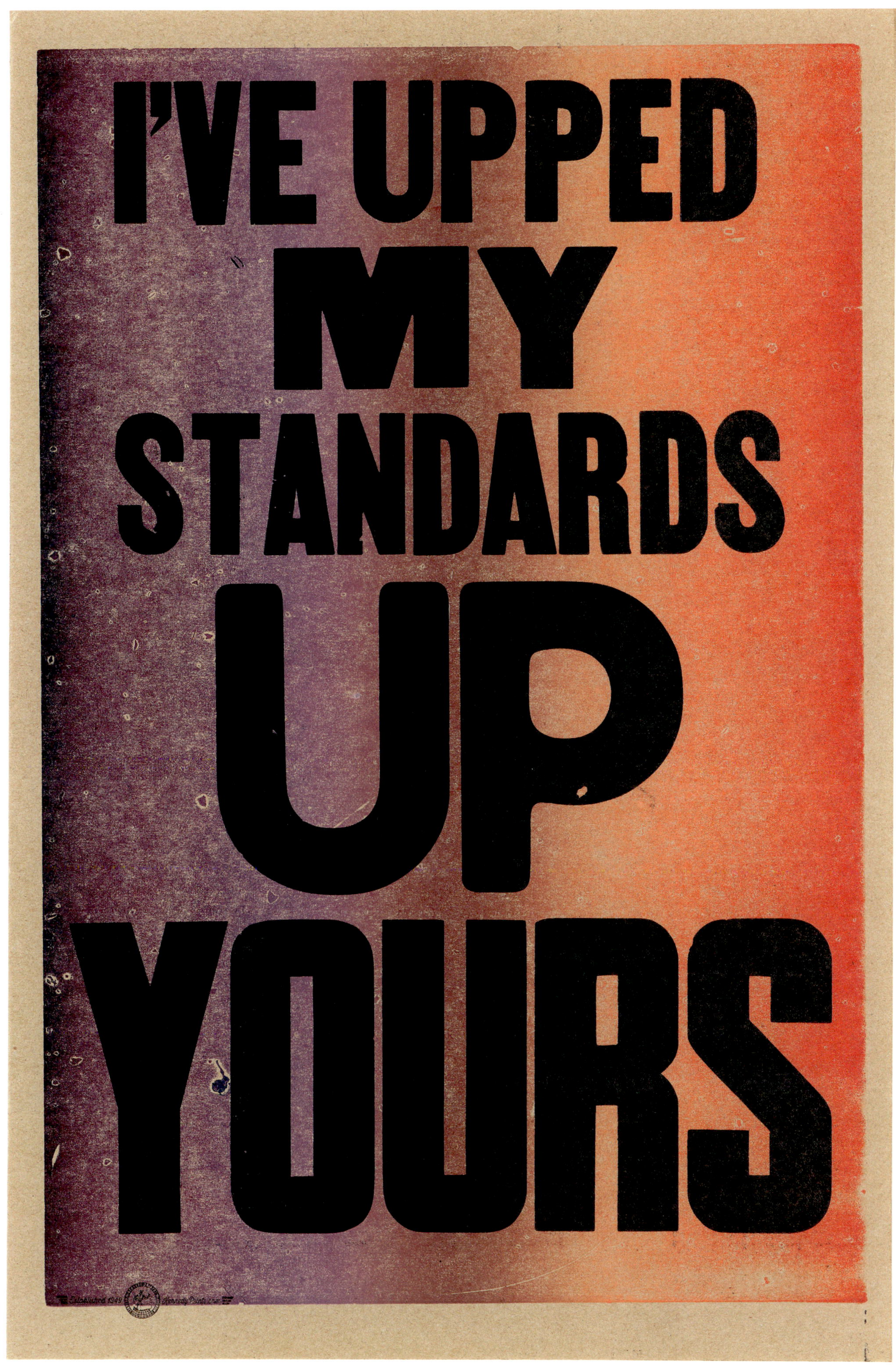
I'VE UPPED
MY
STANDARDS
UP
YOURS

FUCK YOU!

I'LL FUCK MYSELF.

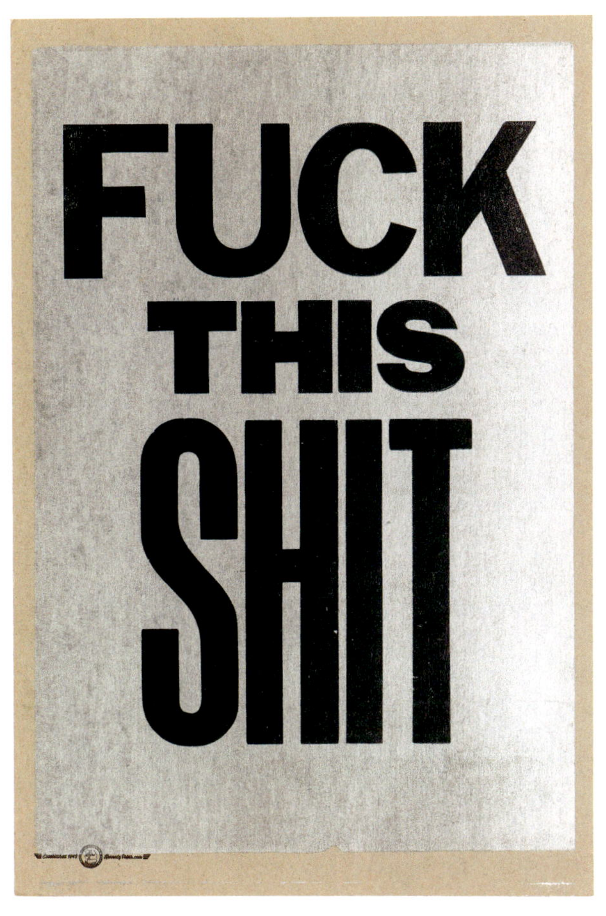
FUCK
THIS
SHIT

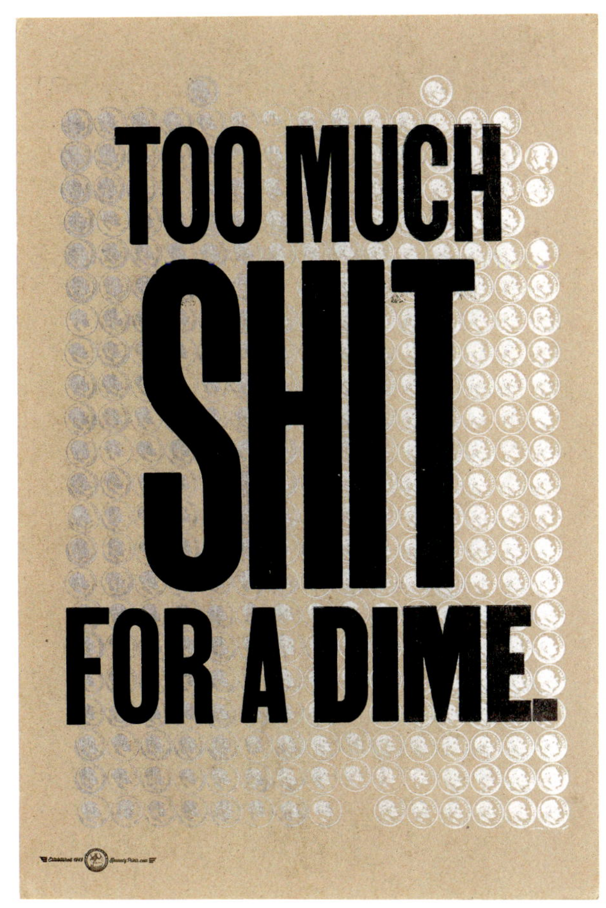
TOO MUCH
SHIT
FOR A DIME.

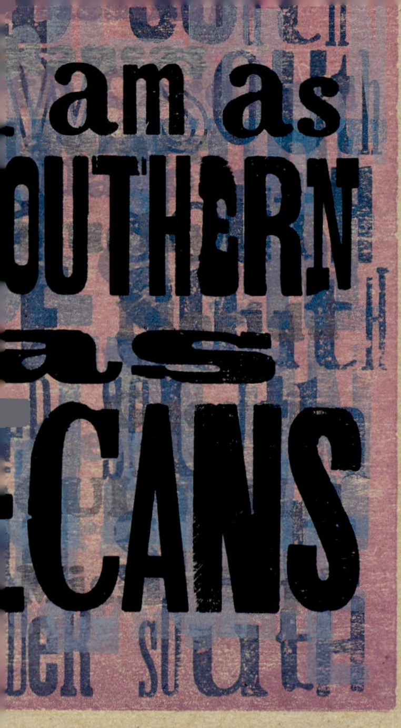

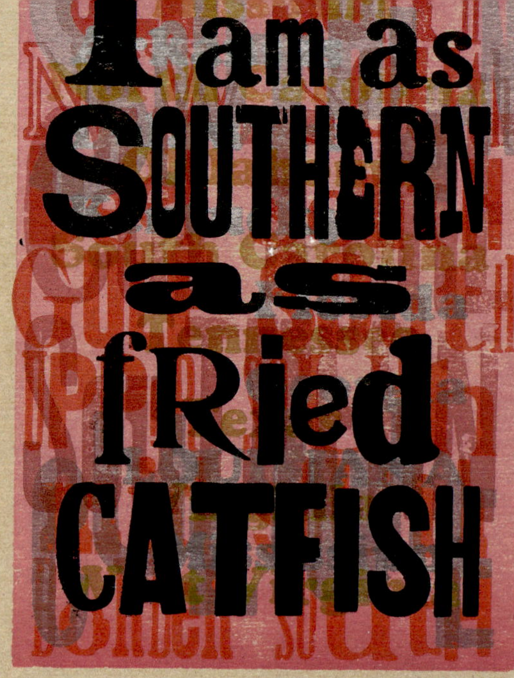

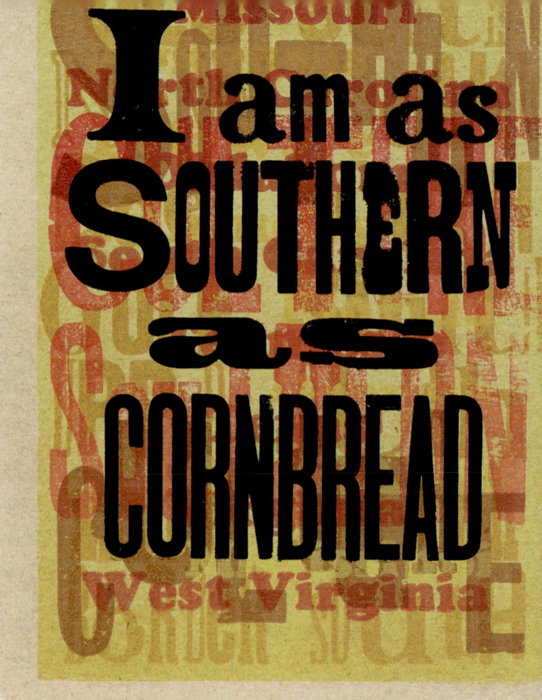

I am as
SOUTHERN
as
WHITE
BREAD

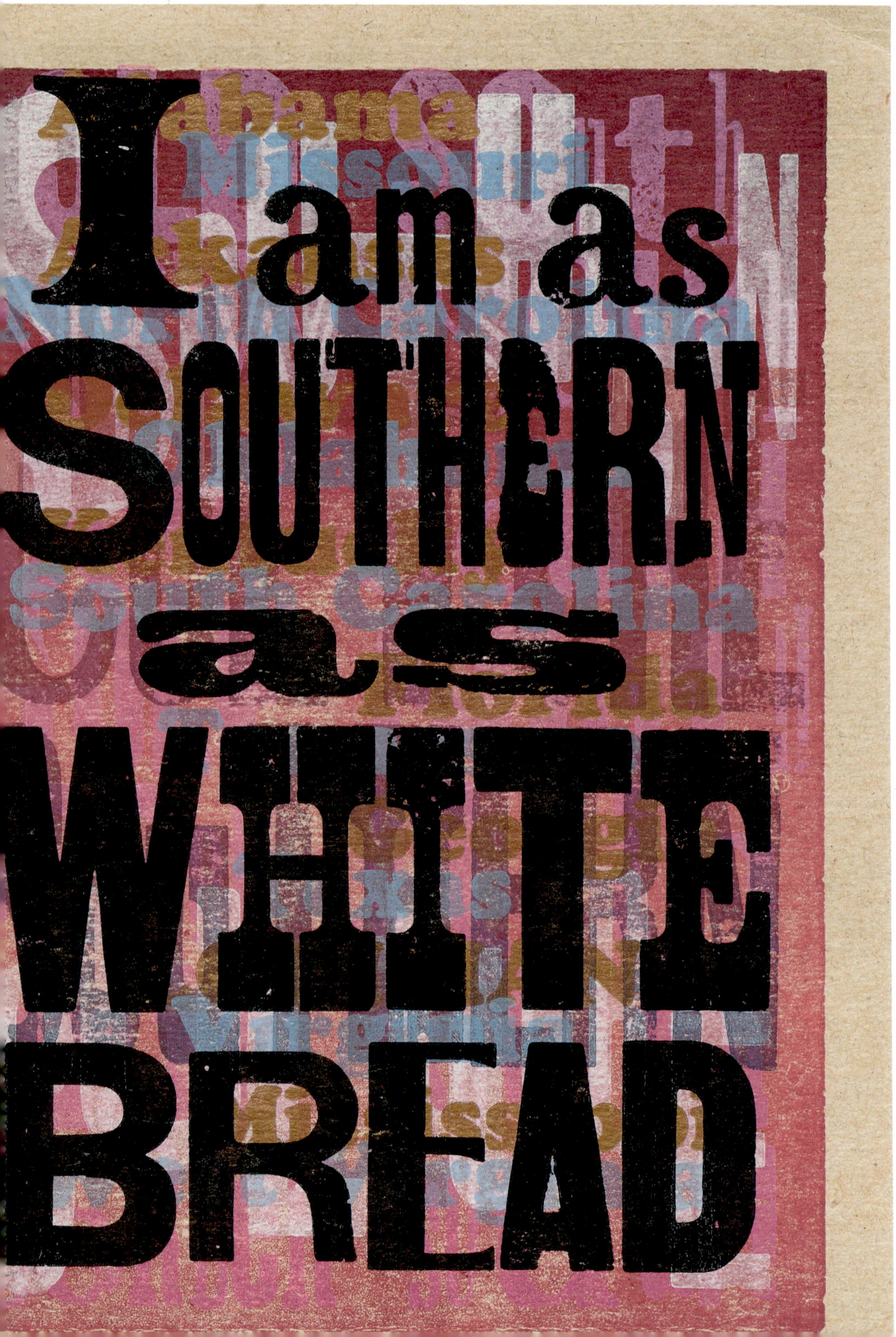

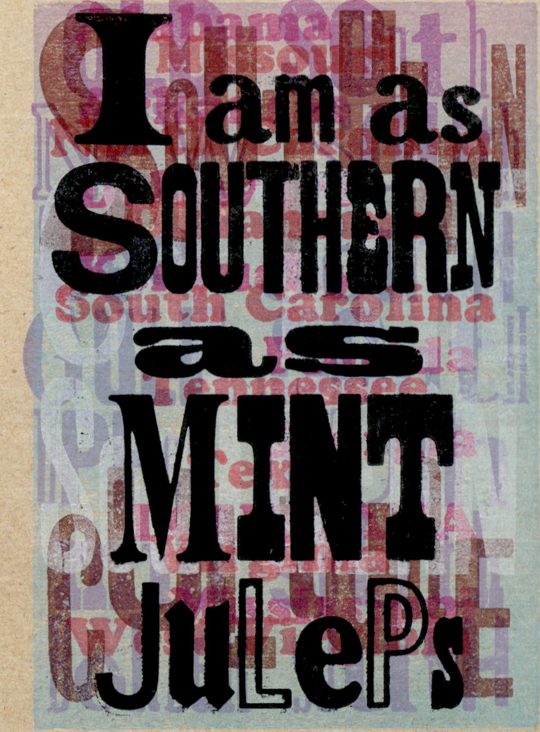

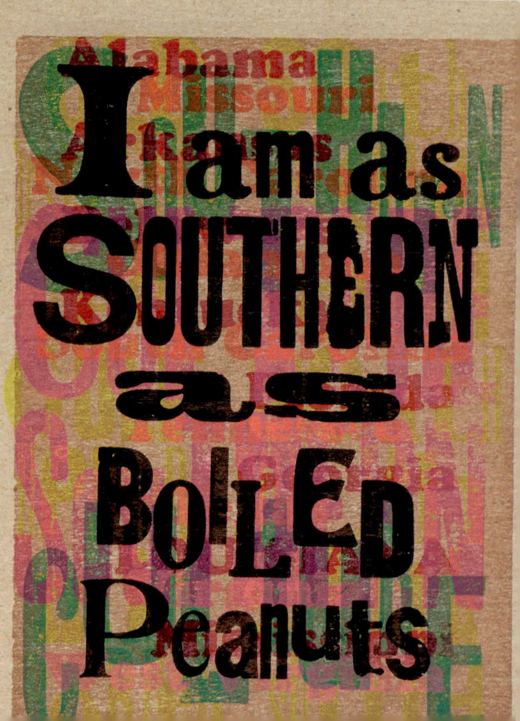

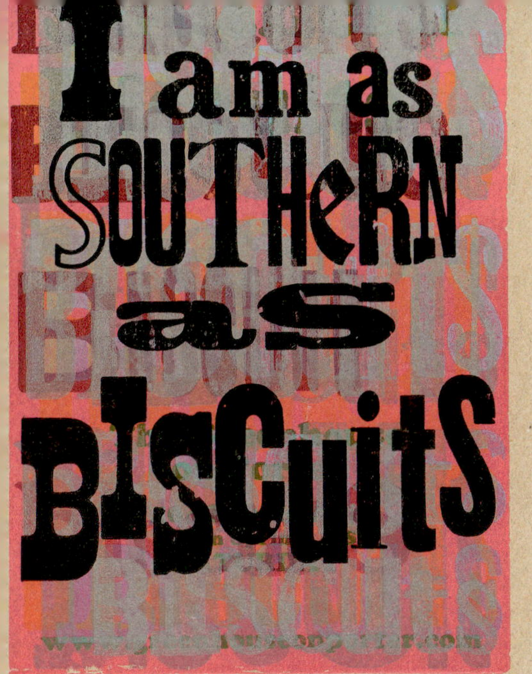

I am as
SOUTHERN
as
BLACK-EYED
PEAS

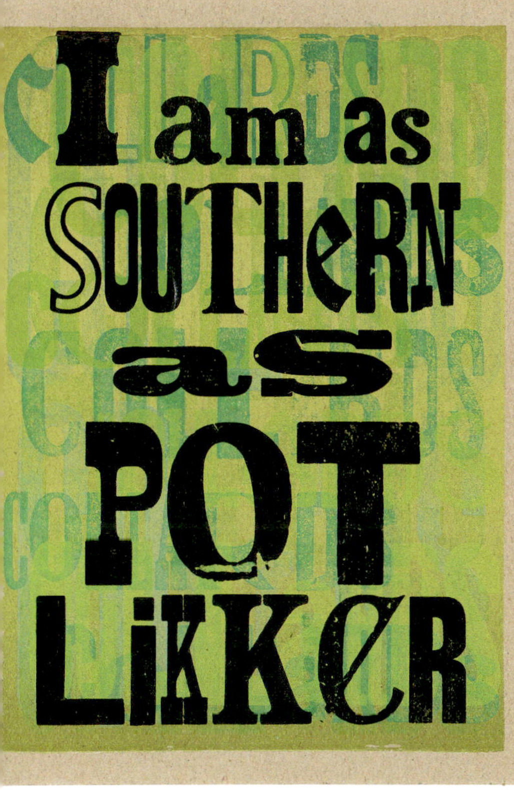

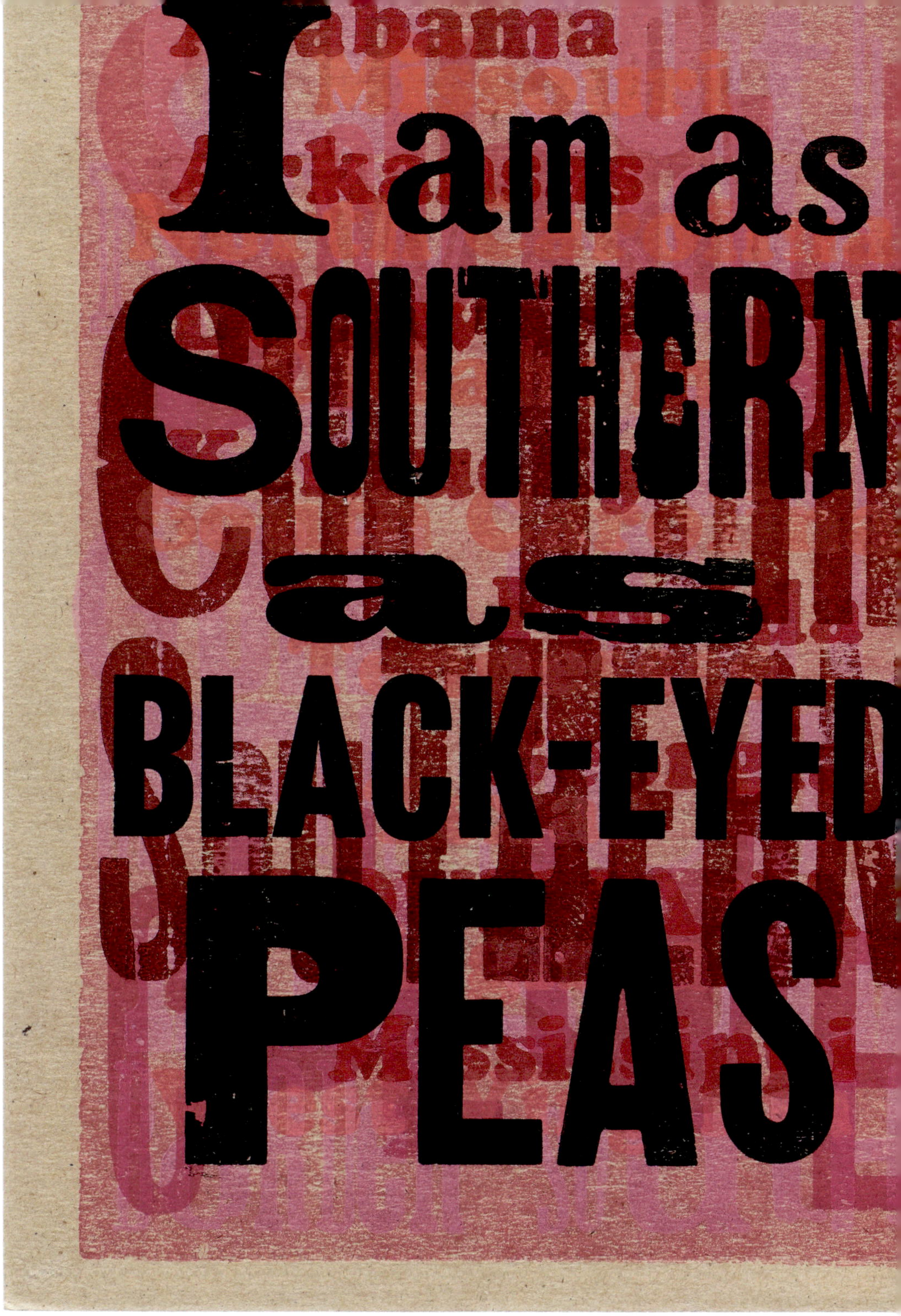

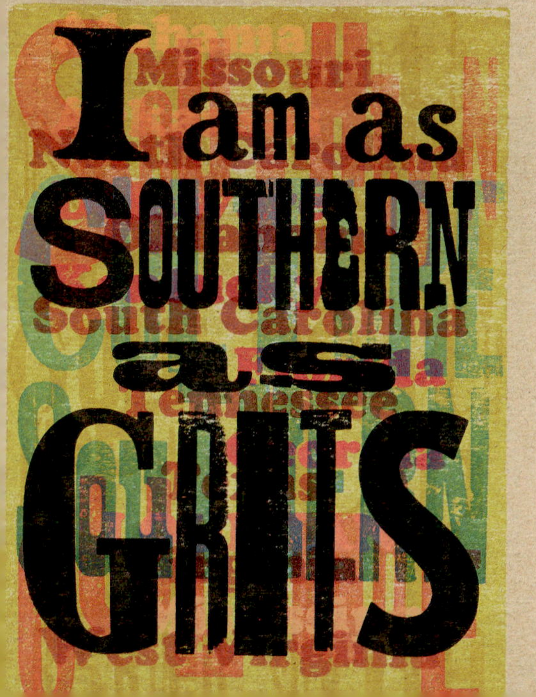

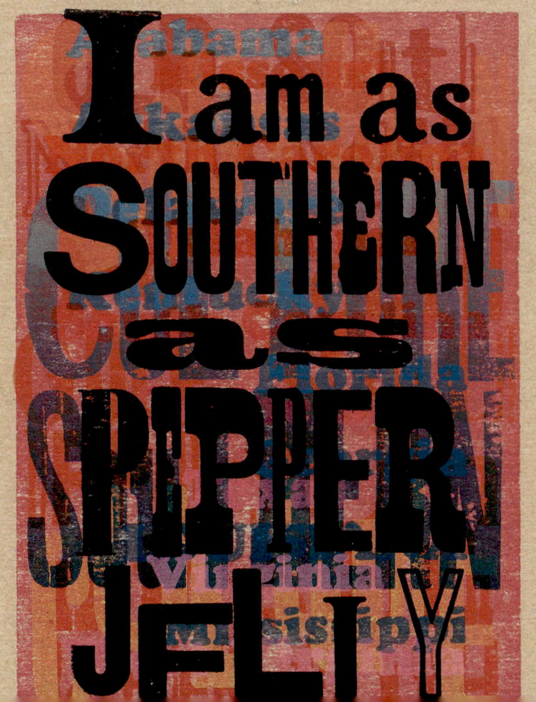

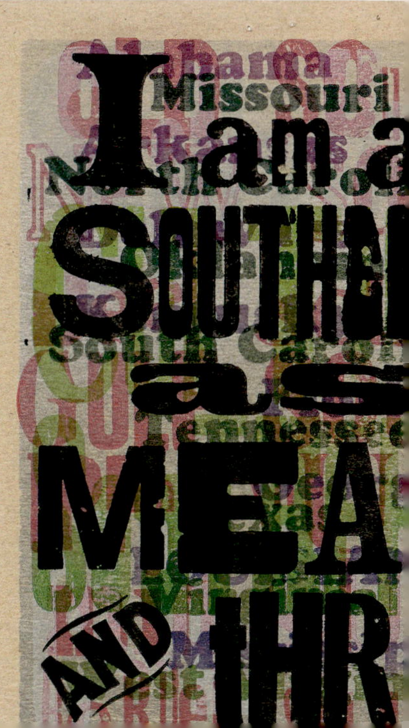

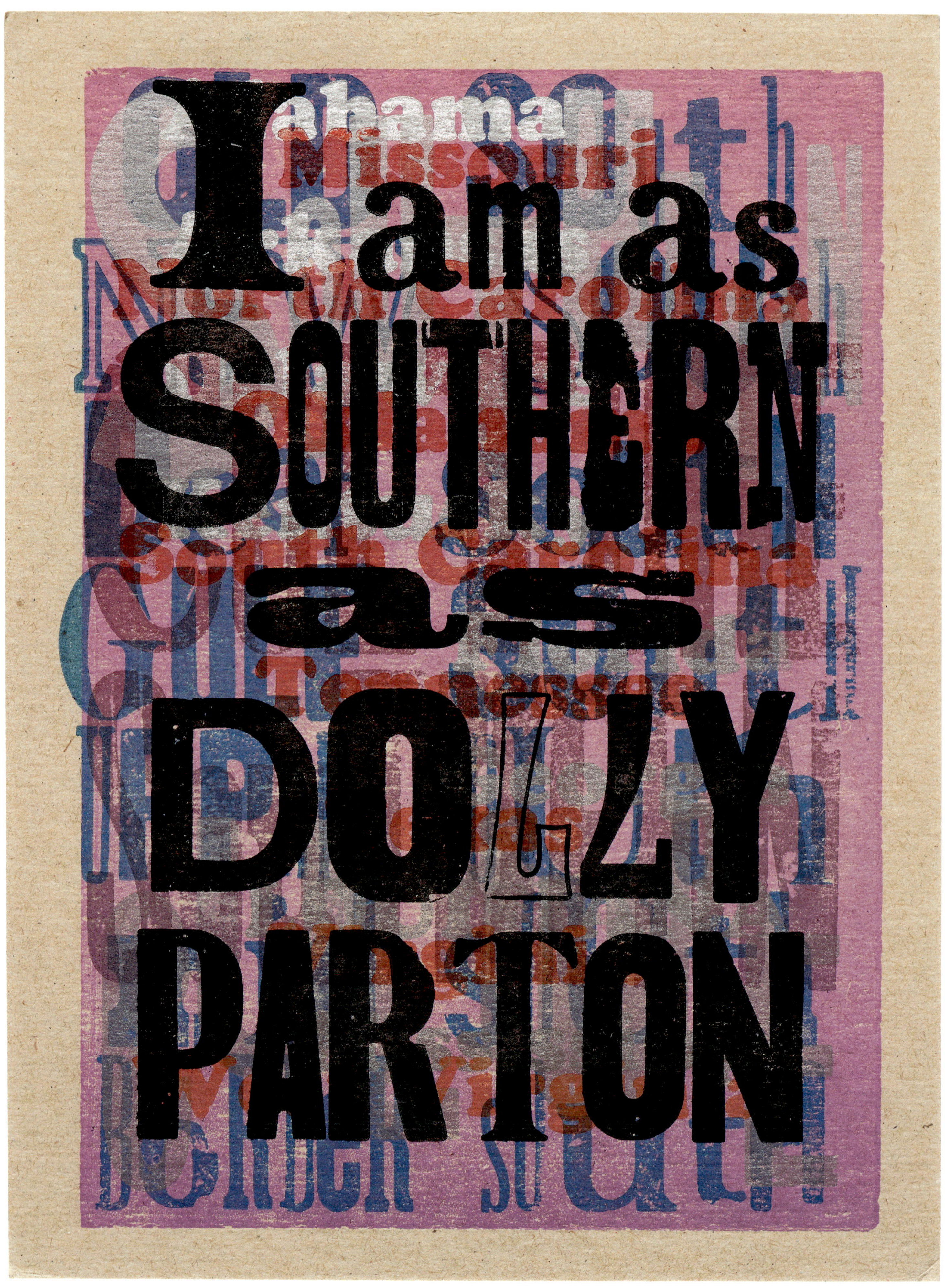
I am as
SOUTHERN
as
DOLLY
PARTON

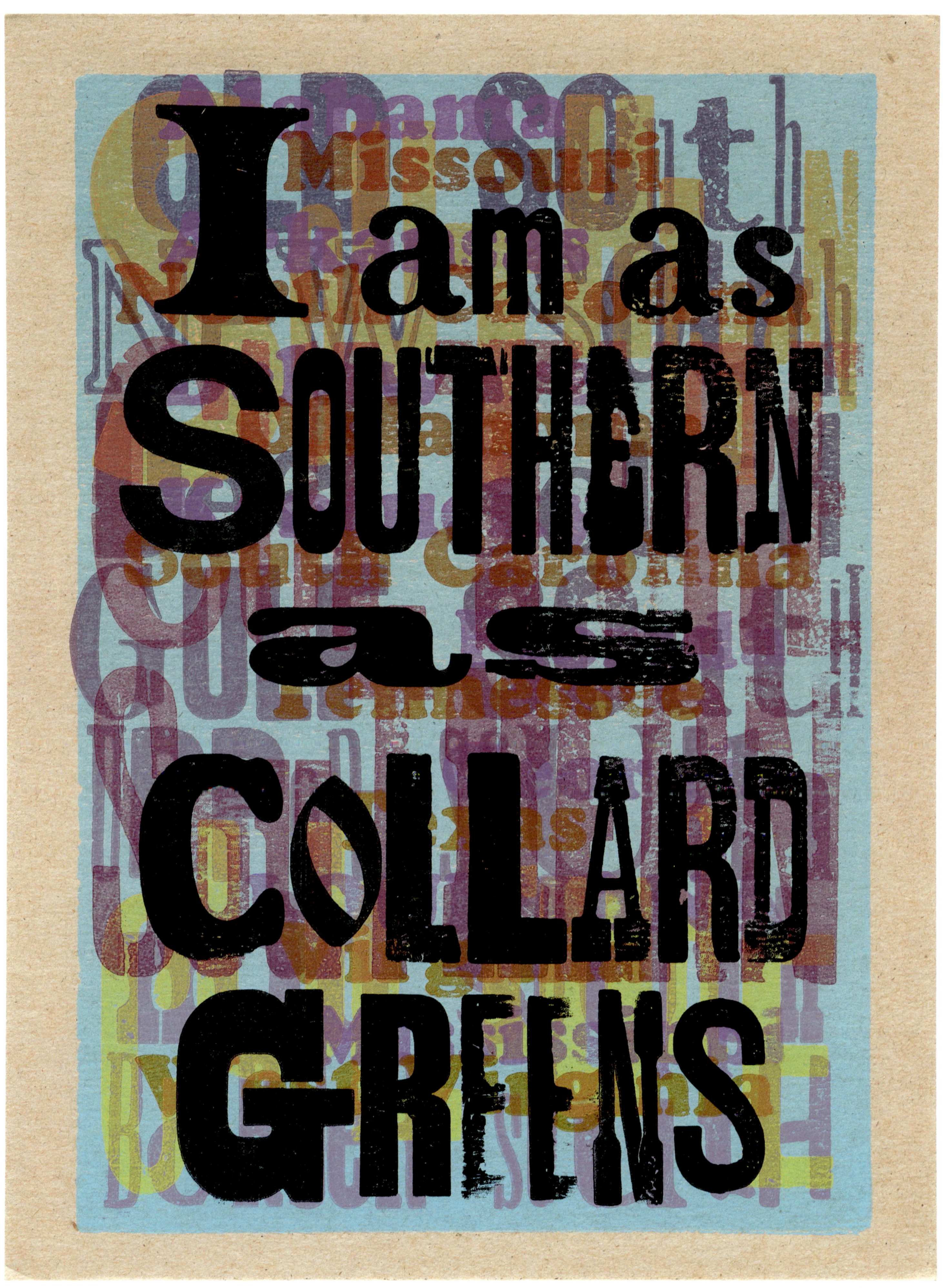
I am as
SOUTHERN
as
COLLARD
GREENS

> “Adults used to say ‘Coffee makes you black’ to deter children from drinking it. But it was a Black pride thing, too: The first time I heard the saying, it came from my mother’s very dark-skinned friend, who joked: ‘And after I have this cup, I’m gonna have another.’”

“By request, I have also printed *Coffee Makes You Queer* and *Coffee Makes you Trans*. I am doing my part to keep this idiom in circulation!”

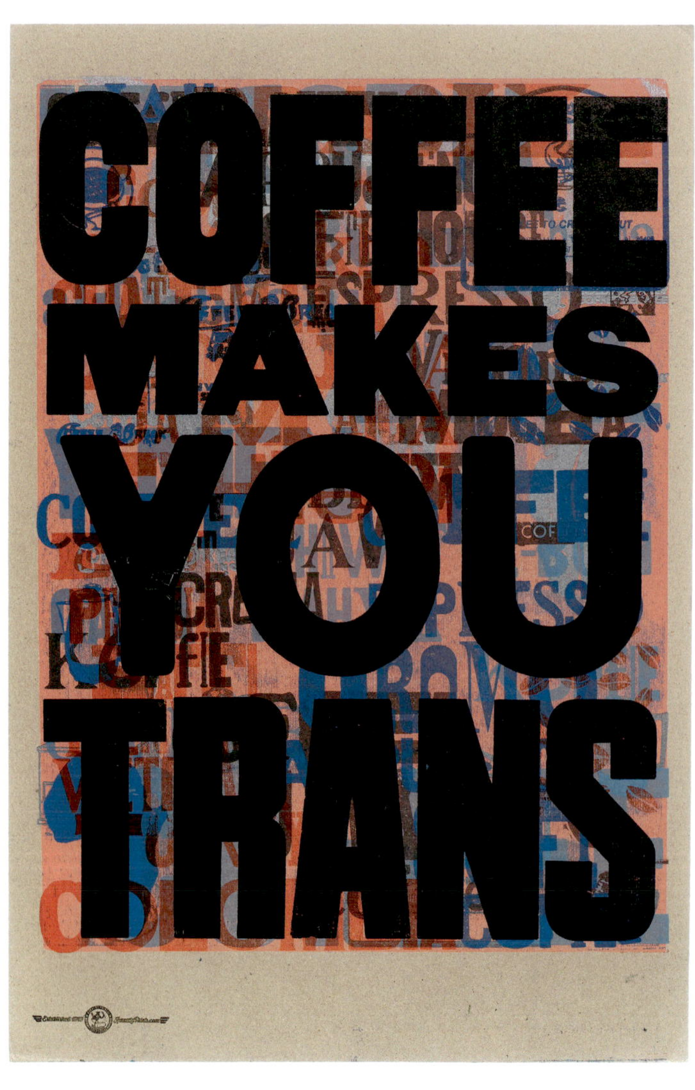

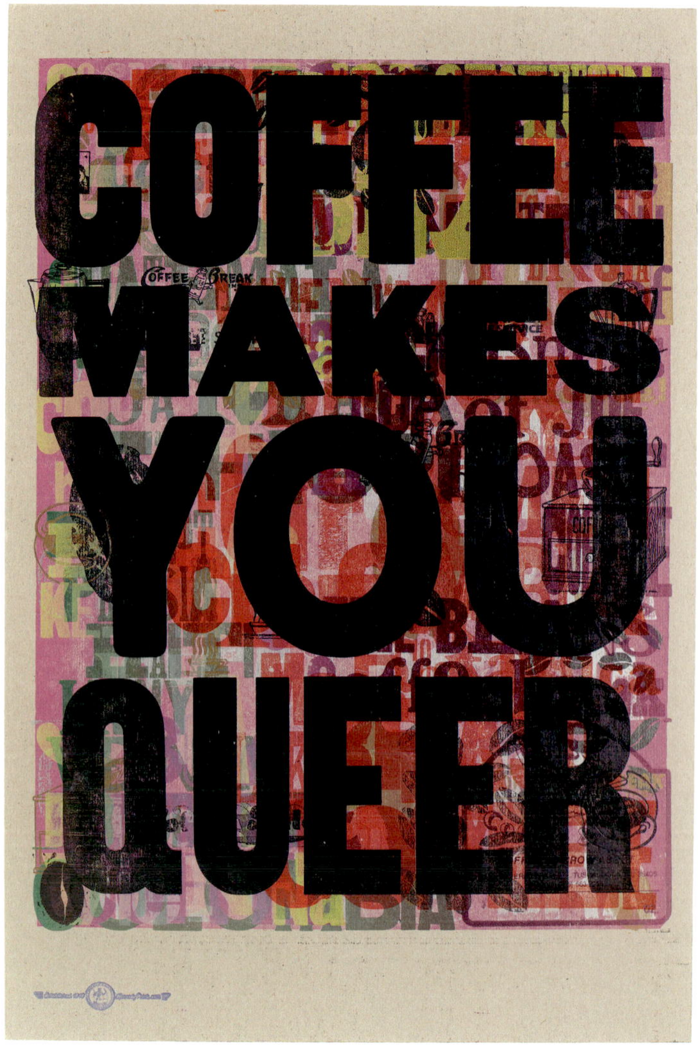

COFFEE
MAKES
YOU
BLACK

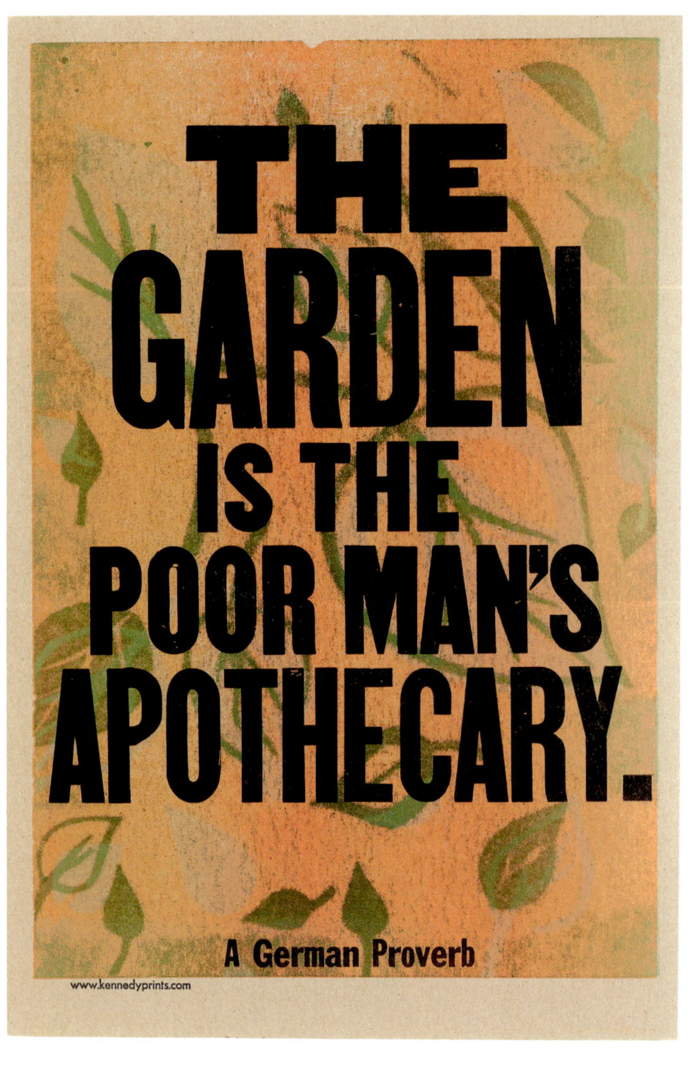
THE
GARDEN
IS THE
POOR MAN'S
APOTHECARY.
A German Proverb
www.kennedyprints.com

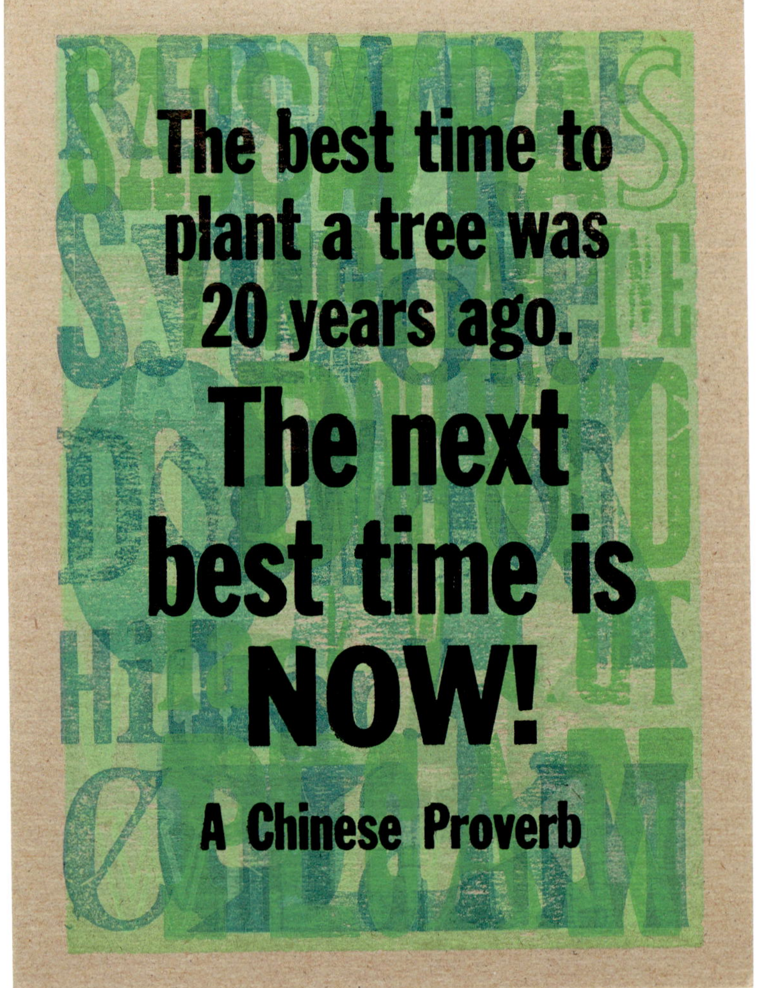
The best time to
plant a tree was
20 years ago.
The next
best time is
NOW!
A Chinese Proverb

IF YOU HAVE A
GARDEN
AND A
LIBRARY
YOU HAVE
EVERYTHING
YOU NEED.
Cicero
www.kennedyprints.com

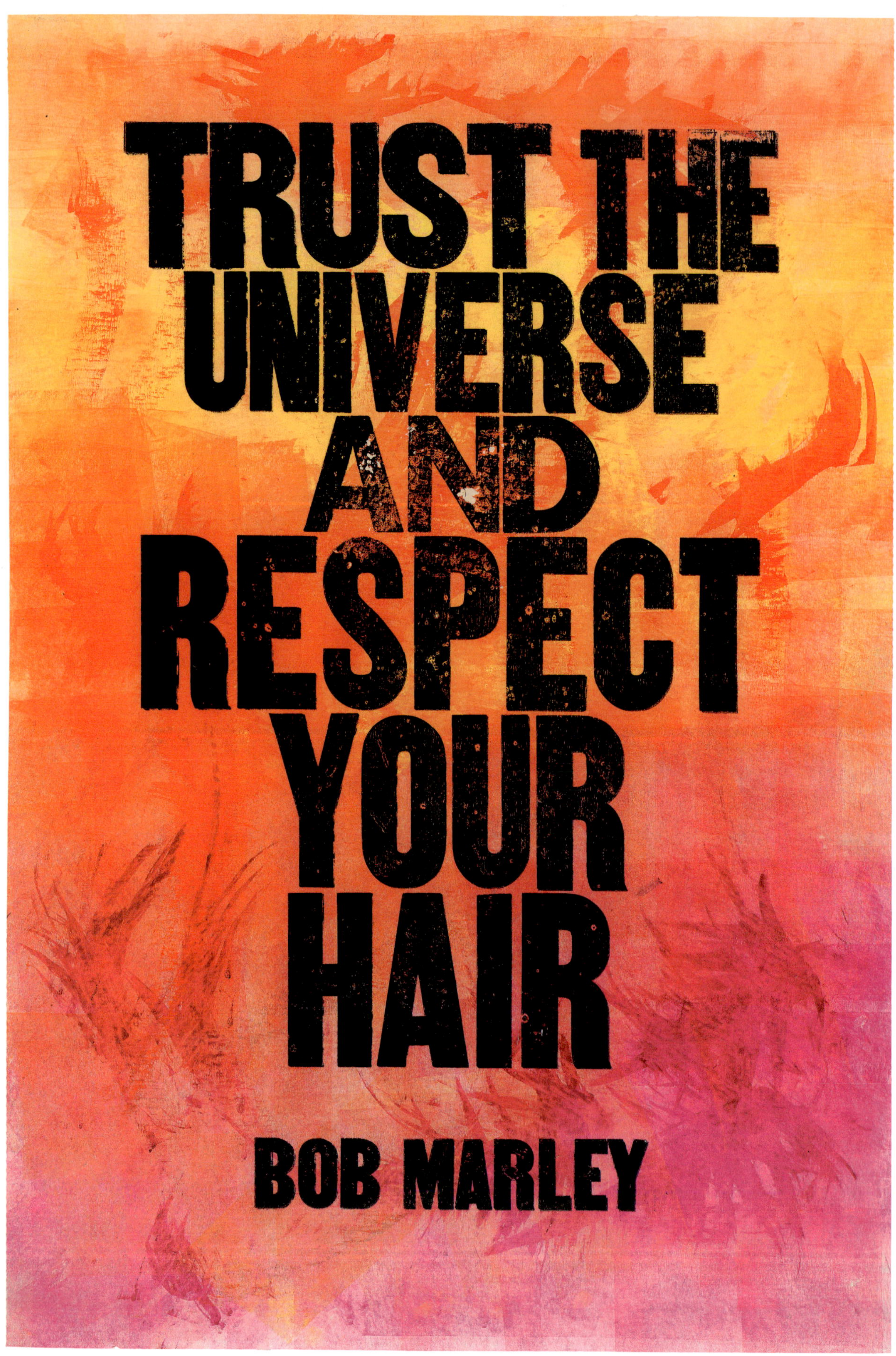
TRUST THE
UNIVERSE
AND
RESPECT
YOUR
HAIR
BOB MARLEY

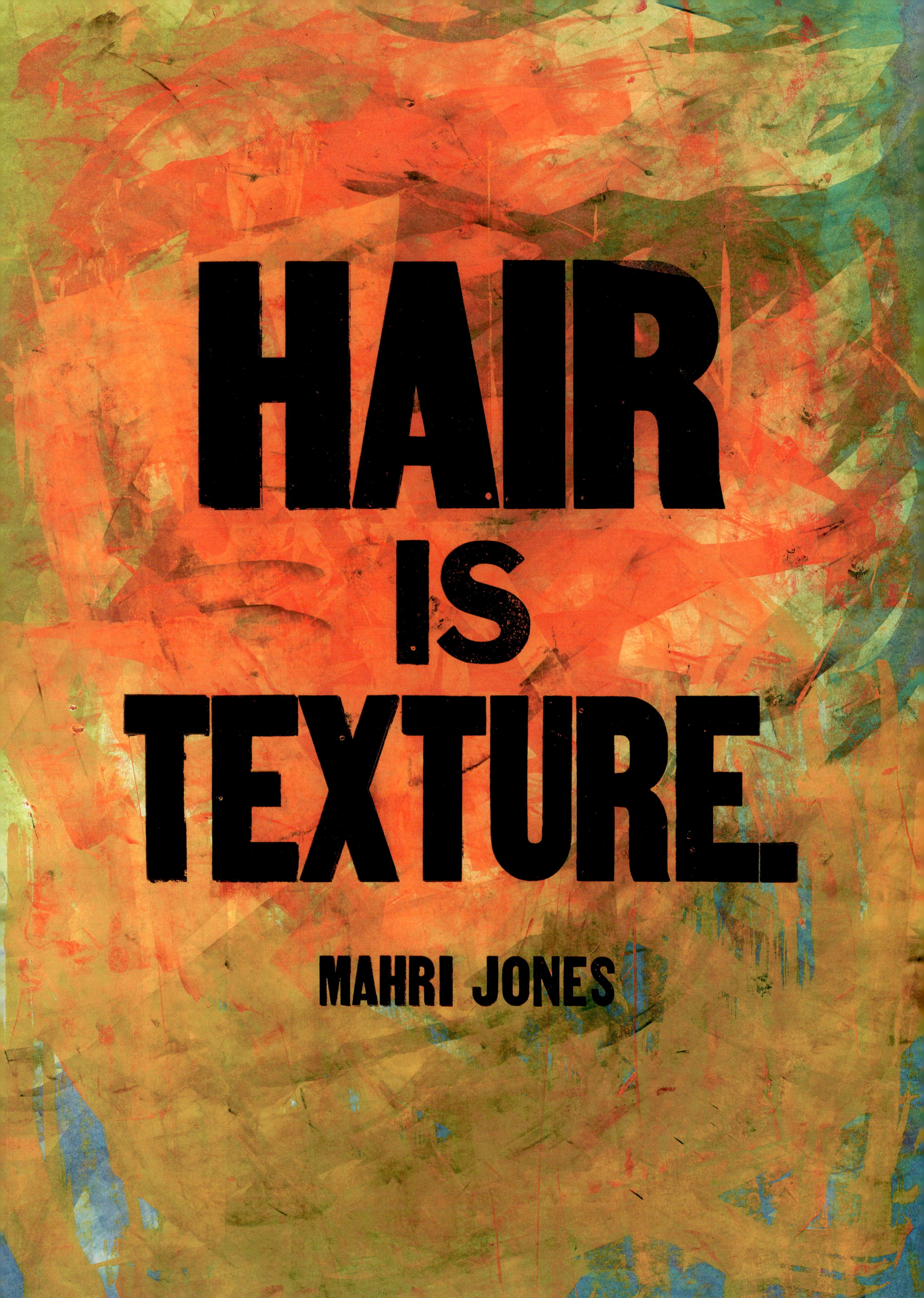
HAIR
IS
TEXTURE.
MAHRI JONES

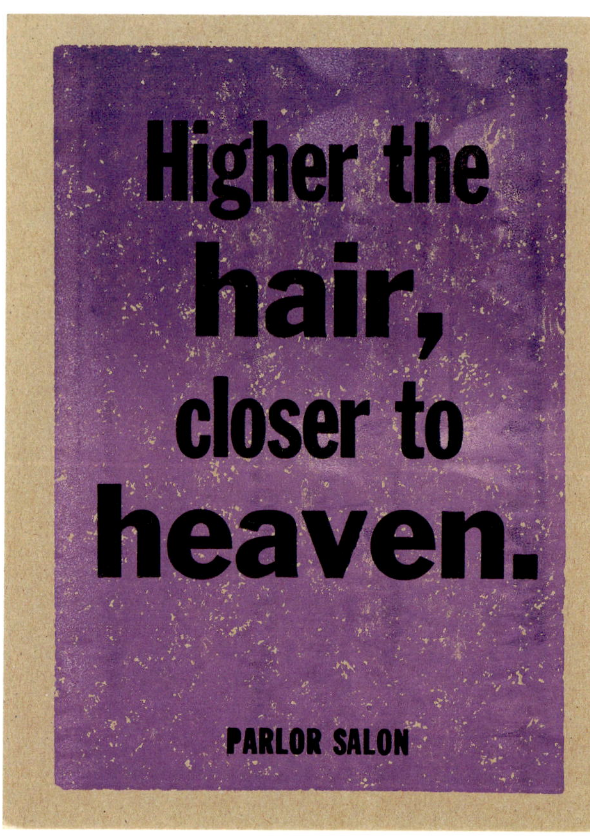
Higher the
hair,
closer to
heaven.
PARLOR SALON

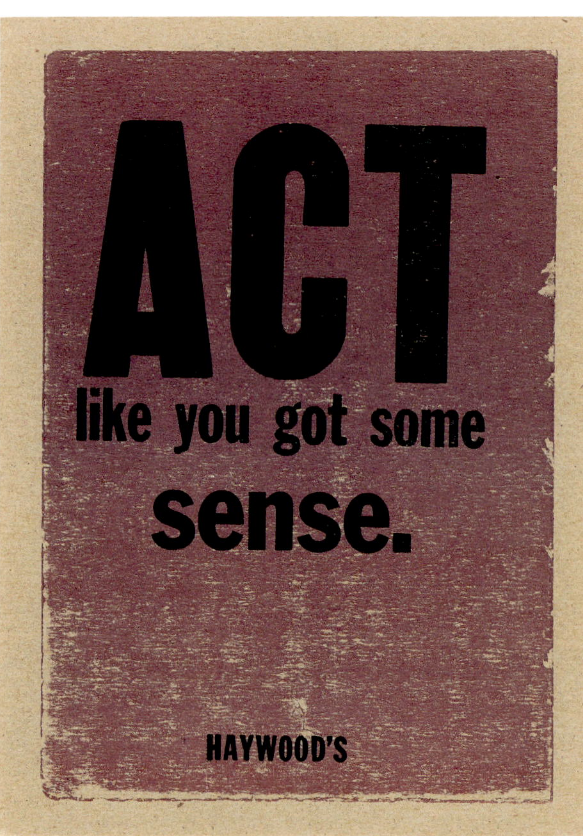
ACT
like you got some
sense.
HAYWOOD'S

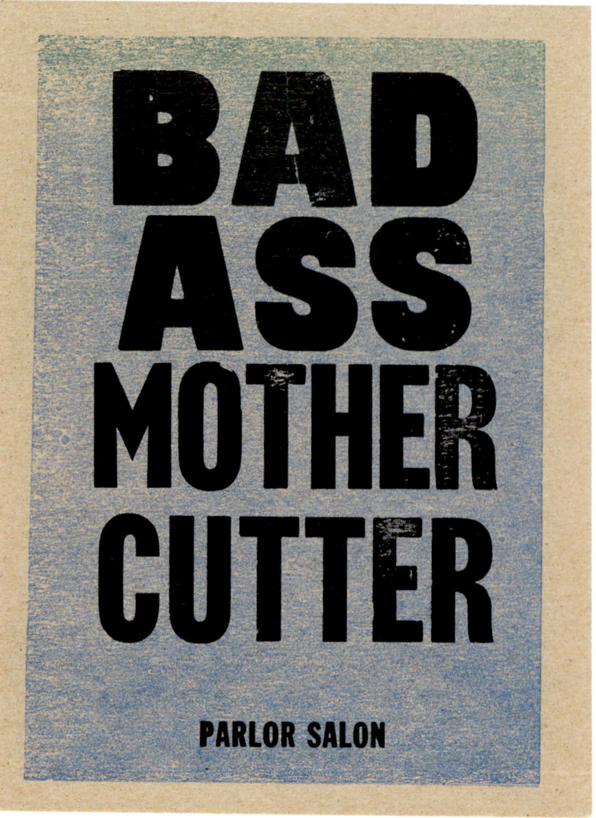
BAD
ASS
MOTHER
CUTTER
PARLOR SALON

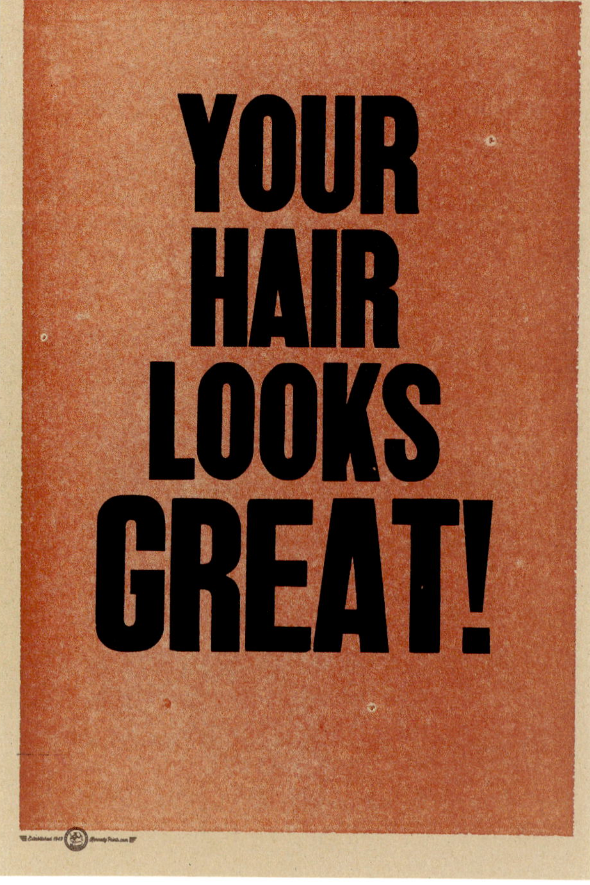
YOUR
HAIR
LOOKS
GREAT!

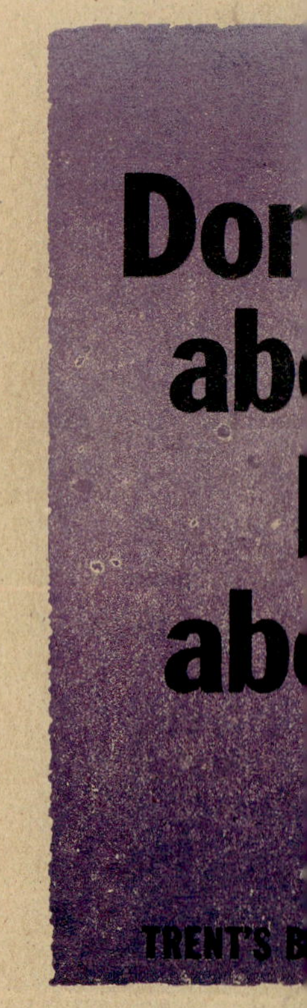
TRENT'S

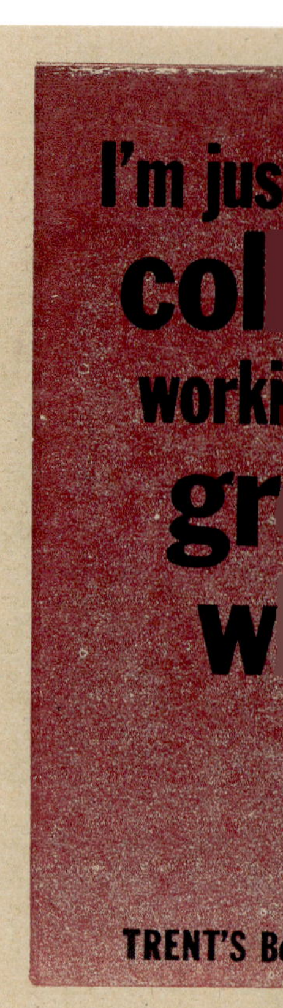
TRENT'S

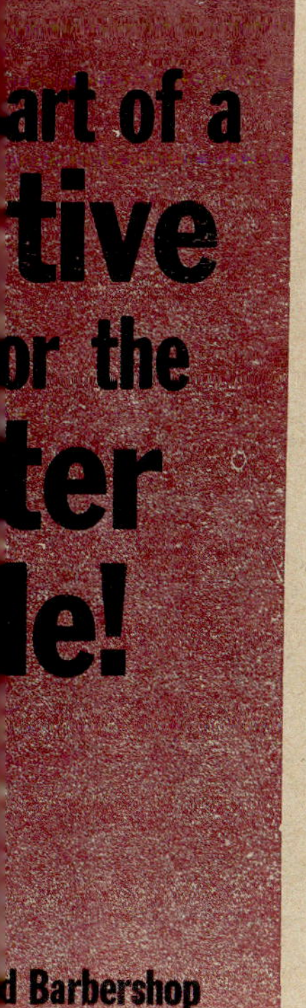
art of a
tive
or the
ter
le!
d Barbershop

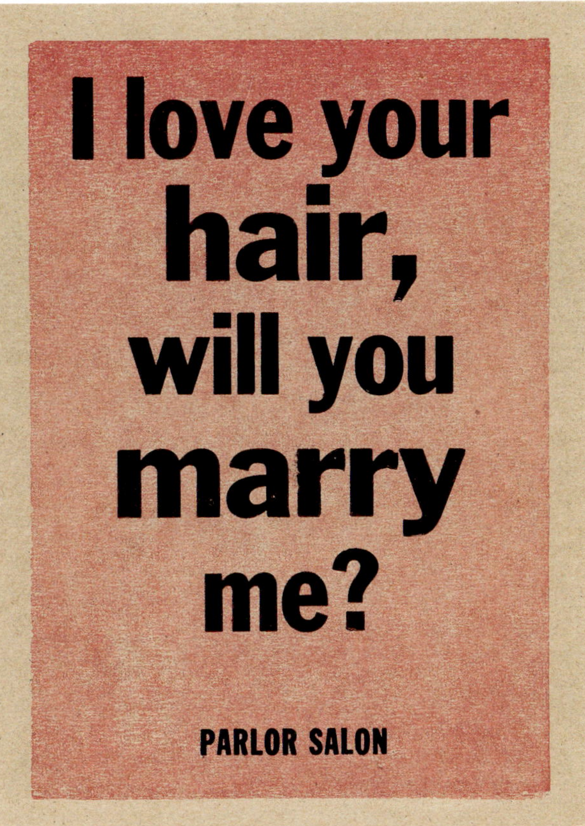
I love your hair, will you marry me?
PARLOR SALON

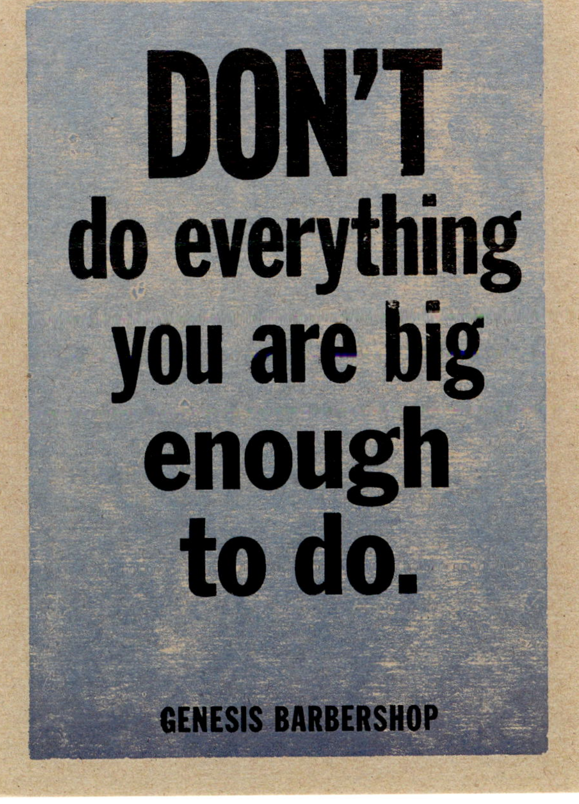
DON'T do everything you are big enough to do.
GENESIS BARBERSHOP

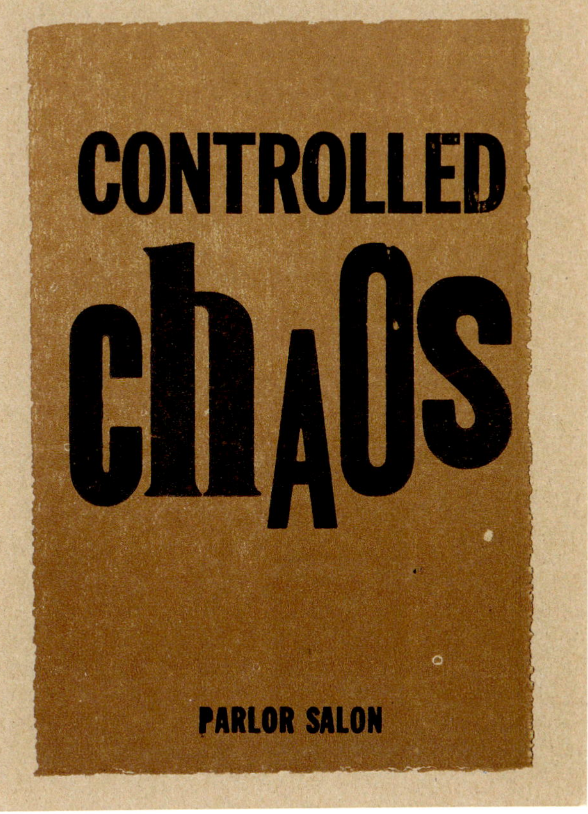
CONTROLLED chAOs
PARLOR SALON

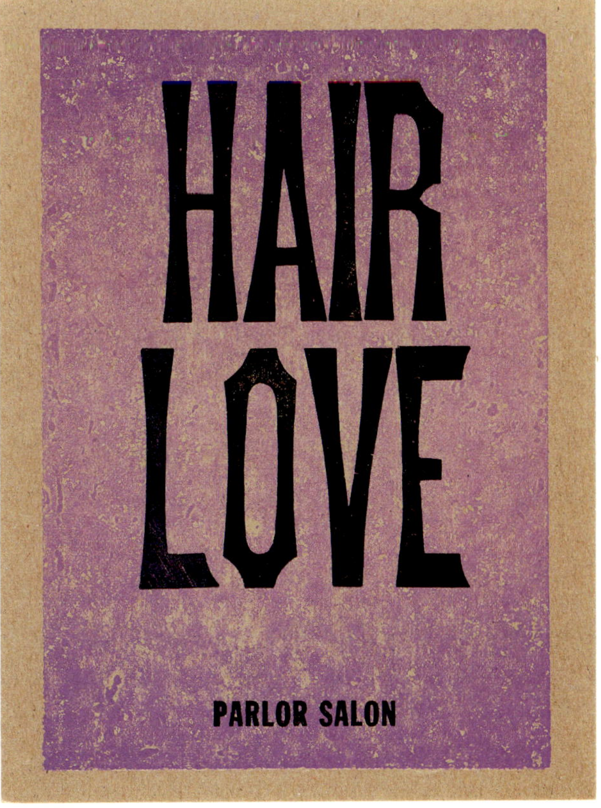
HAIR LOVE
PARLOR SALON

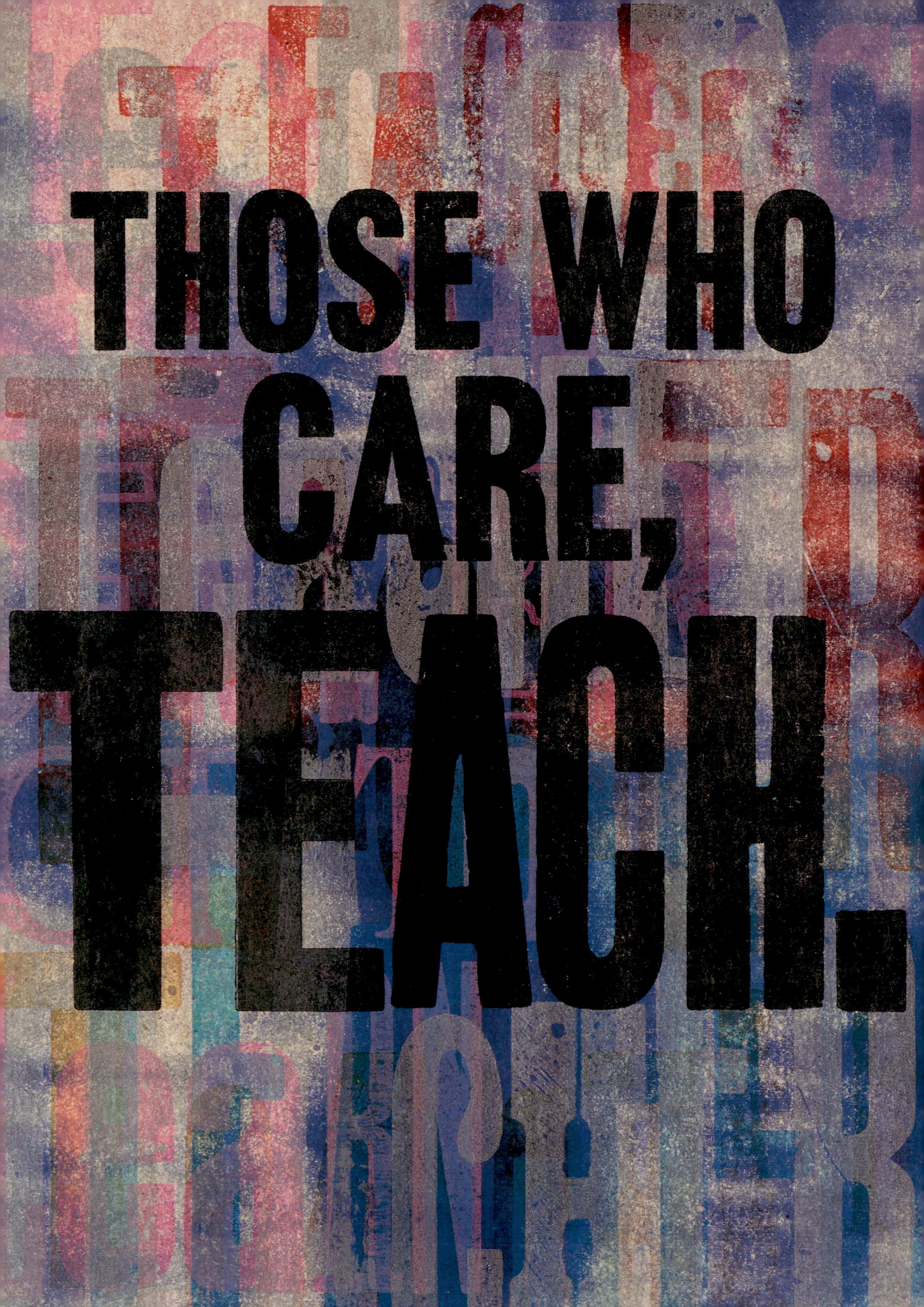
THOSE WHO
CARE,
TEACH.

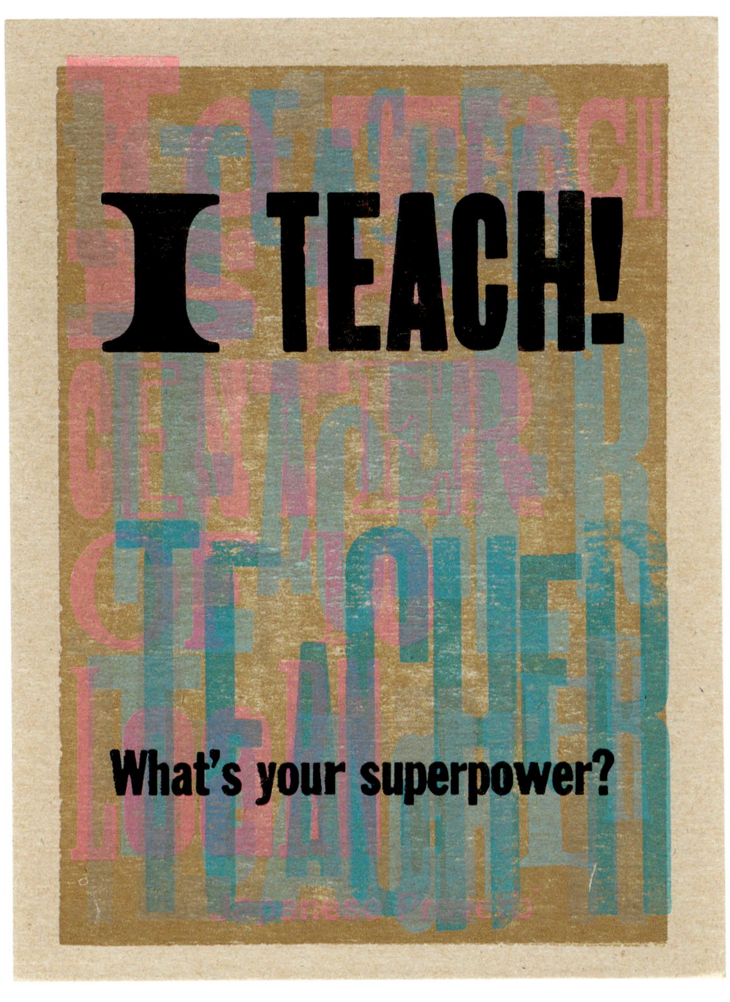
I TEACH!
What's your superpower?

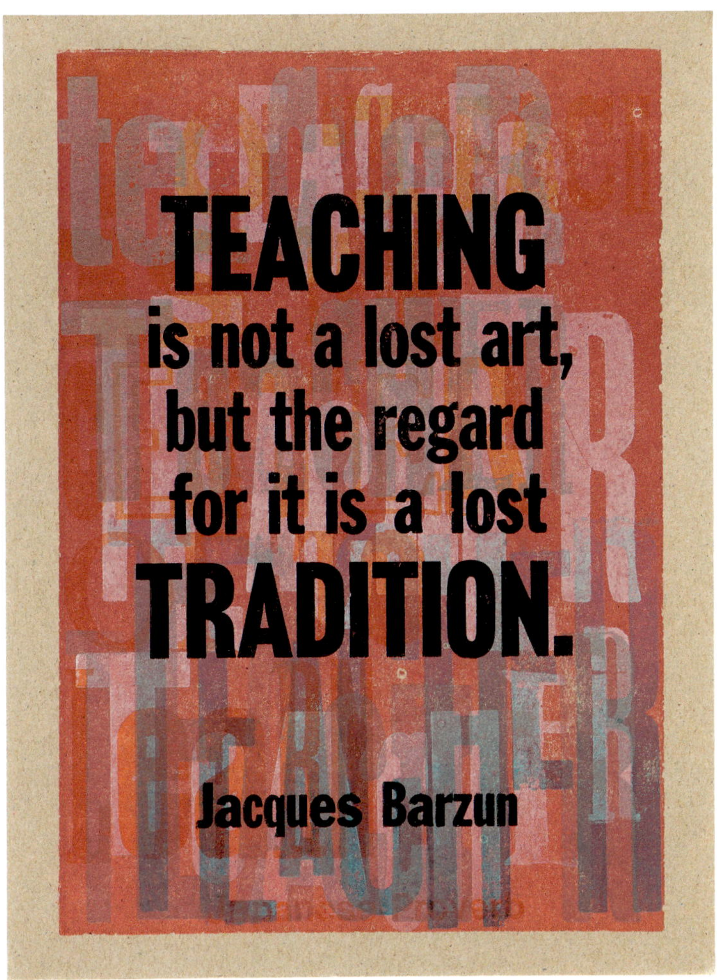
TEACHING
is not a lost art,
but the regard
for it is a lost
TRADITION.
Jacques Barzun

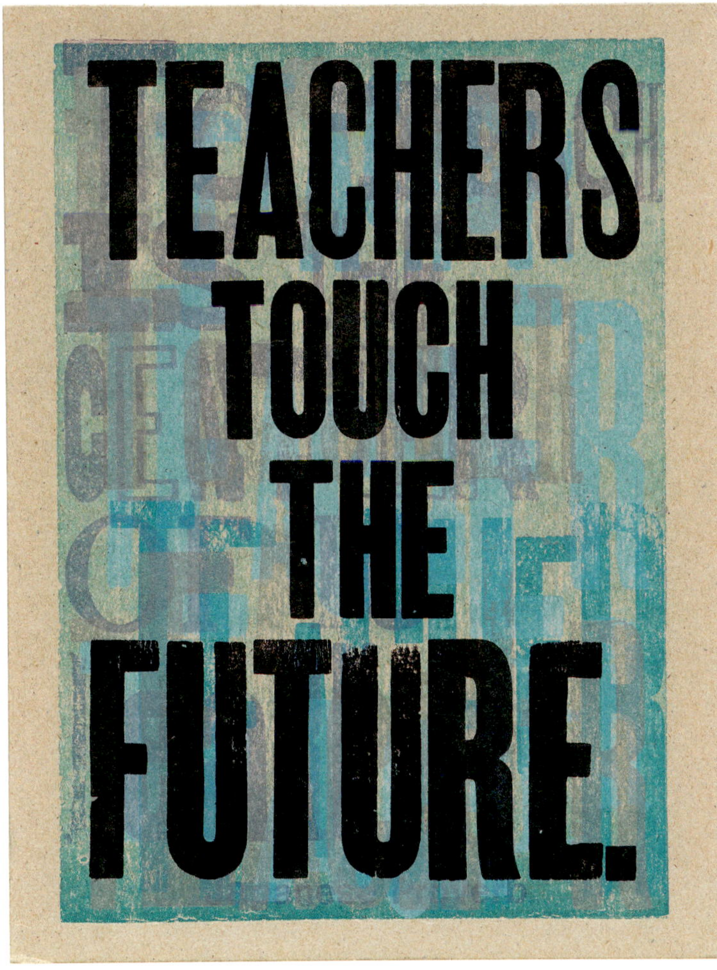
TEACHERS
TOUCH
THE
FUTURE.

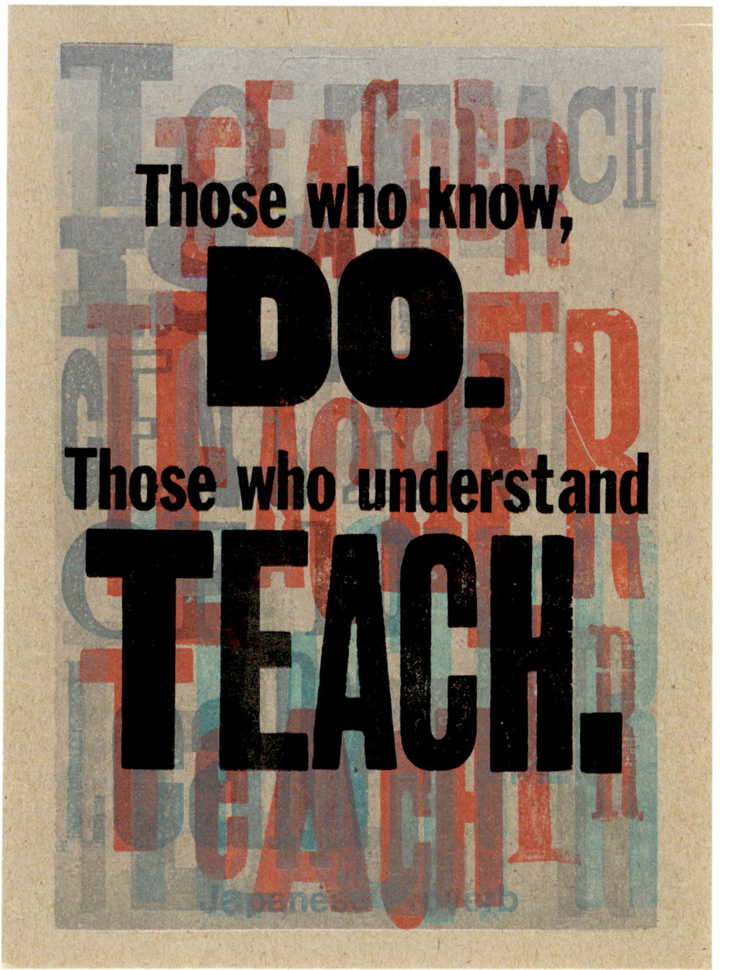
Those who know,
DO.
Those who understand
TEACH.

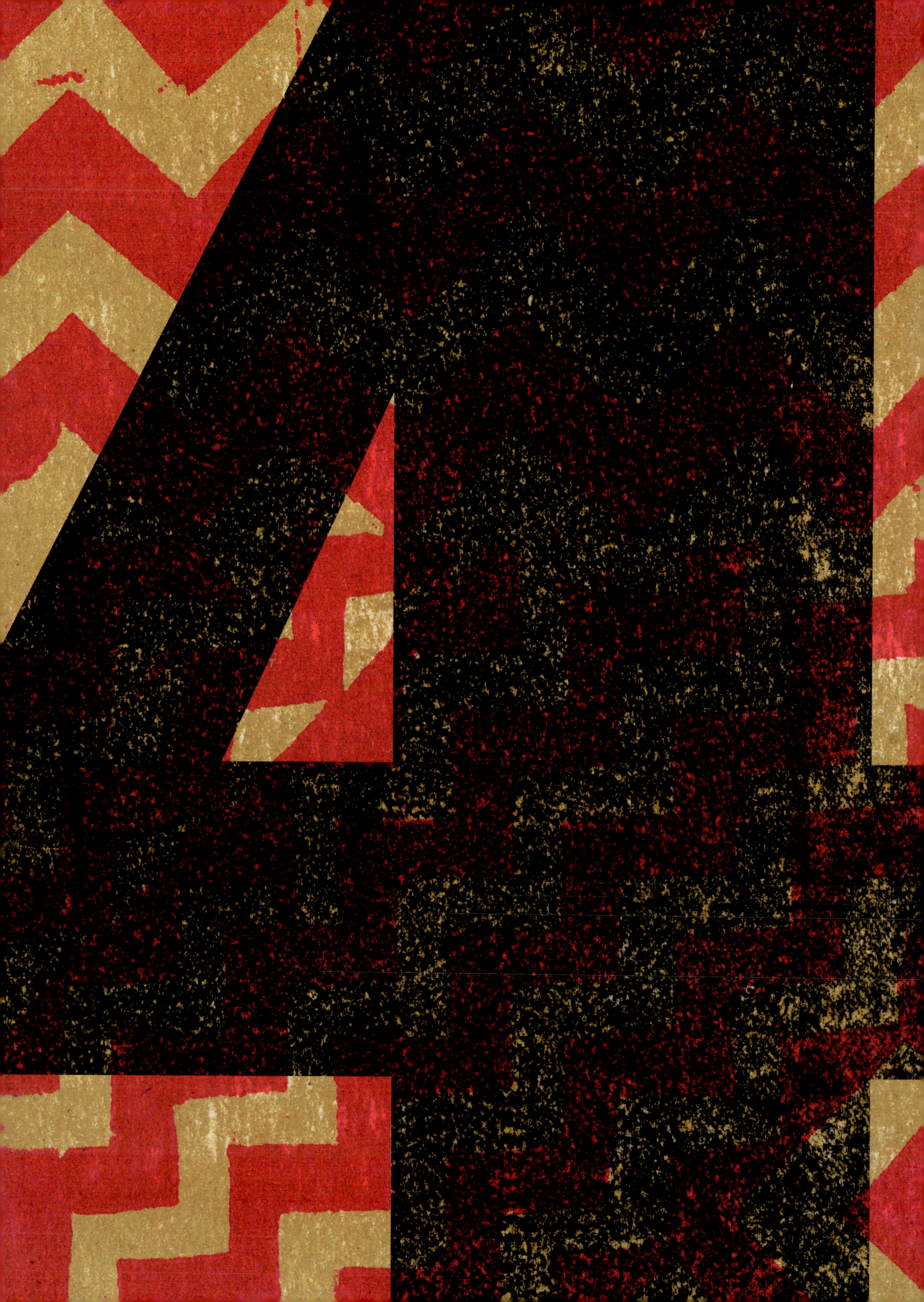
4

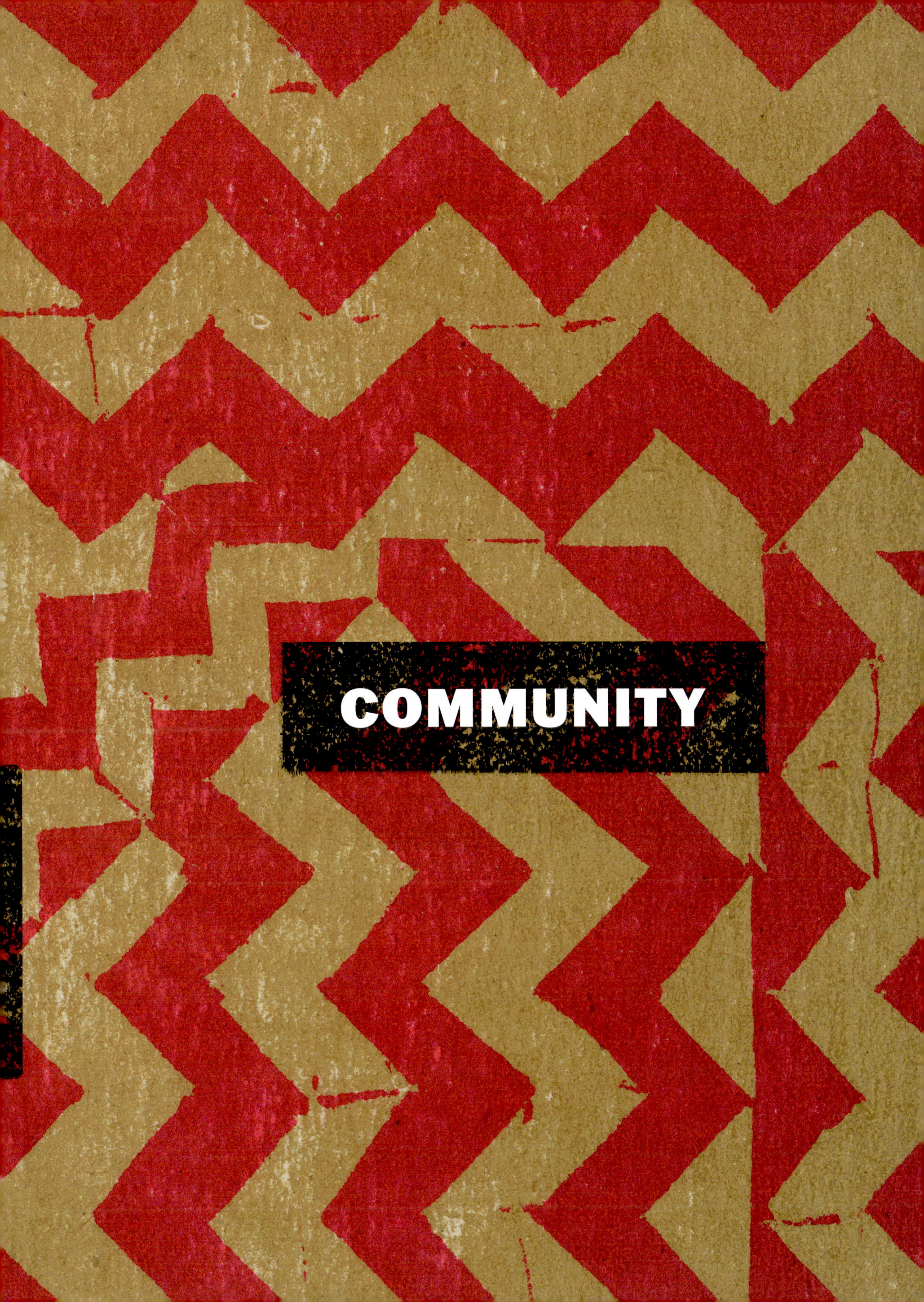
COMMUNITY

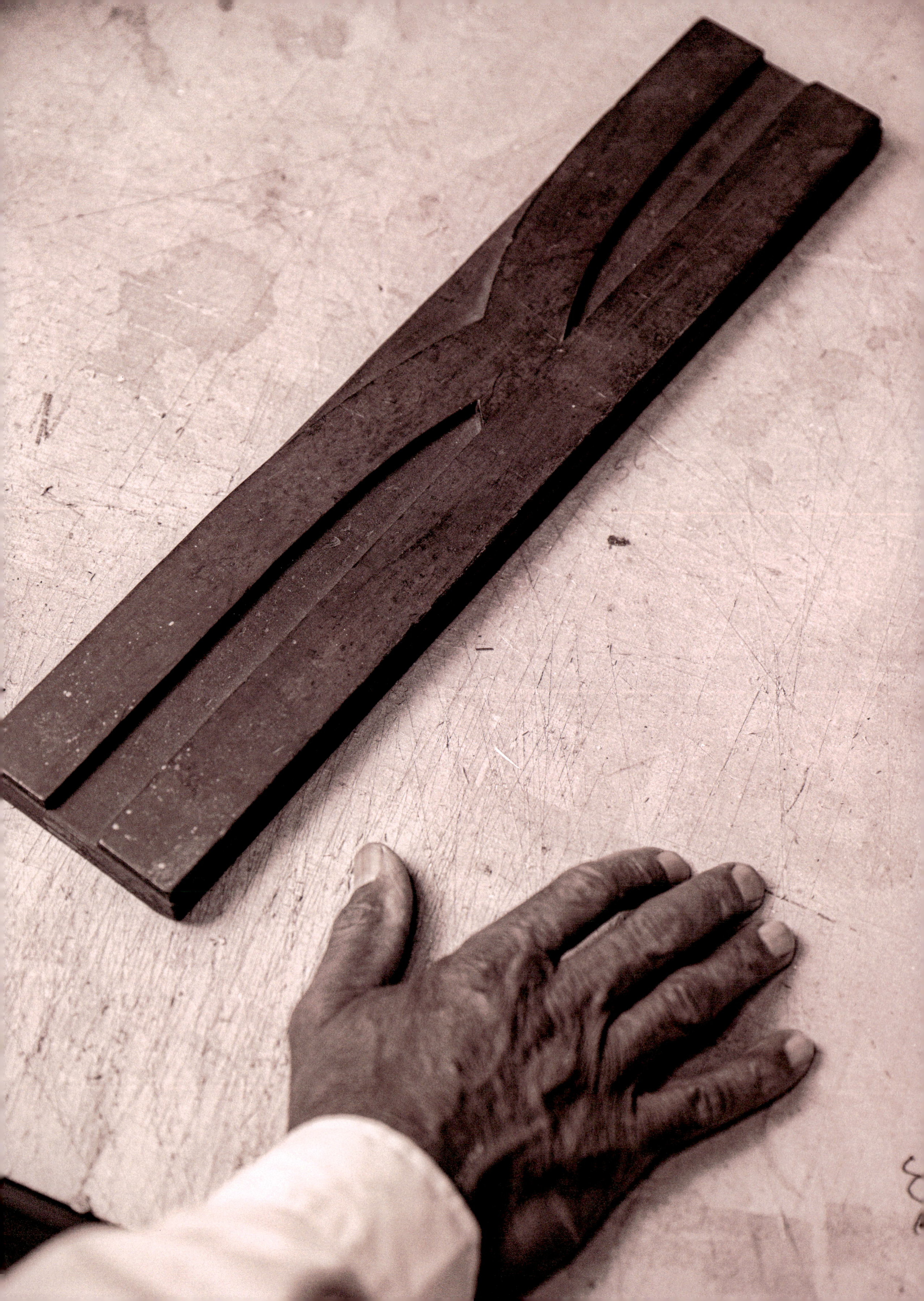

"A **community** consists of all walks of life. It is the bakers, the printers, the mechanics, the poets, the teachers, the farmers. You have to have community in order to survive."

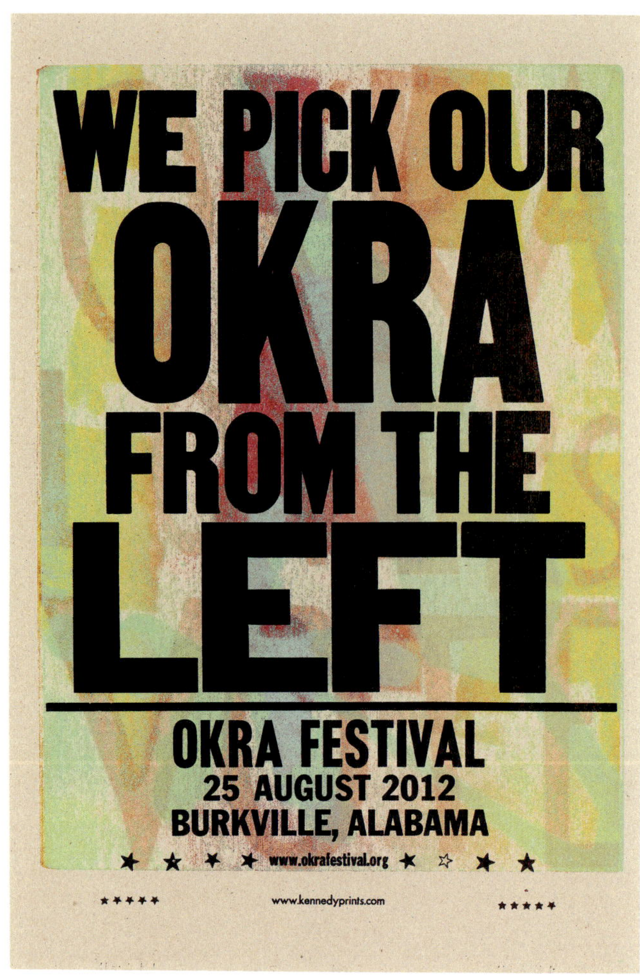
WE PICK OUR
OKRA
FROM THE
LEFT
OKRA FESTIVAL
25 AUGUST 2012
BURKVILLE, ALABAMA
www.okrafestival.org
www.kennedyprints.com

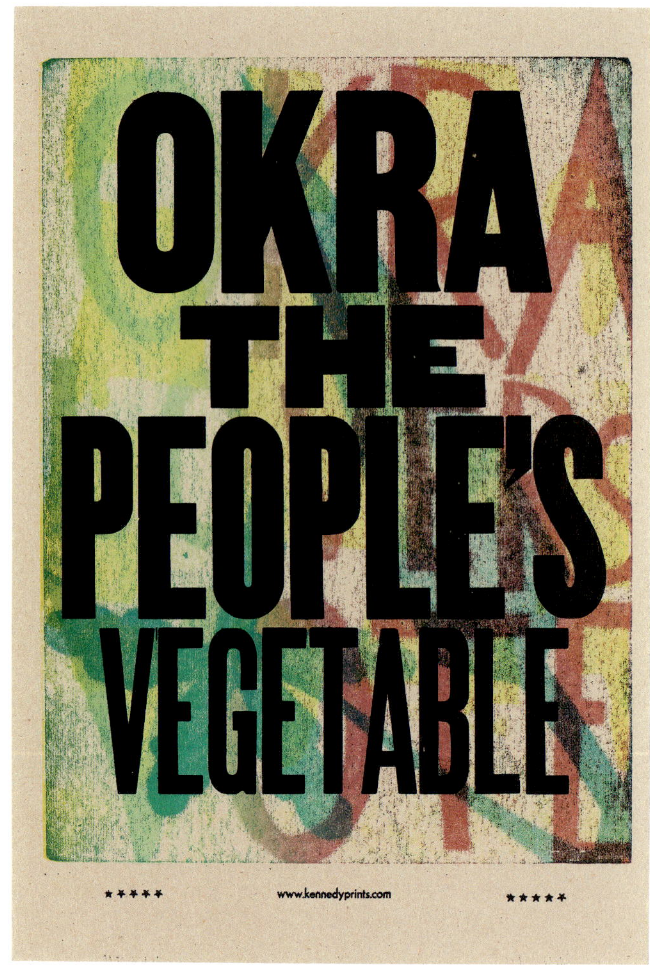
OKRA
THE
PEOPLE'S
VEGETABLE
www.kennedyprints.com

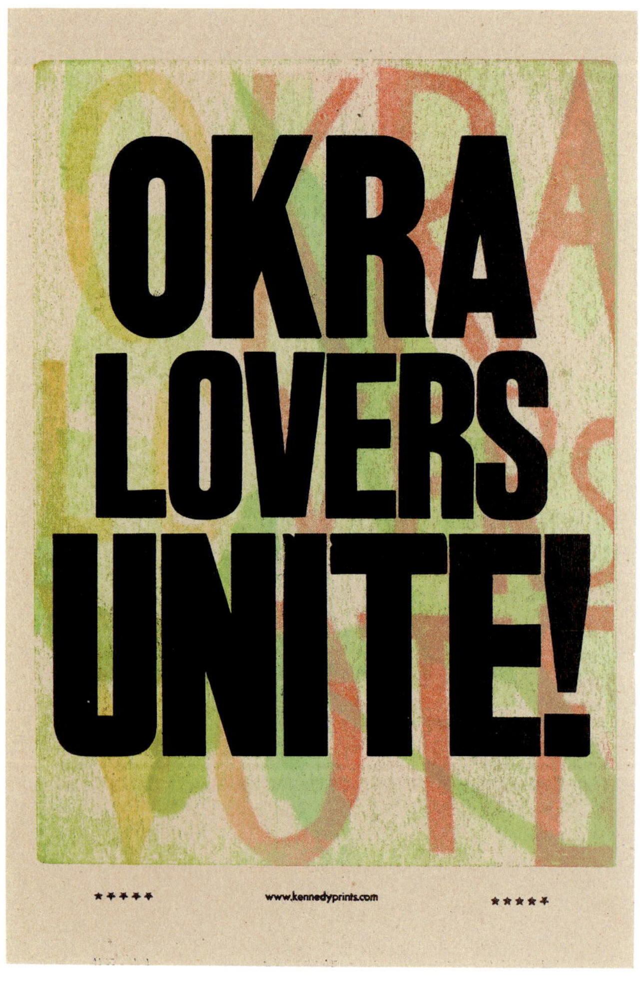
OKRA
LOVERS
UNITE!
www.kennedyprints.com

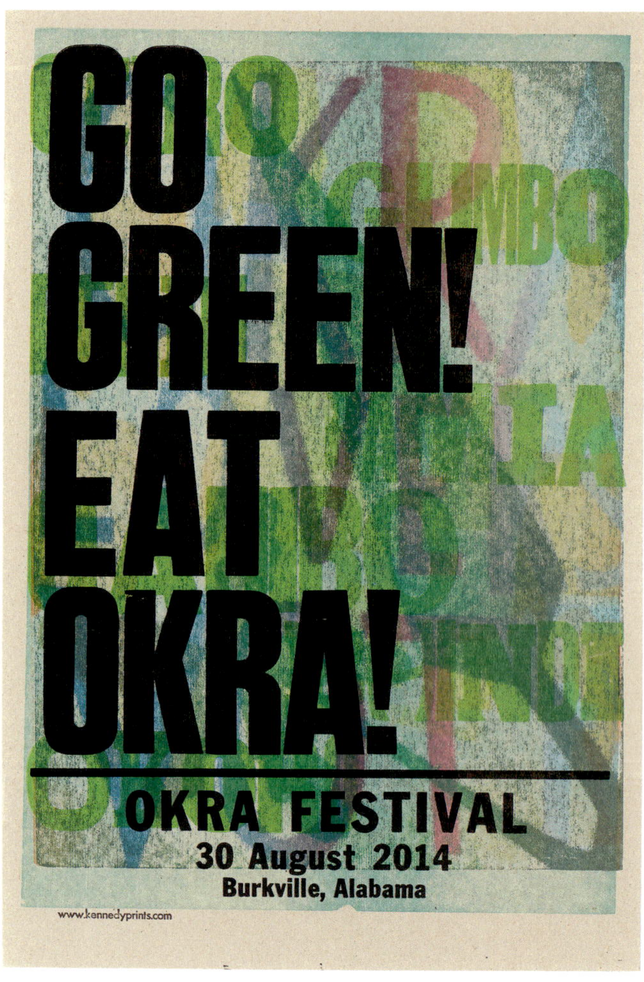
GO
GREEN!
EAT
OKRA!
OKRA FESTIVAL
30 August 2014
Burkville, Alabama
www.kennedyprints.com

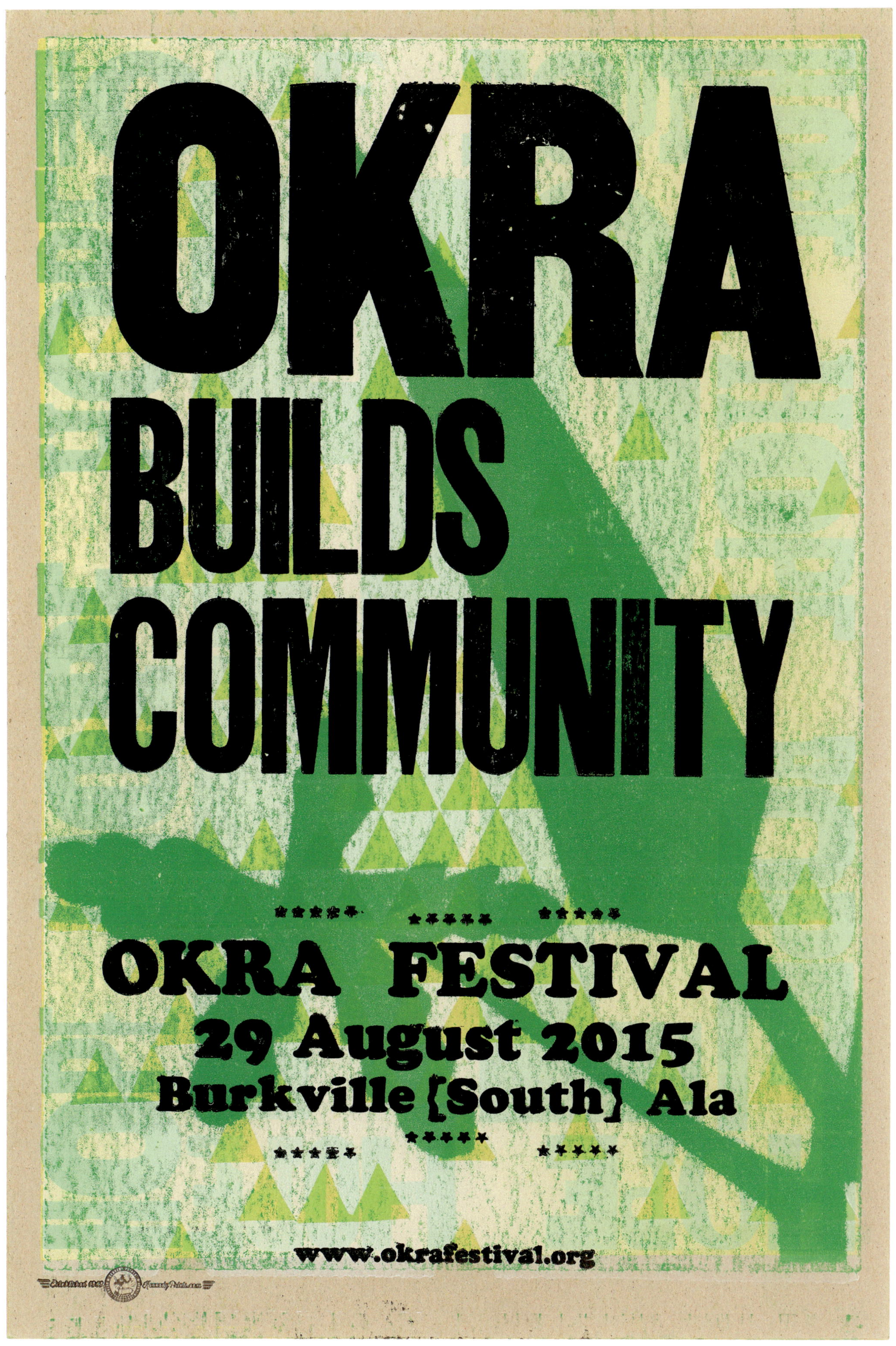
OKRA
BUILDS
COMMUNITY
OKRA FESTIVAL
29 August 2015
Burkville [South] Ala
www.okrafestival.org

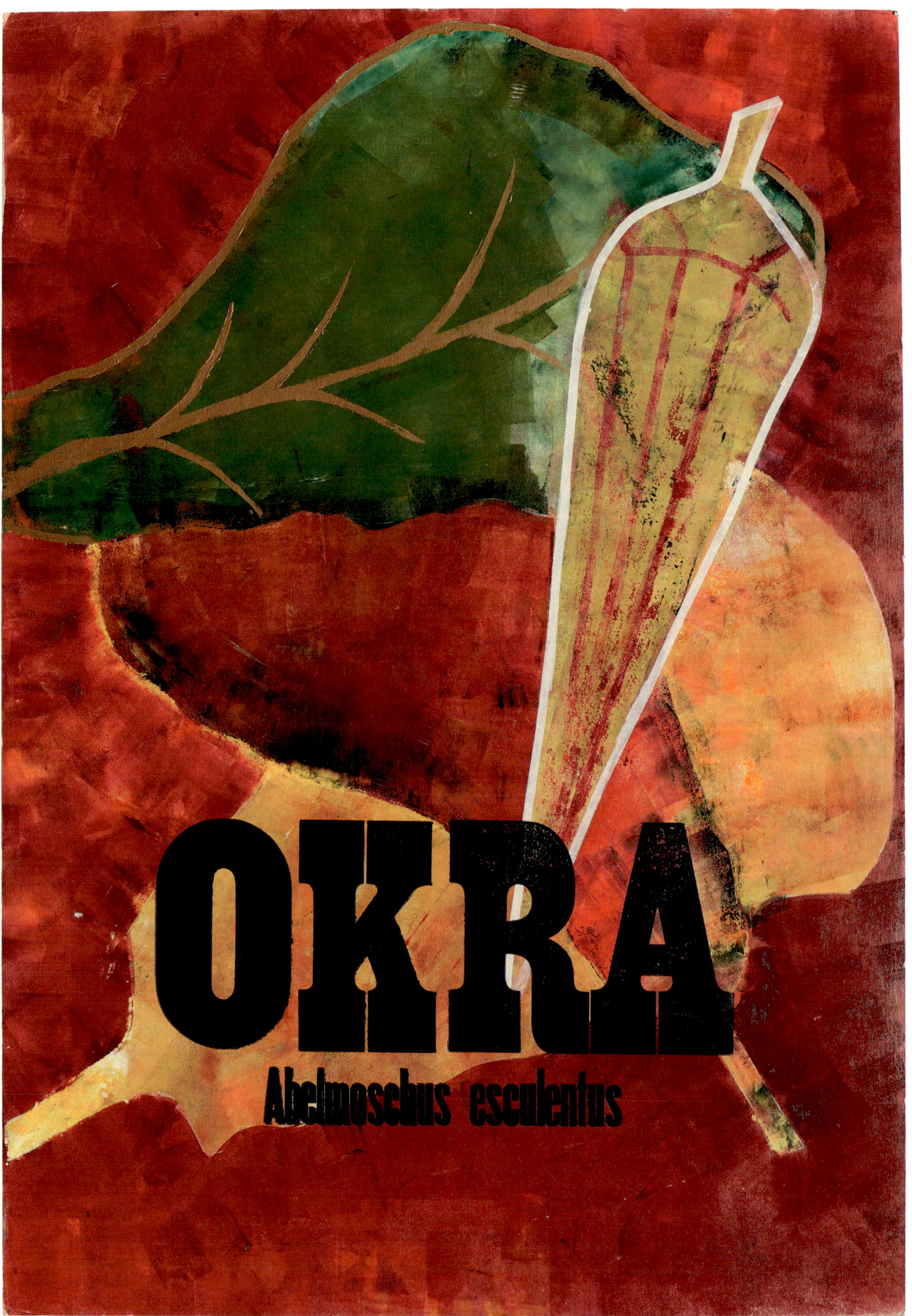
OKRA
Abelmoschus esculentus

"I print because it is the most productive thing I can do for my community. It's how I show up. Don't ask me to run anything or organize anything, but I can print 100 posters for your food drive or festival or lecture or cause, if you're trying to do some good. That's what being a citizen printer means to me."

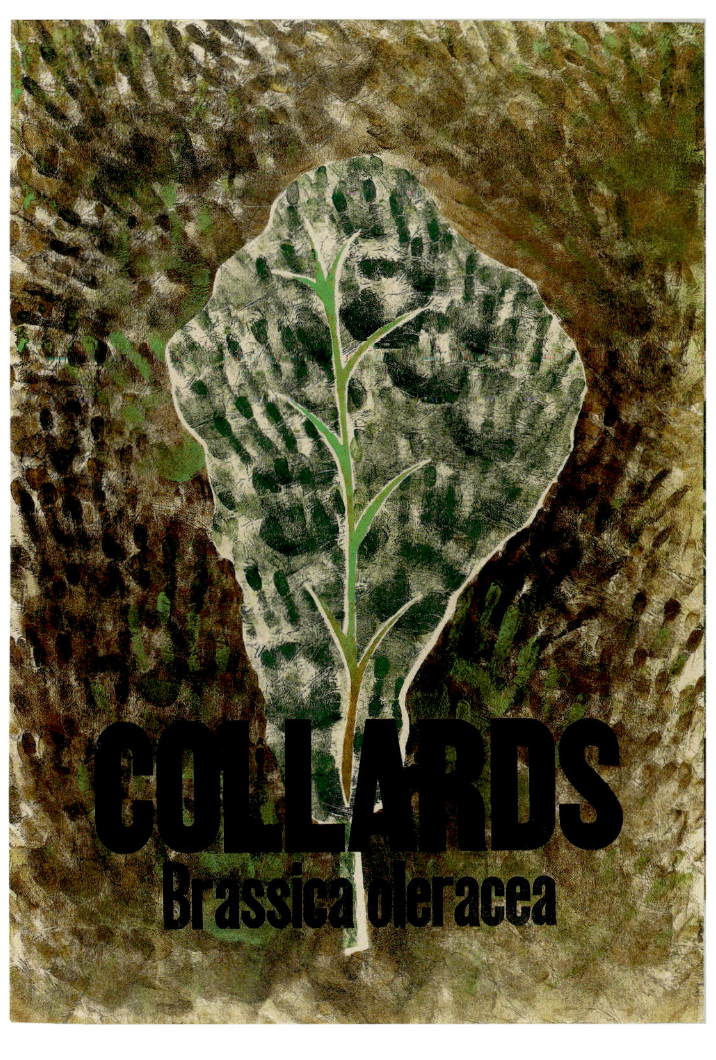

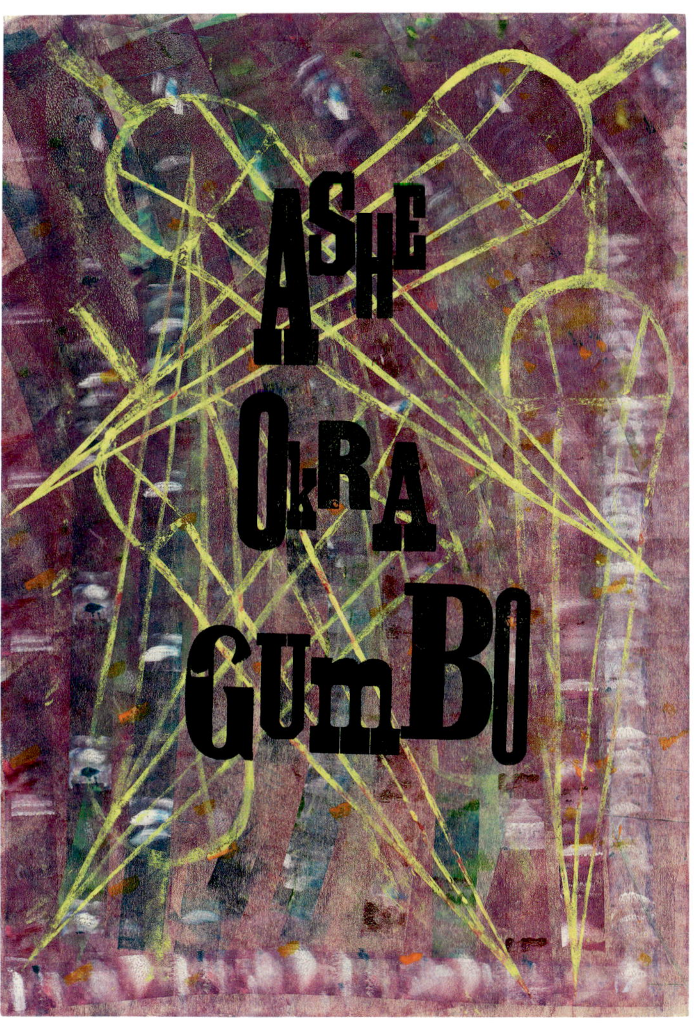

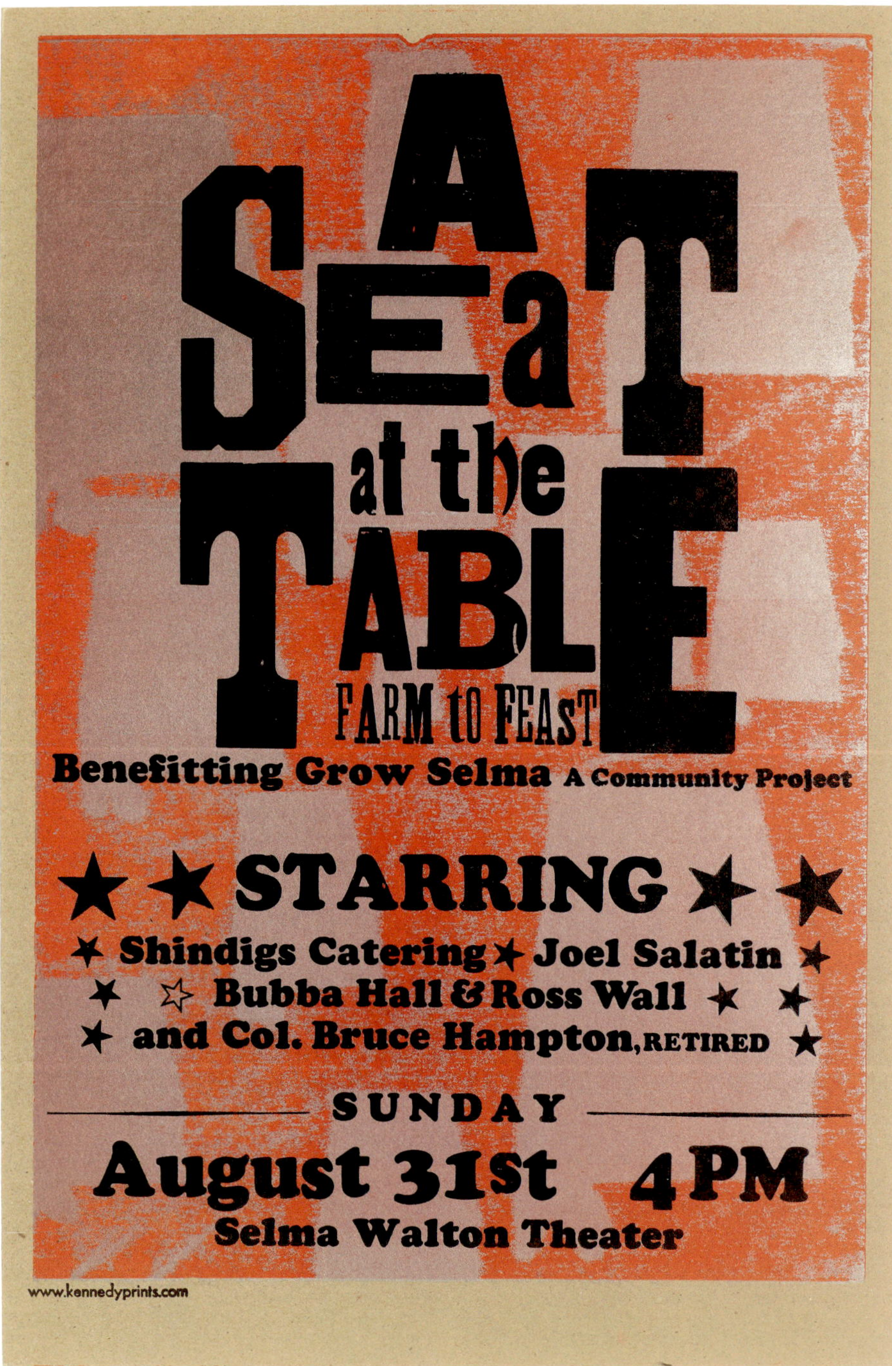
A
Seat
at the
Table
Farm to Feast
Benefitting Grow Selma A Community Project
STARRING
Shindigs Catering Joel Salatin
Bubba Hall & Ross Wall
and Col. Bruce Hampton, RETIRED
SUNDAY
August 31st 4 PM
Selma Walton Theater
www.kennedyprints.com

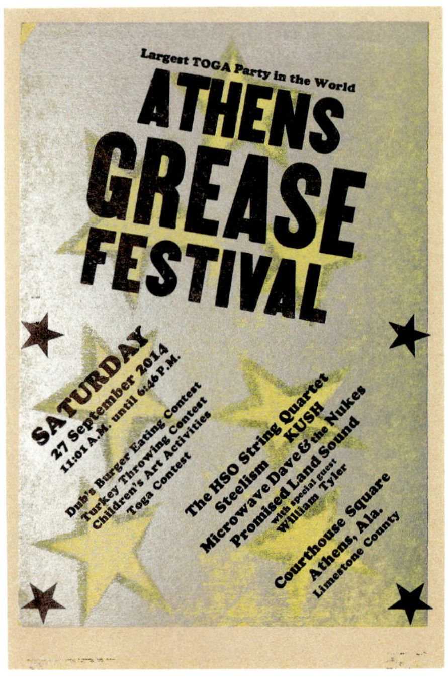
Largest TOGA Party in the World
ATHENS
GREASE
FESTIVAL
SATURDAY
27 September 2014
11:01 A.M. until 6:46 P.M.
Dub's Burger Eating Contest
Turkey Throwing Contest
Children's Art Activities
Toga Contest
The HSO String Quartet
Steelism KUSH
Microwave Dave & the Nukes
Promised Land Sound
with special guest
William Tyler
Courthouse Square
Athens, Ala.
Limestone County

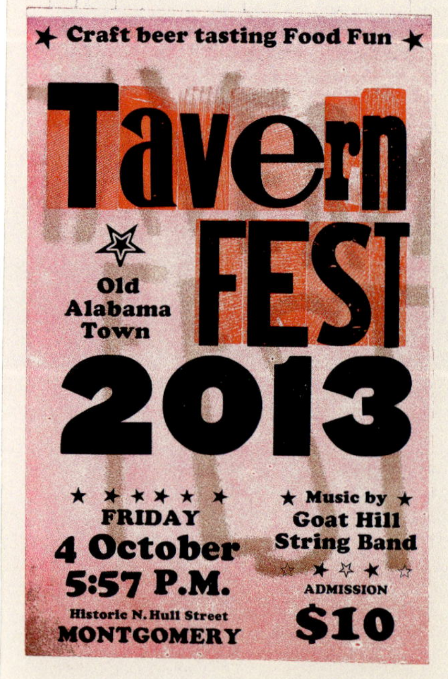
Craft beer tasting Food Fun
Tavern
FEST
Old
Alabama
Town
2013
FRIDAY
4 October
5:57 P.M.
Historic N. Hull Street
MONTGOMERY
Music by
Goat Hill
String Band
ADMISSION
$10

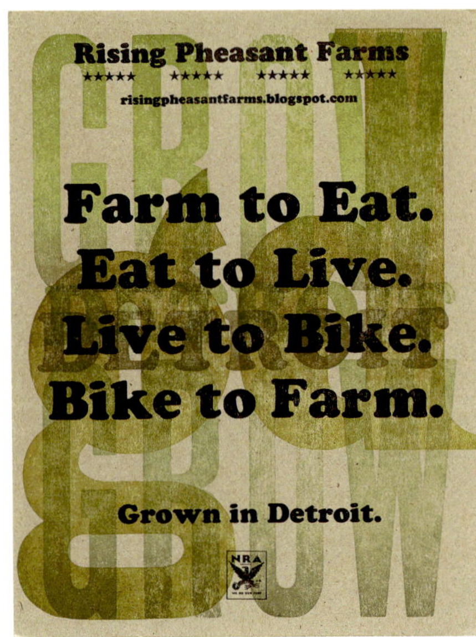
Rising Pheasant Farms
risingpheasantfarms.blogspot.com
Farm to Eat.
Eat to Live.
Live to Bike.
Bike to Farm.
Grown in Detroit.

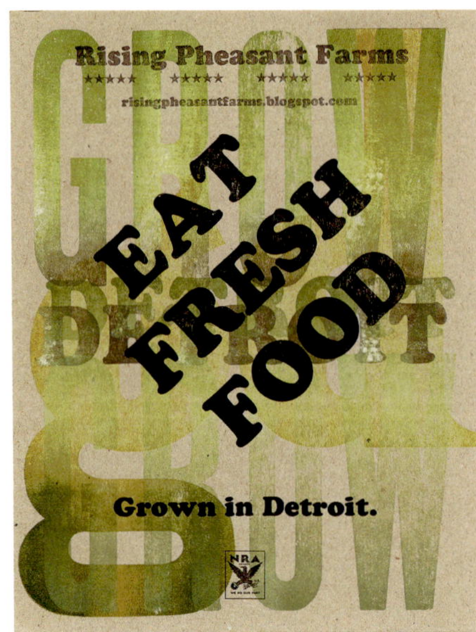
Rising Pheasant Farms
risingpheasantfarms.blogspot.com
EAT
FRESH
FOOD
Grown in Detroit.

Rising Pheasant Farms
risingpheasantfarms.blogspot.com
Support
Urban
Farms
BUY LOCAL

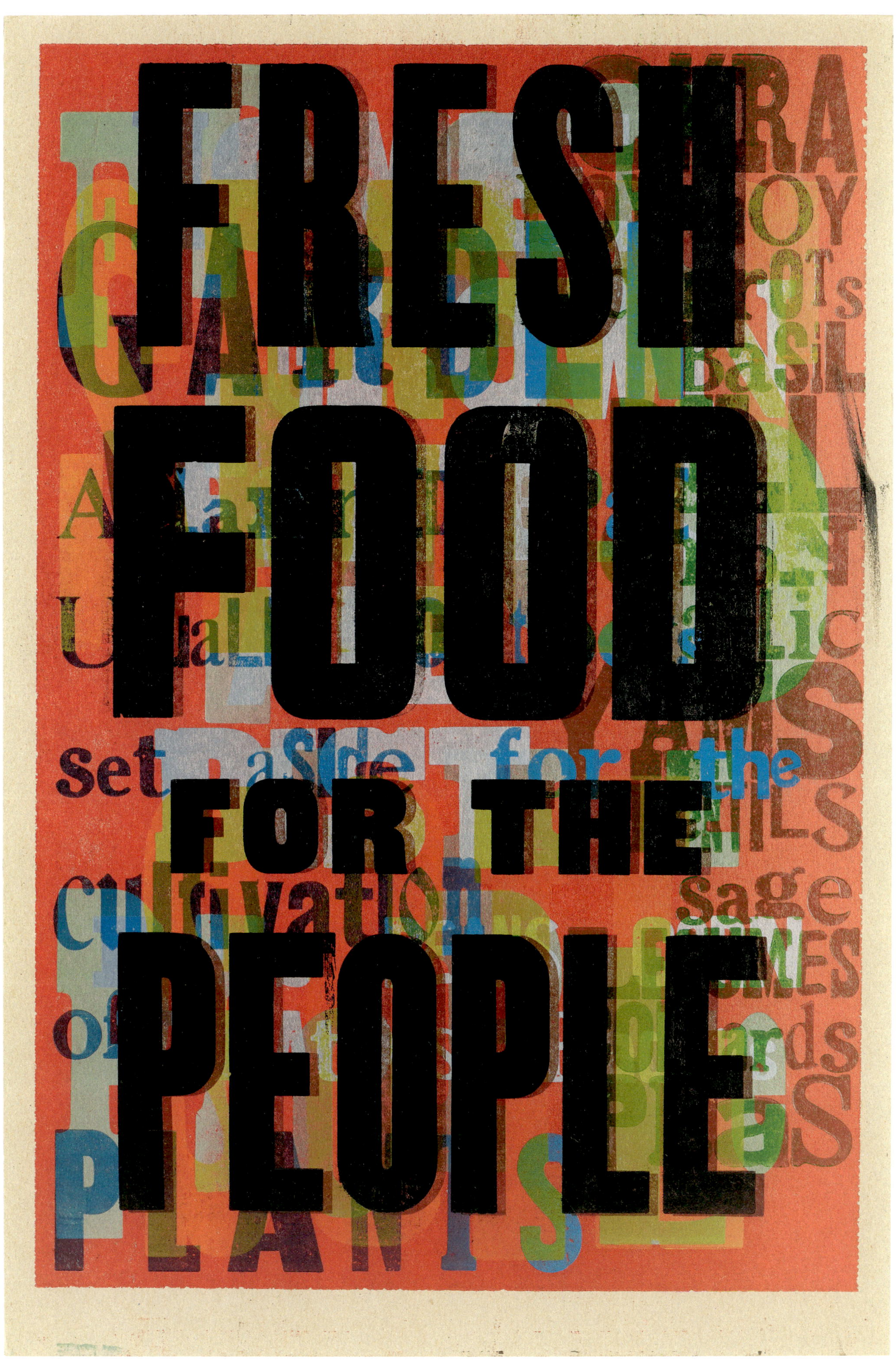
FRESH
FOOD
FOR THE
PEOPLE
set aside for the
cultivation
Sage
Basil

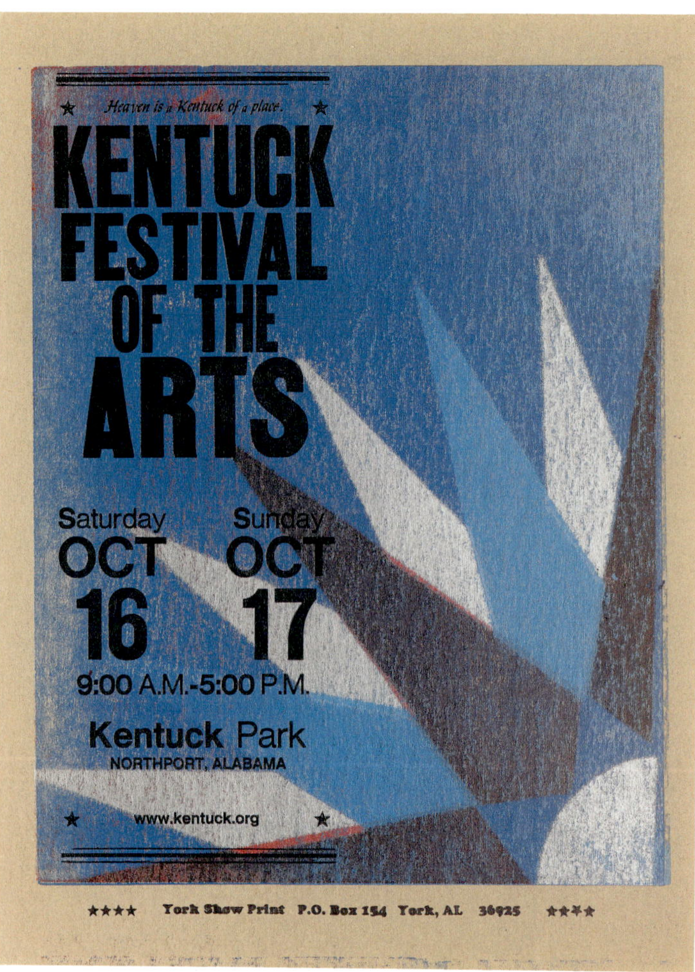
Heaven is a Kentuck of a place.
KENTUCK
FESTIVAL
OF THE
ARTS
Saturday OCT 16
Sunday OCT 17
9:00 A.M.-5:00 P.M.
Kentuck Park
NORTHPORT, ALABAMA
www.kentuck.org
York Show Print P.O. Box 154 York, AL 36925

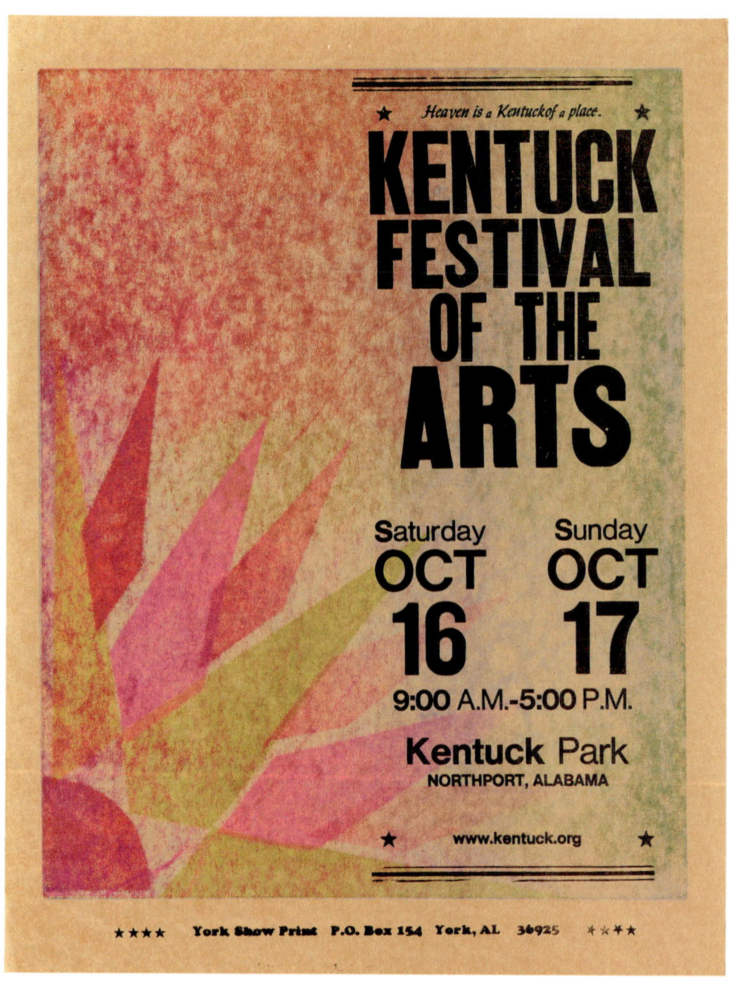
Heaven is a Kentuck of a place.
KENTUCK
FESTIVAL
OF THE
ARTS
Saturday OCT 16
Sunday OCT 17
9:00 A.M.-5:00 P.M.
Kentuck Park
NORTHPORT, ALABAMA
www.kentuck.org
York Show Print P.O. Box 154 York, AL 36925

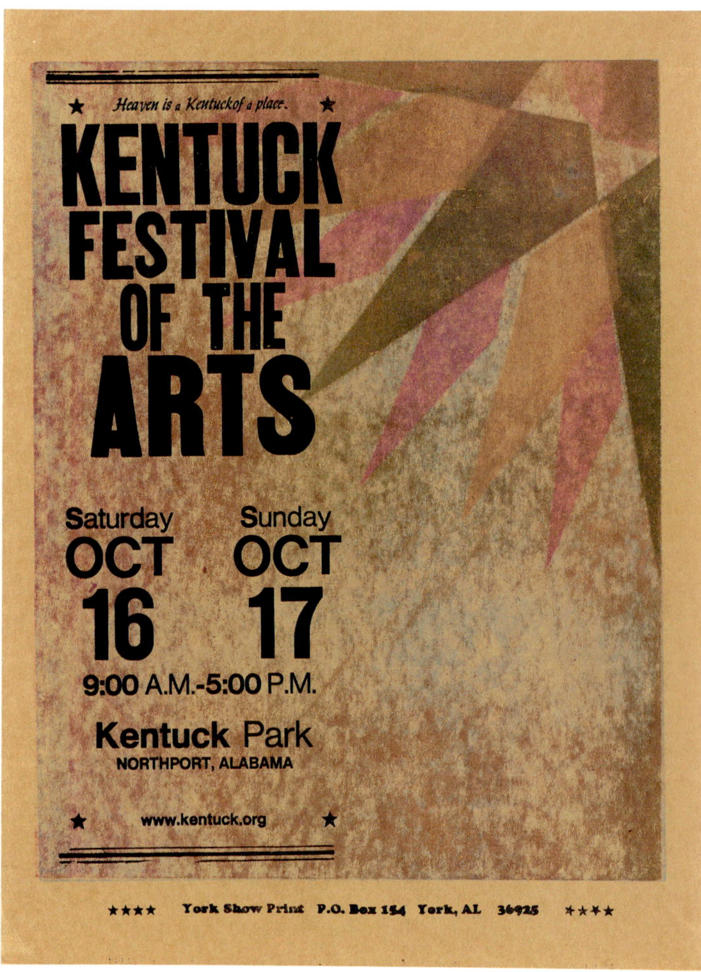
Heaven is a Kentuck of a place.
KENTUCK
FESTIVAL
OF THE
ARTS
Saturday OCT 16
Sunday OCT 17
9:00 A.M.-5:00 P.M.
Kentuck Park
NORTHPORT, ALABAMA
www.kentuck.org
York Show Print P.O. Box 154 York, AL 36925

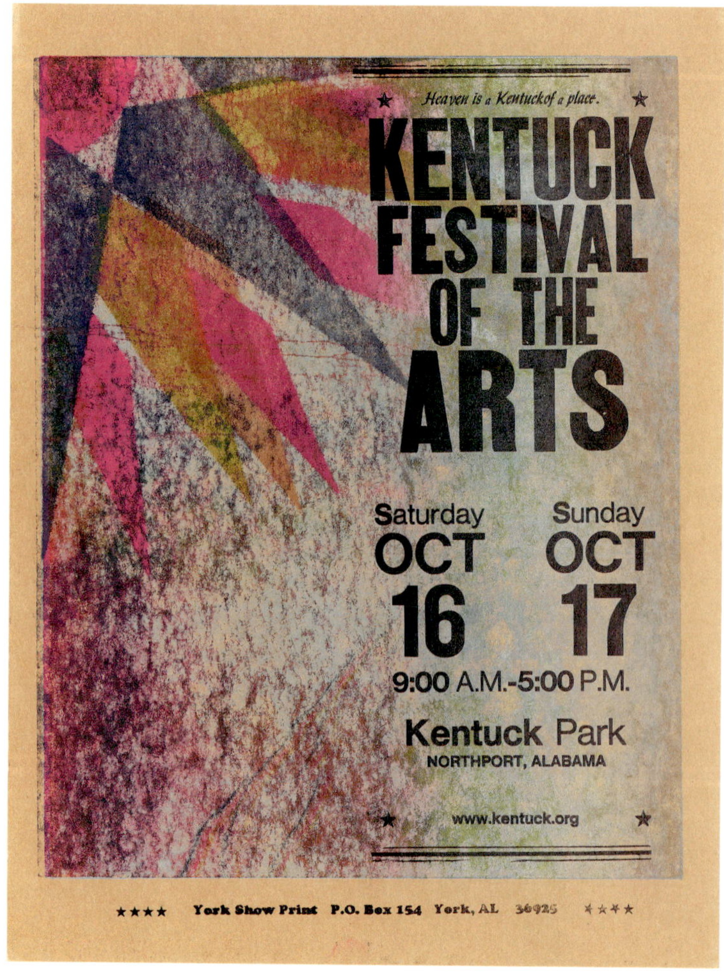
Heaven is a Kentuck of a place.
KENTUCK
FESTIVAL
OF THE
ARTS
Saturday OCT 16
Sunday OCT 17
9:00 A.M.-5:00 P.M.
Kentuck Park
NORTHPORT, ALABAMA
www.kentuck.org
York Show Print P.O. Box 154 York, AL 36925

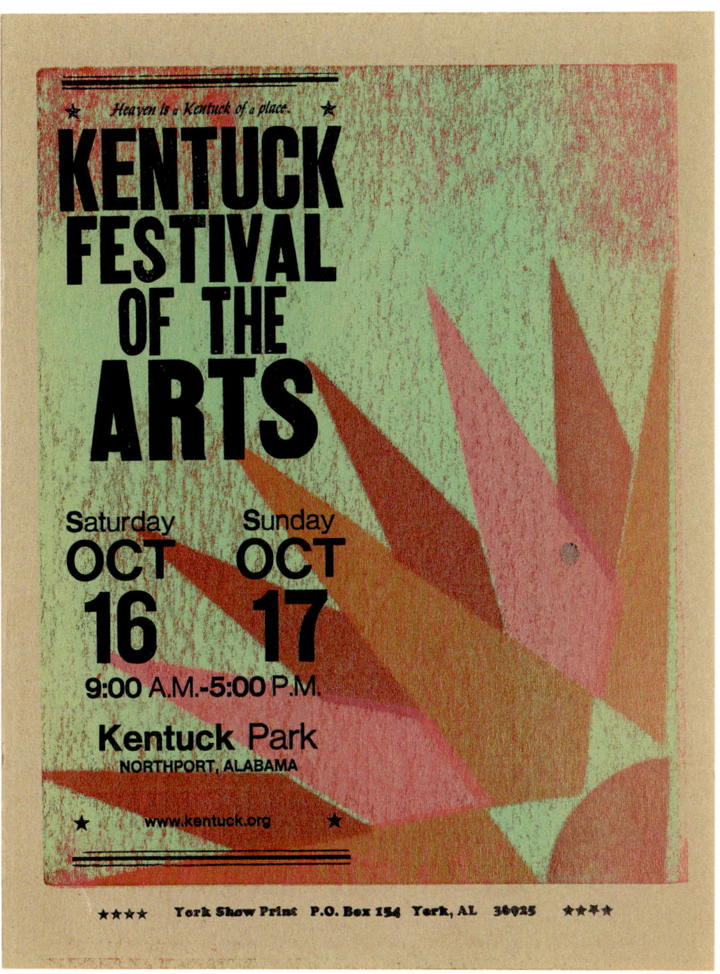

Heaven is a Kentuck of a place.
KENTUCK FESTIVAL OF THE ARTS
Saturday OCT 16
Sunday OCT 17
9:00 A.M.-5:00 P.M.
Kentuck Park
NORTHPORT, ALABAMA
www.kentuck.org
York Show Print P.O. Box 154 York, AL 36925

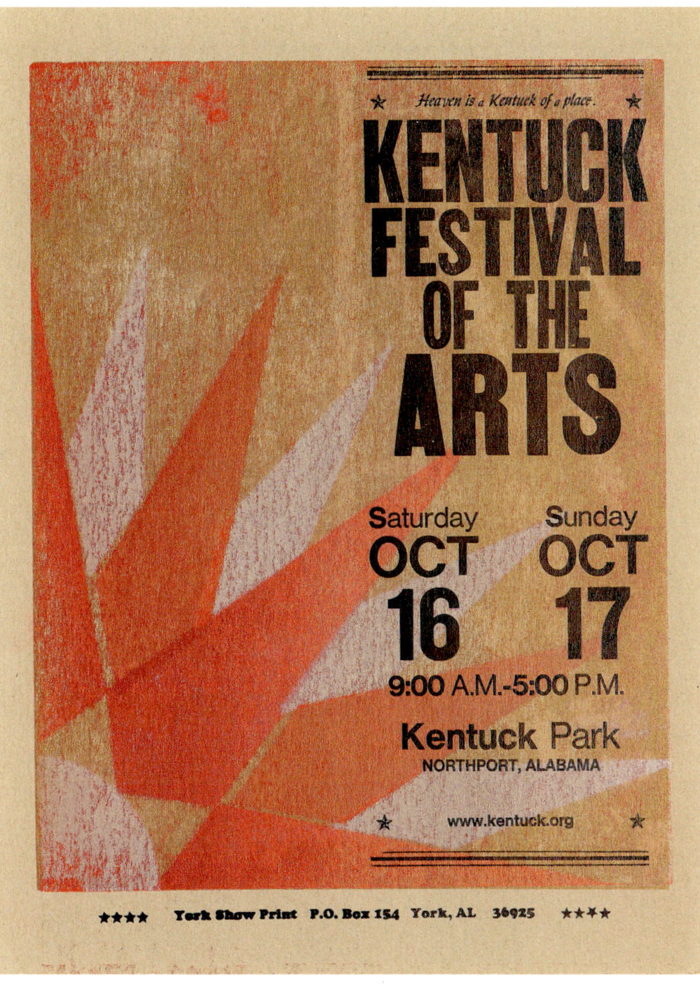

Heaven is a Kentuck of a place.
KENTUCK FESTIVAL OF THE ARTS
Saturday OCT 16
Sunday OCT 17
9:00 A.M.-5:00 P.M.
Kentuck Park
NORTHPORT, ALABAMA
www.kentuck.org
York Show Print P.O. Box 154 York, AL 36925

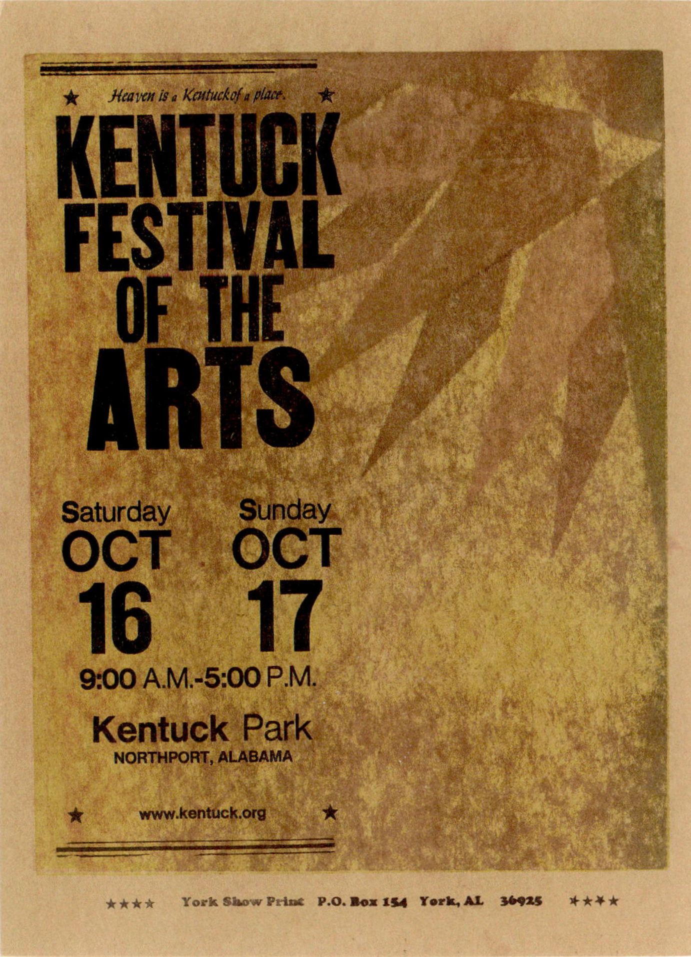

Heaven is a Kentuck of a place.
KENTUCK FESTIVAL OF THE ARTS
Saturday OCT 16
Sunday OCT 17
9:00 A.M.-5:00 P.M.
Kentuck Park
NORTHPORT, ALABAMA
www.kentuck.org
York Show Print P.O. Box 154 York, AL 36925

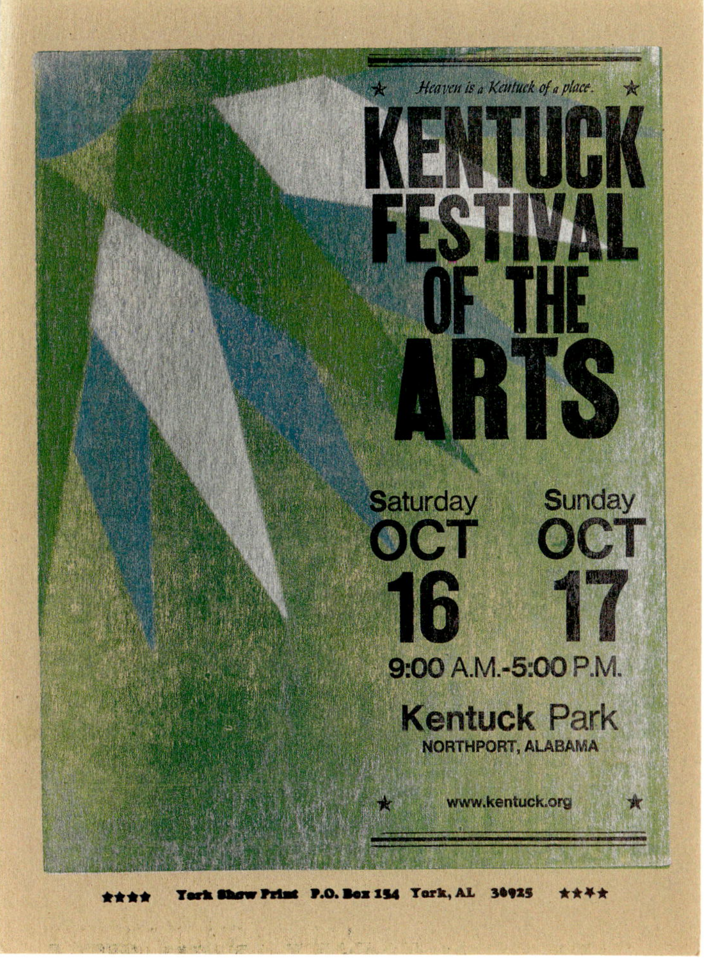

Heaven is a Kentuck of a place.
KENTUCK FESTIVAL OF THE ARTS
Saturday OCT 16
Sunday OCT 17
9:00 A.M.-5:00 P.M.
Kentuck Park
NORTHPORT, ALABAMA
www.kentuck.org
York Show Print P.O. Box 154 York, AL 36925

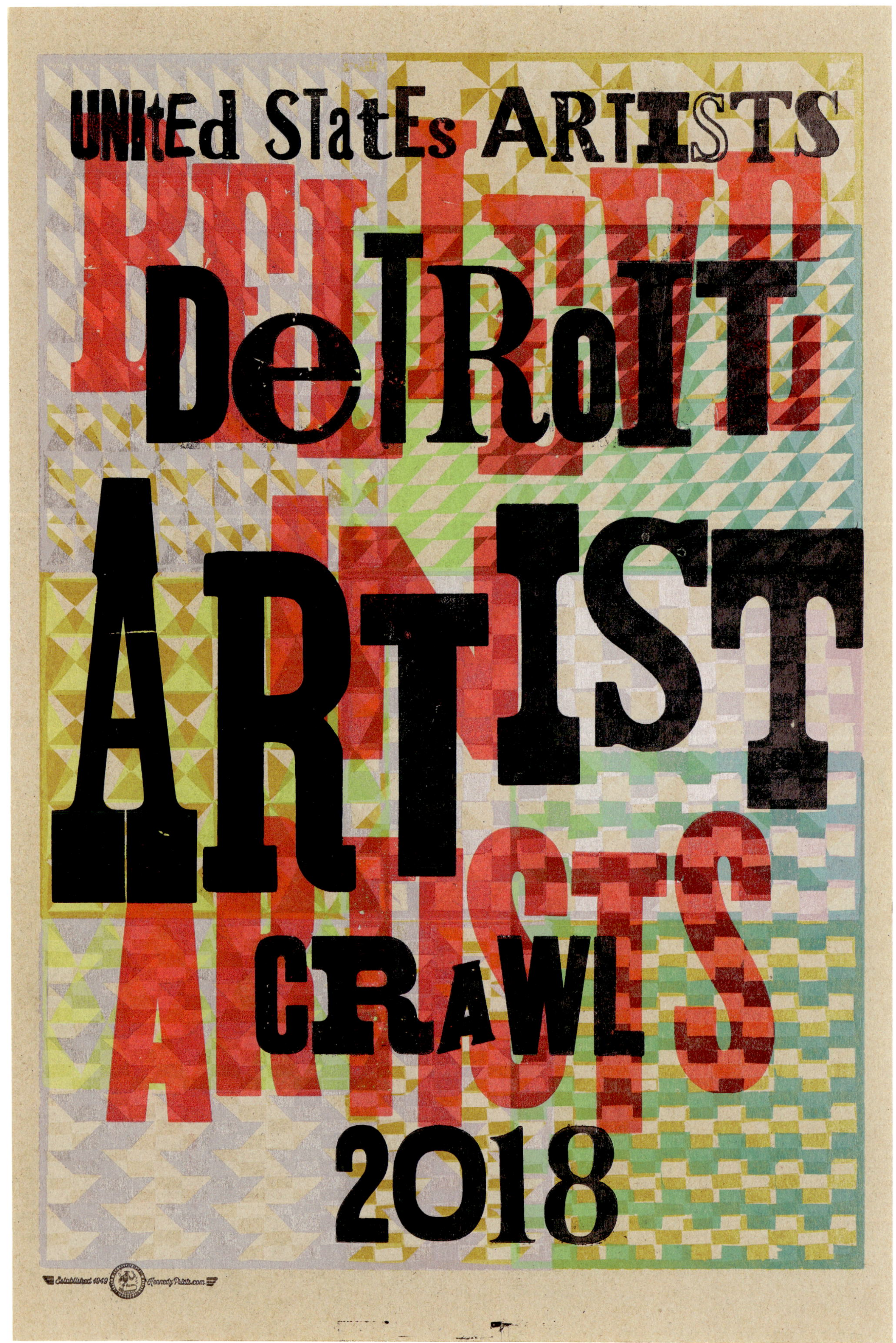
UNItEd StatEs ARTISTS
DEtRoIT
ARTIST
CRAWL
2018
Established 1949
KennedyPrints.com

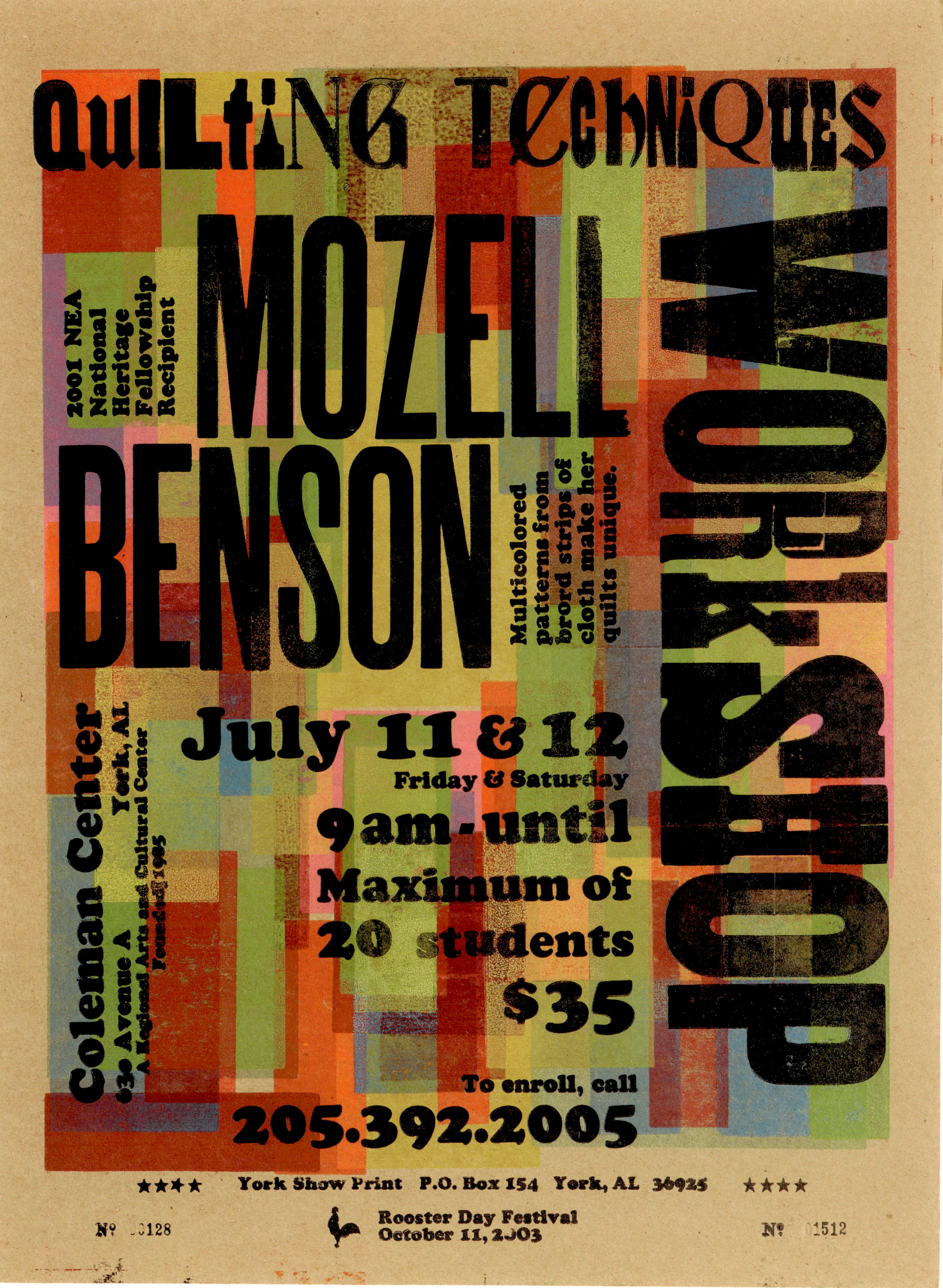
Quilting Techniques
MOZELL BENSON
WORKSHOP
2001 NEA
National
Heritage
Fellowship
Recipient
Multicolored
patterns from
brord strips of
cloth make her
quilts unique.
Coleman Center
630 Avenue A
York, AL
A Regional Arts and Cultural Center
July 11 & 12
Friday & Saturday
9am - until
Maximum of
20 students
$35
To enroll, call
205.392.2005
★★★★ York Show Print P.O. Box 154 York, AL 36925 ★★★★
Rooster Day Festival
October 11, 2003

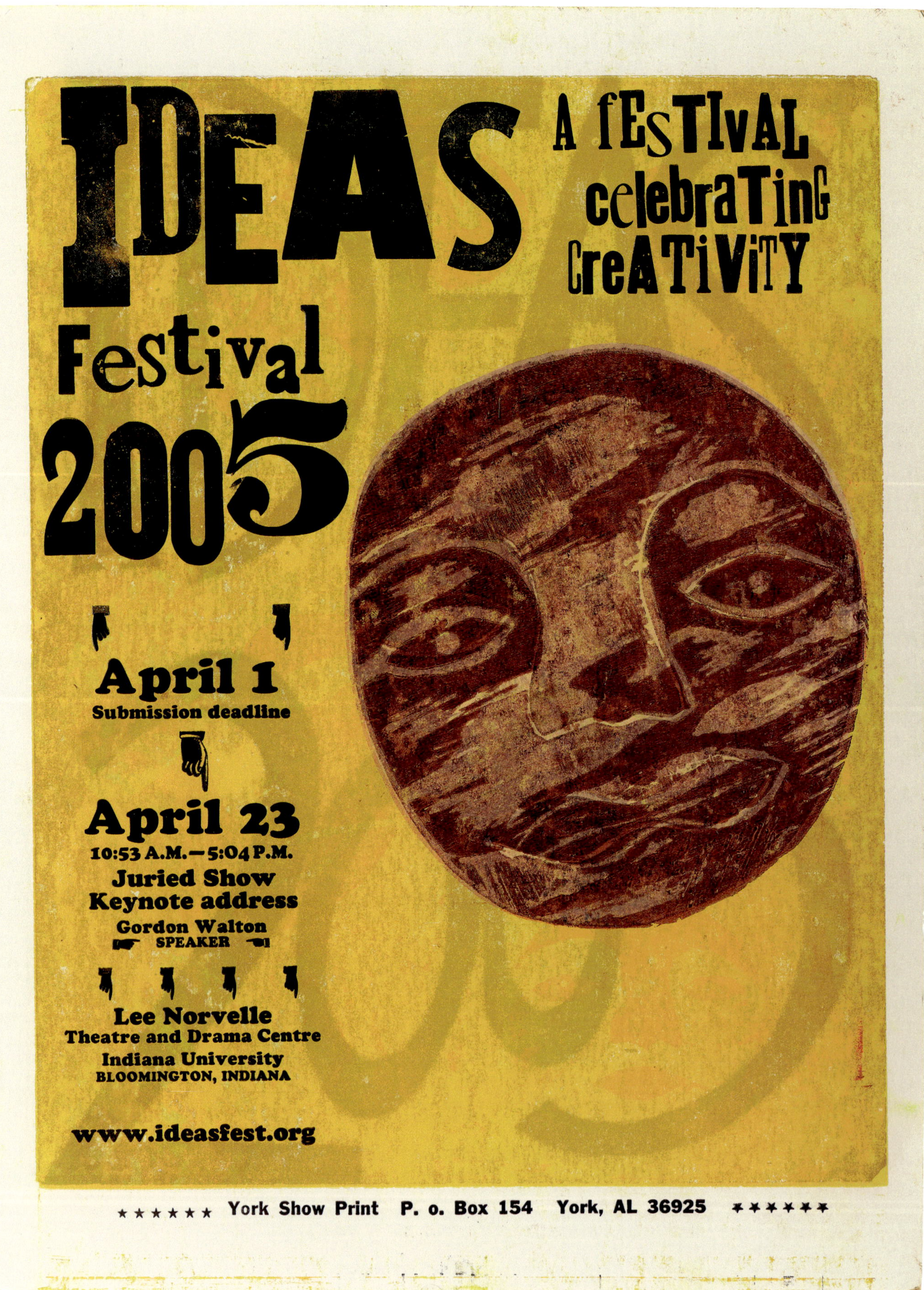
IDEAS
A fEsTIvAL celebraTing CreATiViTY
Festival
2005
April 1
Submission deadline
April 23
10:53 A.M.—5:04 P.M.
Juried Show
Keynote address
Gordon Walton
SPEAKER
Lee Norvelle
Theatre and Drama Centre
Indiana University
BLOOMINGTON, INDIANA
www.ideasfest.org
York Show Print P. o. Box 154 York, AL 36925

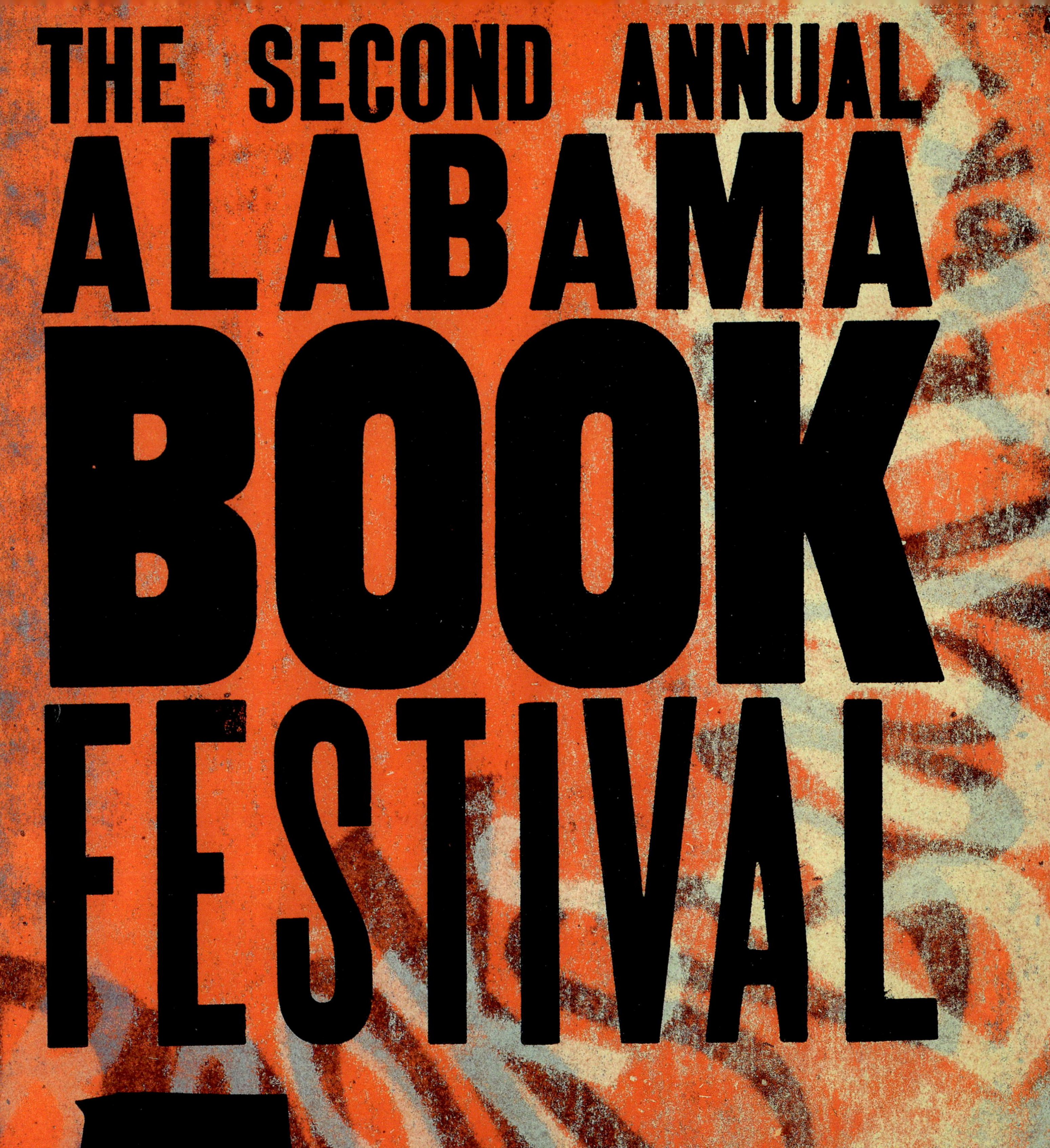

21 April 2007
9:02 a.m.-4:00 p.m.
Old Alabama Town
Montgomery, Alabama

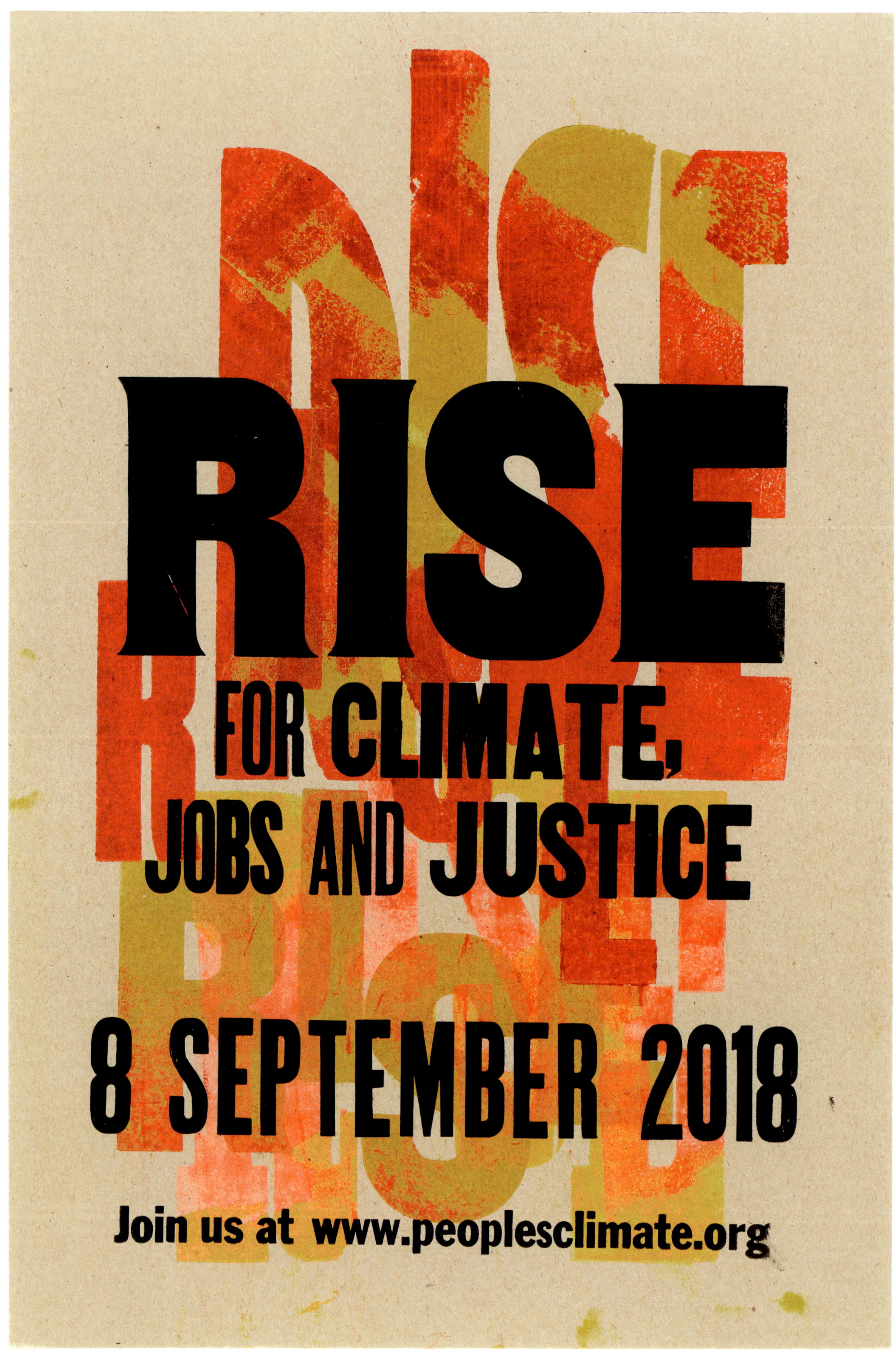
RISE
FOR CLIMATE,
JOBS AND JUSTICE
8 SEPTEMBER 2018
Join us at www.peoplesclimate.org

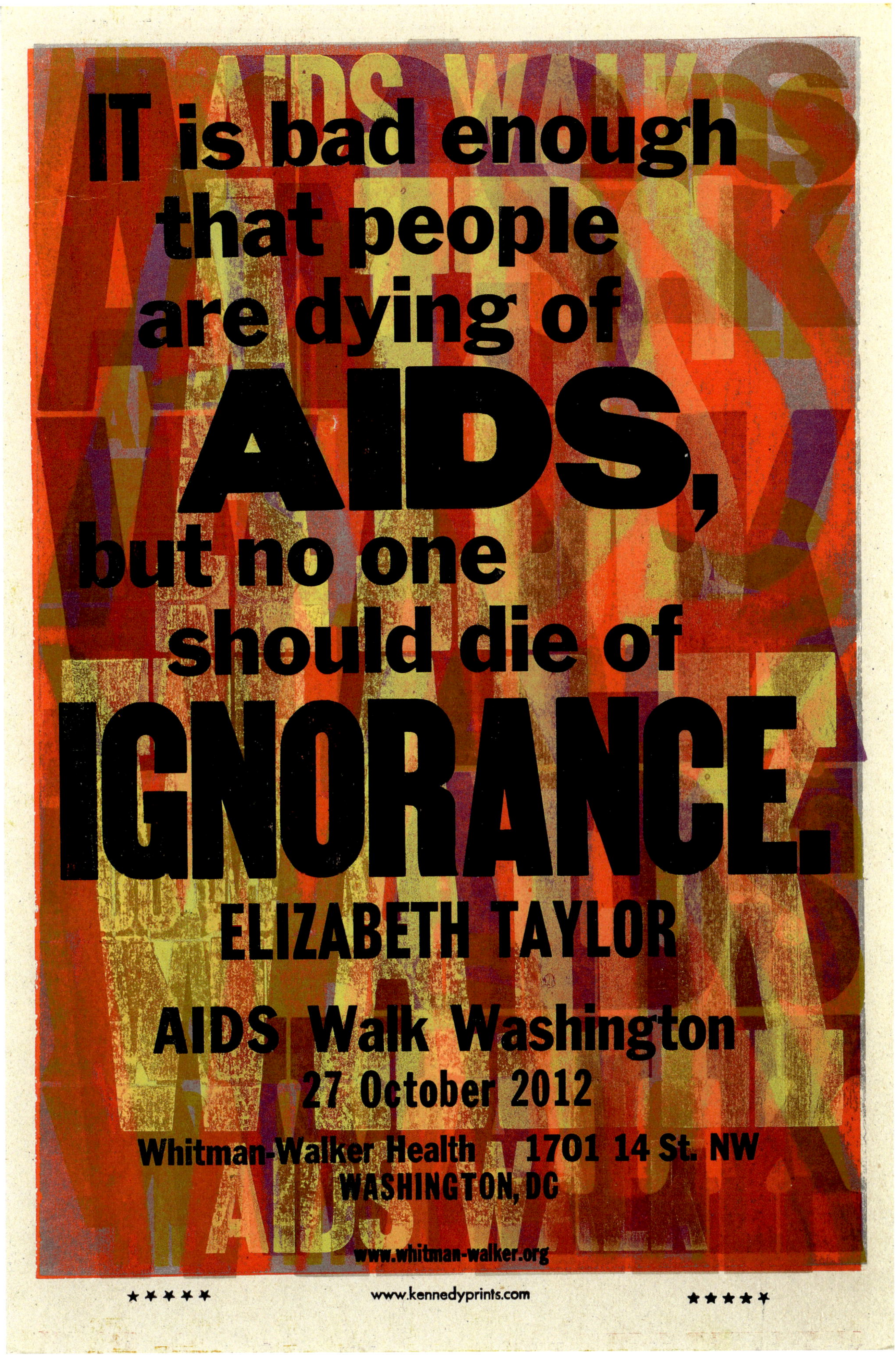
IT is bad enough
that people
are dying of
AIDS,
but no one
should die of
IGNORANCE.
ELIZABETH TAYLOR
AIDS Walk Washington
27 October 2012
Whitman-Walker Health 1701 14 St. NW
WASHINGTON, DC
www.whitman-walker.org
★★★★★ www.kennedyprints.com ★★★★★

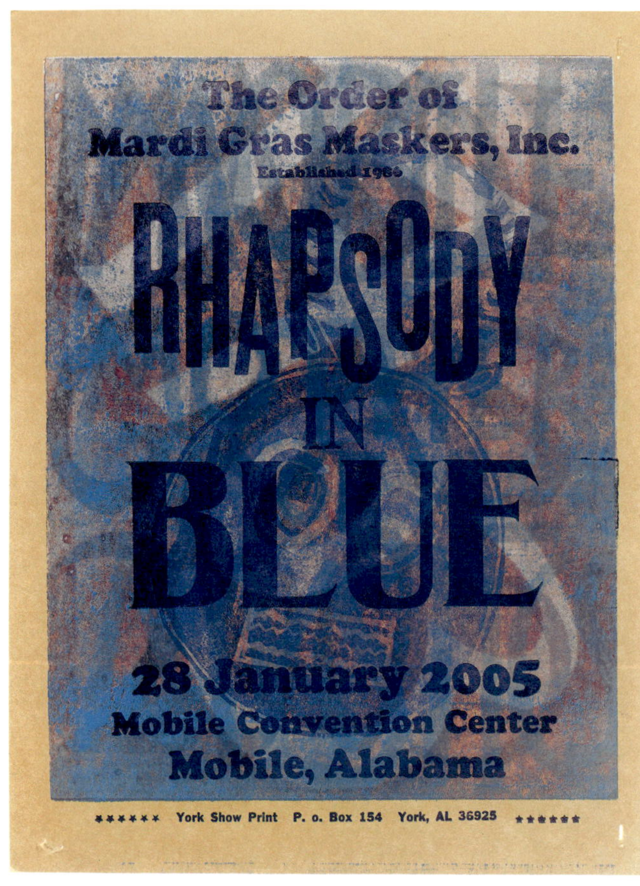
The Order of
Mardi Gras Maskers, Inc.
Established 1980
RHAPSODY
IN
BLUE
28 January 2005
Mobile Convention Center
Mobile, Alabama
****** York Show Print P. o. Box 154 York, AL 36925 ******

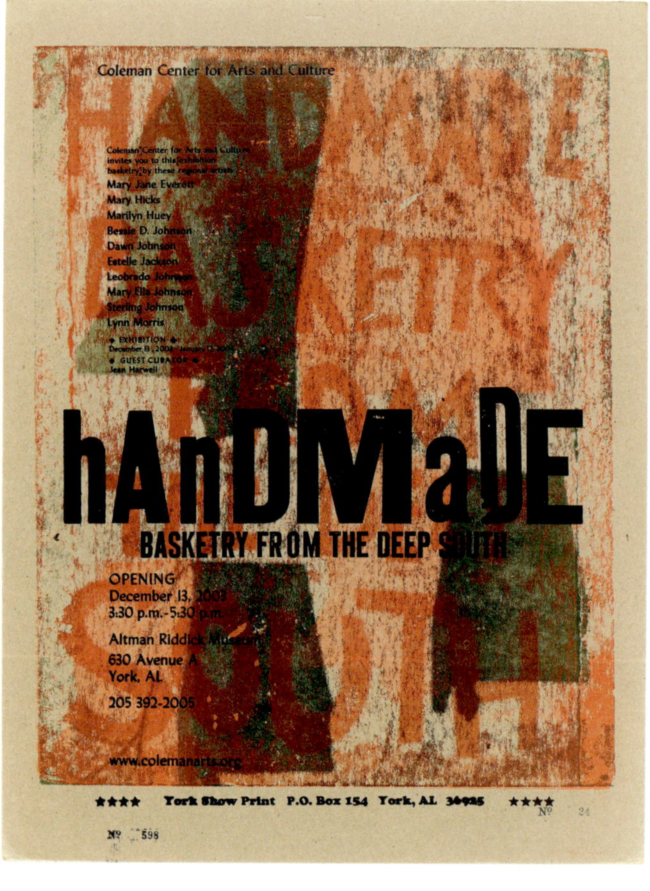
Coleman Center for Arts and Culture
Coleman Center for Arts and Culture
invites you to this exhibition
basketry by these regional artists
Mary Jane Everett
Mary Hicks
Marilyn Huey
Bessie D. Johnson
Dawn Johnson
Estelle Jackson
Leobrado Johnson
Mary Ella Johnson
Sterling Johnson
Lynn Morris
EXHIBITION
GUEST CURATOR
Jean Harwell
hAnDMaDE
BASKETRY FROM THE DEEP SOUTH
OPENING
December 13,
3:30 p.m.-5:30 p.m.
Altman Riddick
630 Avenue A
York, AL
205 392-2005
www.colemanarts.org
**** York Show Print P.O. Box 154 York, AL 36925 ****

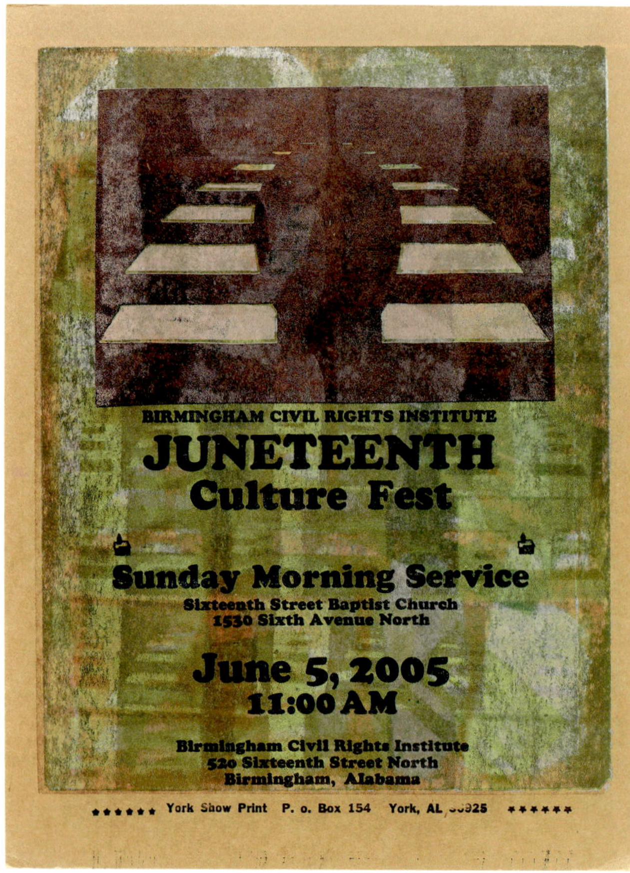
BIRMINGHAM CIVIL RIGHTS INSTITUTE
JUNETEENTH
Culture Fest
Sunday Morning Service
Sixteenth Street Baptist Church
1530 Sixth Avenue North
June 5, 2005
11:00 AM
Birmingham Civil Rights Institute
520 Sixteenth Street North
Birmingham, Alabama
****** York Show Print P. o. Box 154 York, AL ******

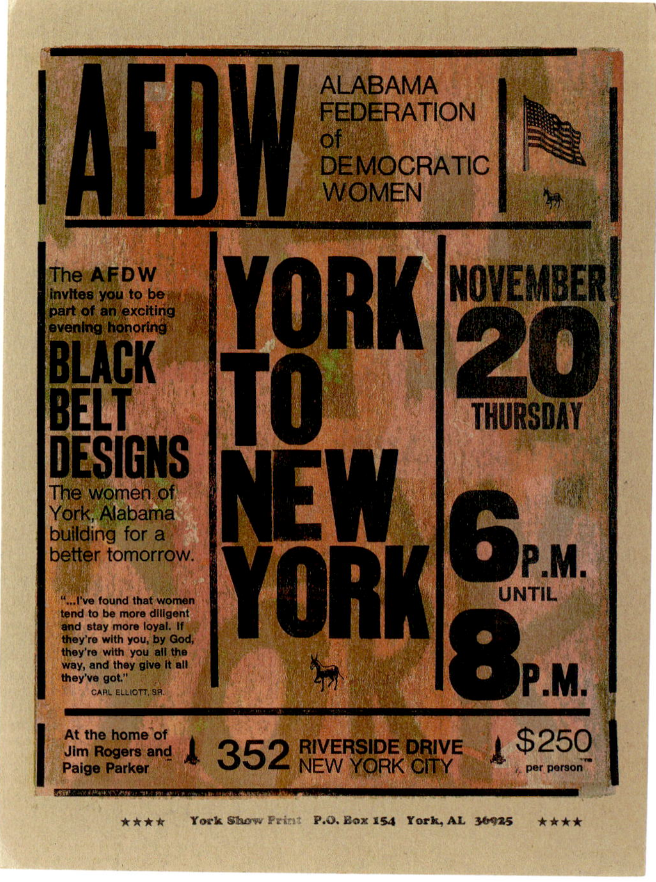
AFDW
ALABAMA
FEDERATION
of
DEMOCRATIC
WOMEN
The AFDW
invites you to be
part of an exciting
evening honoring
BLACK
BELT
DESIGNS
The women of
York, Alabama
building for a
better tomorrow.
"...I've found that women
tend to be more diligent
and stay more loyal. If
they're with you, by God,
they're with you all the
way, and they give it all
they've got."
CARL ELLIOTT, SR.
YORK
TO
NEW
YORK
NOVEMBER
20
THURSDAY
6 P.M.
UNTIL
8 P.M.
At the home of
Jim Rogers and
Paige Parker
352 RIVERSIDE DRIVE
NEW YORK CITY
$250
per person
**** York Show Print P.O. Box 154 York, AL 36925 ****

BLACK

African American Art
from the Corcoran Gallery of Art

13 January - 2 April 2006

Mobile Museum of Art
4850 Museum Drive

 Printed at Kennedy Prints! 

TEE'S LOUNGE

The **21st century** juke joint

LADIES NO FIGHTING IN THE BATHROOM

This is a **GROWN FOLKS** establishment

501 First Avenue York, Alabama

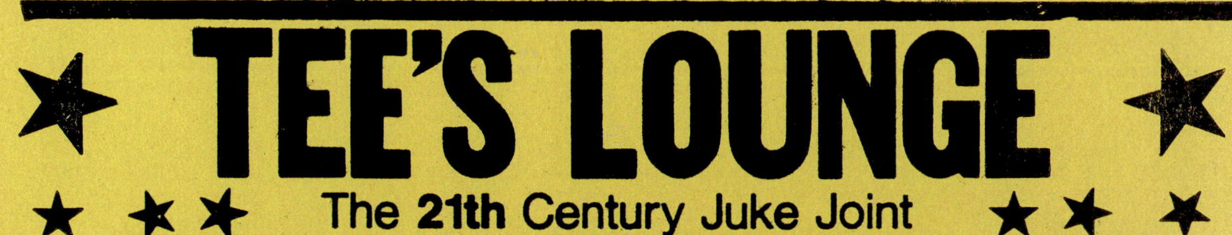

BE NICE OR LEAVE!

This a **GROWN FOLKS** establishment!

501 First Avenue York, Alabama

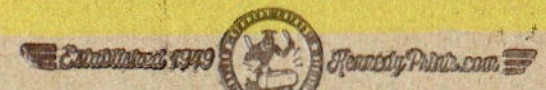

“When I say I want to print negro—that I want to do for printing what the blues did for music—I mean I want to improvise, to syncopate, to interpret musical notation with type, with color, with the rhythm of the letters on the page. For me, printing is like opening up my mouth and singing.”

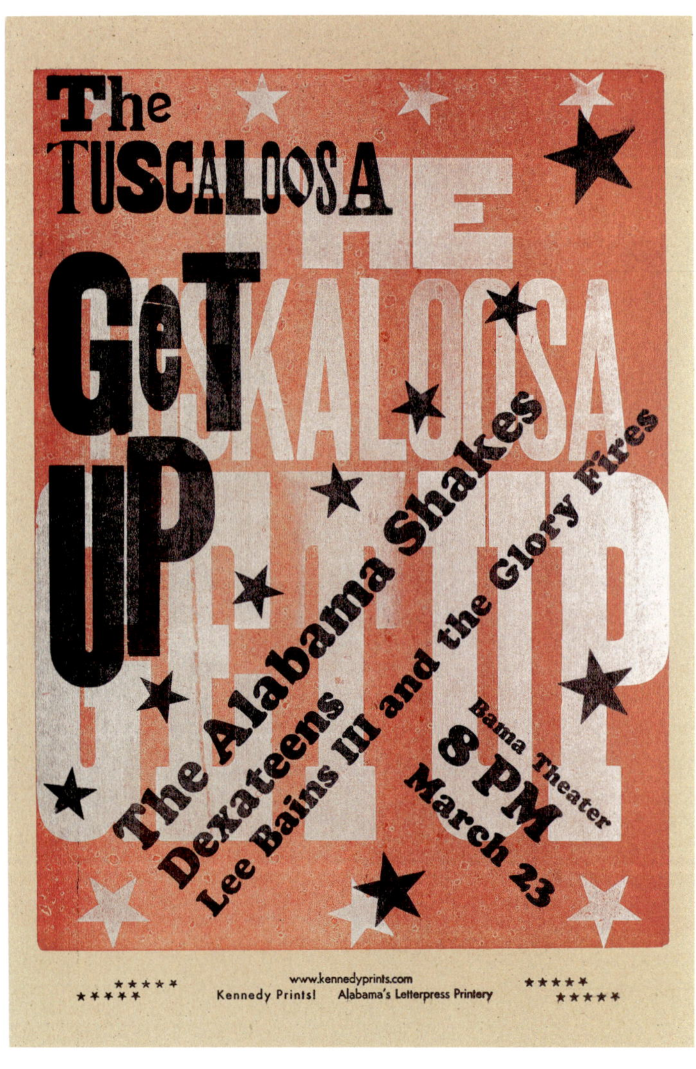

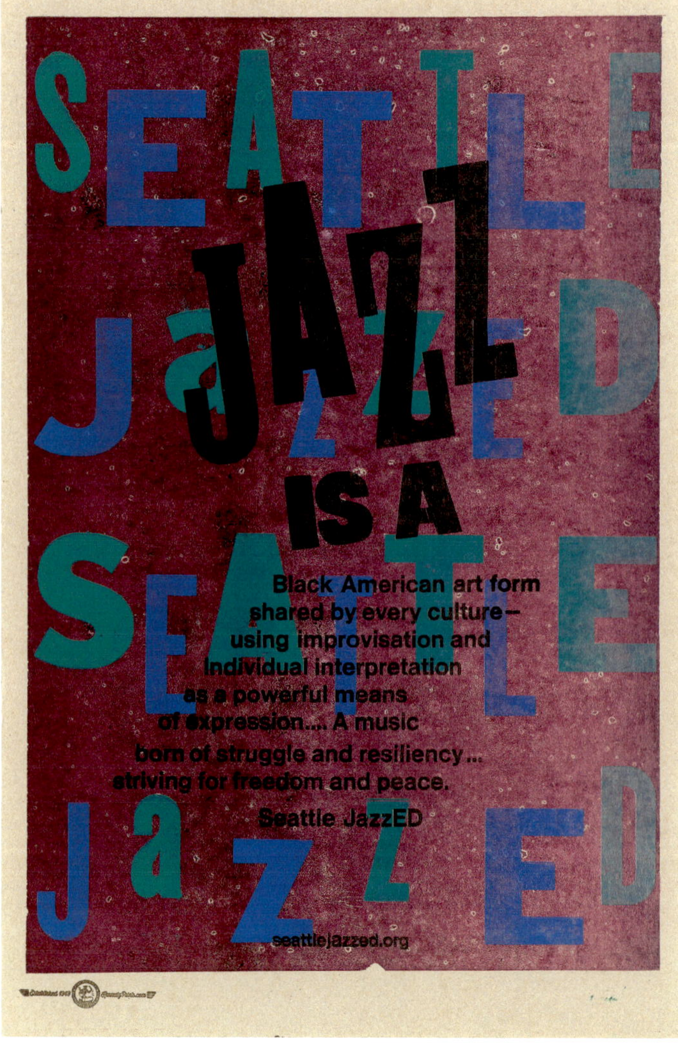

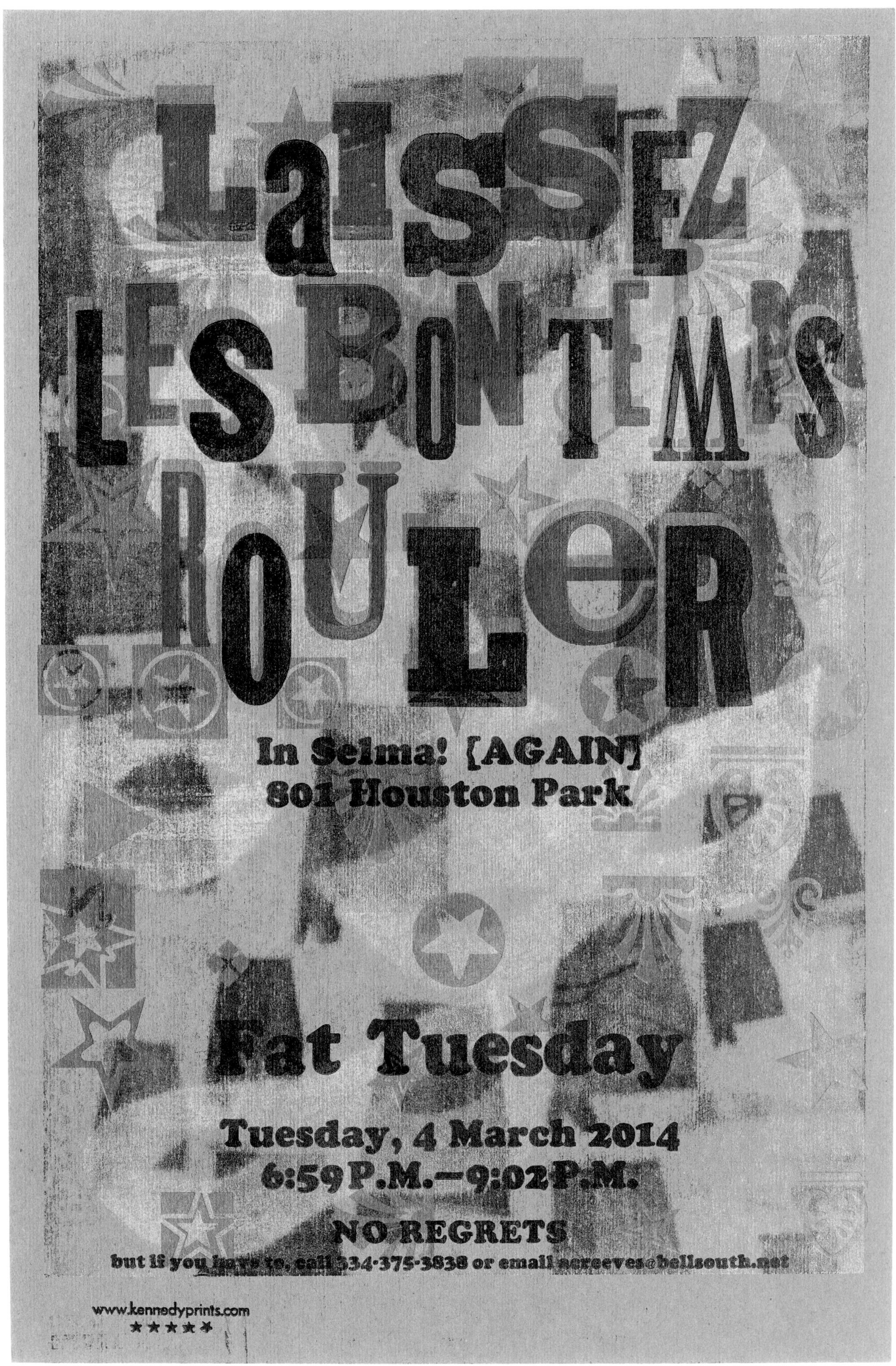
LAISSEZ
LES BONTEMPS
ROULER
In Selma! {AGAIN}
801 Houston Park
Fat Tuesday
Tuesday, 4 March 2014
6:59 P.M.—9:02 P.M.
NO REGRETS
but if you have to, call 334-375-3838 or email acreeves@bellsouth.net
www.kennedyprints.com
★★★★★

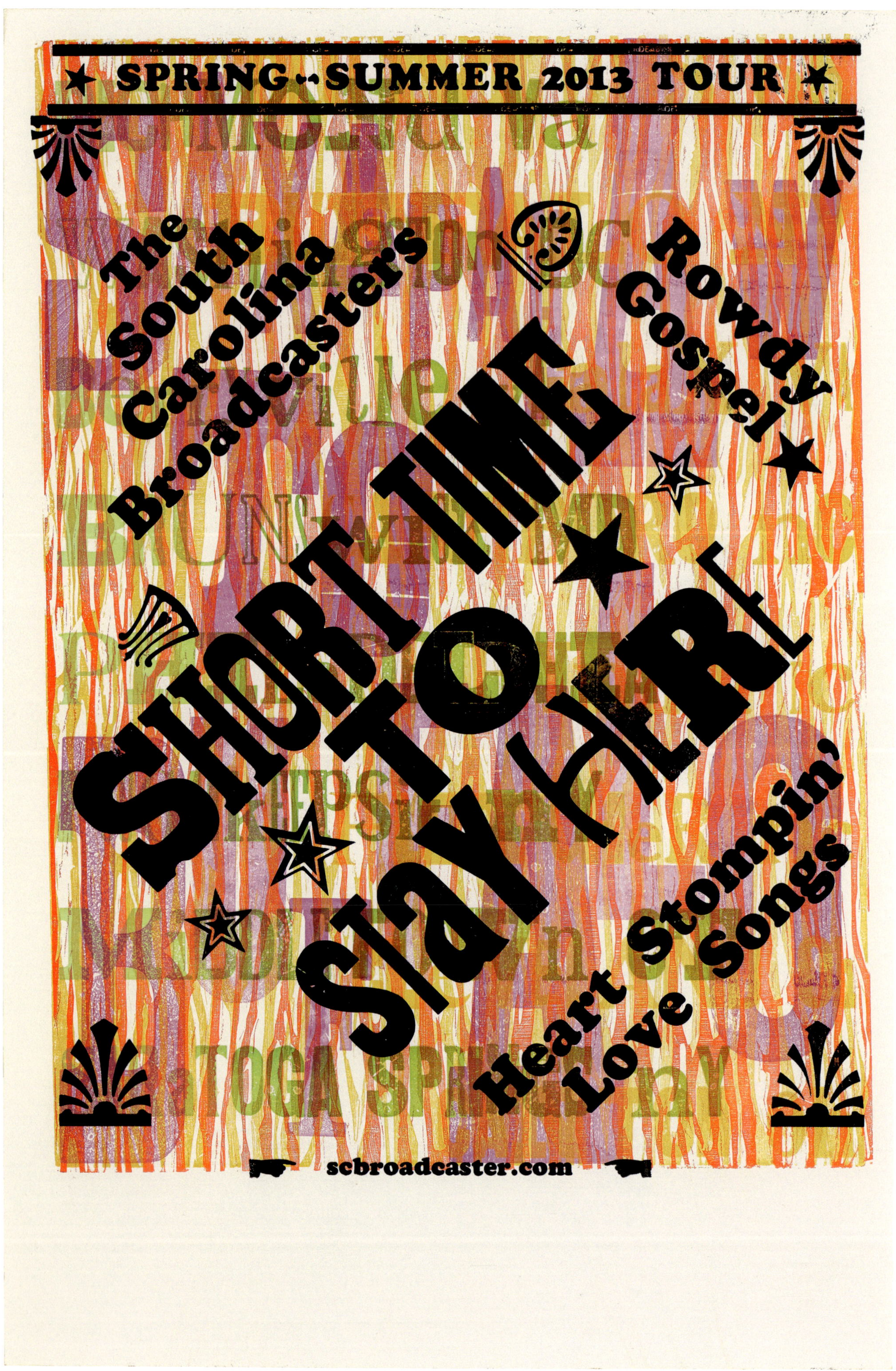
SPRING SUMMER 2013 TOUR
The South Carolina Broadcasters
Rowdy Gospel
SHORT TIME TO STAY HERE
Heart Stompin' Love Songs
scbroadcaster.com

Flying Monkey Arts ★ Lowe Mill

8th annual

Cigar Box Guitar FESTIVAL

Handcrafted instruments, artist market, workshops, documentary film, demos and more

and folk arts sideshow

★ Bill Jehle's Cigar Box Guitar Museum ★

June 1 Friday

★ FREE ★
Concerts on the Dock
6pm-9pm

June 2 Saturday

Jam sessions start at noon and end at 6pm
Flymo Theater Extravaganza
7pm-midnight 15 dollar
with special Special guests
John Lowe and Microwave Dave

Kennedy Prints! We Put Ink On Paper
★★★★★ www.kennedyprints.com ★★★★★

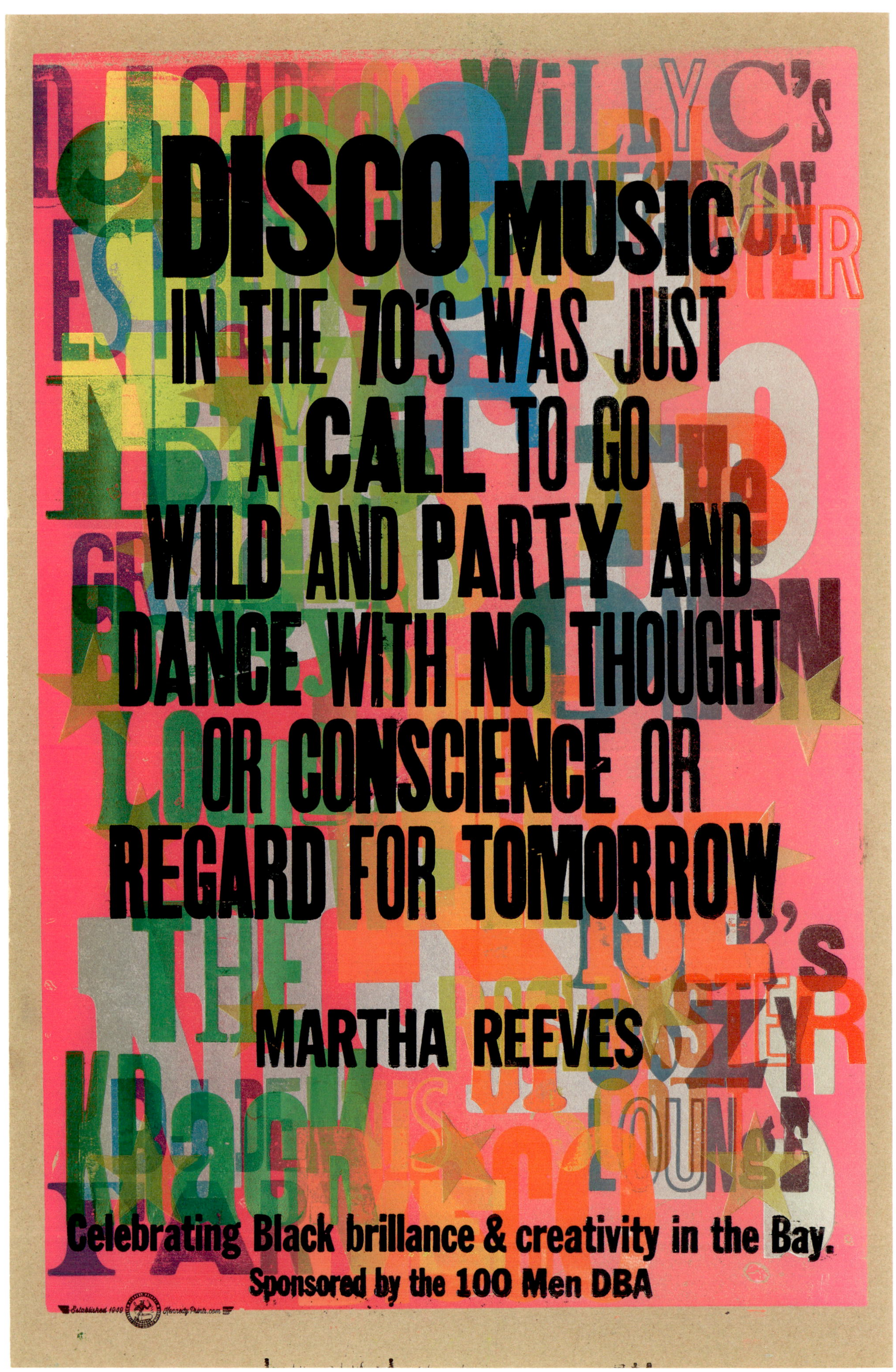
DISCO MUSIC
IN THE 70'S WAS JUST
A CALL TO GO
WILD AND PARTY AND
DANCE WITH NO THOUGHT
OR CONSCIENCE OR
REGARD FOR TOMORROW.
MARTHA REEVES
Celebrating Black brillance & creativity in the Bay.
Sponsored by the 100 Men DBA

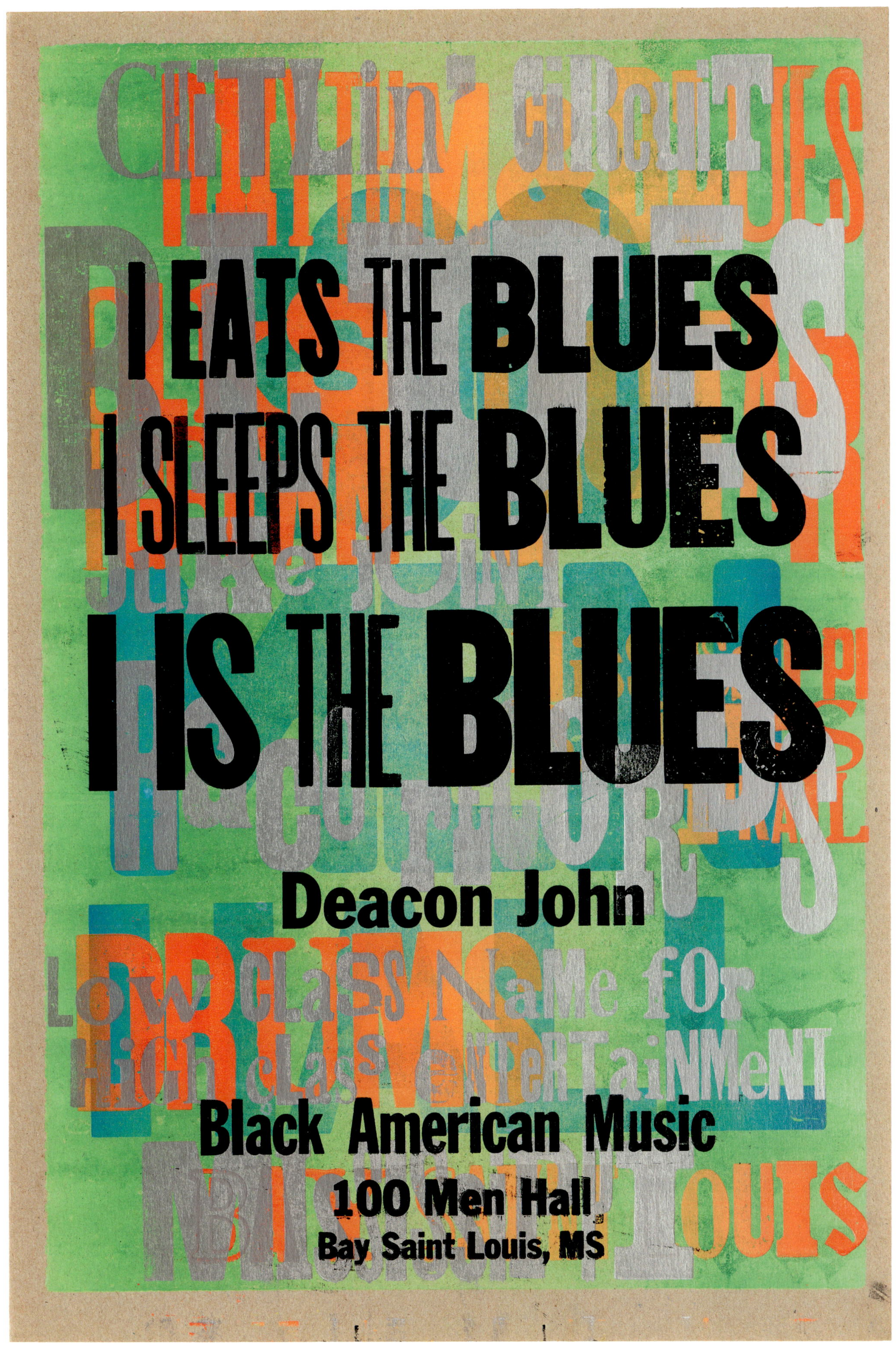
I EATS THE BLUES
I SLEEPS THE BLUES
I IS THE BLUES
Deacon John
Black American Music
100 Men Hall
Bay Saint Louis, MS

Johnny Shines Street Holt, Alabama

Gates open 10:57am MUSIC 12:06pm

SEPT

BECAUSE THeRE's nOthing moRE POweRFuL than A WOMaN SINGING the BLUES

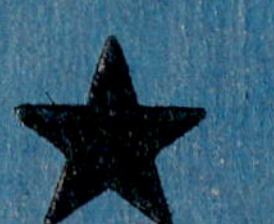 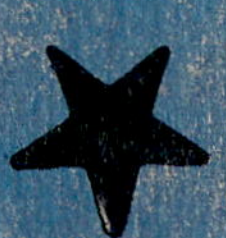 FEATURING  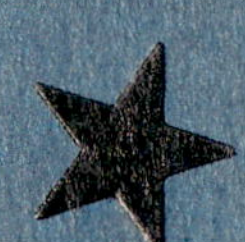

LABAMA ANNIE DEBBIE BOND

IATTIE B RACHEL EDWARDS

ANGA LASTER PORSHA RAY

CARROLINE SHINES

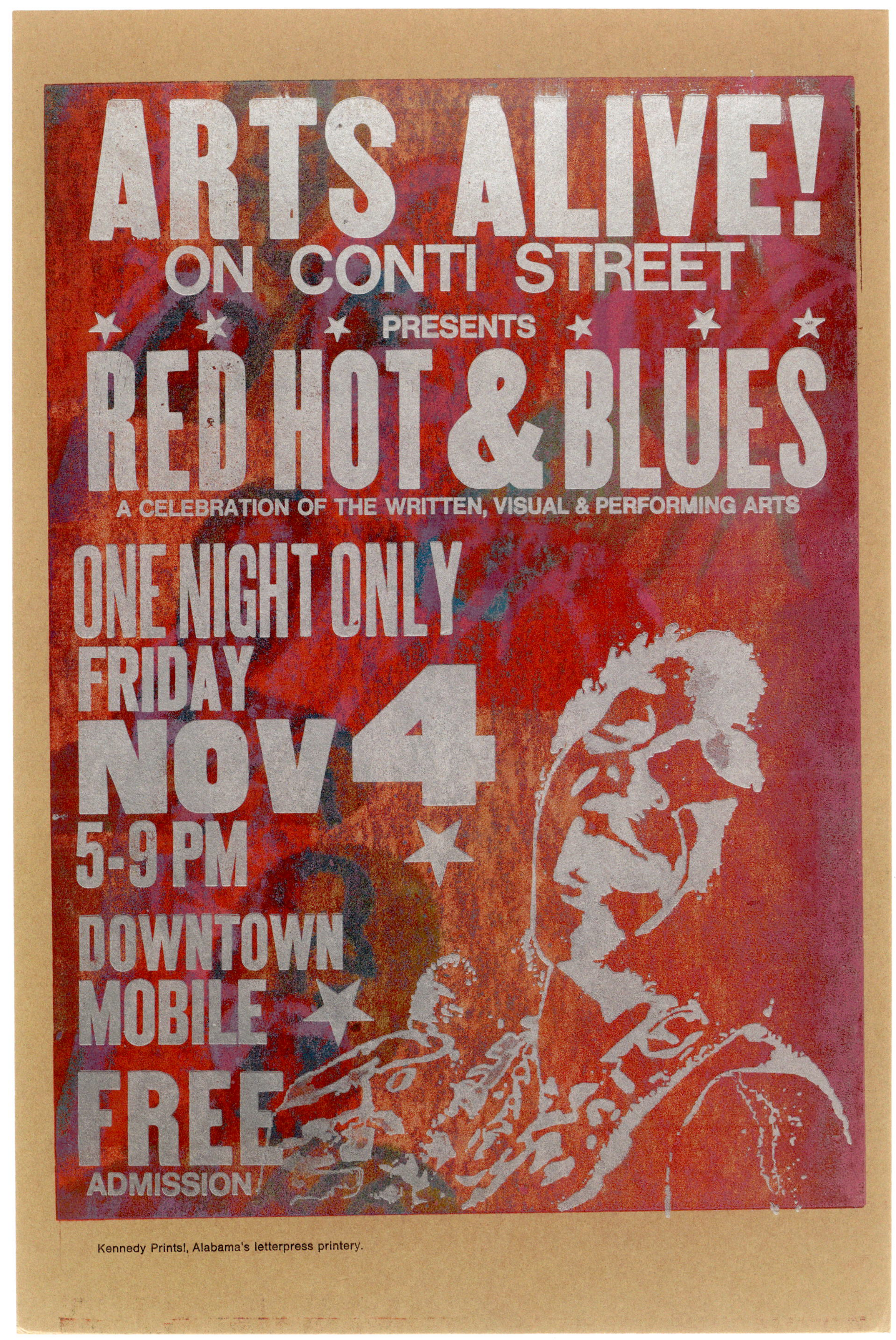

Kennedy Prints!, Alabama's letterpress printery.

MAKE MUSIC
NOLA

STUDENT SPRING CONCERT
WITH THE
ST CECILIA'S ASYLUM CHORUS

FRIDAY
6 MAY 2016
6:30 PM

MARIGNY OPERA HOUSE
725 ST. FERDINAND STREET

www.makemusicnola.org

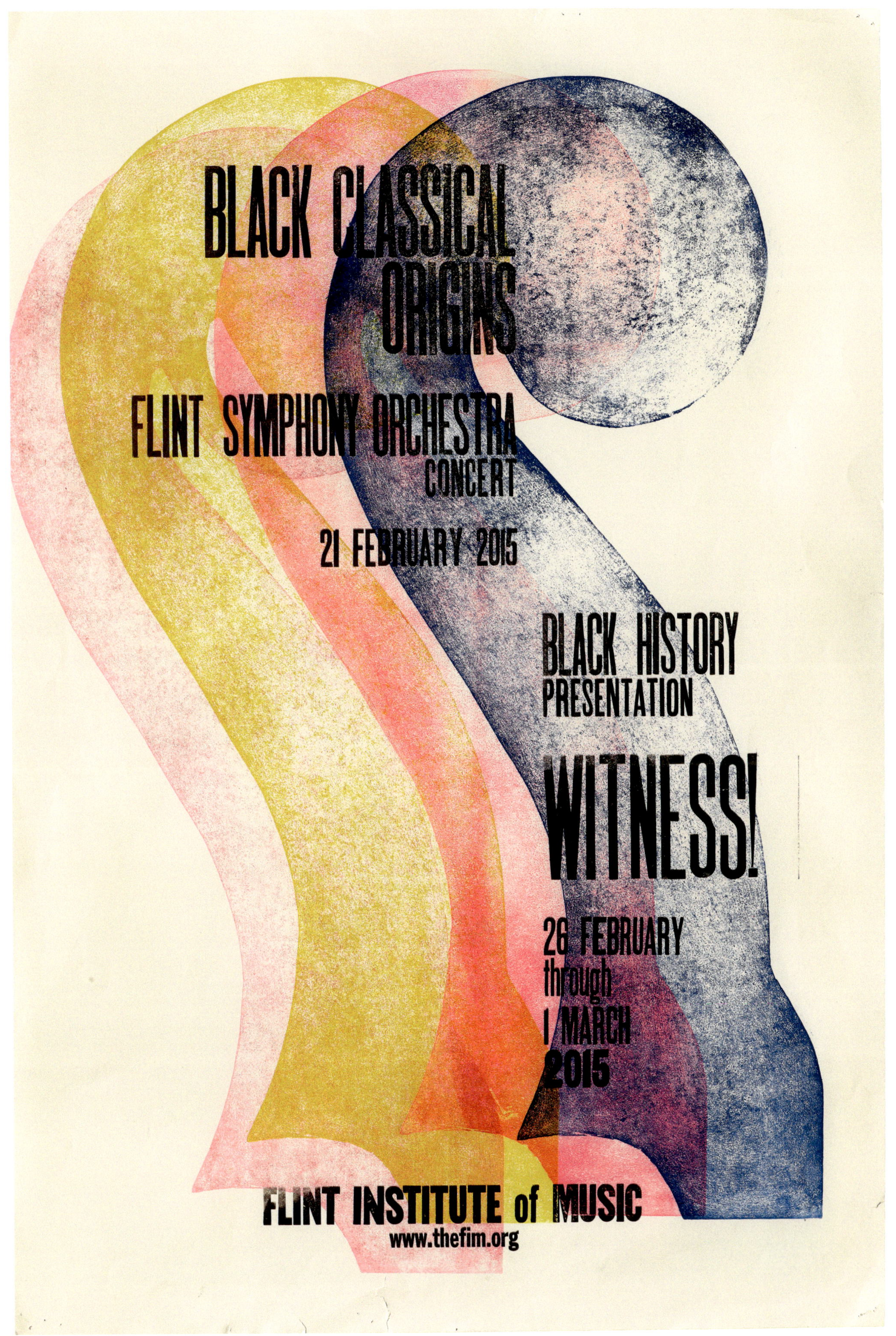
BLACK CLASSICAL ORIGINS
FLINT SYMPHONY ORCHESTRA
CONCERT
21 FEBRUARY 2015
BLACK HISTORY
PRESENTATION
WITNESS!
26 FEBRUARY
through
1 MARCH
2015
FLINT INSTITUTE of MUSIC
www.thefim.org

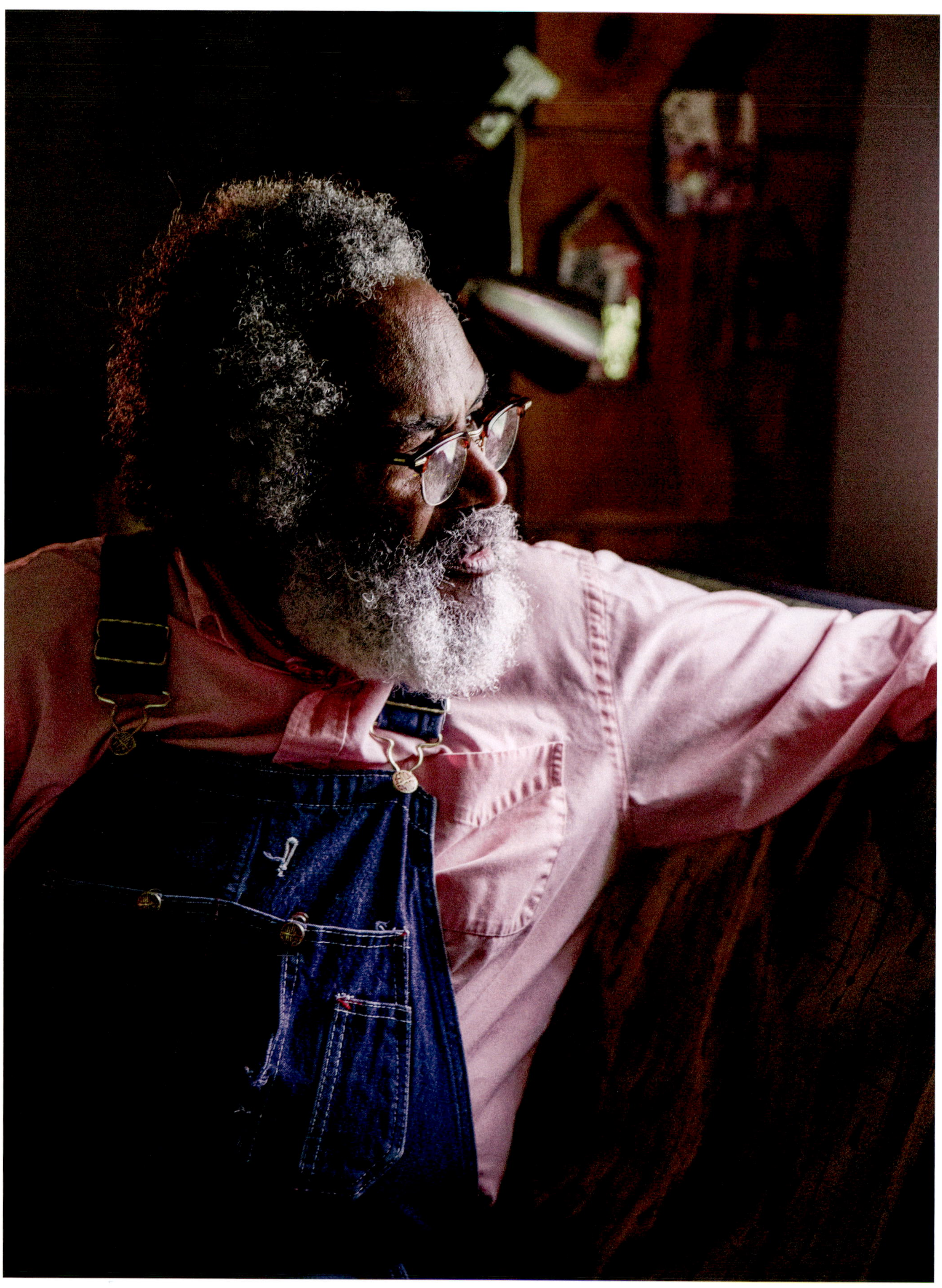

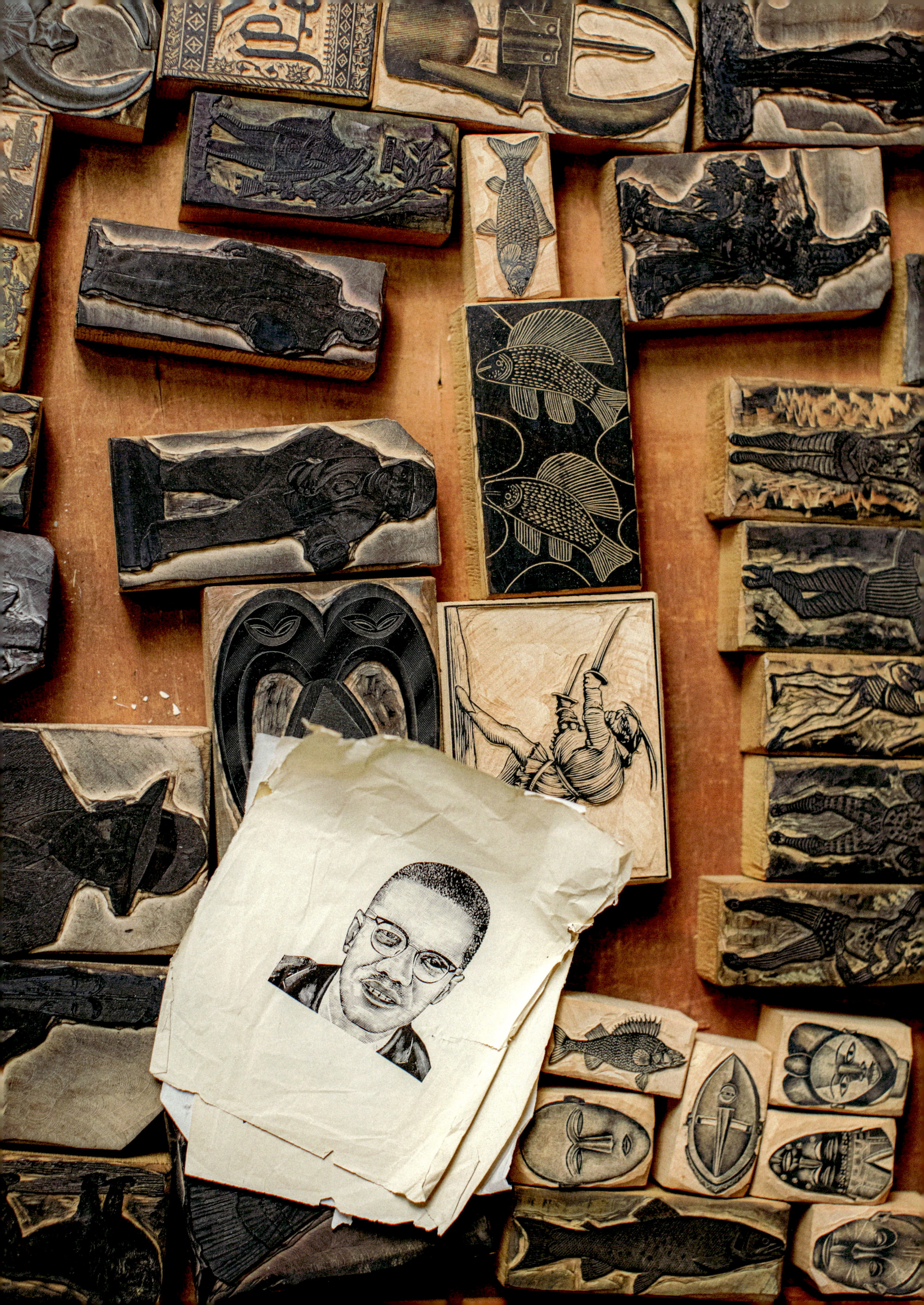

FAIRHOPE
FILM
FESTIVAL

6-9 November 2014

Four days of brilliant, entertaining and award-winning films

www.fairhopefilmfest.org

www.kennedyprints.com

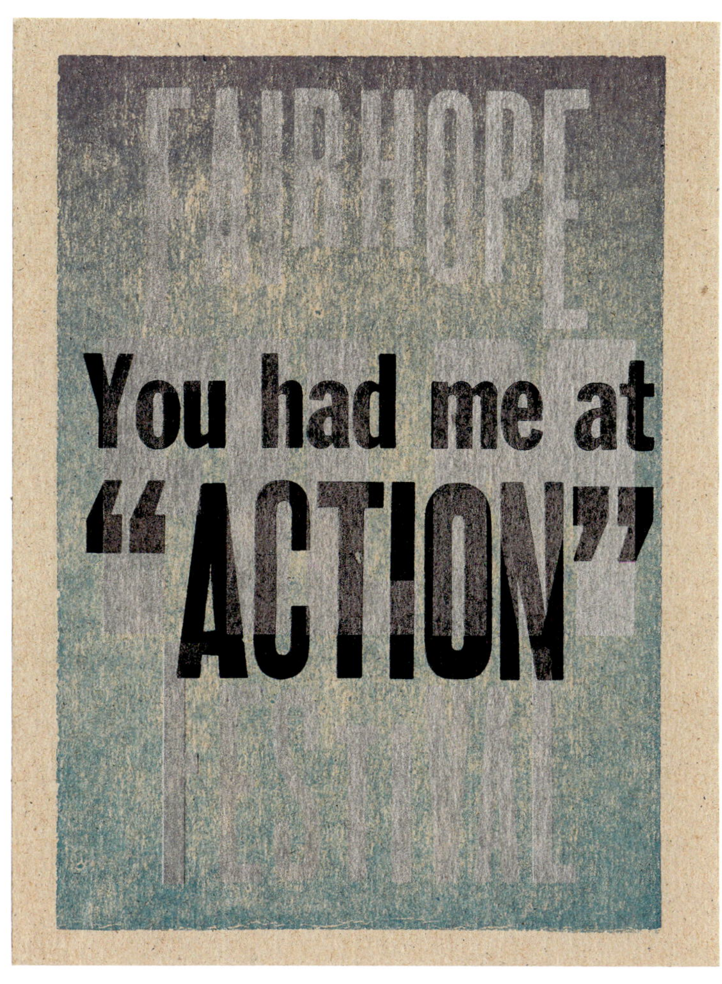

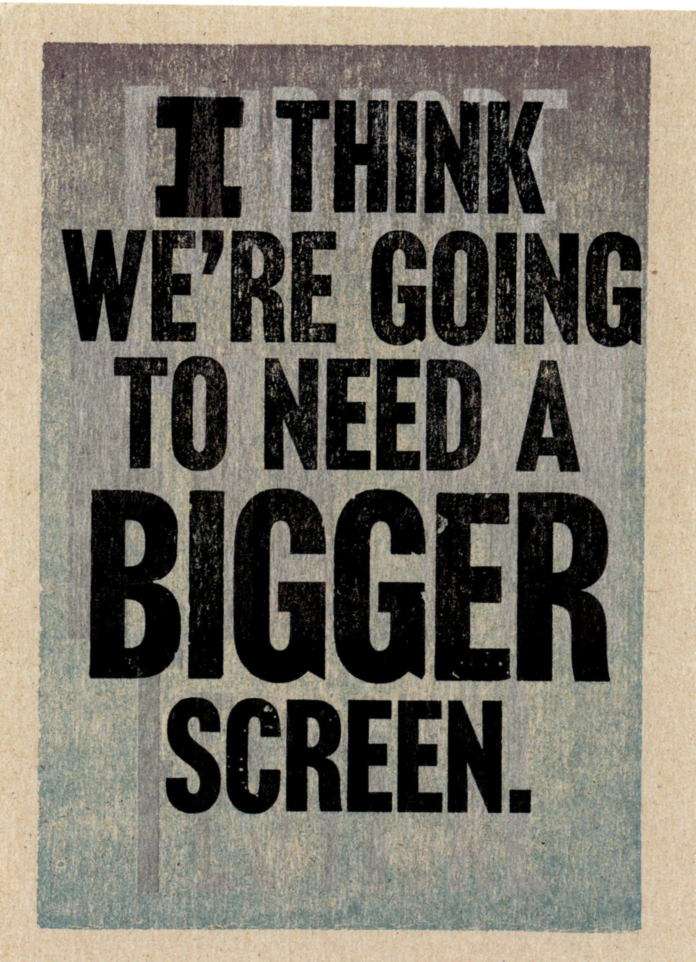

HEY!
I'M
WATCHIN'
HERE.

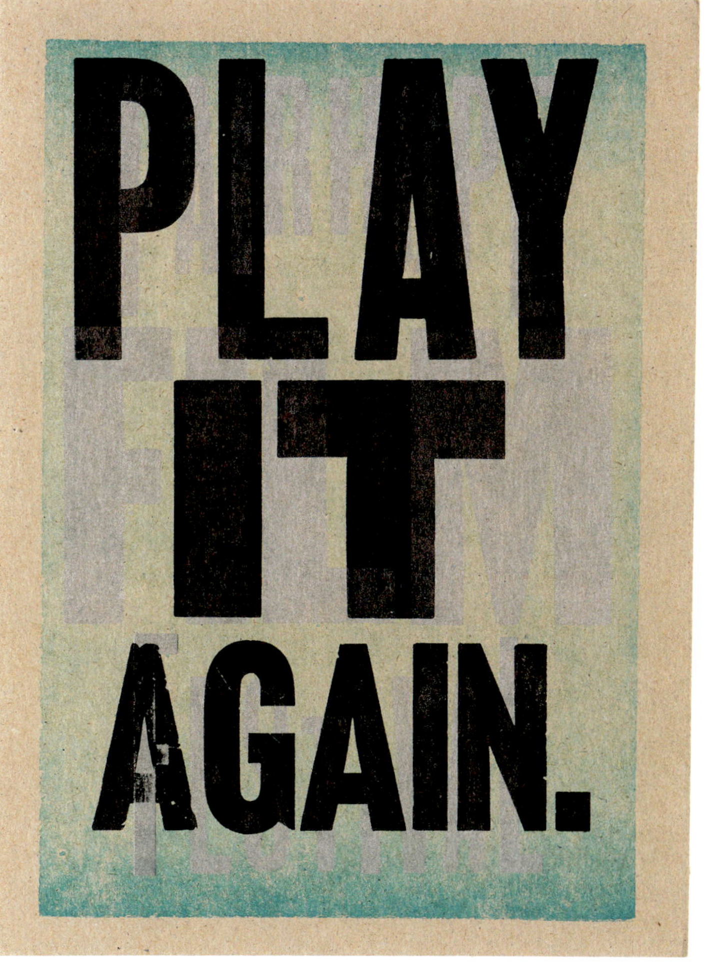

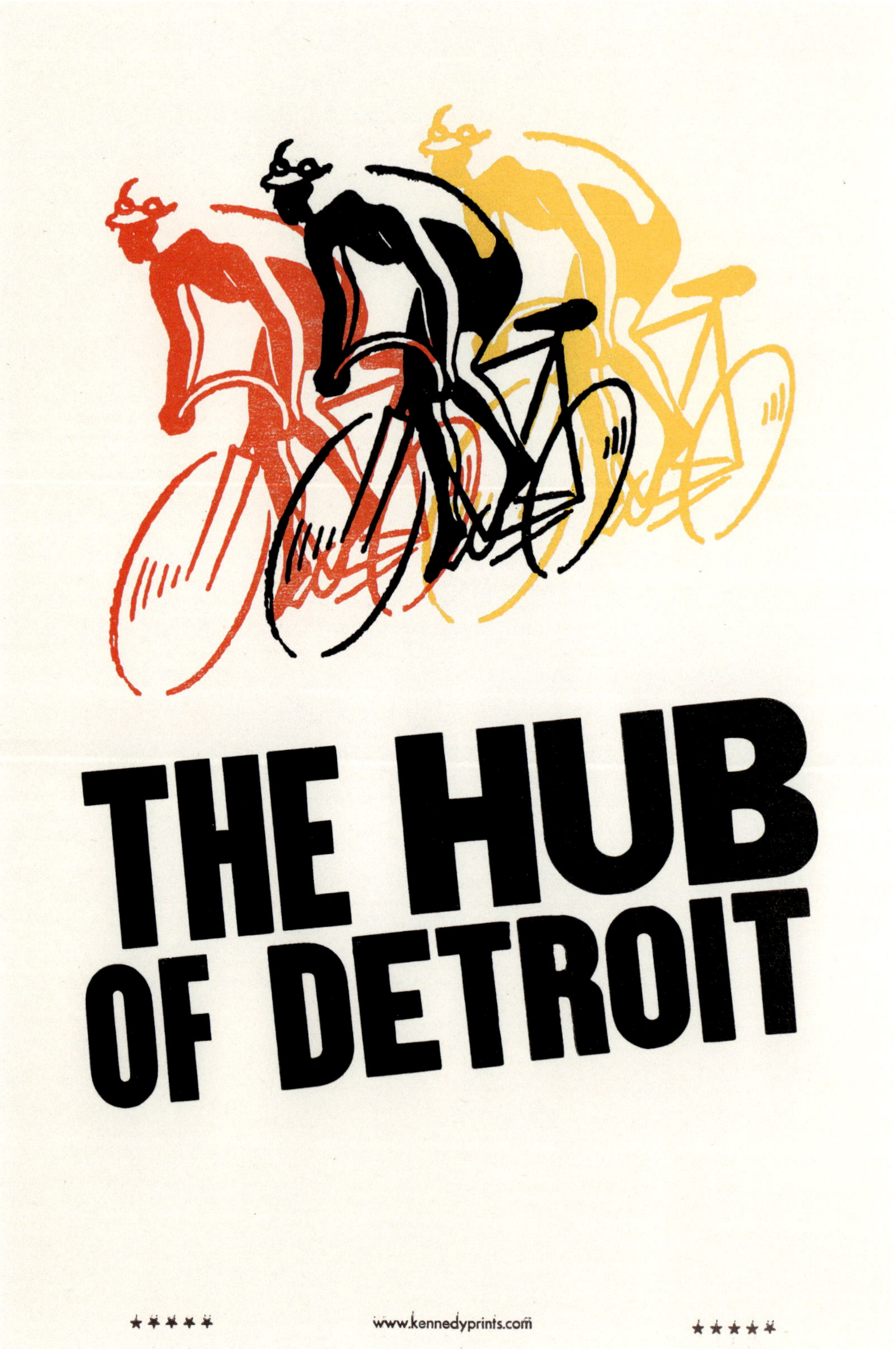

THE HUB
OF DETROIT

★★★★★ www.kennedyprints.com ★★★★★

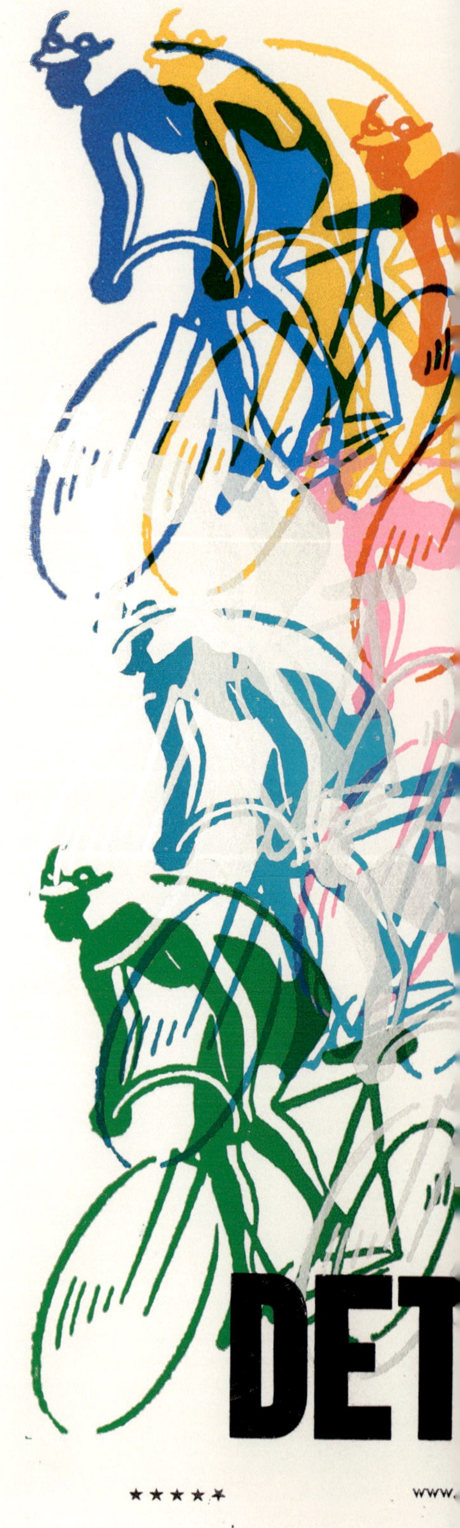

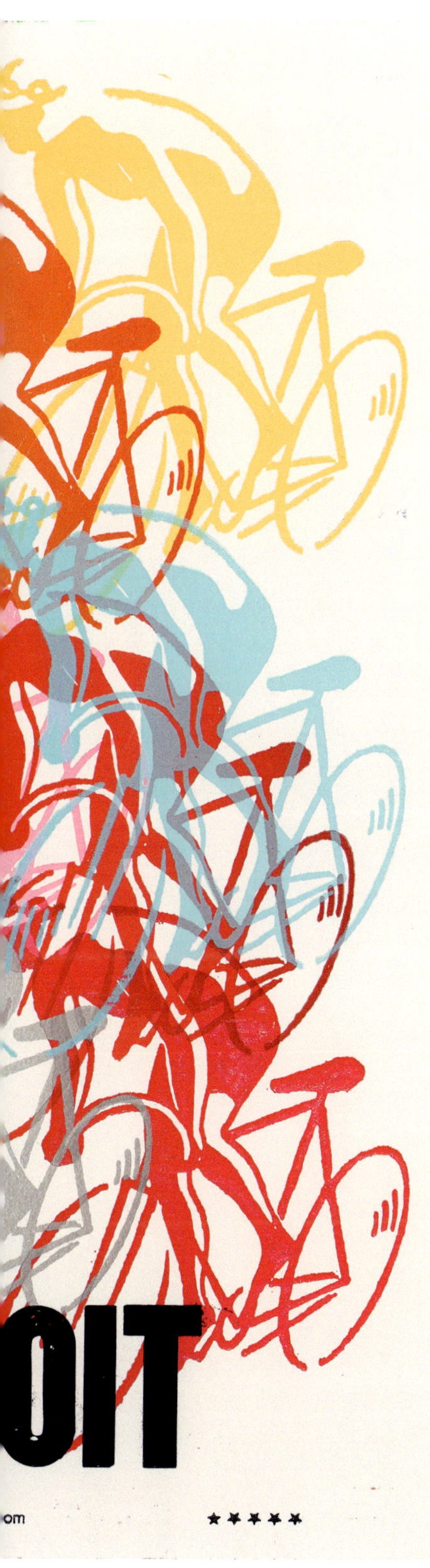

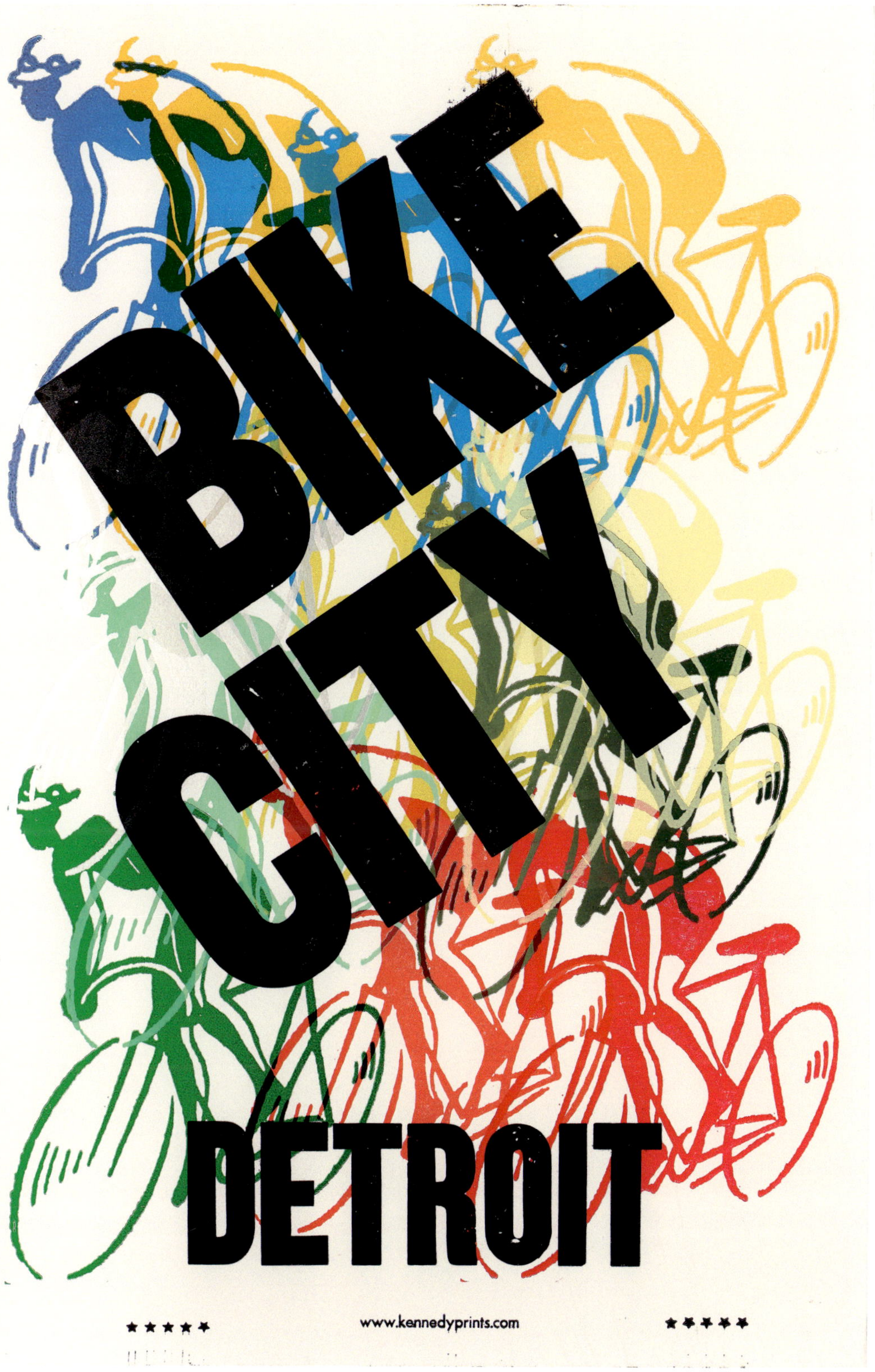

BIKE CITY

DETROIT

www.kennedyprints.com

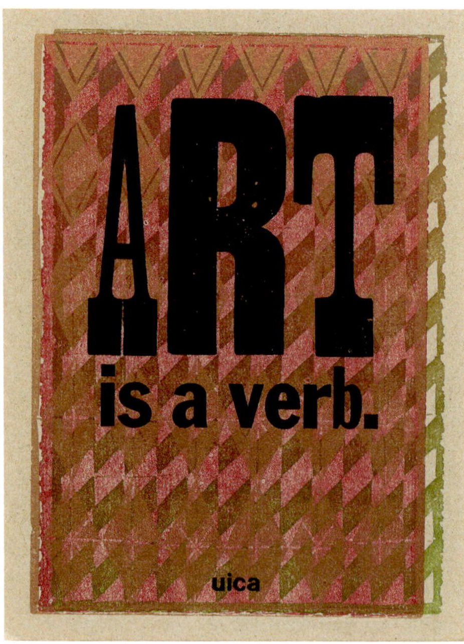
ART
is a verb.
uica

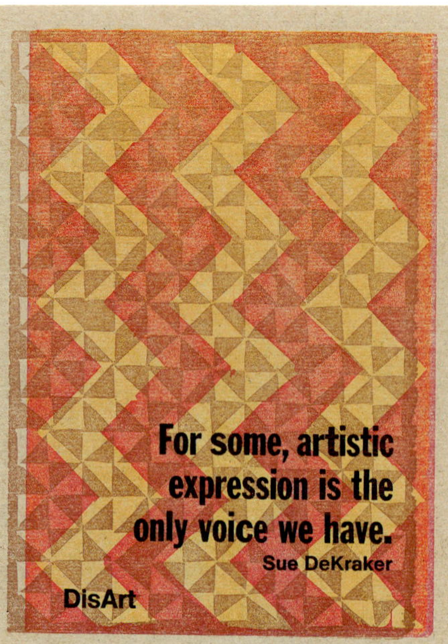
For some, artistic
expression is the
only voice we have.
Sue DeKraker
DisArt

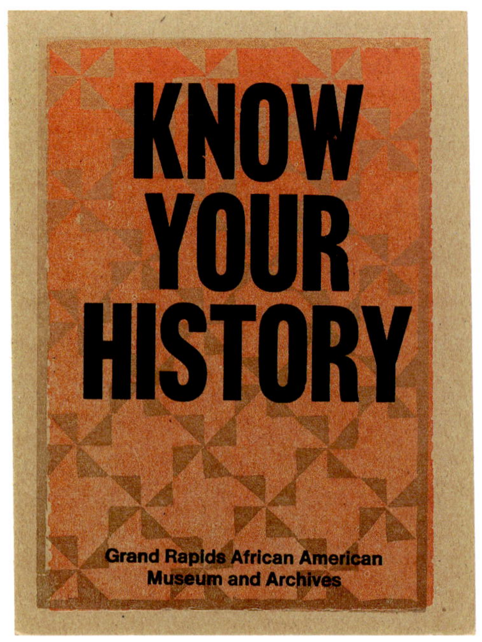
KNOW
YOUR
HISTORY
Grand Rapids African American
Museum and Archives

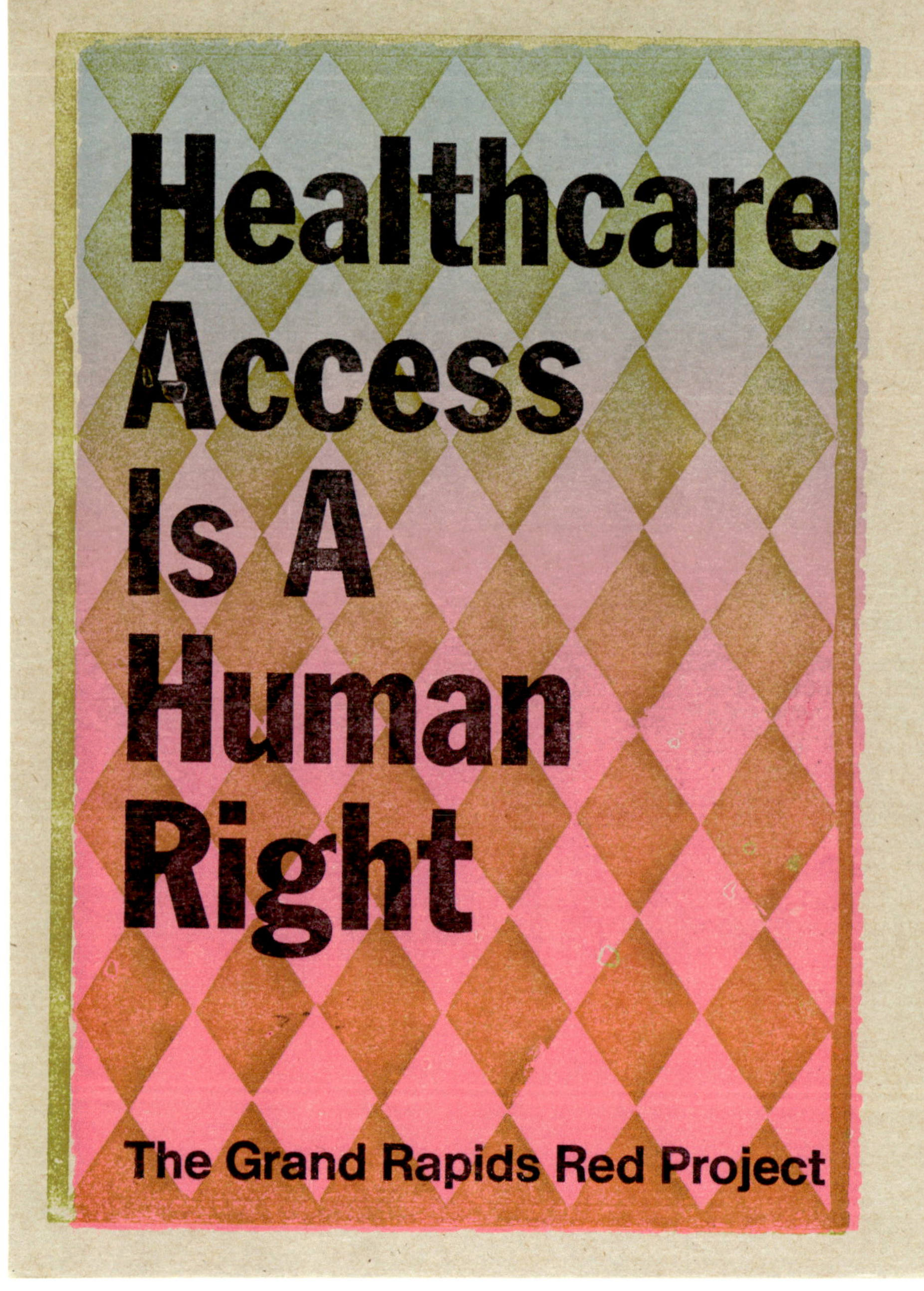
Healthcare
Access
Is A
Human
Right
The Grand Rapids Red Project

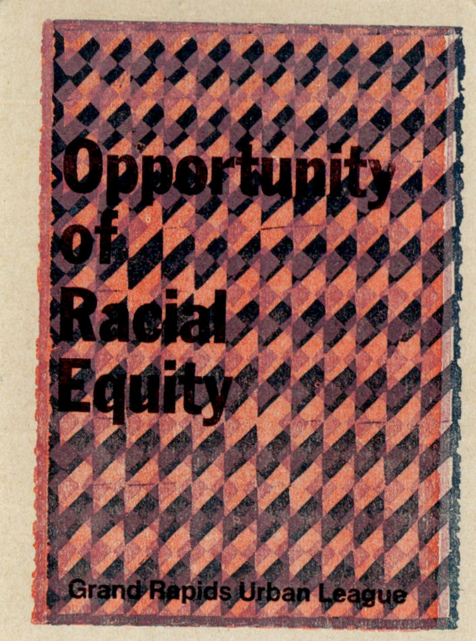
Opportunity
of
Racial
Equity
Grand Rapids Urban League

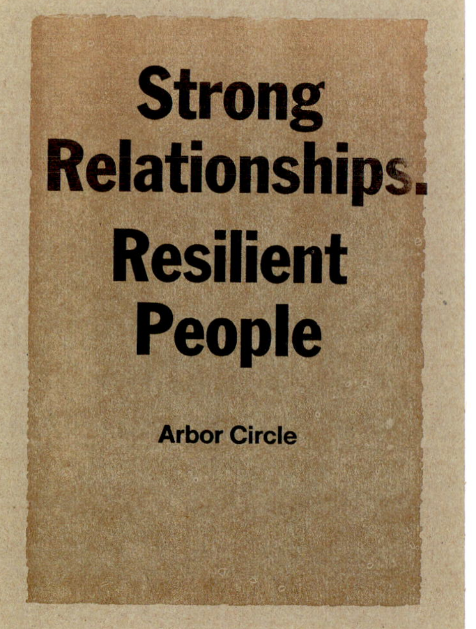
Strong
Relationships.
Resilient
People
Arbor Circle

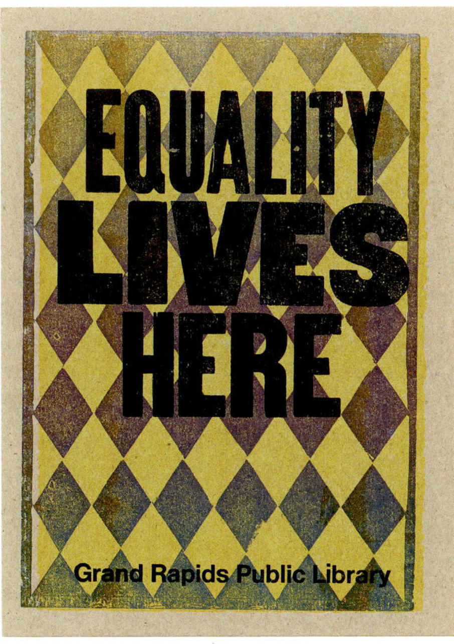
EQUALITY
LIVES
HERE
Grand Rapids Public Library

Good Food.
Transparency.
Stewardship.
Sense of Place.
Fulton Street Farmers Market

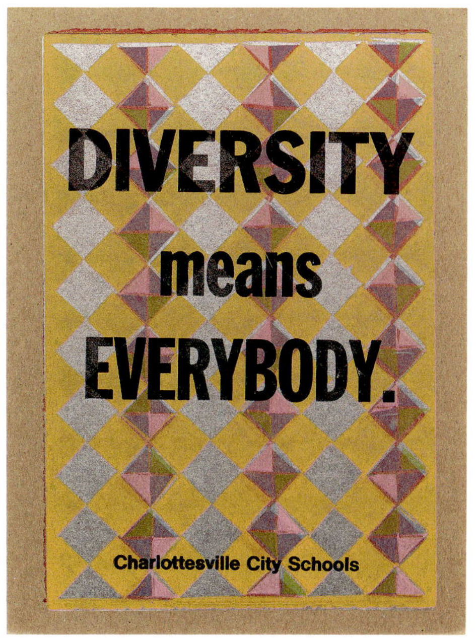
DIVERSITY
means
EVERYBODY.
Charlottesville City Schools

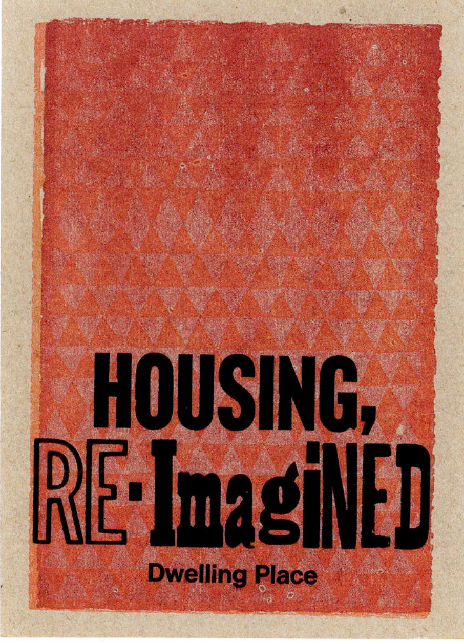
HOUSING,
RE-ImagiNED
Dwelling Place

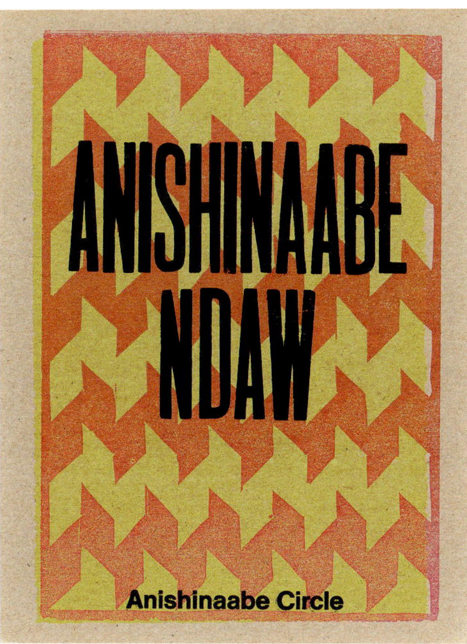
ANISHINAABE
NDAW
Anishinaabe Circle

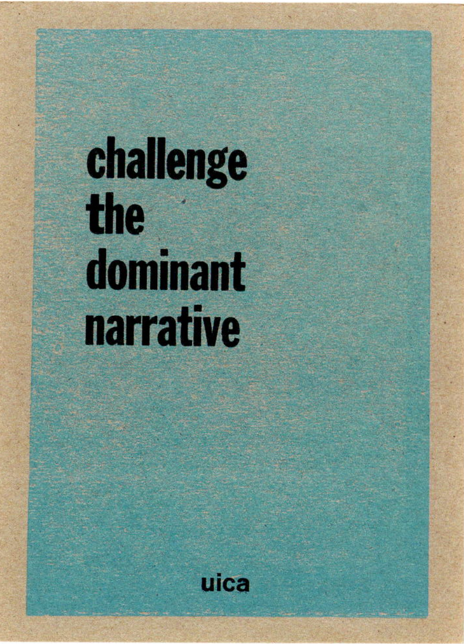
challenge
the
dominant
narrative
uica

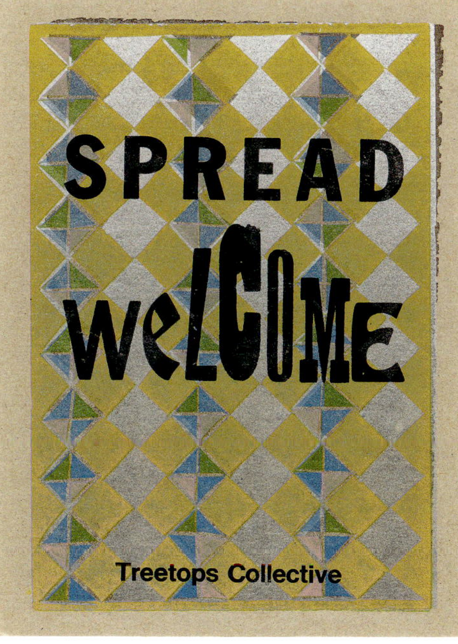
SPREAD
weLCOME
Treetops Collective

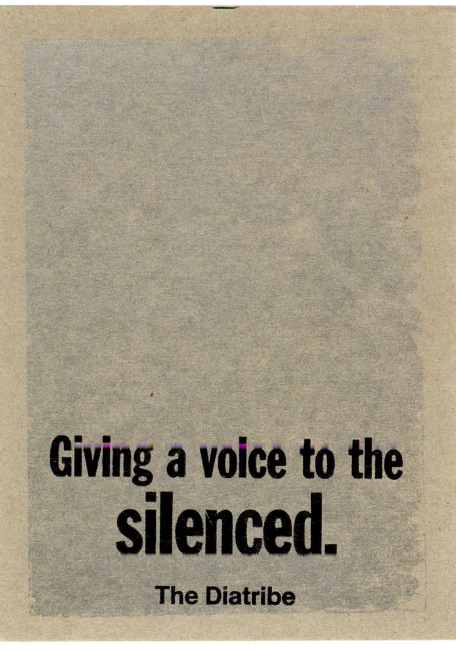
Giving a voice to the
silenced.
The Diatribe

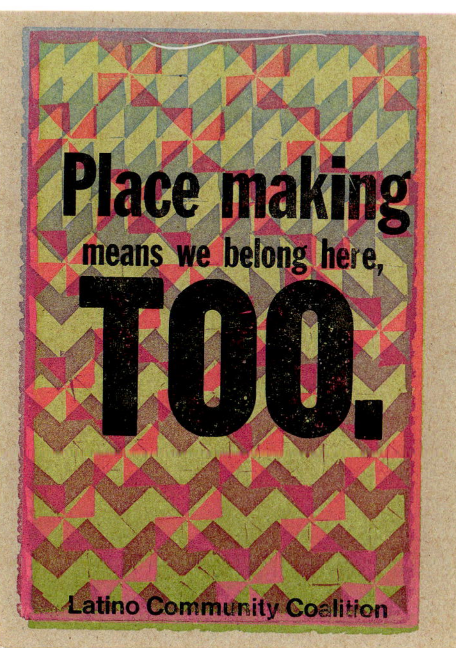
Place making
means we belong here,
TOO.
Latino Community Coalition

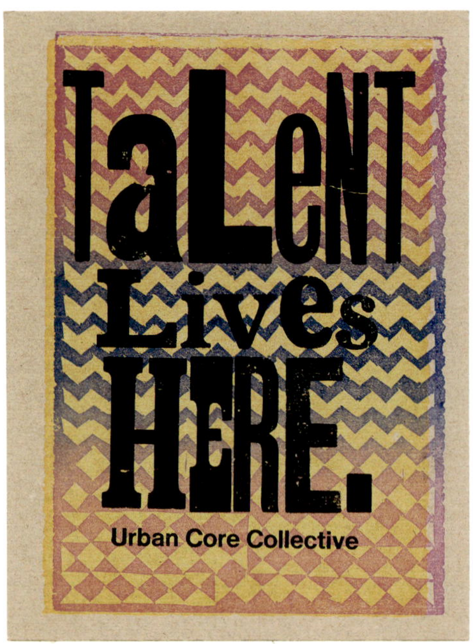
TaLeNT
Lives
HERE.
Urban Core Collective

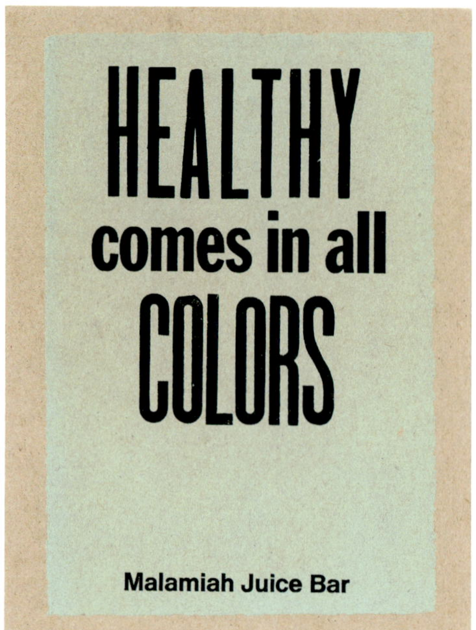
HEALTHY
comes in all
COLORS
Malamiah Juice Bar

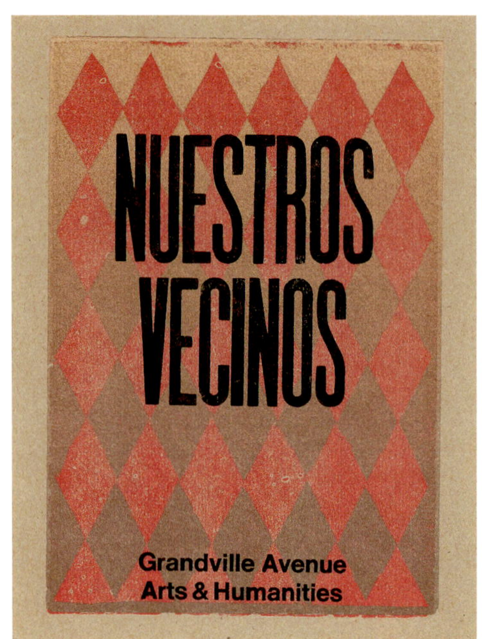
NUESTROS
VECINOS
Grandville Avenue
Arts & Humanities

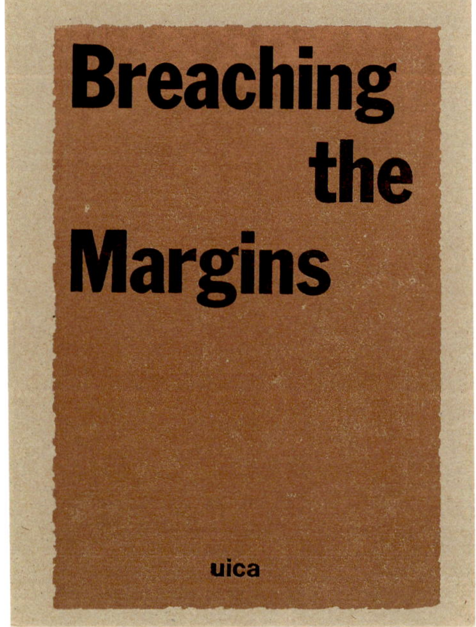
Breaching
the
Margins
uica

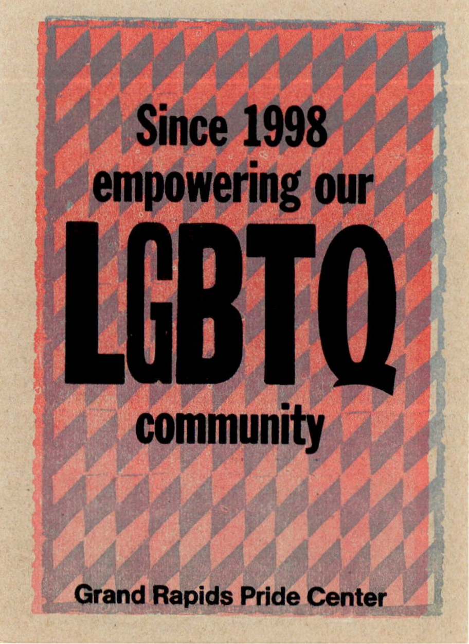
Since 1998
empowering our
LGBTQ
community
Grand Rapids Pride Center

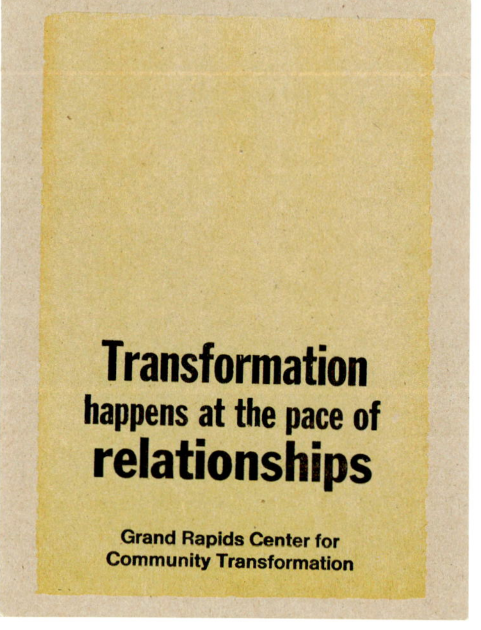
Transformation
happens at the pace of
relationships
Grand Rapids Center for
Community Transformation

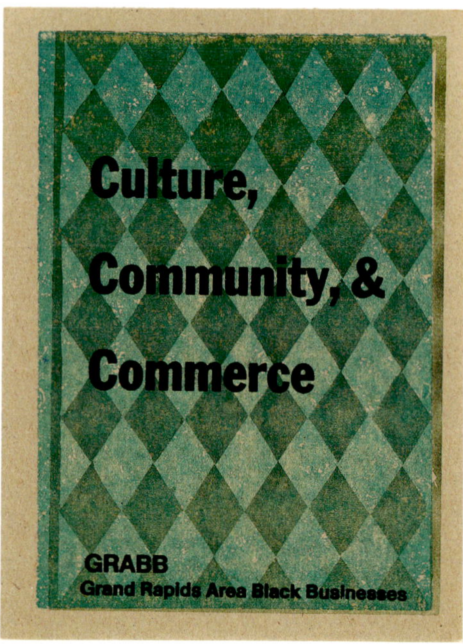
Culture,
Community, &
Commerce
GRABB
Grand Rapids Area Black Businesses

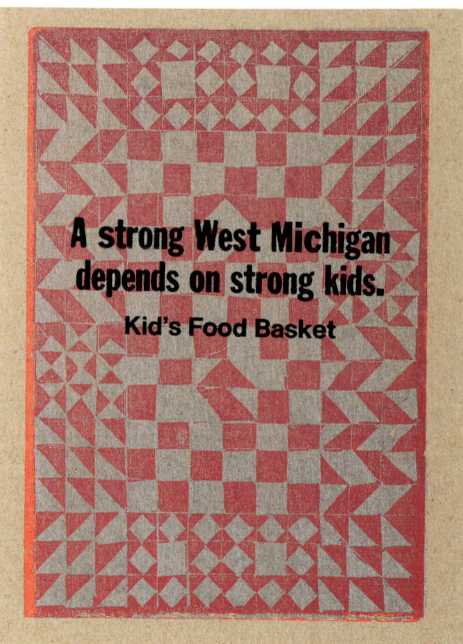
A strong West Michigan
depends on strong kids.
Kid's Food Basket

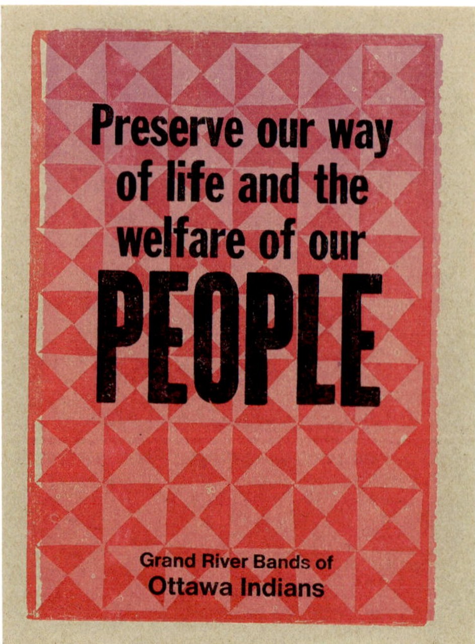
Preserve our way
of life and the
welfare of our
PEOPLE
Grand River Bands of
Ottawa Indians

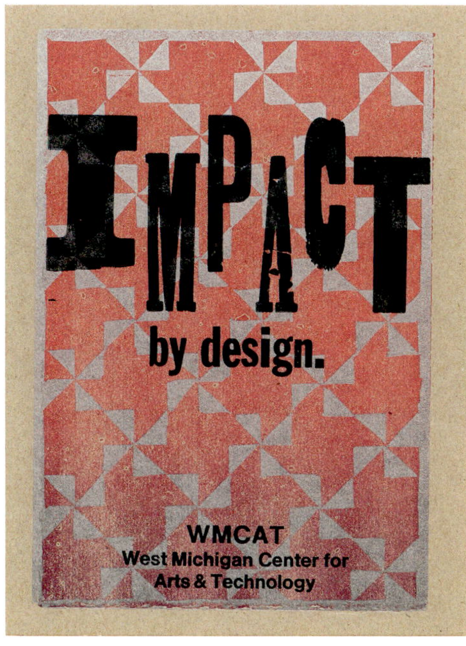
IMPACT
by design.
WMCAT
West Michigan Center for
Arts & Technology

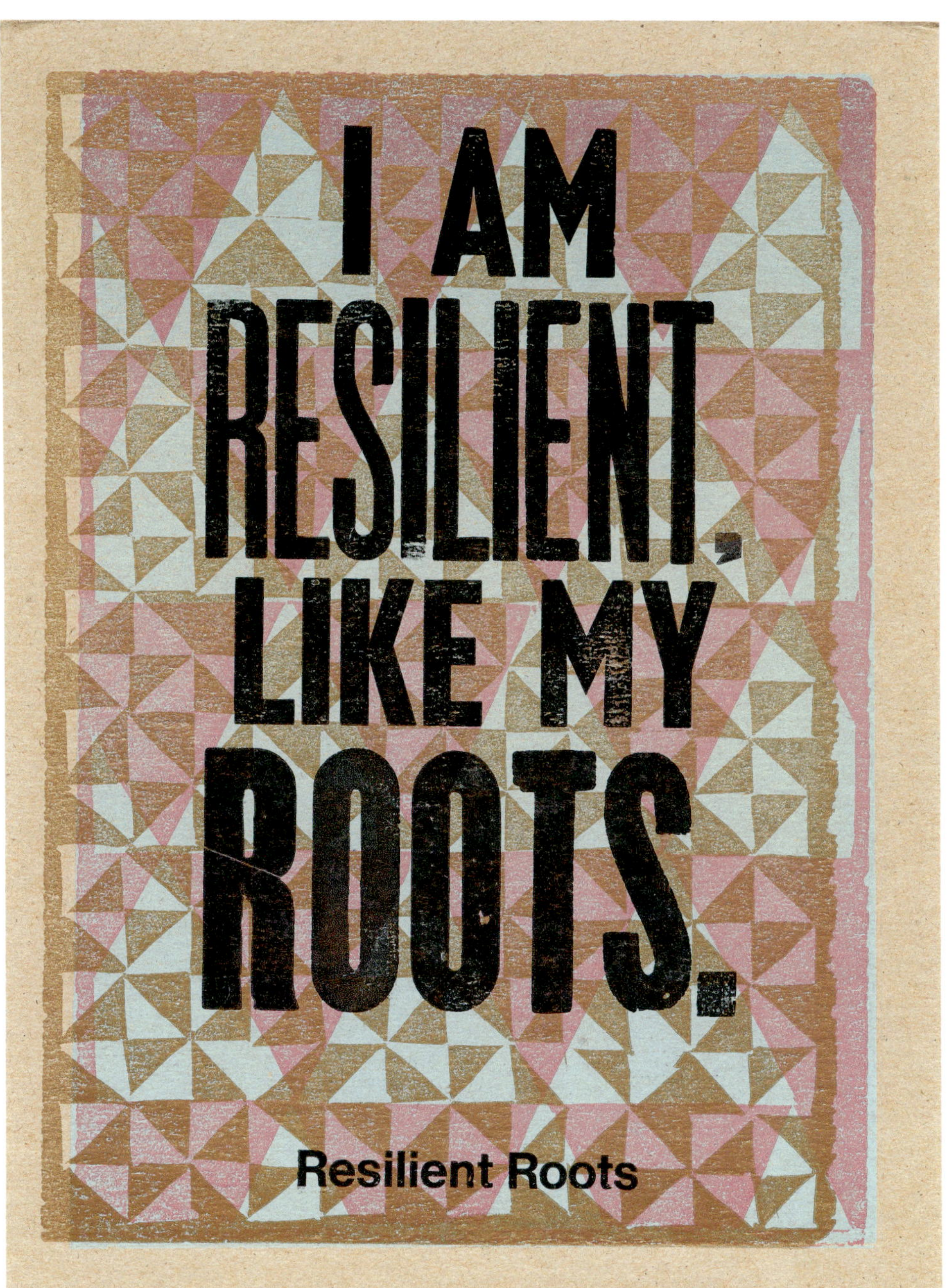
I AM
RESILIENT,
LIKE MY
ROOTS.
Resilient Roots

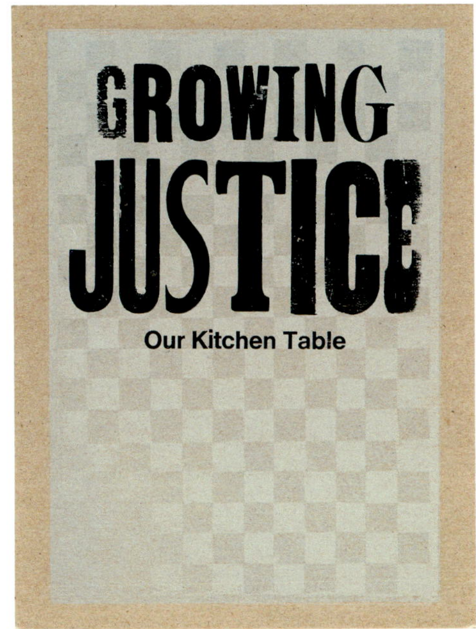
GROWING
JUSTICE
Our Kitchen Table

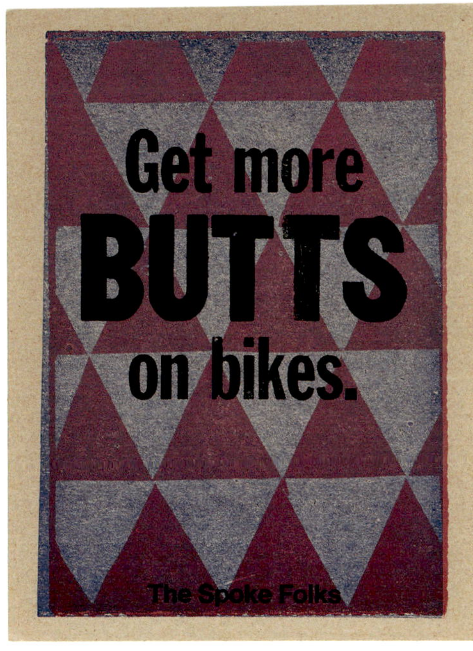
Get more
BUTTS
on bikes.
The Spoke Folks

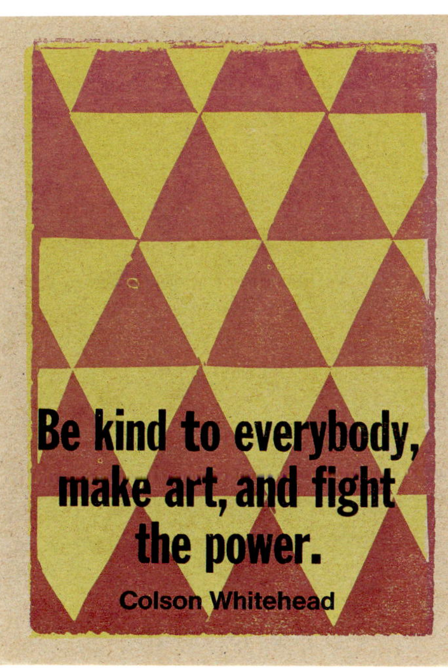
Be kind to everybody,
make art, and fight
the power.
Colson Whitehead

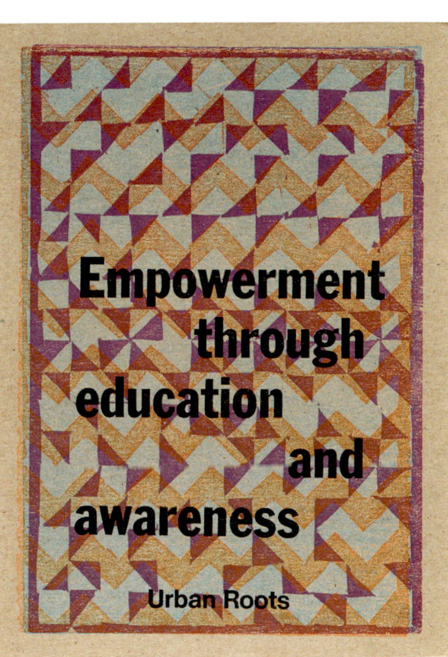
Empowerment
through
education
and
awareness
Urban Roots

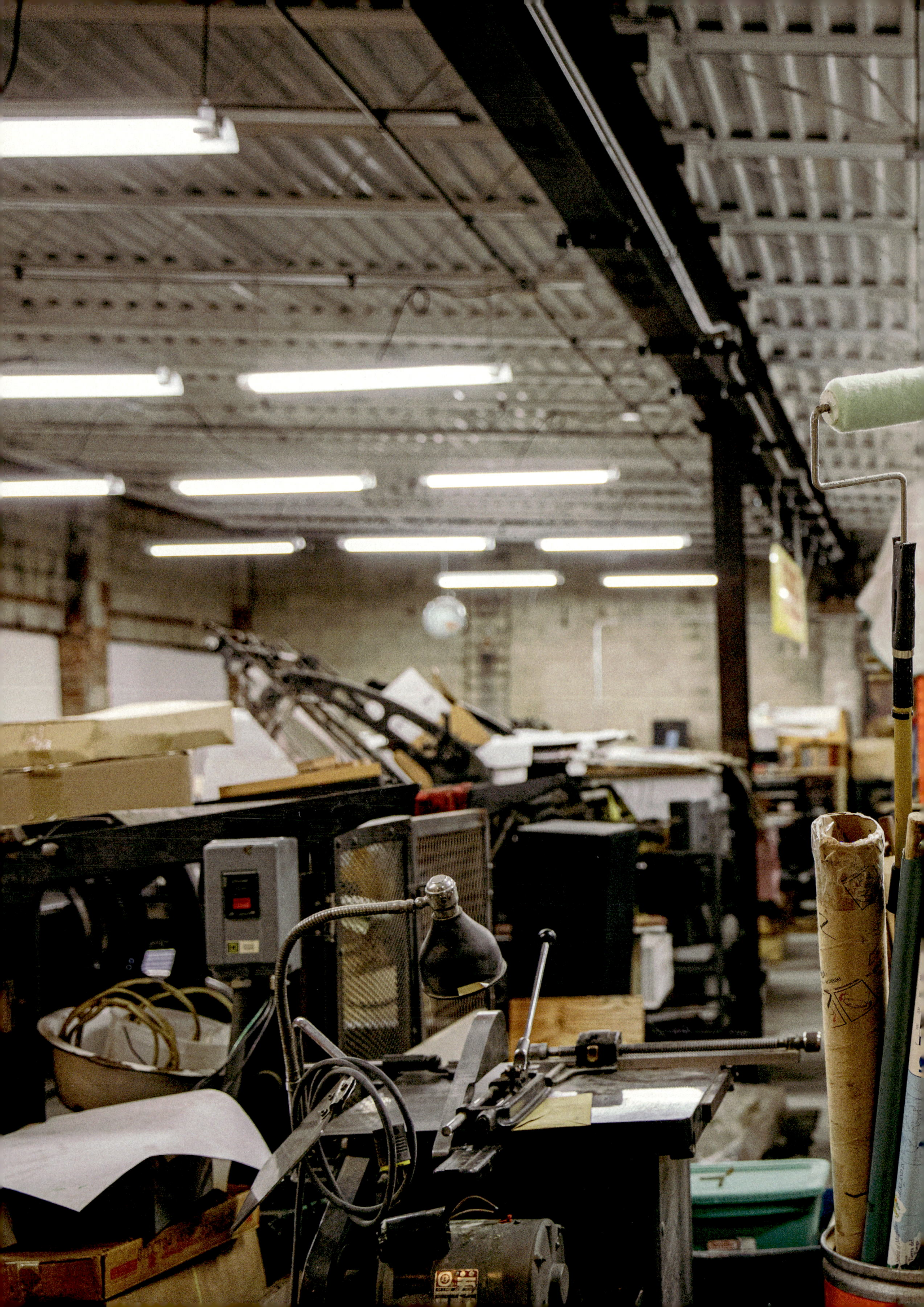

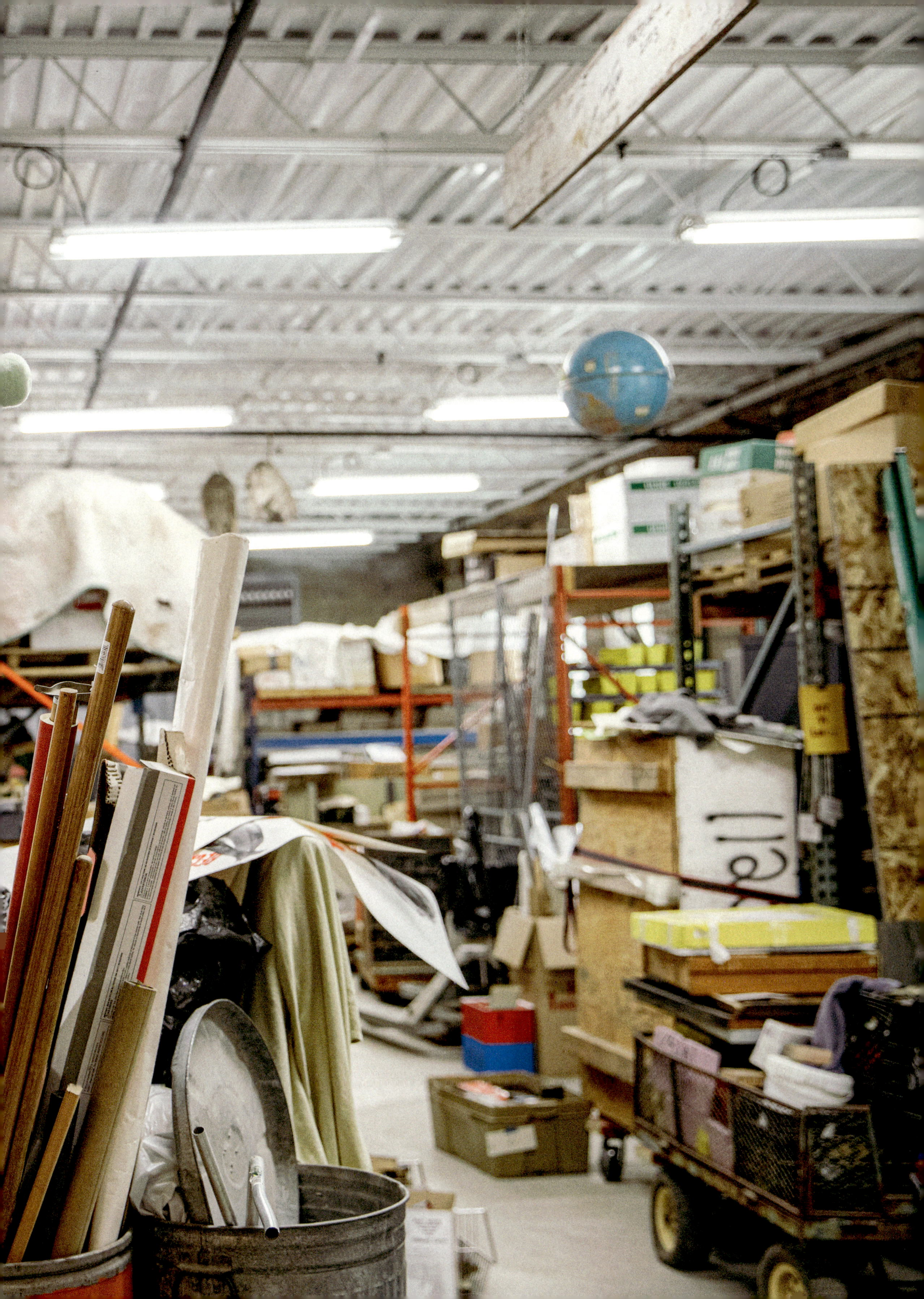

notes

Man of Letters by Austin Kleon

1 "Wendy MacNaughton, Amos Kennedy, and Adobe Stock Artists Talk Diversity," Adobe Max, October 28, 2023, video, 29:17, https://www.adobe.com/max/2021/sessions/graphic-design-with-wendy-macnaughton-and-amos-ken-mb170.html.

Incorrigible Disturber of the Peace! INK & EQUITY! by Myron Beasley

1 James Baldwin, "The Creative Process," *Collected Essays*, ed. Toni Morrison (New York: Library of America, 1998), 669.

2 In the Hebrew Bible, Amos is a force for social justice who condemns the corruption of the Israeli kingdom in the eighth century BCE (Amos 5:24).

3 Henry Louis Gates, Jr., *The Signifying Monkey: A Theory of African-American Literary Criticism* (New York: Oxford University Press, 1989).

4 Under the imprint Pulcinoelefante Edizioni in Osnago, Italy, publisher and letterpress printer Alberto Casiraghi has issued more than 7,000 illustrated chapbooks since 1982, selling them all for 10 euros apiece. Sebastiano Vassalli, "Pulcinoelefante i piccoli libri diventano grandi," *La Stampa*, March 7, 2007: https://web.archive.org/web/20150402144908/http://archivio.lastampa.it/articolo?id=11c28bd4aa31aea14aac09a257bfd59fd24df7ac

5 Tara Donaldson, "Dress and Protest: Fashion Hasn't Been a Bystander in the Black Civil Rights Movement," *WWD*, February 1, 2021, https://wwd.com/feature/protest-fashion-black-civil-rights-black-panthers-blm-1234715312/; Richard Thompson Ford, *Dress Code: How the Laws of Fashion Made History* (New York: Simon & Schuster, 2022); Tanisha C. Ford, "SNCC Women, Denim, and the Politics of Dress," *The Journal of Southern History* 79, no. 3 (August 2013): 625–58; Abena L. Mhoon, "Dressing for Freedom," *Black History Bulletin* 67, nos. 1–4 (January–December 2004): 26–29; Shane White and Graham White, *Stylin': African-American Expressive Culture from Its Beginnings to the Zoot Suit* (Ithaca, NY: Cornell University Press, 1999).

6 Amos Paul Kennedy, Jr., interview by Myron Beasley, October 13, 2020.

7 Kennedy-Beasley interview, October 13, 2020.

8 Amos Paul Kennedy, Jr., interview by Myron Beasley, December 5, 2020.

9 Kennedy-Beasley interview, December 5, 2020.

10 William H. Chafe, et al., *Remembering Jim Crow: African Americans Tell about Life in the Segregated South* (New York: The New Press, in association with Lyndhurst Books of the Center for Documentary Studies of Duke University, 2014); Imani Perry, *South to America: A Journey Below the Mason-Dixon to Understand the Soul of a Nation* (New York: Ecco, 2022).

11 Robert Farris Thompson, *Flash of the Spirit: African and Afro-American Art and Philosophy* (New York: Vintage, 1984).

12 Kennedy-Beasley interview, December 5, 2020.

13 Kennedy-Beasley interview, December 5, 2020.

14 For more on Thomas Ingmire, see his website, Form and Expression, https://www.thomasingmire.com/.

15 Amos Paul Kennedy, Jr., interview by Lucie Parker, October 22, 2023.

16 Amos Paul Kennedy, Jr., interview by Sarah Lange, 2018, transcript 1764, University of Wisconsin–Madison Oral History Program.

17 Kennedy-Lange interview.

18 Kennedy-Parker interview.

19 Kennedy-Beasley interview, December 5, 2020.

20 Kennedy-Lange interview.

21 Hendrik Nicolaas (H. N.) Werkman and Jan Martinet, *Werkman: 'Druksels' en Gebruiksdrukwerk| 'Druksel' Prints and General Printed Matter* (Amsterdam: Stedelijk Museum, 1977); Fridolin Müller, Peter F. Althaus, and Jan Martinet, eds., *H. N. Werkman: Documents in the Visual Arts*, vol. 2 (New York: Hastings House, 1967).

22 Kennedy-Lange interview.

23 Kennedy-Parker interview.

24 Kennedy-Lange interview.

25 Lerone Bennett, Jr., Roland A. Barton, and W. E. B. Du Bois, "What's in a Name? Negro vs. Afro-American vs. Black," *ETC: A Review of General Semantics* 26, no. 4 (December 1969): 399–412, https://www.jstor.org/stable/42574587.

26 Kennedy-Parker interview.

27 David Moos and Gail Trechsler, eds., *Samuel Mockbee and the Rural Studio: Community Architecture* (Birmingham: Birmingham Museum of Art, 2003); Anna G. Goodman, "The Paradox of Representation and Practice in the Auburn University Rural Studio," *Traditional Dwellings and Settlements Review* 25, no. 2 (2014): 39–52.

28 Amos Paul Kennedy, Jr., interview by Myron Beasley, August 22, 2021.

29 Amos Paul Kennedy, Jr., "A Conversation with Amos Kennedy," interview with Angelina Lippert of Poster House, streamed live on March 7, 2023, YouTube video, 1:24, https://www.youtube.com/watch?v=vSyMgmNHsXc.

30 Kennedy-Lippert interview.

31 Kennedy-Lippert interview.

32 Kennedy-Lange interview.

33 Laura Zinger, dir., *Proceed and Be Bold!* (Chicago: 20K Films, 2008), posted November 12, 2012, YouTube video, 1:34:52, https://youtu.be/i251DDffUzY?si=2qtyZR21aNLhuPze.

34 Kennedy-Lange interview.

Amos Paul Kennedy, Jr., & the Legacy of Black Printing in America by Kelly Walters

1 Amos Paul Kennedy, Jr., quoted in Jasmine Liu, "An Exquisite Riddle Book and Thousands of Works by Black Artists at the Met Library," *Hyperallergic*, February 10, 2022, https://hyperallergic.com/710971/thousands-of-works-by-black-artists-at-the-met-library/.

2 Erika Piola, "The Rise of Early American Lithography and Antebellum Visual Culture," *Winterthur Portfolio* 48, no. 2/3 (Summer/Autumn 2014): 125–38.

3 Frederick Douglass, "West India Emancipation Speech," August 4, 1857, Canandaigua, New York, http://hdl.loc.gov/loc.mss/ms000009.mss11879.00388.

4 Amos Paul Kennedy, Jr., interview by Lucie Parker, October 22, 2023.

5 "The Importance of the Slave Narrative Collection," Born in Slavery: Slave Narratives from the Federal Writers' Project, 1936 to 1938, Digital Collections, Library of Congress, https://www.loc.gov/collections/slave-narratives-from-the-federal-writers-project-1936-to-1938/articles-and-essays/introduction-to-the-wpa-slave-narratives/importance-of-the-slave-narratives-collection/.

6 Yuval Taylor, ed., *I Was Born a Slave: An Anthology of Classic Slave Narratives: 1849–1866*, vol. 2, with a foreword by Charles Johnson (Chicago: Lawrence Hill Books, 1999).

7 The Works Progress Administration, which was renamed Works Projects Administration in 1939.

8 Kennedy-Parker interview.

9 Amiri Baraka (LeRoi Jones), *Blues People: The Negro Experience in White America and the Music That Developed from It* (New York: Apollo Editions, 1963), 22.

10 "About This Collection," Frederick Douglass Newspapers, 1847 to 1874, Digital Collections, Library of Congress, https://www.loc.gov/collections/frederick-douglass-newspapers/about-this-collection/; Jane Rhodes, *Mary Ann Shadd Cary: The Black Press and Protest in the Nineteenth Century*, New Edition, (Bloomington, Indiana: Indiana University Press, 2023); Gordon Fraser, "Emancipatory Cosmology: Freedom's Journal, The Rights of All, and the Revolutionary Movements of Black Print Culture," *American Quarterly*, 68, no. 2 (June 2016): 263–86.

11 Malea Walker, "Ida B. Wells and the Activism of Investigative Journalism," Library of Congress Blogs, February 12, 2020, https://blogs.loc.gov/headlinesandheroes/2020/02/ida-b-wells-and-the-activism-of-investigative-journalism/.

12 Kinshasha Holman Conwill, *Dream a World Anew: The African American Experience and the Shaping of America* (Washington, DC: Smithsonian Books, 2016), 178.

13 Kennedy-Parker interview.

14 Melissa Barton, *Gather Out of Star-Dust: A Harlem Renaissance Album* (New Haven, CT: Yale University Press, 2017), 6.

15 Abby Arthur Johnson and Ronald Maberry Johnson, *Propaganda and Aesthetics: The Literary Politics of Afro-American Magazines in the Twentieth Century* (Amherst: University of Massachusetts Press, 1979), 78.

16 Kennedy-Parker interview.

17 "Blackface: The Birth of an American Stereotype," Smithsonian National Museum of African American History and Culture, https://nmaahc.si.edu/explore/stories/blackface-birth-american-stereotype.

18 Henry Louis Gates, Jr., "The Trope of a New Negro and the Reconstruction of the Image of the Black," *Representations*, no. 24 (1988): 133–35.

19 Henry Louis Gates, Jr., *The Black Church: This Is Our Story, This Is Our Song* (New York: Penguin Books, 2022).

20 Charles Reagan Wilson, "Church Fans: Tradition, Modernity, and Mortality," *Southern Quarterly* 53, no. 1 (Fall 2015): 220–22.

21 Nancy Scheper-Hughes, "Anatomy of a Quilt: The Gee's Bend Freedom Quilting Bee," *Southern Cultures* 10, no. 3 (Fall 2004): 88–98.

22 Amos Paul Kennedy, Jr., "A Conversation with Amos Kennedy," interview with Angelina Lippert of Poster House, streamed live on March 7, 2023, YouTube video, 1:24:00, https://www.youtube.com/watch?v=vSyMgmNHsXc.

23 Isabel Wilkerson, *The Warmth of Other Suns: The Epic Story of America's Great Migration* (New York: Vintage Books, 2011).

24 Kennedy-Parker interview.

25 Kennedy-Parker interview.

26 Kristin G. Congdon and Doug Blandy, "Using Zines to Teach about Postmodernism and the Communication of Ideas," *Art Education* 56, no. 3 (May 2003): 46.

27 Congdon and Blandy, "Using Zines."

28 Kennedy-Parker interview.

29 Kennedy-Parker interview.

30 Kennedy-Parker interview.

index

Page numbers in italics refer to images.

Dates, formats, and locations for artworks by Amos Paul Kennedy, Jr., appear below. He often reprints individual titles, making precise dating a challenge. (He also reserves the right to "disremember"!)

Artworks classified as a poster measure approximately 19 × 12½ inches (49 × 32 cm); a handbill, 8 × 6 inches (20.25 × 15.25 cm); oversize, 38 × 26 inches (96.5 × 66 cm) or 40 × 26 inches (101.5 × 66 cm); a map, 43¾ × 30 inches (111 × 76 cm); a postcard, 6 × 4 inches (15.25 × 10 cm); and a portfolio, 21 × 15¾ inches (53 × 40 cm). Artworks with different trim sizes are noted below or in the captions.

A

Abre Libros Abre Fronteras (2017, handbill, Detroit), *200*
Act Like You Got Some Sense (2017, *Parlor* handbill series, Detroit), *236*
Addie Mae Collins (2014, *Bombingham* map series, Detroit), *122–23*
Aeschylus, *182*
Affirmative Action Is a Joke (1998–99, *Nappygrams* postcard series, Bloomington, Indiana), *53*
af Klint, Hilma, *220*
African Proverbs (1996, artist's book, Chicago), 50, *51*
African Proverbs series (2014, posters, Detroit), 55, *176–78*
Afrika Bambaataa, 72
AIDS
  It Is Bad Enough That People Are Dying of AIDS… (2012, poster, Gordo), *257*
Ailey, Alvin, 49
Alabama Federation of Democratic Women York to New York (2005, poster, 19 × 14 inches/49 × 35.5 cm, York), *258*
Allan, Lewis, 52
All Artists Are Political (after 2012, poster, Detroit), *131*
All I Was Doing Was Trying to Get Home from Work (2016, *Quotations of Rosa Louise Parks* portfolio, Detroit), *106*
Always Choose Happy (2013 and 2023 reprint, poster, Detroit), *34–39*
Amiel, Henri Frederic, *189*
And When I Had My Chance to Help Do Something (2022, *Seven Quotations from the Participants in the 1960 Sit-In Movement* portfolio, Detroit), *114*
Anishinaabe Ndaw (2019, handbill, Detroit), *279*
Anticipate the Good… (2014, *African Proverbs* poster series, Detroit), *176*
architecture
  Architects Are, by Nature and Pursuit, Leaders and Teachers (2015, handbill, Detroit), *209*
  Architecture Has to Be Greater… (2015, handbill, Detroit), *209*
  Architecture Is About Shelter for the Spirit! (circa 2005, poster, 14 × 9½ inches/35.5 × 24 cm, Akron), *211*
  The Best Way to Make Real Architecture… (2015, handbill, Detroit), *209*
  Everyone, Rich or Poor, Deserves a Shelter for the Soul (2015, handbill, Detroit), *208*
  I Tell My Students, It's Got to Be Warm, Dry, and Noble (2015, handbill, Detroit), *209*
Armstrong, Louis, 50
art
  All Artists Are Political (after 2012, poster, Detroit), *131*
  Art Is an Act of Total Attention (2023, handbill, Detroit), *220*
  Art Is a Verb (2019, handbill, Detroit), *278*
  The Artist Must Elect to Fight for Freedom (2016, handbill, Detroit), *129*
  Artists Are the Gatekeepers of Truth… (after 2012, poster, Detroit), *130*
  Artists Make Lousy Slaves (after 2012, handbill, Detroit), *45*
  Be Kind to Everybody, Make Art, and Fight the Power (2019, handbill, Detroit), *281*
  Black: African American Art… (2006, poster, Akron), *259*
  For Some, Artistic Expression Is the Only Voice… (2019, handbill, Detroit), *278*
  I Don't Paint Dreams or Nightmares… (2023, handbill, Detroit), *221*
  Kentuck Festival of the Arts (2005, poster, 19 × 14 inches/49 × 35.5 cm, York), *250–51*
  United States Artists Detroit Artist Crawl (2018, poster, Detroit), *252*
Artist Book Works, 48, 50
Ashe Okra Gumbo (2018, oversize, Gordo), *247*
Athens Grease Festival (2014, poster, Detroit), *248*

B

Backed by the Full Faith and Credit… (2009, *Principles of American Capitalism* poster series, Gordo), *154*
Bad Ass Mother Cutter (2017, *Parlor* handbill series, Detroit), *236*
Baker, Ella, 48, 60, *60*, *125*
Baldwin, James, 43, 45, 48, 50, 54, 55
Baraka, Amiri, 49, 63
Barragán, Ro, 19
Barton, Melissa, 64
Barzun, Jacques, *239*
Be a Rebel, Read a Book! (2023, handbill, Detroit), *196*
Be Grown or Be Gone (circa 2002, poster, York; circa 2009 reprint, Gordo), *54*, 55
Be Kind series (circa 2009, posters, Gordo), *188–89*
Be Kind to Everybody, Make Art, and Fight the Power (2019, handbill, Detroit), *281*
Be Nice and… series (circa 2009, posters, Gordo), *188–89*
Be Nice or Leave! (2004, poster, York; after 2012 reprint, Detroit), *261*
Be the Joy That You Seek! (2018, oversize, Detroit), 26, *184*
Be Too Brave to Lie (2017, handbill, Detroit), *202*
Be Too Generous to Cheat (2015, handbill, Detroit), *203*
Beam, Joseph F., *164*
Because There's Nothing More Powerful… (2012, poster, Gordo), *268*
Beecher, Henry Ward, *197*
Bennett, Gwendolyn, 64
Bertozzi, Elana, *204–5*
The Best Time to Plant a Tree… (2014, handbill, Detroit), *232*
The Best Way to Make Real Architecture… (2015, handbill, Detroit), *209*
Biggers, John, 49, *49*
Bike City Detroit (2013, poster, Detroit), *277*
Black: African American Art… (2006, poster, Akron), *259*
Black churches, 66
Black Classical Origins Flint Symphony Orchestra Concert (2015, oversize, Detroit), *271*
Black language, 62–63
Black Lives Matter, 72
The Black Panther (newspaper), 70, *70*
Black pride, 49, 230
  Coffee Makes You Black (2003, poster, York; 2024 reprint, Detroit), *231*
  Every Day I Dream of Black Freedom and Pride (circa 2009, poster, Gordo), *146*
Black printing, legacy of, 12–15, 58, 60–66
Blake, Nathaniel, 46
Blandy, Doug, 71
Bombingham series (2014, maps, Detroit), *122–23*
books. *See also* libraries
  Abre Libros Abre Fronteras (2017, handbill, Detroit), *200*
  Be a Rebel, Read a Book! (2023, handbill, Detroit), *196*
  A Book Is Like a Garden in the Pocket (circa 2005, poster, 14 × 9½ inches/35.5 × 24 cm, Akron), *200*
  Book Lovers Never Go to Bed Alone (after 2012, poster, Detroit), *198*
  Bookstores Are Lonely Forts… (2023, handbill, Detroit), *197*
  Bookstores Save Democracy (2023, handbill, Detroit), *196*
  A Dirty Book Rarely Gets Dusty (after 2012, poster, Detroit), *199*
  The First Thing I Do in Any Town… (2023, handbill, Detroit), *197*
  I Am Fatally Attracted to All Bookstores (2023, handbill, Detroit), *196*
  I Cannot Sleep Unless I Am Surrounded by Books (2023, handbill, Detroit), *197*
  I Love You More than Reading (2017, handbill, Detroit), *200*
  Man Builds No Structure That Outlives a Book (2017, handbill, Detroit), *200*
  Read in Order to Live (2017, handbill, Detroit), *200*
  A Room Without Books… (2017, handbill, Detroit), *201*
  The Second Annual Alabama Book Festival (2007, poster, Akron), *255*
  Wear the Old Coat and Buy the New Book (2017, handbill, Detroit), *200*
  When I Get a Little Money I Buy Books… (2017, poster, Detroit), *200*
  Where Is Human Nature So Weak as in a Bookstore? (2023, handbill, Detroit), *197*
Borges, Jorge Luis, *197*
Breaching the Margins (2019, handbill, Detroit), *280*
Bunce, Bill, 49
Buzbee, Lewis, *196*
By the Time a Fool… (2014, *African Proverbs* poster series, Detroit), *178*

C

Call Me a Nigger but Don't Call Me Non-White (1998–99, *Nappygrams* postcard series, Bloomington, Indiana), *53*
Call No Man Happy Till He Is Dead (circa 2009, *Memento Mori* poster series, Gordo), *182*
Call the Police! (1998–99, *Nappygrams* postcard series, Bloomington, Indiana), *53*
Caring for Myself Is Not Self-Indulgence… (2020, handbill, Detroit), *157*
Carver, George Washington, *202–3*
Casiraghi, Alberto, 45
Challenge the Dominant Narrative (2019, handbill, Detroit), *279*
Checker, Chubby, *54*, 55
Chesnutt, Charles, 17
Children, Tired of Being Harassed by Your Stupid Parents?… (circa 2012, poster, Gordo), *214*
Children of the Same Mother Do Not Always Agree (circa 2002, poster, York), *179*
Cicero, *201*, *233*
Cigar Box Guitar Festival (2012, poster, Gordo), *265*
civil rights movement, 12, 45, 68–70, 72
Coffee Makes You Black (2003, poster, York; 2024 reprint, Detroit), *231*
Coffee Makes You Queer (circa 2009, poster, Gordo; 2024 reprint, Detroit), *230*
Coffee Makes You Trans (2016, poster, Detroit), *230*
Coleman Center for the Arts, 54
Collards Brassica Oleracea (2011, oversize, Gordo), *247*
community, importance of, 243, 247
The Confederate States of America Was a Crime… (2010, flag, 60 × 30 inches/152.5 × 76.25 cm, Gordo), 98, *100–101*
Congdon, Kristin G., 71
Consider Everything an Experiment (2023, handbill, Detroit), *221*
Controlled Chaos (2017, *Parlor* handbill series, Detroit), *237*
Cornwill, Kinshasha, 63–64
Creativity Takes Courage (2023, handbill, Detroit), *221*
Cullen, Countee, 64
Culture, Community, Commerce (2019, handbill, Detroit), *280*

D

dance
  The Dance Dances the Dancer… (2012, poster, Gordo), *204*
  Dance! Fuck Who Is Watching (2018, poster, Detroit), *207*
  Dance Is Eros Incarnate (2012, poster, Gordo), *205*
  Dance Is Making Art (2012, poster, Gordo), *204*
  Dance Is the Body of Emotion (2012, poster, Gordo), *205*
  Dance Is the Embodiment of Play (2012, poster, Gordo), *204*
  The Dancer Feels the Breath of Life… (2012, poster, Gordo), *205*
  The Dancer Moves for All of Us (2012, poster, Gordo), *204*

Rhythm Is the Breath of Dance (2012, poster, Gordo), *205*
She Just Wants to Dance (2018, poster, Detroit), *206*
Deacon John, *267*
de Gaulle, Charles, *182*
Detroit (2013, poster, Detroit), *276–77*
A Dirty Book Rarely Gets Dusty (after 2012, poster, Detroit), *199*
Disco Music in the '70s Was Just a Call... (2023, poster, Detroit), *266*
Diversity Means Everybody (2019, handbill, Detroit), *279*
Don't Be a Credit Card Sharecropper! (circa 2009, poster, Gordo), *151*
Don't Do Everything You Are Big Enough to Do (2017, *Parlor* handbill series, Detroit), *237*
Don't Exercise, Die Early! (circa 2002, poster, York), *191*
Don't Talk About It, Be About It (2017, *Parlor* handbill series, Detroit), *236–37*
Douglas, Aaron, 64, 65
Douglas, Emory, 70
Douglass, Frederick, 17, 58, 59, 62, 63, *103–5*
Du Bois, W. E. B., 52, 64
Dunbar, Paul Laurence, 52

E

Each Person Must Live Their Life as a Model for Others (2016, *Quotations of Rosa Louise Parks* portfolio, Detroit), *108*
Eat Fresh Food (2014, handbill, Detroit), *248*
Edo, *180–81*
education. *See also* books; teaching
Education Is What You Know, Not What's in the Book (2014, *African Proverbs* poster series, Detroit), *176*
Empowerment Through Education and Awareness (2019, handbill, Detroit), *281*
Instruction in Youth Is Like Engraving in Stone (2014, *African Proverbs* poster series, Detroit), *176–77*
Learning Expands Great Souls (2014, *African Proverbs* poster series, Detroit), *176*
To Get Lost Is to Learn the Way (2014, *African Proverbs* poster series, Detroit), *177*
Traveling Is Learning (2014, *African Proverbs* poster series, Detroit), *177*
Elliott, Carl, *200*
Emerson, Ralph Waldo, *188*
Empowerment Through Education and Awareness (2019, handbill, Detroit), *281*
End Slavery Now (2016, handbill, Detroit), *140*
Enthusiasm Is the Electricity of Life (2023, handbill, Detroit), *221*
Equality Is a Special Privilege for Blacks (circa 2002, poster, 18 × 12 inches/ 45.75 × 30.5 cm, York), *136–37*
Equality Lives Here (2019, handbill, Detroit), *279*
Erasmus, Desiderius, *200*
Esquire, Buddy, 71, 72, *72*
Even Though I'm Quiet and Timid... (2019, poster, Detroit), *216*
Every Day I Dream of Black Freedom and Pride (circa 2009, poster, Gordo), *146*
Everyone, Rich or Poor, Deserves a Shelter for the Soul (2015, handbill, Detroit), *208*
An Experiment Combining Bad Printing and Bad Book Binding (2022, artist's book, Colorado Springs, Colorado), 50, *50–51*

F

Fairhope Film Festival (2014, poster and handbill series, Detroit), *274–75*
Fanon, Frantz, 49
fans, 66, *66–67*
Farm to Eat... (2014, handbill, Detroit), *248*
Fire! (2003, artist's book, York), *64–65*, 65
Fire!! (journal), 64, 64–65
The First Thing I Do in Any Town... (2023, handbill, Detroit), *197*
Flaubert, Gustave, *200*
Floyd, George, 72
For Some, Artistic Expression Is the Only Voice... (2019, handbill, Detroit), *278*
Freedom Is Never Given; It Is Won! (2014, handbill, Detroit), *60*
Freedom Quilting Bee, 68
Free Health Care for All (2023, poster, Detroit), 70, *71*
Free Your Mind and Your Ass Will Follow (2018, poster, Detroit), *222*
Fresh Food for the People (2017, poster, Detroit), *249*
Friendship Is Like Peeing on Yourself... (circa 2009, poster, Gordo), *186*
Frost, Robert, *197*
Fuck This Shit (2018, poster, Detroit), *225*
Fuck You! I'll Fuck Myself (circa 2005, poster, Akron), *224*

G

gardens
The Garden Is the Poor Man's Apothecary (circa 2009, poster, Gordo), *232*
If You Have a Garden and a Library... (circa 2009, poster, Gordo), *233*
Gates, Henry Louis, Jr., 66
Gay Pride (2005, poster, Akron), 72, *73*
Gee's Bend quilters, 66, 68
Get More Butts on Bikes (2019, handbill, Detroit), *281*
Giovanni, Nikki, 49
Girls Who Are Strong and Smart and Creative... (2022, poster, Detroit), *159*
Give Light and People Will Find a Way (2014, handbill, Detroit), *60*
Giving a Voice to the Silenced (2019, handbill, Detroit), *279*
God Is Trans (2023, handbill, Detroit), *163*
Goggle Up... (2017, *Smarter Every Day* poster series, Detroit), *194*
Go Green! Eat Okra! (2014, poster, Detroit), *244*
Good Food, Transparency, Stewardship, Sense of Place (2019, handbill, Detroit), *279*
Good History Is the Memory of Freedom and Justice (circa 2009, poster, Gordo), *147*
Goodwin, Jo, *196*
Grandmaster Flash, 72
The Graveyard Is Full of Indispensable Men (circa 2009, *Memento Mori* poster series, Gordo), *182*
Great Migration, 69
Greed Is So Destructive (2016, handbill, Detroit), *156*
Growing Justice (2019, handbill, Detroit), *281*
Gullah people, 62, 63

H

Hair Is Texture (2022, oversize, Detroit), *235*
Hair Love (2017, *Parlor* handbill series, Detroit), *237*
Hamady, Walter, 48, 49
Hamer, Fannie Lou, 60, *132–33*
Hamilton, Philip, 49
Handmade Basketry from the Deep South (2003, poster, 19 × 14 inches/ 49 × 35.5 cm, York), *258*
Harlem Renaissance, 64–66, 72
HBCUs, 46, 49, 63–64
healthcare
Free Health Care for All (2023, poster, Detroit), *71*
Healthcare Access Is a Human Right (2019, handbill, Detroit), *278*
Healthy Comes in All Colors (2019, handbill, Detroit), *280*
Hey, I'm Watching Here (2014, *Fairhope Film Festival* handbill series, Detroit), *275*
Higher the Hair, Closer to Heaven (2017, *Parlor* handbill series, Detroit), *236*
H. N. Werkman School of Bad Printing (2018, oversize, Detroit), *10*
Holiday, Billie, 52
hooks, bell, 11
Hot Printing (Werkman), 50
House of the Turtle (Biggers), 49
Housing, Re-Imagined (2019, handbill, Detroit), *279*
How Can You Know Jesus... (circa 2005, poster, Akron; 2018 reprint, Detroit), *187*
The Hub of Detroit (2013, poster, Detroit), *276*
Hughes, Langston, 64
Hurston, Zora Neale, 64

I

I Ain't Afraid to Live in a World with Trans People... (2023, handbill, Detroit), *163*
I Am as Southern as series (2015, handbills, Detroit), 26, *226–29*
I Am Fatally Attracted to All Bookstores (2023, handbill, Detroit), *196*
I Am Resilient, Like My Roots (2019, handbill, Detroit), *281*
I Cannot Sleep Unless I Am Surrounded by Books (2023, handbill, Detroit), *197*
I Can't Breathe! (2020, oversize, 19¾ × 26 inches/50 × 66 cm, Detroit), *170–71*
Ideas Festival (2005, poster, 19 × 14 inches/ 49 × 35.5 cm, York), *254*
The Idiot Press of Amos Paul Kennedy, Jr., 50
I Don't Paint Dreams or Nightmares... (2023, handbill, Detroit), *221*
I Don't Want a Job, I Want Money (2019, handbill, Detroit), *153*
I Don't Want to Go to Heaven... (2015, poster, Detroit), *193*
I Eats the Blues, I Sleeps the Blues, I Is the Blues (2023, poster, Detroit), *267*
I Fear I Am Integrating My People into a Burning House (after 2012, handbill, Detroit), *138*
If Slavery Is Not Wrong, Nothing Is Wrong (2013, postcard, Detroit), *135*
If There Is No Struggle, There Is No Progress (after 2012, oversize, Detroit), 26, 58, *59*, 62
If the White Man Gives You Anything... (2016, handbill, Detroit), *132*
If Women Want Any Rights... (2013, oversize, Detroit), *102*
If You Are in Debt Somebody Owns a Part of You! (2015, handbill, Detroit), *150*
If You Are Rich, Money Works for You... (2018, handbill, Detroit), *150*
If You Don't Know What's Right, Go with Your Heart (2019, poster, Detroit), *219*
If You Have a Garden and a Library... (circa 2009, poster, Gordo), *233*
I Knew God Was Black, but I Didn't Know They Were Femme! (2018, poster, Detroit), *161*
I Knew God Was Black, but I Didn't Know They Were Trans! (2018, poster, Detroit), *160*
I Knew Someone Had to Take the First Step... (2016, *Quotations of Rosa Louise Parks* portfolio, Detroit), *106*
I Know Who I Am Without Anyone There to Tell Me (2019, poster, Detroit), *216*
I Love You More than Reading (2017, handbill, Detroit), *200*
I Love Your Hair, Will You Marry Me? (2017, *Parlor* handbill series, Detroit), *237*
I'm Going to Sit Here Until They Serve Me (2022, *Seven Quotations from the Participants in the 1960 Sit-In Movement* portfolio, Detroit), *114*
I'm Just a Part of a Collective... (2017, *Parlor* handbill series, Detroit), *236–37*
Impact by Design (2019, handbill, Detroit), *281*
Important that the World Finds Out Whether We've Got a Democracy or Not (2022, *Seven Quotations from the Participants in the 1960 Sit-In Movement* portfolio, Detroit), *114*
I'm Too Old for This Shit (after 2012, poster, Detroit), *213*
In a World of Talkers, Be a Thinker and a Doer (2017, *Smarter Every Day* poster series, Detroit), *194*
Ingmire, Thomas, 47
Instruction in Youth Is Like Engraving in Stone (2014, *African Proverbs* poster series, Detroit), *176–77*
I Teach! What's Your Superpower? (2014, handbill, Detroit), *239*
I Tell My Students, It's Got to Be Warm, Dry, and Noble (2015, handbill, Detroit), *209*
I Think We're Going to Need a Bigger Screen (2014, *Fairhope Film Festival* handbill series, Detroit), *275*
It Is Bad Enough That People Are Dying of AIDS... (2012, poster, Gordo), *257*
It's Fun to Be Weird! (2015, handbill, Detroit), *218*
I've Upped My Standards, Up Yours (circa 2009, poster, Gordo; after 2012 reprint, Detroit), *223*
I Was Just Trying to Let Them Know How I Felt... (2016, *Quotations of Rosa Louise Parks* portfolio, Detroit), *108*
I Would Like to Be Known as a Person Who Is Concerned About Freedom (2016, *Quotations of Rosa Louise Parks* portfolio, Detroit), *110*
I Would Like to Be Remembered... (2016, *Quotations of Rosa Louise Parks* portfolio, Detroit), *108*
I Would Tell You to Go to Hell, but I Work There (2015, poster, Detroit), *193*

J

Jazzy Jay, 72
Jimmie Lee Jackson (circa 2009, *People Died for Your Right to Vote* map series, Gordo), *120*
Johnson, Abby Arthur, 64
Johnson, Ronald Maberry, 64
Jonathan Myrick Daniels (circa 2009, *People Died for Your Right to Vote* map series, Gordo), *121*
Jones, LeRoi. *See* Baraka, Amiri
Jubalee Press, 50
Juneteenth
Juneteenth Culture Fest (2005, poster, 19 × 14 inches/49 × 35.5 cm, York), *258*
When Juneteenth Becomes a National Holiday... (2021, poster, Detroit), *141*

K

Kahlo, Frida, *221*
Kahn, Si, *131*
Kennedy, Amos Paul, Jr. *See also* individual works
academic career of, 52, 54
birth certificate of, *46*
calligraphy and, 47, *48*
childhood of, *44*, 45–46
children of, 46, *47*
as citizen printer, 56, 247
education of, 46–50, 64
exhibitions of, 56
layered approach of, 11, 34, 37
manifesto of, 12–15
in the peace corps, 46, *47*
personality of, 11, 44
process of, 11, 19, 34, 37, 55, 70
self-identification of, as a negro printer, 12, 15, 52, 60, 262
sense of humor of, 11, 45
as social printer, 43, 56

style of, 11, 60–62
type use of, 26, 34–37, 55, 60, 62
uniform of, 45
woodcut collection of, 31, 45, *64*, 65, 66, *273*
Kennedy, Amos Paul, Sr., 46
Kennedy and Sons Fine Printing, 50
Kennedy, Helen Augusta Davis, 46
Kent, Sister Corita, 11, *221*
Kentuck Festival of the Arts (2005, poster, 19 × 14 inches/49 × 35.5 cm, York), *250–51*
Kindness and Your Best Self Even in All Seasons (2019, poster, Detroit), *216*
Kindness Is a Language… (circa 2009, *Be Kind* poster series, Gordo), *189*
King, Martin Luther, Jr., 48, 60, *126–127*, *138–39*
Kitt, Eartha, *156*
Know Justice, Know Peace (2020, poster, Detroit), *72*, *168*
Knowledge Does Not Equal Understanding (2017, *Smarter Every Day* poster series, Detroit), *195*
Know Your History (2019, handbill, Detroit), *278*

L

Ladies, No Fighting in the Bathroom (2003, poster, York; after 2012 reprint, Detroit), 55, *260*
Laissez Les Bon Temps Rouler (2014, poster, Detroit), *263*
Landback (2018, map, 31½ × 20½ inches/80 × 30 cm, Detroit), *118–19*
Lange, Dorothea, *220*
Langston, John M., *148*
Lawrence, Jacob, 49
Learning Expands Great Souls (2014, *African Proverbs* poster series, Detroit), *176*
Learn Politeness from the Impolite (2014, *African Proverbs* poster series, Detroit), *176*
LGBTQIA+ rights, 71, 72
Coffee Makes You Queer (circa 2009, poster, Gordo; 2024 reprint, Detroit), *230*
Coffee Makes You Trans (2016, poster, Detroit), *230*
Gay Pride (2005, poster, Akron), *73*
God Is Trans (2023, handbill, Detroit), *163*
I Ain't Afraid to Live in a World with Trans People… (2023, handbill, Detroit), *163*
I Knew God Was Black, but I Didn't Know They Were Femme! (2021, poster, Detroit), *161*
I Knew God Was Black, but I Didn't Know They Were Trans! (2021, poster, Detroit), *160*
Love Trans Love (2016, poster, Detroit), *162*
Remember Stonewall 1969 (circa 2005, poster, Akron), *165*
Since 1998 Empowering Our LGBTQ Community (2019, handbill, Detroit), *280*
We Are Black Men Who Are Proudly Gay… (2021, poster, Detroit), *164*
libraries. *See also* books
If You Have a Garden and a Library… (circa 2009, poster, Gordo), *233*
A Library Is Not a Luxury… (2017, handbill, Detroit), *200*
Public Libraries Build Community (2017, handbill, Detroit), *200*
A Truly Great Library Contains Something in It to Offend Everyone (2023, handbill, Detroit), *196*
Your Library Is Your Paradise (2017, handbill, Detroit), *200*
Life's Most Persistent and Urgent Question Is… (2009, poster, 22⅜ × 15½ inches/56.75 × 39.25 cm, Gordo), *139*
The Limits of Tyrants Are Prescribed… (2013, oversize, Detroit), *104–5*
Lincoln, Abraham, *135*
Look Closer: Layers of Beauty Are Everywhere (2017, *Smarter Every Day* poster series, Detroit), *195*
Lorde, Audre, *157*
Love Trans Love (2016, poster, Detroit), *162*

M

MacLaren, Ian, *188*
Make Haste to Be Kind (circa 2009, *Be Kind* poster series, Gordo), *189*
Make Music NOLA (2016, oversize, Detroit), *270*
Man Builds No Structure That Outlives a Book (2017, handbill, Detroit), *200*
Marley, Bob, *142–43*, *234*
Mask (2000, artist's book, 17¼ × 11¼ inches/43.75 × 28.5 cm, Bloomington, Indiana), 26, *86–91*
Matisse, Henri, *221*
May I Take Your Order Please? (2022, *Seven Quotations from the Participants in the 1960 Sit-In Movement* portfolio, Detroit), *113*
McKay, Claude, 52
Memento Mori series (circa 2009, posters, Gordo), *182–83*
Memories of Our Lives, of Our Works, and Our Deeds Will Continue (2016, *Quotations of Rosa Louise Parks* portfolio, Detroit), *108*
Mockbee, Samuel (Sambo), 26, 54–55, *208–9*, 210, *211*
The More We Discover the Wonders of Nature… (2023, handbill, Detroit), *220*
Murdered series (2013, fans, Detroit), 66, *66–67*
My Demons Protect the World from Me (2018, poster, Detroit), *190*
My Grandpa Says You Can Be a Strong Man or a Smart One, I Think He's Both (2019, poster, Detroit), *216*

N

Nappygrams series (1998–1999, postcards, Bloomington, Indiana), 52, 53, *53*
A Nation May Lose Its Liberties… (2019, poster, Detroit), *148*
The Nature of the Flower Is to Bloom… (after 2012, map, Detroit), *124*
Negroes: Stolen People Living on Stolen Lands (2018, 18⅞ × 15¾ inches/48 × 40 cm, Detroit), *117*
Newman, Lance, *149*
New Negro movement, 66
Newton, Huey P., 70
Niggers Come in All Colors (2018 and 2023 reprint, poster, Detroit), *144–45*
No (2016, *Quotations of Rosa Louise Parks* portfolio, Detroit), *109*
Nobody's Free Until Everybody's Free (2016, handbill, Detroit), *133*
Non-White? (1998–99, *Nappygrams* postcard series, Bloomington, Indiana), *53*
Nope, I Can't Go to Hell, Satan Still Has that Restraining Order Against Me (circa 2014, poster, Detroit), *193*
Nuestros Vecinos (2019, handbill, Detroit), *280*
Nugent, Richard, 64
NWF (Non-White Folks) (1998–99, *Nappygrams* postcard series, Bloomington, Indiana), *53*

O

Obama, Barack, 69
Okra, the People's Vegetable (2012, poster, Gordo), *244*
Okra Abelmoschus Esculentus (2011, oversize, Gordo), *246*
Okra Builds Community (2015, poster, Detroit), *245*
Okra Festival (2006, poster, Akron), *54*
Okra Lovers Unite! (2012, poster, Gordo), *244*
The Old Forget What the Young Don't Know (2015, handbill, Detroit), *213*
Old Is an Attitude (2018, poster, Detroit), *212*
One Love (circa 2002, poster, York), *143*
The Only Tired I Was, Was Tired of Giving In (2016, *Quotations of Rosa Louise Parks* portfolio, Detroit), *108*
Opportunity of Racial Equity (2019, handbill, Detroit), *278*
Otis, Bass, 61
Our Mistreatment Was Just Not Right and I Was Tired of It (2016, *Quotations of Rosa Louise Parks* portfolio, Detroit), *106*

P

Parks, Gordon, *221*
Parks, Rosa, 60, 69, *106–11*
Parlor series (2017, handbills, Detroit), *236–37*
Peace (2012, poster, Gordo), *166–67*
People Died for Your Right to Vote series (circa 2009, maps, Gordo), *120–21*
People Should Eat in Dignity (2022, *Seven Quotations from the Participants in the 1960 Sit-In Movement* portfolio, Detroit), *115*
Phelps, Austin, *200*
Pig Out, Die Early! (circa 2002, poster, York; 2024 reprint, Detroit), *191*
Pile of Bricks project, 56
Place Making Means We Belong Here, Too (2019, handbill, Detroit), *279*
Plath, Sylvia, *220*
Play It Again (2014, *Fairhope Film Festival* handbill series, Detroit), *275*
police violence, 72
I Can't Breathe! (2020, oversize, 19¾ × 26 inches/50 × 66 cm), Detroit), *170–71*
What Would I Post If You Were Murdered by the Police? (2020, poster, Detroit), *169*
What Would You Post If I Were Murdered by the Police? (2020, poster, Detroit), *169*
Post-Racial, My Ass! (circa 2009, map, 32 × 50 inches/81 × 127 cm, Gordo), *68–69*, 69
Power Concedes Nothing Without a Demand (2013, oversize, Detroit), *103*
Preserve Our Way of Life and the Welfare of Our People (2019, handbill, Detroit), *280*
Principles of American Capitalism series (2009, posters, Gordo), *154–55*
Privatize Profits, Socialize Risks (2009, *Principles of American Capitalism* poster series, Gordo), *154*
The Problem Isn't Racism… (2019, handbill, Detroit), *151*
Proceed and Be Bold! (circa 2002, poster, York; after 2012 reprint, Detroit), 56, *57*
Proceed and Be Bold! (documentary), 56
Public Libraries Build Community (2017, handbill, Detroit), *200*

Q

Quilting Techniques Workshop (2003, poster, York), 66, *253*
Quotations of Rosa Louise Parks: Human Rights Activist (2007, portfolio, Akron; 2016 reprint, Detroit), 69, *106–11*

R

racism, 31, 66, 69, 72, 169
The Problem Isn't Racism… (2019, handbill, Detroit), *151*
Racism, Materialism, Militarism (2014, map, 28 × 40 inches/71 × 101.5 cm, Detroit), *126–27*
Racism Is Still with Us… (2016, *Quotations of Rosa Louise Parks* portfolio, Detroit), *111*
That Until the Basic Human Rights Are Equally Guaranteed to All… (circa 2002, poster, York), *142*
Read in Order to Live (2017, handbill, Detroit), *200*
Red Hot & Blues (circa 2005, poster, Akron), *269*
The Red Summer of 1919 (2019, artist's book, 6¼ × 4¾ inches/15.75 × 12 cm, Colorado Springs, Colorado), *92–93*
Reeves, Martha, *266*
Remember Stonewall 1969 (circa 2005, poster, Akron), *165*
Rev. James Reeb (circa 2009, *People Died for Your Right to Vote* map series, Gordo), *120*
Rhapsody in Blue (2005, poster, 19 × 14 inches/49 × 35.5 cm, Akron), *258*
Rhythm Is the Breath of Dance (2012, poster, Gordo), *205*
Rice, T. D., 65
Riddick, Tut, *187*
Riddle Ma Riddle (1996, artist's book, Milwaukee, Wisconsin), 62, *62–63*
Rise for Climate, Jobs, and Justice (2018, poster, Detroit), *256*
Robeson, Paul, 60, *128–30*
A Room Without Books… (2017, handbill, Detroit), *201*
Ross, Bob, *220*

Sanchez, Sonia, 49
Seale, Bobby, 70
A Seat at the Table (2014, poster, Detroit), *248*
Seattle JazzED (2013, poster, Detroit), *262*
The Second Annual Alabama Book Festival (2007, poster, Akron), *255*
Send Money (2023, poster, Detroit), *152*
Seven Quotations from the Participants in the 1960 Sit-In Movement in Arlington, Virginia (2022, portfolio, Detroit), *112–15*
Shadd, Mary Ann, 63
She Just Wants to Dance (2018, poster, Detroit), *206*
She Who Learns, Teaches (2014, *African Proverbs* poster series, Detroit), *177*
She [Who] Wanders Around by Day a Lot, Learns a Lot (2014, *African Proverbs* poster series, Detroit), *176–77*
Short Time to Stay Here (2013, poster, Detroit), *264*
Simone, Nina, *135*, *156*
Since 1998 Empowering Our LGBTQ Community (2019, handbill, Detroit), *280*
slavery
End Slavery Now (2016, handbill, Detroit), *140*
If Slavery Is Not Wrong, Nothing Is Wrong (2013, postcard, Detroit), *135*
Slavery Has Never Been Abolished… (2013, postcard, Detroit), *135*
Smarter Every Day series (2017, posters, Detroit), *194–95*
Smoke, Die Early! (circa 2002, poster, York), *191*
Sojourner Truth, *102*
Sovereign (2018, map, 20½ × 29⅛ inches/52 × 74 cm, Detroit), *116–17*
Spread Welcome (2019, handbill, Detroit), *279*
Stop Giving Us Homework (2019, poster, Detroit), *215*
Strange Fruit (1994, artist's book, Chicago), 26, 50, 52, *52*, *53*, *94–97*
Strong People Don't Need Strong Leaders (2014, handbill, Detroit), *60*
Strong Relationships, Resilient People (2019, handbill, Detroit), *278*
A Strong West Michigan Depends on Strong Kids (2019, handbill, Detroit), *280*
Support Urban Farms (2014, handbill, Detroit), *248*

T

Talent Lives Here (2019, handbill, Detroit), *280*
Tavern Fest (2013, poster, Detroit), *248*
Taylor, Breonna, 72
Taylor, Elizabeth, *257*
teaching. *See also* education
  I Teach! What's Your Superpower? (2014, handbill, Detroit), *239*
  She Who Learns, Teaches (2014, *African Proverbs* poster series, Detroit), *177*
  Teachers Touch the Future (2014, handbill, Detroit), *239*
  Teaching Is Not a Lost Art (2014, handbill, Detroit), *239*
  Those Who Care, Teach (2014, handbill, Detroit), *238*
  Those Who Know, Do; Those Who Understand, Teach (2014, handbill, Detroit), *239*
Tee's Lounge, 54, 55, 56, *260–61*
Tenure, Housewifery & Slavery… (1998–99, *Nappygrams* postcard series, Bloomington, Indiana), *53*
Terrell, Mary Church, 63
That Until the Basic Human Rights Are Equally Guaranteed to All… (circa 2002, poster, York), *142*
There Is One Thing You Have Got to Learn… (2016, handbill, Detroit), *133*
Thompson, Lemoin. *See* Esquire, Buddy
Those Who Care, Teach (2014, handbill, Detroit), *238*
Those Who Know, Do; Those Who Understand, Teach (2014, handbill, Detroit), *239*
Thurman, Wallace, 64
Till, Emmett, 72
The Time Had Just Come When I Had Been Pushed… (2016, *Quotations of Rosa Louise Parks* portfolio, Detroit), *107*
To Get Lost Is to Learn the Way (2014, *African Proverbs* poster series, Detroit), *177*
Too Big to Fail (2009, *Principles of American Capitalism* poster series, Gordo), *155*
Too Much Shit for a Dime (2018, poster, Detroit), *225*
To Try and Fail Is Not Laziness (2014, *African Proverbs* poster series, Detroit), *177*
Transformation Happens at the Pace of Relationships (2019, handbill, Detroit), *280*
Traveling Is Learning (2014, *African Proverbs* poster series, Detroit), *177*
A Truly Great Library Contains Something in It to Offend Everyone (2023, handbill, Detroit), *196*
Trust the Universe and Respect Your Hair (2022, oversize, Detroit), *234*
The Tuscaloosa Get Up (2012, poster, Gordo), *262*
Twain, Mark, *189*

U

United States Artists Detroit Artist Crawl (2018, poster, Detroit), *252*
Until the Killing of Black Men… (after 2012, map, 36½ × 23½ inches/92.75 × 59.5 cm, Detroit), *125*
Updike, John, *197*

V

van der Looij, Jan-Willem, 19, *75*, *77*, *78*
Viola Gregg Liuzzo (circa 2009, *People Died for Your Right to Vote* map series, Gordo), *121*
Vote (2012, handbill, 7 × 3 inches/18 × 8 cm, Gordo), *134*

W

Walker, Alice, *124*
Wanted Poster Series #14a (White), *49*
Ward, Jesmyn, *159*
Waters, Sheila, *48*, *49*
We Are Black Men Who Are Proudly Gay… (2021, poster, Detroit), *164*
Wear the Old Coat and Buy the New Book (2017, handbill, Detroit), *200*
We Ask for Nothing That Is Not Right… (2016, handbill, Detroit), *128*
We Don't Make Mistakes, Just Happy Little Accidents (2023, handbill, Detroit), *220*
We Have a Belief in Democracy (2022, *Seven Quotations from the Participants in the 1960 Sit-In Movement* portfolio, Detroit), *114*
Wells, Ida B., 63
We Pick Our Okra from the Left (2012, poster, Gordo), *244*
Werkman, Hendrik Nicolaas (H. N.), *10*, 11, 17, 49–50
We've All Been Given a Gift… (2012, handbill, Gordo), *180–81*
Whatever My Individual Desires Were… (2016, from the *Quotations of Rosa Louise Parks* portfolio, Detroit), *111*
What Would I Post If You Were Murdered by the Police? (2020, poster, Detroit), *169*
What Would You Post If I Were Murdered by the Police? (2020, poster, Detroit), *169*
When I Get a Little Money I Buy Books… (2017, poster, Detroit), *200*
When Juneteeth Becomes a National Holiday… (2021, poster, Detroit), *141*
Where Is Human Nature So Weak as in a Bookstore? (2023, handbill, Detroit), *197*
White, Charles W., 49, *49*
Whitehead, Colson, *281*
Why Do a Vast Majority of Black Americans… (2020, poster, Detroit), *141*
Wilde, Oscar, *193*
Wilk, John, 63
Williams, George W., 17
Wilson, Charles Reagan, 66
A Wise Woman Who Knows Proverbs Reconciles Difficulties (2014, *African Proverbs* poster series, Detroit), *178*
Women Have Hot Flashes, I Have Power Surges (2018, poster, Detroit), *158*
The Worst Enemy to Creativity Is Self-Doubt (2023, handbill, Detroit), *220*

Y

You Are Going to Hell and the Devil Is My Bitch (circa 2009, poster, Gordo), *192*
You Cannot Unsay Bad Words (after 2012, handbill, Detroit), *217*
You Can't Open the Gates of Hell… (circa 2014, poster, Detroit), *193*
You Can't Put Old Heads on Young Shoulders (2015, handbill, Detroit), *212*
You Had Me at "Action" (2014, *Fairhope Film Festival* handbill series, Detroit), *275*
You Have to Risk It to Get That Biscuit (2017, *Parlor* handbill series, Detroit), *72*, *73*
You Learned to Deal with Other People in Society… (2019, poster, Detroit), *149*
You Must Never Be Fearful About What You Are Doing When It Is Right (2016, *Quotations of Rosa Louise Parks* portfolio, Detroit), *108*
Your Hair Looks Great! (2017, *Parlor* handbill series, Detroit), *236*
Your Library Is Your Paradise (2017, handbill, Detroit), *200*
You've Got to Learn to Leave the Table When Love's No Longer Being Served (2016, handbill, Detroit), *156*
You Will Not Die Because You Are Sick but Because You Are Alive (circa 2009, *Memento Mori* poster series, Gordo), *183*

Z

zines, 71–72
Zinger, Laura, 56

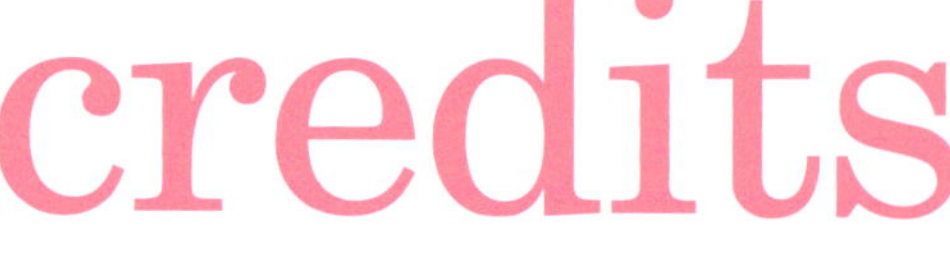

credits

Artwork & Image Credits
All artwork © Amos Paul Kennedy, Jr., unless otherwise noted below.

All artwork collection of Letterform Archive or on loan from Amos Paul Kennedy, Jr. All artwork images © Letterform Archive unless otherwise noted below.

All family snapshots and early portraits courtesy of Amos Paul Kennedy, Jr.

All original portraiture and studio imagery © Aundre Larrow, with photography assistance from Kristle Marshall, unless otherwise noted below.

page 46 map of Louisiana courtesy of David Rumsey Map Center, Stanford Libraries • birth certificate courtesy of Amos Paul Kennedy, Jr. **page 49** John Biggers image courtesy of John Biggers Papers, Emory University Stuart A. Rose Manuscript, Archives, and Rare Book Library; artwork © Estate of John Biggers • Charles W. White image © and courtesy of the Art Institute of Chicago / Art Resource, NY; artwork © the Charles White Archives **page 50** *Hot Printing* by H. N. Werkman **page 53** images © and courtesy of Indiana University **page 54** Chubby Checker concert poster by Globe Poster; reprinted with permission of the Globe Collection and Press at MICA **page 55** image of the *Amos Paul Kennedy, Jr.: Lyrics of My People* exhibition courtesy of the Kennedy Museum of Art, Ohio University **page 56** image © and courtesy of Garrett MacLean **page 61** *Caution* and *Outrage* broadside images courtesy of the Library of Congress, Rare Book and Special Collections Division, Printed Ephemera Collection **page 63** image of the Tuskegee University printshop courtesy of the Tuskegee University Archives • image of the Atlanta University printshop courtesy of the Atlanta University Photographs Collection, Atlanta University Center Robert W. Woodruff Library • image of *The North Star* courtesy of the Library of Congress, Serial and Government Publications Division **page 64** *Fire!!* cover artwork © 2024 Heirs of Aaron Douglas / Licensed by VAGA at Artists Rights Society (ARS), New York **pages 70–71** *The Black Panther* front and back cover artwork © 2024 Emory Douglas / Licensed by AFNYLAW.com **page 71** Getty Images / Robert Sengstacke Abbott **page 72** Buddy Esquire flyer images courtesy of Johan Kugelberg Hip Hop Collection, #8021, Division of Rare and Manuscript Collections, Cornell University Library **pages 75, 77, and 78** *Open 4 No Business*; *If Bad Printing Is Wrong, We Don't Wanna Be Right*; and *Busy Doing Nothing* posters courtesy of Amos Paul Kennedy, Jr., and Jan-Willem van der Looij **pages 255 and 257** images © and courtesy of Poster House, Poster House Permanent Collection

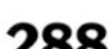

acknowledgments

GAIL ANDERSON is chair of BFA Design and BFA Advertising at the School of Visual Arts and creative director at Visual Arts Press. Gail serves on the Citizens' Stamp Advisory Committee for the U.S. Postal Service and the advisory boards of Poster House and The One Club for Creativity. She is an AIGA Medalist; the 2018 recipient of the Cooper Hewitt, Smithsonian National Design Award for Lifetime Achievement; and a 2022 Art Directors Club Paul Manship Medallion Honoree. Her work is represented in the Library of Congress's permanent collection, the Milton Glaser Design Study Center and Archives, and the National Museum of African American History and Culture.

MYRON M. BEASLEY, PhD, is a professor of American Studies and of Gender and Sexuality Studies at Bates College and the author of *Performance, Art, and Politics in the African Diaspora* (2023). He curated *Print, Protest, Power: The Works of Amos Paul Kennedy, Jr., and Emory Douglas* (2018) for the Able Baker Contemporary in Portland, Maine. He has been recognized with awards and fellowships from the Andy Warhol Foundation for the Visual Arts, the Whiting Foundation, the National Endowment for the Humanities, the Davis Family Foundation, the Ruth and Joseph C. Reed Foundation for the Arts, and the Dorothea and Leo Rabkin Foundation.

AUSTIN KLEON is the *New York Times* bestselling author of a trilogy of illustrated books about creativity in the digital age: *Steal Like an Artist*, *Show Your Work!*, and *Keep Going*. He's also the author of *Newspaper Blackout*, a collection of poems made by redacting the newspaper with a permanent marker. His books have been translated into dozens of languages and have sold more than a million copies worldwide. He's been featured on NPR's *Morning Edition*, *PBS NewsHour*, and in the *New York Times* and the *Wall Street Journal*. He speaks for organizations such as Pixar, Google, SXSW, TEDx, and the *Economist*. He lives in Austin, Texas, with his wife and sons.

AUNDRE LARROW is a Jamaican-born photographer based in Brooklyn, New York. From his time as an Adobe Creative resident exploring stories across the country to working on the set of W. Kamau Bell's *United Shades of America*, Aundre seeks to see the fundamental truth in each human being, regardless of background, culture, or upbringing.

JOE NEWTON is a font-obsessed designer, educator, and illustrator who cut his design teeth during Seattle's grunge explosion, creating posters, videos, and album art for his band, Gas Huffer. He has led creative teams at cult Seattle weekly the *Stranger*, *Rolling Stone*, and Veer (as head of type), and he partnered with Gail to form Anderson Newton Design. Joe served for eight years on the advisory board of the Type Directors Club and teaches typography at the School of Visual Arts. He recently published his first book, collaborating with nationally syndicated sex advice guru Dan Savage.

KELLY WALTERS is an artist, a designer, and the founder of the multidisciplinary design studio Bright Polka Dot. Her ongoing design research interrogates the identity formation and systems of value embedded in Black visual and material culture. Kelly has curated a number of exhibitions, including *Kindred*, *Open Dialogue: Artists + Designers of Afro-Caribbean Descent*, and *Remix: Activating the Archive*. She received a Graham Foundation award for her exhibition *With a Cast of Colored Stars* in 2021. Kelly has written about Black American design historics and the impact of colonization on the construction of the Black image. Her publications include *Black, Brown + Latinx Design Educators: Conversations on Design and Race* and the co-edited anthology *The Black Experience in Design: Identity, Expression & Reflection*. Kelly is currently the director of the BFA Communication Design program and an assistant professor of communications design at Parsons School of Design in New York. She is the curator of the 2024 Letterform Archive exhibition *Amos Paul Kennedy, Jr.: Citizen Printer.*

PUBLISHER ACKNOWLEDGMENTS
Thank you to Kate Long Stellar and Paola Zanol for collections assistance; April Harper and 42-line for artwork digitization; and Kate Bolen, Stephen Coles, Ken DellaPenta, Alan P. Kennedy, Sr., Gail Nelson-Bonebrake, and Chris Westcott for editorial assistance.

AUTHOR ACKNOWLEDGMENTS
I offer gratitude to all the people who enrich my life with the generosity that makes my work possible. This book could not have happened without the kinship of the many communities that nurture me. Thank you to my parents, my siblings, and my sons and their mother for raising me; to my friends for their support; to my fellow printers for sharing both craft and commiseration; to the citizens and museums who have hung my work on the walls of their homes and galleries, as well as the art librarians who have included it in their collections; to my patrons who have allowed me to provide a service to them; to the towns of Grambling, York, Akron, Gordo, and Detroit for giving me space to do my thing; and to the wordsmiths—the ancestors, activists, poets, makers, philosophers, students, and friends—whose words I have inked up (and sometimes misspelled).

And thanks in advance to YOU for becoming the citizen version of whatever role you play best. A citizen is an individual who uses their talent for the benefit of the community. So go find your talent and use it as a citizen would!

Above all, be kind.

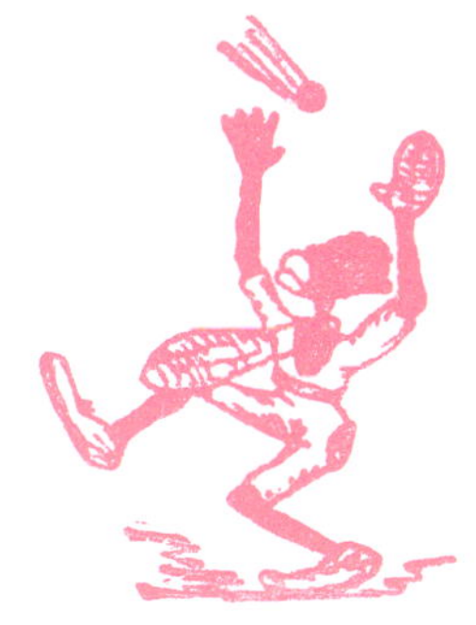

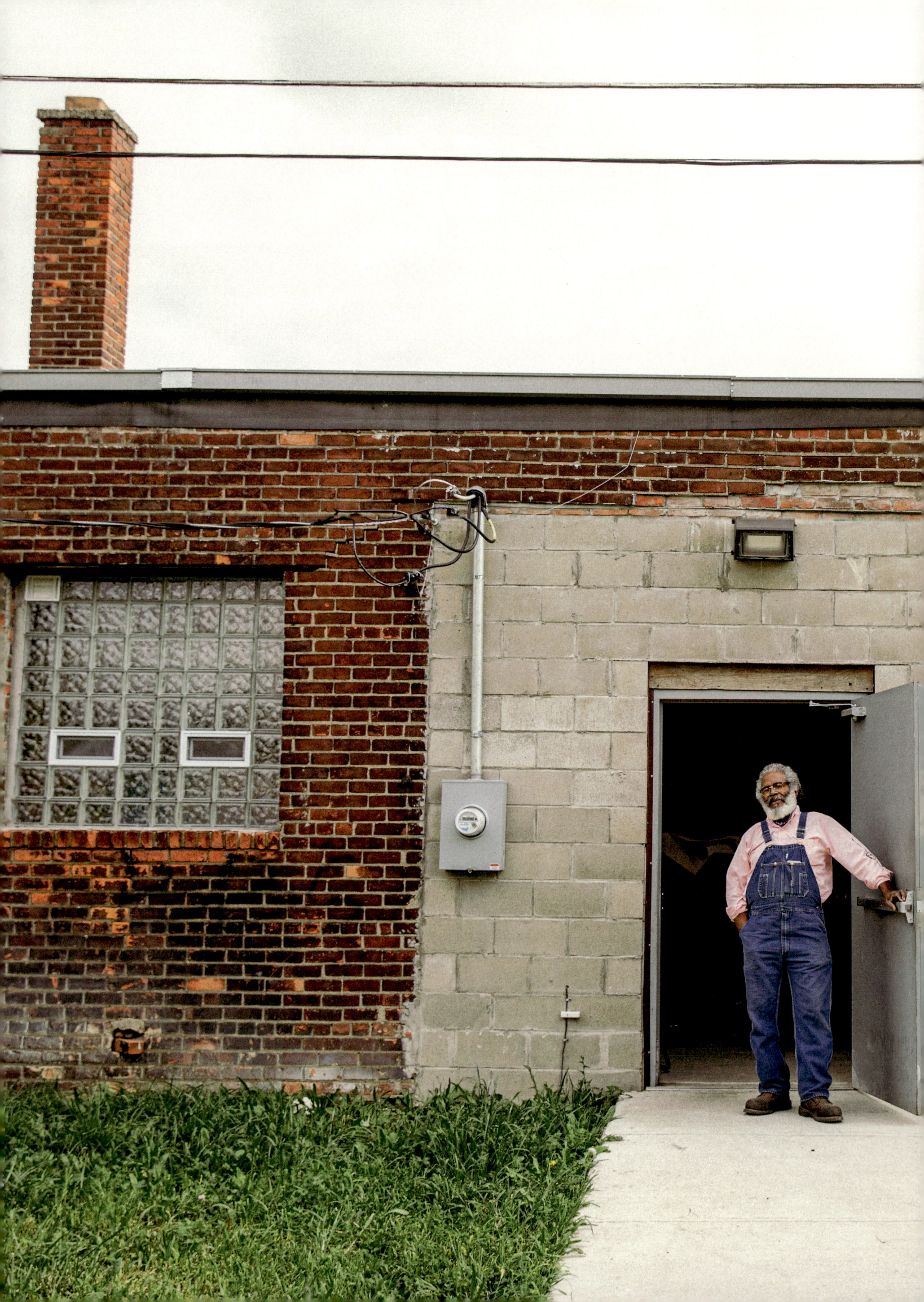

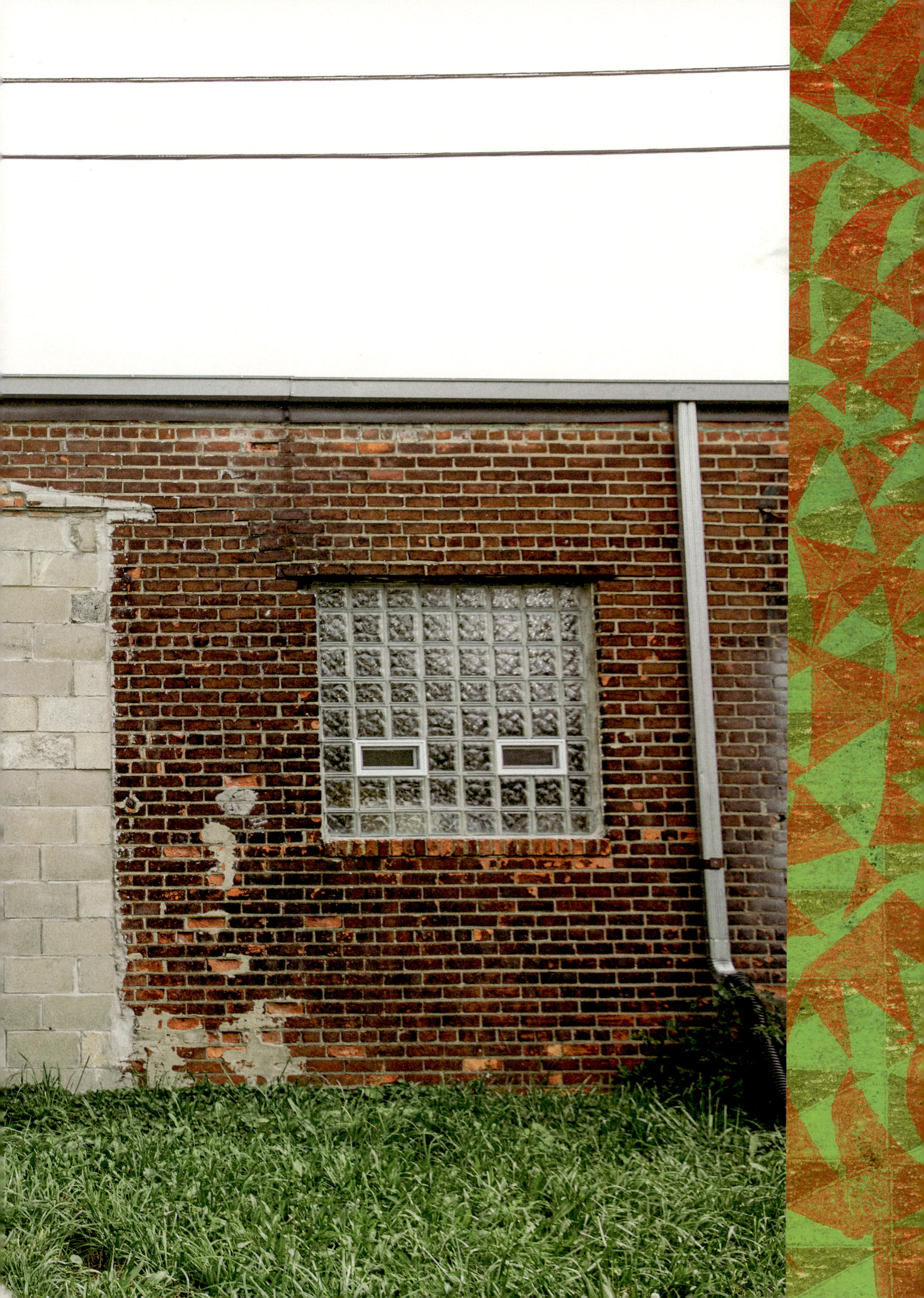

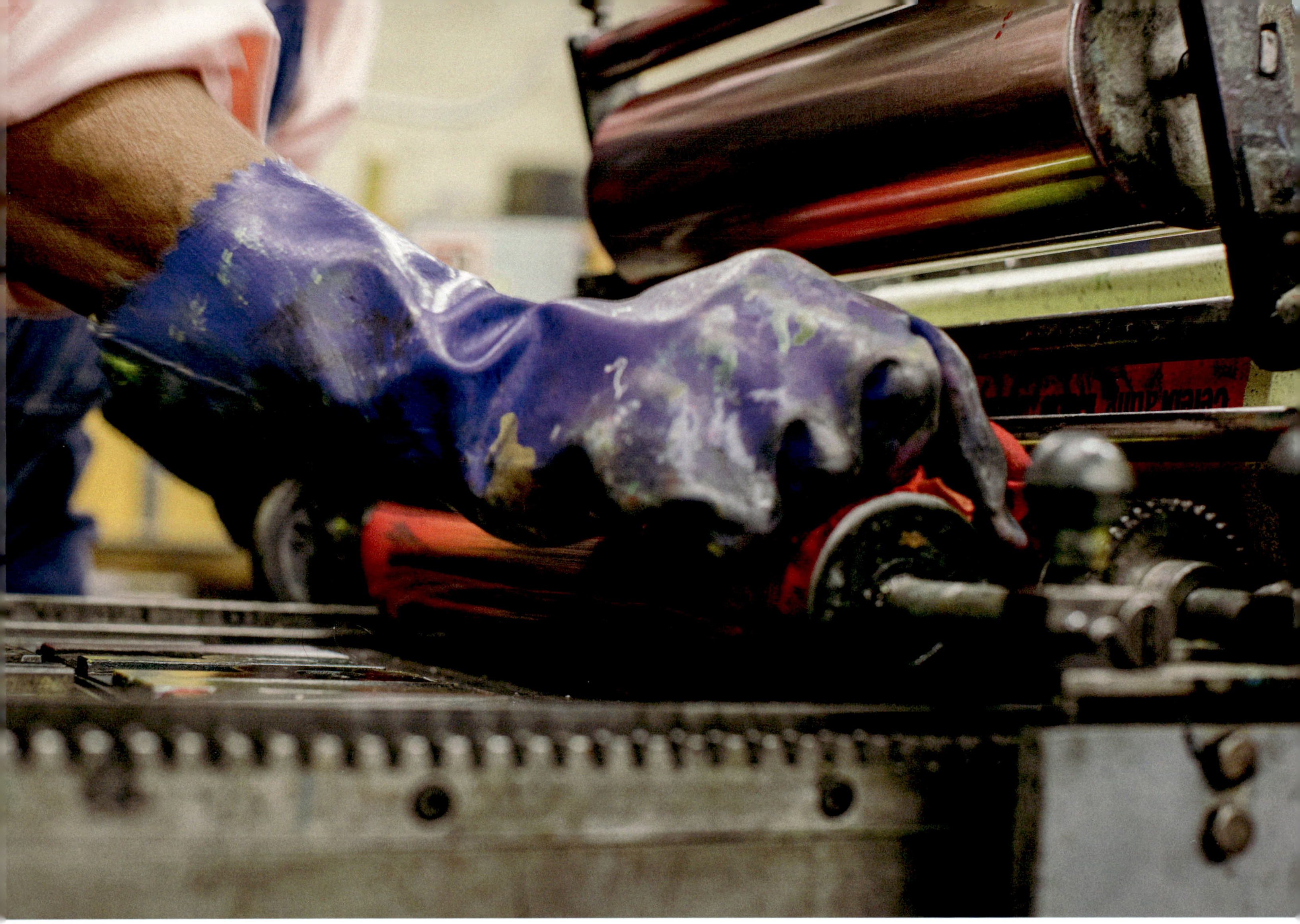

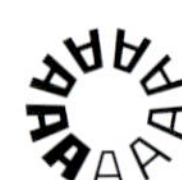

Letterform Archive
2339 Third Street, Floor 4R
San Francisco, CA 94107
letterformarchive.org

PUBLISHER EMERITUS
Rob Saunders

PUBLISHER
Lucie Parker

ASSOCIATE MANAGING EDITOR
Molly O'Neil Stewart

EDITORIAL ASSISTANT
Khoo Zi Yun (Geraldine) Ang

ART DIRECTOR
Alice Chau

DESIGNERS
Gail Anderson and Joe Newton

PHOTOGRAPHER
Aundre Larrow

PRINT PRODUCTION & COLOR MANAGER
Thomas Bollier

Available through ARTBOOK | D.A.P.
75 Broad Street, Suite 630
New York, NY 10004
www.artbook.com

ISBN: 978-1-7368633-8-1

Library of Congress Control Number: 2024933770

10 9 8 7 6 5 4 3 2 1
2024 2025 2026 2027 2028

Printed in China by 1010 Printing

ABOUT LETTERFORM ARCHIVE BOOKS
Founded in 2015 in San Francisco, Letterform Archive is a nonprofit center for design inspiration. Letterform Archive Books produces titles based on its collection of more than 100,000 artifacts spanning the history of graphic design, type design, and lettering.

ABOUT THE ARTWORK REPRODUCTION
Part of Letterform Archive's mission is to preserve and share its collection in print. Collections materials are digitized in-house using state-of-the-art camera equipment and raking light, then referenced alongside proofs to ensure a perfect color match. Printed using high-resolution stochastic screening, the resulting publications feature archive-quality reproductions that faithfully re-create the experience of the originals.

ABOUT THE TYPE
Citizen Printer's main headings and running text are set in New Century Schoolbook, which was designed in 1919 by Morris Fuller Benton for American Type Founders as a textbook typeface legible enough for young readers; it was later revived by Matthew Carter for Linotype in 1980. Captions, running footers, notes, indexes, and credits appear in ATF Franklin Gothic, Mark van Bronkhorst's reinterpretation of Benton's classic 1902 sans serif, while subheadings, quotations, and folios make use of Nick Sherman's HEX Franklin, a 2022 tribute that allows for tight spacing and other stylistic adjustments that provide character and voice. Front matter headings and drop capitals are styled in Thorowgood Egyptian, an 1834 condensed slab serif revived by Greg Gazdowicz and Paul Barnes of Commercial Classics in 2019.

Typeface selections reflect the type choices made by Amos Paul Kennedy, Jr., in his letterpress prints, honoring his preference that type be loud and legible for the masses.

The cover title treatment, excerpts of his manifesto (see pages 12–15), type impressions (see page 26), and historic woodcut impressions (see pages 30–31) were printed by Kennedy himself.

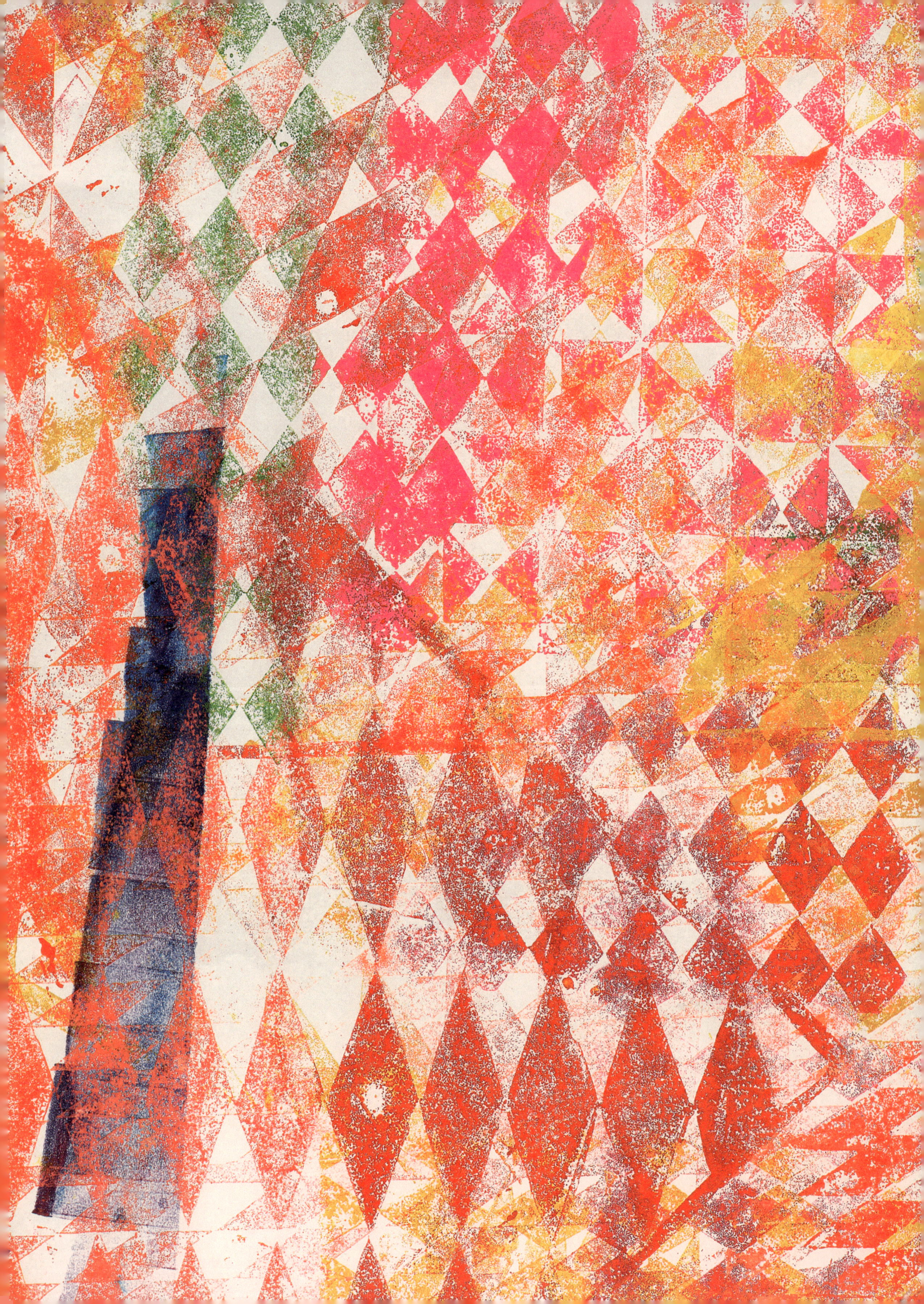